InfoPath 2013 Cookbook 2

121 Codeless Recipes for SharePoint 2013

S.Y.M. Wong-A-Ton

InfoPath 2013 Cookbook 2 – 121 Codeless Recipes for SharePoint 2013

To my loyal readers

Thank you for your support

Table of Contents

Introduction

In *InfoPath 2013 Cookbook: 121 Codeless Recipes for Beginners*, you learned the basics of designing InfoPath 2013 forms and working with controls. *InfoPath 2013 Cookbook 2: 121 Codeless Recipes for SharePoint 2013* is all about taking those basics skills you acquired from *InfoPath 2013 Cookbook* and extending them to working with InfoPath 2013 forms in SharePoint 2013.

InfoPath 2013 has several integration points with SharePoint 2013, but there are four main types of InfoPath forms you can use with SharePoint:

1. SharePoint list forms
2. SharePoint form library forms
3. Workflow forms
4. Document Information Panels

SharePoint list forms are probably the quickest and easiest types of forms to design, but they do have their limitations. Because a SharePoint list form is tightly bound to a SharePoint list, the controls you can place on SharePoint list forms are limited by the data types that are available in SharePoint. For example, because SharePoint has no data structures to accommodate repeating structures such as repeating tables or repeating sections, you cannot use these controls on SharePoint list forms. In addition, InfoPath 2013 does not allow you to write code for SharePoint list forms. Therefore, if you require any of the aforementioned functionality, you must use a SharePoint form library form instead. SharePoint form library forms allow for greater flexibility when designing and publishing InfoPath forms and they also allow you to write code. You will learn more about SharePoint list forms in Chapter 1 and about SharePoint form library forms in Chapter 2.

Because SharePoint lists and libraries are core elements of SharePoint, you may often want to retrieve data from lists or libraries from within any one of the types of InfoPath forms. Chapter 3 offers several solutions for retrieving data from SharePoint lists and libraries, and then using this data in InfoPath forms.

Controls are an integral part of InfoPath forms. While you have already learned to work with several types of controls in *InfoPath 2013 Cookbook: 121 Codeless Recipes for Beginners*, Chapter 4 takes a deeper look into how you can integrate a couple of specific controls such as drop-down list boxes, picture controls, person/group picker controls, and multiple-selection list boxes with SharePoint data.

From the four types of forms, a workflow form is the only type of form that cannot be created from scratch from within InfoPath Designer 2013. Workflow forms are generated by SharePoint Designer 2013 when you publish a SharePoint 2010 workflow to SharePoint. And once generated, you can use InfoPath Designer 2013 to customize them. You will learn how to create workflow initiation forms in Chapter 5. Chapter 5 also shows you how you can go beyond workflow forms to create SharePoint Designer workflows that run on, create, and interact with InfoPath forms stored in a form library.

While document information panel forms are not actually displayed in the browser through SharePoint like the other three types of forms are, their form templates are stored in SharePoint and their fields are related to columns defined on content types. You will learn more about document information panels in Chapter 6.

InfoPath Forms Services is available in SharePoint Server 2013 and is required for InfoPath forms to be displayed in a browser through SharePoint. If you are reading this book, I assume you have already installed InfoPath 2013, Word 2013, Excel 2013, Access 2013, and SharePoint Designer 2013, and that you have a SharePoint Server with InfoPath Forms Services at your disposal. This book does not explain the administrative tasks you need to perform to install and configure SharePoint with InfoPath Forms Services.

Who should read this book?

This book was written for Microsoft Office users who already have basic knowledge of InfoPath 2013 and SharePoint 2013 as separate products, but who are yet to start integrating the two with each other. This book was also written specifically for beginner to intermediate users who are not necessarily programmers. While this book may also be beneficial to programmers, it does not contain any code that would need to be compiled before it can run. In addition, this book does not contain any information on how to administer SharePoint 2013 or InfoPath Forms Services, so is not geared towards SharePoint administrators.

While this book assumes that you already have basic knowledge of SharePoint 2013, you do not need to know anything about the SharePoint components that are related to InfoPath, since that information is covered within the book. For example, you do not need to know how to work with SharePoint form libraries, site content types, or know anything about workflows in SharePoint Designer 2013, because the basics of those topics are explained in the book.

This book follows a practical approach. Almost every chapter first presents a small amount of theory explaining a few key concepts and then slowly builds your InfoPath with SharePoint integration skills with step-by-step recipes (tutorials) that follow a logical sequence and increase in complexity as you progress through the book. Almost every recipe has a discussion section that expands on the steps outlined in the recipe and offers additional information on what you have learned.

You will not find everything you can do with InfoPath and SharePoint explained in this book, because this book is not meant to be used as reference material. The goal of this book is to expand the knowledge you have already acquired from *InfoPath 2013 Cookbook: 121 Codeless Recipes for Beginners* into the SharePoint 2013 realm, and provide you with ideas on how you can integrate InfoPath with SharePoint by using one of four types of InfoPath forms in SharePoint, including the use of SharePoint Designer, Word, Excel, and Access with InfoPath through SharePoint.

How to use this book

This book has been set up in a cookbook-style with 121 recipes. A recipe consists of 3 parts: A description of the problem, a step-by-step outline of the solution, and further discussion highlighting important parts of the recipe, expanding on what you have learned, or providing background information on a specific topic.

Chapters 1 and 2 cover the basics of creating and working with two of the most common types of InfoPath forms in SharePoint, so I recommend you do these chapters in full before going through any other chapter.

Recipes 43 through 46 in Chapter 3 cover the basics of connecting to and using data from SharePoint lists, so I recommend you do these before going through recipes in other chapters. While the recipes in Chapter 4 stand on their own, they make use of techniques discussed in Chapter 3.

For Chapter 5, I recommend you start with recipes 80 through 87 in sequence to learn the basics of SharePoint Designer workflows. After that, you can randomly choose recipes from Chapter 5.

Recipes 97 through 100 in Chapter 6 should be done in sequence. And before you do recipe 101 or 102, ensure that you have gone through the basic recipes in Chapter 5.

Recipes 105, 107, and 108 in Chapter 7 cover the basics of calling Excel Services web service operations from within InfoPath forms, so I recommend doing these three recipes before any other recipe in Chapter 7.

While most of the recipes in this book are ordered in a way to build on each other, any recipe that requires knowledge you should have acquired from previous recipes will reference those recipes so that you can go back and do those recipes if you skipped them.

About the author

My name is S.Y.M. Wong-A-Ton and I have been a software developer since the start of my IT career back in 1997. The first Microsoft products I used as a developer were Visual Basic 4 and SQL Server 6.5. During my IT career I have developed as well as maintained and supported all types of applications ranging from desktop applications to web sites and web services. I have been a Microsoft Certified Professional since 1998 and have held the title of Microsoft Certified Solution Developer for almost as long as I have been in IT.

I was originally trained as a Geophysicist and co-wrote (as the main author) a scientific article while I was still a scientist. This article was published in 1997 in the Geophysical Research Letters of the American Geophysical Union.

I started exploring the first version of InfoPath in 2005 in my spare time and was hooked on it from day one. What I liked most about InfoPath was the simplicity with which I was able to quickly create electronic forms that were like small applications on their own; all this without writing a single line of code!

While exploring InfoPath, I started actively helping other InfoPath users, who were asking questions on the Internet, to come up with innovative solutions. And because the same questions were being asked frequently, I decided to start writing tutorials and articles about InfoPath on my web site *Enterprise Solutions*, which evolved into what is known today as *BizSupportOnline* and can be visited at http://www.bizsupportonline.net.

Shortly after starting to share my knowledge about InfoPath with others, I received recognition from Microsoft in the form of the Microsoft Most Valuable Professional (MVP) award, and have received this award every year since then, which as of writing has been 8 years in a row.

I have worked with SharePoint since its first version was released and while continuing to explore SharePoint throughout the years, I have found many InfoPath with SharePoint solutions, which I have shared with the InfoPath community through free articles, blog posts, and videos.

This book is a continuation of my sharing of knowledge, tips, tricks, and techniques with you, but most importantly, of providing you with codeless solutions for working with InfoPath and SharePoint. So I sincerely hope that you not only enjoy reading this book, but that it also inspires you to extend the solutions it contains to find more integration points between InfoPath and SharePoint without having to write a single line of code.

Support

Every effort has been made to ensure the accuracy of this book. Corrections for this book are provided at http://www.bizsupportonline.com.

If you have comments, questions, suggestions, improvements, or ideas about this book, please send them to bizsupportonline@gmail.com with "InfoPath 2013 Cookbook 2" in the subject line.

Chapter 1: SharePoint List Forms

Every SharePoint list has a set of forms you can use to add, view, or edit list items. These forms are by default SharePoint forms that display the columns of a list as fields on a form. You can use InfoPath Designer 2013 to create SharePoint list forms that replace the default SharePoint list forms and are based on what is called a SharePoint list form template. In this chapter you will learn how to create and work with SharePoint list form templates.

SharePoint list form basics

A customized SharePoint list form is an InfoPath form that is tightly bound to one particular SharePoint list. There are two types of SharePoint list forms:

1. SharePoint list forms with which you can manage one list item at a time.
2. SharePoint list forms with which you can manage multiple list items at a time.

You can use InfoPath Designer 2013, SharePoint 2013, or SharePoint Designer 2013 to start the process of customizing a SharePoint list form in InfoPath Designer 2013 as you will learn from the next recipes.

1 Customize a SharePoint list form from within SharePoint

Problem

You want to create an InfoPath form that can be used to view, add, or edit SharePoint list items.

Solution

You can use one of two methods to customize a SharePoint list form depending on the content type associated with the list. If you want to customize the default content type of an existing SharePoint list, you can use the **Customize Form** command that is available on a SharePoint list to open a new or an existing form template in InfoPath Designer 2013. And if you want to customize a specific content type that is associated with an existing SharePoint list, you can go through the list settings to access the form settings page to open a new or an existing form template in InfoPath Designer 2013.

If you require background information about content types and how to add multiple content types to a SharePoint list, see ***Add existing content types to a SharePoint list*** in the Appendix.

To customize the SharePoint list form for the default content type of a SharePoint list from within SharePoint:

1. In SharePoint, navigate to an existing SharePoint list.
2. Click **List** ➤ **Customize List** ➤ **Customize Form**. This should open InfoPath Designer 2013 with a new form template that is based on the columns of the default content type of the SharePoint list. If the SharePoint list form has already been previously customized, so a list form template already exists for the SharePoint list, the existing form template should open in InfoPath Designer 2013.

Figure 1. Customize List group on the List tab in SharePoint 2013.

3. In InfoPath, customize the form template to suit your needs, and then click **File** ➤ **Info** ➤ **Quick Publish**, click **File** ➤ **Publish** ➤ **SharePoint List**, or click the **Quick Publish** command on the **Quick Access Toolbar** to publish the form template back to SharePoint.

To customize a SharePoint list form for a specific content type that is associated with a SharePoint list from within SharePoint:

1. In SharePoint, navigate to an existing SharePoint list that has multiple content types associated with it.

2. Click **List** ➤ **Settings** ➤ **List Settings**.
3. On the **Settings** page under **General Settings**, click **Form settings**.
4. On the **Form Settings** page, select the content type for which you want to customize its SharePoint list form from the **Content Type** drop-down list box, and click **OK**. This should open InfoPath Designer 2013. Note that the **Content Type** drop-down list box only appears when there are multiple content types associated with a list.

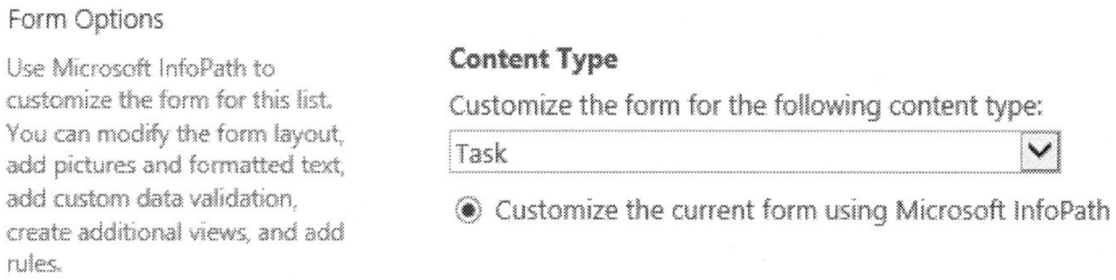

Figure 2. Selecting a specific content type to customize its SharePoint list form.

5. In InfoPath, customize the form template to suit your needs, and then click **File** ➤ **Info** ➤ **Quick Publish**, click **File** ➤ **Publish** ➤ **SharePoint List**, or click the **Quick Publish** command on the **Quick Access Toolbar** to publish the form template back to SharePoint.

In SharePoint, navigate to the SharePoint list for which you customized its form, and then click **Items** ➤ **New** ➤ **New Item** and select the content type for which you customized its SharePoint list form from the drop-down menu that appears. The customized InfoPath form should appear.

Discussion

To be able to create a SharePoint list form template for an existing SharePoint list from within SharePoint, you must have at least **Edit** permission on the site where the SharePoint list is located, **Design** permission on the SharePoint list, and the type of SharePoint list must be customizable.

The methods in this recipe can be used to create a new InfoPath form for a SharePoint list as well as update or modify an existing InfoPath form for a SharePoint list. While it may seem like you used a SharePoint list as the basis for a SharePoint list form, in reality, you used a content type that is associated with that SharePoint list as the basis for a SharePoint list form.

A SharePoint list may or may not have multiple content types associated with it depending on whether management of content types has been enabled or not (also see *Add existing content types to a SharePoint list* in the Appendix). So there are two situations that can take place:

1. If management of content types is not enabled on a SharePoint list, the default content type of that SharePoint list will be used as the basis for the SharePoint list form.
2. If management of content types is enabled on a SharePoint list and there are multiple content types associated with the SharePoint list, you can use any one of those content types to base the SharePoint list form on.

In the solution described above, you used the **Customize Form** command on the Ribbon in SharePoint to customize the InfoPath form that is linked to the default content type of the SharePoint list, and you used the **Form Settings** page, which you accessed via the **Settings** page of the list, to customize the SharePoint list form for a specific content type that was associated with the SharePoint list. Note that you could have also used the **Form Settings** page to start the customization of an InfoPath form linked to the default content type, and that you could have also assigned a different content type to be the default content type and then used the **Customize Form** command to edit the SharePoint list form linked to that content type. So you can use either method for customizing a SharePoint list form for a particular content type. However, you cannot customize the SharePoint list form for all types of lists in SharePoint. For example, the SharePoint list form for a **Calendar** list cannot be customized, because the **Customize Form** button is not present on the Ribbon, neither are the options on the **Form Settings** page.

When you create a SharePoint list form template, the columns of the content type associated with the SharePoint list you use as the basis for the form template along with standard list columns such as **ID**, **Created By**, etc. become fields of the Main data source of the form.

And when you fill out a SharePoint list form, the data you enter into the fields on the form are stored as an item in the SharePoint list. So unlike SharePoint form library forms, which you will learn more about in Chapter

2, SharePoint list forms are not stored as separate XML files within SharePoint, but are rather used as front-end forms that channel data through to a SharePoint list that functions as the data source.

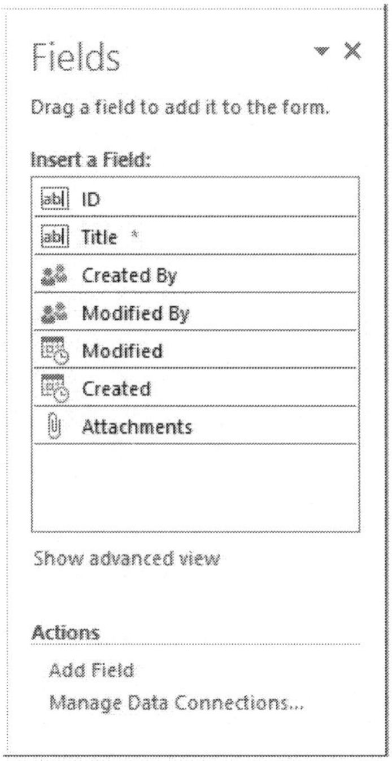

Figure 3. The Fields task pane in InfoPath showing the content type fields.

This also immediately highlights one disadvantage of SharePoint list forms: The types of fields you are allowed to place on a SharePoint list form depend on the data types of columns of the content type associated with a SharePoint list and on whether those data types are supported in InfoPath. Because complex data structures such as repeating or nested data cannot be defined as data types of columns in SharePoint, they are not supported by SharePoint list forms. So if you want to add repeating structures (for example, repeating tables or repeating sections) to a form, you must use a SharePoint form library form instead of a SharePoint list form.

In addition, because a SharePoint list form is tightly bound to its data source, you cannot publish or republish the form template to another location. If you go to the **Publish** tab in InfoPath Designer 2013, you will see that there are no other publishing options available other than the option to publish the form template to the SharePoint list it was originally bound to and an option to export the source files of the form template. So once you have created a SharePoint list form template, you cannot change its (quick) publish location in InfoPath Designer 2013.

Before you customize a SharePoint list form, the SharePoint list uses default ASPX pages as list forms and only the following three items are displayed in the **Form Web Parts** drop-down menu, which you can access via the **List ➤ Customize List ➤ Form Web Parts** command on the Ribbon:

1. Default New Form
2. Default Display Form
3. Default Edit Form

After you customize and publish an InfoPath form template to a SharePoint list, you will see the following three items appear in the **Form Web Parts** command drop-down menu under a **Content Type Forms** section:

1. (Item) New Form
2. (Item) Display Form
3. (Item) Edit Form

The content type name is listed between brackets in front of each one of the forms. If there are multiple content types associated with the SharePoint list, each content type, for which you customized its list form, would have its own set of forms listed under the **Content Type Forms** section of the drop-down menu as shown in the following figure.

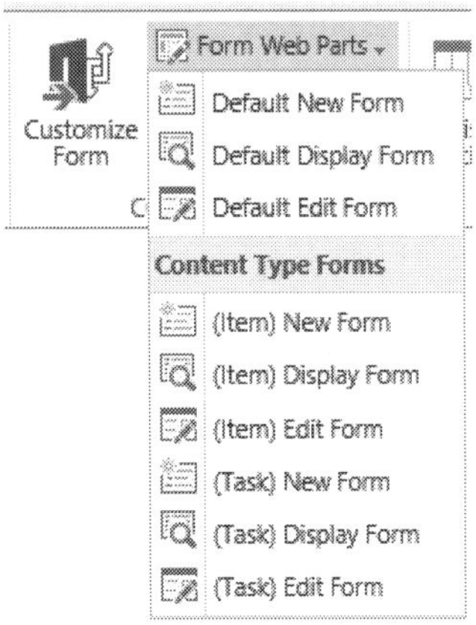

Figure 4. Both the Item and Task content types have customized list forms.

The content type forms are web part pages that host the customized SharePoint list form template you modified in InfoPath. If you click on any one of these three items, a web part page containing an InfoPath form for the corresponding type of form should open in the browser. The InfoPath form on the web part page is embedded in an InfoPath Form Web Part, which you will learn more about in recipe *13 Embed a SharePoint list form on a SharePoint page*. For now, just remember that you can customize this web part page to suit your needs and that the one form template you customized for the content type on the SharePoint list in InfoPath is used for all three types of forms (new, display, and edit).

And finally, you can also use SharePoint Designer 2013 to perform the steps outlined in this recipe as follows:

1. In SharePoint Designer 2013, open the SharePoint site where the SharePoint list for which you want to customize its form is located.
2. In the left **Navigation** pane, click **Lists and Libraries**.
3. On the **Lists and Libraries** page, click the list for which you want to customize its form.
4. On the Ribbon, click **List Settings ➤ Actions ➤ Design Forms in InfoPath** and then select the content type for which you want to customize its form. This should open the SharePoint list form for customization in InfoPath Designer 2013.

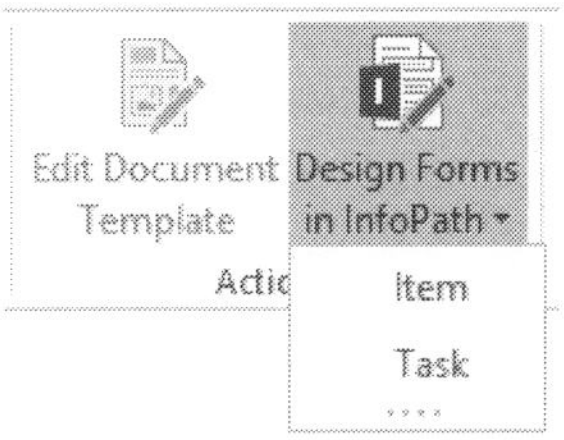

Figure 5. Design Forms in InfoPath command in SharePoint Designer 2013.

5. In InfoPath, customize the form template to suit your needs, and then click **File ➤ Info ➤ Quick Publish**, click **File ➤ Publish ➤ SharePoint List**, or click the **Quick Publish** command on the **Quick Access Toolbar** to publish the form template back to SharePoint.

While you are still in SharePoint Designer 2013, now is also the time to learn where SharePoint stores the customized InfoPath form templates:

1. In the left **Navigation** pane, click **All Files**.
2. On the **All Files** page, click the **Lists** folder.
3. On the **Lists** page, click the SharePoint list for which you want to locate its customized InfoPath form template.
4. On the list's page, click the folder that has the name of the content type for which you want to locate its form template. If the SharePoint list only has a default **Item** content type associated with it, the folder would be called **Item**. Otherwise, the folder should have the same name as the content type.

Once you are in the folder for the content type (for example, the **Item** folder), you should see an InfoPath form template named **template.xsn** and also three ASPX pages (**displayifs.aspx**, **editifs.aspx**, and **newifs.aspx**) that are used as the web part pages to embed the SharePoint list form. Note that from here you could click on the **template.xsn** file to open and modify it in InfoPath Designer 2013.

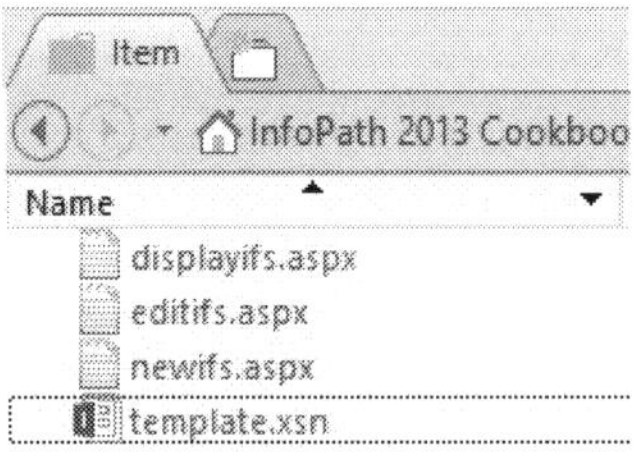

Figure 6. SharePoint list form template and form web part pages in SharePoint Designer.

2 Customize a SharePoint list form from within InfoPath

Create a SharePoint list form for a new SharePoint list

Problem

You want to create an InfoPath form template that is based on a SharePoint list, but you do not yet have a list in SharePoint, so would like to create the SharePoint list through InfoPath when you create the new form template.

Solution

You can create a SharePoint list form template in InfoPath Designer 2013 and specify that you would like to create a new SharePoint list for the form template.

To create a new SharePoint list and SharePoint list form template from within InfoPath:

1. In InfoPath, click **File ➤ New ➤ SharePoint List** under **Popular Form Templates**, and then click **Design Form** to create a new **SharePoint List** form template.

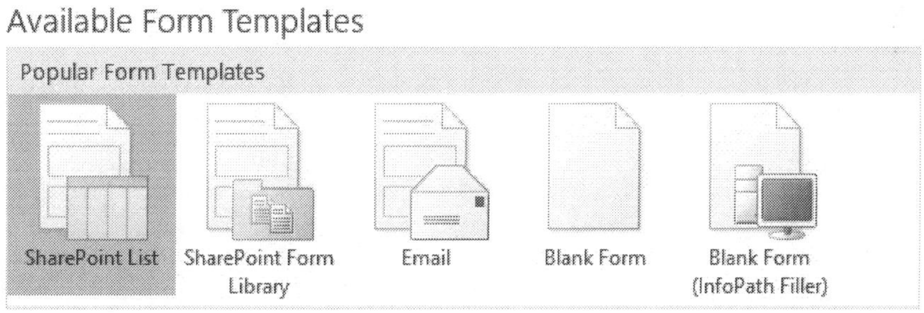

Figure 7. SharePoint List command to create a form template in InfoPath.

2. On the **Data Connection Wizard**, enter the URL of the SharePoint site where you want to create the new SharePoint list, and click **Next**.
3. On the **Data Connection Wizard**, leave the **Create a new SharePoint list** option selected, type a name for the list in the **List**

Name text box, and click **Next**.

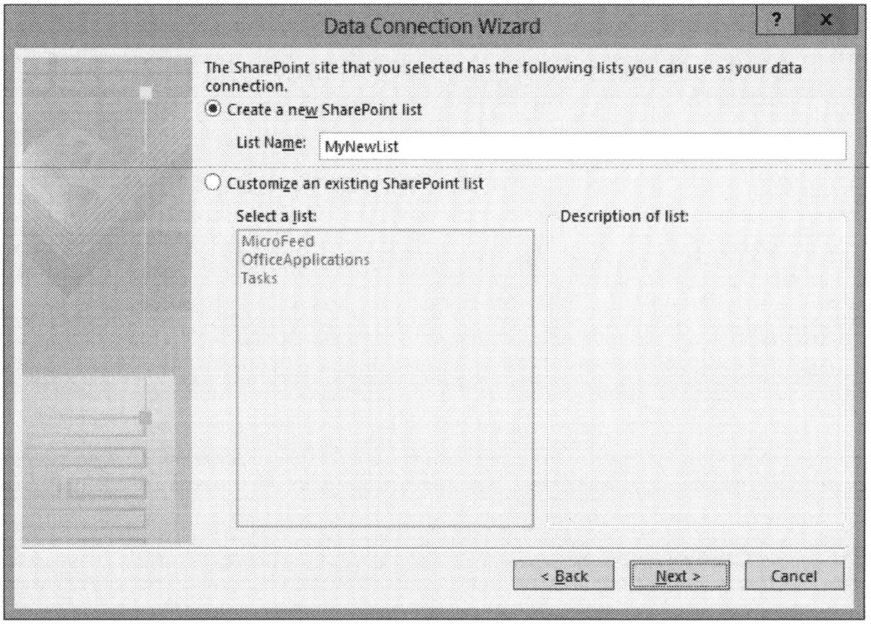

Figure 8. Creating a new SharePoint list in InfoPath Designer 2013.

4. On the **Data Connection Wizard**, leave the **Manage multiple list items with this form** check box deselected, and click **Finish**. InfoPath should create a new list in SharePoint for the form template and place controls for the **Title** and **Attachments** fields on an **Edit item (default)** view of the form template in InfoPath Designer 2013.
5. Customize the form template to suit your needs, and then click **File ➤ Info ➤ Quick Publish**, click **File ➤ Publish ➤ SharePoint List**, or click the **Quick Publish** command on the **Quick Access Toolbar** to publish the form template back to SharePoint.

In SharePoint, navigate to the SharePoint list for which you customized its form, and add a new item. The customized InfoPath form should appear.

Discussion

To be able to create a new SharePoint list, design, and then publish its list form template from within InfoPath Designer 2013, you must have **Design** permission on the site where you want to create the SharePoint list.

Once you have created a form template that is bound to a new SharePoint list, you can add controls to the view of the form template or fields to the Main data source of the form (see recipe *4 Add a new field to a SharePoint list through InfoPath*). And once you publish the form template to SharePoint, the fields that you added in InfoPath Designer 2013 should become columns of the content type associated with the SharePoint list the form template is linked to.

Create a SharePoint list form for an existing SharePoint list

Problem

You want to use InfoPath Designer 2013 to design a form template and create a form with which users can view, add, or edit SharePoint list items.

Solution

You can use the **SharePoint List** form template in InfoPath Designer 2013 to design a form template and create a form with which you can view, add, or edit SharePoint list items.

Suppose you have a SharePoint list named **OfficeApplications** that contains the following data:

Title	Color
Word	Blue
Excel	Green
Access	Red
PowerPoint	Orange
OneNote	Purple
InfoPath	Purple
Publisher	Blue

To customize a SharePoint list form for an existing SharePoint list from within InfoPath:

1. In InfoPath, click **File ➤ New ➤ SharePoint List** under **Popular Form Templates**, and then click **Design Form** to create a new **SharePoint List** form template.
2. On the **Data Connection Wizard**, enter the URL of the SharePoint site where the **OfficeApplications** SharePoint list is located, and click **Next**.
3. On the **Data Connection Wizard**, select the **Customize an existing SharePoint list** option, select **OfficeApplications** in the **Select a list** list box, and click **Next**.

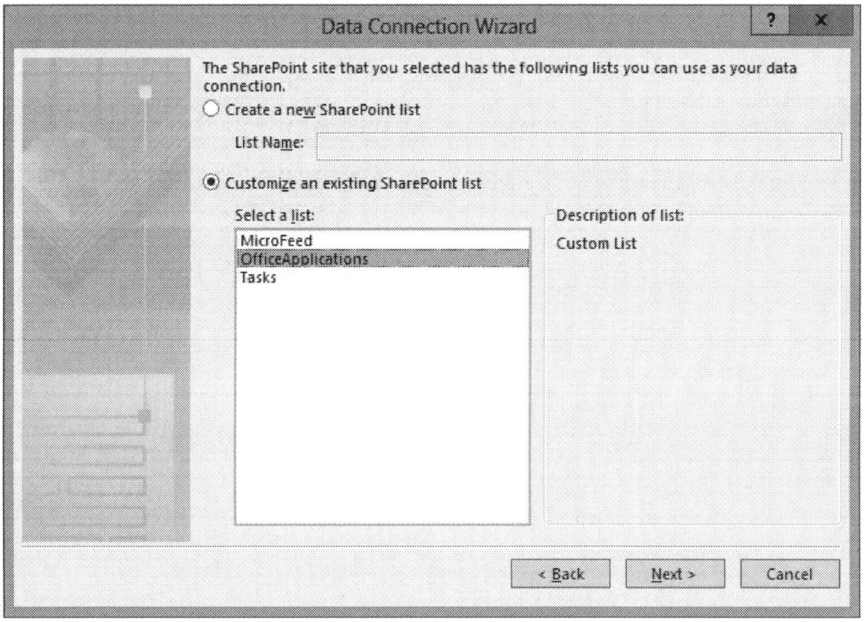

Figure 9. Customizing the list form for an existing SharePoint list in InfoPath.

4. If the **OfficeApplications** SharePoint list does not have multiple content types associated with it, you would go directly to step 5 after step 3. If the **OfficeApplications** SharePoint list has multiple content types associated with it, InfoPath should display an extra screen where you can select the content type for which you want to customize its SharePoint list form, and then click **Next**.

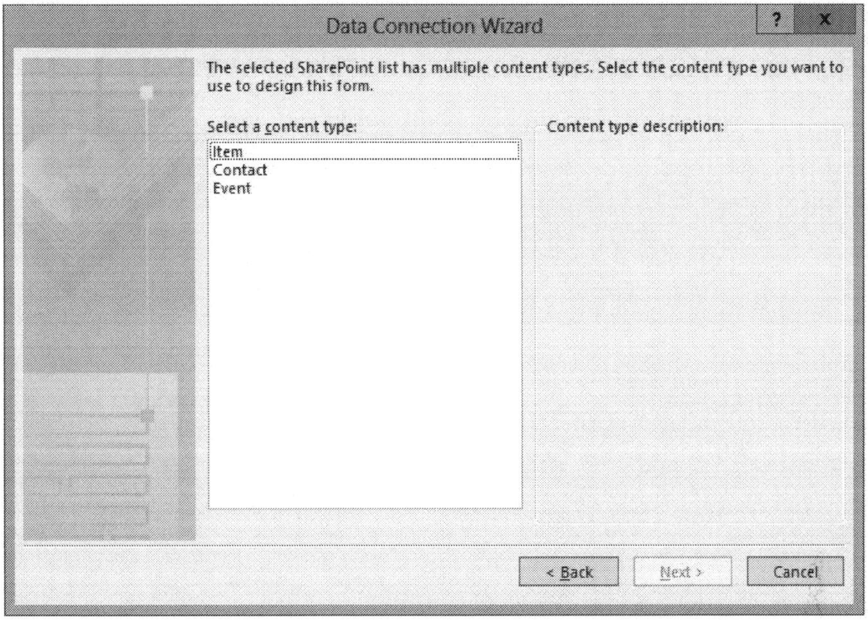

Figure 10. Selecting the content type to use to design a SharePoint list form.

5. On the **Data Connection Wizard**, leave the **Manage multiple list items with this form** check box deselected, and click **Finish**. InfoPath should create the form template and place controls on an **Edit item (default)** view. If the InfoPath form for the SharePoint list has already been customized previously, InfoPath should open the existing, already customized InfoPath form template, instead of creating a new one.
6. Customize the form template to suit your needs, and then click **File ➤ Info ➤ Quick Publish**, click **File ➤ Publish ➤ SharePoint List**, or click the **Quick Publish** command on the **Quick Access Toolbar** to publish the form template back to SharePoint.

In SharePoint, navigate to the SharePoint list for which you customized its form, and add a new item. The customized InfoPath form should appear.

Discussion

To be able to create a SharePoint list form template for an existing SharePoint list from within InfoPath Designer 2013, you must have at least **Contribute** permission on the site where the SharePoint list is located and **Design** permission on the SharePoint list.

SharePoint lists that are not customizable using InfoPath are not listed in the **Select a list** list box on the **Data Connection Wizard** where you can choose a SharePoint list to customize.

When you create a SharePoint list form template, InfoPath displays the fields of the Main data source of the form by default in **basic view** mode on the **Fields** task pane. **Basic view** mode does not display the structure of the Main data source and only displays fields with which you can add, edit, or display (not query) data.

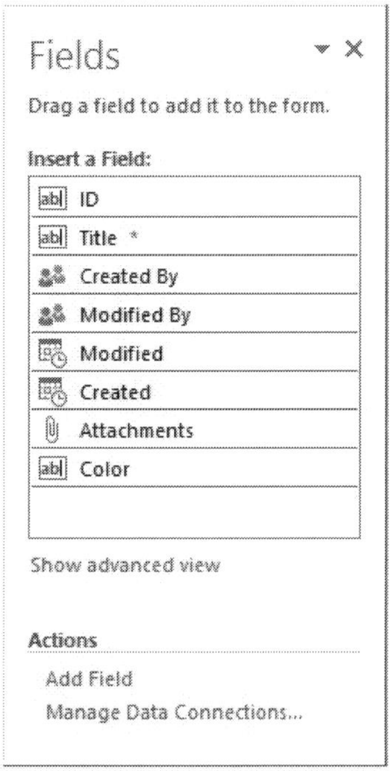

Figure 11. Fields task pane in basic view mode.

To see the structure of the Main data source, on the **Fields** task pane, click **Show advanced view** at the bottom of the **Fields** task pane. The Main data source in **advanced view** mode consists of two main group nodes:

1. queryFields
2. dataFields

The **queryFields** group node contains fields that can be used to query (search for or filter) data in the SharePoint list, while the **dataFields** group node contains fields that can be used to display data from the SharePoint list. The fields under the **dataFields** group node are also used to submit data to the SharePoint list through the main data connection of the form. The main data connection of a SharePoint list form submits data to the SharePoint list the form is connected to, and it cannot be changed to submit data to another SharePoint list or to multiple SharePoint lists.

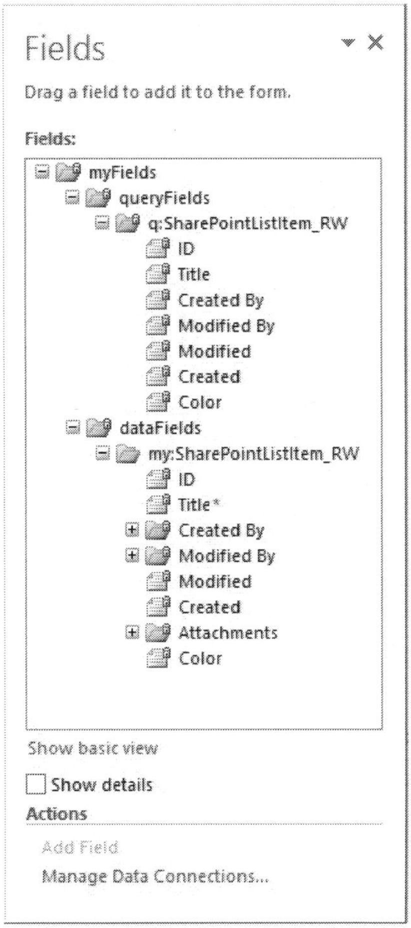

Figure 12. Fields task pane in advanced view mode.

The controls that InfoPath placed on the view of the form template when you created it are bound to fields that are located under the **dataFields** group node. Because those controls are used to edit a list item, they are placed on a view named **Edit item (default)** (see **Page Design ➤ Views ➤ View**). To verify that the fields bound to those controls are indeed located under the **dataFields** group node, click on any of the fields on the view and then look which field is highlighted on the **Fields** task pane.

You can add new controls to the view of the form template or new fields to the Main data source (see recipe *4 Add a new field to a SharePoint list through InfoPath*), and once you publish the form template, those fields should become columns of the content type associated with the SharePoint list the form template is linked to.

3 Create a SharePoint list form to manage multiple list items

Problem

You want to create an InfoPath form with which users can add, edit, or delete one or more SharePoint list items through that form.

Solution

You can use the **SharePoint List** form template in InfoPath Designer 2013 to design a form template and create a form with which you can manage multiple list items.

Suppose you have a SharePoint list named **OfficeApplications** as described in *Create a SharePoint list form for an existing SharePoint list* in recipe *2 Customize a SharePoint list form from within InfoPath*.

To create a SharePoint list form with which you can manage multiple list items:

1. In InfoPath, click **File** ➤ **New** ➤ **SharePoint List** under **Popular Form Templates**, and then click **Design Form** to create a new **SharePoint List** form template.
2. On the **Data Connection Wizard**, enter the URL of the SharePoint site where the **OfficeApplications** SharePoint list is located, and click **Next**.
3. On the **Data Connection Wizard**, select the **Customize an existing SharePoint list** option, select **OfficeApplications** in the **Select a list** list box, and click **Next**.

4. If the **OfficeApplications** SharePoint list does not have multiple content types associated with it, you would go directly to step 5 after step 3. If the **OfficeApplications** SharePoint list has multiple content types associated with it, InfoPath should display an extra screen where you can select the content type for which you want to customize its SharePoint list form, and then click **Next**.
5. On the **Data Connection Wizard**, select the **Manage multiple list items with this form** check box, and click **Finish**. InfoPath should create the form template and place controls in a repeating section on the **Edit item (default)** view. Note that if the check box is missing, it means that the SharePoint list form has already been previously customized to allow for single item viewing and editing. Once you have customized a SharePoint list form, you cannot change it from managing multiple items to managing one item or vice versa, unless you first delete the list form as described in recipe *6 Restore the default form of a SharePoint list* and then customize the form again to manage either one or multiple items.

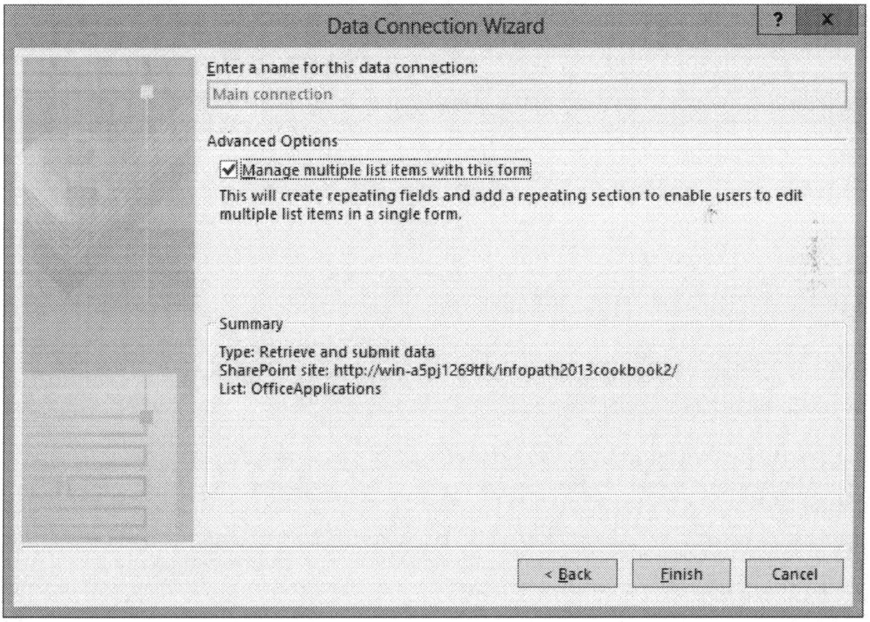

Figure 13. Selecting the 'Manage multiple list items with this form' check box.

6. Customize the form template to suit your needs, and then click **File ➤ Info ➤ Quick Publish**, click **File ➤ Publish ➤ SharePoint List**, or

click the **Quick Publish** command on the **Quick Access Toolbar** to publish the form template back to SharePoint.

In SharePoint, navigate to the SharePoint list for which you customized its form, and add a new item. The customized InfoPath form with which you can manage multiple list items should appear.

Discussion

In the solution described above you saw that enabling a SharePoint list form to manage multiple items is a matter of selecting the **Manage multiple list items with this form** check box on the last screen of the **Data Connection Wizard**. While you customized the form for an existing SharePoint list in this recipe, the check box should also be available when you create a new SharePoint list (step 4 in *Create a SharePoint list form for a new SharePoint list* in recipe *2 Customize a SharePoint list form from within InfoPath*).

Adding or editing multiple SharePoint list items instead of one works just like adding or editing one SharePoint list item, which means that you can apply the same techniques to both where querying and refreshing data are concerned. The only difference is that when you enable management of multiple list items, the form fields are stored under a **my:SharePointListItem_RW** repeating group node

Figure 14. SharePointListItem_RW is a repeating group for a multi-itemed form.

instead of a non-repeating group node as is the case for a SharePoint list form that manages a single item.

Figure 15. SharePointListItem_RW is a non-repeating group for a single-itemed form.

This also means that any fields you drag-and-drop onto the view, should be placed within a repeating table or a repeating section control. By default, InfoPath places controls within a repeating section control when you enable management of multiple items, but you could also place the controls in a repeating table control as follows:

1. Right-click the repeating section control and select **Change Control ➤ Repeating Table** from the context menu that appears.
2. Delete any fields you want to delete from the view by selecting their respective columns within the repeating table and pressing **Backspace** on your keyboard or by selecting **Table Tools ➤ Layout ➤ Rows & Columns ➤ Delete ➤ Columns** on the Ribbon.

You can add new controls to the repeating section or repeating table on the view of the form template or new fields under the **my:SharePointListItem_RW** repeating group node in the Main data source of the form (see recipe *4 Add a new field to a SharePoint list through InfoPath*), and once you publish the form template, those fields should become part of the content type associated with the SharePoint list the form template is linked to.

4 Add a new field to a SharePoint list through InfoPath

Problem

You have a SharePoint list form template open in InfoPath Designer 2013 and want to add a new field to the SharePoint list the form template is linked to, from within InfoPath.

Solution

When designing a SharePoint list form template in InfoPath, you can add fields or controls to the form template, which will then automatically be added to the content type associated with the SharePoint list when you publish the form template.

To add a new field to a SharePoint list through InfoPath by adding a control to the form template:

1. In InfoPath, create a new SharePoint list form template or open an existing one as described in recipe *1 Customize a SharePoint list form from within SharePoint* or recipe *2 Customize a SharePoint list form from within InfoPath*.
2. Click on the view of the form template to place the cursor where you want to insert a new control, and then from the **Controls** group on the **Home** tab, click on the control you want to add.
3. With the control still selected, change the **Name** of the field on the **Properties** tab under the **Properties** group to a name that is suitable to be used as a SharePoint list column.

In InfoPath, on the **Fields** task pane, click **Show advanced view**. The **queryFields** and **dataFields** group nodes in the Main data source should appear. Verify that a new field has been added under the **my:SharePointListItem_RW** group node under the **dataFields** group node. At this point, the new field exists in the form template, but not yet in SharePoint. You must publish the form template for the field to also be added in SharePoint.

You can also add a new field to a SharePoint list by adding it directly to the Main data source and not binding it to any control on the view.

To add a new field to a SharePoint list through InfoPath by adding a field to the Main data source of the form:

1. In InfoPath, create a new SharePoint list form template or open an existing one as described in recipe *1 Customize a SharePoint list form from within SharePoint* or recipe *2 Customize a SharePoint list form from within InfoPath*.
2. On the **Fields** task pane:
   a. If **basic view** is being shown, under **Actions** at the bottom of the **Fields** task pane, click **Add Field**.
   b. If **advanced view** is being shown, expand the **dataFields** group node, right-click the **my:SharePointListItem_RW** group node, and select **Add** from the drop-down menu that appears.

3. On the **Add Field or Group** dialog box, enter a **Display Name** and a **Name** for the field (InfoPath automatically generates a **Name** based on the **Display Name** you enter, but you can change the generated **Name** if you wish), select the data type from the **Data type** drop-down list box, and click **OK**. The new field should appear under the **my:SharePointListItem_RW** group node under the **dataFields** group node in the Main data source.

When you publish the form template to SharePoint, the new field should be added as a new column to the content type associated with the SharePoint list the form template is linked to.

Discussion

SharePoint list forms do not support the full range of controls that is available in InfoPath, because they are limited by the types of fields you can add to a SharePoint list. If you expand the list of controls in InfoPath, you will notice that a few controls such as repeating tables and repeating sections are not available when you are designing a SharePoint list form template, and that the amount of controls that is available is less than for example when you create a **Blank Form** or **SharePoint Form Library** template.

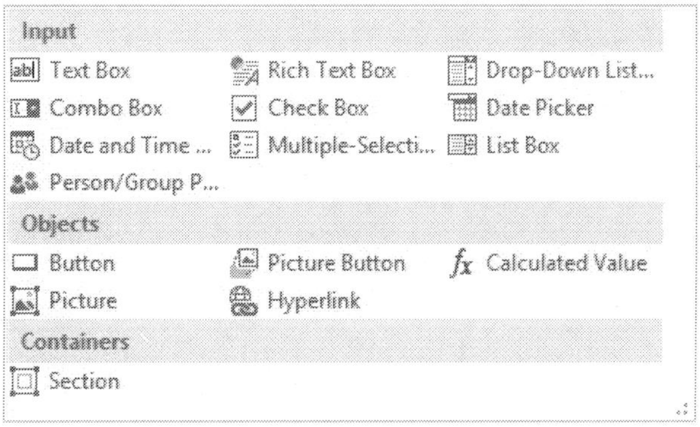

Figure 16. InfoPath controls you can place on a SharePoint list form.

So if you know that you may need to use controls that are not available for SharePoint list form templates, you may want to consider creating a SharePoint form library form template (see Chapter 2) instead of a SharePoint list form template.

Perform the steps from the second method described in the solution above again, and when you are on the **Add Field or Group** dialog box, go through the list of data types. As you select each data type, you may see other data entry options being enabled or disabled on the dialog box. For example, if you choose any of the **Choice** data types, an **Edit Choices** button with which you can enter a list of choices, is enabled.

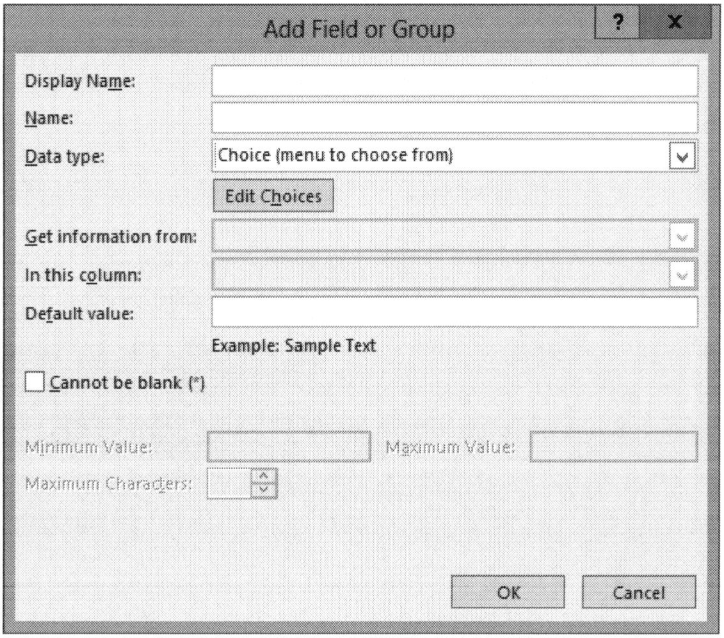

Figure 17. Selecting a Choice data type on the Add Field or Group dialog box in InfoPath.

If you choose **Currency** as the data type, the **Minimum Value** and **Maximum Value** text boxes are enabled. If you choose **Single line of text** as the data type, you can change the maximum amount of characters that the field should support. You can also select **Lookup** as the data type and select where the information should come from.

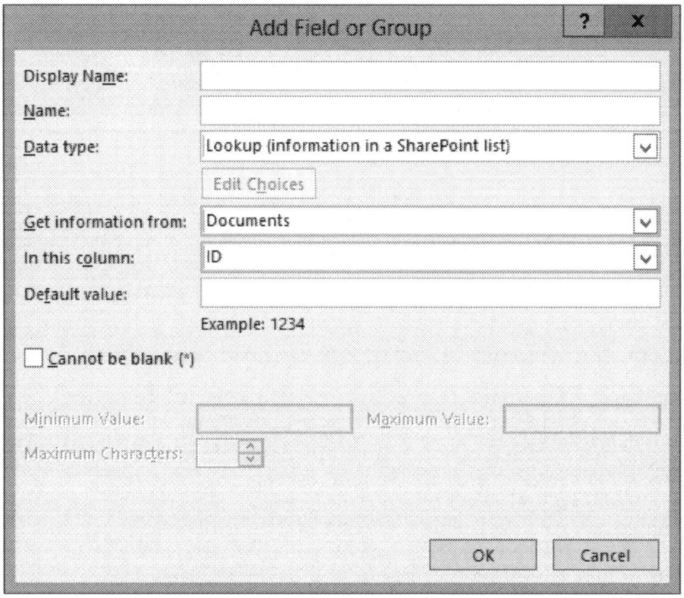

Figure 18. Selecting a Lookup data type on the Add Field or Group dialog box in InfoPath.

Once you publish the form template to SharePoint, the new fields you added to the form template will be locked and their data types cannot be changed anymore. You can see whether a field is locked by the small padlock that appears in the top-right corner of the field's icon on the **Fields** task pane.

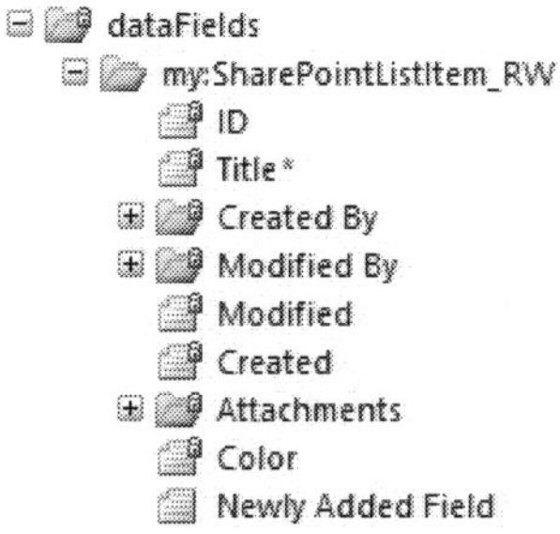

Figure 19. Newly Added Field has not yet been added to the SharePoint list.

In the figure above, all of the fields except for **Newly Added Field** have a padlock icon on them, which means that **Newly Added Field** does not yet exist on the content type associated with the SharePoint list in SharePoint. Once you publish the form template, **Newly Added Field** should appear as a column in the SharePoint list and then also get a padlock icon in InfoPath Designer 2013.

The solution described above adds a field to a SharePoint list from within InfoPath, so the direction is from InfoPath to SharePoint. But you could also go in the opposite direction by first adding a column to the SharePoint list (or content type) and then updating the Main data source in InfoPath to contain a new field that corresponds to the new SharePoint column.

To update the Main data source in InfoPath after you have added a new column to a SharePoint list (or content type) while you had the form template open in InfoPath Designer 2013, click **Data ➤ SharePoint Form Data ➤ Refresh Fields**.

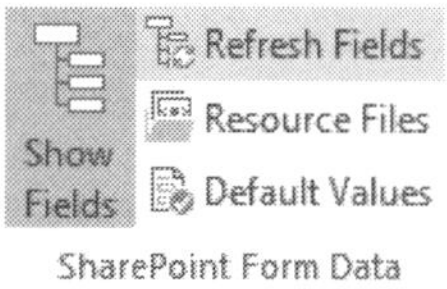

Figure 20. The Refresh Fields command in InfoPath Designer 2013.

5 Delete a field from a SharePoint list through InfoPath

Problem

You have a SharePoint list form template open in InfoPath and want to delete fields from the SharePoint list the form template is linked to, from within InfoPath.

Solution

You must delete a field from the Main data source of a SharePoint list form template and publish the form template in order for the field to be deleted from the content type associated with the SharePoint list.

To delete a field from a SharePoint list through InfoPath:

1. In InfoPath, create a new SharePoint list form template or open an existing one as described in recipe *1 Customize a SharePoint list form from*

within SharePoint or recipe *2 Customize a SharePoint list form from within InfoPath*.

2. On the **Fields** task pane, right-click the field you want to delete, and select **Delete** from the drop-down menu that appears.
3. Read what the message says on the message box that appears, and then click **Yes**.
4. If a control was previously bound to the field you deleted, it will remain unbound on the view of the form template unless you delete it. So select that control on the view and press **Delete** on your keyboard to delete the control from the view.
5. Click **File ➤ Info ➤ Quick Publish**, click **File ➤ Publish ➤ SharePoint List**, or click the **Quick Publish** command on the **Quick Access Toolbar** to publish the form template back to SharePoint.

In SharePoint, navigate to the SharePoint list for which you customized its list form and verify that the column does not exist anymore on the list or on the content type associated with the list.

Discussion

In the solution described above you used the **Fields** task pane to delete a field and consequently also a column from a SharePoint list (or content type) once the form template was published to SharePoint. It is important to remember that when you delete a control from a view of a form template, you do not automatically also delete the field that that control is bound to from the Main data source of the form, so neither from the content type or SharePoint list. So you must use the **Fields** task pane to delete fields.

You can also delete a field from the content type or from the SharePoint list in SharePoint via the **Settings** page of the SharePoint list instead of from within InfoPath. If you delete a field via SharePoint, you can click **Data ➤ SharePoint Form Data ➤ Refresh Fields** in InfoPath Designer 2013 afterwards to remove the deleted field from the list of fields in the Main data source of the form.

6 Restore the default form of a SharePoint list

Problem

You customized the list form for a content type associated with a SharePoint list, but now you want to revert back to the original default form that SharePoint creates for a SharePoint list.

Solution

You can change the type of form used by a SharePoint list through the **Settings** page of the list.

To restore the default form of a SharePoint list:

1. In SharePoint, navigate to the SharePoint list for which you want to restore its list form, and click **List ➤ Settings ➤ List Settings**.
2. On the **Settings** page under **General Settings**, click **Form settings**.
3. On the **Form Settings** page, select the **Use the default SharePoint form** option, select the **Delete the InfoPath Form from the server** check box, and click **OK**. If you do not select the **Delete the InfoPath Form from the server** check box, the customized SharePoint list form will remain on the server and will be used as the starter form template if you ever decide to customize the form again in the future. Note that if a SharePoint list has multiple content types associated with it, SharePoint will display a drop-down list box on the **Form Settings** page from which you can choose the content type for which you want to revert back to its default SharePoint form.

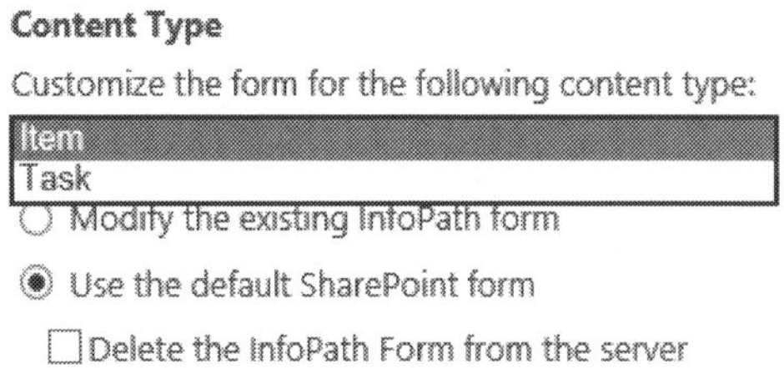

Figure 21. Drop-down list box with two content types on the Form Settings page.

In SharePoint, add a new item to the list or edit an existing item from the list to verify that the InfoPath form is not being used anymore as the SharePoint list form. Note that if you get an error message saying that *The webpage cannot be found*, close and reopen the browser and then try again.

The InfoPath-related options under the **Form Web Parts** command on the Ribbon (**List ➤ Customize List**) should also be gone.

Discussion

In the solution described above, you learned that you can select the **Delete the InfoPath Form from the server** check box on the form settings page when restoring the forms back to the default SharePoint forms. By doing this, you would delete all of the files (ASPX and XSN files) that are located in the content type's folder (see the discussion section of recipe *1 Customize a SharePoint list form from within SharePoint*). If you do not choose to delete the InfoPath form from the server, the next time you customize the list form, the old InfoPath form template would be retrieved and used for customization.

7 Hide the Ribbon for a SharePoint list form

Problem

You want to hide all of the commands that appear on the Ribbon for SharePoint forms when you have a list form open in SharePoint.

Solution

You can hide the Ribbon for a SharePoint list form by configuring an option via the **Form Options** dialog box in InfoPath.

To hide the Ribbon for a SharePoint list form:

1. In InfoPath, create a new SharePoint list form template or open an existing one as described in recipe *1 Customize a SharePoint list form from within SharePoint* or recipe *2 Customize a SharePoint list form from within InfoPath*.

2. Click **File** ➤ **Info** ➤ **Form Options**.
3. On the **Form Options** dialog box, ensure that **Web Browser** is selected in the **Category** list, and then deselect the **Show InfoPath commands in Ribbon or toolbar** check box.

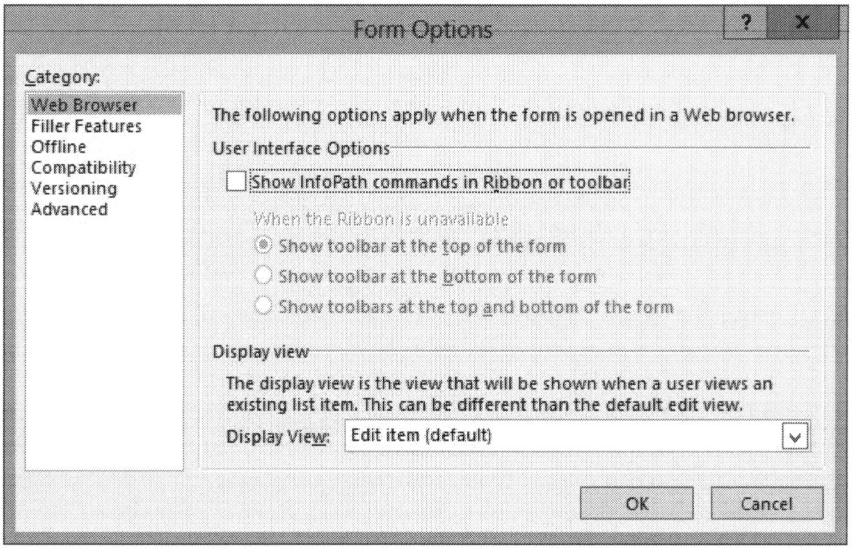

Figure 22. Form Options dialog box screen to hide the Ribbon.

4. On the **Form Options** dialog box, click **OK**.
5. Click **File** ➤ **Info** ➤ **Quick Publish**, click **File** ➤ **Publish** ➤ **SharePoint List**, or click the **Quick Publish** command on the **Quick Access Toolbar** to publish the form template back to SharePoint.

In SharePoint, navigate to the SharePoint list for which you customized its form. Add a new item or open an existing item and verify that the Ribbon is not present anymore.

Discussion

When filling out a SharePoint list form, **Save**, **Close**, **Paste**, **Copy**, and **Cut** commands are displayed on the Ribbon by default.

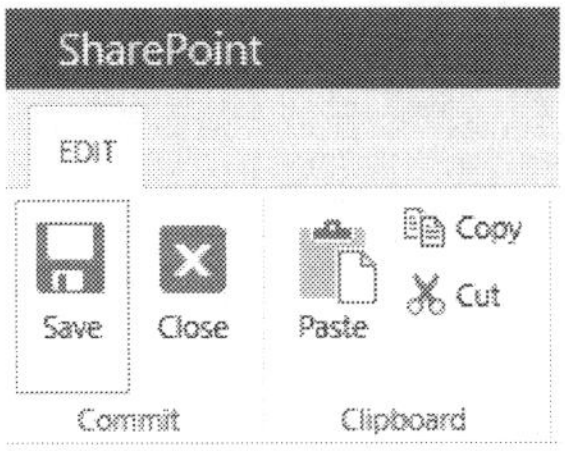

Figure 23. Ribbon commands for a SharePoint list form in SharePoint 2013.

If you have added a custom **Save** button on a SharePoint list form as described in recipe *8 Add a custom Save button to a SharePoint list form*, you may want to prevent users from using the commands on the Ribbon. You can hide the Ribbon through the **Form Options** dialog box in InfoPath as described in the solution above.

8 Add a custom Save button to a SharePoint list form

Method 1: Add an Action rule to a button

Problem

You want users to be able to click a button on a SharePoint list form to be able to save a list item instead of using the standard commands that are present on the Ribbon or in cases where the Ribbon has been hidden as described in recipe *7 Hide the Ribbon for a SharePoint list form*.

Solution

You can add a **Submit data** action rule to a button on a SharePoint list form to save an item back to the SharePoint list.

To add a custom **Save** button to a SharePoint list form:

1. In InfoPath, create a new SharePoint list form template or open an existing one as described in recipe *1 Customize a SharePoint list form from within SharePoint* or recipe *2 Customize a SharePoint list form from within InfoPath*.

2. Add a **Button** control to the view of the form template and label it **Save Item**.
3. Add an **Action** rule to the button control with an action that says:

```
Submit using a data connection: Main Data Connection
```

4. Click **File** ➤ **Info** ➤ **Quick Publish**, click **File** ➤ **Publish** ➤ **SharePoint List**, or click the **Quick Publish** command on the **Quick Access Toolbar** to publish the form template back to SharePoint.

In SharePoint, navigate to the SharePoint list for which you customized its form, and add a new item. Enter some data and then click the **Save Item** button you added. Click the **Close** command on the Ribbon to close the form. The new item you added should be present in the list.

Discussion

In the solution described above, the form will not automatically close once an item has been saved. To have the form automatically close, you would have to add a second action to the **Save Item** button that says:

```
Close this form: No Prompt
```

Or add a separate **Close** button that has an **Action** rule set on it to close the form.

Method 2: Configure the Action property of a button

Problem

You want users to be able to click a button on a SharePoint list form to be able to save a list item instead of using the standard commands that are present on the Ribbon or in cases where the Ribbon has been hidden as described in recipe *7 Hide the Ribbon for a SharePoint list form*.

Solution

You can add a button that has a **Submit** action defined on it that will run actions to save an item back to the SharePoint list and then close the form.

To add a custom **Save** button to a SharePoint list form:

1. In InfoPath, create a new SharePoint list form template or open an existing one as described in recipe *1 Customize a SharePoint list form from within SharePoint* or recipe *2 Customize a SharePoint list form from within InfoPath*.
2. Add a **Button** control to the view of the form template.
3. On the **Properties** tab under the **Button** group, select **Submit** from the **Action** drop-down list box. The label of the button should automatically change to **Submit**.
4. On the **Properties** tab under the **Button** group in the **Label** text box, replace **Submit** with **Save Item** to change the label of the button.

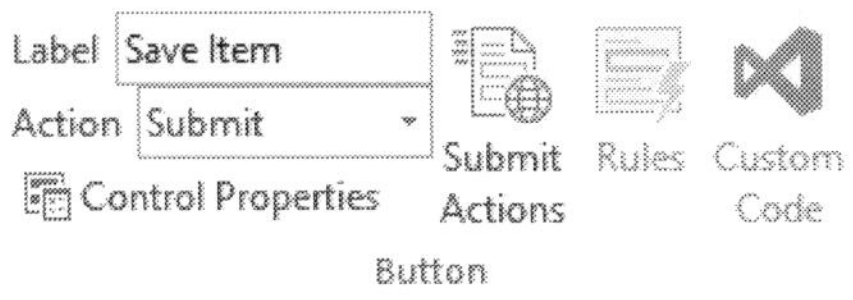

Figure 24. Commands under the Button group on the Properties tab in InfoPath.

5. Click **File ➤ Info ➤ Quick Publish**, click **File ➤ Publish ➤ SharePoint List**, or click the **Quick Publish** command on the **Quick Access Toolbar** to publish the form template back to SharePoint.

In SharePoint, navigate to the SharePoint list for which you customized its form, and add a new item. Enter some data and then click the **Save Item** button you added. The form should automatically close and the new item you added should be present in the list.

Discussion

The **Submit** button action performs the actions that have been defined on the **Submit Options** dialog box, which you can open via **Data ➤ Submit Form ➤ Submit Options** or via **Properties ➤ Button ➤ Submit Actions**. The default actions for a SharePoint list form are to send the data to a SharePoint list and then close the form.

Note that you can select **Leave the form open** in the **After submit** drop-down list box on the **Submit Options** dialog box to leave the form open after the item has been saved, or you can select **Open a new form** to open a new form immediately after an item has been saved.

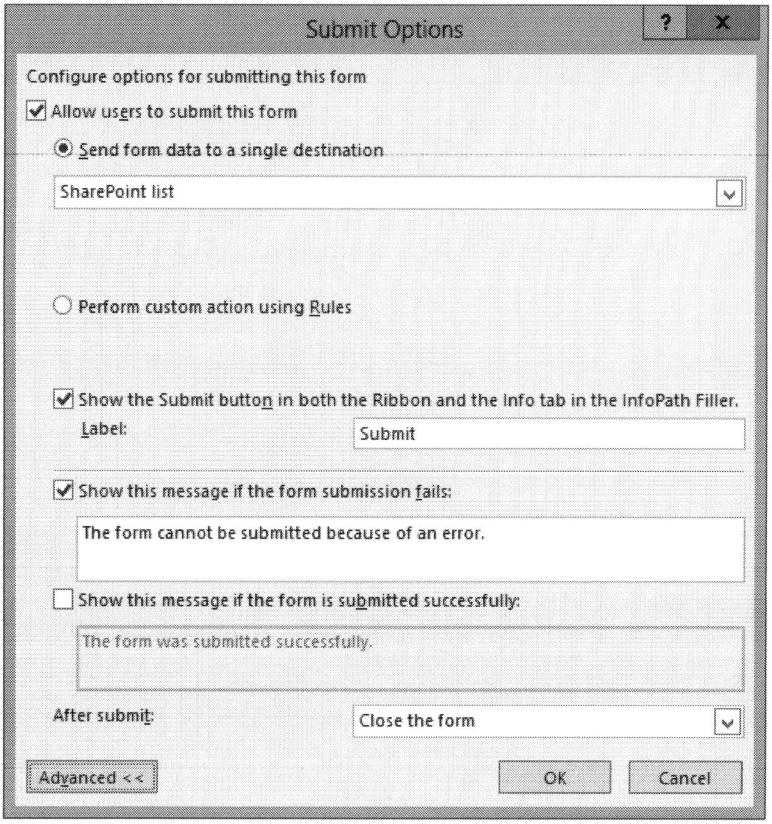

Figure 25. The Submit Options dialog box as configured by default for a list form.

Query data through SharePoint list forms

The main data connection of a SharePoint list form not only submits data to the SharePoint list the form is connected to, but it also supports retrieving data from the SharePoint list through querying. The recipes in this section show you how to run queries on SharePoint list forms to retrieve specific data from a SharePoint list.

9 Add query functionality to a SharePoint list form

Problem

You have a SharePoint list form with which you can view, add, or edit one SharePoint list item at a time. You want to be able to type the name of a specific list item in a text box, and then retrieve data for that particular item, so that you can edit it.

Solution

You can use the fields that are located under the **queryFields** group node in the Main data source to search for an existing SharePoint list item and populate the form with its data.

To add query functionality to a SharePoint list form:

1. In InfoPath, create a new SharePoint list form template or open an existing one as described in recipe *1 Customize a SharePoint list form from within SharePoint* or recipe *2 Customize a SharePoint list form from within InfoPath*.
2. On the **Fields** task pane, click **Show advanced view** if **basic view** is being shown. This should display the **queryFields** and **dataFields** group nodes in the Main data source.
3. On the **Fields** task pane, expand the **queryFields** group node, expand the **q:SharePointListItem_RW** group node, and then drag-and-drop the **Title** field onto the view of the form template to automatically bind it to a text box control.
4. Add a **Button** control to the view of the form template, and change its **Action** property from **Rules** to **Run Query**.

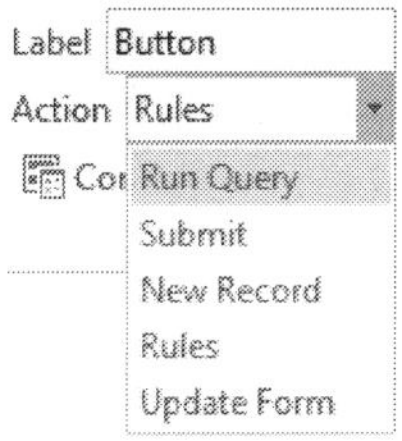

Figure 26. Selecting the Run Query action for a button in InfoPath Designer 2013.

5. Publish the form template to SharePoint.

In SharePoint, navigate to the SharePoint list for which you customized its form, and add a new item. When the form opens, click the **Run Query** button. The data for the first item in the list should be retrieved and displayed on the form. Note that if you created a SharePoint list form that manages multiple list items as described in recipe *3 Create a SharePoint list form to manage multiple list items*, all of the SharePoint list items would be retrieved and displayed on the form. Type the title for an existing item in the query text box for the **Title** field, and click the **Run Query** button. The form should be populated with data for that specific item from the SharePoint list.

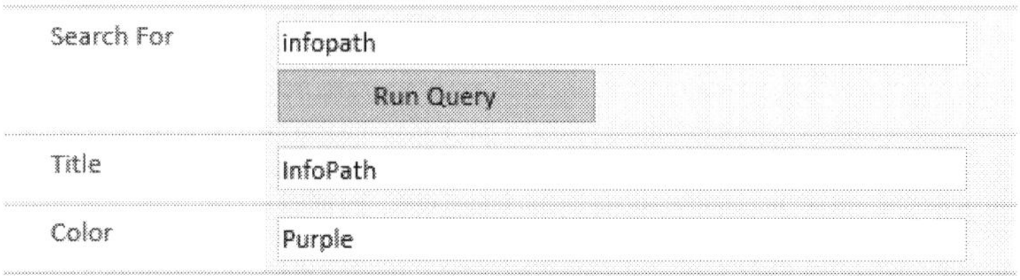

Figure 27. The InfoPath form displaying the query results for a search on 'infopath'.

Discussion

In general, when you are editing SharePoint list items directly in a SharePoint list, you can open a specific item without performing a query to find the right item to edit. Therefore, the solution described above is better suited for scenarios where you do not want to have users access a SharePoint list directly, but rather place an InfoPath form on a web page, so that they can search for and edit items through a web page (also see recipe *13 Embed a SharePoint list form on a SharePoint page*).

When you add a button control to a SharePoint list form, you can set the button to perform one of the following actions:

- Run Query – Runs a query on the main data connection.
- Submit – Submits data to the SharePoint list.
- New Record – Clears all of the fields on the form for entering new data.

- Rules – Allows you to add custom rules to a button.
- Update Form – Updates form data in an incremental manner.

When you set the **Action** property of a button to anything other than **Rules**, you are only allowed to add additional formatting rules to the button, but no custom action rules. If you want to add custom action rules to a button, you must set the **Action** property of the button to **Rules**.

There is an additional button action named **Refresh** with which you can refresh one or all of the secondary data sources in an InfoPath form using the corresponding data connections. This action only appears in the list of button actions when you add one or more secondary data sources to a form template.

If you want to retrieve all of the data contained in a SharePoint list without filtering it, you can add a button to the view of the form template and set its **Action** property to **Run Query**. This is the quickest way to create a "query and return all" button. A second way is to add a button to the form template and set its **Action** property to **Rules**, and then add an **Action** rule to the button that has a **Query for data** action that queries the main data connection of the form.

10 Query for multiple items in a SharePoint list form

Problem

You created a SharePoint list form with which you can manage multiple list items. Because the list is fairly long, you want to be able to query for specific items in the list, so that you can quickly retrieve and edit them.

Solution

You can add query functionality to a multi-itemed SharePoint list form by using the fields that are located under the **queryFields** group node in the Main data source of the form.

Suppose you have a SharePoint list named **OfficeApplications** as described in *Create a SharePoint list form for an existing SharePoint list* in recipe *2 Customize a SharePoint list form from within InfoPath* and you want to be able to search on either the **Title** or the **Color** field. You can add a drop-down list box to the form template that switches between searching on **Title** or **Color**, and then use the selected item in the drop-down list box to set the value of the **Title** or **Color** field that is located under the **q:SharePointListItem_RW** group node under the **queryFields** group node in the Main data source of the form before running the query.

Because you must bind a drop-down list box to a field and there is no field in the Main data source that provides the names of fields, you can use a secondary data source that contains the field names as a helper data source. Note that if you add a field to the Main data source to bind the drop-down list box to, it would create an unnecessary column (a column that does not really have anything to do with storing data for a list item) in the SharePoint list. To avoid this, you can make use of a secondary data source, because data from secondary data sources is not permanently stored in the form itself unless you opt to store a copy of the data in the form template when you create the data connection. In any case, a secondary data source does not affect the structure of the Main data source of the form, so also does not add unnecessary columns to the SharePoint list.

To create a drop-down list box that contains the names of fields you want to query on, you can create an XML file named **FilterColumns.xml** that has the following contents:

```
<filtercolumns>
  <selectedvalue/>
  <columns>
    <column>Title</column>
    <column>Color</column>
  </columns>
</filtercolumns>
```

To query for multiple items in a SharePoint list form:

1. In InfoPath, create a new SharePoint list form that manages multiple items as described in recipe *3 Create a SharePoint list form to manage multiple list items.*

2. Select **Data ➤ Get External Data ➤ From Other Sources ➤ From XML File** and follow the instructions to add an XML data connection for the **FilterColumns.xml** file to the form template. Name the data connection **FilterColumns** and leave the **Automatically retrieve data when form is opened** check box selected.
3. Click **Insert ➤ Tables ➤ Custom Table**, and add a custom table with one row and two columns above the repeating section on the view of the form template.
4. On the **Fields** task pane, click **Show advanced view** if **basic view** is being shown, and then select **FilterColumns (Secondary)** from the drop-down list box.
5. Right-click the **selectedvalue** field, drag it to the view of the form template, drop it in the first column of the custom table, and select **Drop-Down List Box** from the context menu that appears.
6. Open the **Drop-Down List Box Properties** dialog box, and configure the list box choices to come from the **FilterColumns** data source, with the **Entries** property set to be equal to the **column** repeating field under the **columns** group node, and both the **Value** and **Display name** properties set to be equal to a dot (**.**), which represents the **column** repeating field. Click **OK** when you are done.

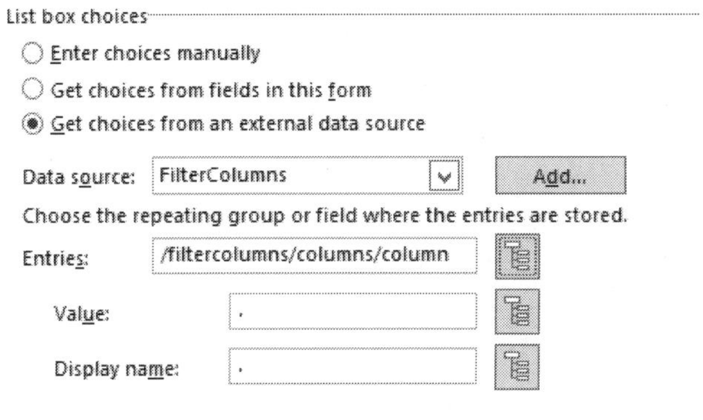

Figure 28. Configuration settings for the drop-down list box.

7. On the **Fields** task pane, select **Main** from the drop-down list box.
8. On the **Fields** task pane, expand the **queryFields** group node, expand the **q:SharePointListItem_RW** group node, drag-and-drop the **Title** field in the second column of the custom table, and then drag-and-drop

the **Color** field and place it below the text box for the **Title** field in the second column of the custom table.

9. Add a **Button** control below the custom table on the view of the form template and set its **Action** property to **Run Query**.
10. Add an **Action** rule to the **selectedvalue** drop-down list box with the following 2 actions that say:

```
Set a field's value: Title = ""
Set a field's value: Color = ""
```

where **Title** and **Color** are fields that are located under the **q:SharePointListItem_RW** group node under the **queryFields** group node in the Main data source. This rule clears any text you previously entered in either the **Title** or **Color** query text boxes.

11. Add a **Formatting** rule to the **Title** query text box that has a **Condition** that says:

```
selectedvalue ≠ "Title"
or
selectedvalue is blank
```

and that has a formatting of **Hide this control**. Here, **selectedValue** is the **selectedValue** field in the **FilterColumns** secondary data source and **Title** is a static piece of text. This rule hides the **Title** query text box if no item has been selected in the drop-down list box or if **Title** has not been selected in the drop-down list box.

12. Add a **Formatting** rule to the **Color** query text box that has a **Condition** that says:

```
selectedvalue ≠ "Color"
or
selectedvalue is blank
```

and that has a formatting of **Hide this control**. Here, **selectedValue** is the **selectedValue** field in the **FilterColumns** secondary data source and **Color** is a static piece of text. This rule hides the **Color** query text box if no item has been selected in the drop-down list box or if **Color** has not been selected in the drop-down list box.

13. Publish the form template to SharePoint.

In SharePoint, navigate to the SharePoint list for which you customized its form, and add a new item. When the form opens, select a field to search on from the drop-down list box, for example, **Title**. The query text box for the **Title** field should appear. Type a piece of text into the text box, for example, **Word**, and click the **Run Query** button. The SharePoint list item containing **Word** in its **Title** field should appear. Repeat these steps and search for items that have the same color (if your SharePoint list does not have any such items, add a few items). Multiple items that have the same color should appear in the repeating section. Select the empty item from the drop-down list box, and then click the **Run Query** button. All of the items from the SharePoint list should appear.

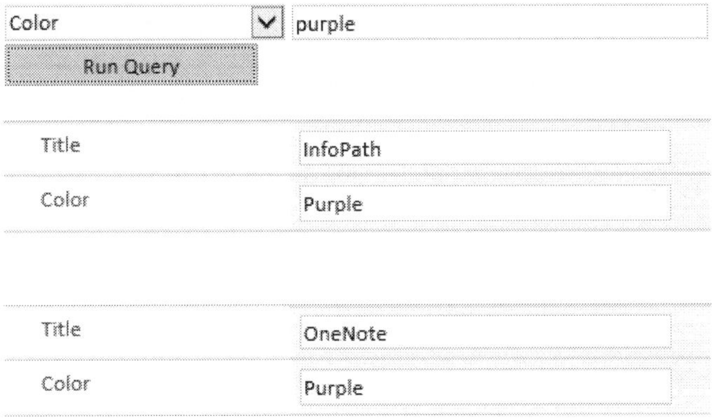

Figure 29. The InfoPath form displaying Office applications that have a 'purple' color.

Discussion

The solution described above made use of an XML file that provided data for a drop-down list box. This XML file contained a field (**selectedvalue**) which you used to bind the drop-down list box to, as well as the items (**column** repeating field) to fill the drop-down list box. Adding this XML file to the form template and then binding the drop-down list box to a field in the secondary data source for the XML file helped you avoid having to add unnecessary fields to the underlying SharePoint list (or content type) of the form for the sole purpose of adding query functionality.

Drop-down list boxes can also be populated with static values. But in the case of SharePoint list forms, as soon as you try to add a drop-down list box via the **Controls** task pane or the **Controls** group on the **Home** tab, you are prompted to enter choices manually or look up the choices in a SharePoint list. Selecting either option would create a field in the Main data source and in the underlying SharePoint list (or content type) of the form.

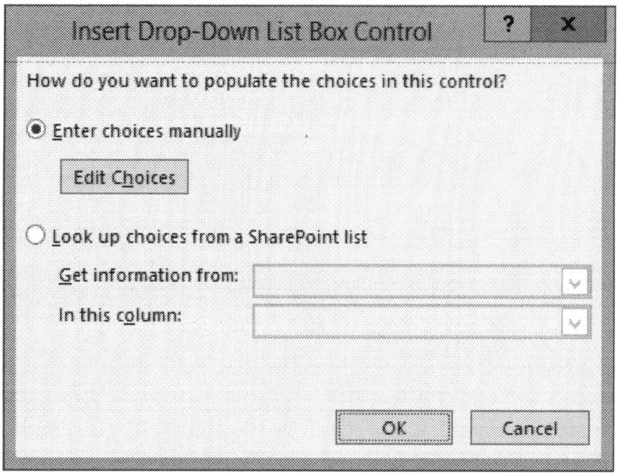

Figure 30. Dialog box to select choices for a drop-down list box on a SharePoint list form.

Tip:

> If you ever need fields to provide supporting functionality in a SharePoint list form, but do not want to add those fields as columns to the SharePoint list (or content type), you can create an XML file that contains the supporting fields and then add that XML file as a secondary data source to the form.

11 Perform wildcard searches with a SharePoint list form

Problem

You created a SharePoint list form with which you can manage multiple list items. You want to be able to type a piece of text into a text box, and then have the SharePoint list items that match part of, or the entire search term, appear on the form.

Solution

You can use conditional formatting on the repeating section or repeating table that displays the SharePoint list items in combination with the **contains()** and **translate()** functions to be able to perform filtering on items in a SharePoint list.

Suppose you have a SharePoint list named **OfficeApplications** as described in *Create a SharePoint list form for an existing SharePoint list* in recipe *2 Customize a SharePoint list form from within InfoPath* and you want to be able to perform a wildcard search on the **Title** field.

Because you require a separate field in which a user can type a search term and because any fields you add to the Main data source of the form will also be added to the underlying SharePoint list, you can make use of a secondary data source in order not to add unnecessary columns to the SharePoint list. For the latter you can use the **FilterColumns.xml** file you used in recipe *10 Query for multiple items in a SharePoint list form*.

To perform wildcard searches with a SharePoint list form:

1. In InfoPath, create a new SharePoint list form that manages multiple items as described in recipe *3 Create a SharePoint list form to manage multiple list items*.
2. Select **Data ➤ Get External Data ➤ From Other Sources ➤ From XML File** and follow the instructions to add an XML data connection for the **FilterColumns.xml** file. Name the data connection **FilterColumns** and leave the **Automatically retrieve data when form is opened** check box selected.
3. On the **Fields** task pane, click **Show advanced view** if **basic view** is being shown, and then select **FilterColumns (Secondary)** from the drop-down list box.
4. Drag-and-drop the **selectedvalue** field onto the view of the form template just above the repeating section. It should automatically get bound to a text box control.

5. Add a **Button** control to the view of the form template and set its **Action** property to **Run Query**.
6. Add a **Formatting** rule to the repeating section control (the **my:SharePointListItem_RW** repeating group node) that has a **The expression** condition that says:

```
not(contains(translate(my:Title, "ABCDEFGHIJKLMNOPQRSTUVWXYZ",
"abcdefghijklmnopqrstuvwxyz"),
translate(xdXDocument:GetDOM("FilterColumns")/filtercolumns/sel
ectedvalue, "ABCDEFGHIJKLMNOPQRSTUVWXYZ",
"abcdefghijklmnopqrstuvwxyz")))
```

   with a formatting of **Hide this control**. Here, **selectedValue** is the **selectedValue** field in the **FilterColumns** secondary data source and **Title** is the **Title** field that is located under the **my:SharePointListItem_RW** group node under the **dataFields** group node in the Main data source. This rule hides any section in the repeating section control if the **Title** field does not contain the piece of text entered in the **selectedvalue** text box.
7. Publish the form template to SharePoint.

In SharePoint, navigate to the SharePoint list for which you customized its form, and add a new item. When the form opens, click the **Run Query** button. All of the items from the SharePoint list should appear. Type a piece of text in the **selectedvalue** text box, and then click the **Run Query** button. A section should appear for each SharePoint list item that has the piece of text you searched for in its **Title** field.

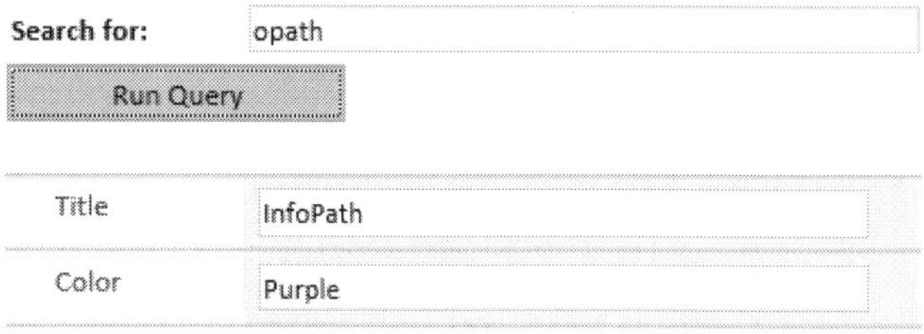

Figure 31. SharePoint list form to perform a wildcard search on items in a SharePoint list.

Discussion

The solution described above made use of an XML file so that you could bind a field to a text box control on the form without having to add this field to the underlying SharePoint list for the sole purpose of adding search and filter functionality to the form (also see the discussion section of recipe *10 Query for multiple items in a SharePoint list form*).

In addition, you made use of the **translate()** function in a condition of a formatting rule to be able to perform non-case-sensitive filtering on the data in the repeating section.

12 Add new record functionality to a SharePoint list form

Problem

You have a SharePoint list form, which you would like to use to add new items to a SharePoint list.

Solution

You can add a button that has its **Action** property set to **New Record** to the view of the form template to clear the form in preparation for entering new data for a new SharePoint list item.

To add new record functionality to a SharePoint list form:

1. In InfoPath, create a new SharePoint list form template or open an existing one as described in recipe *1 Customize a SharePoint list form from within SharePoint* or recipe *2 Customize a SharePoint list form from within InfoPath*.
2. Add a **Button** control to the view of the form template and set its **Action** property to **Run Query**. You will use this button to populate the form with data from the first item in the SharePoint list for testing purposes.
3. Add a second **Button** control to the view of the form template and set its **Action** property to **New Record**. The **Label** for the button should automatically change to the text **New Record**.
4. Publish the form template to SharePoint.

In SharePoint, navigate to the SharePoint list for which you customized its form, and add a new item. When the form opens, click the **Run Query** button. The form should get populated with data (if did not, populate it with some data by manually filling out the fields). Click the **New Record** button. The fields on the form should get cleared. Now you can enter fresh data and then click **Save** to submit the data as a new item to the SharePoint list.

Figure 32. The first item in the list being shown after clicking the Run Query button.

Figure 33. The InfoPath form with cleared fields after clicking the New Record button.

Discussion

The **New Record** button action clears a form in preparation for entering data for a new record or list item as shown in the solution described above. Note that you can only add formatting rules to a **New Record** button, and that you cannot add any validation or action rules to it.

Display SharePoint list forms

SharePoint list forms are by default displayed embedded in an InfoPath Form Web Part on three web part pages that are used for viewing, adding, or editing SharePoint list data (also see the discussion section of recipe *1 Customize a SharePoint list form from within SharePoint*). While you can customize these web part pages to further suit your needs, you can also use the InfoPath Form Web Part on other pages within a SharePoint site to display a SharePoint list form. The recipes in this section show you how to do the latter.

13 Embed a SharePoint list form on a SharePoint page

Problem

You want to place the InfoPath form for a SharePoint list on a page in a SharePoint site so that users can easily fill out the form without having to navigate to the SharePoint list.

Solution

You can use an **InfoPath Form Web Part** to embed an InfoPath form on a page in SharePoint.

To embed a SharePoint list form in an InfoPath Form Web Part on a SharePoint page:

1. In InfoPath, create a new SharePoint list form template or open an existing one as described in recipe *1 Customize a SharePoint list form from within SharePoint* or recipe *2 Customize a SharePoint list form from within InfoPath*, customize it to suit your needs, and publish it to SharePoint.
2. In SharePoint, navigate to the page on which you want to embed the SharePoint list form, and then click **Page ➤ Edit ➤ Edit** or click the small **Edit** command on the Ribbon. Note that you can select **Add a page** from the **Settings** menu (the gear icon in the top-right corner) to add a new page to a site if you do not already have a page.
3. Click anywhere on the page where you want to embed the InfoPath form, and then click **Insert ➤ Parts ➤ Web Part**.

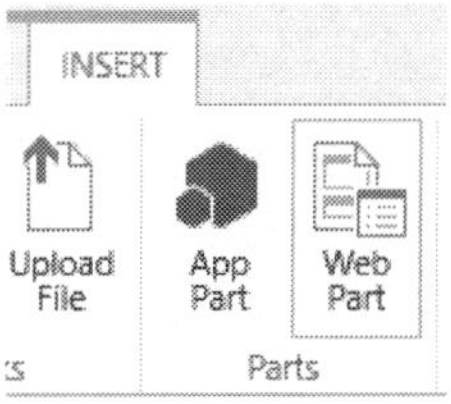

Figure 34. Inserting a web part on a SharePoint page.

4. At the top of the page, select **Forms** in the **Categories** list, select **InfoPath Form Web Part** in the **Parts** list, and click **Add**.

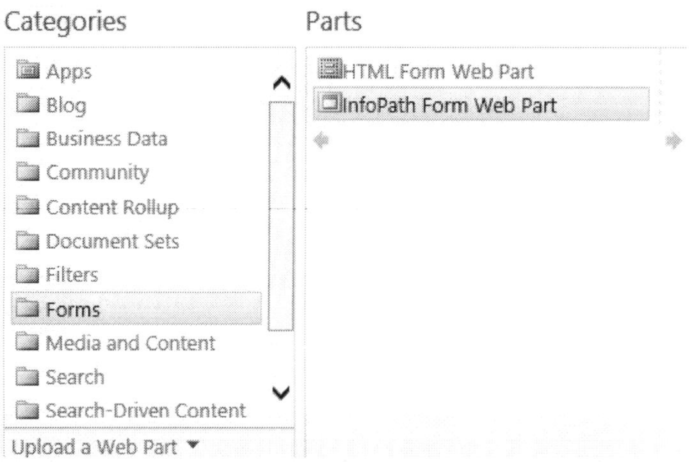

Figure 35. Selecting the InfoPath Form Web Part in SharePoint 2013.

5. Once the web part has been added to the page, you must configure it to display the SharePoint list form. So on the web part, click on the text that says **Click here to open the tool pane**.

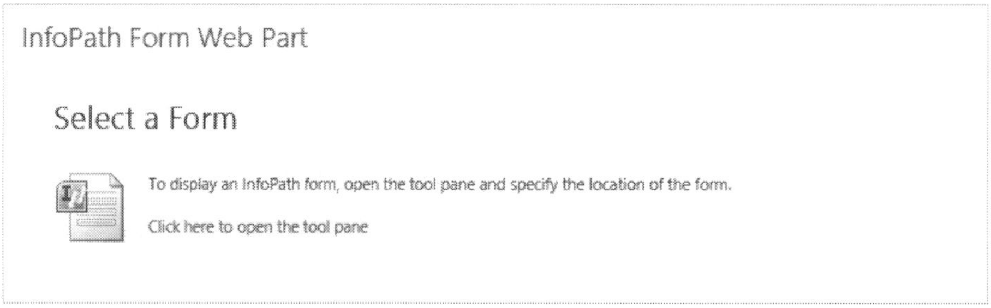

Figure 36. InfoPath Form Web Part on a SharePoint page.

6. On the web part tool pane on the right-hand side of the page, select the SharePoint list that is connected to the SharePoint list form you want to embed from the **List or Library** drop-down list box.
7. On the web part tool pane, select the content type for which you want to display its SharePoint list form from the **Content Type** drop-down list box. The content types that have InfoPath forms associated with them, so for which you have customized their SharePoint list forms, are listed in the **Content Type** drop-down list box. So if a SharePoint list is associated with more than one content type that has a customized

SharePoint list form, multiple content types should be listed in the drop-down list box.

8. If you want to display a read-only form for a list item when the form initially opens, you can select the **Display a read-only form (lists only)** check box on the web part tool pane. Users would then have to click the **Edit Item** command on the Ribbon before they can edit and save a list item. Leave this check box deselected for now; this should display an editable form for a list item as soon as the form opens.

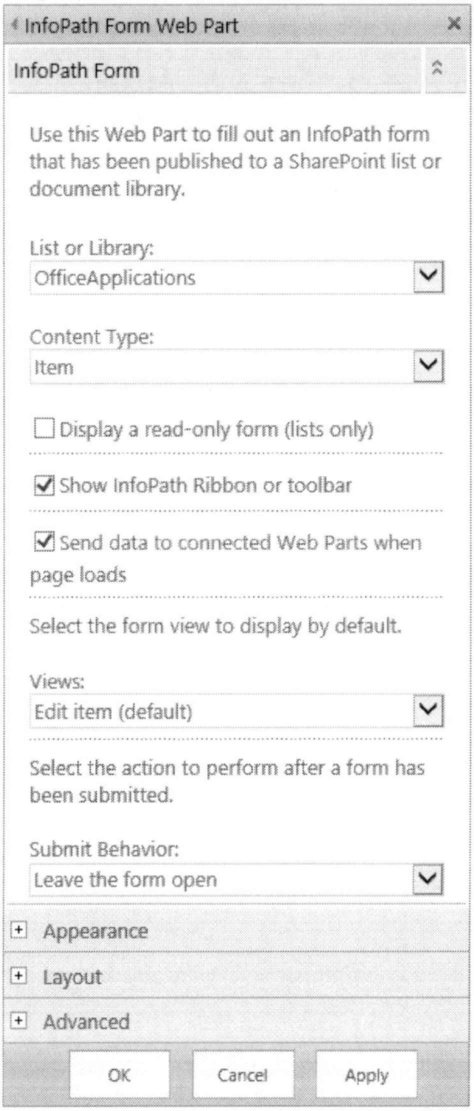

Figure 37. Settings on the web part tool pane in SharePoint 2013.

Note that you can choose what to do with the form once the list item has been saved by selecting the **Close the form**, **Open a new form**, or **Leave the form open** option from the **Submit Behavior** drop-down list box on the web part tool pane. Also note that these options are not linked to the **After submit** options that you can select on the **Submit Options** dialog box in InfoPath Designer 2013, and that the embedded SharePoint list form behaves according to the web part settings.

9. On the web part tool pane, expand **Appearance** and change the **Title** of the web part to a suitable title (for example **Office Applications**).
10. On the web part tool pane, configure any other options you would like to configure, and then click **OK**.
11. Click **Page ➤ Edit ➤ Save** or click the small **Save** command on the Ribbon to save and stop editing the page.

The InfoPath form should now be embedded in the web part on the page and you should be able to fill it out and save it.

Figure 38. The InfoPath form embedded on a SharePoint page.

Note that to save the list item, you must select the **Edit** tab to bring forward the Ribbon commands for the InfoPath form, and then click **Save**. To make the **Edit** tab appear, click anywhere on the form.

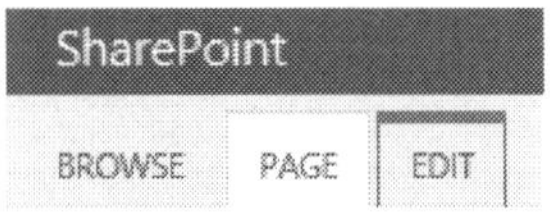

Figure 39. The Edit tab that appears when an InfoPath form has the focus on a page.

14 Master/detail with two linked SharePoint lists

Problem

You have two related SharePoint lists and you want to use the display form of the base SharePoint list to edit an item, but also display its related items from the related SharePoint list and access any of those items for editing.

Solution

You can add a filtered list for the related list to the **Display Form** web part page of the base SharePoint list to create master/detail functionality.

Suppose you have a base SharePoint list named **SoftwareCategories** with the following contents:

Title
Servers
Office Applications
Development Tools

and a second SharePoint list named **SoftwareProducts** that is related to the **SoftwareCategories** list through a **Category** lookup column (linked to the **Title** column in the **SoftwareCategories** list) and that has the following contents:

Title	**Category (Lookup in Title in SoftwareCategories)**
SQL Server	Servers
Word	Office Applications
Excel	Office Applications
Visual Studio	Development Tools

Additional Column Settings

Specify detailed options for the type of information you selected.

Description:

Require that this column contains information:

 ○ Yes ◉ No

Enforce unique values:

 ○ Yes ◉ No

Get information from:

 [SoftwareCategories ∨]

In this column:

 [Title ∨]

 ☐ Allow multiple values

Add a column to show each of these additional fields:

 ☐ ID
 ☐ Title
 ☐ Modified
 ☐ Created
 ☐ Version
 ☐ Title (linked to item)

 ☑ Add to default view

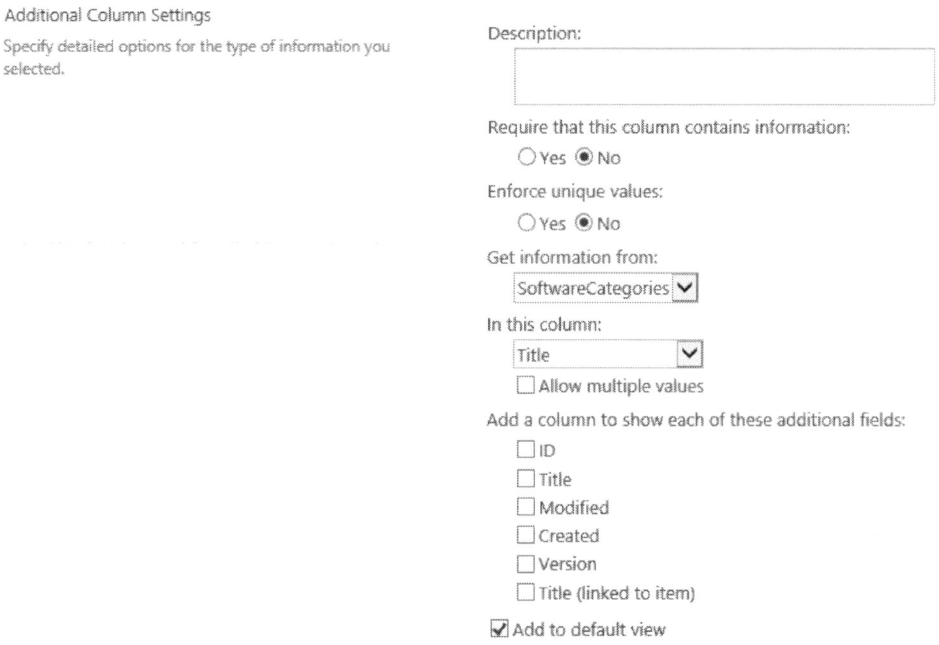

Figure 40. Additional column settings for the Category lookup column.

To modify the **Display Form** web part page that is used to display the **SoftwareCategories** SharePoint list to be able to create master/detail functionality between two linked SharePoint lists:

1. Customize the SharePoint list form for the **SoftwareCategories** list as described in recipe *1 Customize a SharePoint list form from within SharePoint* and publish the form template to SharePoint.

2. In SharePoint, navigate to the **SoftwareCategories** list, and select **List ➤ Customize List ➤ Form Web Parts ➤ (Item) Display Form**.

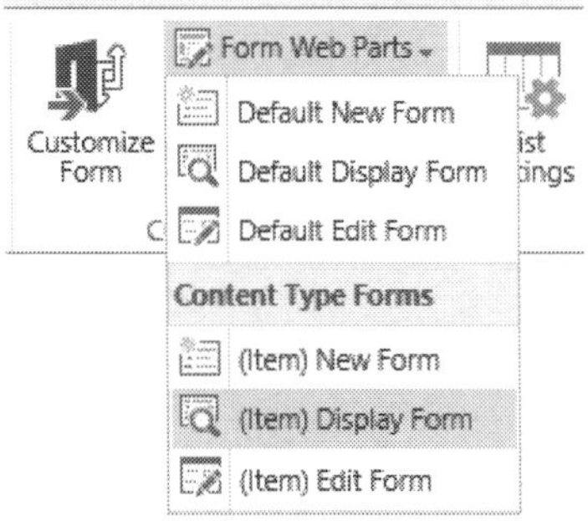

Figure 41. Selecting to edit the Display Form of a content type of a SharePoint list.

This should open the web part page of the **Display Form** in edit mode. Note that the text **(Item)** may vary in your case depending on the content types you have associated with the list. Also note that the SharePoint list form is embedded in an InfoPath Form Web Part on the web part page.

3. On the **Display Form** web part page, click **Add a Web Part**.
4. At the top of the page, select **Apps** in the **Categories** list, select **SoftwareProducts** in the **Parts** list, and click **Add**. This should add a list web part above the InfoPath Form Web Part for the **SoftwareCategories** list that was already present on the page.
5. Rearrange the web parts by dragging-and-dropping the **SoftwareProducts** list web part to a location below the InfoPath Form Web Part for the **SoftwareCategories** list.
6. Hover over the **SoftwareProducts** list web part, click the drop-down arrow that appears in the top-right corner of the web part, and select **Connections ➤ Get Filter Values From ➤ InfoPath Form Web Part**.

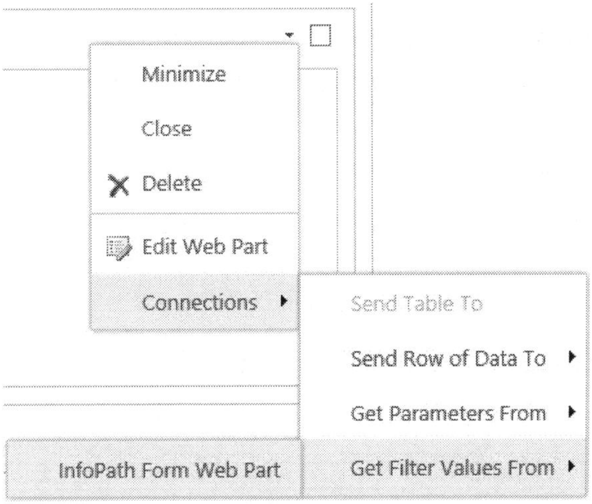

Figure 42. Initiating the configuration of a web part connection.

7. On the **Configure Connection** webpage dialog, leave **ID** selected in the **Provider Field Name** drop-down list box, select **Category** from the **Consumer Field Name** drop-down list box, and click **Finish**.

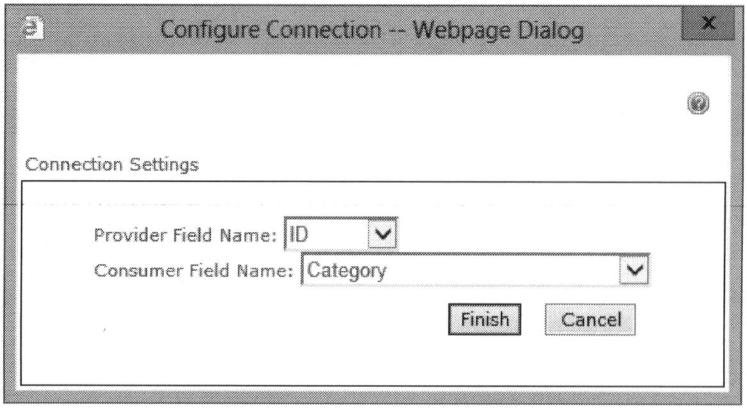

Figure 43. Configuring the web part filter connection in SharePoint 2013.

With this you have configured the **SoftwareProducts** list web part to be filtered by the **ID** of the item displayed in the **SoftwareCategories** InfoPath Form Web Part.

8. Click **Page ➤ Edit ➤ Stop Editing** on the Ribbon.

In SharePoint, navigate to the **SoftwareCategories** SharePoint list and click on an item in the list. When the display page opens, the software products corresponding to the category you selected should appear below the form with which you can view the information for the category.

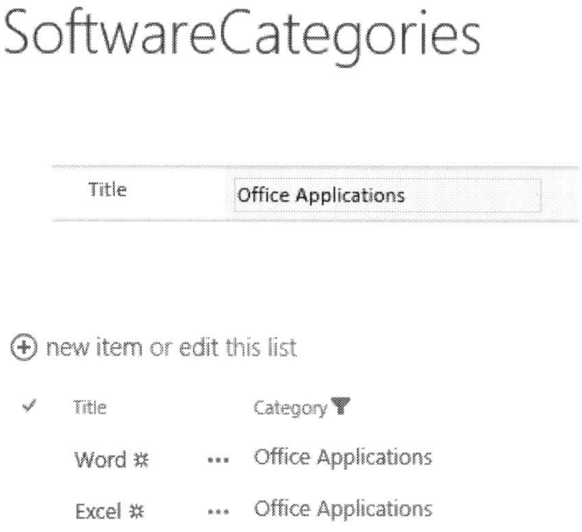

Figure 44. The Display Form for a SharePoint list item showing related items.

Click **new item** to add another software product for the category. Enter the details for the new software product, ensure that you relate the new software product to the software category you currently have open, and then save the item. The new software product should appear in the software products list. If you want to edit any details for the category itself, you must click on the form for the category to make the **View** tab appear, and then click **View ➤ Manage ➤ Edit Item** on the Ribbon. If you want to edit the details for an existing software product, you can click on the software product you want to edit to open its display page.

Discussion

Once you have customized a form for a SharePoint list, that form is embedded in an InfoPath Form Web Part on web part pages for the new, edit, and display pages of a SharePoint list item. You can open and edit these web part pages via the **Form Web Parts** command under the **Customize List** group on the **List** tab on the Ribbon. And once you are in edit mode for the web part page, you can treat the page like any other web part page by adding and removing web parts, customizing the web parts to suit your needs, and setting up web part connections.

In the solution described above, you modified the **Display Form** web part page to include an extra SharePoint list web part that used a filter to display only those items that were linked to the item displayed by the InfoPath form. A caveat of this solution is that when you click to add a new detail item, the drop-down list box that contains the names of the software categories for the detail item does not automatically select the correct category pertaining to the master item, so the category must be manually selected.

15 Master/detail between a SharePoint list and an InfoPath form

Problem

You customized the form of a SharePoint list. Now you want to only display the **Title** column of the list in a web part on the left-hand side of a page and then when you select an item from the list, display the selected item's details in an InfoPath form on the right-hand side of the page.

Solution

You can create a SharePoint view for the SharePoint list, embed the SharePoint list in a web part, and then use web part connections to connect the SharePoint list web part to an InfoPath Form Web Part that displays the details for a list item.

Suppose you have a SharePoint list named **OfficeApplications** as described in *Create a SharePoint list form for an existing SharePoint list* in recipe *2 Customize a SharePoint list form from within InfoPath*.

To use an InfoPath form as the detail view for items in a master SharePoint list on a page:

1. Customize the SharePoint list form for the **OfficeApplications** list as described in recipe *1 Customize a SharePoint list form from within SharePoint* and publish the form template to SharePoint.
2. In SharePoint, navigate to the **OfficeApplications** list, and click **List ➤ Manage Views ➤ Create View**.
3. On the **View Type** page, click **Standard View**.
4. Because you want to display only the titles of Office applications in a list on the left-hand side of a page, you must create a separate view for the **OfficeApplications** list that only contains the **Title** column and that can be selected to be used as the view for a list embedded in a web part. So on the **Create View** page, enter a **View Name** (for example **TitleOnlyView**), deselect all of the check boxes under the **Display** column except for the check box for the **Title** column, and click **OK**.

5. Select **Add a page** from the **Settings** menu (the gear icon in the top-right corner).
6. On the **Add a page** dialog, enter **OfficeApplicationsDetails** in the **New page name** text box, and then click **Create**.
7. When the page opens, select **Format Text ➤ Layout ➤ Text Layout ➤ Two columns**.
8. Place the cursor in the left column on the page, and then click **Insert ➤ Parts ➤ Web Part**.
9. At the top of the page, select **Apps** in the **Categories** list, select **OfficeApplications** in the **Parts** list, and click **Add**.
10. Hover over the web part, click the drop-down arrow that appears in the top-right corner of the **OfficeApplications** web part, and select **Edit Web Part** from the drop-down menu that appears.
11. On the web part tool pane, select **TitleOnlyView** from the **Selected View** drop-down list box, click **OK** on the message box that appears, and then click **OK** to close the web part tool pane.

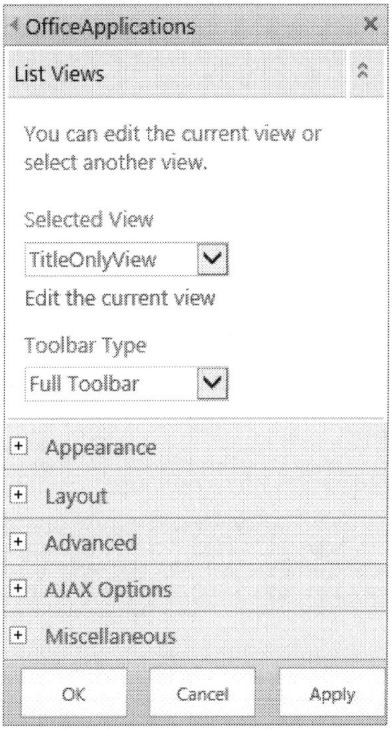

Figure 45. Selecting the view to use on the web part tool pane.

12. Place the cursor in the right column on the page, and then click **Insert ➤ Parts ➤ Web Part**.
13. At the top of the page, select **Forms** in the **Categories** list, select **InfoPath Form Web Part** in the **Parts** list, and click **Add**.
14. Hover over the InfoPath Form Web Part, click the drop-down arrow that appears in the top-right corner of the web part, and select **Edit Web Part** from the drop-down menu that appears.
15. Click the drop-down arrow in the top-right corner of the InfoPath Form Web Part again, and select **Connections ➤ Get Form From ➤ OfficeApplications** from the drop-down menu that appears.

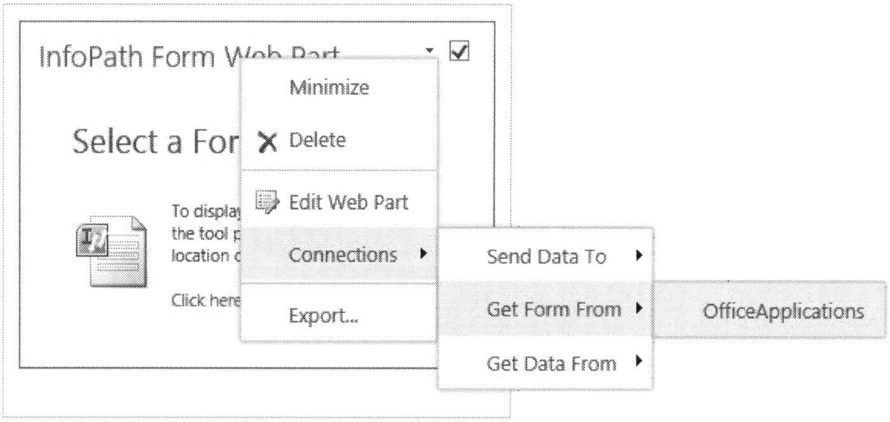

Figure 46. Configuring the InfoPath Form Web Part to use the customized list form.

With this you have set the InfoPath Form Web Part to use and display the **Edit Form** SharePoint list form of the **OfficeApplications** list.

16. On the web part tool pane, click **OK**.
17. Click **Page ➤ Edit ➤ Save** or click the small **Save** command on the Ribbon to save and stop editing the page.

In SharePoint, navigate to the **OfficeApplicationsDetails** page. Click on an arrow in the **Select** column of any item in the SharePoint list web part. The details corresponding to the item you selected on the left should appear in the InfoPath Form Web Part on the right. Edit the data in the form that is embedded in the InfoPath Form Web Part, and then click **Edit ➤ Commit ➤ Save** to save the changes.

Figure 47. InfoPath form connected to a SharePoint list on a page.

Discussion

In the solution described above, you learned how to connect an InfoPath Form Web Part to a SharePoint list web part, so that the InfoPath Form Web Part could use the customized list form of the SharePoint list. Note that when you connect an InfoPath Form Web Part to use the form that has been defined on a SharePoint list, you will be unable to change the web part to use a different list or library through the web part tool pane unless you first disconnect the InfoPath Form Web Part from the current list through its web part connections by deselecting the check box in front of the web part connection and confirming that you want to delete the connection.

An item is by default displayed as editable whenever you embed a SharePoint list form in an InfoPath Form Web Part. If you want an item to be displayed as read-only, you must select the **Display a read-only form (lists only)** check box on the web part tool pane of the InfoPath Form Web Part, or customize the SharePoint list form to include a read-only view, which you can then select from the **Views** drop-down list box on the web part tool pane when you configure the InfoPath Form Web Part. Note that if you choose to create and use a read-only view for a SharePoint list form to completely prevent users from editing data, you should not select the **Display a read-only form (lists only)** check box, since the latter would still allow users to click the **Edit Item** command on the Ribbon to initiate editing data.

16 Use 2 different InfoPath forms to enter data in one SharePoint list

Problem

You want users to be able to select from one of two types of forms to enter data into a SharePoint list.

Solution

You can add two different content types to a SharePoint list and then customize the InfoPath form for each content type so that users are able to use two different InfoPath forms to enter data into the SharePoint list.

Suppose you want to use an InfoPath form for a SharePoint list to add list items that only have first name and last name fields, and a second InfoPath form for the same SharePoint list to add items that have first name, last name, city, and country fields.

To use two different InfoPath forms to enter data in one SharePoint list:

1. In SharePoint, select **Site settings** from the **Settings** menu (the gear icon in the top-right corner).
2. On the **Site Settings** page under **Web Designer Galleries**, click **Site content types**.
3. On the **Site Content Types** page, click **Create**.
4. On the **New Site Content Type** page, type **CustomerWithAddress** in the **Name** text box, select **List Content Types** from the **Select parent content type from** drop-down list box, select **Item** from the **Parent Content Type** drop-down list box, leave **Custom Content Types** selected in the **Existing group** drop-down list box, and click **OK**.
5. On the **Site Content Type** page under **Columns**, click **Add from existing site columns**.

6. On the **Add Columns** page, leave **All Groups** selected in the **Select columns from** drop-down list box, hold the **Ctrl** key pressed down while selecting **City** and **Country/Region** from the **Available columns** list, click **Add**, and then click **OK**.

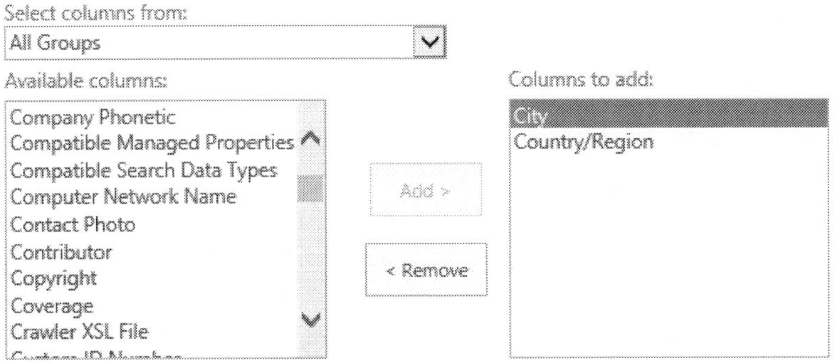

Figure 48. Selecting columns to add to a content type in SharePoint.

7. Select **Add an app** from the **Settings** menu (the gear icon in the top-right corner).
8. On the **Site Contents** page, click **Custom List**.
9. On the **Adding Custom List** dialog, type **Customers** in the **Name** text box, and then click **Create**.
10. On the **Site Contents** page, hover over the newly created **Customers** SharePoint list, click the ellipsis button that appears behind the list's name, and then click **Settings** on the context menu that appears.
11. On the **Settings** page under **General Settings**, click **Advanced settings**.
12. On the **Advanced Settings** page, select the **Yes** option for **Allow management of content types**, and click **OK**.

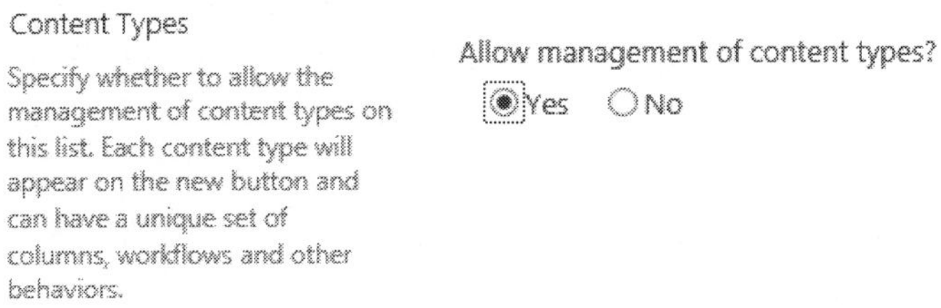

Figure 49. Enabling management of content types on a SharePoint list.

13. On the **Settings** page under **Content Types**, click **Add from existing site content types**.
14. On the **Add Content Types** page, select **Custom Content Types** from the **Select site content types from** drop-down list box, select **CustomerWithAddress** in the **Available Site Content Types** list box, click **Add**, and then click **OK**. With this you have added a second content type to the SharePoint list.
15. On the **Settings** page under **Content Types**, click the **Item** content type.
16. On the **List Content Type** page under **Settings**, click **Name and description**.
17. On the **Content Type Settings** page, change the text in the **Name** text box to **Customer**, change the description to say **Create a new Customer**, and then click **OK**. Users should now be able to go to the SharePoint list, click **Items ➤ New ➤ New Item**, and select either **Customer** or **CustomerWithAddress** to create a list item.

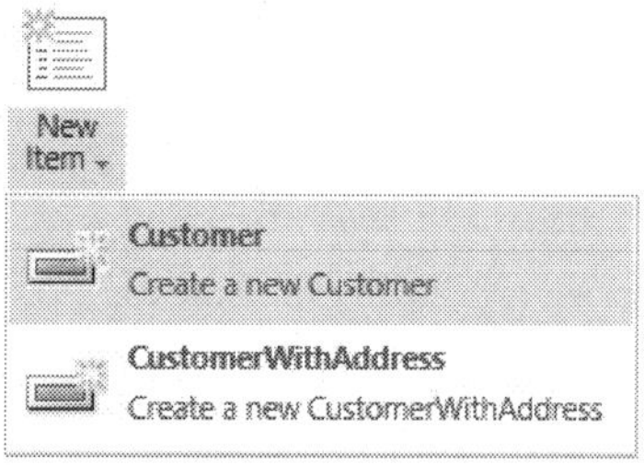

Figure 50. Adding a new SharePoint list item based on one of two content types.

18. On the **List Content Type** page, click **Settings** in the breadcrumb trail to navigate back to the **Settings** page of the SharePoint list.
19. On the **Settings** page under **Columns**, click **Create column**.
20. On the **Create Column** page, type **Last Name** in the **Column name** text box, leave the **Single line of text** option selected, and then click **OK**.
21. Repeat the previous step to add a column named **First Name** to the SharePoint list. If you look at the **Columns** on the **Settings** page, you should see that the **First Name**, **Last Name**, and **Title** columns are now being used by both content types, and that the **City** and

Country/Region columns are only used by the **CustomerWithAddress** content type.

Column (click to edit)	Type	Used in
City	Single line of text	CustomerWithAddress
Country/Region	Single line of text	CustomerWithAddress
Created	Date and Time	
First Name	Single line of text	Customer, CustomerWithAddress
Last Name	Single line of text	Customer, CustomerWithAddress
Modified	Date and Time	
Title	Single line of text	Customer, CustomerWithAddress
Created By	Person or Group	
Modified By	Person or Group	

Figure 51. Columns being shared by two content types.

22. Once you have the SharePoint list with content types set up, you can customize the InfoPath form for each one of the content types. So follow the instructions in recipe *1 Customize a SharePoint list form from within SharePoint* or recipe *2 Customize a SharePoint list form from within InfoPath* to customize the SharePoint list form for the **Customer** and **CustomerWithAddress** content types of the SharePoint list.

In SharePoint, navigate to the **Customers** SharePoint list, click **Items ➤ New ➤ New Item**, and then select **Customer** from the drop-down menu that appears. The InfoPath form for the **Customer** content type should appear. Enter some data and then click **Save**. Click **Items ➤ New ➤ New Item**, and then select **CustomerWithAddress** from the drop-down menu that appears. The InfoPath form for the **CustomerWithAddress** content type should appear. Enter some data and then click **Save**.

Discussion

In the solution described above, you shared two list columns (**Last Name** and **First Name**) between the two content types associated with the SharePoint list, so that those columns would only appear once for both content types in the SharePoint list. Note that when you added the columns to the SharePoint list, they were automatically copied onto the list content types that were already associated with the SharePoint list. You could have also used site columns instead of list columns to achieve the same result.

Chapter 2: SharePoint Form Library Forms

Unlike SharePoint list forms, SharePoint form library forms are forms that are physically stored as XML files in SharePoint form libraries. And while the process for designing and publishing SharePoint form library form templates is slightly more involved than that for desiging and publishing SharePoint list form templates, SharePoint form library form templates offer more flexibility where the availability of controls, the data structure of a form, and form deployment options are concerned.

Creating SharePoint form library form templates is a two-step process:

1. You must create and design a browser-compatible form template in InfoPath Designer 2013.
2. You must publish the form template to a form library or as a site content type, and browser-enable the form template when you publish it.

The recipes in this chapter are intended to guide you through these steps.

Design SharePoint form library form templates

While you can create SharePoint form library form templates that are not browser-compatible, this book provides instructions for forms that should be filled out through a browser via SharePoint. InfoPath offers two starter form templates you can use to create browser-compatible form templates that can be used for creating forms that are stored in SharePoint form libraries:

1. Blank Form
2. SharePoint Form Library

The main difference between these two form templates is that a **SharePoint Form Library** form template starts with a built-in layout on its default view, while a **Blank Form** template starts with a standard blank page layout on its default view. You can use the same types of controls on both form templates, both form templates have their compatibility set to **Web Browser Form**, and both form templates require InfoPath Forms Services, which is part of SharePoint Server, to be able to fill out forms through a browser. If InfoPath Forms Services is not available, InfoPath Filler 2013 must be installed locally on users' computers to be able to fill out web forms.

InfoPath also offers a non-browser-compatible form template named **Blank Form (InfoPath Filler)** you can use to create forms that can be stored in SharePoint form libraries, but which can only be filled out through InfoPath Filler 2013. Unlike the other two types of form templates, if you design a **Blank Form (InfoPath Filler)** template, you have the full range of controls that is available in InfoPath at your disposal. The only limitation with regards to SharePoint is that while users can navigate to a SharePoint form library in their browser to open a form, the form will always open in InfoPath Filler 2013 instead of the browser. This also means that all users who fill out forms based on this type of form template must have InfoPath Filler 2013 installed locally on their computers.

The following table lists the functionality offered by the aforementioned types of form templates.

	SharePoint Form Library	**Blank Form**	**Blank Form (InfoPath Filler)**
Start with a built-in layout	✓		
Publish to SharePoint	✓	✓	✓
Fill out forms via the browser	✓	✓	
Users must install InfoPath locally			✓

While InfoPath Filler 2013 may or may not be required to fill out InfoPath forms depending on the form type, you must always install InfoPath 2013 if you want to design and publish InfoPath form templates.

17 Create a SharePoint form library form template

Problem

You want to design an InfoPath form template that can be published to SharePoint and used to create forms that can be filled out through a browser and stored in a SharePoint form library.

Solution

You can use either the **SharePoint Form Library** template or the **Blank Form** template in InfoPath Designer 2013 to create and design forms that can be stored in a SharePoint form library.

To create a SharePoint form library form template:

1. Open InfoPath Designer 2013.
2. On the **New** tab under **Popular Form Templates**, select either **SharePoint Form Library** or **Blank Form**, and click **Design Form**.

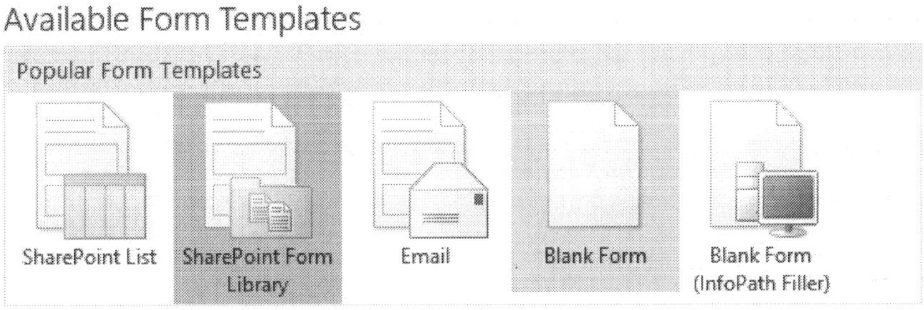

Figure 52. SharePoint Form Library and Blank Form templates in InfoPath.

3. Design the form template to suit your needs by adding views, controls, and rules to the form template as described in *InfoPath 2013 Cookbook: 121 Codeless Recipes for Beginners.*

Once you are done designing the form template, the next step would be to publish the form template to a SharePoint form library, which you will learn how to do in for example recipe *19 Publish a form template to a form library*.

Discussion

Form templates that are based on the **Blank Form** or **SharePoint Form Library** starter form templates are browser-compatible form templates with which you can create forms that when saved in SharePoint, are saved as physical XML files in a SharePoint form library; not as SharePoint list items as is the case when you save a SharePoint list form (see Chapter 1).

The main difference between SharePoint list forms and SharePoint form library forms is that the schema (or Main data source) of a SharePoint list form depends on the columns of a content type associated with a SharePoint list, while the schema of a SharePoint form library form is independent of the columns defined on a SharePoint form library. Therefore, while you cannot use nested or repeating data structures in a SharePoint list form, you have no such limitation with SharePoint form library forms. So SharePoint form library forms offer far more flexibility where defining the structure of your forms and the use of controls are concerned.

You can verify that the **Blank Form** and the **SharePoint Form Library** form templates are browser-compatible form templates by checking the **Form type** that is located under the **Compatibility** category on the **Form Options** dialog box (**File ➤ Info ➤ Form Options**) and which should be set to **Web Browser Form** by default when you create a browser-compatible form template from within InfoPath Designer 2013. Note that the **Web Browser Form (InfoPath 2010)** and **Web Browser Form (InfoPath 2007)** form types also exist for backward compatibility with SharePoint 2010 and 2007.

Browser-compatible form templates have a couple of limitations when you compare them to InfoPath Filler form templates. In addition to having fewer controls available in the **Controls** section on the Ribbon and task pane, you are also not able to display message boxes via browser forms. For example, when you use a **Close the form** action in a rule on a button, you cannot prompt the user to save the form when closing it.

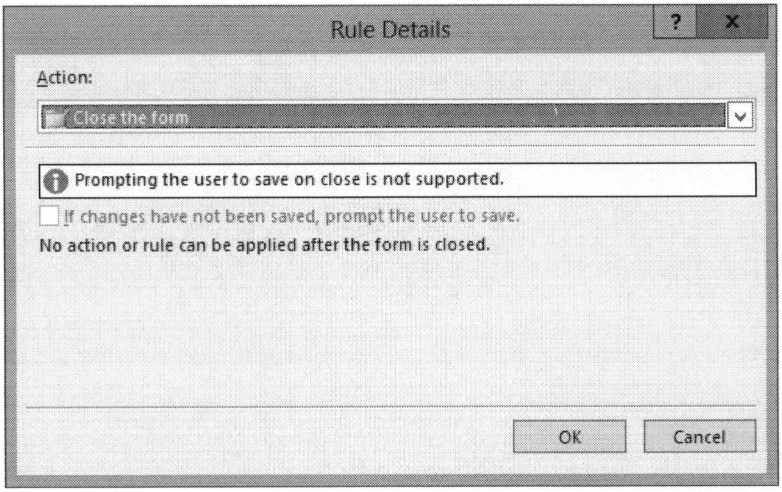

Figure 53. Prompting the user to save on close is not supported in browser forms.

User roles (**Data ➤ Roles ➤ User Roles**) are also not available in browser-compatible form templates.

Because browser-compatible form templates are generally hosted and displayed through InfoPath Forms Services in SharePoint, you must ensure that whatever controls or business logic you add to a form template are supported by InfoPath Forms Services in SharePoint, because any incompatibilities at design time may result in the form template producing errors or the form template not being able to be browser-enabled on the server when you publish it.

There are a few things you can do to ensure that browser-compatible form templates you design will work in InfoPath Forms Services and the web browser. The first thing is to use the **Design Checker** task pane to find incompatibilities. You can open the **Design Checker** task pane via **File ➤ Info ➤ Design Checker**. Click **Refresh** on the **Design Checker** task pane to find incompatibilities, and if there are any issues, you should resolve them before publishing the form template.

Figure 54. The Design Checker task pane in InfoPath Designer 2013.

The second thing you can do is verify that the form template will work correctly on the server where you are going to publish it. For this you can select the **Verify on server** check box on the **Design Checker** task pane, and click **Refresh** to resolve any browser optimization issues you find. Note that for the **Verify on server** option of the **Design Checker** to work, you must specify the URL of the server to use via the **Form Options** dialog box. You can click **Change settings** on the **Design Checker** task pane, or open the **Form Options** dialog box via **File ➤ Info ➤ Form Options** and select **Compatibility** in the **Category** list, to set the server URL.

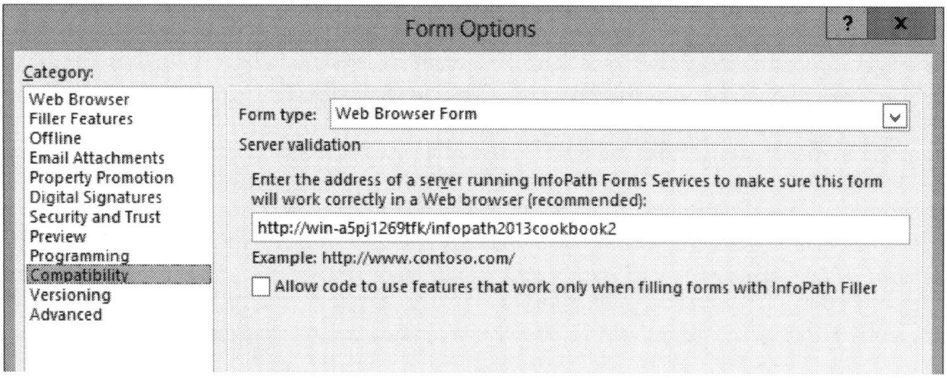

Figure 55. Setting the URL to validate the form on the server.

The final thing to note is that InfoPath offers a few browser-specific features such as the **Browser forms** tab on the **Properties** dialog box for controls. This tab allows you to select when data should be sent back to the server.

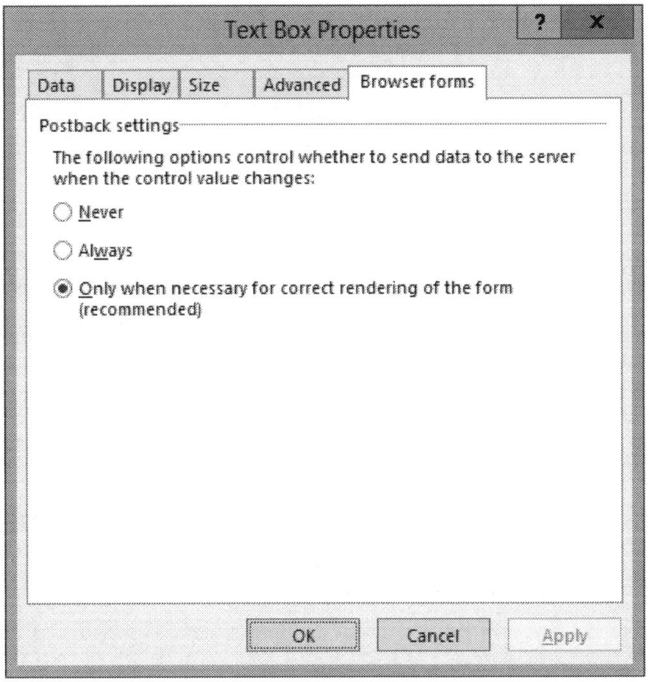

Figure 56. Browser forms tab on the Properties dialog box for a control in InfoPath 2013.

The **Postback settings** are set by default on **Only when necessary for correct rendering of the form (recommended)**, but you could also select the **Never** or **Always** option. If you select the **Always** option, be aware that this could degrade the performance of forms.

In addition, InfoPath Forms Services allows a maximum of 75 postbacks per session by default, so a user could hit that target very quickly if you selected the **Always** option. After the maximum amount of postbacks allowed is hit, the user will see the following message appear:

This session has exceeded the amount of allowable resources

If a user gets this error, you must either modify your form template in such a way to reduce the amount of unnecessary postbacks, or increase the maximum amount of postbacks for InfoPath Forms Services in SharePoint.

Your administrator can change the maximum amount of postbacks in SharePoint Central Administration via **General Application Settings ➤ InfoPath Forms Services ➤ Configure InfoPath Forms Services ➤ Thresholds**.

Thresholds
Specify the thresholds at which to end user sessions and log error messages.
Number of postbacks per session: 75
Number of actions per postback: 200

Figure 57. Configuring thresholds for InfoPath Forms Services in SharePoint.

Another browser-specific feature is a button action called **Update Form**, which you can select from the **Action** drop-down list box on the **General** tab of the **Button Properties** dialog box or on the **Properties** tab on the Ribbon. When you select this action, the button is only shown on web browser forms (so not in InfoPath Filler 2013 or in preview mode in InfoPath Designer 2013).

You can use the **Update Form** button action to refresh data and send data to the server on demand. This helps improve performance of forms. For example, instead of selecting the **Always** option as discussed earlier, you could place an **Update Form** button on a form, so that users can manually perform postbacks whenever they require form data to be refreshed or if form data fails to refresh despite having set the postback setting to **Always**. The **Update Form** button action works similar to the **Update** command that is located on a form's Ribbon. This button is disabled by default, but you can enable it to appear on the Ribbon through the **Form Options** dialog box (also see recipe *33 Hide or show Ribbon commands for a form*).

18 Create a form library and edit its form template

Problem

You want to edit an InfoPath form template that belongs to an existing SharePoint form library.

Solution

You can edit the template that is linked to the **Form** content type of the SharePoint form library. This will open the form template in InfoPath Designer 2013, so that you can modify it.

Before you can modify the form template of a form library, you must have a form library at your disposal. You can use an existing form library or create a new form library as the steps in this solution will demonstrate. Before you create a form library, you must ensure that you have the proper rights on the SharePoint site where you want to create the form library.

To manually create a SharePoint form library:

1. In SharePoint, navigate to the site on which you want to create a form library, and select **Add an app** from the **Settings** menu (the gear icon in the top-right corner).

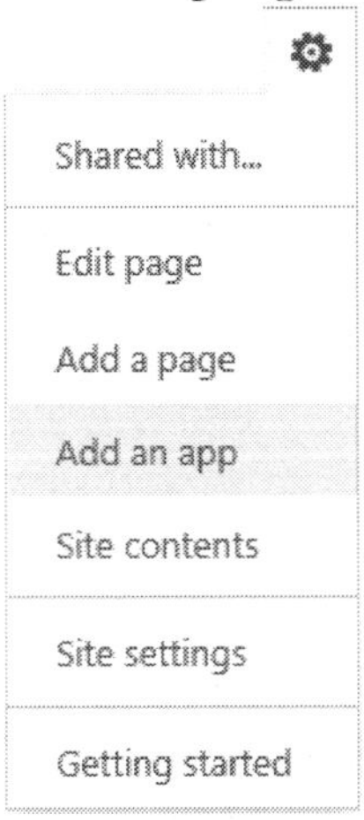

Figure 58. 'Add an app' menu item on the Settings menu in SharePoint 2013.

2. On the **Your Apps** page, click **Form Library**.

Figure 59. The Form Library app on the Your Apps page in SharePoint.

3. On the **Adding Form Library** dialog, enter a name for the form library in the **Name** text box, and then click **Create**.

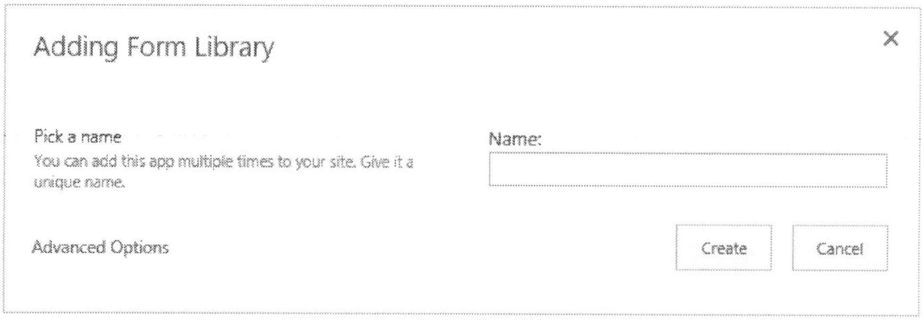
Adding Form Library
Pick a name
You can add this app multiple times to your site. Give it a unique name.
Name:
Advanced Options
Create
Cancel

Figure 60. The Adding Form Library dialog in SharePoint 2013.

SharePoint should create the form library and redirect you to the **Site Contents** page.

To edit the form template of a form library:

1. In SharePoint, navigate to the form library for which you want to edit its form template, and click **Library ➤ Settings ➤ Library Settings**, or if you are still on the **Site Contents** page, hover over the newly created form library, click the ellipsis button that appears behind the form library's name, and then click **Settings** on the context menu that appears.
2. On the **Settings** page under **General Settings**, click **Advanced settings**.
3. On the **Advanced Settings** page under **Document Template**, you should see a **Template URL** listed, and beneath that an **Edit Template** link. Click **Edit Template** to open the form template in InfoPath Designer 2013 for editing.

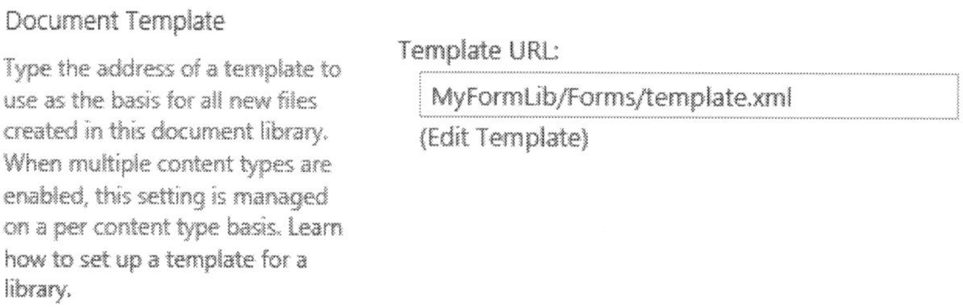
Document Template
Type the address of a template to use as the basis for all new files created in this document library. When multiple content types are enabled, this setting is managed on a per content type basis. Learn how to set up a template for a library.
Template URL:
MyFormLib/Forms/template.xml
(Edit Template)

Figure 61. Document Template section on the Advanced Settings page.

Note: The **Edit Template** link is not present when management of content types is enabled.

4. In InfoPath, design the form template to suit your needs by adding views, controls, and rules to the form template as described in *InfoPath 2013 Cookbook: 121 Codeless Recipes for Beginners*.

Once you are done designing the form template, the next step would be to publish the form template back to the same form library as described in recipe *20 Republish a form template*.

In SharePoint, on the **Advanced Settings** page, click **Cancel**. If you navigate back to the **Advanced Settings** page, you should see that the **Template URL** changed from **template.xml** to **template.xsn**, which means that the document library template is now an InfoPath form template.

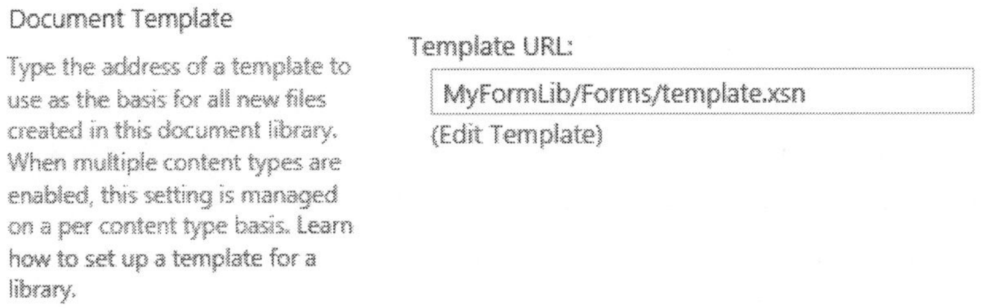
Document Template
Type the address of a template to use as the basis for all new files created in this document library. When multiple content types are enabled, this setting is managed on a per content type basis. Learn how to set up a template for a library.
Template URL:
MyFormLib/Forms/template.xsn
(Edit Template)

Figure 62. Form library now pointing to a form template as its document template.

Discussion

To be able to create a new form library, you must have at least **Edit** permission on the site where you want to create the form library. However, if your intention is to create a new form library, modify its form template, and then republish it as described in the solution above, you must have **Design** permission on the site. If you are modifying the form template of an existing form library, you require at least **Contribute** permission on the site and **Design** permission on the form library.

One of the main differences between a form library and other types of libraries is that a form library is designed to store InfoPath forms, i.e. XML files that contain processing instructions for InfoPath. And just like other lists and libraries in SharePoint, a form library can be associated with one or more content types, and is typically associated with content types that inherit from the **Form** content type. If you need background information about content types, refer to *Content types and site columns* in the Appendix.

Note that you do not always have to manually create a form library to be able to edit an InfoPath form template. You can also let InfoPath Designer 2013 create a new form library when you publish a form template as described in recipe *19 Publish a form template to a form library*.

By default, when you create a new form library, SharePoint creates an XML file and places it in the **Forms** folder under the form library (see step 3). When you publish a form template from within InfoPath Designer 2013 to a SharePoint form library, the **template.xml** file is replaced by the form template and gets the name **template.xsn**. With this you now also know that if you see **template.xml** listed as the document template of a form library, it is highly likely that a valid form template has yet to be published to the form library. The form template that is created when you click **Edit Template** in SharePoint is equivalent to a **Blank Form** template with its compatibility set to **Web Browser Form (InfoPath 2010)**.

When you created the form library in SharePoint, you only had to enter the name of the form library to be able to create it. But there are more options you could have selected and chosen to fill out when creating a form library. Had you clicked the **Advanced Options** link on the **Adding Form Library** dialog, the **New** page would have offered the ability to enter a name and a description for the form library, and to enable versioning on forms in the form library. You are not required to select these options when creating a form library, because you can always change or set them afterwards via the **Settings** page of the form library.

In SharePoint, go back to the **Settings** page of the form library. You can use the **Settings** page to perform management tasks and set permissions for the form library. Take a moment to familiarize yourself with all of the links on this page; the links are pretty self-explanatory.

To go back to the form library, click on the form library name in the breadcrumb trail at the top of the page.

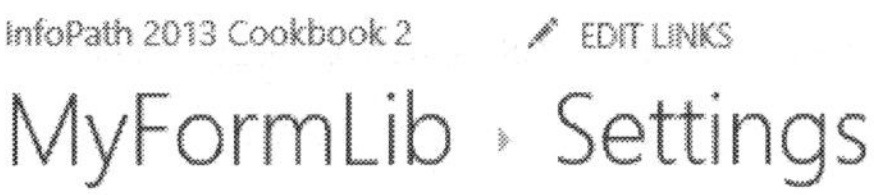

Figure 63. Using the breadcrumb trail to navigate back to the form library in SharePoint.

Or if there is a link in the **Quick Launch** menu on the left-hand side of the page, you can access the form library from there too. Once you are on the form library page, you will see a link that says **new document**.

Figure 64. 'new document' link in a SharePoint form library.

If you click the **new document** link immediately after you create the new form library but before you edit and publish the form template of the form library, InfoPath Filler 2013 will open and prompt you to select a form template through the **Open With Form Template** dialog box.

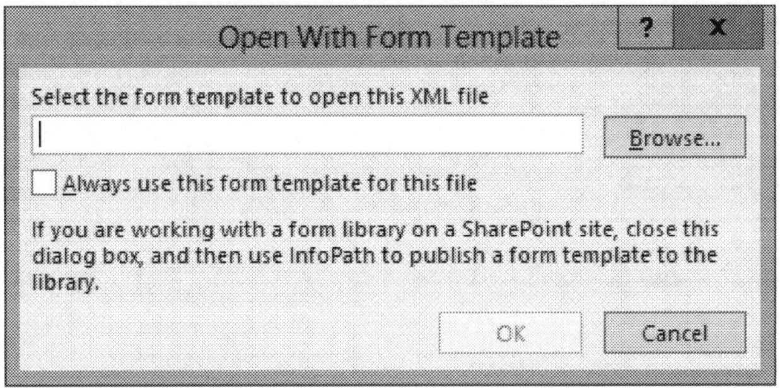

Figure 65. The Open With Form Template dialog box in InfoPath Filler 2013.

This is because while you have manually created a form library, the form library does not yet have a valid InfoPath form template it can use to create forms. A newly and manually created form library is always linked to an XML file; not an XSN file. So for the **new document** link to work properly, you must first publish a form template to the form library from within InfoPath as described in *Publish a form template to a form library* or *Publish a form template as a site content type* in this chapter.

When you click **new document** in a form library, SharePoint uses what is called the default content type that is set on the form library to create a document. SharePoint allows you to configure more than one content type on lists and libraries (also see recipe *27 Create different types of forms in one form library*). This is what enables you to use one form library to create more than one type of form. So if you have not enabled management of content types and only have one form template configured on a form library, you can click **new document** to create a new form that is based on that form template. But if you have configured a form library to use more than one form template, you must click **Files** ➤ **New** ➤ **New Document** and then select the form template you want to use from the drop-down menu that appears. If you look at the **New Document** command drop-down menu for a newly and manually created form library, you should only see one item listed.

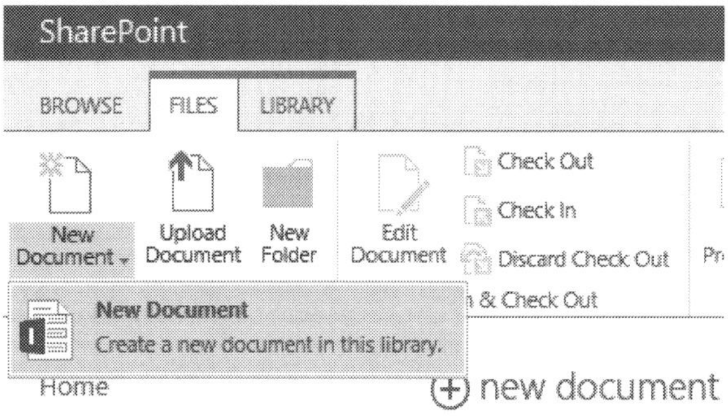

Figure 66. New Document command under the New group on the Files tab in SharePoint.

Publish a form template to a form library

Once you are done designing a browser-compatible form template, you can publish it to SharePoint to make it available to users for creating forms from it. From within InfoPath Designer 2013, you can either publish user form templates to SharePoint or prepare form templates for publishing by an administrator. User form templates are form templates that can be published directly by users to either a SharePoint form library or as a site content type. User form templates do not require Full Trust to run.

Throughout this book you will be creating user form templates, so will not go through the administrator-approved publishing process for InfoPath form templates.

19 Publish a form template to a form library

Problem

You designed a form template and want to publish it to a form library on a SharePoint site.

Solution

You can use the **Publishing Wizard** in InfoPath to publish a form template to a SharePoint form library.

To publish a form template to a SharePoint form library:

1. In InfoPath, create a new SharePoint form library form template or use an existing one.
2. Click **File ➤ Publish ➤ SharePoint Server** to start publishing the form template. InfoPath may prompt you to save the form template.
3. On the **Publishing Wizard**, enter the URL of the SharePoint site to which you want to publish the form template, and click **Next**.

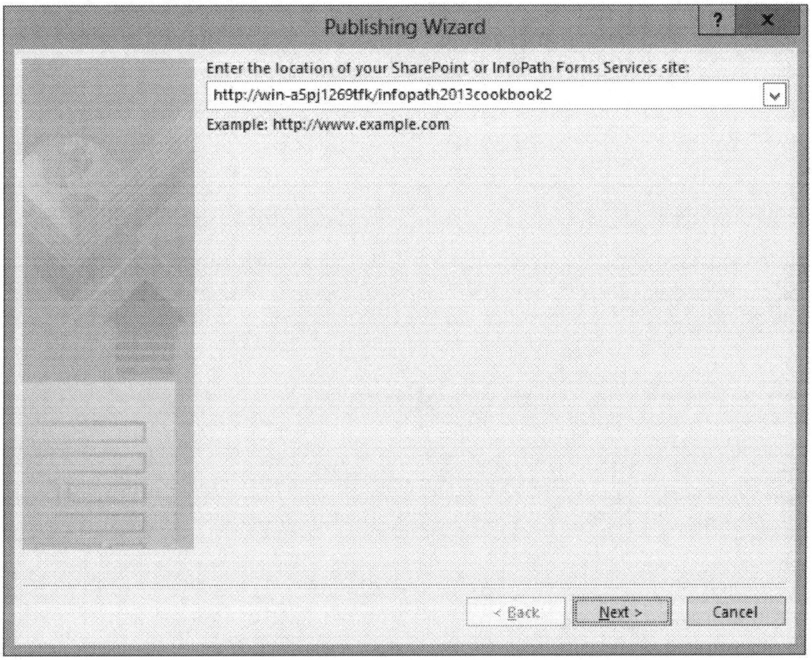

Figure 67. Entering a SharePoint site URL on the Publishing Wizard.

4. On the **Publishing Wizard**, ensure that the **Form Library** option is selected, ensure that the **Enable this form to be filled out using a browser** check box is selected, and click **Next**.

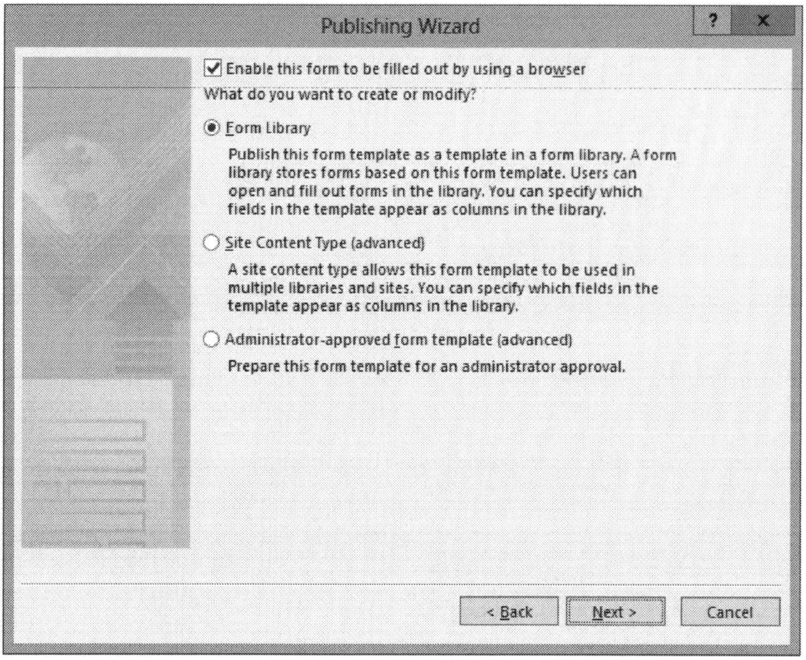

Figure 68. Selecting Form Library on the Publishing Wizard in InfoPath 2013.

5. On the **Publishing Wizard**, ensure that the **Create a new form library** option is selected, and click **Next**. Note that if you want to update an existing form library instead of create a new form library, you would have to select the **Update the form template in an existing form library** option instead, and then select an existing form library to update.

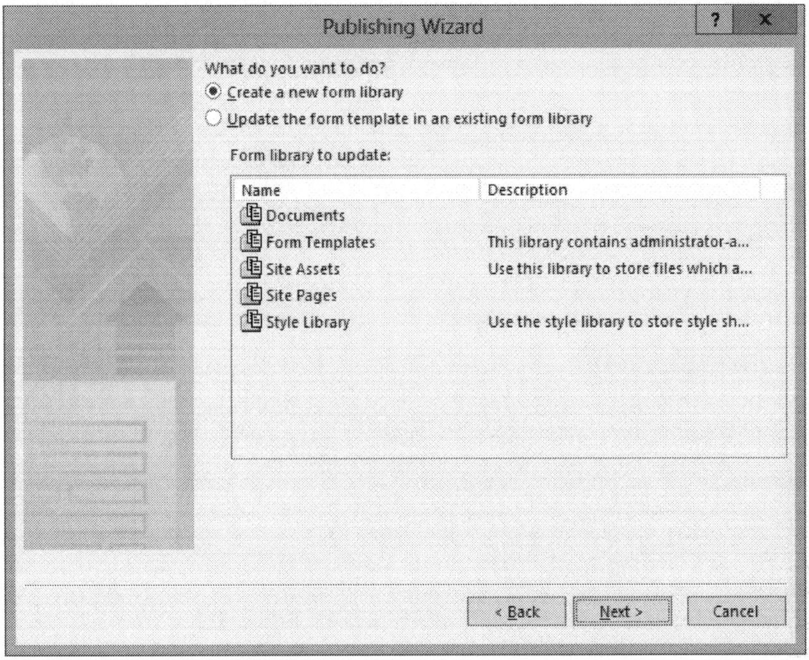

Figure 69. Selecting to create a new form library on the Publishing Wizard in InfoPath 2013.

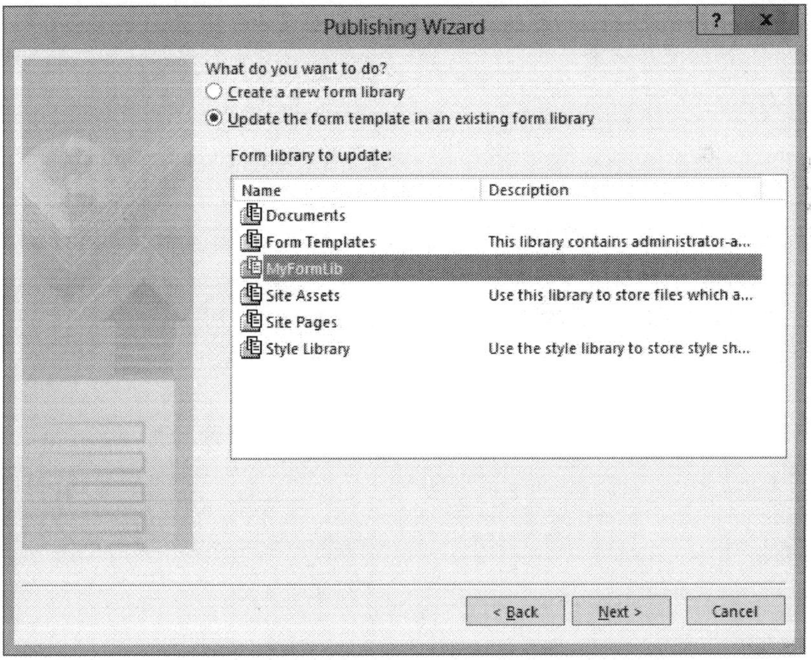

Figure 70. Selecting an existing form library to update on the Publishing Wizard.

6. Only if you are publishing a form template to a new form library: On the **Publishing Wizard**, enter a name for the new form library, and click **Next**.

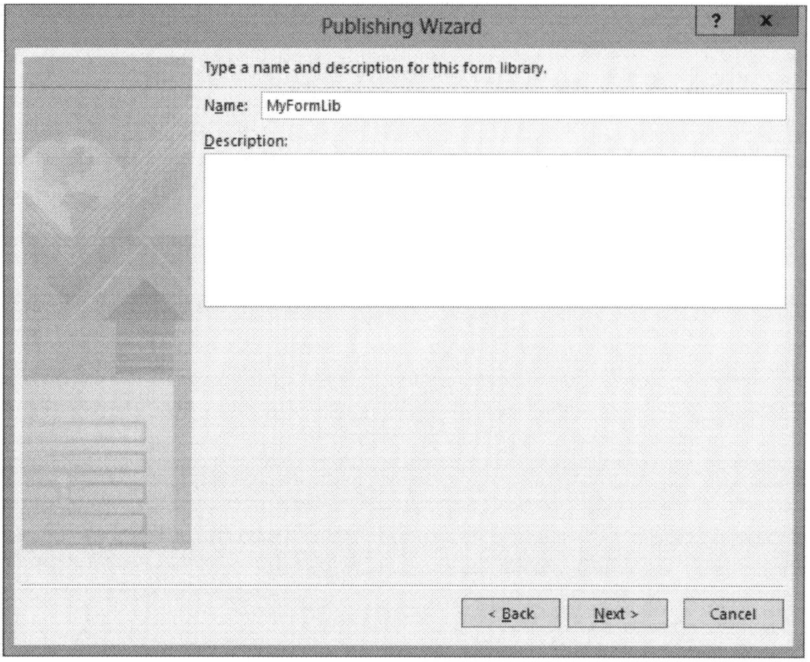

Figure 71. Entering a name for the new form library on the Publishing Wizard.

7. The following screen is for adding fields you want to promote to SharePoint or Outlook as columns (see for example recipe *22 Promote form fields to columns of a form library*) and for adding fields you want to use as parameters in web part connections (see for example recipe *41 Master/detail across two forms linked through one field*). On the **Publishing Wizard**, click **Next**.

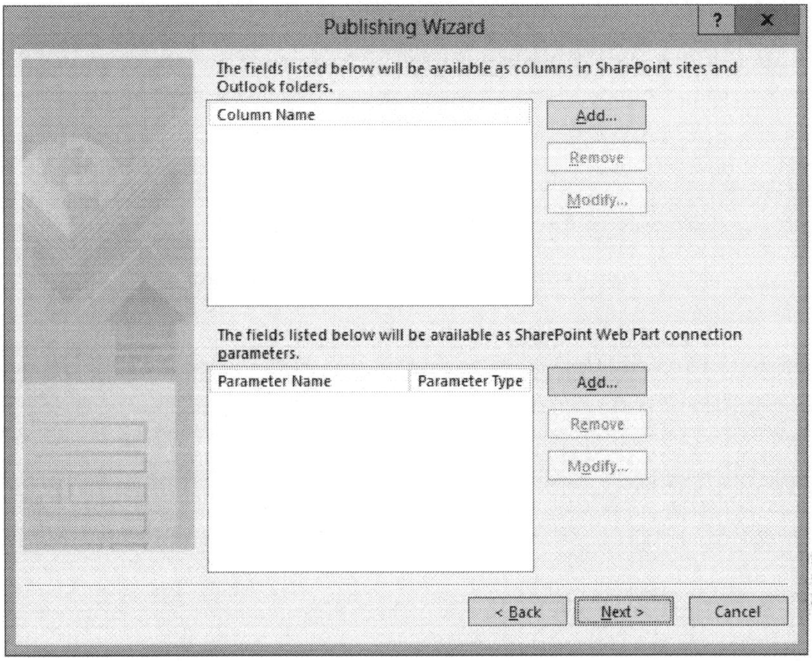

Figure 72. Publishing Wizard screen to promote fields and add parameters.

8. On the **Publishing Wizard**, click **Publish**.
9. On the **Publishing Wizard**, click **Close**.

In SharePoint, navigate to the form library where you published the form template, and then click **new document** to create and add an InfoPath form to the form library. An InfoPath form should open in the browser.

Tip:

> Always pay close attention to any warnings InfoPath displays on the very last screen of the **Publishing Wizard** after you click **Publish** and after the form template has been published, since this screen may contain additional information that could indicate that the form template was not successfully published or for example that the form cannot be filled out through a browser for one reason or another.

Discussion

To be able to publish a form template to a new form library, you must have **Design** permission on the site to which you want to publish the form template. And if you want to publish a form template to an existing form library, you must have at least **Contribute** permission on the site and **Design** permission on the form library.

When you publish a form template directly to a form library as described in the solution above, a **Form** content type is automatically associated with the form library and the InfoPath form template you published becomes the document template of the form library. Publishing a form template directly to a form library updates the default content type (the first content type listed) for the form library (also see recipe *27 Create different types of forms in one form library* and recipe *28 Configure a form library to create a certain type of form by default*).

The following two steps are an absolute must when you want to publish an InfoPath form template that creates forms that can be filled out through a browser and stored in a form library:

1. You must have used one of the browser-compatible form templates (**SharePoint Form Library** or **Blank Form**) when creating the form template; or ensure that the **Compatibility** of the form template has been set to **Web Browser Form** via the **Form Options** dialog box.
2. You must browser-enable the form template when publishing the form template to SharePoint through the **Publishing Wizard**.

If you skip one or both of these steps, your InfoPath forms will fail to open in the browser. The terms browser-compatible and browser-enabled tend to confuse form template designers who are new to InfoPath, so let us first look at what they mean.

A form template that is browser-compatible is a form template that is suitable to create forms that can be displayed and filled out through the browser as well as through InfoPath Filler 2013.

A form template that is browser-enabled is a form template in which a "switch" has been turned on that says that the form template has been enabled to create forms on a particular SharePoint site via the browser. This "switch" is turned on during the form template publishing process in InfoPath Designer 2013.

While you take care of making a form template browser-compatible in InfoPath Designer 2013, the SharePoint server you publish the form template to dictates whether the form template can or cannot be browser-enabled. Always remember that designing and publishing browser-compatible form templates to SharePoint is not something you only do in InfoPath Designer 2013. The publishing process requires teamwork between InfoPath and SharePoint. For example, if you are failing to successfully browser-enable or publish a form template to SharePoint, or if you are getting any other types of errors, you must ensure that everything is working and is configured properly both in InfoPath as well as in SharePoint. This includes ensuring that you have the required permissions on SharePoint to publish form templates.

On the second screen of the **Publishing Wizard**, there is a check box with the label **Enable this form to be filled out by using a browser**. You must select this check box to browser-enable a form template. If you do not see the check box, but instead see a message that says:

This form template is browser-compatible, but it cannot be browser-enabled on the selected site.

InfoPath Forms Services in SharePoint may not be configured to allow form templates to be browser-enabled.

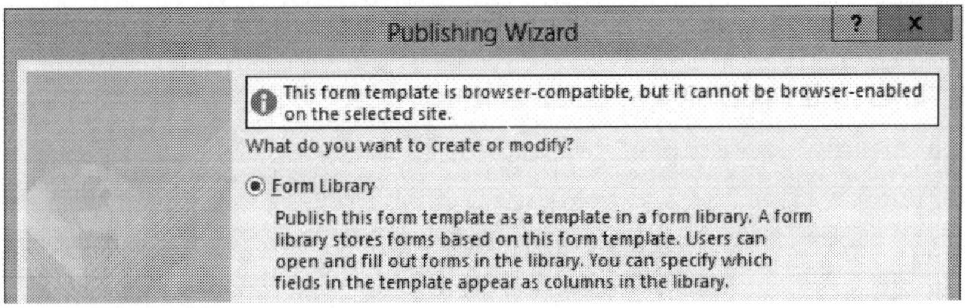

Figure 73. Browser-enable check box is missing from the Publishing Wizard.

Before you can browser-enable a form template from within InfoPath Designer 2013, an administrator must configure the following setting for InfoPath Forms Services in SharePoint Central Administration under

General Application Settings ➤ InfoPath Forms Services ➤ Configure InfoPath Forms Services ➤ User Browser-enabled Form Templates:

- **Allow users to browser-enable form templates** – This option is selected by default, but if an administrator deselects it, you will only be able to publish form templates that are not browser-enabled, so the forms will open in InfoPath Filler 2013 instead of the browser.

The **Allow users to browser-enable form templates** setting only gives form template designers the ability to publish browser-compatible form templates to SharePoint and browser-enable them during the publishing process. An administrator must also enable the following setting for InfoPath Forms Services in SharePoint Central Administration under **General Application Settings ➤ InfoPath Forms Services ➤ Configure InfoPath Forms Services ➤ User Browser-enabled Form Templates** for forms to open in a browser:

- **Render form templates that are browser-enabled by users** – This option is selected by default, but if an administrator deselects it, users will not be able to use the browser to fill out browser-enabled forms, so will be forced to use InfoPath Filler 2013 to open and fill out forms.

And finally, when you create a SharePoint form library, it is automatically set to open forms in the browser, but it can also be set to force forms to open in InfoPath Filler 2013. If a SharePoint form library has been set to open InfoPath forms in InfoPath Filler 2013, you can change it to open InfoPath forms in the browser by selecting either the **Open in the browser** option or the **Use the server default (Open in the browser)** option on the **Advanced Settings** page of the form library, which you can access via the **Settings** page of the form library.

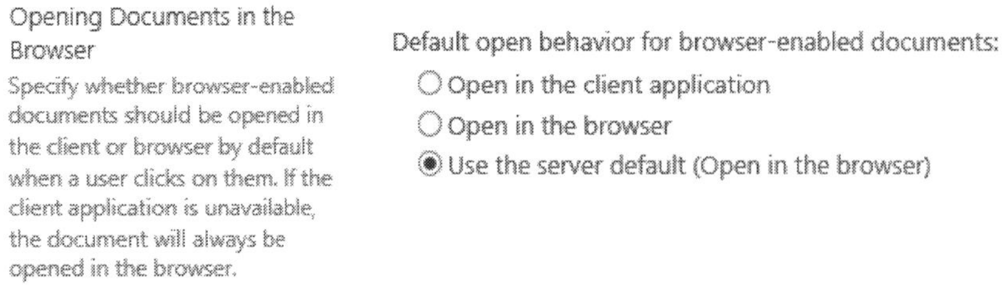
Opening Documents in the Browser
Specify whether browser-enabled documents should be opened in the client or browser by default when a user clicks on them. If the client application is unavailable, the document will always be opened in the browser.
Default open behavior for browser-enabled documents:
Open in the client application
Open in the browser
Use the server default (Open in the browser)

Figure 74. The 'Opening Documents in the Browser' setting of a SharePoint form library.

The following three publishing options are shown on the second screen of the **Publishing Wizard**:

1. **Form Library** – Select this option to publish the form template directly to a SharePoint form library.
2. **Site Content Type (advanced)** – Select this option to publish the form template as a content type on a SharePoint site. You will have to perform extra steps afterwards to add the content type to one or more form libraries (also see recipe *25 Create a content type for an InfoPath form from within InfoPath* and recipe *27 Create different types of forms in one form library*), which is why the text **advanced** has been placed in brackets behind this option.
3. **Administrator-approved form template (advanced)** – Select this option to prepare the form template to be published by an administrator. You must use this option if the form template contains code and cannot be published as a sandboxed solution, if the form template needs Full Trust to run, or if the form template contains links to centrally managed data connections. Because this book teaches you how to create codeless form templates that do not access centrally managed data connections or require Full Trust to run, you can ignore this option for now and choose one of the other two options.

20 Republish a form template

Problem

You previously published a form template to a form library and now you want to republish it to the same or to a different form library.

Solution

You can use the **Quick Publish** command to republish a form template to the same location it was previously published to; or you must use the **SharePoint Server** command on the **File ➤ Publish** tab and not the **Quick Publish** command if you want to republish a form template to a different location.

To republish a form template to the same form library it was previously published to:

1. In InfoPath, open a previously published form template.
2. Click the small **Quick Publish** command on the **Quick Access Toolbar**, click **File ➤ Info ➤ Quick Publish**, or click **File ➤ Publish ➤ Quick Publish**.

Figure 75. Quick Publish command on the Quick Access Toolbar in InfoPath.

To republish a form template to a different form library than the one it was previously published to:

1. In InfoPath, open a previously published form template.
2. Click **File ➤ Publish ➤ SharePoint Server**, follow the instructions on the **Publishing Wizard** as described in recipe *19 Publish a form template to a form library*, and select a different form library to publish the form template to while publishing the form template.

Discussion

When you successfully publish a form template for the first time, InfoPath stores the publish location and uses it as the default publish location the next time you republish the form template. This allows you to use the **Quick Publish** functionality in InfoPath to quickly publish a previously published form template to the same location. The **Quick Publish** command is meant to save time, because you only have to click once to republish the form template.

However, if you want to republish a form template to a different location, you must go through all of the steps of the **Publishing Wizard** again to republish the form template. After you have done this, InfoPath will once again use the new publish location for all subsequent publishing attempts when you click the **Quick Publish** command.

If you are republishing a form template to a different location (for example republishing a form template to a different site collection or server), InfoPath may detect this and then display a check box to adjust data connections on the last screen of the **Publishing Wizard**.

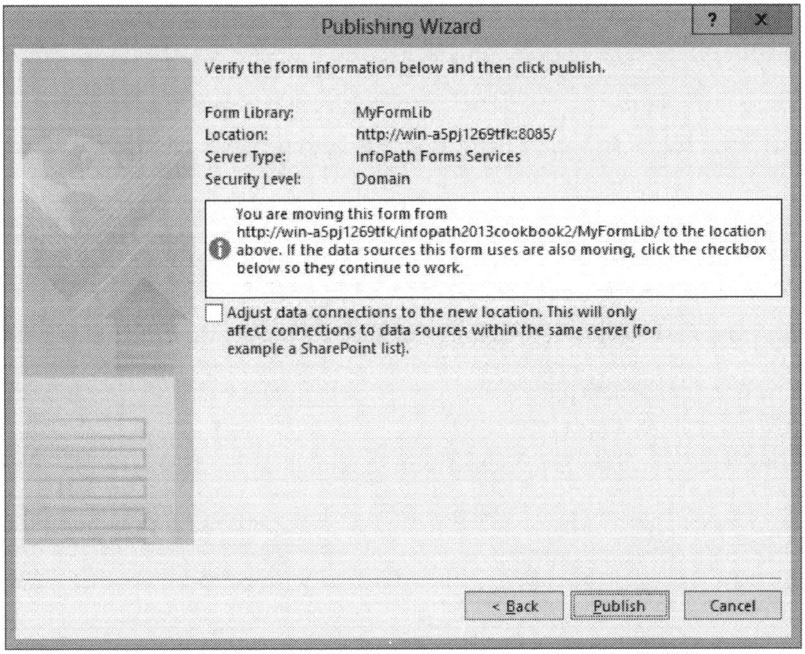

Figure 76. Republishing a form template to another site collection.

Note:

InfoPath does not allow you to change the publish location for certain types of form templates; not even through the **Publishing Wizard**. For example, SharePoint list forms (see Chapter 1) and workflow forms (see Chapter 5) are tightly bound to a list or workflow, so their form templates cannot be republished to a different list or workflow.

21 Find and update a template that was published to a form library

Problem

You have a form library that makes use of a form template that does not contain code and that was previously published to a form library, but that cannot be found anywhere on disk. You want to update the form template to contain extra functionality.

Solution

You can open the form template that is being used by the form library from within SharePoint, update it to suit your needs, and then republish it.

To update a form template that was published to a form library:

1. In SharePoint, navigate to the form library where the form template was published, and click **Library** ➤ **Settings** ➤ **Library Settings**.
2. On the **Settings** page under **General Settings**, click **Advanced settings**.
3. On the **Advanced Settings** page under **Document Template**, click **Edit Template**.

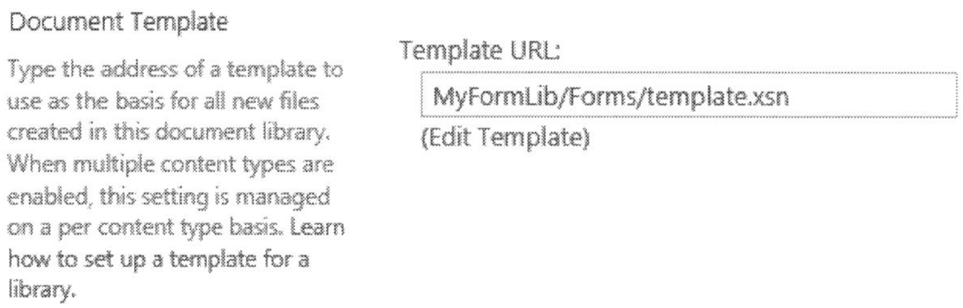
Document Template
Type the address of a template to use as the basis for all new files created in this document library. When multiple content types are enabled, this setting is managed on a per content type basis. Learn how to set up a template for a library.
Template URL:
MyFormLib/Forms/template.xsn
(Edit Template)

Figure 77. The Document Template section on the Advanced Settings page.

4. In InfoPath, apply the changes you want to apply to the form template, and when you are done, republish the form template by clicking the small **Quick Publish** command on the **Quick Access Toolbar**, clicking **File** ➤ **Info** ➤ **Quick Publish**, clicking **File** ➤ **Publish** ➤ **Quick Publish**, or clicking **File** ➤ **Publish** ➤ **SharePoint Server**

thereby accepting the settings that were previously set when the form template was last published.

5. In SharePoint, on the **Advanced Settings** page, click **OK**.

In SharePoint, navigate to the form library, add a new form, and verify that the changes you made to the form template were applied. For example, if you added new controls, you should see those controls appear on the form you opened.

Discussion

If the latest version of a form template was saved to disk, you can just open that form template in InfoPath, apply the changes you want to apply, and then republish it as described in recipe *20 Republish a form template*. The solution described above is good for situations in which a codeless form template was lost, but is still fully functional in SharePoint. It is also good to use if you are unsure whether a form template that you have found on disk is the latest version, no code has been written for that form template, and the form template that is currently working in SharePoint is the form template that should be updated.

Note: If **Edit Template** is not present on the **Advanced Settings** page, see recipe *30 Find and update a template that was published as a content type*.

22 Promote form fields to columns of a form library

Problem

You want to be able to fill out a couple of fields in a form that is stored in a SharePoint form library through a datasheet view or properties page in SharePoint, so without having to open the InfoPath form itself.

Solution

You can promote form fields to columns of a form library to enable data to be entered through a datasheet view of the form library or through the properties page of an item in the form library.

To promote form fields to columns of a form library:

1. In InfoPath, create a new SharePoint form library form template or use an existing one.
2. Add a **Text Box** control named **fullName** to the view of the form template.
3. Start publishing the form template to a SharePoint form library as described in recipe *19 Publish a form template to a form library*, and when you reach the columns and parameters configuration screen of the **Publishing Wizard** as shown in the figure below, click **Add** on the right-hand side of the list box at the top of the dialog box.

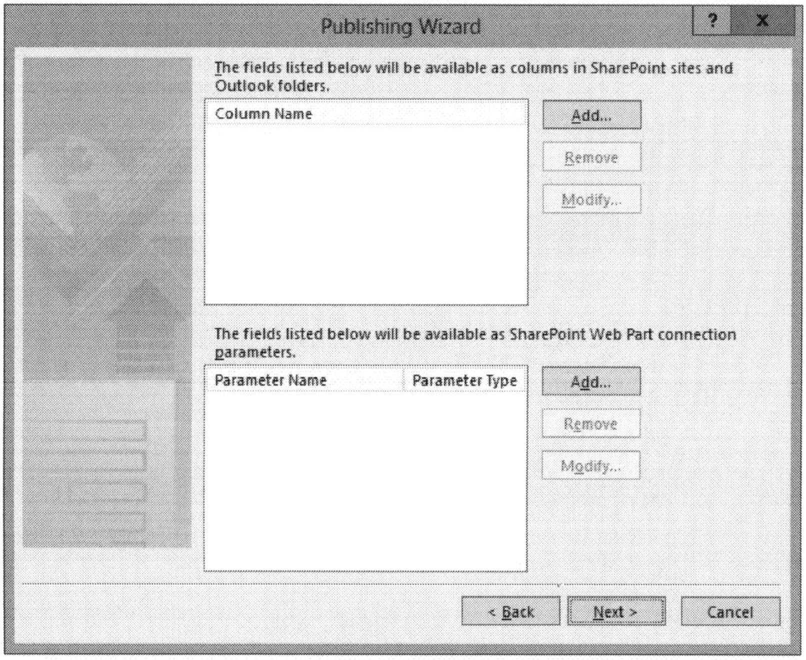

Figure 78. Property promotion screen of the Publishing Wizard.

4. On the **Select a Field or Group** dialog box, select the field you want to promote (**fullName** in this case) in the **Field to display as column** tree view.

5. On the **Select a Field or Group** dialog box, select one of the following items from the **Site column group** drop-down list box:
   a. **(None: Create new column in this library)**, if you want to create a new column in the form library, and then type the name of the column in the **Column name** text box or accept the default name.
   b. **(This form library)**, if you want to use an existing column in the form library, and then select the existing column from the **Column name** drop-down list box. Note that the **Column name** drop-down list box is empty when you are publishing a form template to a new form library. To see column names appear in the drop-down list box, you must publish the form template to an existing form library that has columns.
6. On the **Select a Field or Group** dialog box, select the **Allow users to edit data in this field by using a datasheet or properties page** check box, and click **OK**.

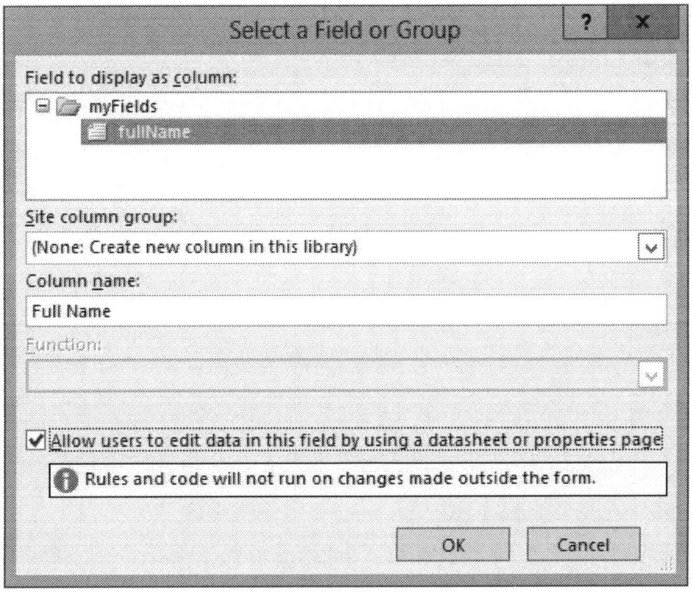

Figure 79. Dialog box to promote a form field to a column in SharePoint.

7. On the **Publishing Wizard**, click **Add** to add another field and go through steps 4 through 6 again, click **Modify** to change the settings for an existing promoted field and go through steps 4 through 6 again, click **Remove** to delete an existing promoted field, or click **Next** to continue publishing the form template.

In SharePoint, navigate to the form library where you published the form template. You should see the fields you promoted displayed as columns of the form library. Add a form to the form library, enter data, save, and then close the form. Open the properties page of the form by selecting the check box in front of the form and then clicking **Files ➤ Manage ➤ Edit Properties**; or click on the ellipsis behind the form, click on the ellipsis behind **Share** on the context menu that appears, and then select **Edit Properties** from the drop-down menu that appears.

Name *	form01	.xml
Full Name	S.Y.M. Wong-A-Ton	

Created at 2/11/2014 10:20 AM by ☐ Jane Doe
Last modified at 2/11/2014 10:20 AM by ☐ Jane Doe

[Save] [Cancel]

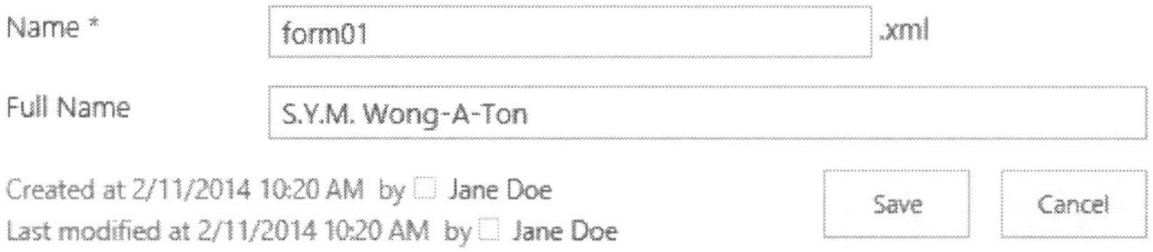

Figure 80. The properties page of an InfoPath form in SharePoint 2013.

You should be able to change the values of the fields you promoted on the properties page of the form. Change the value of a field you promoted and click **Save**. Then open the InfoPath form in the browser by clicking on its name in the form library and verify that the changes you made on the properties page were written to the form itself.

Discussion

In the solution described above you learned how to promote an InfoPath field to a column of a form library in SharePoint. Promoting fields to columns of a SharePoint form library is a two-step process:

1. You must map the field you want to promote either to a new or an existing column.
2. You must select whether the field should be editable through a datasheet or properties page.

Note that when you publish a form template as a site content type as described in recipe *25 Create a content type for an InfoPath form from within InfoPath*, the options to promote a field are slightly different than the ones you get when you publish a form template to a form library, but the process remains the same.

When you publish a form template to a form library, you can promote a field to:

1. A new column of the form library.
2. An existing column of the form library.
3. An existing site column on the site.

When you publish a form template as a site content type, you can promote a field to:

1. An existing column of the content type.
2. A new site column on the site (and of the content type).
3. An existing site column on the site.

You can preconfigure the column names for fields you want to promote via the **Property Promotion** screen of the **Form Options** dialog box (**File ➤ Info ➤ Form Options ➤ Property Promotion**).

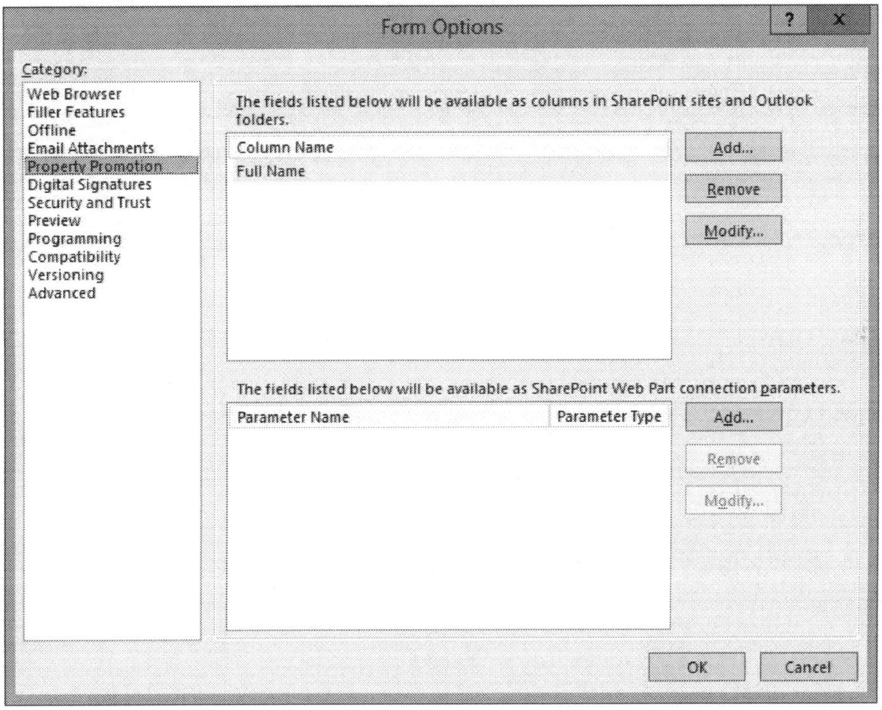

Figure 81. Configuring property promotion via the Form Options dialog box.

Any column names you enter through the **Form Options** dialog box will automatically be used to create new columns on the form library when you publish the form template to a form library, or to create new site columns on the site and content type when you publish the form template as a site content type. If you want to promote fields to existing columns of a form library, of a content type, or on a site, you must configure property promotion through the **Publishing Wizard** when you publish the form template instead of through the **Form Options** dialog box.

Note that not all types of fields can be promoted. For example, fields bound to file attachment and picture controls that have the data type **Picture or File Attachment (base64)** cannot be promoted. However, you can promote a picture that has been included in the form as a link, so which has the **Hyperlink (anyURI)** data type. In addition, whenever you promote a field to an existing column, you must ensure that the data type of the field in InfoPath matches that of the column in SharePoint. The following table lists the matching of data types in InfoPath 2013 with data types in SharePoint 2013 when you promote a field.

Data Types in InfoPath 2013	Data Types in SharePoint 2013
Text (string)	Single line of text
Rich Text (XHTML)	Multiple lines of text (plain text)
Whole Number (integer)	Integer
Decimal (double)	Number
True/False (Boolean)	Yes/No
Hyperlink (anyURI)	Hyperlink or Picture
Date (date)	Date and Time
Time (time)	Date and Time

Data Types in InfoPath 2013	Data Types in SharePoint 2013
Date and Time (dateTime)	Date and Time
Picture or File Attachment (base64)	Not supported

Table 1. Property promotion data type matching between InfoPath and SharePoint.

In addition, repeating groups and repeating fields are aggregated to display only one value when you promote them to columns in SharePoint. Repeating fields are single fields that are child nodes of a repeating group node, such as for example the fields in a repeating table; or repeating fields that are child nodes of a single group node, such as for example the repeating field of a multiple-selection list box.

InfoPath provides an extra **Function** drop-down list box containing the following functions you can choose from when promoting repeating fields:

- first
- last
- count
- merge
- sum
- average
- min
- max

From the list above, the **sum**, **average**, **min**, and **max** functions are displayed in the **Function** drop-down list box, only if the data type of a repeating field is a number (**Whole Number** or **Decimal**).

When you promote a repeating group of a repeating table or a repeating section, you can only select the **count** function. The **count** function promotes the field as the total number of groups or sections. When promoted to SharePoint, the data type assigned is **Integer**.

The **first** and **last** functions promote only the first or last nodes in a group of nodes. When promoted to SharePoint, the data type assigned depends on the data type of the node.

The **merge** function promotes a repeating field as a concatenation of all of the fields that have the same name and that repeat. When promoted to SharePoint, the data type assigned is **Multiple lines of text** and each field is displayed on a separate line in a concatenated string.

If you change the data type of a field in InfoPath after you publish a form template and after already having promoted that field once before, and you try to republish the form template, InfoPath should display a message saying that you must remove or modify the column.

You can remove or modify a column through one of the following two methods:

1. Open the **Form Options** dialog box, select **Property Promotion** in the **Category** list, remove the column for the promoted field, add the column for the promoted field back again, and then republish the form template.
2. Go through the **Publishing Wizard** steps again, on the property promotion screen, remove and then add the column for the promoted field back again or map the promoted field to a different column, and then continue republishing the form template.

If either or both methods described above fail to update the column in SharePoint, remove the column for the promoted field in InfoPath, republish the form template, add the column for the promoted field back in InfoPath, and then republish the form template again.

And finally, in the solution described above, you selected the **Allow users to edit data in this field by using a datasheet or properties page** check box, because you wanted to be able to edit data through a datasheet or properties page in SharePoint. If you only want to display data from forms in columns of a form library and not edit the data through a datasheet or properties page, you can leave this check box deselected when promoting fields.

23 Promote form fields to existing site columns

Problem

You want to promote fields on an InfoPath form to site columns, so that you are able to fill out fields on a form that is stored in the form library to which those same site columns have been added, without having to open the form itself.

Solution

You can promote form fields to site columns instead of list columns when you publish a form template.

To promote form fields to existing site columns:

1. In SharePoint, create a new **Single line of text** site column as described in *Create a new site column* in the Appendix or choose an existing one to use.
2. In InfoPath, create a new SharePoint form library form template or use an existing one.
3. Add a **Text Box** control named **fullName** to the view of the form template.
4. Start publishing the form template to a SharePoint form library (see recipe *19 Publish a form template to a form library*) or as a site content type (see recipe *25 Create a content type for an InfoPath form from within InfoPath*), and when you reach the columns and parameters configuration screen of the **Publishing Wizard**, click **Add** on the right-hand side of the list box at the top of the dialog box.
5. On the **Select a Field or Group** dialog box, select the field you want to promote (**fullName** in this case) in the **Field to display as column** tree view.
6. On the **Select a Field or Group** dialog box, select the site column group that contains the site column you want to use from the **Site column group** drop-down list box. Typically if you created a site column as described in *Create a new site column* in the Appendix, the site column group to select would be **Custom Columns**.

7. On the **Select a Field or Group** dialog box, select the site column you want to promote the field to from the **Column name** drop-down list box. When selecting a site column you must ensure that the data type of the field you want to promote matches that of the site column you select. For example, you cannot promote a date field to a column that only accepts Boolean values (see the data type matching table in the discussion section of recipe *22 Promote form fields to columns of a form library* for more details). If you try to promote fields to columns that do not have matching data types, InfoPath will display the following message:

   The data type of the selected site column does not match the data type of the field to promote.

8. On the **Select a Field or Group** dialog box, select the **Allow users to edit data in this field by using a datasheet or properties page** check box, and click **OK**.
9. On the **Publishing Wizard**, click **Add** to add another field and go through steps 5 through 8 again, click **Modify** to change the settings for an existing promoted field and go through steps 5 through 8 again, click **Remove** to delete an existing promoted field, or click **Next** to continue publishing the form template.

In SharePoint, navigate to the form library where you published the form template. You should see the fields you promoted displayed as columns of the form library. Add a form to the form library, enter data, save, and then close the form. Open the properties page of the form by selecting the check box in front of the form and then clicking **Files ➤ Manage ➤ Edit Properties**; or click on the ellipsis behind the form, click on the ellipsis behind **Share** on the context menu that appears, and then select **Edit Properties** from the drop-down menu that appears. You should be able to change the values of the fields you promoted on the properties page of the form. Change the value of a field you promoted and click **Save**. Then open the InfoPath form in the browser by clicking on its name and verify that the changes you made on the properties page were written to the form itself.

Discussion

In the solution described above you learned how to promote an InfoPath field to an existing site column in SharePoint. Because you cannot preconfigure property promotion of fields to existing site columns through the **Form Options** dialog box, you must use the **Publishing Wizard** when promoting form fields to existing site columns. And once you select a site column to promote a field to, you cannot reselect that same site column to promote another field to it, because InfoPath removes it from the list of site columns you can select. In addition, if you promote a field to a site column that does not already exist on a form library (if you are publishing the form template to a form library) or on a content type (if you are publishing the form template as a site content type), that site column will be added to the form library or content type when you publish the form template.

24 Delete a column linked to a promoted field

Problem

You promoted an InfoPath form field to a column in SharePoint, and now you want to delete this column from the form library or content type in SharePoint.

Solution

You can remove the field from the list of promoted fields in InfoPath and republish the form template to delete the column from the form library or content type in SharePoint.

To delete a column linked to a promoted field:

1. In InfoPath, open the form template you published to a form library or as a site content type, and used to promote the field to a column in SharePoint.
2. Click **File** ➤ **Info** ➤ **Form Options**.
3. On the **Form Options** dialog box, select **Property Promotion** in the **Category** list.

4. On the **Form Options** dialog box, select the column you want to delete in the list box that displays fields that have been made available as columns in SharePoint or Outlook (the top-most list box), click **Remove**, and then click **OK**.
5. Republish the form template as described in recipe *20 Republish a form template*.

In SharePoint, navigate to the form library that had the column for the promoted field assigned to it and check whether the column has been removed. If you published the form template as a site content type, navigate to the **Site Content Types** page, click on the content type, and verify that the column has been removed.

Discussion

In the solution described above you deleted a column for a promoted field from within InfoPath Designer 2013. You could have also deleted the column from within SharePoint itself. However, doing so would not remove the field promotion from the InfoPath form template, so a column may wind up being recreated when you republish the form template in the future. And while you used the **Form Options** dialog box to delete a promoted field and the **Quick Publish** command to republish the form template, you could have also gone through the steps of the **Publishing Wizard** again to remove the promoted field and then republish the form template.

Note:

> Removing promoted columns from a form library or content type does not affect the actual data stored within existing InfoPath forms in the form library or forms that are based on the content type. This action only removes public access to InfoPath form fields. However, you should still be able to edit the values of form fields by opening the InfoPath form, unless you have deleted the fields from the form template itself.

Publish a form template as a site content type

25 Create a content type for an InfoPath form from within InfoPath

Problem

You have an InfoPath form template which you want to use to create InfoPath forms that are stored in multiple SharePoint form libraries on sites in a site collection.

Solution

You can publish the InfoPath form template as a site content type to SharePoint so that you can use it across multiple form libraries.

To publish an InfoPath form template as a site content type:

1. In InfoPath, create a new SharePoint form library form template or use an existing one.
2. Click **File ➤ Publish ➤ SharePoint Server** to start publishing the form template. InfoPath may prompt you to save the form template.
3. On the **Publishing Wizard**, enter the URL of the SharePoint site to which you want to publish the form template, and click **Next**.
4. On the **Publishing Wizard**, ensure that the **Enable this form to be filled out by using a browser** check box is selected, select **Site Content Type (advanced)**, and click **Next**.

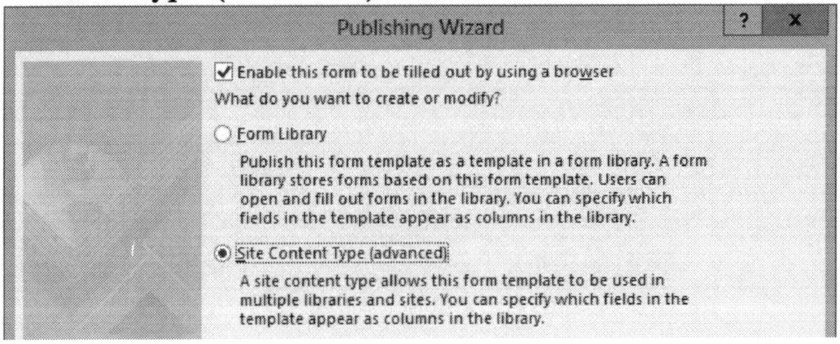

Figure 82. Selecting to publish a form template as a site content type in InfoPath 2013.

5. On the **Publishing Wizard**, leave the **Create a new content type** option selected, leave **Form** selected as the content type to base the new content type on, and click **Next**. Note that if you were republishing the form template or wanted to update the document template of an existing content type, you would have to select the **Update an existing site content type** option as described in recipe *30 Find and update a template that was published as a content type* instead of the **Create a new content type** option.

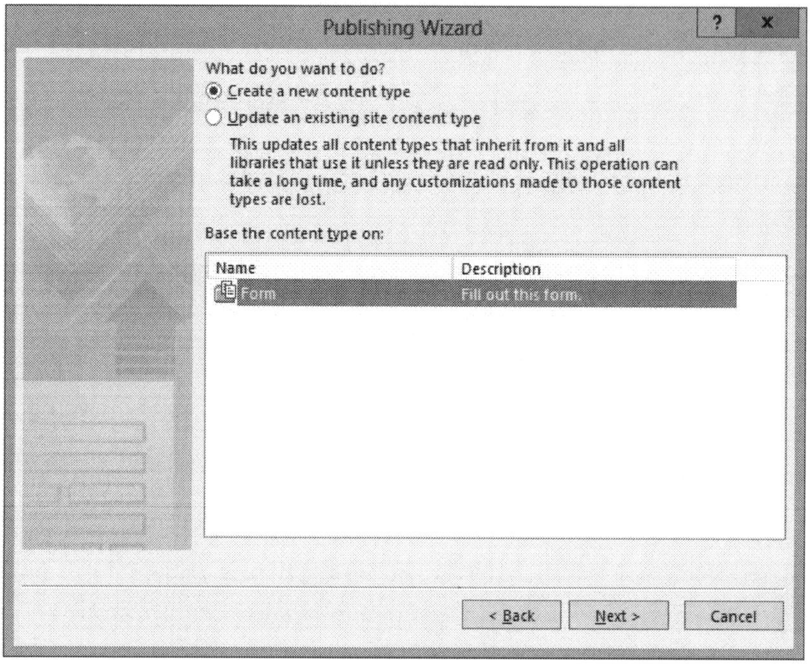

Figure 83. Creating a new content type based on the Form content type.

6. On the **Publishing Wizard**, enter a name for the content type, and click **Next**.
7. On the **Publishing Wizard**, click **Browse**.
8. On the **Browse** dialog box, browse to and select a SharePoint document library (on the site to which the form template is being published) in which you want to store the form template, enter a **File name** for the form template, and then click **Save**.

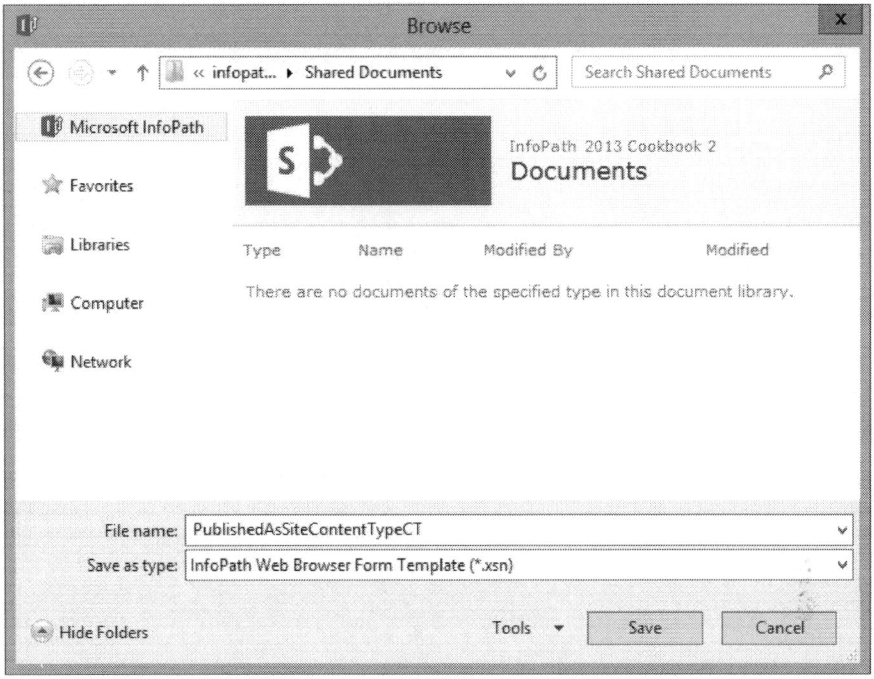

Figure 84. Saving the form template for the content type in a document library.

9. On the **Publishing Wizard**, click **Next**.
10. On the **Publishing Wizard**, promote any fields you want to promote as described in recipe *22 Promote form fields to columns of a form library* or recipe *23 Promote form fields to existing site columns*, and click **Next**.
11. On the **Publishing Wizard**, click **Publish**.
12. On the **Publishing Wizard**, click **Close**.

The form template should have been published as a site content type on the SharePoint site you specified through the **Publishing Wizard**. In SharePoint, navigate to the site where you published the form template. Select **Site settings** from the **Settings** menu (the gear icon in the top-right corner), and then on the **Site Settings** page under **Web Designer Galleries**, click **Site content types**. On the **Site Content Types** page, verify that the new site content type is listed under the **Microsoft InfoPath** group. Now the form template is ready to be added as a content type to form libraries (see recipe *27 Create different types of forms in one form library*).

Discussion

In the solution described above, you published a form template as a site content type. When you publish a form template as a site content type, a site content type is created on the site you specified through the **Publishing Wizard** and the InfoPath form template you published becomes the document template of that content type. You can publish an InfoPath form template as a site content type whenever you want to reuse a form template across several SharePoint form libraries that reside on the same site or on a subsite of the site to which you publish the form template. After you publish a form template as a site content type, it is not ready for use yet. The next step would be to add the content type to a SharePoint form library as described in recipe *27 Create different types of forms in one form library*.

When you publish a form template as a site content type, you do not need permissions to create or access a form library, but you do need permissions to:

1. Access the SharePoint site on which you want to publish the form template.
2. Query the content types on the site.
3. Create or update a content type.

Typically, this would require **Design** permission on the site to which you want to publish the form template.

26 Create a content type for an InfoPath form from within SharePoint

Problem

You want to create a content type in SharePoint that can be used to generate InfoPath forms.

Solution

You can manually create a content type in SharePoint, and then update that content type from within InfoPath to set an InfoPath form template to be its document template.

To create a content type for an InfoPath form from within SharePoint:

1. In SharePoint, select **Site settings** from the **Settings** menu (the gear icon in the top-right corner).
2. On the **Site Settings** page under **Web Designer Galleries**, click **Site content types**.
3. On the **Site Content Types** page, click **Create**.
4. On the **New Site Content Type** page, enter a **Name** for the content type (for example **SPInfoPathCT**), select **Document Content Types** from the **Select parent content type from** drop-down list box, select **Form** from the **Parent Content Type** drop-down list box, leave **Custom Content Types** selected in the **Existing group** drop-down list box, and click **OK**.

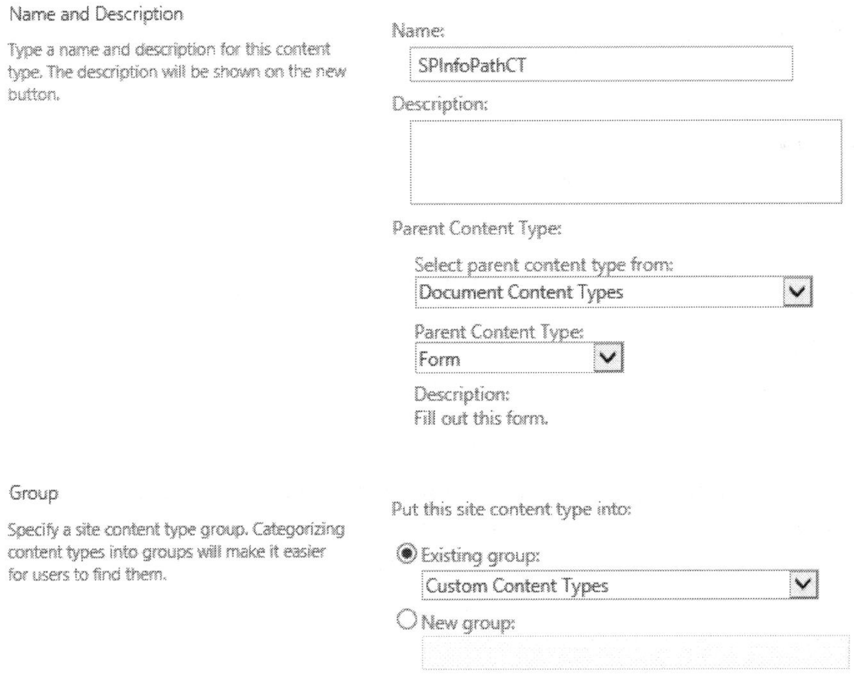
Name and Description
Type a name and description for this content type. The description will be shown on the new button.
Name:
SPInfoPathCT
Description:
Parent Content Type:
Select parent content type from:
Document Content Types
Parent Content Type:
Form
Description:
Fill out this form.
Group
Specify a site content type group. Categorizing content types into groups will make it easier for users to find them.
Put this site content type into:
Existing group:
Custom Content Types
New group:

Figure 85. Creating a new Form content type in SharePoint 2013.

5. In InfoPath, create a new SharePoint form library form template or use an existing one.
6. Follow steps 2 through 4 of recipe *25 Create a content type for an InfoPath form from within InfoPath*.
7. On the **Publishing Wizard**, select the **Update an existing site content type** option, select **SPInfoPathCT** in the list of site content types, and click **Next**.

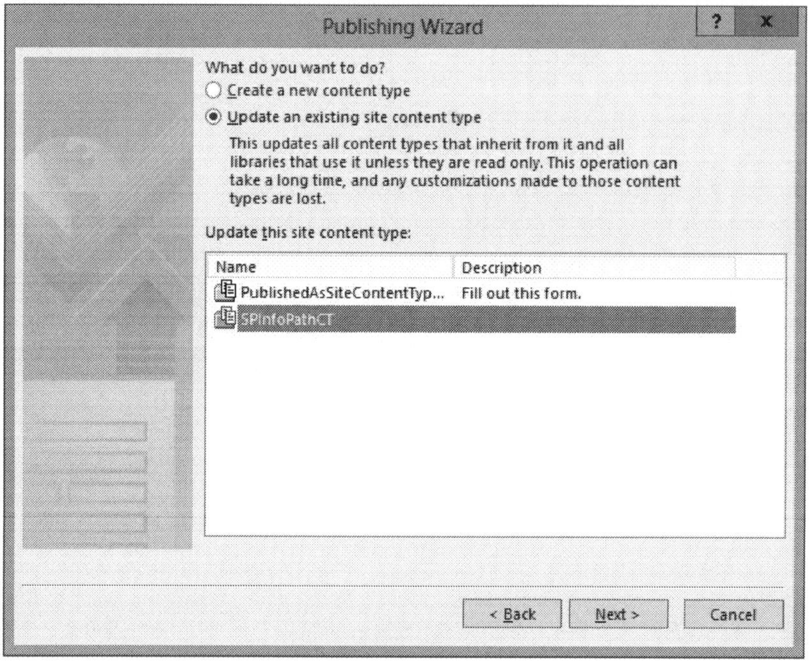

Figure 86. Updating an existing content type.

8. Follow steps 7 through 12 of recipe *25 Create a content type for an InfoPath form from within InfoPath*.

The form template should have been published to SharePoint and linked to the existing site content type as its document template. In SharePoint, navigate to the site where you published the form template. Select **Site settings** from the **Settings** menu (the gear icon in the top-right corner), and then on the **Site Settings** page under **Web Designer Galleries**, click **Site content types**. On the **Site Content Types** page, locate the **SPInfoPathCT** site content type under the **Microsoft InfoPath** group, and click it. On the **Site Content Type** page under **Settings**, click **Advanced settings**. On the **Advanced Settings** page, you should see the form template you published specified under **Document Template**.

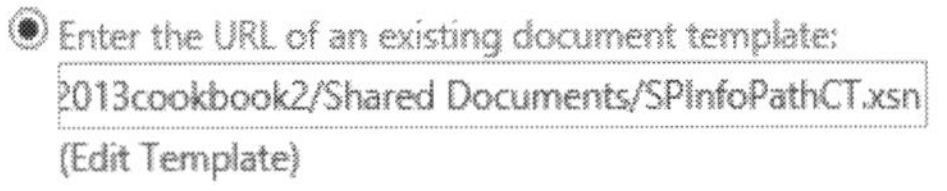

Figure 87. The form template specified as the document template of the content type.

Now the content type is ready to be associated with form libraries so that InfoPath forms can be created (see recipe *27 Create different types of forms in one form library*).

Discussion

In recipe *25 Create a content type for an InfoPath form from within InfoPath*, you published an InfoPath form template as a site content type from within InfoPath, thereby creating a new content type in SharePoint. In this recipe, you started in SharePoint by creating a content type and then afterwards updated that content type from within InfoPath.

Note that for a content type to appear in the list of content types in InfoPath Designer 2013, you must base that content type on the **Form** parent content type when you create it.

Also note that when you first created the content type in SharePoint, you placed it under a group named **Custom Content Types**, and that after you updated the content type from within InfoPath, the content type was automatically moved and placed under the group named **Microsoft InfoPath** on the **Site Content Types** page.

27 Create different types of forms in one form library

Problem

You want users to be able to select from one of several form templates that can be used to create different types of InfoPath forms in one form library.

Solution

You can enable management of content types on a form library and then add all of the content types for the form templates, which you want users to use to create different types of InfoPath forms in the form library, to the form library.

To create different types of InfoPath forms in one SharePoint form library:

1. In InfoPath, create a new SharePoint form library form template or use an existing one, and publish it as a site content type as described in recipe *25 Create a content type for an InfoPath form from within InfoPath*.
2. In SharePoint, create a new form library as described in recipe *18 Create a form library and edit its form template* without editing its form template, or use an existing one.
3. Navigate to the form library which you want to use to create different types of forms, and click **Library** ➤ **Settings** ➤ **Library Settings**.
4. On the **Settings** page, you must enable management of content types to be able to add the content type for each InfoPath form you want to create. So under **General Settings**, click **Advanced settings**.
5. On the **Advanced Settings** page, select the **Yes** option for **Allow management of content types**, and click **OK**.

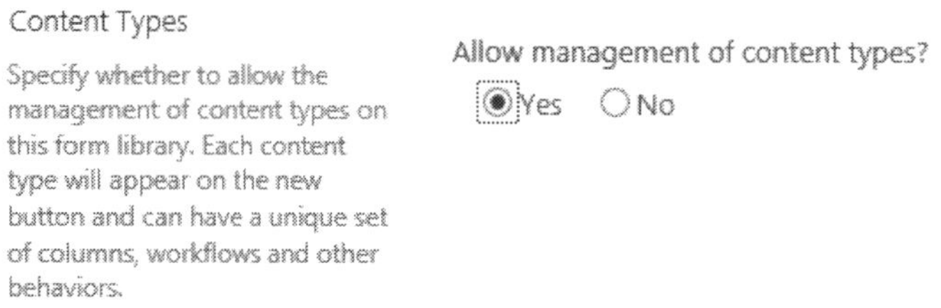

Figure 88. Content Types section on the Advanced Settings page.

6. Back on the **Settings** page, you should now see a **Content Types** section present on the page. Click the **Add from existing site content types** link under the **Content Types** section to add an existing site content type to the form library.

Content Types

This document library is configured to allow multiple content types. Use content types to specify the information you want to display about an item, in addition to its policies, workflows, or other behavior. The following content types are currently available in this library:

Content Type	Visible on New Button	Default Content Type
Form	✓	✓

▫ Add from existing site content types

▫ Change new button order and default content type

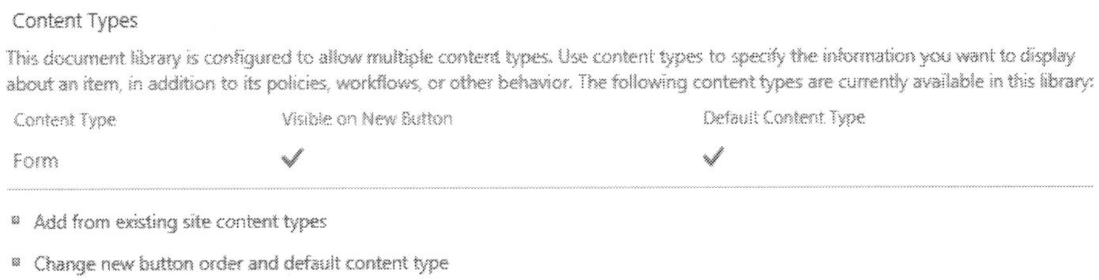

Figure 89. Content Types section on the Settings page of the form library.

7. On the **Add Content Types** page, select **Microsoft InfoPath** from the **Select site content types from** drop-down list box, select the content type you want to add to the form library (this would be the content type pertaining to the form template you published as a site content type) in the **Available Site Content Types** list box, click **Add** to add it to the **Content types to add** list box, and then click **OK**. Note that if you want to add more than one content type to the form library, you can select multiple content types at once by holding the **Ctrl** key pressed down on your keyboard while you click to select the content types you want to add.

Select site content types from:
Microsoft InfoPath

Available Site Content Types:

Content types to add:
PublishedAsSiteContentTypeCT

Add >

< Remove

Description:
Fill out this form.

Group: Microsoft InfoPath

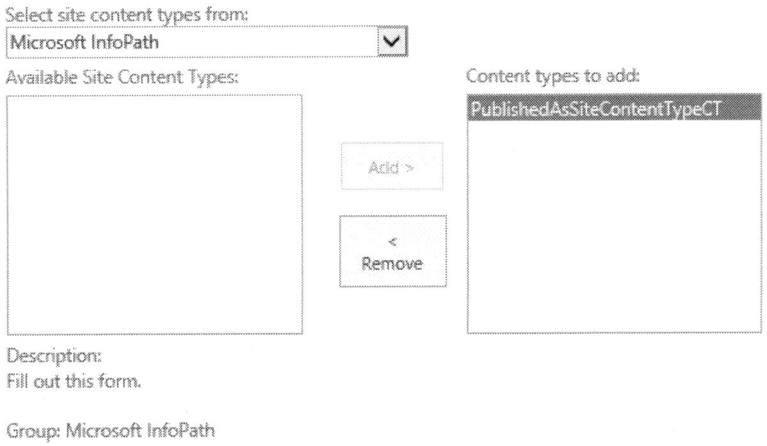

Figure 90. Selecting a content type to add to a form library.

The content type for the InfoPath form template should now appear under the **Content Types** section on the **Settings** page.

Content Types

This document library is configured to allow multiple content types. Use content types to specify the information you want to display about an item, in addition to its policies, workflows, or other behavior. The following content types are currently available in this library:

Content Type	Visible on New Button	Default Content Type
Form	✓	✓
PublishedAsSiteContentTypeCT	✓	

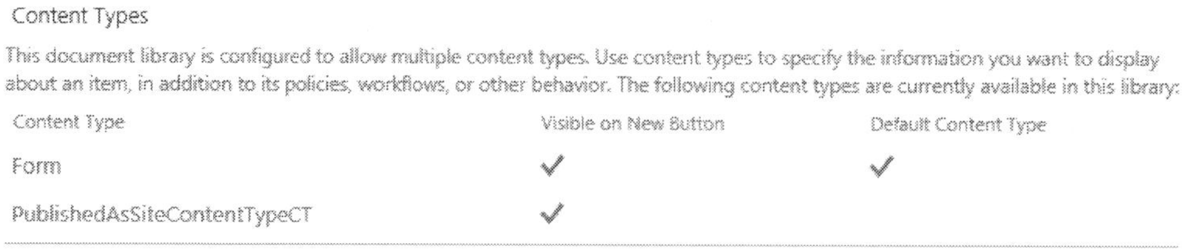

Figure 91. Content Types section after the content type has been added to the form library.

And when you go to the form library and select **Files ➤ New ➤ New Document**, the content type should be listed as a menu item on the **New Document** command drop-down menu, where users can now select from one or more form templates to create different types of InfoPath forms.

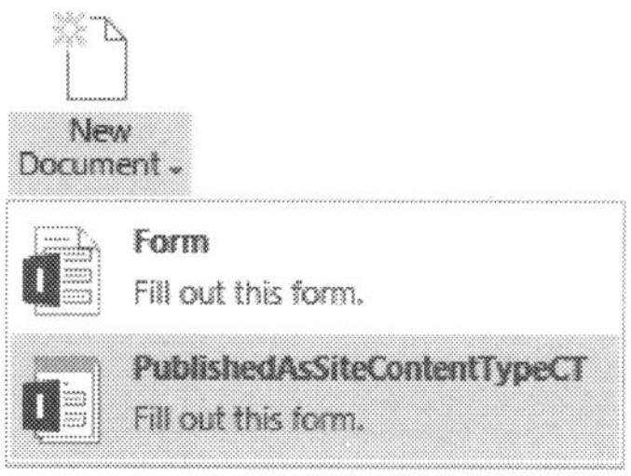

Figure 92. Content type listed on the New Document command drop-down menu.

Discussion

In the solution described above, you learned how to add one site content type to a form library. That site content type was linked to a particular form template you published as a site content type to SharePoint. If you want a form library to allow users to choose from several InfoPath form templates with which they can create different types of forms, you must repeat step 6 to add the site content types that are linked to the form templates you want to add to the form library, or add multiple content types when performing step 7.

Go back to the **Settings** page of the form library. Under the **Content Types** section, you should see a content type named **Form** listed with two check marks: One for **Visible on New Button** and another one for **Default Content Type**. If a content type has a check mark in the **Default Content Type** column, that content type is the content type that will be used to create forms when you click the **new document** link in the form library as well as the content type that is listed as first on the **New Document** command drop-down menu on the Ribbon. So when you have more than one content type listed under the **Content Types** section, you can set another content type to be the default content type (also see recipe *28 Configure a form library to create a certain type of form by default*), and therefore also set which form template is used to create forms whenever a user clicks **new document** in the form library.

28 Configure a form library to create a certain type of form by default

Problem

You have configured a SharePoint form library to create and store different types of InfoPath forms. Now you want to configure the form library to create one of those InfoPath forms by default when a user clicks the **new document** link in the form library.

Solution

After you have added one or more content types to a form library, you can set a form template to be the default form template that is used to create new forms in the form library by making the content type that is linked to that form template the default content type of the form library.

To configure a form library to create a certain type of form by default:

1. In InfoPath, create a new SharePoint form library form template or use an existing one, and publish it as a site content type as described in recipe *25 Create a content type for an InfoPath form from within InfoPath*.
2. In SharePoint, add the site content type for the form template you published, to a new or an existing form library as described in recipe *27 Create different types of forms in one form library*.
3. On the **Settings** page of the form library under **Content Types**, click **Change new button order and default content type**.

4. On the **Change New Button Order** page, select **1** from the **Position from Top** drop-down list box for the content type you want to make the default content type, and click **OK**. Note that the positions of all of the other content types associated with the form library should automatically rearrange themselves.

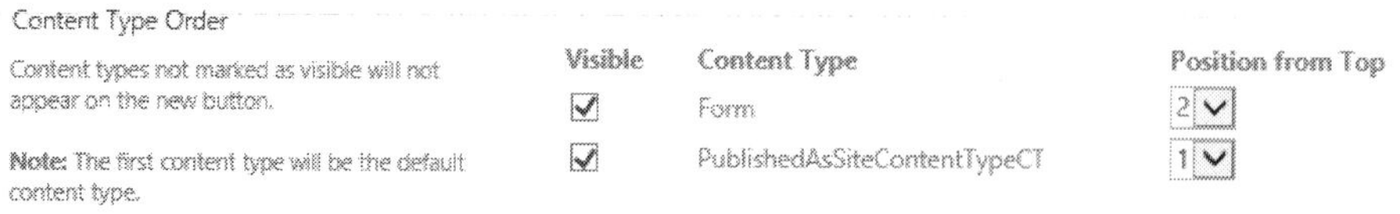

Figure 93. Setting the content type order in SharePoint 2013.

In SharePoint, navigate to the form library, and verify that the changes were successful by clicking the **new document** link in the SharePoint form library and by checking the order of form templates listed on the **New Document** command drop-down menu on the Ribbon.

Discussion

The default content type of a form library is the first content type that is listed on the **New Document** command drop-down menu on the Ribbon and also the content type that SharePoint uses by default when a user clicks the **new document** link in a form library.

In the solution described above, you learned how to use the **Change New Button Order** page to make a particular content type the default content type of a form library. If you have more than two content types associated with a form library, you can use the **Position from Top** setting to rearrange the order in which the form templates that are linked to those content types should appear on the **New Document** command drop-down menu.

Once you have made a content type the default content type of a form library, users can click the **new document** link in the form library to quickly add forms to the form library instead of having to use the **New Document** command on the Ribbon.

You can also use the **Change New Button Order** page to make a content type invisible by deselecting the **Visible** check box for that content type. This action should remove the content type from the **New Document** command drop-down menu, but not from the form library itself.

29 Rename items listed on the New Document menu of a form library

Problem

You published an InfoPath form template as a site content type and added it to a form library, but the newly added form template appears on the **New Document** command drop-down menu with the same name you gave the site content type. You want to rename the form template that appears on the **New Document** command drop-down menu, so that it displays a name that is meaningful to users.

Solution

To rename a form template that is listed on the **New Document** command drop-down menu on the Ribbon, you must first enable management of content types on the form library, and then rename the content type linked to the form template via the **List Content Type** page.

To rename items that are listed on the **New Document** command drop-down menu on the Ribbon:

1. In InfoPath, create a new SharePoint form library form template or use an existing one, and publish it as a site content type as described in recipe *25 Create a content type for an InfoPath form from within InfoPath*.
2. In SharePoint, add the site content type for the form template to a new or an existing form library as described in recipe *27 Create different types of forms in one form library*.
3. On the **Settings** page of the form library under **Content Types**, click on the name of the content type you want to rename.
4. On the **List Content Type** page under **Settings**, click **Name and description**.
5. On the **Content Type Settings** page, enter a new name in the **Name** text box, change the **Description** if you wish (the text you enter here will appear below the menu item name on the **New Document** command drop-down menu on the Ribbon), and click **OK**.

In SharePoint, navigate to the form library that is linked to the renamed content type. Click **Files** ➤ **New** ➤ **New Document** and verify that the new name (and description) you entered appear on the **New Document** command drop-down menu.

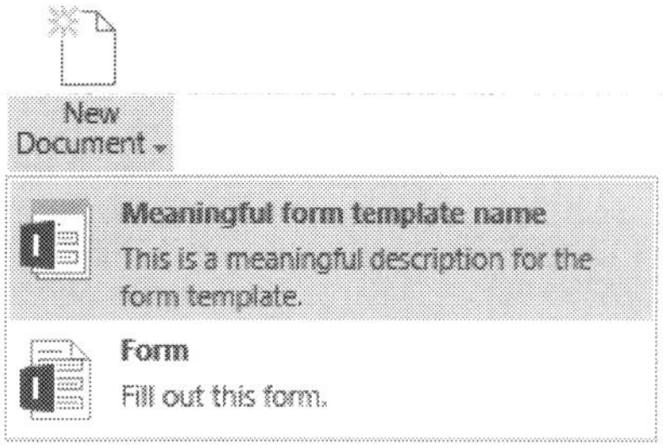

Figure 94. Form template with a user-friendly name on the New Document menu.

Discussion

The solution described above assumed that you published a form template as a site content type as described in recipe *25 Create a content type for an InfoPath form from within InfoPath* or recipe *26 Create a content type for an InfoPath form from within SharePoint*, and then added that content type to a form library as described in recipe *27 Create different types of forms in one form library*. In doing so, the **Content Types** section would be present on the **Settings** page of the form library. If you did not take this route to publish a form template, but rather published a form template directly to a form library as described in recipe *19 Publish a form template to a form library*, the **Content Types** section would be missing from the **Settings** page of the form library. In the latter case, you would have to enable management of content types as described in steps 4 and 5 of recipe *27 Create different types of forms in one form library* to have the **Content Types** section appear on the **Settings** page. Once you have enabled management of content types, you can click on the **Form** content type listed under the **Content Types** section and follow steps 4 and 5 of the solution described above to rename the menu item. Note that before you enable management of content types on a form library, the menu item has the name **New Document**. This menu item name should change to **Form** after you enable management of content types on the form library.

30 Find and update a template that was published as a content type

Update a form template that was stored locally on disk

Problem

You have a form library that makes use of a form template that was published as a site content type. You want to update the form template to contain extra functionality.

Solution

You can use the **Update an existing site content typ**e option on the **Publishing Wizard** to update the form template used by a particular content type.

Important:

> This solution assumes that the form template being updated is the latest version. If you are unsure whether a form template that has been stored on disk is the latest version, no code has been written for that form template, and the form template that is currently working in SharePoint is the form template that should be updated, you may want to use the second method described in this recipe.

To update a form template that was published as a content type:

1. In InfoPath, apply the changes you want to apply to the form template, and when you are done, follow steps 2 through 4 of recipe *25 Create a content type for an InfoPath form from within InfoPath*.
2. On the **Publishing Wizard**, select the **Update an existing site content type** option, select the content type you want to update in the list of site content types, and click **Next**.

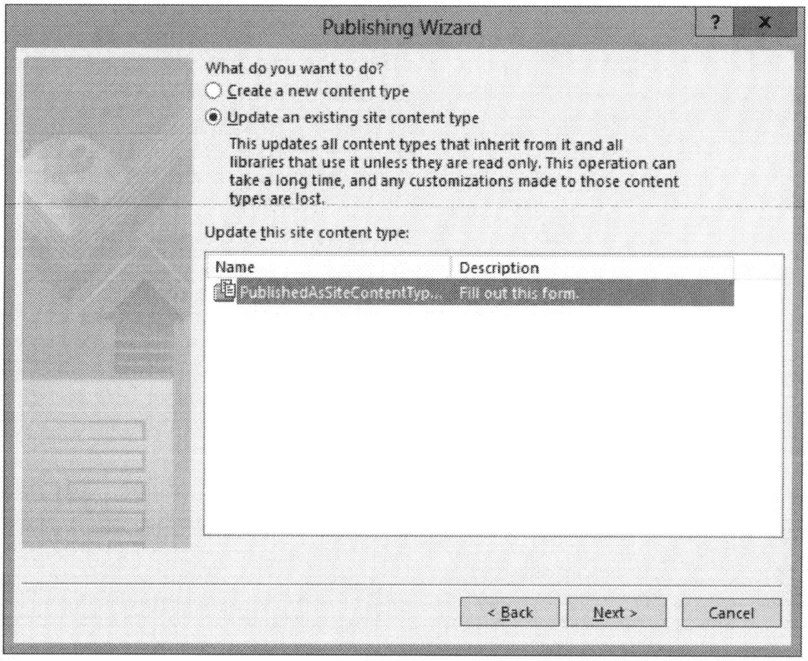

Figure 95. Updating an existing content type.

3. Follow steps 7 through 12 of recipe *25 Create a content type for an InfoPath form from within InfoPath*.

In SharePoint, navigate to the form library that makes use of the content type you updated and add a new form. When the form opens, verify that the changes you made to the form template were applied. For example, if you added new controls, you should see those controls appear on the form you opened.

Update a form template that cannot be found on disk

Problem

You have a form library that makes use of a form template that does not contain code and that was published as a site content type, but that cannot be found anywhere on disk. You want to update the form template to contain extra functionality.

Solution

You can retrieve the form template that is being used by the content type that was created via InfoPath from within SharePoint, open it in InfoPath, and then update it to suit your needs.

To update a form template that was published as a content type:

1. In SharePoint, navigate to the form library that makes use of the content type for the form template you want to update.
2. Click **Library ➤ Settings ➤ Library Settings**.
3. On the **Settings** page under **Content Types**, click the name of the content type that makes use of the form template you want to update.
4. On the **List Content Type** page under **Settings**, click **Advanced settings**.
5. On the **Advanced Settings** page under **Document Template**, you should see the URL of the form template being used by the content type. Click **Edit Template** to open the form template in InfoPath Designer 2013.
6. In InfoPath, apply the changes you want to apply to the form template, and when you are done, republish the form template by clicking **File ➤ Info ➤ Quick Publish**, **File ➤ Publish ➤ Quick Publish**, or **File ➤ Publish ➤ SharePoint Server** thereby accepting the settings that were previously set when the form was last published. Note that InfoPath may prompt you to save the form template before republishing it.
7. Close InfoPath.
8. In SharePoint, on the **Advanced Settings** page, click **Cancel**.

In SharePoint, navigate to the form library and add a new form. When the form opens, verify that the changes you made to the form template were applied. For example, if you added new controls, you should see those controls appear on the form you opened.

Discussion

In the second solution described above, you updated the document template of a list content type associated with a form library. Note that you could have also updated the site content type that was originally created when the form template was published to SharePoint for the first time. However, because in the example above, both the list content type and the site content type are pointing to the same form template that was stored somewhere central (the **Documents** library on the site), updating either content type would have updated all of the content types that made use of the form template.

Note that the second solution is perfect for cases in which a codeless form template was lost on disk, but is still fully functional in SharePoint.

31 Delete the content type for a form template from a form library

Problem

You want to remove a form template that is currently associated with a form library through a content type, from that form library.

Solution

You can delete the content type that is linked to the form template you want to delete from a form library through the **List Content Type** page. Proceed with caution.

Warning:

> Never delete any site content types that are part of a default SharePoint installation.

To delete the content type for a form template from a form library:

1. In SharePoint, navigate to the form library from which you want to delete the content type, and ensure that the form library does not contain any forms that were created using the content type you want to delete. Tip: You can select **Libray ➤ Manage Views ➤ Current View ➤ Relink Documents** to switch to the **Relink Documents** view of the form library and look at the **Content Type** column to identify forms that are linked to a particular content type.

2. Click **Library ➤ Settings ➤ Library Settings**, and enable management of content types as described in steps 4 and 5 of recipe *27 Create different types of forms in one form library* if it is not already enabled.
3. On the **Settings** page under **Content Types**, click on the name of the content type for the form template you want to delete.
4. On the **List Content Type** page under **Settings**, click **Delete this content type**.

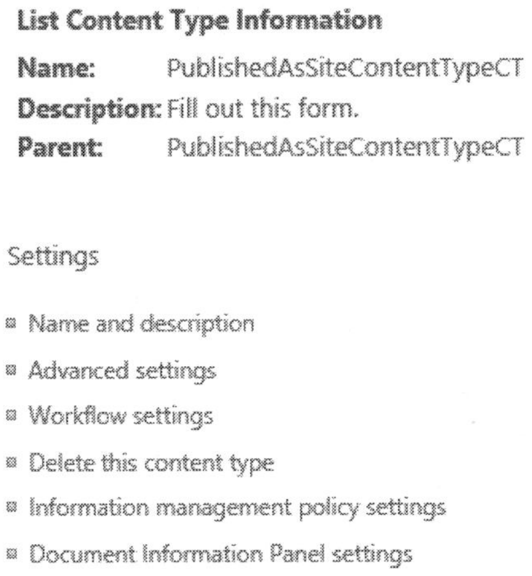

Figure 96. Content type settings on the List Content Type page.

5. Click **OK** on the message box that asks you whether you are sure you want to delete the list content type.

The content type should not be listed anymore under the **Content Types** section on the **Settings** page or on the **New Document** command drop-down menu of the form library.

Discussion

A form template, when published as a site content type to SharePoint, becomes the document template of that content type. So if you want to delete a form template from a form library, you must delete the content type for that form template from the form library. But you can only delete or disassociate a content type from a form library if the form library does not contain forms that are linked to the form template of that content type. If there are forms that are still linked to the form template of the content type you are trying to delete from the form library, SharePoint should display an error that says:

Content Type is still in use

In addition, when you disassociate a content type from a form library, you only delete the content type that has been copied onto the form library, i.e. the list content type. The original site content type from which the list content type was initially created when you associated the site content type with the form library remains intact, so theoretically speaking you could re-add the content type to the form library at a later stage.

You can verify that the site content type has not been deleted by going to the **Site Content Types** page, which is accessible through **Site settings ➤ Site content types**, and verify that the content type is still listed under the **Microsoft InfoPath** group. If you also want to delete the site content type, you must click on its name, and then on the **Site Content Type** page under **Settings**, click **Delete this site content type**. If you get the message

The content type is in use.

it means that list content types that were created from the site content type may still be associated with one or more libraries. You would have to delete those list content types before trying to delete the site content type.

You could also delete the **Form** list content type that is automatically updated when you publish a form template directly to a form library, in which case you would not have an original site content type to restore the list content type from; you would have to republish the form template to have that content type restored.

Also note that you would have to manually add a **Form** content type back to the form library (click **Add from existing site content types** and then select the **Form** site content type from under the **Document Content Types** group), make the newly added **Form** list content type the default content type of the form library (see recipe *28 Configure a form library to create a certain type of form by default*), and then republish the form template from within InfoPath Designer 2013. These steps are necessary, because when you publish a form template directly to a form library, the document template of the default content type of the form library is updated. So if you have another content type listed as the default content type, that content type would be updated instead of the **Form** list content type.

If you want to perform a total cleanup of a form template that you have previously published to SharePoint as a site content type, you can perform the following steps:

1. In SharePoint, navigate to each form library that is making use of the content type and delete all of the forms that are based on the content type from each form library.
2. Navigate to the **Settings** page of each form library that is associated with the content type and delete the content type as described in the solution above. This action deletes the list content type from each form library.
3. Navigate to the **Site Content Types** page, locate the site content type you want to delete, click on it to go to its **Site Content Type** page, and then under **Settings**, click **Delete this site content type** to delete the site content type. This action deletes the original site content type that was published to SharePoint. Important: Never delete the original **Form** site content type that is installed by default when a SharePoint site collection is created.
4. Navigate to the document library where you stored the form template for the site content type, and delete the form template.
5. Navigate to the **Recycle Bin** of the site, and delete the forms and the form template.

32 Use one form library column for data from two different forms

Problem

You want to be able to use one form library to create two different types of forms. You also want a field that has the same name on the two types of forms to appear only once in the form library, so to share one column in the form library and not have the column appear twice with the same name in the form library.

Solution

You can use site columns and promote fields of two different InfoPath form template to those columns, so that the two form templates can store data in the same columns in a form library and so that columns are not duplicated in the form library.

To use one form library column for data from two different forms:

1. While SharePoint comes with site columns for names you could reuse (**First Name** and **Last Name Phonetic**), you are going to create your own site columns in this solution. So in SharePoint, navigate to the site to which you will be publishing the form templates and then follow the instructions in *Create a new site column* in the Appendix to add two **Single line of text** site columns named **Employee First Name** and **Employee Last Name** to the site. Place the site columns in the default **Custom Columns** group.
2. In InfoPath, create a new SharePoint form library form template.
3. Add four **Text Box** controls named **firstName**, **lastName**, **city**, and **country**, respectively, to the view of the form template. Note that **city** and **country** will not be shared between the two InfoPath forms in the form library.
4. Follow steps 2 through 6 of recipe *19 Publish a form template to a form library* to start publishing the form template to a new form library named **EmployeesLib**.
5. On the **Publishing Wizard**, click the top-most **Add** button.
6. On the **Select a Field or Group** dialog box, select **firstName** in the **Field to display as column** tree view, select **Custom Columns** from the **Site column group** drop-down list box, select **Employee First Name** from the **Column name** drop-down list box, and then click **OK**. This will add the **Employee First Name** site column to the form library.
7. Repeat steps 5 and 6, but then select **lastName** and **Employee Last Name** instead.
8. On the **Publishing Wizard**, click the top-most **Add** button.
9. On the **Select a Field or Group** dialog box, select **city** in the **Field to display as column** tree view, select **(None: Create new column in**

this library) from the **Site column group** drop-down list box, leave **City** in the **Column name** text box, and then click **OK**. This will create a new list column in the form library.

10. Repeat steps 8 and 9, but then select **country** instead.
11. On the **Publishing Wizard**, click **Next**.
12. On the **Publishing Wizard**, click **Publish**.
13. On the **Publishing Wizard**, click **Close**.
14. In InfoPath, create another new SharePoint form library form template.
15. Add three **Text Box** controls named **firstName**, **lastName**, and **city**, respectively, to the view of the form template. Note that **city** will not be shared between the two InfoPath forms in the form library.
16. Because you already published the previous form template directly to the form library (so as the default content type), you must publish this form template to SharePoint as a site content type and then add the content type manually to the **EmployeesLib** form library. So follow steps 2 through 9 of recipe *25 Create a content type for an InfoPath form from within InfoPath* to start publishing the form template as a new site content type named **EmployeeCT**.
17. On the **Publishing Wizard**, click the top-most **Add** button.
18. On the **Select a Field or Group** dialog box, select **firstName** in the **Field to display as column** tree view, select **Custom Columns** from the **Site column group** drop-down list box, select **Employee First Name** from the **Column name** drop-down list box, and then click **OK**. This will add the **Employee First Name** site column to the content type.
19. Repeat steps 17 and 18, but then select **lastName** and **Employee Last Name** instead.
20. On the **Publishing Wizard**, click the top-most **Add** button.
21. On the **Select a Field or Group** dialog box, select **city** in the **Field to display as column** tree view, select **Core Contact and Calendar Columns** from the **Site column group** drop-down list box, select **City** from the **Column name** drop-down list box, and then click **OK**. This will add the **City** site column to the content type.
22. On the **Publishing Wizard**, click **Next**.

23. On the **Publishing Wizard**, click **Publish**.
24. On the **Publishing Wizard**, click **Close**.
25. In SharePoint, navigate to the **EmployeesLib** form library, and then add the **EmployeeCT** content type to the form library as described in recipe *27 Create different types of forms in one form library*. Once you have added the content type, on the **Settings** page under **Columns**, you should see that the **Employee First Name** and **Employee Last Name** columns are being shared by the **Form** content type (default content type) and the **EmployeeCT** content type, and that **City** appears twice in the form library, which means that **City** is not being shared by the two content types.

Columns

A column stores information about each document in the document library. Because this document library allows multiple content types, some column settings, such as whether information is required or optional for a column, are now specified by the content type of the document. The following columns are currently available in this document library:

Column (click to edit)	Type	Used in
City	Single line of text	EmployeeCT
City	Single line of text	Form
Country	Single line of text	Form
Created	Date and Time	Form, EmployeeCT
Employee First Name	Single line of text	Form, EmployeeCT
Employee Last Name	Single line of text	Form, EmployeeCT
Modified	Date and Time	Form, EmployeeCT
Title	Single line of text	
Created By	Person or Group	
Modified By	Person or Group	
Checked Out To	Person or Group	

Figure 97. Columns defined on the form library after adding the content type.

In SharePoint, navigate to the **EmployeesLib** form library and click **new document** to add a new form that is based on the default content type. Fill out the form and then save it back to the form library. The first and last names you entered in the form should be visible in the **Employee First Name** and **Employee Last Name** columns of the form library. Select **Files ➤ New ➤ New Document ➤ EmployeeCT** to add a new form that is based on the **EmployeeCT** content type. Fill out the form and then save it back to the form library. The first and last names you entered in the second form should be visible in the same **Employee First Name** and

Employee Last Name columns of the form library as the first form. Note that you would have to add the **City** field that is linked to the **EmployeeCT** content type to the **All Documents** view of the form library for it to become visible in the form library.

Discussion

The solution described above is a good example of how you can combine techniques from previous recipes in this chapter and use content types with form libraries.

Submit forms to a form library

Submitting InfoPath forms to a form library is optional. Where browser forms in SharePoint are concerned, you can either save a form to a form library or submit it to a form library. When you save an InfoPath form in SharePoint, you are presented with a **Save As** dialog.

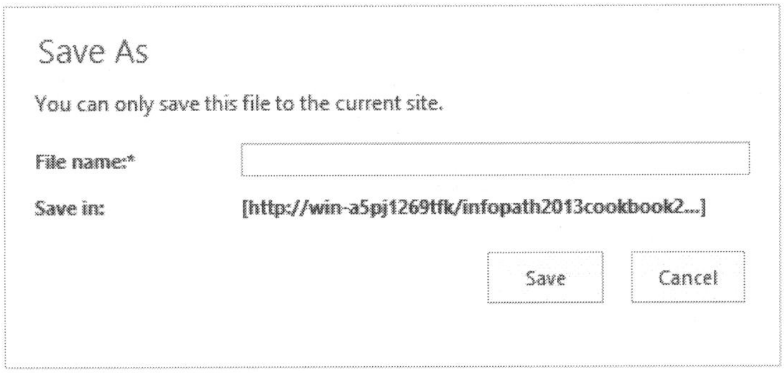

Figure 98. Save As dialog in SharePoint 2013.

You can then enter a name and click **Save** to save the form back to the form library; not to your local disk drive. If you want to save a copy locally, you must use the **Download a Copy** command on the Ribbon or on the context menu of a form after you have selected a form to download.

At this stage, you as a user are in control of the name you assign to the form. If a form with the same name already exists in the form library, you will be prompted with a message asking whether you want to replace the existing file or not; no error takes place.

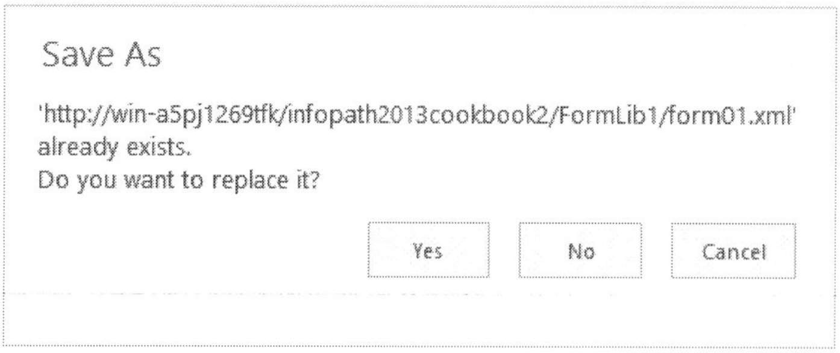
Save As
'http://win-a5pj1269tfk/infopath2013cookbook2/FormLib1/form01.xml'
already exists.
Do you want to replace it?
Yes
No
Cancel

Figure 99. Save As message box prompting to replace an existing form in a form library.

One final thing to note is that once you save the form you must manually close it by clicking the **Close** command on the Ribbon.

When you submit a form in SharePoint, the form can be submitted to a form library, but does not have to be. You could configure the form to be submitted to another destination such as for example a web service. You could even configure the form to be submitted to multiple destinations, for example to a form library and a web service. The latter is not possible when saving a form.

Where the assigning of file names to forms is concerned, when submitting a form, users are not able to enter a name for the form unless you provide them with an InfoPath form field in which they can enter a file name and then use this field in the submit data connection for the form library. So the form template designer is pretty much in control of configuring the form template to generate a unique file name when submitting a form to a form library. Therefore, if you do not want users to enter their own names for forms saved to form libraries, you must configure those forms to be submitted instead of saved.

In addition, you must also ensure that form names you generate are unique or that you configure forms to be overwritten if their names already exist in a form library, otherwise users will be presented with a warning that the form cannot be submitted because of an error. The exact message would say:

The form cannot be submitted to the specified SharePoint document library. The document library already contains a file with the same name. A value in the form may be used to specify the file name. If you know what that value is, modify it and try submitting the form again.

When a user receives this message, she is genuinely stuck and cannot proceed with submitting or saving the form, especially if you have disabled the save functionality by removing the commands from the Ribbon as described in recipe *33 Hide or show Ribbon commands for a form*.

And finally, where having to manually close a form after saving it is concerned, when you configure a form to be submitted, you can also configure it to automatically close, to remain open, or to have a new form be opened after the form has been submitted. These options are not available when you manually save a form.

So while there may be genuine scenarios in which you would want to give users total flexibility when saving forms, there may be times when you may want to take control of saving the forms or want to perform actions that are just not available when saving forms. In the latter cases, you may want to submit a form instead of save it.

33 Hide or show Ribbon commands for a form

Problem

You want to hide a few or all of the commands that appear on the Ribbon when you have a form open in SharePoint.

Solution

You can hide Ribbon commands for a form by deselecting the commands through the **Form Options** dialog box in InfoPath.

To hide or show Ribbon commands for a form:

1. In InfoPath, open the form template for which you want to remove commands from the Ribbon, and click **File** ➤ **Info** ➤ **Form Options**.
2. On the **Form Options** dialog box, ensure that **Web Browser** is selected in the **Category** list, and then deselect the check boxes for the commands corresponding to the commands you want to remove (**Submit**, **Save**, **Save As**, **Close**, **Views**, **Print Preview**, or **Update**).

You could also hide the entire Ribbon by deselecting the **Show InfoPath commands in Ribbon or toolbar** check box.

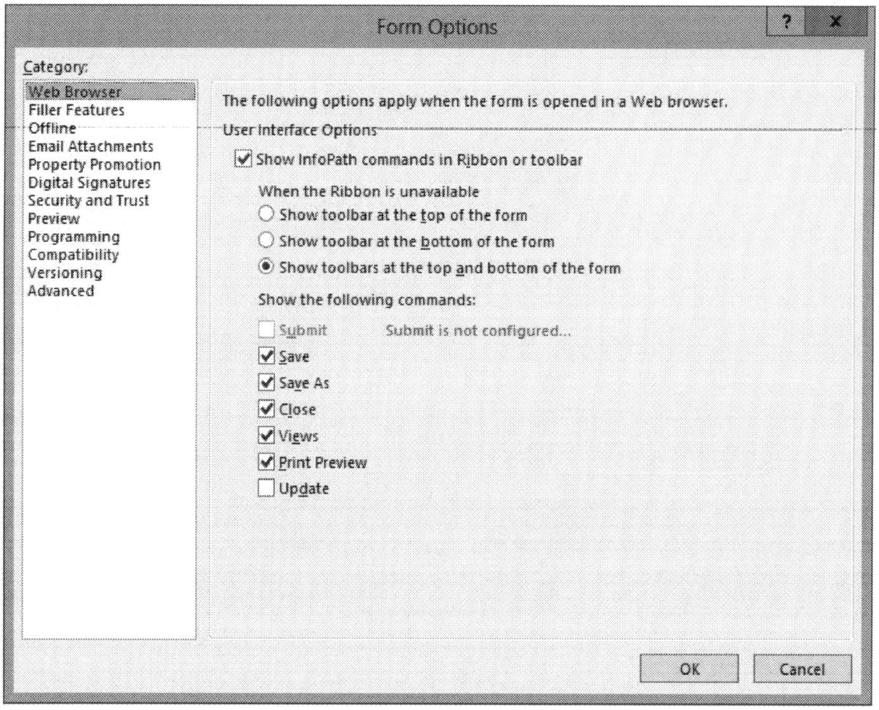

Figure 100. Form Options dialog box screen to hide or show Ribbon commands.

3. On the **Form Options** dialog box, click **OK**.
4. Publish the form template to a SharePoint form library as described in recipe *19 Publish a form template to a form library*.

In SharePoint, navigate to the form library where you published the form template and add a new form. When the form opens, verify that the commands you deselected in InfoPath Designer 2013 are not present on the Ribbon.

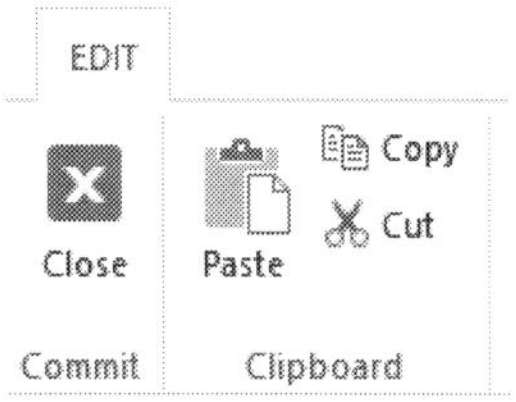

Figure 101. The Ribbon commands for a browser form with only the Close button enabled.

Discussion

When filling out a browser form in SharePoint, a context Ribbon is displayed with the following commands: **Submit**, **Save**, **Save As**, **Close**, **Views**, **Print Preview**, and **Update**. You can hide one or all of these commands through the **Form Options** dialog box in InfoPath.

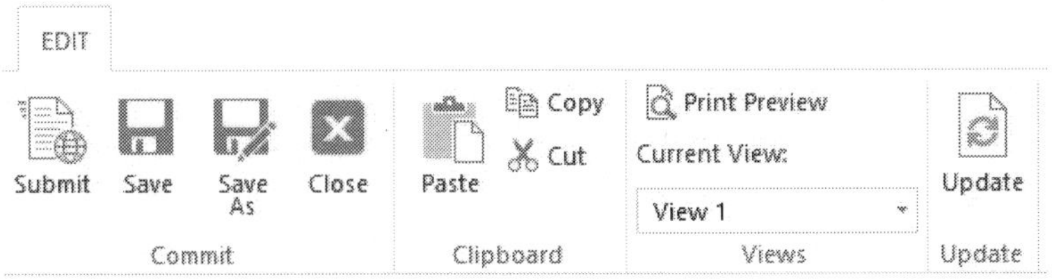

Figure 102. The full array of Ribbon commands available for a browser form.

If you have configured a submit data connection for a form template, it makes sense not to allow users to manually save forms that are based on that form template. Therefore, you should consider removing the **Save** and **Save As** commands from the Ribbon if you are displaying the **Submit** command. Note that the check box for showing the **Submit** command is disabled by default and that you can only show or hide the **Submit** command after you have configured a submit data connection for the form template.

When submitting forms, you have the option to use either the **Submit** command on the Ribbon, or a custom submit button on the form with its **Action** property set to **Submit** or with a **Submit data** action rule set on it. While the **Submit** command on the Ribbon is quick and easy to configure and show, you may want to use a custom submit button on a form for example if you want to conditionally show the submit button. You do not have much control over the **Submit** command on the Ribbon other than either showing or hiding it by configuring this statically when you design the form template, and not dynamically when a form is being filled out. The latter is only possible when you use a custom submit button.

The **Current View** drop-down list box on the Ribbon becomes available only if you have enabled the **Views** options on the **Form Options** dialog box and if the form template has more than one (visible) view.

The **Update** command is not enabled by default, but you can enable it to allow users to force sending data to the server and thereby refresh data in the form. You may want to use this command for example if you have disabled automatic postbacks on controls to minimize the amount of postbacks and therefore need a way to allow users to refresh form data on demand as was discussed in recipe *17 Create a SharePoint form library form template*.

34 Submit a form to a form library and then close it

Problem

You want to be able to submit a form to a form library and then close the form immediately afterwards.

Solution

You can add a form library submit connection to the form template, which by default has an action to close the form after it has been submitted.

To submit a form to a form library and then close it:

1. In InfoPath, create a new SharePoint form library form template or use an existing one.
2. Click **Data ➤ Submit Form ➤ Submit Options**.
3. On the **Submit Options** dialog box, select the **Allow users to submit this form** check box. This should enable the rest of the options on the dialog box.
4. On the **Submit Options** dialog box, leave the **Send form data to a single destination** option selected, and select **SharePoint document library** from the drop-down list box below it. Note: If you want to submit the form to multiple destinations as you will do in recipe *35 Submit a form to a folder in a form library based on a condition* you must select to submit the form using either rules or code.
5. Because you have not yet configured a submit data connection for the form template, the drop-down list box below the label that says

Choose a data connection for submit is disabled. So on the **Submit Options** dialog box, click **Add**.

6. Before performing this step you must already have a form library present on a SharePoint site, or you must first publish the form template thereby creating a new form library, and then use its URL to create the data connection. Note that the form library you submit forms to need not be the same as the form library you publish the form template to. On the **Data Connection Wizard**, enter the URL of the form library to which you want to submit the form. The URL should have the following format:

   ```
   http://servername/sitename/libraryname
   ```

   where **servername** is the name of the SharePoint server and **sitename** is the name of the site where a form library named **libraryname** is located. Ensure that you do not append **/Forms** behind **libraryname**, so do not use an URL such as

   ```
   http://servername/sitename/libraryname/Forms
   ```

   because this would make the form submit to the **Forms** folder of the form library. The **Forms** folder is used to store ASPX files for the form library as well as an InfoPath form template (if you published a form template directly to the form library). The **Forms** folder is invisible when you are looking at the contents of a form library in SharePoint, so any forms you submit to this folder will also remain invisible to users.

7. On the **Data Connection Wizard**, click the formula button behind the **File name** text box.

8. On the **Insert Formula** dialog box, construct a formula that generates a unique form name, such as for example:

   ```
   concat("Form - ", userName())
   ```

   or

   ```
   concat("Form - ", now())
   ```

   and click **OK**. Note that the first formula uses the user's logon name and the second formula uses the current date and time to generate a file name for the form using the **concat()** function. Also note that this would mean that when a form that uses the first formula is resubmitted, the form would have to be overwritten (unless another user resubmits the form), while a new name would automatically be generated for a form that uses the second formula every time the form is resubmitted.

The formula you choose to use depends largely on how you want to deal with the resubmission of existing forms. If you want a new file name to be generated for a form every time a form is submitted to the form library, you can construct a formula that is similar to the second formula using a date and time. If you want an existing form to be overwritten every time that form is resubmitted, you can use a formula that is similar to the first formula (the user name does not change every second, but it is unique to each user), but then you must also select the **Allow overwrite if file exists** check box on the **Data Connection Wizard**, so that the user is not shown an error message when the form is resubmitted and a form that has the same name already exists in the form library.

Note: If you want to allow a user to specify a file name upon submitting the form and not automatically generate a file name based on a date or a user name, you could add a text box control to the view of the form template and then use the **Insert Field or Group** button on the **Insert Formula** dialog box to select the field that is bound to the text box, and add it to the formula that generates the file name for the submitted form. And if you do not want a user to be able to change the file name anymore after a form has already been submitted once before, you must perform a check whether the form is an existing form (see for example recipe *59 Determine whether a form is new or already exists*), add conditional formatting to the text box to disable the field in which the file name is stored if the form is not new and the value of the field is not blank, and then also select the **Allow overwrite if file exists** check box on the **Data Connection Wizard** to avoid getting an error message if the form already exists when it is resubmitted to the form library (also see recipe *60 Autonumber a form when it is submitted to a form library* and recipe *61 Create separate add and edit views in a form* for examples of how you could go about setting up conditional form submission).

9. On the **Data Connection Wizard**, select the **Allow overwrite if file exists** check box depending on your scenario (see the discussion in the previous step), and click **Next**.
10. On the **Data Connection Wizard**, name the data connection **SubmitToFormLibrary**, and click **Finish**.
11. On the **Submit Options** dialog box, click **Advanced**, and ensure that **Close the form** is selected in the **After submit** drop-down list box. This is the default selection, so if you are setting up the form submit for the first time you do not have to check it.
12. On the **Submit Options** dialog box, click **OK**.
13. Publish the form template to a SharePoint form library as described in recipe *19 Publish a form template to a form library*. Note that the form library you publish the form template to need not be the same as the form library to which you submit forms.

In SharePoint, navigate to the form library where you published the form template and add a new form. When the form opens, fill out the form and then click **Submit**. The form should close after you submit it. In SharePoint, navigate to the form library that you used for the submit data connection and verify that the form has indeed been submitted to the form library with the file name from the formula you used in step 8.

Discussion

There are two ways to submit a form to a form library:

1. Submit a form and generate a new name every time the form is submitted or resubmitted.
2. Submit a form with a specific name and use this name every time the form is resubmitted.

Depending on how you want to handle resubmitting a form, you might have to select the **Allow overwrite if file exists** check box as discussed in step 8 of the solution described above.

In the solution described above you added a submit data connection while configuring submit options. In the next recipe, you will first add submit data connections and then afterwards configure submit options.

You can extend the solution described above by removing the **Save**, **Save As**, and **Close** commands from the Ribbon as described in recipe *33 Hide or show Ribbon commands for a form*, because you do not really need to display them when you configure a form to be submitted and closed.

Note that users must be granted permissions to a site and to the form library on the site to be able to save or submit forms. This typically involves having at least **View Only** permission on the site on which the form library is located and **Contribute** permission on the form library itself.

35 Submit a form to a folder in a form library based on a condition

Problem

You have a form which you want to submit either to the root folder of a form library or to another folder in the form library based on an option that has been selected.

Solution

You can add multiple submit data connections to a form template and then use action rules to submit a form based on conditions.

To submit a form to a folder in a form library based on a condition:

1. In SharePoint, manually create a new form library named **TwoFolderLib** as described in recipe *18 Create a form library and edit its form template* without editing its form template.
2. Navigate to the **TwoFolderLib** form library, and click **Files ➤ New ➤ New Folder** to create a new folder.
3. On the **Create a new folder** dialog, type **Folder1** in the **Name** text box, and then click **Save**.
4. Repeat the steps 2 and 3 to create a second folder named **Folder2**.
5. In InfoPath, create a new SharePoint form library form template or use an existing one.

6. Add an **Option Button** control that has 3 options and the name **folder** to the view of the form template.
7. Label the option buttons **Root Folder**, **Folder 1**, and **Folder 2**, respectively.
8. Open the **Option Button Properties** dialog box for the first option button, and then on the **Data** tab, select the **This button is selected by default** check box, and click **OK**.
9. Click **Data ➤ Submit Form ➤ To SharePoint Library**.
10. On the **Data Connection Wizard**, enter the URL of the form library to which you want to submit a form (**TwoFolderLib** in this case). The URL should have the following format:

    ```
    http://servername/sitename/TwoFolderLib
    ```

    where **servername** is the name of the SharePoint server and **sitename** is the name of the site where the **TwoFolderLib** form library is located. Because the URL is pointing to the form library itself, this **Submit** data connection will be used to submit a form to the root folder of the form library. Ensure that you do not append **/Forms** behind **TwoFolderLib**, so do not use an URL such as

    ```
    http://servername/sitename/TwoFolderLib/Forms
    ```

    because this would make the form submit to the **Forms** folder of the form library.
11. On the **Data Connection Wizard**, click the formula button behind the **File name** text box.
12. On the **Insert Formula** dialog box, enter a formula that generates a unique name for the form submitted based on the current date and time, for example:

    ```
    concat("Form - ", now())
    ```

    and click **OK** (also see the discussion in step 8 of recipe *34 Submit a form to a form library and then close it*).
13. On the **Data Connection Wizard**, leave the **Allow overwrite if file exists** check box deselected, and click **Next**.

14. On the **Data Connection Wizard**, name the data connection **RootFolderSubmit**, leave the **Set as the default submit connection** check box selected, and click **Finish**.
15. Click **Data ➤ Submit Form ➤ To SharePoint Library**.
16. On the **Data Connection Wizard**, enter the URL of the **Folder1** folder in the form library in the **Document Library** text box. The URL should have the following format:

    ```
    http://servername/sitename/TwoFolderLib/Folder1
    ```

    where **servername** is the name of the SharePoint server, **sitename** is the name of the site where the **TwoFolderLib** form library is located, and **Folder1** is the name of the first folder in the **TwoFolderLib** form library. Because the URL is pointing to a folder, this **Submit** data connection will be used to submit a form to the **Folder1** folder in the form library.
17. On the **Data Connection Wizard**, click the formula button behind the **File name** text box.
18. On the **Insert Formula** dialog box, enter a formula that generates a unique name for the form submitted based on the current date and time, for example:

    ```
    concat("Form - ", now())
    ```

    and click **OK**.
19. On the **Data Connection Wizard**, leave the **Allow overwrite if file exists** check box deselected, and click **Next**.
20. On the **Data Connection Wizard**, name the data connection **Folder1Submit**, leave the **Set as the default submit connection** check box deselected, and click **Finish**.
21. Repeat steps 15 through 20 to add a submit data connection for the **Folder2** folder in the form library. Ensure that you use the correct URL for the folder, for example:

    ```
    http://servername/sitename/TwoFolderLib/Folder2
    ```

    and that you name the data connection **Folder2Submit**.

22. Click **Data ➤ Submit Form ➤ Submit Options**.
23. On the **Submit Options** dialog box, you should see the default submit connection already configured as the submit connection for the form. Because you want to submit to either the root folder or another folder, and not only to the root folder of the form library, you must configure the form to be submitted to multiple destinations based on conditions. Therefore you must use rules, so select the **Perform custom action using Rules** option, and click **OK**. This should open the **Rules** task pane for the **Form Submit** event.
24. On the **Rules** task pane, you should see an **Action** rule already added for the default submit connection. The action should say:

    ```
    Submit using a data connection: RootFolderSubmit
    ```

    You must now add a condition to this rule so that the action only runs if the first option button is selected. So on the **Rules** task pane, select **Rule 1**, click the text under **Condition**, and add a condition that says:

    ```
    folder = "1"
    ```

    where **folder** is the field that is bound to the option button control and **1** is the value of the first option button.
25. On the **Rules** task pane, add a second **Action** rule with a **Condition** that says:

    ```
    folder = "2"
    ```

    and with an action that says:

    ```
    Submit using a data connection: Folder1Submit
    ```

    This action rule submits the form to the **Folder1** folder in the form library if the second option button has been selected.
26. On the **Rules** task pane, add a third **Action** rule with a **Condition** that says:

    ```
    folder = "3"
    ```

    and with an action that says:

    ```
    Submit using a data connection: Folder2Submit
    ```

This action rule submits the form to the **Folder2** folder in the form library if the third option button has been selected.

27. Publish the form template to the **TwoFolderLib** form library as described in recipe *19 Publish a form template to a form library* thereby selecting to update the **TwoFolderLib** form library instead of creating a new form library.

In SharePoint, navigate to the **TwoFolderLib** form library and add a new form. When the form opens, select the second option (to submit to the **Folder1** folder in the form library), and click **Submit**. Click on **Folder1** in the form library to open the folder and verify that the form was stored in it. Repeat the process for the other options and verify that the forms were stored in the correct root or subfolder.

Discussion

In the solution described above, you learned how to submit a form to multiple destinations based on conditions. To make this possible, you had to:

1. Create three submit data connections to submit the form to your destinations of choice.
2. Enable submitting the form to multiple destinations using rules.
3. Add action rules to submit the form to each destination based on a condition.

This technique of using rules to submit a form is not limited to form library submit data connections, but can be used with any type and number of submit data connections. And whenever a scenario calls for submitting a form based on one or more conditions, you must use rules (or code) to submit that form.

36 Submit a form and switch to a 'Thank You' view

Problem

You want to be able to submit a form to a form library and then switch to a 'Thank You' view after the form has been submitted.

Solution

You can submit a form using a rule with two actions that will first submit the form to a form library and then switch views.

To submit a form to a form library and then switch views to display a 'Thank You' view:

1. In InfoPath, create a new SharePoint form library form template or use an existing one.
2. Click **Page Design** ➤ **Views** ➤ **New View**.
3. On the **Add View** dialog box, type **ThankYouView** in the **New view name** text box, and click **OK**.
4. Open the **View Properties** dialog box for the **ThankYouView** view, and then on the **General** tab, deselect the **Show on the View menu when filling out this form** check box, and click **OK**.
5. Type a piece of text on the view, for example "Thank you for filling out this form."
6. Add a **Button** control to the **ThankYouView** view and label it **Close Form**.
7. Add an **Action** rule to the **Close Form** button with an action that says:

   ```
   Close this form: No Prompt
   ```

   This action rule closes the form without prompting the user to save any changes.
8. Follow steps 2 through 10 of recipe *34 Submit a form to a form library and then close it*.
9. On the **Submit Options** dialog box, click **Advanced**, and then select **Leave the form open** from the **After submit** drop-down list box. Because you want to switch to the **ThankYouView** view after you

submit the form and not close the form, you must change the submit options so that the form remains open after it has been submitted.

10. Because you want to submit the form and then switch to display the **ThankYouView** view, you must execute two actions upon submitting the form, so you must run an **Action** rule instead of just running one submit action by sending the form to the form library. So on the **Submit Options** dialog box, select the **Perform custom action using Rules** option, and click **OK**. This should open the **Rules** task pane for the **Form Submit** event.
11. On the **Rules** task pane, there should already be one rule present with an action that submits the form to the form library. Add a second action to this rule to switch to the **ThankYouView** view. So the two actions on the rule should now say:

    ```
    Submit using a data connection: SubmitToFormLibrary
    Switch to view: ThankYouView
    ```

    The first action submits the form to the form library and the second action switches to display the **ThankYouView** view.
12. Publish the form template to a SharePoint form library as described in recipe *19 Publish a form template to a form library*. Note that the form library you publish the form template to need not be the same as the form library to which you submit forms.

In SharePoint, navigate to the form library where you published the form template and add a new form. When the form opens, fill out the form and then click **Submit**. The form should remain open and switch to display the **ThankYouView** view. Click the **Close Form** button. The form should close.

Discussion

You can extend the solution described above by removing the **Save**, **Save As**, and **Close** commands from the Ribbon as described in recipe *33 Hide or show Ribbon commands for a form*, since users would be submitting the form by clicking on the **Submit** command on the Ribbon and then closing the form using the **Close Form** button on the **ThankYouView** view.

37 Send an alert when a new form is added to a form library

Problem

You want to be able to receive an email whenever a new form is added to a particular SharePoint form library.

Solution

You can add an alert to a form library and configure it to send you an email whenever a new form is added to the form library.

To send an alert when a new form is added to a form library:

1. In InfoPath, create a new SharePoint form library form template or use an existing one, and publish it to a form library as described in recipe *19 Publish a form template to a form library*.
2. In SharePoint, navigate to the form library where you published the form template, click **Library** ➤ **Share & Track** ➤ **Alert Me**, and then select **Set alert on this library** from the drop-down menu that appears.

Figure 103. Selecting to set an alert on a form library in SharePoint 2013.

3. On the **New Alert** dialog, your email address should automatically appear under the **Delivery Method** section.

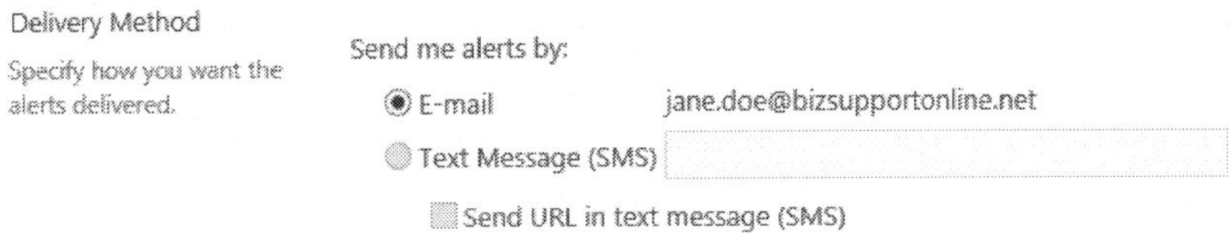

Figure 104. Email address to send alerts to.

Note that if you have full control of the form library, a section named Send Alerts To should appear on the New Alert dialog where you can configure an alert to be sent to multiple users.

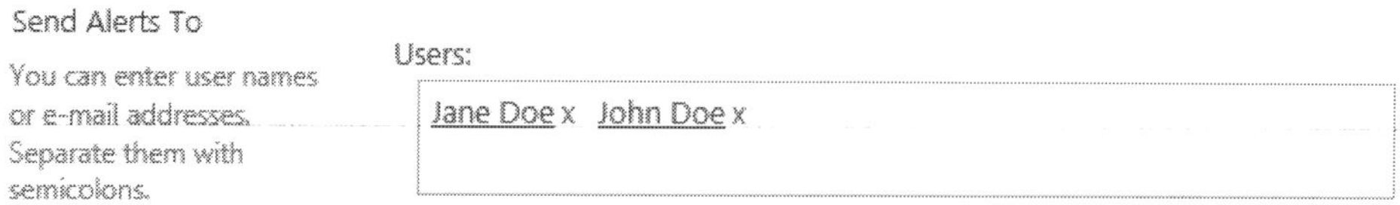
Send Alerts To
You can enter user names or e-mail addresses. Separate them with semicolons.
Users:
Jane Doe x John Doe x

Figure 105. Configuring an alert to be sent to multiple users.

4. On the **New Alert** dialog under **Change Type**, select the **New items are added** option, and then click **OK**.

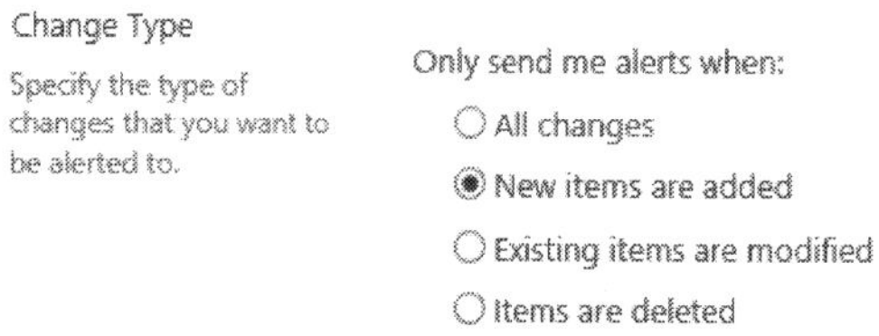
Change Type
Specify the type of changes that you want to be alerted to.
Only send me alerts when:
All changes
New items are added
Existing items are modified
Items are deleted

Figure 106. Selecting to send alerts for new items that are added to the form library.

Now whenever a new form is saved or submitted to the form library, you should receive an email.

Discussion

In the solution described above, you saw how to configure a form library to send an email whenever a new form is saved or submitted to the form library. While this is the easiest way to subscribe to email alerts on a form library, it does not offer much flexibility in terms of configuring the email message that is sent out. If you want to send a customized email message to users, you could make use of a SharePoint workflow as described in recipe *88 Send a form's link in an email to selected users at workflow startup*. And if you want to select users in an InfoPath form and then send an email when that form is submitted, you could use a people picker as described in recipe *74 Get email addresses from a person/group picker* and actions in the form submit event to first switch to a view that has been customized to display a message and then call an email submit data connection to send the active view of the form in an email, or you could use a SharePoint workflow as described in recipe *90 Send an email to a list of people in a people picker*.

Note that an administrator must configure SharePoint to send emails for the solution to work.

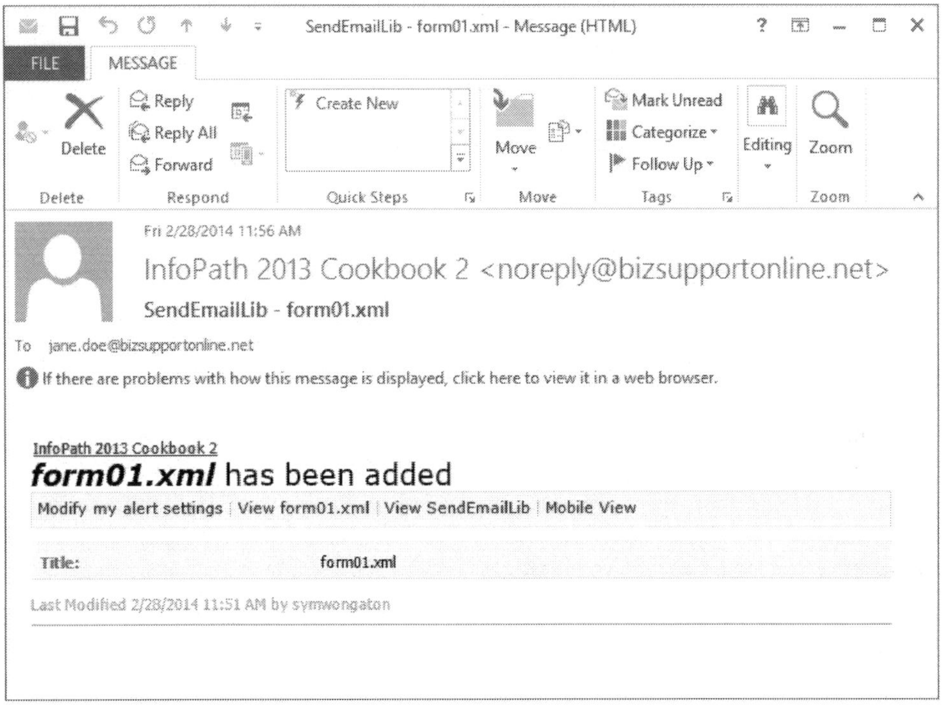

Figure 107. Email message that was sent as an alert when a new form was added.

To delete a previously added alert:

1. In SharePoint, log on as the user for whom you want to delete an alert, click **Page ➤ Share & Track ➤ Alert Me**, and then select **Manage My Alerts** from the drop-down menu that appears.

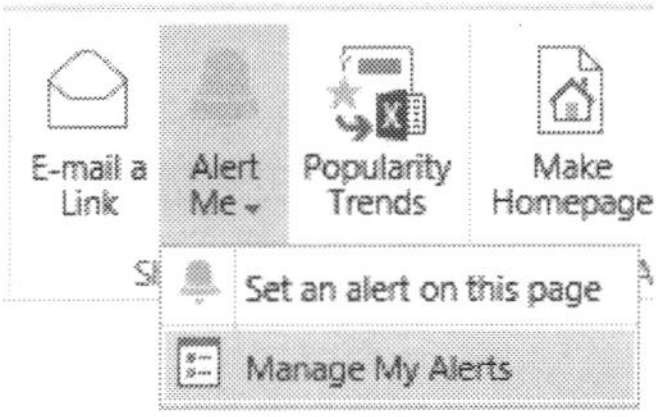

Figure 108. Selecting to manage alerts in SharePoint 2013.

2. On the **My Alerts on this Site** page, select the check box in front of the form library for which you want to delete an alert, and the click **Delete Selected Alerts**. Click **OK** on the message box that appears to confirm deleting the selected alert.

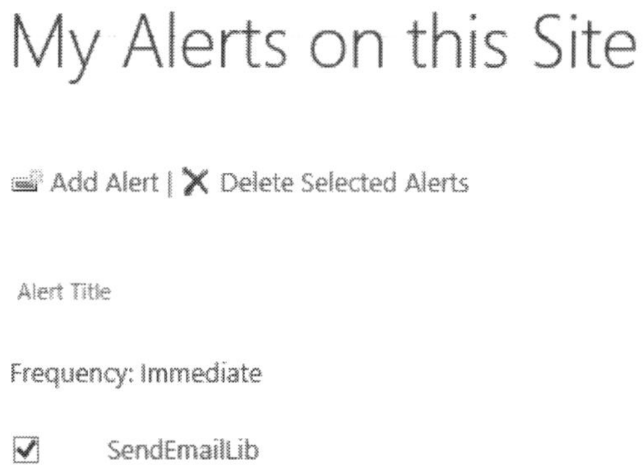

Figure 109. Deleting an alert on a form library in SharePoint 2013.

Display SharePoint form library forms

SharePoint form library forms can be displayed via the standard **FormServer.aspx** page of InfoPath Forms Services, embedded in InfoPath Form Web Parts, or shown as links on SharePoint pages.

The recipes in this section will guide you through a couple of scenarios for displaying SharePoint form library forms in the browser.

38 Add a link to open a form from a SharePoint page

Problem

You want to add a link to a web page on a SharePoint site to be able to click it to open and fill out a new InfoPath form. When the form is closed, saved, or submitted, you want the user to be redirected back to the page on which the link is located.

Solution

You can add a hyperlink to a SharePoint page to open a new InfoPath form.

To add a link to open a form from a SharePoint page:

1. In InfoPath, create a new SharePoint form library form template or use an existing one, and publish it to a SharePoint form library.
2. In SharePoint, navigate to the SharePoint page on which you want to place a link, and copy its URL from the browser's address bar. Open Notepad and temporarily paste the URL in Notepad. If you do not have a page, you can add a new one by selecting **Add a page** from the **Settings** menu (the gear icon in the top-right corner).
3. Navigate to the form library where you published the form template and add a new form. When the form opens, copy the URL from the browser's address bar, paste it in Notepad, and then modify it by changing the value of the **Source** query string parameter to point to the URL of the SharePoint page instead of that of the form library. For example, you should change an URL that looks like the following:

```
http://servername/sitename/_layouts/15/FormServer.aspx?XsnLocat
ion=http://servername/sitename/formlibraryname/Forms/template.x
sn&SaveLocation=http%3A%2F%2Fservername%2Fsitename%2Fformlibrar
yname&ClientInstalled=true&DefaultItemOpen=1&Source=http%3A%2F%
2Fservername%2Fsitename%2Fformlibraryname%2FForms%2FAllItems%2E
aspx
```

   into an URL that looks like the following:

```
http://servername/sitename/_layouts/15/FormServer.aspx?XsnLocat
ion=http://servername/sitename/formlibraryname/Forms/template.x
sn&SaveLocation=http%3A%2F%2Fservername%2Fsitename%2Fformlibrar
yname&ClientInstalled=true&DefaultItemOpen=1&Source=http%3A%2F%
2Fservername%2Fsitename%2FSitePages%2Fpagename.aspx
```

   where the value of the **Source** query string parameter has been set to be equal to the URL of a page named **pagename.aspx** that is located in the **SitePages** document library. Note that all slashes (/) in the URL for the page have been replaced by **%2F** and the colon by **%3A**.

   Close the form without saving or submitting it. Note: If you want a user to be redirected back to the form library and not to the page where the form's link is located, you must leave the entire URL intact and not modify the **Source** query string parameter.

4. Navigate to the SharePoint page on which you want to place a link, and click **Page** ➤ **Edit** ➤ **Edit** or click the small **Edit** command on the Ribbon.
5. Once the page is in edit mode, click anywhere on the page where you want to place the link, and then select **Insert** ➤ **Links** ➤ **Link** ➤ **From Address** on the Ribbon.

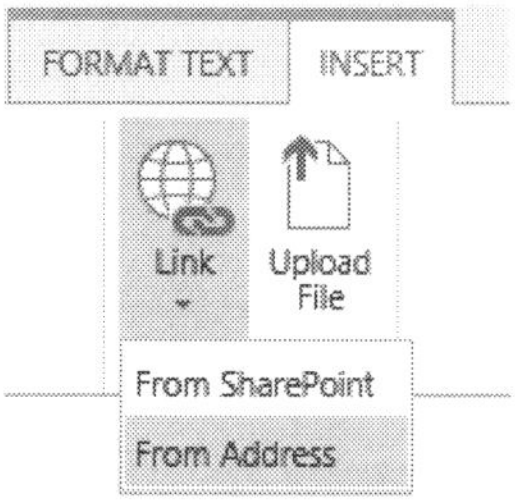

Figure 110. Inserting a link on a page in SharePoint 2013.

6. On the **Insert Hyperlink** dialog, enter the text that should be displayed for the link in the **Text to display** text box, copy the URL of the form you constructed in step 3 from Notepad, paste it into the **Address** text box, and then click **OK**.

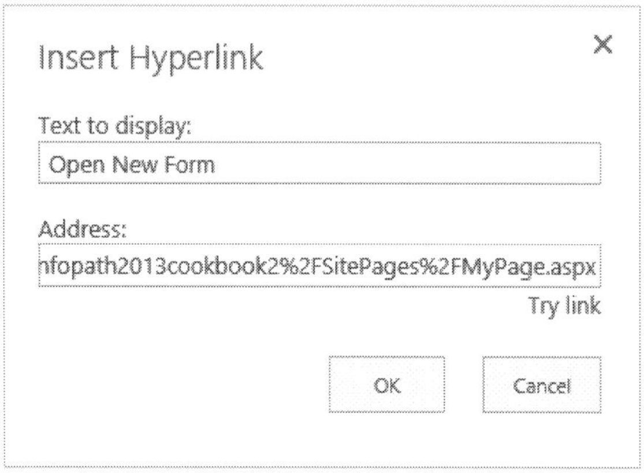

Figure 111. Entering the text and URL for a link in SharePoint 2013.

7. Click **Page** ➤ **Edit** ➤ **Save** or click the small **Save** command on the Ribbon to save and stop editing the page.

You should now be able to click on the link to open a new form. After you fill out, save or submit, and close the form, you should be redirected back to the page where the link is located, and not to the form library. Navigate to the form library and verify that the new form was added to it.

Discussion

In the solution described above you used the URL of a new form to add a link to a SharePoint page. You also changed the value of the **Source** query string parameter, so that users would be redirected back to the location where the link is located when the form is closed.

There are more query string parameters in the URL of a browser form you can modify to manipulate the behavior of a form. A few of them worth mentioning are:

- **SaveLocation** – Specifies the URL of a folder in a form library on a site in the site collection where the form should be saved. The folder can be the root folder or a subfolder of a form library.
- **Source** – Specifies a location to which the user should be redirected when the form is closed. This location must be in the same site collection as where the form or form template is opened.
- **XmlLocation** – Specifies the URL of an existing form that should be opened. **XmlLocation** and **XsnLocation** are mutually exclusive, which means you should not specify both in the URL.
- **XsnLocation** – Used to open a new form that is based on a form template.
- **DefaultItemOpen** – This query string parameter is overridden by the **OpenIn** query string parameter.

  ```
  DefaultItemOpen = 0
  ```

  is equivalent to

  ```
  OpenIn = PreferClient
  ```

  and

  ```
  DefaultItemOpen = 1
  ```

is equivalent to

```
OpenIn = Browser
```

- **OpenIn** – Specifies whether a form should be opened in the browser, in InfoPath, or in the web page used for rendering on mobile devices. If you do not specify the **OpenIn** or the **DefaultItemOpen** query string parameter in the URL of a link to a form or form template:
    - **PreferClient** will be the default value for the **OpenIn** query string parameter, if you specify both the **XsnLocation** and **Source** query string parameters in the URL. To force a new form to open in the browser, set **OpenIn** to **Browser**.
    - The form template will be downloaded instead of a new form opened in InfoPath Filler 2013, if you only specify the **XsnLocation** parameter in the URL.
- **NoRedirect** – If set to **true** and **XmlLocation** is specified, the actual XML file for the form will be downloaded instead of the form being displayed in the browser. Its default value is **false**. This query string parameter does not have any effect when used in the URL of a link. The following applies to links:
    - If you want to open a form in the browser, you must specify the **XmlLocation** and **OpenIn** query string parameters in the URL, and set the value of the **OpenIn** query string parameter to **Browser**. For example:

      ```
      http://servername/sitename/_layouts/15/FormServer.aspx
      ?XmlLocation=/sitename/formlibraryname/XMLFileName.xml
      &OpenIn=Browser
      ```

    - If you want to download the actual XML file for a form, you must specify only the **XmlLocation** query string parameter in the URL and/or set the **OpenIn** query string parameter to **PreferClient**. For example:

      ```
      http://servername/sitename/_layouts/15/FormServer.aspx
      ?XmlLocation=/sitename/formlibraryname/XMLFileName.xml
      ```

      or

```
http://servername/sitename/_layouts/15/FormServer.aspx
?XmlLocation=/sitename/formlibraryname/XMLFileName.xml
&OpenIn=PreferClient
```

You can find the full list of parameters and descriptions of their behavior when used in combination with form libraries in the article entitled *How to: Use Query Parameters to Invoke Browser-Enabled InfoPath Forms* on MSDN.

Once you have added a link to a page, you can go back to modify that link or delete it if you want to.

To modify the link you added:

1. In SharePoint, navigate to the page where the link is located, and click **Page ➤ Edit ➤ Edit** or click the small **Edit** command on the Ribbon.
2. Once the page is in edit mode, click on the text for the link you want to modify. This should make the **Link** tab appear on the Ribbon.

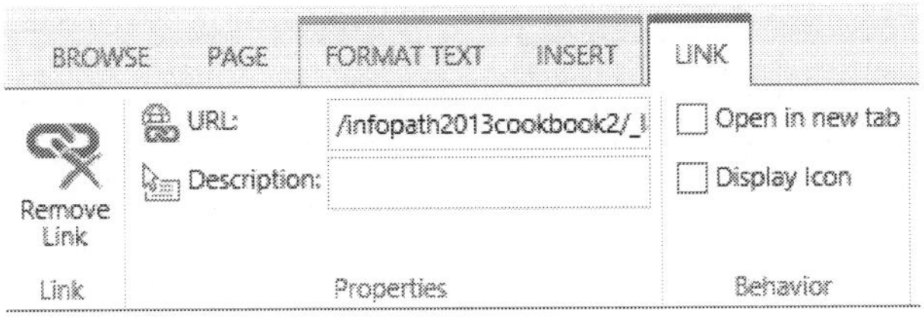

Figure 112. Commands on the Link tab in SharePoint 2013.

3. On the **Link** tab, modify the link as you see fit by changing its URL, its description, its behavior, or by removing the link, and then click **Page ➤ Edit ➤ Save** or click the small **Save** command on the Ribbon to save and stop editing the page.

39 Add a link to open a form from the Quick Launch menu

Problem

You want to add a link for an InfoPath browser form to the Quick Launch menu of a SharePoint site.

Solution

You can edit the look and feel of a site to add a link with which you can open a form, to the Quick Launch menu of a site.

To add a link to open a form from the Quick Launch menu:

1. In InfoPath, create a new SharePoint form library form template or use an existing one, and publish it to a SharePoint form library.
2. In SharePoint, navigate to the form library where you published the form template and add a new form. Save the form back to the form library, and then click on the form to open it in the browser.
3. Copy the URL of the form from the browser's address bar, and then close the form. Paste the URL in Notepad, and remove `&ClientInstalled=true` from the URL. For example, you should change an URL that looks like the following:

    ```
    http://servername/sitename/_layouts/15/FormServer.aspx?XmlLocat
    ion=http://servername/sitename/libraryname/formname.xml&ClientI
    nstalled=true&DefaultItemOpen=1&Source=http%3A%2F%2Fservername%
    2Fsitename%2Flibraryname%2FForms%2FAllItems%2Easpx
    ```

    into an URL that looks like the following:

    ```
    http://servername/sitename/_layouts/15/FormServer.aspx?XmlLocat
    ion=http://servername/sitename/libraryname/formname.xml&Default
    ItemOpen=1&Source=http%3A%2F%2Fservername%2Fsitename%2Flibraryn
    ame%2FForms%2FAllItems%2Easpx
    ```

    where **servername** is the name of the SharePoint server and **sitename** is the name of the site where a form named **formname.xml** is located in a form library named **libraryname**. You could also remove the server name from the URL as follows:

    ```
    /sitename/_layouts/15/FormServer.aspx?XmlLocation=/sitename/lib
    raryname/formname.xml&DefaultItemOpen=1&Source=/sitename/librar
    yname/Forms/AllItems.aspx
    ```

    Note that if you do not want the form library's page to be shown after the form is closed, you must change the value of the **Source** parameter in the URL to point to the location where the user should be redirected to after she closes the form. When you are done modifying the URL, copy the modified URL to the Windows clipboard.

4. Navigate to the SharePoint site on which you want to add a link to the Quick Launch menu, and select **Site settings** from the **Settings** menu (the gear icon in the top-right corner).
5. On the **Site Settings** page under **Look and Feel**, click **Quick launch**.
6. On the **Quick Launch** page, click **New Heading**.
7. On the **New Heading** page, type the URL of the SharePoint site on which the form library is located in the **Type the Web address** text box, type a title for the new heading (for example **Custom Links**) in the **Type the description** text box, and click **OK**.
8. On the **Quick Launch** page, click **New Navigation Link**.
9. On the **New Navigation Link** page, paste the URL of the InfoPath form in the **Type the Web address** text box, type a title for the new navigation link (for example **InfoPath Form**) in the **Type the description** text box, select the heading you added earlier from the **Heading** drop-down list box, and click **OK**.

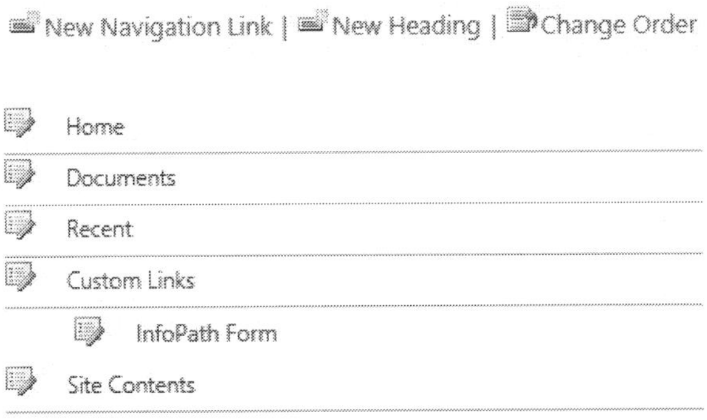

Figure 113. Link added to the Quick Launch menu in SharePoint 2013.

You should now see both the heading and the link listed in the Quick Launch menu. Click on the link to verify that the InfoPath form can be opened.

Discussion

In the solution described above, you copied the full URL of an InfoPath form, modified its parameters (also see the discussion section of recipe *38 Add a link to open a form from a SharePoint page* for a list of parameters you can use in the URL of a form), and added it as a link to the Quick Launch menu to be able to open an existing form.

Because the **Type the Web address** text box on the **New Navigation Link** or **Edit Navigation Link** page accepts a maximum of 255 characters, you cannot use a very long URL for a form, so you must find ways to reduce the length of the URL. Therefore, if you want to link to for example a new form in a form library, you can remove the **ClientInstalled** query string parameter and the server name from the URL. So an URL for a new form such as the following:

```
http://servername/sitename/_layouts/15/FormServer.aspx?XsnLocation=
http://servername/sitename/libraryname/Forms/template.xsn&SaveLocat
ion=http%3A%2F%2Fservername%2Fsitename%2Flibraryname&ClientInstalle
d=true&DefaultItemOpen=1&Source=http%3A%2F%2Fservername%2Fsitename%
2Flibraryname%2FForms%2FAllItems%2Easpx
```

would become:

```
/sitename/_layouts/15/FormServer.aspx?XsnLocation=/sitename/library
name/Forms/template.xsn&SaveLocation=/sitename/libraryname&DefaultI
temOpen=1&Source=/sitename/libraryname/Forms/AllItems.aspx
```

If you want to edit a previously added link, you must go back to the **Quick Launch** page and click the **Edit** command in front of the link you want to edit. You can delete a previously added link by clicking the **Delete** button on the **Edit Navigation Link** page.

40 Embed an InfoPath form on a SharePoint page

Problem

You want to place an InfoPath form on a SharePoint page so that users can easily access and fill out the form.

Solution

You can use the **InfoPath Form Web Part** that comes with SharePoint to embed an InfoPath form on a SharePoint page.

To embed an InfoPath form in an InfoPath Form Web Part on a SharePoint page:

1. In InfoPath, create a new SharePoint form library form template or use an existing one, and publish it to a SharePoint form library.
2. In SharePoint, navigate to the page on which you want to embed the InfoPath form, and click **Page ➤ Edit ➤ Edit** or click the small **Edit** command on the Ribbon.
3. Click anywhere on the page where you want to embed the InfoPath form, and then click **Insert ➤ Parts ➤ Web Part**.
4. At the top of the page, select **Forms** in the **Categories** list, select **InfoPath Form Web Part** in the **Parts** list, and click **Add**.

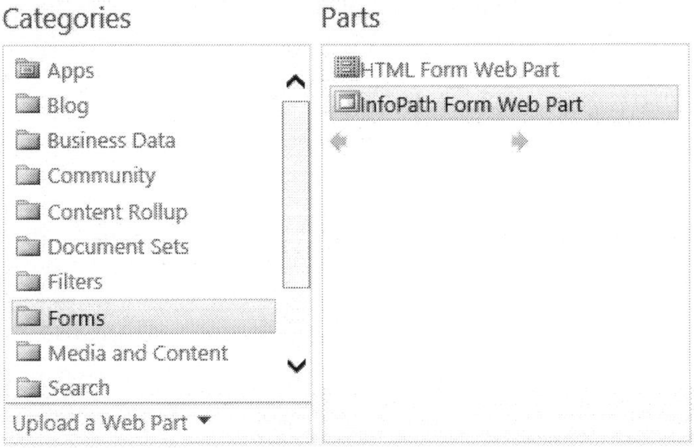

Figure 114. Selecting the InfoPath Form Web Part in SharePoint 2013.

5. Once the web part has been added to the page, you must configure it to display a specific InfoPath form. So on the web part, click on the text that says **Click here to open the tool pane**.

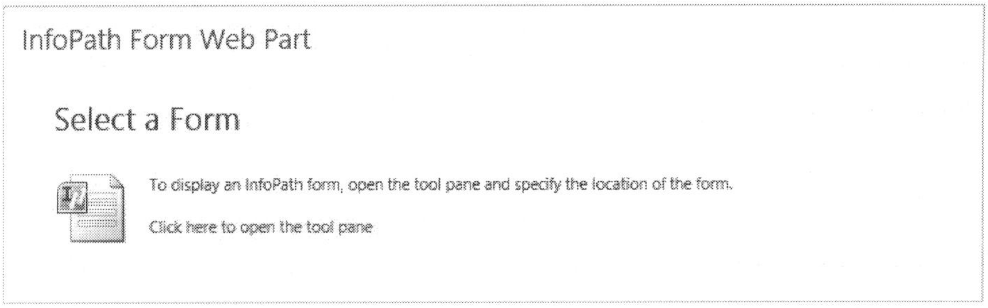

Figure 115. InfoPath Form Web Part on a SharePoint page.

6. On the web part tool pane, select the form library you published the InfoPath form template to from the **List or Library** drop-down list box.
7. On the web part tool pane, select the content type that should be used to create the form from the **Content Type** drop-down list box. Typically, if you associated multiple content types with a form library as described in recipe *27 Create different types of forms in one form library*, this drop-down list box should contain those content types. However, if you published the form template to a form library without adding any additional content types, only a **Form** content type should be listed in the drop-down list box.
8. On the web part tool pane, select the view to use when the form is opened from the **Views** drop-down list box. If the form has multiple views, all of those views would be listed in this drop-down list box.
9. On the web part tool pane, expand the **Appearance** section, change the **Title** of the web part to a suitable title, configure any other options you would like to configure, and then click **OK**.
10. Click **Page ➤ Edit ➤ Save** or click the small **Save** command on the Ribbon to save and stop editing the page.

The InfoPath form should now be embedded in the web part on the page and you should be able to fill it out and then click **Edit ➤ Commit ➤ Save** or **Edit ➤ Commit ➤ Submit** on the Ribbon to save or submit the form. Note that the **Edit** tab on the Ribbon appears when you click on the form or in a field on the form that is embedded in the web part.

Discussion

Once you have configured an **InfoPath Form Web Part**, you can change its settings by going into edit mode for the page, hovering over the web part, clicking on the drop-down arrow that appears in the top-right corner of the web part, and then selecting **Edit Web Part** from the drop-down menu that appears.

You can use an **InfoPath Form Web Part** not only to embed an InfoPath form on a SharePoint page, but also to set up web part connections between two InfoPath forms as you will see in the next two recipes.

41 Master/detail across two forms linked through one field

Problem

You have a SharePoint list containing information about project managers. You want to create an InfoPath form to enter project information. The form should contain a repeating table that has one column in which a drop-down list box is located. The drop-down list box should be populated with the names of the project managers from the SharePoint list. You want to give users the ability to not only select and add managers to a project, but also modify the SharePoint list data for a selected manager if required.

Solution

You can create a SharePoint list form for the project managers list, create a SharePoint form library form to enter project information, and then use InfoPath Form Web Parts and web part connections to set up passing data between the two forms.

To create master/detail functionality across a SharePoint form library form and a SharePoint list form and link the two forms through one field:

1. In SharePoint, create a SharePoint list named **ProjectManagers**. Add a column named **ManagerName** and any other relevant columns you require to the list. Populate the list with data.
2. Start customizing the form for the **ProjectManagers** SharePoint list as described in recipe *1 Customize a SharePoint list form from within SharePoint*.
3. In InfoPath, add an **Action** rule to the **ID** field that is located under the **my:SharePointListItem_RW** group node under the **dataFields** group node with the following 2 actions:

```
Set a field's value: ID = ID
Query using a data connection: Main Data Connection
```

where the first **ID** is the **ID** field that is located under the **q:SharePointListItem_RW** group node under the **queryFields** group node and the second **ID** is the **ID** field that is located under the

my:SharePointListItem_RW group node under the **dataFields** group node in the Main data source. This rule sets up the query fields for the SharePoint list form to retrieve data for a particular ID. The SharePoint form library form will send an ID of a manager to the ID field that is located under the **my:SharePointListItem_RW** group node under the **dataFields** group node in the Main data source of the SharePoint list form. The second action refreshes the data in the form by executing the query on the SharePoint list.

4. Publish the form template to SharePoint.
5. Create a new SharePoint form library form template or use an existing one.
6. Click **Data ➤ Get External Data ➤ From SharePoint List** and follow the instructions to add a **Receive** data connection to the **ProjectManagers** SharePoint list (also see *Use a SharePoint list data connection* in recipe *43 2 Ways to retrieve data from a SharePoint list*). Ensure that you select the **ID** and **ManagerName** fields as fields to include in the secondary data source and that you leave the **Automatically retrieve data when form is opened** check box selected.
7. Add a **Repeating Table** with two columns to the view of the form template. Change the first text box in the repeating table into a **Drop-Down List Box** control, and replace the second text box with a **Button** control (delete the field that is bound to the second text box control from the Main data source). Name the field that is bound to the drop-down list box **managerID** and label the button **Open Manager Form**.
8. Populate the drop-down list box with entries from the **ProjectManagers** secondary data source. Select the **ID** field for the **Value** property and the **ManagerName** field for the **Display name** property.

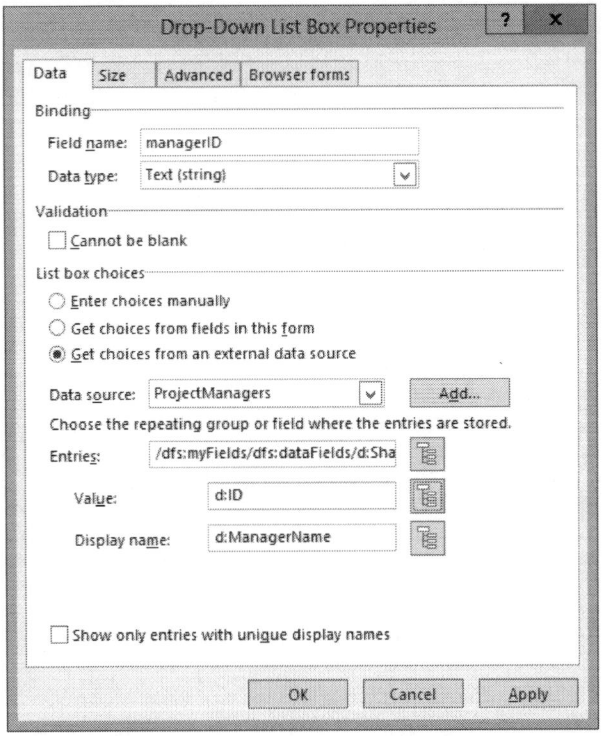

Figure 116. Filling the drop-down list box with data from the ProjectManagers list.

9. Add a hidden **Field (element)** of type **Text (string)** named **selectedManagerID** to the Main data source of the form. This field will store the ID of the manager that is selected from the repeating table when you click the **Open Manager Form** button.
10. Add an **Action** rule to the **Open Manager Form** button that has the following action:

    ```
    Set a field's value: selectedManagerID = managerID
    ```

    where **selectedManagerID** is the hidden field and **managerID** is the field that is bound to the drop-down list box in the repeating table.
11. Add an **Action** rule to the **selectedManagerID** hidden field that has the following action:

    ```
    Send data to Web Part
    ```

    and then on the **Rule Details** dialog box, click **Property Promotion**.

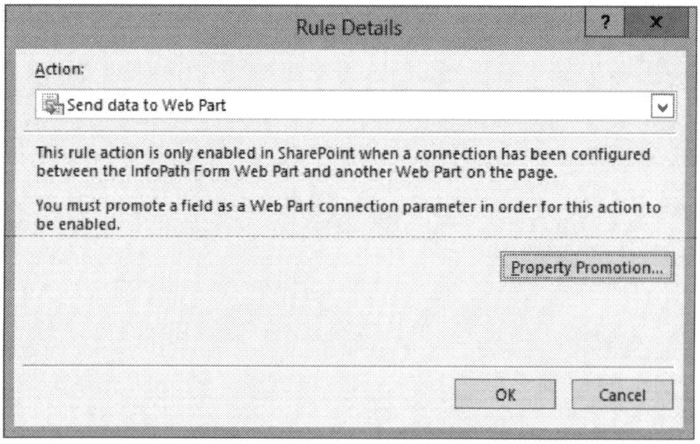

Figure 117. Adding a Send data to Web Part action in InfoPath Designer 2013.

12. On the **Form Options** dialog box, click **Add** in the section for managing SharePoint web part connection parameters (the bottom section).
13. On the **Select a field** dialog box, select **selectedManagerID** in the **Field to use as Web Part Connection Parameter** tree view, type **SelectedManagerID** in the **Parameter name** text box, select the **Output** option, and click **OK**. With this you have set the **selectedManagerID** to send data to a web part whenever its value changes.

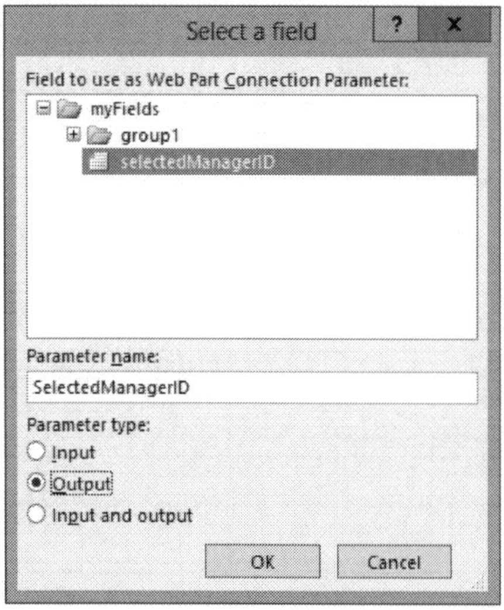

Figure 118. Promoting the selectedManagerID field as an output web part parameter.

14. On the **Form Options** dialog box, click **OK**.
15. On the **Rule Details** dialog box, click **OK**.
16. Publish the form template to a SharePoint form library named **ProjectsLib**.
17. In SharePoint, navigate to the site where you published the form template, and then select **Add a page** from the **Settings** menu (the gear icon in the top-right corner).
18. On the **Add a page** dialog, type **ProjectAndManagers** in the **New page name** text box, and click **Create**.
19. When the **ProjectAndManagers** page opens in edit mode, select **Format Text ➤ Layout ➤ Text Layout ➤ Two columns**.
20. Click to place the cursor in the left column and then click **Insert ➤ Parts ➤ Web Part**.
21. At the top of the page, select **Forms** in the **Categories** list, select **InfoPath Form Web Part** in the **Parts** list, and click **Add**.
22. Repeat the steps 20 and 21 to add an **InfoPath Form Web Part** in the right column.
23. Once you have added the two web parts to the page, you must configure them to display InfoPath forms from the **ProjectsLib** form library and **ProjectManagers** SharePoint list. So on the left web part, click on the text that says **Click here to open the tool pane**.
24. On the web part tool pane on the right-hand side of the page, select the **ProjectsLib** form library from the **List or Library** drop-down list box, expand the **Appearance** section, change the **Title** to **Project**, and then click **OK**.
25. On the right web part, click on the text that says **Click here to open the tool pane**.
26. On the web part tool pane on the right-hand side of the page, select the **ProjectManagers** SharePoint list from the **List or Library** drop-down list box, expand the **Appearance** section, change the **Title** to **Project Manager**, and then click **OK**.
27. Hover over the left web part, click the drop-down arrow that appears in the top-right corner of the web part, and then select **Edit Web Part** from the drop-down menu that appears.

28. Click the drop-down arrow in the top-right corner of the web part again, and select **Connections ➤ Send Data To ➤ Project Manager** from the drop-down menu that appears.

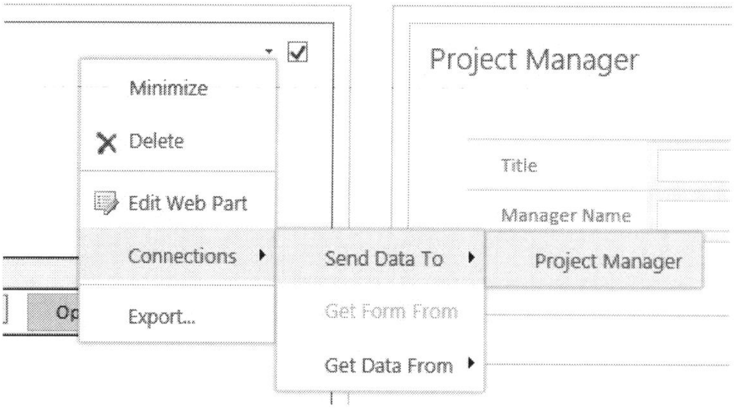

Figure 119. Configuring web part connections in SharePoint 2013.

29. On the **Configure Connection** webpage dialog, leave **SelectedManagerID** selected in the **Provider Field Name** drop-down list box, select **ID** from the **Consumer Field Name** drop-down list box, and then click **Finish**. With this you have configured the **Project** web part to send data from the **SelectManagerID** field to the **ID** field of the **Project Manager** web part.

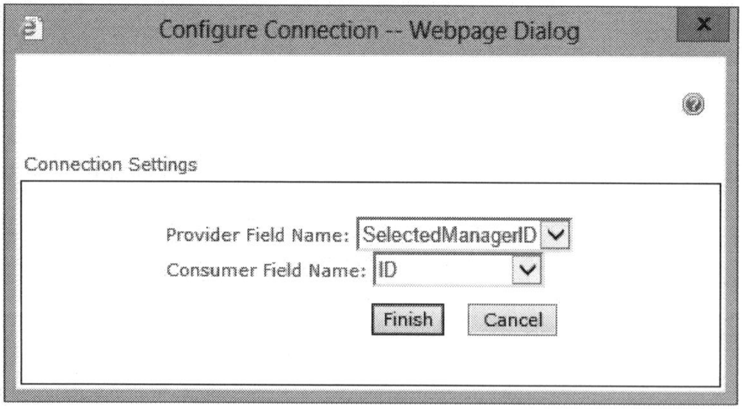

Figure 120. The Configure Connection webpage dialog in SharePoint 2013.

30. Click **Page ➤ Edit ➤ Save** or click the small **Save** command on the Ribbon to save and stop editing the page.

In SharePoint, navigate to the **ProjectAndManagers** page. Select a manager from the drop-down list box in the repeating table. Add a second row to the repeating table and select a different manager. Click the **Open Manager Form** button behind the second drop-down list box. The SharePoint list form should display the details for the manager you selected. Edit the manager details in the SharePoint list form and then click **Edit ➤ Commit ➤ Save** on the Ribbon. Finish entering data in the project form and then click **Edit ➤ Commit ➤ Save** on the Ribbon. Save the project form back to the **ProjectsLib** form library. Navigate to the **ProjectManagers** SharePoint list and verify that the data you changed was saved. Navigate to the **ProjectsLib** form library and verify that the form was saved.

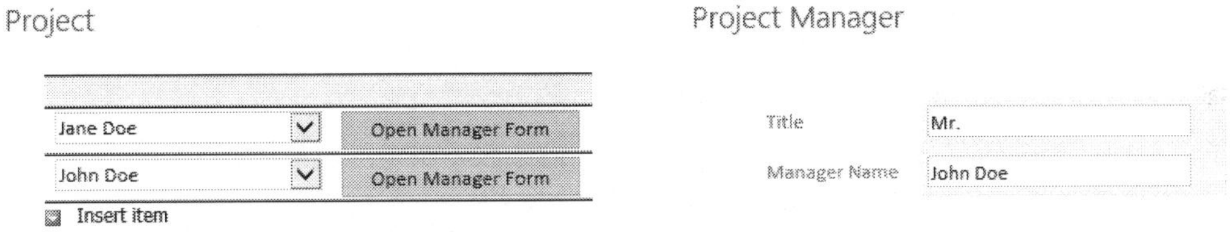

Figure 121. Passing data between a form library form and a list form in SharePoint.

Discussion

In the solution described above you learned how to connect a SharePoint form library form to a SharePoint list form to be able to modify data that is used as read-only data in the SharePoint form library form. You also used a hidden field as a temporary storage location for a selected ID to enable passing the ID of the selected manager as an output web part connection parameter, because fields inside repeating groups are not supported as web part connection parameters.

There are three types of web part connection parameters you can define:

1. Input
2. Output
3. Input and Output

A field that has been configured as an **Input** parameter can receive data from a field in another web part. A field that has been configured as an

Output parameter can send data to a field in another web part. And a field that has been configured as an **Input and Output** parameter can both send and receive data.

You can configure web part connection parameters via the **Form Options** dialog box, when you add a **Send data to Web Part** action to a rule by clicking the **Property Promotion** button, or when you publish a form template through the **Publishing Wizard**. While you cannot configure web part connection parameters on a SharePoint list form template, you can still configure an InfoPath Form Web Part that hosts a SharePoint list form to send or receive data as you have seen in the solution described above.

And finally, you used a **Send data to Web Part** action in a rule on the hidden field to send a selected ID to any consumer web parts, in this case to an InfoPath Form Web Part containing a SharePoint list form, whenever the value of the **selectedManagerID** field changed.

Note: The solution described above should work for SharePoint 2013 Service Pack 1. Without Service Pack 1 installed, you may receive an error when trying to query the Main Data Connection of the SharePoint list form when you use an action as described in step 3. If this is the case, you must remove the **Query for data** action from the rule and add a **Button** control to the view of the form template that has its **Action** property set to **Run Query**. You can change the label of the button to **Retrieve Selected Manager**. The user must then click this button to retrieve the data of the selected manager after she has clicked the **Open Manager Form** in the repeating table.

42 Pass data from a selected row in a repeating table to another form

Problem

You have two InfoPath forms that are embedded on the same page in SharePoint. You want to select data from a row in a repeating table on the first form, click on a button, and then pass this data to the second form.

Solution

You can set up web part connection parameters in InfoPath form templates and use a **Send data to Web Part** action in one form to send data to another form. In addition, you must use SharePoint Designer 2013 to set up the web part connections.

For this recipe, you will create two form templates. The first form template sends data and the second form template receives data.

To design the first form template:

1. In InfoPath, create a new SharePoint form library form template or use an existing one.
2. Add a **Repeating Table** control with two columns to the view of the form template. Name the first text box in the repeating table **title**, and the second text box **color**.
3. Add two hidden fields of type **Text (string)** to the Main data source of the form. Name the fields **selectedTitle** and **selectedColor**, respectively.
4. Click anywhere in the second column of the repeating table, and then select **Table Tools ➤ Layout ➤ Rows & Columns ➤ Insert Right**. This should insert a column to the right of the second column. If a third text box was added to the repeating table, delete it from the view and delete its corresponding field from the Main data source.
5. Add a **Button** control to the third column of the repeating table and label it **Select**.
6. Add an **Action** rule to the **Select** button with the following 3 actions:

   ```
   Set a field's value: selectedTitle = title
   Set a field's value: selectedColor = color
   Send data to Web Part
   ```

   This action rule sets the values of the **selectedTitle** and **selectedColor** hidden fields to be equal to the values of the **title** and **color** fields that are located in the same row in which the **Select** button was clicked, and then sends the data to any consumer web parts.

7. To be able to have a form send data to another web part, you must set up **Output** web part connection parameters. So click **File ➤ Info ➤ Form Options**.
8. On the **Form Options** dialog box, select **Property Promotion** in the **Category** list, and then in the section to add SharePoint web part connection parameters (the bottom section), click **Add**.
9. On the **Select a field** dialog box, select **selectedTitle** in the **Field to use as Web Part Connection Parameter** tree view, leave **Selected Title** as the **Parameter name**, select **Output** as the **Parameter type**, and click **OK**.
10. Repeat steps 8 and 9 to add a **Selected Color** parameter that is linked to the **selectedColor** field as an **Output** web part connection parameter.
11. On the **Form Options** dialog box, click **OK**.
12. Publish the form template to a SharePoint form library named **SourceFormLib**.

To design the second form template:

1. In InfoPath, create a new SharePoint form library form template or use an existing one.
2. Add two **Text Box** controls to the view of the form template and name them **title** and **color**, respectively. The values of these two fields will be set by the other form.
3. To be able to have a form receive data from another web part, you must set up **Input** web part connection parameters. So click **File ➤ Info ➤ Form Options**.
4. On the **Form Options** dialog box, select **Property Promotion** in the **Category** list, and then in the section to add SharePoint web part connection parameters (the bottom section), click **Add**.
5. On the **Select a field** dialog box, select **title** in the **Field to use as Web Part Connection Parameter** tree view, leave **Title** as the **Parameter name**, select **Input** as the **Parameter type**, and click **OK**.
6. Repeat steps 4 and 5 to add a **Color** parameter that is linked to the **color** field as an **Input** web part connection parameter.

7. On the **Form Options** dialog box, click **OK**.
8. Publish the form template to a SharePoint form library named **DestinationFormLib**.

Once you have designed and published the form templates, you must embed them on a SharePoint page.

To embed the forms on a SharePoint page:

1. In SharePoint, navigate to the site where you published the form templates, and select **Add a page** from the **Settings** menu (the gear icon in the top-right corner).
2. On the **Add a page** dialog, type **PassMultipleParams** in the **New page name** text box, and then click **Create**.
3. When the **PassMultipleParams** page opens in edit mode, select **Format Text ➤ Layout ➤ Text Layout ➤ Two columns**.
4. Place the cursor in the left column on the page, and then follow steps 3 through 9 of recipe *40 Embed an InfoPath form on a SharePoint page* to insert and configure an **InfoPath Form Web Part** that displays the form from the **SourceFormLib** form library. Set the **Title** of the web part to **Source Form**.
5. Place the cursor in the right column on the page, and then follow steps 3 through 9 of recipe *40 Embed an InfoPath form on a SharePoint page* to insert and configure an **InfoPath Form Web Part** that displays the form from the **DestinationFormLib** form library. Set the **Title** of the web part to **Destination Form**.
6. Click **Page ➤ Edit ➤ Save** or click the small **Save** command on the Ribbon to save and stop editing the page.

Once you have embedded the InfoPath forms on a page, you must set up web part connections for the forms from within SharePoint Designer 2013, because you can only set up single connections from within SharePoint's browser interface.

To set up web part connections in SharePoint Designer 2013:

1. In SharePoint Designer 2013, click **File ➤ Sites ➤ Open Site**.
2. On the **Open Site** dialog box, browse to and select the site on which the **PassMultipleParams** page is located, and click **Open**.

3. Once the site has opened, click **Site Pages** in the left **Navigation** pane.
4. On the **Site Pages** page, click **PassMultipleParams.aspx**.
5. On the **PassMultipleParams.aspx** page under **Customization**, click **Edit file**.
6. Click **Code View Tools** ➤ **Edit** ➤ **Editing** ➤ **Find** on the Ribbon.
7. On the **Find and Replace** dialog box, type **Source Form** in the **Find what** text box, click **Find Next**, and then click **Close**. This should place the cursor on the code for the first web part in the file.
8. Click **Web Part Tools** ➤ **Format** ➤ **Connections** ➤ **Add Connection** on the Ribbon.

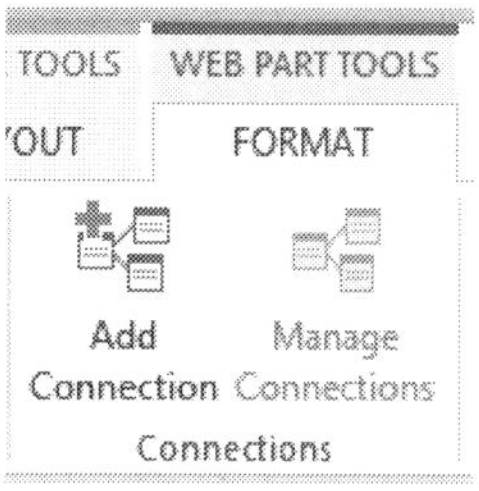

Figure 122. Add Connection command on the Ribbon in SharePoint Designer 2013.

9. On the **Web Part Connections Wizard**, select **Send Data To**, and click **Next**.

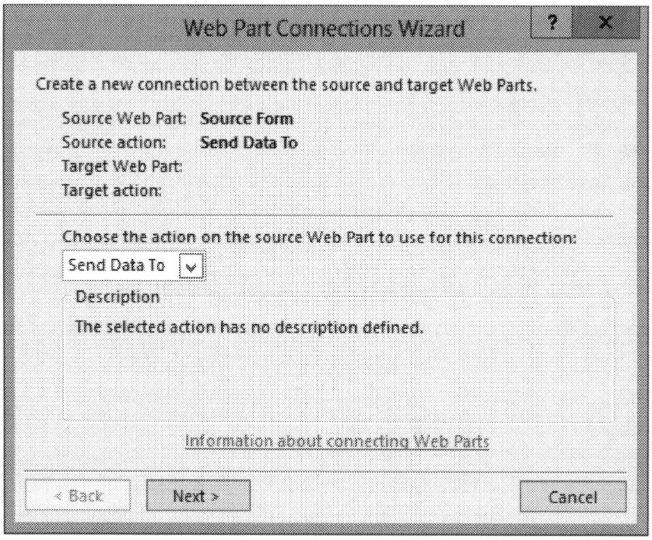

Figure 123. Web Part Connections Wizard in SharePoint Designer 2013.

10. On the **Web Part Connections Wizard**, leave the **Connect to a Web Part on this page** option selected, and click **Next**.

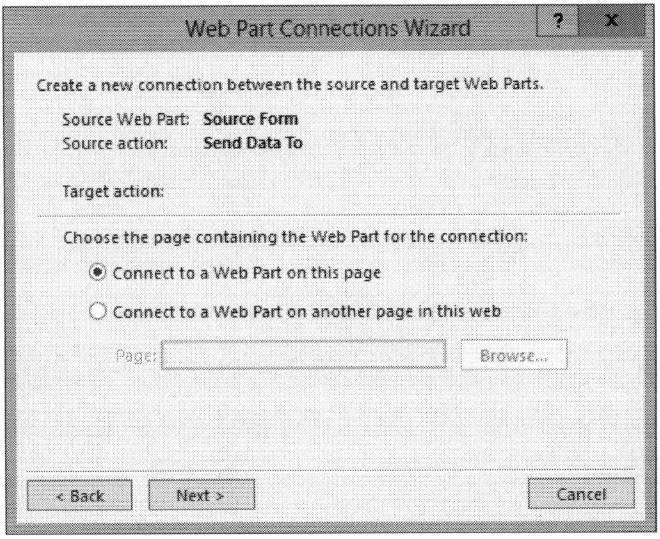

Figure 124. Selecting to connect to a web part on the same page.

11. On the **Web Part Connections Wizard**, leave **Destination Form** selected in the **Target Web Part** drop-down list box, leave **Get Data From** selected in the **Target action** drop-down list box, and click **Next**.

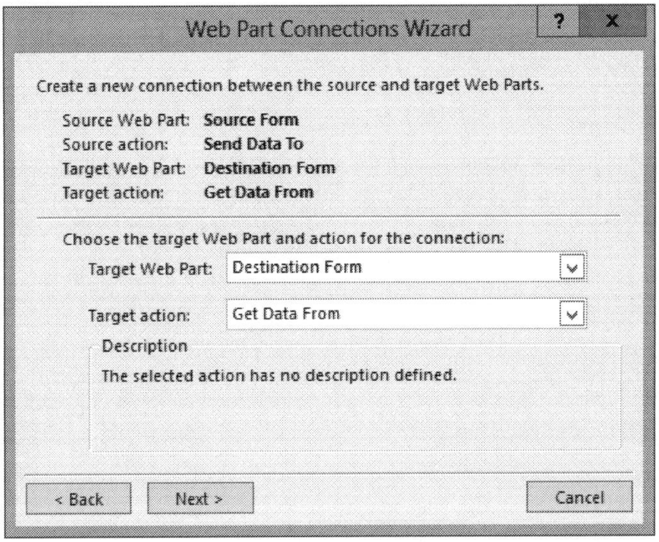

Figure 125. Selecting the web part to connect to.

12. On the **Web Part Connections Wizard**, select **Selected Color** in the **Columns in Source Form** list on the same row as **Color** in the **Inputs to Destination Form** list, select **Selected Title** in the **Columns in Source Form** list on the same row as **Title** in the **Inputs to Destination Form** list, and then click **Next**.

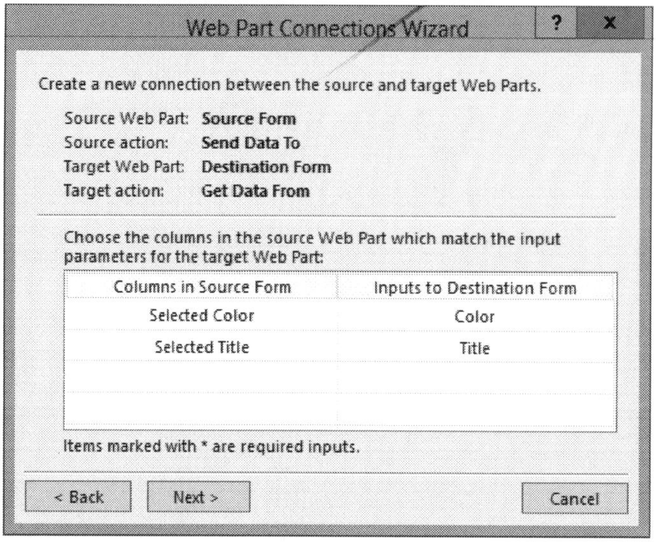

Figure 126. Setting up the parameters for the web part connections.

13. On the **Web Part Connections Wizard**, review the information, and then click **Finish**.

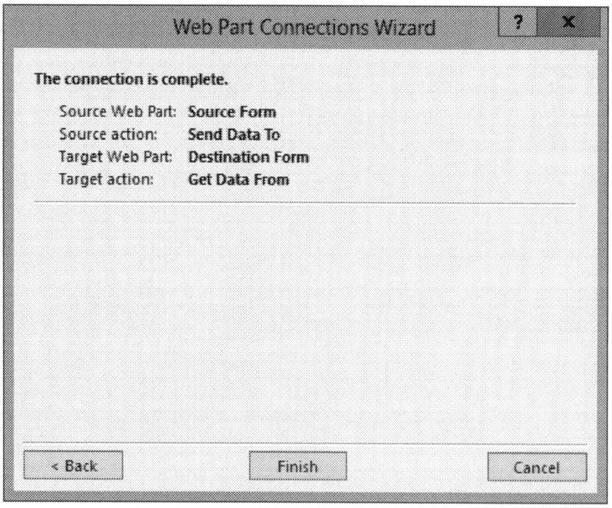

Figure 127. Last screen of the Web Part Connections Wizard.

14. Click **Save** on the **Quick Access Toolbar** at the top of SharePoint Designer 2013 to save the page. Click **Yes** on the message box that appears.

In SharePoint, navigate to the **PassMultipleParams** page. Populate the repeating table with a couple of rows of data. Click the **Select** button in one of the rows and verify that the data from the fields in the row in which the **Select** button is located was copied over to the second form.

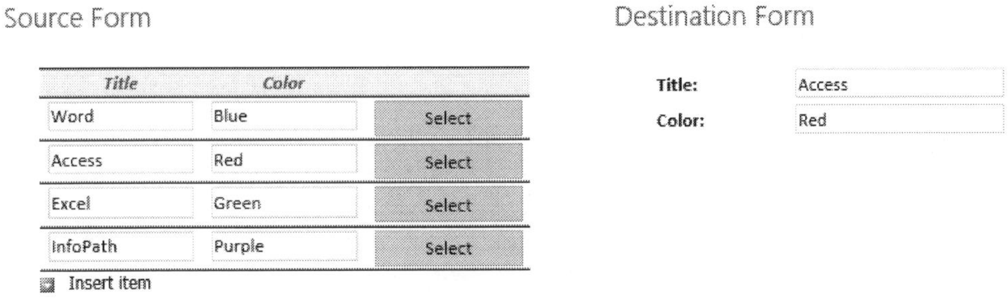

Figure 128. Passing data between two form library forms on a SharePoint page.

Discussion

While the solution described above used a repeating table in the Main data source of a form to pass a row of data to another form, you could have also retrieved data from a secondary data source such as a SharePoint list, bound this secondary data source to a repeating table and then added a select button to each row (see *Use a Select button in a repeating table* in recipe *45 3 Ways to copy SharePoint list data to form fields*) to be able to select and pass data from a row of the repeating table to the other form.

In recipe *41 Master/detail across two forms linked through one field* you used SharePoint's browser interface to set up web part connections between two InfoPath Form Web Parts. However, whenever you want to set up more than one web part connection, you must use SharePoint Designer 2013 to do so, because SharePoint's browser interface allows you to set up only one web part connection between two web parts, and not multiple.

Chapter 3: Work with SharePoint List Data

A common task when designing InfoPath forms is to retrieve and display data from SharePoint lists. InfoPath 2013 comes with 3 data connections you can use to connect to and retrieve data from SharePoint lists:

1. SharePoint list or library data connections
2. Web Service data connections
3. XML data connections

The commands to create the aforementioned types of data connections can be found under the **Get External Data** group on the **Data** tab on the Ribbon in InfoPath Designer 2013.

Figure 129. Ribbon commands to add data connections to retrieve data in InfoPath 2013.

You will learn several ways to retrieve, sort, filter, and work with SharePoint list or library data as you progress through the recipes in this chapter.

Retrieve and display SharePoint list data

SharePoint list data connections are probably the easiest to use when it comes to retrieving data from a SharePoint list or library. They offer simple sort functionality and you can use them to retrieve data from Excel, Access, or SQL Server through SharePoint. REST Web Service data connections are probably the most flexible to use as they offer filter and sort functionality that is not available on the other types of data connections.

The recipes in this section will show you how to use SharePoint list data connections and Web Service data connections to retrieve data from

SharePoint lists, and also discuss when it would make sense to use each method.

43 2 Ways to retrieve data from a SharePoint list

Use a SharePoint list data connection

Problem

You have a SharePoint list which contains data you want to display as read-only on an InfoPath form.

Solution

You can use a SharePoint list data connection to retrieve data from a SharePoint list and use this data within an InfoPath form.

Suppose you have a SharePoint list named **OfficeApplications** as described in *Create a SharePoint list form for an existing SharePoint list* in recipe *2 Customize a SharePoint list form from within InfoPath*.

To retrieve data from this SharePoint list using a SharePoint list data connection:

1. In InfoPath, create a new browser-compatible form template or use an existing one.
2. Click **Data ➤ Get External Data ➤ From SharePoint List**.
3. On the **Data Connection Wizard**, enter the URL of the SharePoint site where the SharePoint list you want to connect to (**OfficeApplications** in this case) is located, and click **Next**.

Figure 130. Entering the URL of the SharePoint site where the list is located.

4. On the **Data Connection Wizard**, select the list you want to connect to (**OfficeApplications** in this case) from the **Select a list or library** list box, and click **Next**.

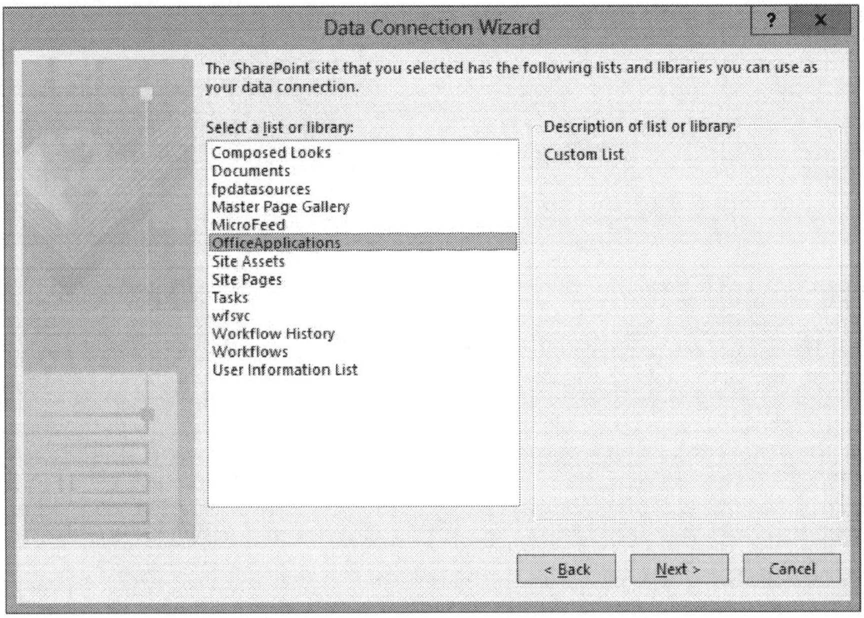

Figure 131. Selecting the SharePoint list to connect to.

5. On the **Data Connection Wizard**, select any fields (for example, **Title** and **Color**) that you want to include in the secondary data source that will be created for the SharePoint list in InfoPath, and click **Next**.

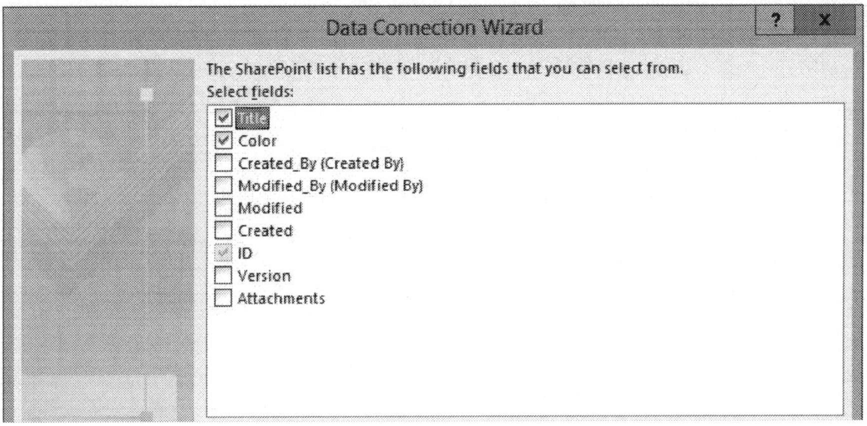

Figure 132. Selecting the fields to include in the data source.

6. On the **Data Connection Wizard**, click **Next**. Note that if you wanted to save data from the SharePoint list within the form template for offline use, you could select the **Store a copy of the data in the form template** check box before clicking **Next**.

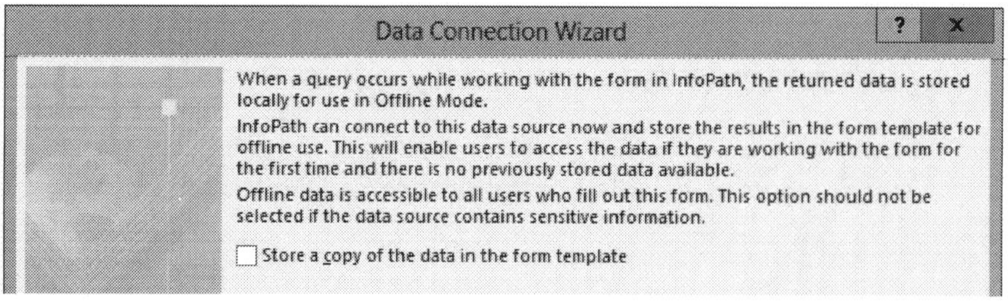

Figure 133. Choosing not to store a copy of the data in the form template.

7. On the **Data Connection Wizard**, enter a name for the data connection or accept the default name InfoPath generates based on the name of the SharePoint list, leave the **Automatically retrieve data when form is opened** check box selected, and click **Finish**.

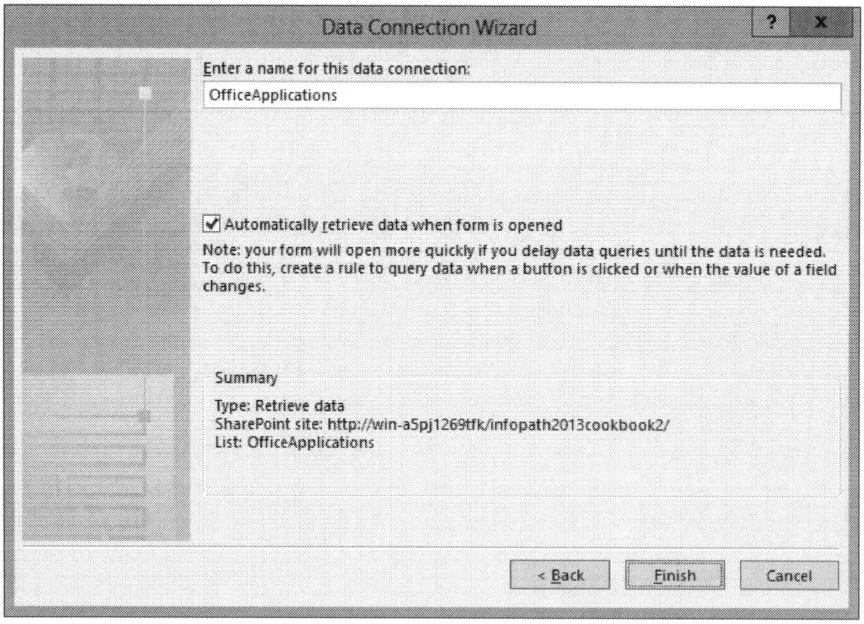

Figure 134. The last screen of the Data Connection Wizard in InfoPath Designer 2013.

You should now be able to use the data connection to get data from the SharePoint list and use it in your InfoPath form for example to populate a drop-down list box. The data that is returned is located under the **SharePointListItem_RW** repeating group node under the **dataFields** group node in the secondary data source for the SharePoint list.

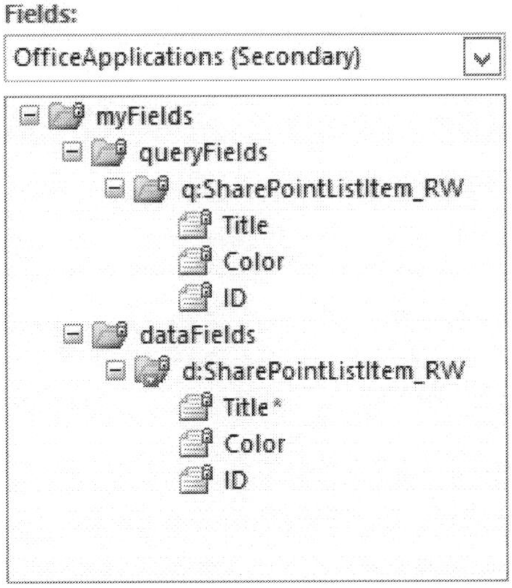

Figure 135. The data source for the SharePoint list on the Fields task pane.

Discussion

If you click **Data ➤ Get External Data ➤ Data Connections**, you should see the data connection listed on the **Data Connections** dialog box (see Figure 136). At the bottom of the **Data Connections** dialog box you can get more details about the data connection, such as for example that its type is **Retrieve data**, that it is a **Secondary data source**, and that it connects to a SharePoint site.

In the solution described above, you left the **Automatically retrieve data when form is opened** check box selected on the last screen of the **Data Connection Wizard**. It is not a best practice to leave this check box selected especially if you expect a SharePoint list to contain many items, since loading all of the data from the SharePoint list when the form opens could negatively impact the performance of the form.

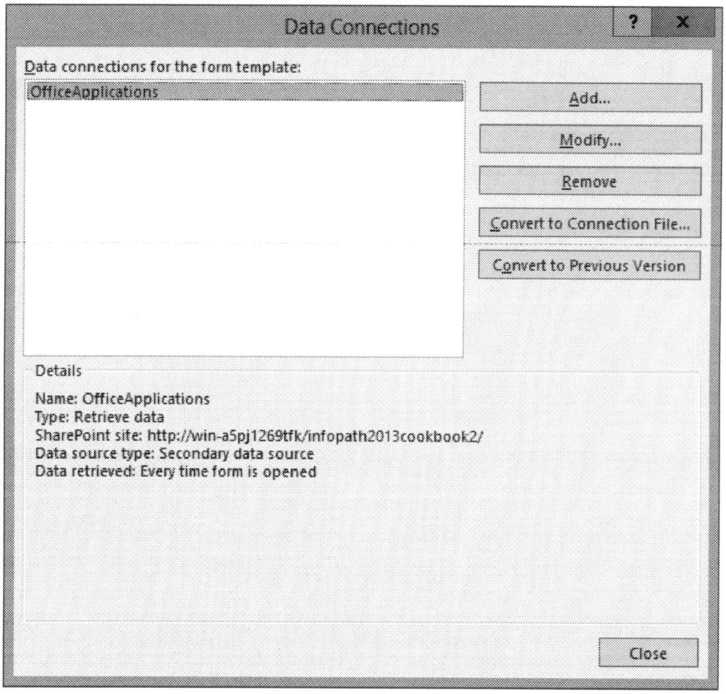

Figure 136. Data Connections dialog box in InfoPath Designer 2013.

Just like the Main data source of SharePoint list forms (see the discussion section of *Create a SharePoint list form for an existing SharePoint list* in recipe *2 Customize a SharePoint list form from within InfoPath*), a secondary data source for a SharePoint list consists of a **queryFields** and a **dataFields** group node. The **queryFields** group node contains fields that can be used to query (look up) data in the SharePoint list, while the **dataFields** group node contains fields that can be used to display data from the SharePoint list.

In cases where you want to retrieve data on demand instead of automatically when a form opens, it is best to deselect the **Automatically retrieve data when form is opened** check box on the last screen of the **Data Connection Wizard** and then use the fields under the **queryFields** group node in the secondary data source for the SharePoint list to retrieve data as shown in recipe *50 Filter SharePoint list data on an exact match*.

Use SharePoint's REST interface for querying list data

Problem

You have a SharePoint list which contains data you want to display as read-only on an InfoPath form.

Solution

You can use a data connection to SharePoint's REST interface for querying list data to retrieve data from a SharePoint list and display this data within an InfoPath form.

Suppose you have a SharePoint list named **OfficeApplications** as described in *Create a SharePoint list form for an existing SharePoint list* in recipe *2 Customize a SharePoint list form from within InfoPath*.

To retrieve data from this SharePoint list using SharePoint's REST interface:

1. In InfoPath, create a new browser-compatible form template or use an existing one.
2. Select **Data ➤ Get External Data ➤ From Web Service ➤ From REST Web Service**.
3. On the **Data Connection Wizard**, enter the URL of SharePoint's REST interface for querying list data, for example:

   ```
   http://servername/sitename/_api/web/lists/getbytitle('OfficeApp
   lications')/items
   ```

   and click **Next**. Here, **servername** is the name of the SharePoint server and **sitename** is the name of the site where the **OfficeApplications** SharePoint list is located. Tip: Always test a REST Web Service URL in the browser to see whether it returns valid XML data before using the URL in InfoPath.

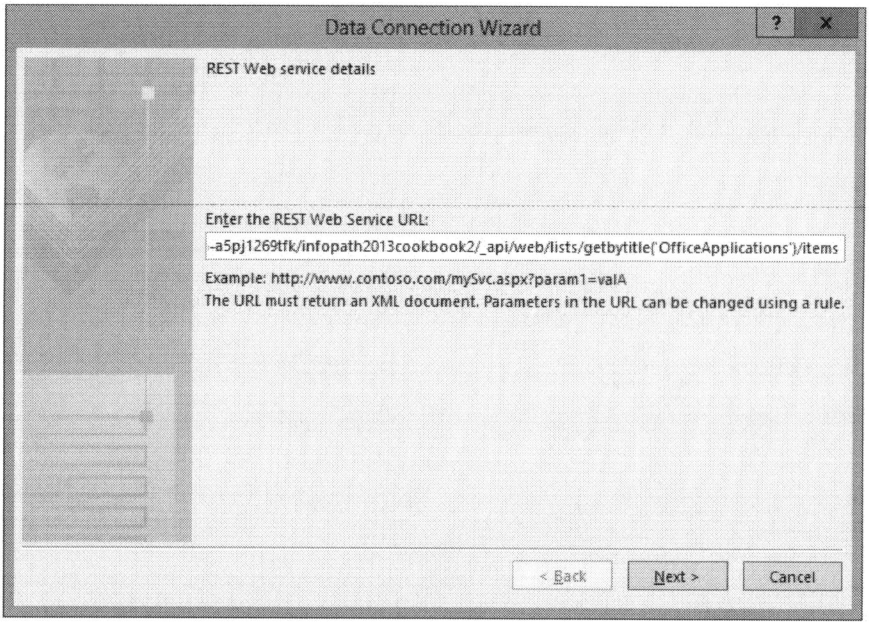

Figure 137. Entering the REST Web Service URL on the Data Connection Wizard.

4. On the **Data Connection Wizard**, enter a name for the data connection (for example **OfficeApplicationsREST**), leave the **Automatically retrieve data when form is opened** check box selected, and click **Finish**. Note: If your SharePoint environment is configured to use Claims Based authentication as opposed to Windows Classic authentication and the form is going to be filled out through the browser, you must set up UDC authentication for the data connection that makes the web service call as described in *Configure a web service data connection for a web browser form* in the Appendix.

You should now be able to use the data connection to get data from the SharePoint list and use it in your InfoPath form for example to populate a drop-down list box. The data returned for each item in the data source is located under the **entry** repeating group node and the **m:properties** group node in the secondary data source for the REST web service.

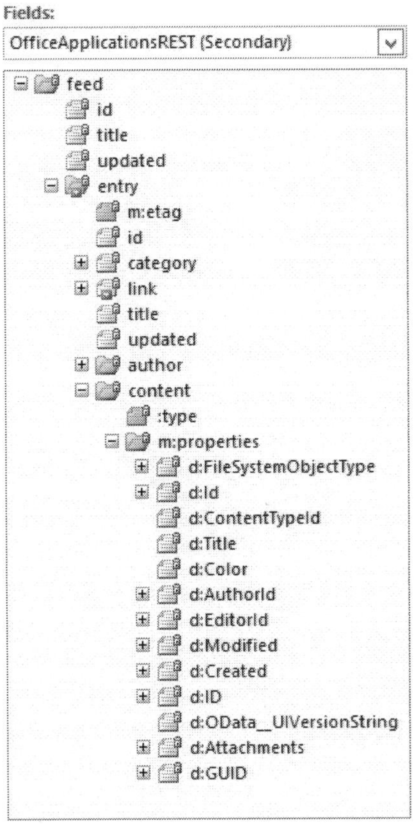

Figure 138. The data source for the REST web service on the Fields task pane.

Discussion

The advantage of using a REST web service data connection compared to a SharePoint list data connection as described in *Use a SharePoint list data connection* in this recipe is the ability to sort SharePoint list data on multiple fields instead of just one field and the flexibility when setting up filters to filter SharePoint list data.

Note that if you do not know where the data you want to use is located in the data source for a REST web service, enter the REST URL in the browser and check the data there to find the corresponding XML nodes to use in InfoPath. To have Internet Explorer return XML for a REST URL, open the **Internet Options** dialog box, select the **Content** tab, click **Settings** under **Feeds and Web Slices**, and then on the **Feeds and Web**

Slice Settings dialog box, deselect the **Turn on feed reading view** check box.

44 Display SharePoint list data in a repeating table

Problem

You have added a SharePoint list data connection to a form template and want to display the data from the SharePoint list in a repeating table.

Solution

You can bind the secondary data source for a SharePoint list to a repeating table to be able to display its data in the repeating table.

Suppose you have a SharePoint list named **OfficeApplications** as described in *Create a SharePoint list form for an existing SharePoint list* in recipe *2 Customize a SharePoint list form from within InfoPath*.

To display data from this SharePoint list in a repeating table:

1. In InfoPath, create a new SharePoint form library form template or use an existing one.
2. Add a **Receive** data connection to the **OfficeApplications** SharePoint list to the form template as described in *Use a SharePoint list data connection* in recipe *43 2 Ways to retrieve data from a SharePoint list*.
3. On the **Fields** task pane, select **OfficeApplications (Secondary)** from the drop-down list box.

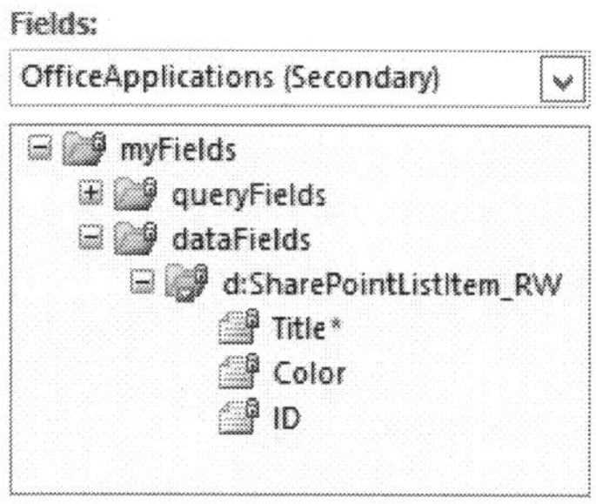

Figure 139. The OfficeApplications secondary data source in InfoPath Designer 2013.

4. On the **Fields** task pane, expand the **dataFields** group node, click the **d:SharePointListItem_RW** repeating group node, drag it to the view of the form template, drop it, and select **Repeating Table** from the context menu that appears when you drop it.
5. Publish the form template to a SharePoint form library.

In SharePoint, navigate to the form library where you published the form template and add a new form. When the form opens, all of the data from the SharePoint list should appear in the repeating table.

Discussion

In the solution described above, you bound a repeating group node under the **dataFields** group node in the secondary data source for the SharePoint list to a repeating table control. Note that if you used SharePoint's REST web service to retrieve SharePoint list data as described in recipe *43 2 Ways to retrieve data from a SharePoint list*, you would have had to bind the repeating table fields to a different repeating group node within the secondary data source for the SharePoint list.

If you look at the structure of the secondary data source for the SharePoint list on the **Fields** task pane, you should see two group nodes under the **myFields** root node:

1. queryFields
2. dataFields

The **queryFields** group node contains fields that can be used to query (look up and/or filter) data in the SharePoint list, while the **dataFields** group node contains fields that contain the data from the SharePoint list after you have run a query on the data connection. You can use the fields under the **dataFields** group node to display data from the SharePoint list on the InfoPath form.

Unlike the **dataFields** group node in the Main data source of a SharePoint list form (see the discussion section of *Create a SharePoint list form for an existing SharePoint list* in recipe *2 Customize a SharePoint list form from within InfoPath*), in the case of a **Receive** data connection for a SharePoint list, you can only use the fields under the **dataFields** group node to display data, and not to add or edit data in the SharePoint list. The data in the fields under the **dataFields** group node is read-only. This also means that when you bind these fields to controls in a repeating table, you cannot modify the data that is displayed in the repeating table. For example, if you click on any one of the text box controls within the repeating table and try to set the default value of the field, you will see that the **Default Value** option has been disabled. So if you want to work with and change data that comes from a **Receive** data connection for a SharePoint list, you must find a way to copy the data from the secondary data source over to other fields on the InfoPath form that are modifiable. The next recipe shows you ways to copy data from a SharePoint list to fields in the Main data source of a form.

45 3 Ways to copy SharePoint list data to form fields

Auto-populate fields when an item in a drop-down list box is selected

Problem

You have added a SharePoint list data connection to a form template and populated a drop-down list box with the data from the SharePoint list data source. You want users to be able to select an item from the drop-down list box and then automatically populate other fields on the form with data corresponding to the selected item in the drop-down list box.

Solution

You can use filters on the data in the secondary data source for the SharePoint list to look up and copy the information you require to other fields on the InfoPath form.

Suppose you have a SharePoint list named **OfficeApplications** as described in *Create a SharePoint list form for an existing SharePoint list* in recipe *2 Customize a SharePoint list form from within InfoPath*.

To auto-populate form fields with data from this SharePoint list when an item in a drop-down list box is selected:

1. In InfoPath, create a new SharePoint form library form template or use an existing one.
2. Add a **Receive** data connection to the **OfficeApplications** SharePoint list to the form template as described in *Use a SharePoint list data connection* in recipe *43 2 Ways to retrieve data from a SharePoint list*. Ensure that you select **Title** and **Color** as fields to include in the data source, and that you leave the **Automatically retrieve data when form is opened** check box selected.
3. Add a **Drop-Down List Box** control to the view of the form template, name it **selectedOfficeApplication**, and populate it with entries from the **OfficeApplications** secondary data source. Use the **ID** field for the **Value** and the **Title** field for the **Display name** of the items in the drop-down list box.

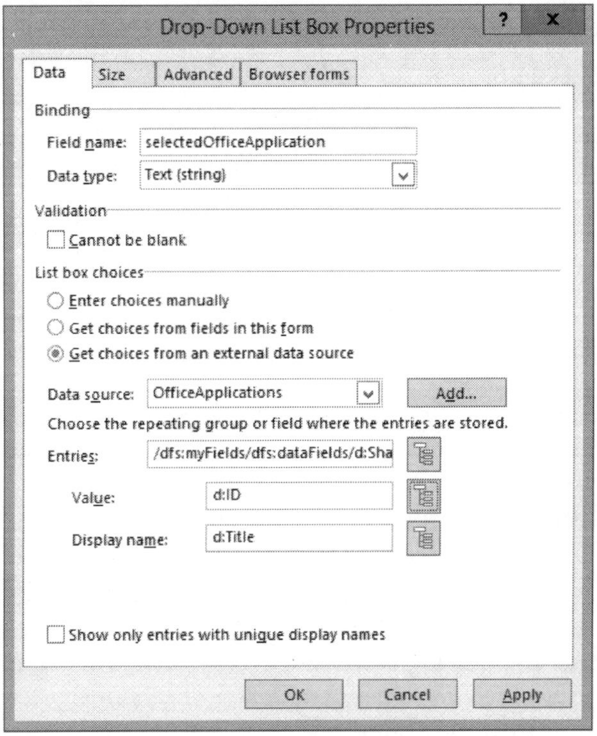

Figure 140. Populating the drop-down list box with SharePoint list items.

4. Add two **Text Box** controls to the view of the form template and name them **title** and **color**, respectively.

5. Add an **Action** rule to the drop-down list box with the following 2 actions:

```
Set a field's value: title = Title[ID =
selectedOfficeApplication]
Set a field's value: color = Color[ID =
selectedOfficeApplication]
```

where **title**, **color**, and **selectedOfficeApplication** are located in the Main data source of the form; and **ID**, **Title**, and **Color** are located under the **d:SharePointListItem_RW** repeating group node under the **dataFields** group node in the **OfficeApplications** secondary data source. The values of both the **Title** and **Color** fields in the secondary data source are filtered by the value of the **ID** field in the secondary data source being equal to the selected value in the drop-down list box (`[ID = selectedOfficeApplication]`). To add the first action:

a. On the **Rules** task pane, select **Add ➤ Set a field's value**.

b. On the **Rule Details** dialog box, click the button behind the **Field** text box.

c. On the **Select a Field or Group** dialog box, leave **Main** selected in the drop-down list box, select **title**, and click **OK**.

d. On the **Rule Details** dialog box, click the button behind the **Value** text box.

e. On the **Insert Formula** dialog box, click **Insert Field or Group**.

f. On the **Select a Field or Group** dialog box, select **OfficeApplications (Secondary)** from the drop-down list box, expand the **dataFields** group node, expand the **d:SharePointListItem_RW** repeating group node, select **Title**, and click **Filter Data**.

g. On the **Filter Data** dialog box, click **Add**.

h. On the **Specify Filter Conditions** dialog box, select **ID** from the first drop-down list box, leave **is equal to** selected in the second drop-down list box, and then select **Select a field or group** from the third drop-down list box.

i. On the **Select a Field or Group** dialog box, select **Main** from the drop-down list box, select **selectedOfficeApplication**, and click **OK**.

j. Click **OK** when closing all dialog boxes.

This rule performs data lookups in the secondary data source of the SharePoint list based on the selected item in the drop-down list box, and then sets the values of the text box controls accordingly.

6. Publish the form template to a SharePoint form library.

In SharePoint, navigate to the form library where you published the form template and add a new form. When the form opens, select an item from the drop-down list box, and verify that the corresponding values for title and color appear in the text boxes.

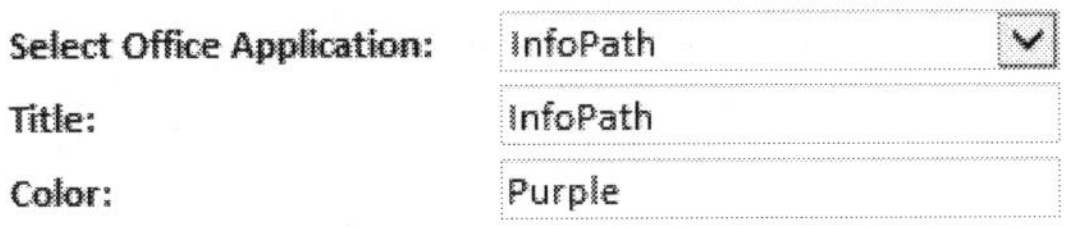

Figure 141. The form displaying the title and color for a selected Office application.

Discussion

In the solution described above, all of the data from the secondary data source was retrieved as soon as the form opened. This is mainly because you needed to populate the drop-down list box with initial data, so that users would have something to select from. But if your scenario entails a user knowing an **ID** or **Title** they could enter, you could change the solution to allow users to explicitly enter this data into a text box, and then run a query that made use of that **ID** or **Title** to retrieve corresponding data. In such a solution you would first have to set the value of the **ID** or **Title** field under the **queryFields** group node in the secondary data source to be equal to the value the user typed into the text box, run a **Query for data** action on the secondary data source, and then use a **Set a field's value** action to populate form fields based on the data that was returned in the fields located under the **dataFields** group node in the secondary data source. You would not have to use the **Filter Data** command for such a solution, since filtering would have already taken place when you ran the query (also see recipe *50 Filter SharePoint list data on an exact match*).

Use a Select button in a repeating table

Problem

You have bound a secondary data source for a SharePoint list to a repeating table control on an InfoPath form. Now you want to be able to copy the data from one of the rows of the repeating table to other fields on the InfoPath form.

Solution

You can add an extra column with a button to a repeating table that is bound to the secondary data source for a SharePoint list and then use action rules on the button to set values of other fields on the form.

Suppose you have a SharePoint list named **OfficeApplications** as described in *Create a SharePoint list form for an existing SharePoint list* in recipe *2 Customize a SharePoint list form from within InfoPath*.

To copy data from this SharePoint list to form fields using a button to select data from a repeating table row:

1. In InfoPath, create a new SharePoint form library form template or use an existing one.
2. Add a **Receive** data connection to the **OfficeApplications** SharePoint list to the form template as described in *Use a SharePoint list data connection* in recipe *43 2 Ways to retrieve data from a SharePoint list*. Ensure that you select **Title** and **Color** as fields to include in the data source, and that you leave the **Automatically retrieve data when form is opened** check box selected.
3. Bind the **d:SharePointListItem_RW** repeating group node under the **dataFields** group node in the **OfficeApplications** secondary data source to a repeating table on the view of the form template as described in recipe *44 Display SharePoint list data in a repeating table*.
4. Click anywhere in the header of the right-most column of the repeating table to place the cursor, and then select **Table Tools ➤ Layout ➤**

Rows & Columns ➤ Insert Right to add a new column to the repeating table.

5. Add a **Button** control to the cell of the new column of the repeating table and label the button **Select**.
6. Add two **Text Box** controls to the view of the form template and name them **title** and **color**, respectively.
7. Add an **Action** rule to the **Select** button with the following 2 actions:

```
Set a field's value: title = Title
Set a field's value: color = Color
```

   where **title** and **color** are located in the Main data source of the form and **Title** and **Color** are located under the **d:SharePointListItem_RW** repeating group node under the **dataFields** group node in the **OfficeApplications** secondary data source.

8. Publish the form template to a SharePoint form library.

In SharePoint, navigate to the form library where you published the form template and add a new form. When the form opens, click on the **Select** button in any row of the repeating table. The values of the **Title** and **Color** fields in the same row of the repeating table in which the **Select** button is located, should appear in the corresponding **title** and **color** text boxes on the form.

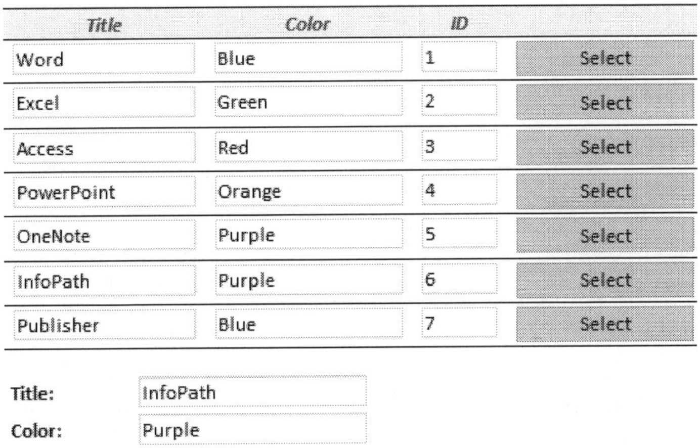

Figure 142. The InfoPath form with the title and color of InfoPath selected.

Discussion

A repeating table that is bound to a secondary data source is not modifiable, meaning that you cannot add any fields to it. The data source is locked; you can see that it is at the padlocks that have been placed on the fields and groups in the secondary data source on the **Fields** task pane. However, you are allowed to add buttons to rows of the repeating table, because buttons do not have to be bound to fields in the data source. The solution described above makes use of the latter.

By adding a button to each row of the repeating table, you enable the data in each individual row to be selected through the button that is located in that same row. Copying data from the secondary data source for the SharePoint list then simply becomes a matter of adding an action rule to the button to set the values of fields that are located elsewhere on the form.

Copy data to a row of a repeating table on insert

Problem

You have a repeating table control on an InfoPath form. Every time a user clicks to add a row to the repeating table, you want to copy values that correspond to an item selected in a drop-down list box to that specific row of the repeating table.

Solution

You can configure fields in a repeating table to pull data from a SharePoint list whenever a new row is added to the repeating table.

Suppose you have a SharePoint list named **OfficeApplications** as described in *Create a SharePoint list form for an existing SharePoint list* in recipe *2 Customize a SharePoint list form from within InfoPath*.

To copy data from this SharePoint list to fields in the repeating table when a new row is added to the repeating table:

1. In InfoPath, create a new SharePoint form library form template or use an existing one.

2. Add a **Receive** data connection to the **OfficeApplications** SharePoint list to the form template as described in *Use a SharePoint list data connection* in recipe *43 2 Ways to retrieve data from a SharePoint list*. Ensure that you select **Title** and **Color** as fields to include in the data source, and that you leave the **Automatically retrieve data when form is opened** check box selected.
3. Add a **Drop-Down List Box** control to the view of the form template, name it **selectedOfficeApplication**, and populate it with entries from the **OfficeApplications** secondary data source. Use the **ID** field for the **Value** and the **Title** field for the **Display name** of the items in the drop-down list box.
4. Add a **Repeating Table** control with 3 columns to the view of the form template, and rename the fields in the repeating table to **id**, **title**, and **color**, respectively.
5. Click **Data ➤ Form Data ➤ Default Values**, and then on the **Edit Default Values** dialog box, deselect the check box in front of the **group2** repeating group node, and click **OK**. This should remove the first empty row from the repeating table when a new form is created.

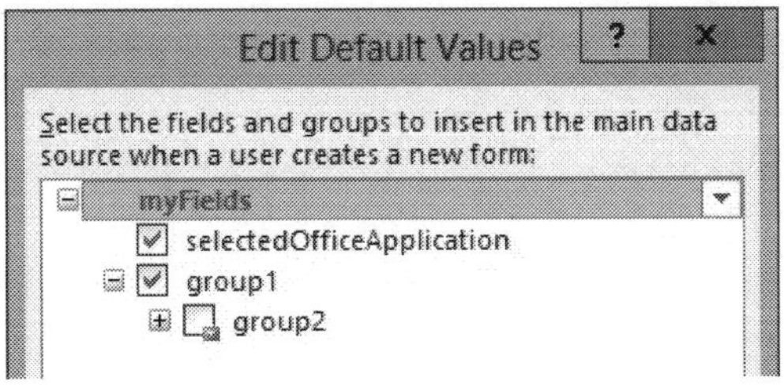

Figure 143. A cleared check box in front of the group2 repeating group node.

6. Set the **Default Value** of the **id** field in the repeating table to be equal to the following formula:

```
xdXDocument:GetDOM("OfficeApplications")/dfs:myFields/dfs:dataF
ields/d:SharePointListItem_RW/d:ID[. = xdXDocument:get-
DOM()/my:myFields/my:selectedOfficeApplication]
```

This formula filters the secondary data source for the SharePoint list on the **ID** of the selected Office application in the drop-down list box, and then returns the **ID** of the item found. Deselect the **Refresh value when formula is recalculated** check box on the **Field or Group**

Properties dialog box, so that the **id** fields in all of the other rows of the repeating table are not refreshed every time a new row is added to the repeating table.

7. Set the **Default Value** of the **title** field in the repeating table to be equal to the following formula:

```
xdXDocument:GetDOM("OfficeApplications")/dfs:myFields/dfs:dataF
ields/d:SharePointListItem_RW/d:Title[../d:ID =
xdXDocument:get-DOM()/my:myFields/my:selectedOfficeApplication]
```

This formula filters the secondary data source for the SharePoint list on the **ID** of the selected Office application in the drop-down list box, and then returns the **Title** of the item found. Deselect the **Refresh value when formula is recalculated** check box on the **Field or Group Properties** dialog box, so that the **title** fields in all of the other rows of the repeating table are not refreshed every time a new row is added to the repeating table.

8. Set the **Default Value** of the **color** field in the repeating table to be equal to the following formula:

```
xdXDocument:GetDOM("OfficeApplications")/dfs:myFields/dfs:dataF
ields/d:SharePointListItem_RW/d:Color[../d:ID =
xdXDocument:get-DOM()/my:myFields/my:selectedOfficeApplication]
```

This formula filters the secondary data source for the SharePoint list on the **ID** of the selected Office application in the drop-down list box, and then returns the **Color** of the item found. Deselect the **Refresh value when formula is recalculated** check box on the **Field or Group Properties** dialog box, so that the **color** fields in all of the other rows of the repeating table are not refreshed every time a new row is added to the repeating table.

9. Publish the form template to a SharePoint form library.

In SharePoint, navigate to the form library where you published the form template and add a new form. When the form opens, select an item from the drop-down list box, and then click **Insert item** on the repeating table. A row that contains SharePoint list data that corresponds to the selected item in the drop-down list box should appear in the newly added row in the repeating table.

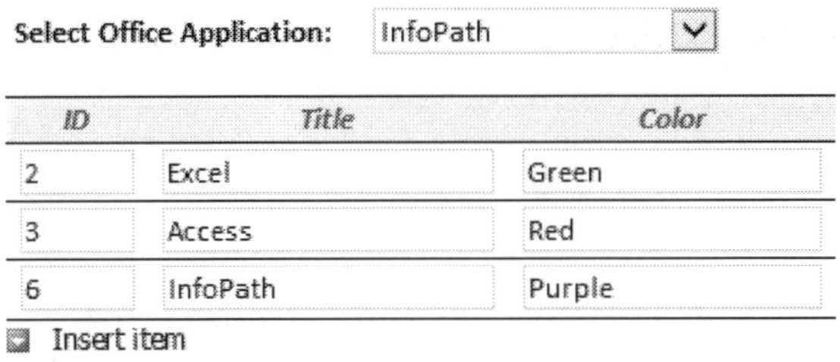

Figure 144. The form with 3 applications selected and inserted into the repeating table.

Discussion

In the solution described above you saw how to use default values on fields in a repeating table to pull data from a secondary data source for a SharePoint list. In the next recipe you will learn how you can use a similar technique of pulling data to populate rows of a repeating table with data from a SharePoint list.

46 Map rows of a repeating table to SharePoint list items

Problem

You want to copy data from a SharePoint list to a repeating table on an InfoPath form.

Solution

You can pre-add a number of rows to a repeating table (as many rows as you think you would need or that would be suitable for displaying items from the SharePoint list), and then automatically map the fields in the repeating table to the corresponding items in the SharePoint list by using the **count()** function and **preceding-sibling** XPath axis in an XPath filter expression.

Suppose you have a SharePoint list named **OfficeApplications** as described in *Create a SharePoint list form for an existing SharePoint list* in recipe *2 Customize a SharePoint list form from within InfoPath*.

To copy data from this SharePoint list to a repeating table that has 5 fixed rows:

1. In InfoPath, create a new SharePoint form library form template or use an existing one.
2. Add a **Receive** data connection to the **OfficeApplications** SharePoint list to the form template as described in *Use a SharePoint list data connection* in recipe *43 2 Ways to retrieve data from a SharePoint list.* Ensure that you select **Title** and **Color** as fields to include in the data source, and that you leave the **Automatically retrieve data when form is opened** check box selected.
3. Add a **Repeating Table** control with 3 columns to the view of the form template, and rename the fields in the repeating table to **id**, **title**, and **color**, respectively.
4. Click **Data ➤ Form Data ➤ Default Values** and add 4 additional default rows (**group2** nodes) to the repeating table for a total of 5 default rows.
5. Set the **Default Value** of the **id** field in the repeating table to be equal to the following formula:

   ```
   xdXDocument:GetDOM("OfficeApplications")/dfs:myFields/dfs:dataF
   ields/d:SharePointListItem_RW[count(current()/../preceding-
   sibling::my:group2) + 1]/d:ID
   ```

   This formula counts the amount of **group2** group nodes that precede the **group2** group node of the current context node, which is the **id** field in the current row of the repeating table, and then uses this amount as a filter on the **OfficeApplications** secondary data source to find the one item in the SharePoint list that is positioned at the same index number as the current row is. For example, **[1]** corresponds to the first item, **[2]** to the second item, etc. That is the trick to making this solution work. Note: You must leave the **Refresh value when formula is recalculated** check box on the **Field or Group Properties** dialog box selected for the default value to be refreshed.
6. Set the **Default Value** of the **title** field in the repeating table to be equal to the following formula (Tip: You can copy the formula from the **id** field and change **d:ID** to **d:Title** to save time):

   ```
   xdXDocument:GetDOM("OfficeApplications")/dfs:myFields/dfs:dataF
   ields/d:SharePointListItem_RW[count(current()/../preceding-
   ```

```
sibling::my:group2) + 1]/d:Title
```

Note: You must leave the **Refresh value when formula is recalculated** check box on the **Field or Group Properties** dialog box selected for the default value to be refreshed.

7. Set the **Default Value** of the **color** field in the repeating table to be equal to the following formula (Tip: You can copy the formula from the **id** field and change **d:ID** to **d:Color** to save time):

```
xdXDocument:GetDOM("OfficeApplications")/dfs:myFields/dfs:dataF
ields/d:SharePointListItem_RW[count(current()/../preceding-
sibling::my:group2) + 1]/d:Color
```

Note: You must leave the **Refresh value when formula is recalculated** check box on the **Field or Group Properties** dialog box selected for the default value to be refreshed.

8. Publish the form template to a SharePoint form library.

In SharePoint, navigate to the form library where you published the form template and add a new form. When the form opens, data from the first 5 items in the SharePoint list should appear in the first 5 rows of the repeating table. Click **Insert item** to insert a new row in the repeating table. The new row should be populated with data from the 6th item in the SharePoint list, if there is a 6th item present in the SharePoint list.

ID	Title	Color
1	Word	Blue
2	Excel	Green
3	Access	Red
4	PowerPoint	Orange
5	OneNote	Purple

Insert item

Figure 145. The InfoPath form displaying the first 5 items from the SharePoint list.

Discussion

As mentioned in step 5 of the solution described above, the trick to making this solution work lies in having a reference number for each row in the repeating table and then using this number as a filter on the data in the

SharePoint list to find the correct data for each row in the repeating table. Because there are no rules in InfoPath with which you can set values in a repeating table, you can use this technique where a repeating table pulls its own data in from another data source to set the values of its fields. And because there are also no rules in InfoPath with which you can add rows to a repeating table, you must pre-add a fixed amount of rows by adding default rows to the repeating table. So while the solution described above is not the perfect solution for copying data to a repeating table or a repeating section, it provides a couple of techniques to work around a few limitations of InfoPath.

Caveat: A repeating table must not contain too many fields with default values set on them, since SharePoint may then display an error message that says:

Default values, rules or code may be running in an infinite loop. To prevent this, ensure that the default value, rule action or event handler does not update the data which causes the same rule action or event handler to execute.

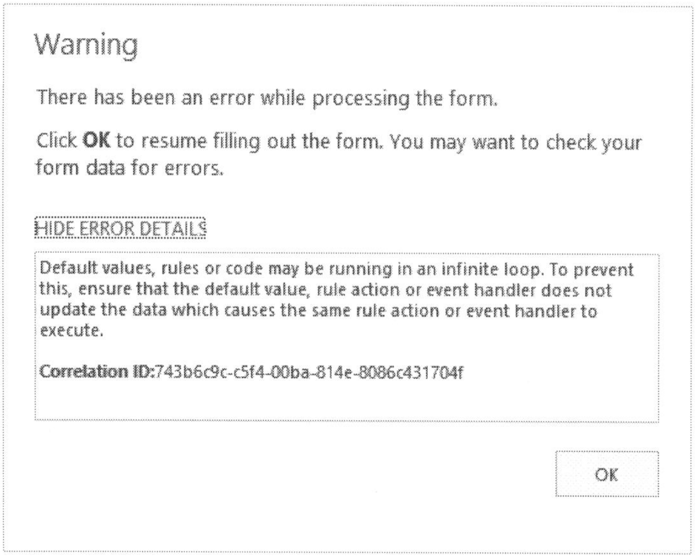

Figure 146. Infinite loop error message in SharePoint 2013.

47 Master/detail data with linked SharePoint lists

Problem

You have two SharePoint lists that are linked to each other through a lookup column. You want to be able to display data from the master list in a drop-down list box on an InfoPath form, select an item from the drop-down list box, and then have the related detail items appear in a repeating table.

Solution

You can use fields under the **queryFields** group node of a SharePoint list data source to query and retrieve data on demand, including related data.

Suppose you have two SharePoint lists named **SoftwareCategories** and **SoftwareProducts** as described in recipe *14 Master/detail with two linked SharePoint lists*.

To display master/detail functionality using two linked SharePoint lists:

1. In InfoPath, create a new SharePoint form library form template or use an existing one.
2. Add a **Receive** data connection to the **SoftwareCategories** SharePoint list as described in *Use a SharePoint list data connection* in recipe *43 2 Ways to retrieve data from a SharePoint list*. Ensure that you select **Title** as a field to include in the data source, and that you leave the **Automatically retrieve data when form is opened** check box selected.
3. Add a **Receive** data connection to the **SoftwareProducts** SharePoint list. Ensure that you select **Title** and **Category** as fields to include in the data source, and that you deselect the **Automatically retrieve data when form is opened** check box.
4. Add a **Drop-Down List Box** control to the view of the form template, name it **category**, and populate it with entries from the **SoftwareCategories** secondary data source. Select the **ID** field for the **Value** property and the **Title** field for the **Display name** property of the drop-down list box.

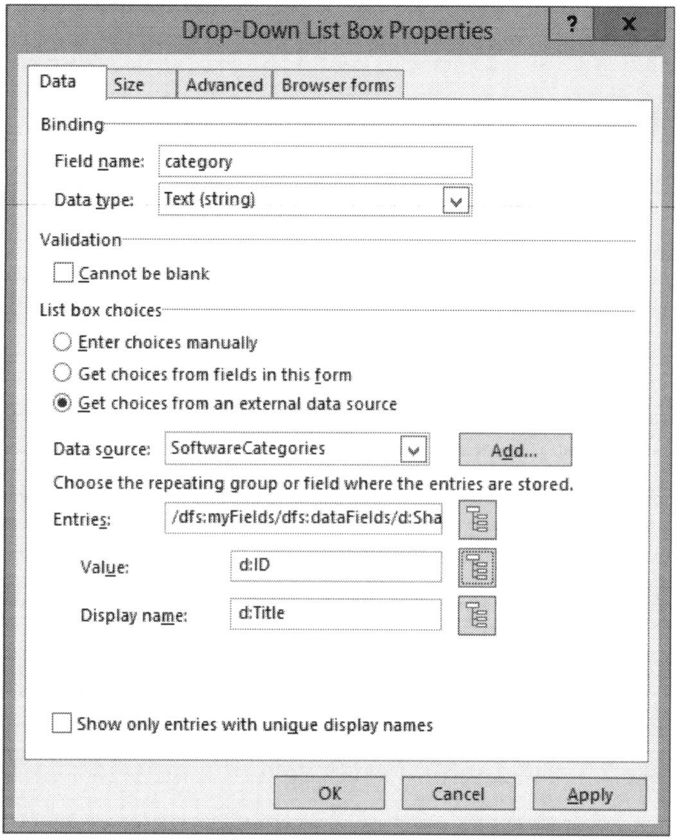

Figure 147. Populating the drop-down list box with items from the SharePoint list.

5. Bind the **SoftwareProducts** secondary data source to a repeating table control on the view of the form template as described in recipe *44 Display SharePoint list data in a repeating table*.
6. Add an **Action** rule to the **category** drop-down list box with the following 2 actions:

```
Set a field's value: Category = .
Query using a data connection: SoftwareProducts
```

where **Category** is the **Category** field that is located under the **q:SharePointListItem_RW** group node under the **queryFields** group node in the **SoftwareProducts** secondary data source, and the dot (**.**) represents the **category** field in the Main data source. This rule sets up a query for the **SoftwareProducts** secondary data source and then executes that query to retrieve filtered data.

7. Publish the form template to a SharePoint form library.

In SharePoint, navigate to the form library where you published the form template and add a new form. When the form opens, select a category from the drop-down list box. The corresponding software products should appear in the repeating table.

Office Applications ☑	

Product	*Category*
Word	2
Excel	2

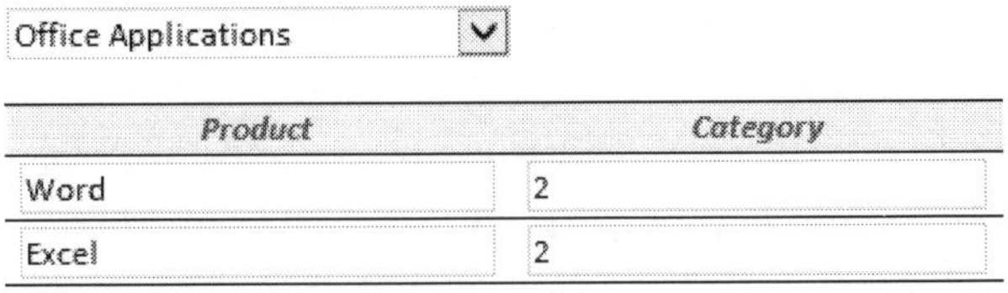

Figure 148. Data in the repeating table filtered by the Office Applications category.

Discussion

In the solution described above, you learned how to use query fields of a SharePoint list data connection to filter and retrieve related SharePoint list items. This technique works well if you have large lists from which you want to retrieve data.

48 Display a list of people from the current user's department

Problem

You want to be able to display a list of users who are in the same department as the user who is currently filling out the form.

Solution

You can use the **User Information List** SharePoint list to look up the department of the current user and then perform a second search to find all of the people who are in that same department. The **Department** property in SharePoint user profiles must have already been populated with values for this solution to work.

To display a list of people who are in the same department as the current user:

1. In InfoPath, create a new SharePoint form library form template or use an existing one.
2. Add a **Text Box** control to the view of the form template and name it **myDepartment**.
3. Add a **Receive** data connection to the **User Information List** SharePoint list as described in *Use a SharePoint list data connection* in recipe *43 2 Ways to retrieve data from a SharePoint list*. Ensure that you select **Department** and **User_name (User name)** as fields to include in the data source, that you deselect the **Automatically retrieve data when form is opened** check box, and that you accept the default name for the data connection (**User Information List**).

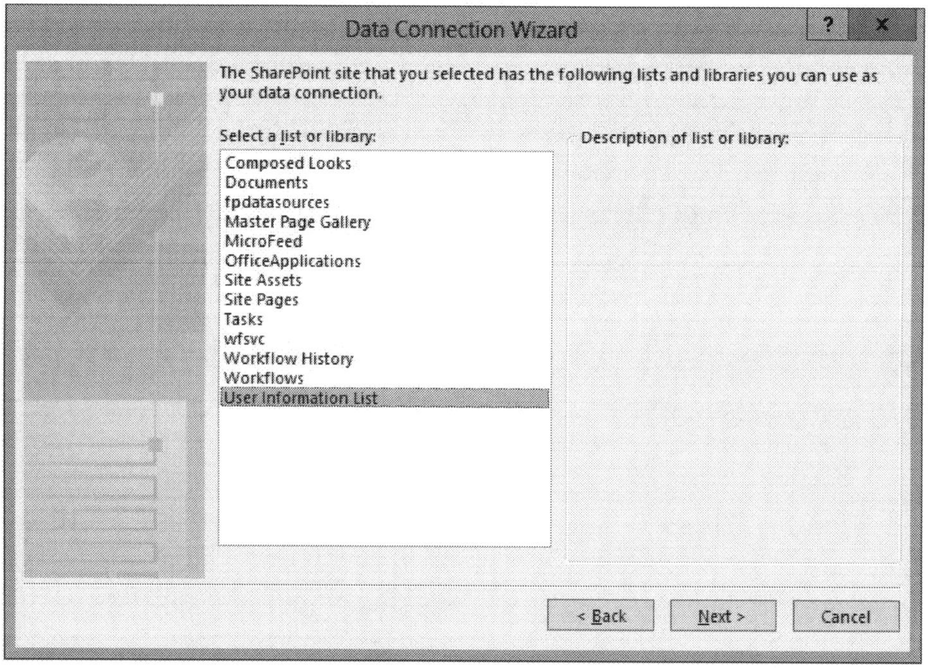

Figure 149. Selecting to connect to the User Information List.

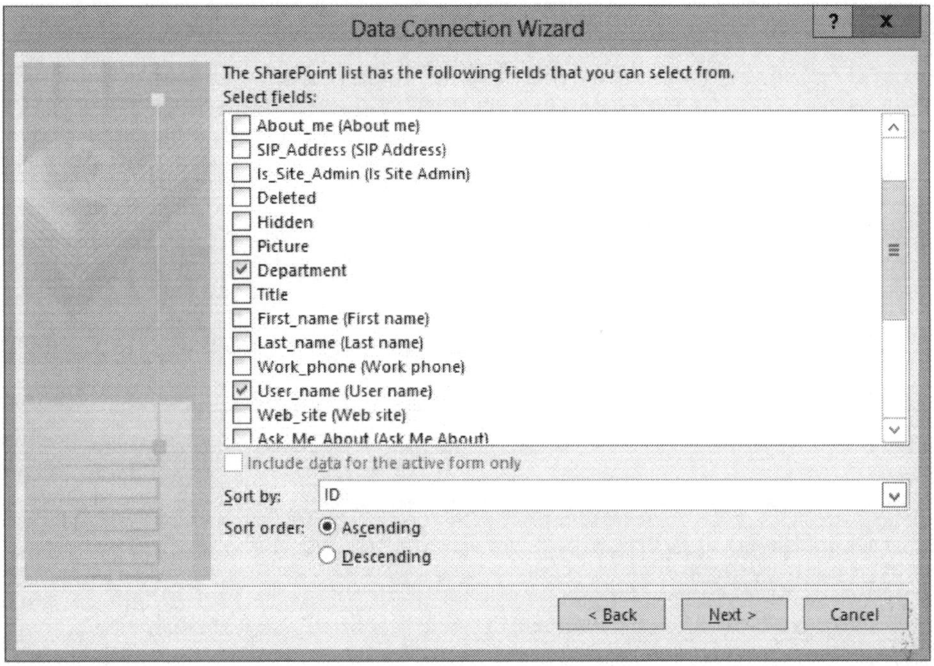

Figure 150. Selecting fields to include in the data source.

4. Bind the **d:SharePointListItem_RW** repeating group node under the **dataFields** group node in the **User Information List** secondary data source to a repeating table on the view of the form template as described in recipe *44 Display SharePoint list data in a repeating table*.
5. You can either add a button to the view to query the **User Information List** or as in this solution, query the **User Information List** when the form loads. So click **Data ➤ Rules ➤ Form Load** to open the **Rules** task pane.
6. Add an **Action** rule to the **Form Load** event that has the following 6 actions:

```
Set a field's value: UserName = substring-after(userName(),
"\")
```

where **UserName** is the **User name** field that is located under the **q:SharePointListItem_RW** group node under the **queryFields** group node in the **User Information List** secondary data source and **userName()** is the InfoPath function that retrieves the user name of the person filling out the form. The **substring-after()** function is used to return the string that comes after the backslash (\ ) in the value of the **userName()** function, which should be equal to the user name in the **User Information List** secondary data source. Note that if you will be publishing the form template to a Windows Classic environment, you must use the **userName()** function without the **substring-after()** function (see the discussion section).

```
Query using a data connection: User Information List
```

This action queries the secondary data source to retrieve the user profile information for the current user.

```
Set a field's value: myDepartment = Department
```

where **myDepartment** is the field that is bound to the text box and that is located in the Main data source of the form, and **Department** is the **Department** field that is located under the **d:SharePointListItem_RW** repeating group node under the **dataFields** group node in the **User Information List** secondary data source. This action retrieves the result of the query that just ran and stores it in the **myDepartment** field.

```
Set a field's value: UserName = ""
```

where **UserName** is the **User name** field that is located under the **q:SharePointListItem_RW** group node under the **queryFields** group node in the **User Information List** secondary data source. This action clears the value you set earlier so that you can retrieve the user profile information for all users instead of just one.

```
Set a field's value: Department = myDepartment
```

where **Department** is the **Department** field that is located under the **q:SharePointListItem_RW** group node under the **queryFields** group node in the **User Information List** secondary data source and **myDepartment** is located in the Main data source. This action sets the value of the department for which all users must be retrieved by the query.

```
Query using a data connection: User Information List
```

This action queries the **User Information List** data connection to retrieve the user profile information for all users who have the same department as the current user.

7. Add a **Formatting** rule to the repeating table that is bound to the **User Information List** secondary data source (the **d:SharePointListItem_RW** repeating group node) with a **Condition** that says:

```
translate(d:UserName, "ABCDEFGHIJKLMNOPQRSTUVWXYZ",
"abcdefghijklmnopqrstuvwxyz") = translate(substring-
after(xdUser:get-UserName(), "\"),
"ABCDEFGHIJKLMNOPQRSTUVWXYZ", "abcdefghijklmnopqrstuvwxyz")
```

   where **d:UserName** is the **User name** field that is located under the **d:SharePointListItem_RW** repeating group node under the **dataFields** group node in the **User Information List** secondary data source and **xdUser:get-UserName()** is the **userName()** InfoPath function that retrieves the user name of the person filling out the form. Note that the **translate()** function is used in the formula above to ensure that both user names are lower case when they are compared with each other so that the comparison does not the fail to find records due to non-matching cases. Also note that if you will be publishing the form template to a Windows Classic environment, you must remove the **substring-after()** function from the expression for the condition (see the discussion section).

   Select a formatting of **Hide this control**. This formatting rule hides the row in the repeating table that corresponds to the current user, so that the current user is excluded from the list of users in the department.

8. Publish the form template to a SharePoint form library.

In SharePoint, navigate to the form library where you published the form template and add a new form. When the form opens, check whether the people who are listed in the repeating table have the same department as the currently logged on user. Log on as a different user who is in a different department. Add a new form and check whether the list of users is correct.

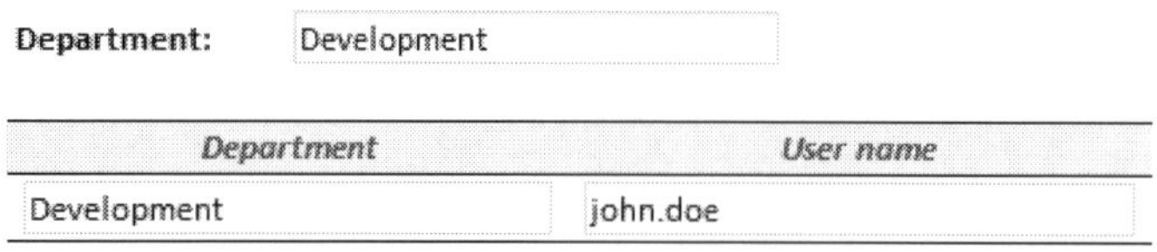

Figure 151. Form displaying users who are in the same department as the current user.

Discussion

In the solution described above you used fields under the **queryFields** group node in the data source for the SharePoint list to first query the User Information List to find the department of the person who is filling out the form, and then used the department returned to query the User Information List for a second time to find all of the users from that department.

The User Information List displays the users on a particular SharePoint site and gets its information from SharePoint user profiles. You can use the User Information List to look up a limited amount of information for a particular user such as for example first and last name, email address, phone number, department, etc. Since the User Information List does not contain all of the properties of a user's profile, if you want to retrieve properties that are not contained in the User Information List, you can use the User Profile Service to retrieve that information (see recipe *75 Get the details of the manager of a selected person in a people picker* for an example of how to use the User Profile Service).

Because the **userName()** function returns user names such as for example

```
i:0#.w|corp\jane.doe
```

in browser-forms that are filled out through SharePoint with Claims Based authentication (where **corp** is the domain name and **jane.doe** is the user name), when comparing user names that are stored in the User Information List with user names returned by the **userName()** function, you must ensure that they have the same format for the comparison not to fail. In the solution described above, you used the **substring-after()** function to perform a correction on the user name returned by the **userName()** function.

```
substring-after(userName(), "\")
```

If you are creating a form template for a Windows Classic environment, you must not use the **substring-after()** function. The formula above should just be:

```
userName()
```

and the condition for the formatting rule in step 7 should be:

```
translate(d:UserName, "ABCDEFGHIJKLMNOPQRSTUVWXYZ",
"abcdefghijklmnopqrstuvwxyz") = translate(xdUser:get-UserName(),
"ABCDEFGHIJKLMNOPQRSTUVWXYZ", "abcdefghijklmnopqrstuvwxyz")
```

Sort and filter SharePoint list data

Filtering SharePoint list data is particularly useful when you have a SharePoint list that contains a large amount of data and you want to use this data in an InfoPath form, but do not want the data retrieval to negatively impact the performance of the form. InfoPath 2013 offers filtering on SharePoint list data connections through fields that are located under the **queryFields** group node in the secondary data source for a SharePoint list. The recipes in this section provide examples of how to sort and filter SharePoint list data in InfoPath.

49 Sort SharePoint list data on one field

Problem

You want to retrieve data from a SharePoint list and have that data appear sorted when it is displayed on an InfoPath form.

Solution

You can use the **Sort by** option on the **Data Connection Wizard** when setting up the data connection for a SharePoint list to sort the list's data by a chosen field in the list in an ascending or a descending order.

To sort SharePoint list data on one field:

1. In InfoPath, create a new browser-compatible form template or use an existing one.
2. Click **Data** ➤ **Get External Data** ➤ **From SharePoint List**.
3. On the **Data Connection Wizard**, enter the URL of the SharePoint site where the SharePoint list you want to connect to is located, and click **Next**.
4. On the **Data Connection Wizard**, select the list you want to connect to from the **Select a list or library** list box, and click **Next**.
5. On the **Data Connection Wizard**, select any fields from the SharePoint list that you want to include in the data source. Below the list of fields, you should see a **Sort by** drop-down list box and **Sort order** option buttons.

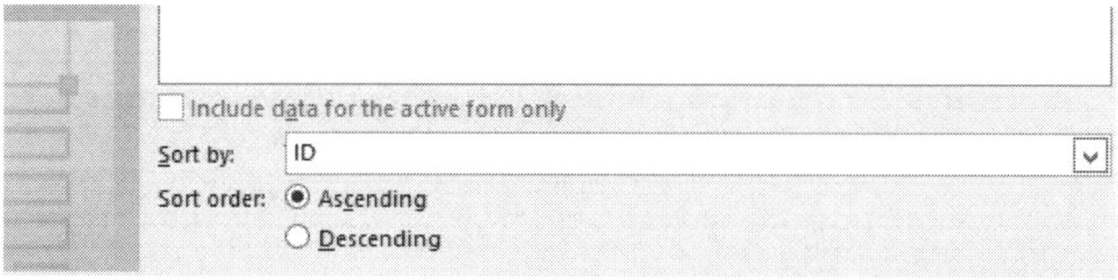

Figure 152. Sort by and Sort order options on the Data Connection Wizard.

   Use the drop-down list box to select the field you want to use to sort the list data by and use the option buttons to select whether to sort the data in an ascending or a descending order.

6. Click **Next**, and finish creating the data connection.

If you now use the data connection to retrieve data from the SharePoint list, the data returned should be sorted by the field you specified through the **Data Connection Wizard**. For example, you could bind the secondary data source for the SharePoint list to a repeating table control as described in recipe *44 Display SharePoint list data in a repeating table* or populate a drop-down list box control with this data, and then preview the form to see whether the data has been sorted.

Discussion

Using the **Sort by** drop-down list box on the **Data Connection Wizard** is the quickest and easiest way to retrieve and sort data from a SharePoint list. However, there are two disadvantages to using this method for sorting SharePoint list data:

1. You can only set the field to sort the data by through the **Data Connection Wizard** at design time, which means that you cannot allow users to select a different field to sort the data by when they are filling out the form at runtime.
2. You can only choose one field by which to sort the data.

Note that sorting data through a SharePoint list data connection sorts the data on the server when it is retrieved and not locally in the InfoPath form.

50 Filter SharePoint list data on an exact match

Problem

You have a repeating table on a form that displays data from a SharePoint list. You want to be able to retrieve and display only those items from the SharePoint list that are an exact match for the data you are looking for.

Solution

You can use fields that are located under the **queryFields** group node in a secondary data source and an action rule on a button to look up and retrieve data from a SharePoint list you want to display in a repeating table.

Suppose you have a SharePoint list named **OfficeApplications** as described in *Create a SharePoint list form for an existing SharePoint list* in recipe *2 Customize a SharePoint list form from within InfoPath* and you want to be able to type a color into a text box and return only those Office applications that have that color specified in their **Color** field.

To filter SharePoint list data on an exact match:

1. In InfoPath, create a new SharePoint form library form template or use an existing one.

2. Add a **Receive** data connection to the **OfficeApplications** SharePoint list as described in *Use a SharePoint list data connection* in recipe *43 2 Ways to retrieve data from a SharePoint list*, but then deselect the **Automatically retrieve data when form is opened** check box on the last screen of the **Data Connection Wizard**.
3. Bind the **d:SharePointListItem_RW** repeating group node under the **dataFields** group node in the **OfficeApplications** secondary data source to a repeating table control on the view of the form template as described in recipe *44 Display SharePoint list data in a repeating table*.
4. On the **Fields** task pane, select **OfficeApplications (Secondary)** from the drop-down list box, expand all of the nodes under the **queryFields** group node, select the **Color** field, and drag-and-drop it onto the view of the form template. It should automatically get bound to a text box control.
5. Add a **Button** control to the view of the form template and label the button **Filter**.
6. With the button control still selected, select **Home ➤ Rules ➤ Add Rule ➤ When This Button Is Clicked ➤ Query for Data**.
7. On the **Rule Details** dialog box, select **OfficeApplications** from the **Data connection** drop-down list box, and click **OK**.
8. Publish the form template to a SharePoint form library.

In SharePoint, navigate to the form library where you published the form template and add a new form. When the form opens, type a color, for example **Purple**, into the color text box, and click **Filter**. OneNote and InfoPath should appear in the repeating table. If you empty the color text box and click **Filter**, all of the items from the **OfficeApplications** SharePoint list should appear in the repeating table.

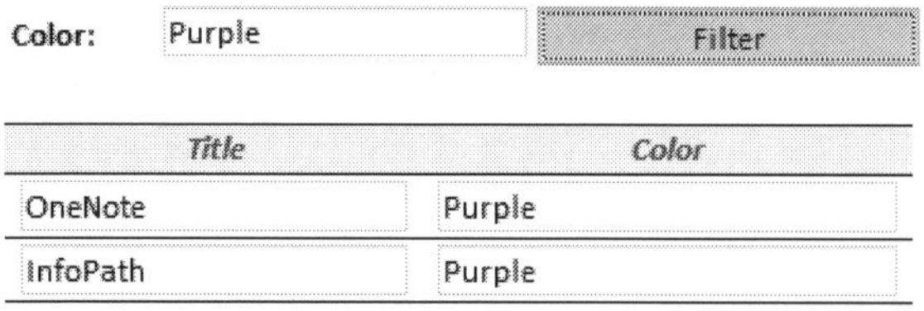

Figure 153. The repeating table displaying items that have the color 'Purple'.

Discussion

The **queryFields** group node contains fields that can be used to query (look up) data in a SharePoint list, and the **dataFields** group node contains fields that can be used to display data from the SharePoint list. Since fields under the **queryFields** group node only accept values but not additional operators to query a list on, you can only use them to perform filtering that returns exact match data. Note that case is ignored when performing a query.

In the solution described above, you used a field that was located under the **queryFields** group node to search for data that matched the color you entered into a text box control. You also used a **Query for data** action rule on a button to query a data connection for a SharePoint list to retrieve items from that list. Note that instead of a **Query for data** action rule on the button, you could have also used the **Refresh** button action of the button to query the data source.

51 Retrieve the first X amount of items from a SharePoint list

Problem

You want to retrieve the first 5 items from a SharePoint list to populate a drop-down list box when a form opens.

Solution

You can use the **$top** query option in the REST web service URL of a SharePoint list to filter data and return only the first X amount of entries from the feed.

Suppose you have a SharePoint list named **OfficeApplications** as described in *Create a SharePoint list form for an existing SharePoint list* in recipe *2 Customize a SharePoint list form from within InfoPath*.

To retrieve the first X amount of items from that SharePoint list:

1. In InfoPath, create a new SharePoint form library form template or use an existing one.

2. Select **Data ➤ Get External Data ➤ From Web Service ➤ From REST Web Service**.

3. On the **Data Connection Wizard**, enter the REST Web Service URL for the SharePoint list, for example:

```
http://servername/sitename/_api/web/lists/getbytitle('OfficeApp
lications')/items?$select=Title,Color&$top=5
```

and click **Next**. Here, **servername** is the name of the SharePoint server and **sitename** is the name of the site where the **OfficeApplications** SharePoint list is located. The URL selects the **Title** and **Color** fields and returns the first 5 items from the list.

4. On the **Data Connection Wizard**, name the data connection **GetFirst5OfficeApplications**, leave the **Automatically retrieve data when form is opened** check box selected, and click **Finish**.

5. Add a **Drop-Down List Box** control to the view of the form template, and populate it with items from the **GetFirst5OfficeApplications** secondary data source. Select the **entry** repeating group node for the **Entries** property of the drop-down list box, and the **Title** field under the **m:properties** group node under the **content** group node for both the **Value** and the **Display name** properties of the drop-down list box.

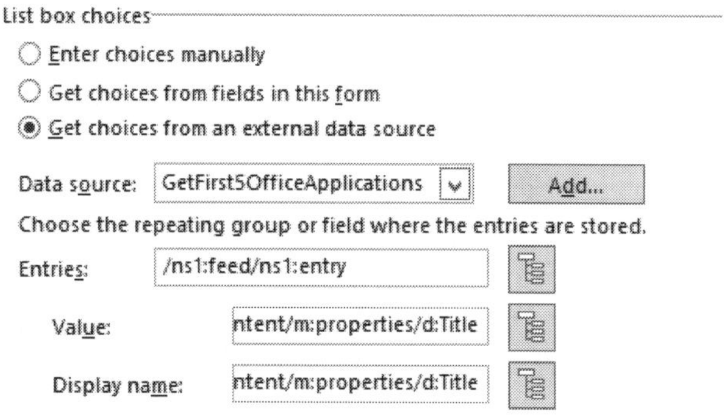

Figure 154. Drop-down list box settings using the data source for the web service.

6. If your SharePoint environment is configured to use Claims Based authentication as opposed to Windows Classic authentication and the form is going to be filled out through the browser, you must set up UDC authentication for the **GetFirst5OfficeApplications** data connection that makes the web service call as described in *Configure a web service data connection for a web browser form* in the Appendix. But

before you do this, test the form in InfoPath Filler 2013 to ensure that the functionality is working properly.

7. Publish the form template to a SharePoint form library.

In SharePoint, navigate to the form library where you published the form template and add a new form. When the form opens, the drop-down list box should display the first 5 items from the SharePoint list.

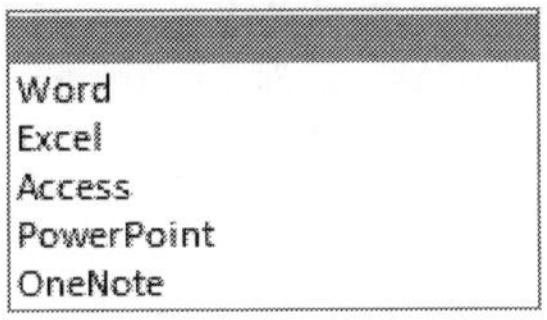

Figure 155. The InfoPath form displaying the first 5 items from the SharePoint list.

Discussion

In the solution described above, you used the **$top** query option to return the first 5 items from a SharePoint list. The **$top** query option returns entries from the top of the feed. For example:

```
http://servername/sitename/_api/web/lists/getbytitle('OfficeApplica
tions')/items?$select=Title,Color&$top=2
```

returns the first two items starting from the top of the feed. And if you entered no number or a number greater than the total amount of items in the SharePoint list, all of the items from the SharePoint list would be returned.

You could extend the solution to return a certain amount of sorted items from a SharePoint list by adding the **$orderby** query option to the URL as follows:

```
http://servername/sitename/_api/web/lists/getbytitle('OfficeApplica
tions')/items?$select=Title,Color&$top=2&$orderby=Title,Color
```

In the URL shown above, the SharePoint list items are first sorted by **Title** and then by **Color**, before the first 2 items in the SharePoint list are returned.

For more information about the use of query options refer to the article entitled *Open Data Protocol by Example* on MSDN.

Validate data entered in SharePoint list forms

Often before submitting data to a SharePoint list through a SharePoint list form, you may want to validate the data to prevent users from adding erroneous data to the list. You can use a SharePoint list data connection to the same list the data is being submitted to, to be able to check existing data against the data being entered by a user and stop submission of incorrect data through validation rules. The recipes in this section provide examples of how to do this.

52 Prevent duplicate items from being added to a SharePoint list

Problem

You have a SharePoint list that contains data in two columns. You want to be able to use an InfoPath form to add data to this list, but then prevent users from adding an item that already exists in the SharePoint list. In essence, you want the data in the two columns combined to be unique for each item entered into the SharePoint list.

Solution

You can use data validation to prevent duplicate items from being entered into a SharePoint list.

Suppose you have a SharePoint list named **OfficeApplications** as described in *Create a SharePoint list form for an existing SharePoint list* in recipe *2 Customize a SharePoint list form from within InfoPath*.

To prevent duplicate items from being added to that SharePoint list:

1. In InfoPath, create a new SharePoint list form template that is based on the **OfficeApplications** SharePoint list as described in recipe *1*

Customize a SharePoint list form from within SharePoint or recipe *2 Customize a SharePoint list form from within InfoPath*.

2. Add a **Receive** data connection to the **OfficeApplications** SharePoint list to the form template as described in *Use a SharePoint list data connection* in recipe *43 2 Ways to retrieve data from a SharePoint list*. Ensure that you select **ID**, **Title**, and **Color** as fields to include in the data source, and that you leave the **Automatically retrieve data when form is opened** check box selected.
3. On the **Fields** task pane, click **Show advanced view** if **Basic view** is being shown. This is to prevent you from having to click **Show advanced view** on dialog boxes when setting up validation rules.
4. Add a **Validation** rule to the **Title** text box, and then click the text **None** under **Condition**.
5. On the **Condition** dialog box, select **Use a formula** from the third drop-down list box.
6. On the **Insert Formula** dialog box, click **Insert Field or Group**.
7. On the **Select a Field or Group** dialog box, select **OfficeApplications (Secondary)** from the drop-down list box, expand the **dataFields** group node, select the **d:SharePointListItem_RW** repeating group node, and then click **Filter Data**.
8. On the **Filter Data** dialog box, click **Add**.
9. On the **Specify Filter Conditions** dialog box, construct 3 conditions that say:

```
Title is equal to Title
and
Color is equal to Color
and
ID is not equal to ID
```

where the first **Title**, **Color**, and **ID** fields are located under the **d:SharePointListItem_RW** repeating group node under the **dataFields** group node in the **OfficeApplications** secondary data source, and the second **Title**, **Color**, and **ID** fields are located under the **my:SharePointListItem_RW** group node under the **dataFields** group node in the Main data source. These conditions check whether the combination of title and color for a new list item already exists in the **OfficeApplications** SharePoint list. Note that the last condition (`ID ≠ ID`) ensures that only new items are validated.

10. On the **Specify Filter Conditions** dialog box, click **OK**.
11. On the **Filter Data** dialog box, click **OK**.
12. On the **Select a Field or Group** dialog box, click **OK**.
13. On the **Insert Formula** dialog box, manually modify the formula by placing the **count()** function around it as follows:

    ```
    count([constructed formula goes here]) > 0
    ```

    The final fomula should look something like the following when you select the **Edit XPath (advanced)** check box:

    ```
    count(xdXDocument:GetDOM("OfficeApplications")/dfs:myFields/dfs
    :dataFields/d:SharePointListItem_RW[d:Title = xdXDocument:get-
    DOM()/dfs:myFields/dfs:dataFields/my:SharePointListItem_RW/my:T
    itle and d:Color = xdXDocument:get-
    DOM()/dfs:myFields/dfs:dataFields/my:SharePointListItem_RW/my:C
    olor and d:ID != xdXDocument:get-
    DOM()/dfs:myFields/dfs:dataFields/my:SharePointListItem_RW/my:I
    D]) > 0
    ```

    This formula checks whether the amount of existing items that have the same title and color as those that were entered into the form is greater than 0.

14. On the **Insert Formula** dialog box, select the **Edit XPath (advanced)** check box, select the entire text for the formula, copy it to the Windows clipboard, and then click **Cancel**.
15. On the **Condition** dialog box, select **The expression** from the first drop-down list box, select all of the text in the text box that appears, press **Delete**, paste the text for the formula you copied earlier into the text box, and then click **OK**.

16. On the **Rules** task pane, enter a **ScreenTip** that says: "Title and color combination already exists".
17. Add a **Validation** rule to the **Color** text box, and then click the text **None** under **Condition**.
18. On the **Condition** dialog box, select **The expression** from the first drop-down list box, select all of the text in the text box that appears, press **Delete**, paste the text for the formula you copied earlier into the text box, and then click **OK**.
19. On the **Rules** task pane, enter a **ScreenTip** that says: "Title and color combination already exists".
20. Publish the form template back to the SharePoint list.

In SharePoint, navigate to the **OfficeApplications** SharePoint list and add a new item to the list. Enter a title and color combination that already exists in the SharePoint list and click away from the text boxes. The validation errors should appear. Open an existing item for editing and verify that the validation rules do not get triggered unless you change the data to be the same as that of an existing item.

Discussion

The solution described above checks the combined values of fields and makes sure that that combination is unique. However, you could still enter an Office application by assigning a different color to it. To prevent an Office application from being added twice to the SharePoint list, you would have to add a second validation rule to the **Title** field that checks the uniqueness of the value of the **Title** field by itself. So you would have to repeat steps 4 through 16, but then change the condition in step 9 to say:

```
Title is equal to Title
and
ID is not equal to ID
```

and change the message in step 16 to say "Title already exists".

The comparison being made in the solution described above is case-sensitive, meaning that if you enter for example "word" as the **Title** and "Blue" as the **Color**, the validation rules will not be triggered, since "Word" is not the same as "word".

You can use the **translate()** function to make the comparison case-insensitve as follows:

1. Change the expressions of the conditions on the validation rules for the **Title** and **Color** text boxes to be the following formula:

```
count(xdXDocument:GetDOM("OfficeApplications")/dfs:myFields/d
fs:dataFields/d:SharePointListItem_RW[translate(d:Title,
"ABCDEFGHIJKLMNOPQRSTUVWXYZ", "abcdefghijklmnopqrstuvwxyz") =
translate(xdXDocument:get-
DOM()/dfs:myFields/dfs:dataFields/my:SharePointListItem_RW/my
:Title, "ABCDEFGHIJKLMNOPQRSTUVWXYZ",
"abcdefghijklmnopqrstuvwxyz") and translate(d:Color,
"ABCDEFGHIJKLMNOPQRSTUVWXYZ", "abcdefghijklmnopqrstuvwxyz") =
translate(xdXDocument:get-
DOM()/dfs:myFields/dfs:dataFields/my:SharePointListItem_RW/my
:Color, "ABCDEFGHIJKLMNOPQRSTUVWXYZ",
"abcdefghijklmnopqrstuvwxyz") and d:ID != xdXDocument:get-
DOM()/dfs:myFields/dfs:dataFields/my:SharePointListItem_RW/my
:ID]) > 0
```

   where you wrap the **translate()** function around each **Title** and **Color** field in the formula.

2. Republish the form template and test the solution.
3. If both validation rules are not being triggered when either one of the fields changes:
   a. In Notepad, create an XML file named **Helper.xml** that has the following contents:

```
<helper>
  <updating>0</updating>
  <value/>
</helper>
```

   b. In InfoPath, select **Data ➤ Get External Data ➤ From Other Sources ➤ From XML File** and follow the instructions to add an XML data connection for the **Helper.xml** file to the form template. Ensure that you leave the **Automatically retrieve data when form is opened** check box selected on the data connection and that you name the data connection **Helper**.

c. Add an **Action** rule to the **Title** text box with a **Condition** that says:

```
updating = "0"
```

and that has 5 actions that say:

```
Set a field's value: updating = "1"
Set a field's value: value = Color
Set a field's value: Color = ""
Set a field's value: Color = value
Set a field's value: updating = "0"
```

where **value** and **updating** are located in the **Helper** secondary data source and **Color** is located under the **my:SharePointListItem_RW** group node under the **dataFields** group node in the Main data source. This rule ensures that a change is simulated on the **Color** field when the value of the **Title** field changes to trigger the validation rule on the **Color** field. The **updating** field ensures that the action rule does not wind up in a loop.

d. Add an **Action** rule to the **Color** text box with a **Condition** that says:

```
updating = "0"
```

and that has 5 actions that say:

```
Set a field's value: updating = "1"
Set a field's value: value = Title
Set a field's value: Title = ""
Set a field's value: Title = value
Set a field's value: updating = "0"
```

where **value** and **updating** are located in the **Helper** secondary data source and **Title** is located under the **my:SharePointListItem_RW** group node under the **dataFields** group node in the Main data source. This rule ensures that a change is simulated on the **Title** field when the value of the **Color** field changes to trigger the validation rule on the **Title** field.

e. Republish the form template and test the solution.

53 Prevent overlapping periods when adding items to a SharePoint list

Problem

You have a SharePoint list in which room reservations are registered and you want to prevent rooms from being double-booked.

Solution

You can use validation rules and a secondary data source for a SharePoint list to validate whether a selected time period for a particular room is invalid, because that room has already been booked for a time period in which the start date and/or end date of the selected time period would fall.

Suppose you have a SharePoint list named **RoomReservations** that has the following columns:

Column	Data Type
RoomNumber	Number
StartDateTime	Date and Time (with the **Date & Time** format)
EndDateTime	Date and Time (with the **Date & Time** format)
BookedBy	Single line of text

To prevent overlapping date and time periods in a SharePoint list:

1. In InfoPath, create a new SharePoint list form template that is based on the **RoomReservations** SharePoint list as described in recipe *1 Customize a SharePoint list form from within SharePoint* or recipe *2 Customize a SharePoint list form from within InfoPath*.
2. If **StartDateTime** and **EndDateTime** appear as date picker controls on the view of the form template (this would be the case if you selected

Date Only as the format for the columns in SharePoint), change the date pickers into **Date and Time Picker** controls.

3. Add a **Receive** data connection to the **RoomReservations** SharePoint list to the form template as described in *Use a SharePoint list data connection* in recipe *43 2 Ways to retrieve data from a SharePoint list*. Ensure that you select **ID**, **RoomNumber**, **StartDateTime**, and **EndDateTime** as fields to include in the data source, that you sort the data source by **StartDateTime**, and that you leave the **Automatically retrieve data when form is opened** check box selected.
4. On the **Fields** task pane, click **Show advanced view** if **Basic view** is being shown, and then bind the **d:SharePointListItem_RW** repeating group node under the **dataFields** group node in the **RoomReservations** secondary data source to a repeating table on the view of the form template as described in recipe *44 Display SharePoint list data in a repeating table*. Change the date and time pickers that are located in the repeating table into normal text boxes that have their data format set to **None (display XML value)**.
5. Add a **Validation** rule to the **StartDateTime** date and time picker with a **Condition** that says:

```
StartDateTime ≥ EndDateTime
and
EndDateTime is not blank
```

and a **ScreenTip** that says: "Enter a date and time before EndDateTime". Here, both **StartDateTime** and **EndDateTime** are located under the **my:SharePointListItem_RW** group node under the **dataFields** group node in the Main data source. This rule ensures that the start date and time entered always falls before the end date and time.

6. Add a **Validation** rule to the **EndDateTime** date and time picker with a **Condition** that says:

```
EndDateTime ≤ StartDateTime
and
StartDateTime is not blank
```

and a **ScreenTip** that says: "Enter a date and time after

StartDateTime". Here, both **StartDateTime** and **EndDateTime** are located under the **my:SharePointListItem_RW** group node under the **dataFields** group node in the Main data source. This rule ensures that the end date and time entered always falls after the start date and time.

7. Add a second **Validation** rule to the **StartDateTime** date and time picker.
8. On the **Rules** task pane, click the text **None** under **Condition**.
9. On the **Condition** dialog box, select **Use a formula** from the third drop-down list box.
10. On the **Insert Formula** dialog box, click **Insert Field or Group**.
11. On the **Select a Field or Group** dialog box, select **RoomReservations (Secondary)** from the drop-down list box, expand the **dataFields** group node, select the **d:SharePointListItem_RW** repeating group node, and then click **Filter Data**.
12. On the **Filter Data** dialog box, click **Add**.
13. On the **Specify Filter Conditions** dialog box, construct 6 conditions that say:

```
StartDateTime is not blank
and
EndDateTime is not blank
and
StartDateTime is greater than or equal to StartDateTime
and
EndDateTime is less than or equal to EndDateTime
and
RoomNumber is equal to RoomNumber
and
ID is not equal to ID
```

where **StartDateTime** and **EndDateTime** in the first 2 conditions are fields that are located under the **my:SharePointListItem_RW** group node under the **dataFields** group node in the Main data source; and the first **StartDateTime**, **EndDateTime**, **RoomNumber**, and **ID** fields in the last 4 conditions are located under the **d:SharePointListItem_RW** repeating group node under the

dataFields group node in the **RoomReservations** secondary data source; and the second **StartDateTime**, **EndDateTime**, **RoomNumber**, and **ID** fields in the last 4 conditions are located under the **my:SharePointListItem_RW** group node under the **dataFields** group node in the Main data source. Note that you must combine the first two conditions in one expression to be able to add the 6 conditions to the rule. These conditions check whether the date and time period entered for a new list item contains any date and time periods of items that are already present in the **RoomReservations** SharePoint list. Note that the last condition (`ID ≠ ID`) ensures that only new items are validated.

14. On the **Specify Filter Conditions** dialog box, click **OK**.
15. On the **Filter Data** dialog box, click **OK**.
16. On the **Select a Field or Group** dialog box, click **OK**.
17. On the **Insert Formula** dialog box, manually modify the formula by placing the **count()** function around it as follows:

```
count([constructed formula goes here]) > 0
```

The final fomula should look something like the following when you select the **Edit XPath (advanced)** check box:

```
count(xdXDocument:GetDOM("RoomReservations")/dfs:myFields/dfs:d
ataFields/d:SharePointListItem_RW[xdXDocument:get-
DOM()/dfs:myFields/dfs:dataFields/my:SharePointListItem_RW/my:S
tartDateTime != "" and xdXDocument:get-
DOM()/dfs:myFields/dfs:dataFields/my:SharePointListItem_RW/my:E
ndDateTime != "" and msxsl:string-compare(d:StartDateTime,
xdXDocument:get-
DOM()/dfs:myFields/dfs:dataFields/my:SharePointListItem_RW/my:S
tartDateTime) >= 0 and msxsl:string-compare(d:EndDateTime,
xdXDocument:get-
DOM()/dfs:myFields/dfs:dataFields/my:SharePointListItem_RW/my:E
ndDateTime) <= 0 and d:RoomNumber = xdXDocument:get-
DOM()/dfs:myFields/dfs:dataFields/my:SharePointListItem_RW/my:R
oomNumber and d:ID != xdXDocument:get-
DOM()/dfs:myFields/dfs:dataFields/my:SharePointListItem_RW/my:I
D]) > 0
```

This formula checks whether the amount of existing time periods that fall within the period defined by the start date and end date entered is greater than 0 (also see the discussion section for how to construct the conditons for the rules in words by using an image of invalid date ranges).

18. On the **Insert Formula** dialog box, select the **Edit XPath (advanced)** check box, select the entire text for the formula, copy it to the Windows clipboard, and then click **Cancel**.
19. On the **Condition** dialog box, select **The expression** from the first drop-down list box, select all of the text in the text box that appears, press **Delete**, paste the text for the formula you copied earlier into the text box, and then click **OK**.
20. On the **Rules** task pane, enter a **ScreenTip** that says: "Existing periods fall within the selected date and time range".
21. Once you know how to use InfoPath's dialog boxes to construct the formula for the condition, you can either continue adding the rest of the rules using the dialog boxes or as demonstrated in this step, manually modify the formula you constructed earlier and then directly set the formula for the expression. So add a third **Validation** rule to the **StartDateTime** date and time picker with a **The expression** condition that uses the following formula:

```
count(xdXDocument:GetDOM("RoomReservations")/dfs:myFields/dfs:d
ataFields/d:SharePointListItem_RW[xdXDocument:get-
DOM()/dfs:myFields/dfs:dataFields/my:SharePointListItem_RW/my:S
tartDateTime != "" and xdXDocument:get-
DOM()/dfs:myFields/dfs:dataFields/my:SharePointListItem_RW/my:E
ndDateTime != "" and msxsl:string-compare(d:StartDateTime,
xdXDocument:get-
DOM()/dfs:myFields/dfs:dataFields/my:SharePointListItem_RW/my:S
tartDateTime) <= 0 and msxsl:string-compare(d:EndDateTime,
xdXDocument:get-
DOM()/dfs:myFields/dfs:dataFields/my:SharePointListItem_RW/my:E
ndDateTime) >= 0 and d:RoomNumber = xdXDocument:get-
DOM()/dfs:myFields/dfs:dataFields/my:SharePointListItem_RW/my:R
oomNumber and d:ID != xdXDocument:get-
DOM()/dfs:myFields/dfs:dataFields/my:SharePointListItem_RW/my:I
D]) > 0
```

and with a **ScreenTip** that says: "The selected date and time range falls within an existing period".

22. Add a fourth **Validation** rule to the **StartDateTime** date and time picker with a **The expression** condition that uses the following formula:

```
count(xdXDocument:GetDOM("RoomReservations")/dfs:myFields/dfs:d
ataFields/d:SharePointListItem_RW[xdXDocument:get-
DOM()/dfs:myFields/dfs:dataFields/my:SharePointListItem_RW/my:S
tartDateTime != "" and xdXDocument:get-
DOM()/dfs:myFields/dfs:dataFields/my:SharePointListItem_RW/my:E
ndDateTime != "" and msxsl:string-compare(d:StartDateTime,
xdXDocument:get-
DOM()/dfs:myFields/dfs:dataFields/my:SharePointListItem_RW/my:S
tartDateTime) <= 0 and msxsl:string-compare(d:EndDateTime,
xdXDocument:get-
DOM()/dfs:myFields/dfs:dataFields/my:SharePointListItem_RW/my:S
tartDateTime) >= 0 and msxsl:string-compare(d:EndDateTime,
xdXDocument:get-
DOM()/dfs:myFields/dfs:dataFields/my:SharePointListItem_RW/my:E
ndDateTime) <= 0 and d:RoomNumber = xdXDocument:get-
DOM()/dfs:myFields/dfs:dataFields/my:SharePointListItem_RW/my:R
oomNumber and d:ID != xdXDocument:get-
DOM()/dfs:myFields/dfs:dataFields/my:SharePointListItem_RW/my:I
D]) > 0
```

and with a **ScreenTip** that says: "The selected start date and time falls within an existing period".

23. Add a fifth **Validation** rule to the **StartDateTime** date and time picker with a **The expression** condition that uses the following formula:

```
count(xdXDocument:GetDOM("RoomReservations")/dfs:myFields/dfs:d
ataFields/d:SharePointListItem_RW[xdXDocument:get-
DOM()/dfs:myFields/dfs:dataFields/my:SharePointListItem_RW/my:S
tartDateTime != "" and xdXDocument:get-
DOM()/dfs:myFields/dfs:dataFields/my:SharePointListItem_RW/my:E
ndDateTime != "" and msxsl:string-compare(d:StartDateTime,
xdXDocument:get-
DOM()/dfs:myFields/dfs:dataFields/my:SharePointListItem_RW/my:S
tartDateTime) >= 0 and msxsl:string-compare(d:StartDateTime,
xdXDocument:get-
DOM()/dfs:myFields/dfs:dataFields/my:SharePointListItem_RW/my:E
```

```
ndDateTime) <= 0 and msxsl:string-compare(d:EndDateTime,
xdXDocument:get-
DOM()/dfs:myFields/dfs:dataFields/my:SharePointListItem_RW/my:E
ndDateTime) >= 0 and d:RoomNumber = xdXDocument:get-
DOM()/dfs:myFields/dfs:dataFields/my:SharePointListItem_RW/my:R
oomNumber and d:ID != xdXDocument:get-
DOM()/dfs:myFields/dfs:dataFields/my:SharePointListItem_RW/my:I
D]) > 0
```

and with a **ScreenTip** that says: "The selected end date and time falls within an existing period".

24. Repeat steps 7 through 23 for the **EndDateTime** date and time picker with the same conditions and the same **ScreenTip** messages as the validation rules on the **StartDateTime** date and time picker.

25. Because the validation rules you added only get triggered when the **StartDateTime** and **EndDateTime** date and time picker values change and because both validation rules depend on the value of the **RoomNumber** field and the validation rules are not triggered when you change the value of the **RoomNumber** field, you must find a way to force the validation rules to be triggered. For this, you are going to temporarily store the values of the date and time pickers in a secondary data source, empty the values of the date and time pickers, and then repopulate the date and time pickers to simulate a change by using a rule. So in Notepad, create an XML file named **Helper.xml** that has the following contents:

```
<helper>
  <value/>
</helper>
```

You are going to use this XML file to force fields to revalidate themselves when a room number is selected.

26. Select **Data ➤ Get External Data ➤ From Other Sources ➤ From XML File** and follow the instructions to add an XML data connection for the **Helper.xml** file to the form template. Ensure that you leave the **Automatically retrieve data when form is opened** check box selected and that you name the data connection **Helper**.

27. Add an **Action** rule to the **RoomNumber** text box with the following 6 actions:

```
Set a field's value: value = StartDateTime
Set a field's value: StartDateTime = ""
Set a field's value: StartDateTime = value
Set a field's value: value = EndDateTime
Set a field's value: EndDateTime = ""
Set a field's value: EndDateTime = value
```

where **value** is located in the **Helper** secondary data source and both **StartDateTime** and **EndDateTime** are located under the **my:SharePointListItem_RW** group node under the **dataFields** group node in the Main data source.

28. Because SharePoint might not always trigger the validation rules when either the value of **StartDateTime** or **EndDateTime** changes, you can force revalidation of both fields in the **Form Submit** event just before the form is saved. So click **Data ➤ Submit Form ➤ Submit Options**.
29. On the **Submit Options** dialog box, select the **Perform custom action using Rules** option, and then click **OK**.
30. Click the **RoomNumber** text box to select it, and then on the **Rules** task pane, right-click its rule and select **Copy Rule** from the drop-down menu that appears.
31. Click **Data ➤ Rules ➤ Form Submit** to switch to the **Form Submit** event on the **Rules** task pane.
32. On the **Rules** task pane, click the **Paste** command to paste the rule.
33. On the **Rules** task pane, right-click the newly pasted rule, and select **Move Up** from the drop-down menu that appears to move the rule up, so that it runs before the rule that submits the form.
34. Publish the form template back to the SharePoint list.

In SharePoint, navigate to the **RoomReservations** SharePoint list and add a couple of reservations with time periods to the list. Then add a new reservation with dates that fall within time periods that already exist for reservations in the SharePoint list. Verify that the validation errors are displayed. Open an existing reservation for editing and verify that the validation rules do not get triggered.

Discussion

In the solution described above, you used two key techniques:

1. Perform a lookup in the SharePoint list that a SharePoint list form is associated with to be able to validate data entered into the SharePoint list through the InfoPath form.
2. Because validation rules only run when the value of the field the validation rule has been defined on changes, you had to implement a workaround for changing the value of the field the validation rule has been defined on when the value of another field on the form changes to be able to trigger the validation rule.

The conditions for the validation rules might be a bit hard to construct, so it might help to try to visualize the conditions.

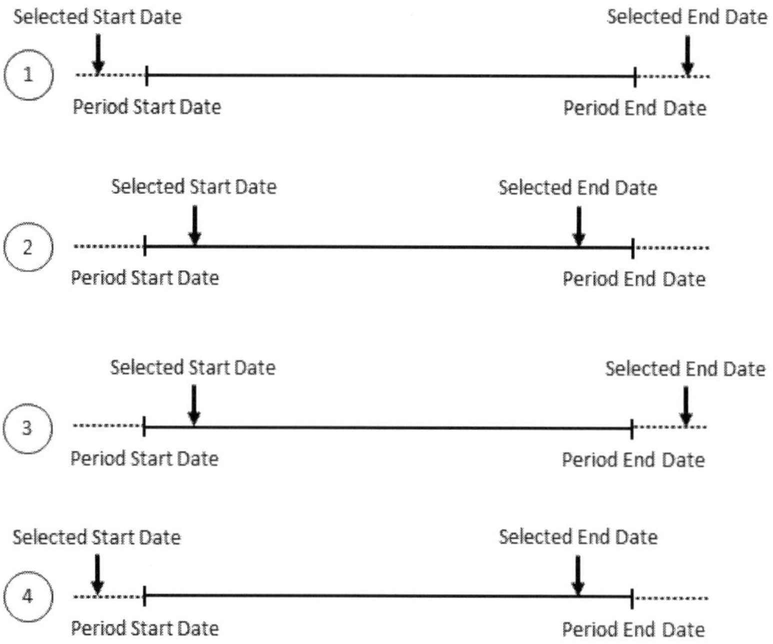

Figure 156. Visualization of invalid date ranges for constructing conditions for rules.

In Figure 156:

- The Period Start Date and Period End Date belong to an existing item in the SharePoint list.

- The Selected Start Date and Selected End Date are dates that are being entered for a new item that should be saved to the SharePoint list.
- For the first rule: If the Period Start Date is greater than or equal to the Selected Start Date and the Period End Date is less than or equal to the Selected End Date, it means that an existing period falls within the selected date range, so a validation error should be shown.
- For the second rule: If the Period Start Date is less than or equal to the Selected Start Date and the Period End Date is greater than or equal to the Selected End Date, it means that the selected date range falls within an existing period, so a validation error should be shown.
- For the third rule: If the Period Start Date is less than or equal to the Selected Start Date and the Period End Date is greater than or equal to the Selected Start Date and the Period End Date is less than or equal to the Selected End Date, it means that the Selected Start Date lies within an existing period, so a validation error should be shown.
- For the fourth rule: If the Period Start Date is greater than or equal to the Selected Start Date and the Period Start Date is less than or equal to the Selected End Date and the Period End Date is greater than or equal to the Selected End Date, it means that the Selected End Date lies within an existing period, so a validation error should be shown.

By putting the conditions into words like this, you should now be able to easily construct the conditions for the validation rules in InfoPath.

Note that you could extend the solution described above by creating a SharePoint list in which the room numbers are stored, add a data connection for that SharePoint list to the form template, and then populate a drop-down list box with room numbers from the SharePoint list instead of letting users manually enter numbers.

Retrieve and display forms stored in a form library

A SharePoint form library is a specialized type of SharePoint list, so you can use similar methods to retrieve and display InfoPath forms as you used for retrieving and displaying SharePoint list items.

The recipes in this section are meant to guide you through a few scenarios for retrieving and working with InfoPath forms from within an InfoPath form.

54 Retrieve a list of forms from a form library

Problem

You want to display a list of all of the forms that are present in a SharePoint form library.

Solution

You can create a **Receive** data connection to a SharePoint list, but connect it to a SharePoint form library instead of a SharePoint list to retrieve a list of the forms from a form library.

To retrieve a list of forms from a form library:

1. In SharePoint, ensure that you have a form library that contains a couple of forms.
2. In InfoPath, create a new SharePoint form library form template or use an existing one.
3. Add a **Receive** data connection to a SharePoint list to the form template as described in *Use a SharePoint list data connection* in recipe *43 2 Ways to retrieve data from a SharePoint list*. Ensure that you select the SharePoint form library that contains the forms you want to display from the list of SharePoint lists or libraries you can connect to, select the **Title** field to be included in the data source, and leave the **Automatically retrieve data when form is opened** check box selected. Note that the **Title** field contains the file name (including the XML file extension) of an InfoPath form in the form library.
4. Bind the secondary data source for the SharePoint form library to a repeating table on the view of the form template as described in recipe *44 Display SharePoint list data in a repeating table*.
5. Publish the form template to a SharePoint form library.

In SharePoint, navigate to the form library where you published the form template and add a new form. When the form opens, all of the file names of the InfoPath forms that are stored in the SharePoint form library that the data connection you added to the form template connects to, should appear in the **Title** column of the repeating table.

Discussion

In the solution described above you created a SharePoint list data connection to a SharePoint form library instead of a SharePoint list, to be able to retrieve data from a library instead of a list.

One reason to connect to a SharePoint form library instead of a SharePoint list would be to open InfoPath forms from within another InfoPath form. But for this you would have to use URLs of the forms contained in the form library. InfoPath does not allow you to modify fields that are located in a secondary data source. This includes setting the **Default Value** of such fields. So while you can retrieve data from a form library, you cannot do much with this data unless you copy values from the secondary data source to other fields on the form (see recipe *45 3 Ways to copy SharePoint list data to form fields* or recipe *46 Map rows of a repeating table to SharePoint list items*) where you can for example prepend the URL of the form library to the file name of the form, so that you can set the constructed full URL of the form as the value of a hyperlink field to be able to click and open a form from the form library from within the InfoPath form (see for example the technique described in recipe *57 Open a form in the browser from another form*).

When you connect a SharePoint list data connection to a library instead of a list, you will see a check box with the label **Include data for the active form only** enabled on the screen of the **Data Connection Wizard** where you can select fields to include in the data source.

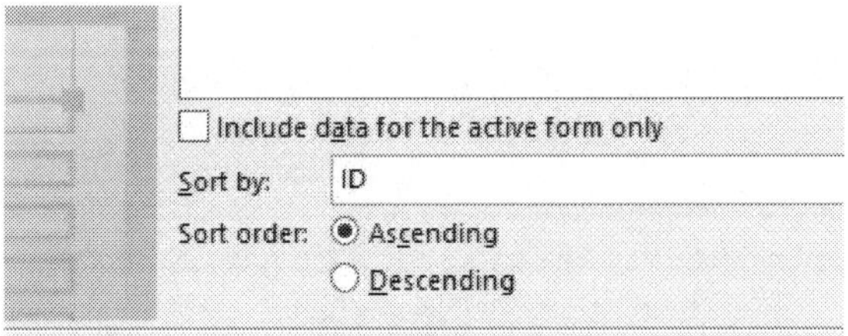

Figure 157. The 'Include data for the active form only' check box.

It only makes sense to select this check box if you have added a SharePoint list data connection to the form library to which the current form will be saved or submitted, and you would like to have the ability to access form library field values for the current form only. For example if you want to retrieve the value of the status of a workflow that is running or has run on a form and use this value in the form to for example show/hide fields, or if you want to retrieve the name of the person who created the (existing) form in the form library (see recipe *55 Display the name of the user who created a form on the form*), you could select the **Include data for the active form only** check box on the **Data Connection Wizard** when you are setting up the data connection to the form library in which the form is stored, to get access to the workflow status or the **CreatedBy** field for that specific form from within the form itself.

55 Display the name of the user who created a form on the form

Problem

You want to display the name of the user who created a form on the form itself.

Solution

You can create a **Receive** data connection to a SharePoint list, but connect it to the SharePoint form library that contains an existing form a user has opened instead of to a SharePoint list, to retrieve information about that form.

To display the name of the user who created a form on the form itself:

1. In InfoPath, create a new SharePoint form library form template or use an existing one.
2. Design the form template as you wish and then publish it to a form library.
3. Add a **Receive** data connection to a SharePoint list to the form template as described in *Use a SharePoint list data connection* in recipe *43*

2 Ways to retrieve data from a SharePoint list. Ensure that you select the SharePoint form library you published the form template to in step 2 from the list of SharePoint lists or libraries you can connect to, select the **Created_By (Created By)** field to be included in the data source, select the **Include data for the active form only** check box, leave the **Automatically retrieve data when form is opened** check box selected, and name the data connection **CreatedByUser**.

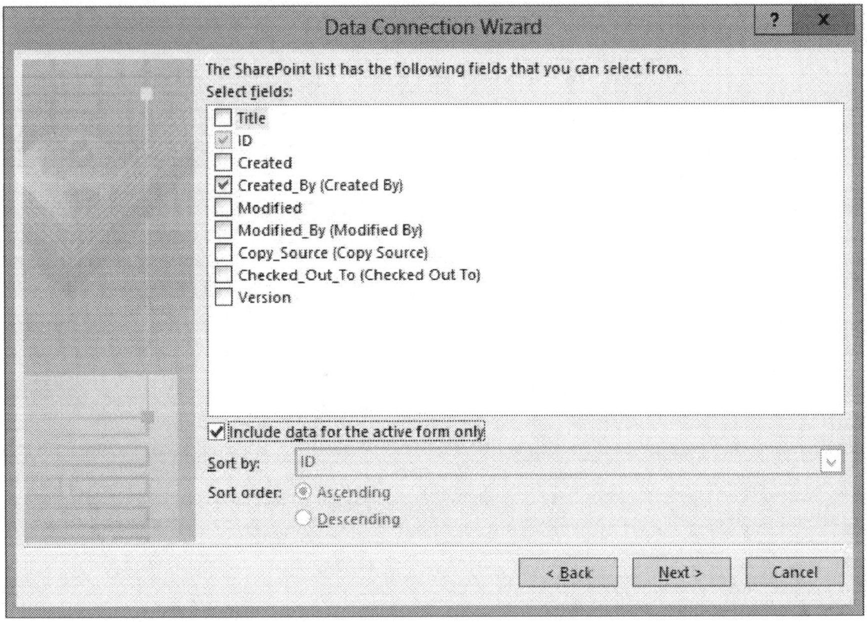

Figure 158. Selecting the 'Include data for the active form only' check box.

4. On the **Fields** task pane, select **CreatedByUser (Secondary)** from the drop-down list box, expand the **dataFields** group node, expand the **d:SharePointListItem_RW** repeating group node, expand the **Created By** group node, expand the **pc:Person** repeating group node, and then drag-and-drop the **DisplayName** field onto the view of the form template. The field should automatically get bound to a text box.
5. Right-click the **DisplayName** text box and then select **Change Control ➤ Calculated Value** from the context menu that appears to change the text box into a calculated value control so that the name of the user who created the form becomes read-only.
6. Republish the form template to the SharePoint form library.

In SharePoint, navigate to the form library where you published the form template and add a new form. When the form opens, you should not see a name of a user, since the form is a new form. Save or submit the form back to the form library, close, and then reopen the form you saved. You should now see your user name displayed on the form as the person who created the form.

Discussion

In the solution described above you created a SharePoint list data connection to a SharePoint form library instead of to a SharePoint list, to be able to retrieve data about a specific form when that form was opened.

When you connect a SharePoint list data connection to a library instead of a list, you should see a check box with the label **Include data for the active form only** enabled on the screen of the **Data Connection Wizard** where you can select fields to include in the data source.

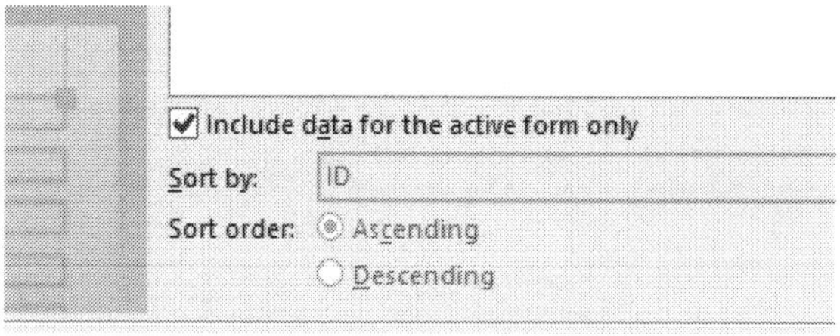

Figure 159. The 'Include data for the active form only' check box.

You can select this check box if you have created a SharePoint list data connection to the form library to which the current form will be saved or submitted, and you would like to have the ability to access form library field values for the current form only. In the solution described above, you selected this check box to get access to the **CreatedBy** field for a specific form from within the form itself.

Note that while the **DisplayName** field was placed within a repeating section when you dragged-and-dropped it onto the view of the form template, it will only display one section once a form has been saved and reopened.

56 Retrieve a list of forms created by the current user from a library

Problem

You want to create an InfoPath form that displays a list of InfoPath forms that are stored in another form library and that were created by the user who opened the form.

Solution

You can use the **userName()** function in InfoPath to retrieve the logon name of the user who is filling out a form, use this logon name to look up a corresponding account name in the **User Information List** SharePoint list, and then use the account name found as a filter to query the SharePoint list data connection for the form library containing the user's forms.

To retrieve a list of forms created by the current user from a form library:

1. In SharePoint, ensure that you have a form library that contains a couple of forms created by different users.
2. In InfoPath, create a new SharePoint form library form template or use an existing one.
3. Add a **Receive** data connection to the **User Information List** SharePoint list (also see *Use a SharePoint list data connection* in recipe *43 2 Ways to retrieve data from a SharePoint list*), ensure that you select **Name** and **User_name (User name)** as fields to include in the data source, accept the default data connection name of **User Information List**, and deselect the **Automatically retrieve data when form is opened** check box.
4. Add a **Receive** data connection to the SharePoint form library that contains the forms you want to display on the InfoPath form (also see recipe *54 Retrieve a list of forms from a form library*), ensure that you select **Title** and **Created_By (Created By)** as fields to include in the data source, give the data connection a suitable name such as for example **GetUserForms**, and deselect the **Automatically retrieve data when form is opened** check box.

5. Bind a repeating table control to the **GetUserForms** secondary data source as described in recipe *44 Display SharePoint list data in a repeating table*.

6. To retrieve only those forms that were created by the user who opened the form, you must use the **userName()** function to retrieve the logon name of the user who opened the form, use this logon name to search for a corresponding display name in the **User Information List** SharePoint list, and then use the display name found to filter the data from the **GetUserForms** secondary data source on the value of its **Created By** field. In this solution, you will retrieve the user's forms when the form opens. So click **Data ➤ Rules ➤ Form Load** and add an **Action** rule to the **Form Load** event with the following 4 actions:

```
Set a field's value: UserName = substring-after(userName(),
"\")
```

where **UserName** refers to the **User name** field under the **q:SharePointListItem_RW** group node under the **queryFields** group node in the **User Information List** secondary data source. This action sets up a query for the **User Information List** secondary data source to be able to retrieve the **User Information List** item for the one user where the user name in the **User Information List** is equal to the string that comes after the backslash (\ ) in the value returned by the **userName()** function. Note that if you will be publishing the form template to a Windows Classic environment, you must use the **userName()** function without the **substring-after()** function (see the discussion section).

```
Query using a data connection: User Information List
```

This action populates the **User Information List** secondary data source based on the logon name of the current user that was passed to it through its query fields.

```
Set a field's value: Author = Title
```

where **Author** refers to the **CreatedBy** field under the **q:SharePointListItem_RW** group node under the **queryFields** group node in the **GetUserForms** secondary data source, and **Title** refers to the **Name** field under the **d:SharePointListItem_RW** repeating group node under the **dataFields** group node in the **User Information List** secondary data source. This action sets up a query for the **GetUserForms** secondary data source to be able to retrieve only those forms where the display name of the person who created the form in the **GetUserForms** secondary data source is equal to the display name of the user in the **User Information List**.

```
Query using a data connection: GetUserForms
```

This action populates the **GetUserForms** secondary data source based on the value of the **CreatedBy** field that was passed to it through its query fields.

7. Publish the form template to a SharePoint form library.

In SharePoint, navigate to the form library where you published the form template and add a new form. When the form opens, verify that only the forms you created are being displayed in the repeating table on the form. Log on as a different user, add a new form again, and verify that only the forms for the user you are signed in as are being displayed on the form.

Discussion

In the solution described above you used a standard SharePoint list data connection to retrieve the forms that were created by the current user. You thereby had to use a **Query for data** action twice in a rule. The reason why the double querying was required is because the **CreatedBy** field under the **queryFields** group node in the **GetUserForms** secondary data source accepts the display name of an account rather than the actual user name as its value. And because the **userName()** function in InfoPath returns the user name (logon name) of the person filling out the form, you must use this user name to look up the display name in the **User Information List** data source (see the discussion section of recipe *48 Display a list of people from the current user's department* for more information about the **User Information List** SharePoint list), and then pass this to the fields under the **queryFields** group node in the **GetUserForms** secondary data source to retrieve the forms that were created by the current user.

Because the **userName()** function returns user names such as for example

```
i:0#.w|corp\jane.doe
```

in browser-forms that are filled out through SharePoint with Claims Based authentication (where **corp** is the domain name and **jane.doe** is the user name), when comparing user names that are stored in the **User Information List** with user names returned by the **userName()** function, you must ensure that they have the same format for the comparison not to fail. In the solution described above, you used the **substring-after()** function to perform a correction on the user name returned by the **userName()** function.

```
substring-after(userName(), "\")
```

If you are creating a form template for a Windows Classic environment, you must not use the **substring-after()** function. The formula above should just say:

```
userName()
```

57 Open a form in the browser from another form

Problem

You want to retrieve all of the forms contained in a form library, select one of those forms, and then open the selected form in the browser.

Solution

You can use a hyperlink control to open an existing form from a form library in the browser.

To open a form in the browser by clicking on a link in another form:

1. In SharePoint, ensure that you have a form library that contains a couple of forms.
2. In InfoPath, create a new SharePoint form library form template or use an existing one.

3. Add a **List Box** control to the view of the form template and name it **selectedForm**.
4. Add a **Hyperlink** control to the view of the form template. Name the hyperlink's field element **formUrl** and the field attribute under it **formTitle**.

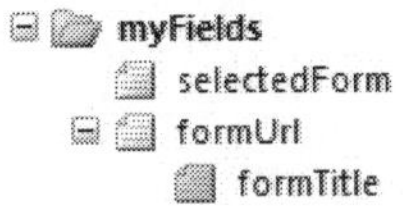

Figure 160. Main data source of the form in InfoPath Designer 2013.

5. Add a **Receive** data connection to the SharePoint form library from step 1 as described in *Use a SharePoint list data connection* in recipe *43 2 Ways to retrieve data from a SharePoint list*. Ensure that you select the **Title** field to be included in the data source, and that you leave the **Automatically retrieve data when form is opened** check box selected. Note that the **Title** field contains the file name (including the XML file extension) of an InfoPath form in the form library.
6. Open the **List Box Properties** dialog box, and configure it to get its entries from the secondary data source for the SharePoint form library. Leave the **Value** and **Display name** properties set to be equal to the **Title** field in the secondary data source.
7. While the **List Box Properties** dialog box is still open, select the **Browser forms** tab, select the **Always** option, and then click **OK**.
8. Add a **Formatting** rule to the hyperlink control with a **Condition** that says:

```
selectedForm is blank
```

and with a formatting of **Hide this control**. This formatting rule hides the hyperlink control when the empty item in the list box is selected.

9. Add an **Action** rule to the list box control with an action that says:

```
Set a field's value: formUrl = concat(SharePointSiteUrl(),
"_layouts/15/FormServer.aspx?", "XmlLocation=",
SharePointSiteUrl(), "MyFormsLib/", .,
"&OpenIn=Browser&Source=", SharePointSiteUrl())
```

where **formUrl** is the field that is bound to the hyperlink control and the dot (**.**) represents the field that is bound to the list box control. Note that you must replace **MyFormsLib** with the name of the form library from step 1. This action sets the value of the hyperlink control to be equal to the URL of the selected form in the list box control.

10. Add a second action to the rule on the list box control that says:

```
Set a field's value: @formTitle = .
```

where **formTitle** is the attribute of the field that is bound to the hyperlink control and the dot (**.**) represents the field that is bound to the list box control. This action sets the value of the title of the hyperlink control to be equal to the title of the selected form in the list box control.

11. Publish the form template to a SharePoint form library.

In SharePoint, navigate to the form library where you published the form template and add a new form. When the form opens, the list box should contain the titles of the InfoPath forms that are stored in the form library from step 1. Select one of the form titles in the list box. The hyperlink control should get populated with the details of the selected form. Click the hyperlink. The InfoPath form should open in a new browser window.

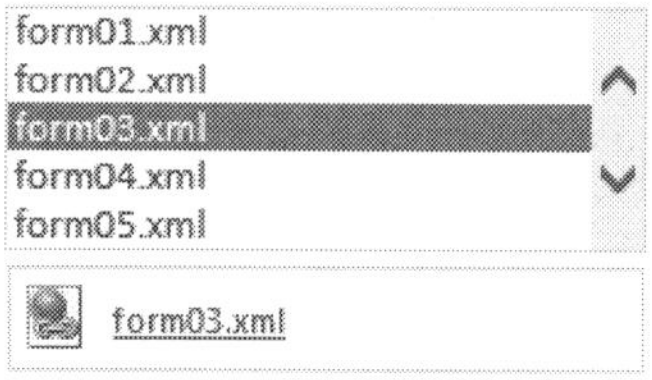

Figure 161. The hyperlink control displaying the link for the selected form.

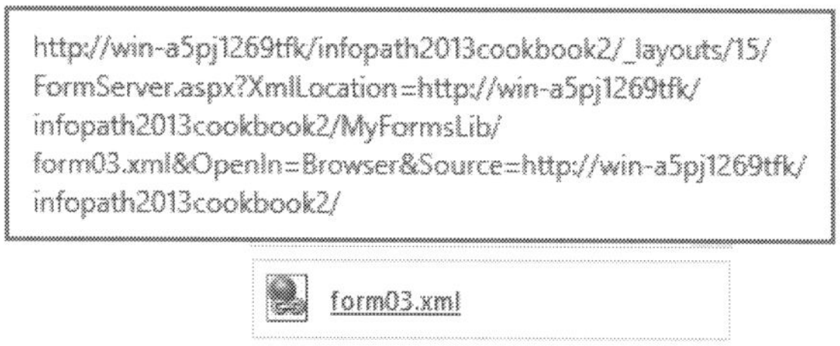

Figure 162. The form's URL as displayed when you hover over the hyperlink.

Discussion

In the solution described above you used the **SharePointSiteUrl()** function to retrieve the URL of the site on which the form is located.

InfoPath functions with which you can retrieve SharePoint-related URL information include:

- **SharePointListUrl** – Returns the address of the SharePoint list where the form is hosted (InfoPath 2010 and greater).
- **SharePointServerRootUrl** – Returns the address of the SharePoint server where the form is hosted (SharePoint 2010 and greater).
- **SharePointSiteCollectionUrl** – Returns the address of the SharePoint site collection where the form is hosted (InfoPath 2010 and greater).
- **SharePointSiteUrl** – Returns the address of the SharePoint site where the form is hosted (InfoPath 2010 and greater).

Note that these functions only work in browser forms and not in forms that are filled out through InfoPath Filler 2013. If you want your forms to work in both the browser and InfoPath Filler 2013, use static URLs instead of the aforementioned functions.

And finally, the URL of each form was constructed using the **concat()** function to generate a valid URL that included the **FormServer.aspx** page of InfoPath Forms Services and the **OpenIn=Browser** query string parameter to be able to force the forms to open in the browser (also see the discussion section of recipe *38 Add a link to open a form from a SharePoint page*).

58 Display a list of the form libraries on a SharePoint site

Problem

You want to be able to display the names of all of the form libraries on a particular SharePoint site in a multiple-selection list box.

Solution

You can use the **SiteData** web service of SharePoint to retrieve and display the names of all of the form libraries on a SharePoint site.

To display a list of the form libraries on a SharePoint site:

1. In InfoPath, create a new SharePoint form library form template or use an existing one.
2. Add a **Multiple-Selection List Box** control to the view of the form template and name its repeating field **formLibrary**.
3. Select **Data ➤ Get External Data ➤ From Web Service ➤ From SOAP Web Service**.
4. On the **Data Connection Wizard**, enter the URL of the **SiteData** web service that is located on the same site from which you want to retrieve a list of form libraries and where you will be publishing the InfoPath form template, for example:

   ```
   http://servername/sitename/_vti_bin/SiteData.asmx
   ```

   and click **Next**. Here, **servername** is the name of the SharePoint server and **sitename** is the name of the site from which you want to retrieve a list of form libraries.
5. On the **Data Connection Wizard**, select **GetListCollection** in the list of operations, and click **Next**.
6. On the **Data Connection Wizard**, leave the **Store a copy of the data in the form template** check box deselected, and click **Next**.
7. On the **Data Connection Wizard**, leave the name of the data connection as **GetListCollection**, leave the **Automatically retrieve data when form is opened** check box selected, and click **Finish**.
8. Open the **Multiple-Selection List Box Properties** dialog box.
9. On the **Multiple-Selection List Box Properties** dialog box, select the **Get choices from an external data source** option, select **GetListCollection** from the **Data source** drop-down list box, and then click the button behind the **Entries** text box.

10. On the **Select a Field or Group** dialog box, expand all of the group nodes, select the **_sList** repeating group node, and then click **Filter Data**.
11. On the **Filter Data** dialog box, click **Add**.
12. On the **Specify Filter Conditions** dialog box, construct two conditions that say:

```
BaseType = "DocumentLibrary"
and
BaseTemplate = "XMLForm"
```

    where both **BaseType** and **BaseTemplate** are located under the **_sList** repeating group node in the **GetListCollection** secondary data source, and **DocumentLibrary** and **XMLForm** are static pieces of text.
13. On the **Specify Filter Conditions** dialog box, click **OK**.
14. On the **Filter Data** dialog box, click **OK**.
15. On the **Select a Field or Group** dialog box, click **OK**.
16. On the **Multiple-Selection List Box Properties** dialog box, configure both the **Value** and the **Display name** properties to get their values from the **Title** field that is located under the **_sList** repeating group node in the **GetListCollection** secondary data source, and then click **OK**.
17. If your SharePoint environment is configured to use Claims Based authentication as opposed to Windows Classic authentication and the form is going to be filled out through the browser, you must set up UDC authentication for the **GetListCollection** data connection that makes the web service call as described in *Configure a web service data connection for a web browser form* in the Appendix. But before you do this, test the form in InfoPath Filler 2013 to ensure that the functionality is working properly.
18. Publish the form template to a SharePoint form library.

In SharePoint, navigate to the form library where you published the form template and add a new form. When the form opens, the multiple-selection list box should contain the names of all of the form libraries on the SharePoint site.

Discussion

In the solution described above, you used the **GetListCollection** operation of the **SiteData** web service with a filter on the **BaseType** and **BaseTemplate** fields to be able to retrieve a list of all of the form libraries on a particular SharePoint site for display in a multiple-selection list box.

Note that you can drag-and-drop the **_sList** repeating group that is located under the **vLists** group node under the **GetListCollectionResponse** group node under the **dataFields** group node in the **GetListCollection** secondary data source onto the view, temporarily bind the **_sList** repeating group node to a repeating table, and then preview the form to view the data that is returned by the web service operation as a way of finding out what kind of filters you would have to use to retrieve the data you want to retrieve.

Check if a form exists in a form library on load or on submit

You can use a data connection to a SharePoint form library to check for the existence of a particular form in the form library before submitting that form to the form library. Doing so allows you to dynamically set the name of a form based on whether it already exists or not in the form library.

The recipes in this section are meant to guide you through a few scenarios for submitting forms to a SharePoint form library thereby checking whether they already exist in the form library.

59 Determine whether a form is new or already exists

Problem

As soon as a form opens you want to be able to determine whether it is a new form or whether it already exists in a form library.

Solution

You can use the **Include data for the active form only** setting of a SharePoint list data connection to the form library where a form is stored and the **Title** of the form to be able to check whether a form is new or not.

To determine whether a form is new or already exists:

1. In InfoPath, create a new SharePoint form library form template or use an existing one.
2. Design the form template as you wish and then publish it to a form library named **NewOrNotLib**.
3. Click **Data ➤ Get External Data ➤ From SharePoint List**.
4. On the **Data Connection Wizard**, enter the URL of the SharePoint site where the **NewOrNotLib** form library is located, and click **Next**.
5. On the **Data Connection Wizard**, select **NewOrNotLib** in the **Select a list or library** list box, and click **Next**.
6. On the **Data Connection Wizard**, select the **Title** field in the **Select fields** list box, select the **Include data for the active form only** check box, and click **Next**.

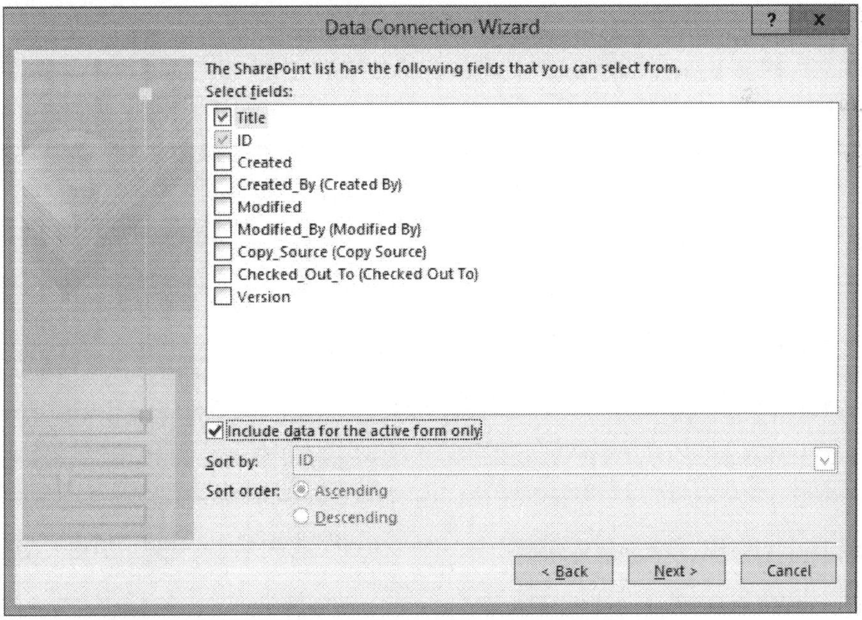

Figure 163. Selecting the fields to include in the data source.

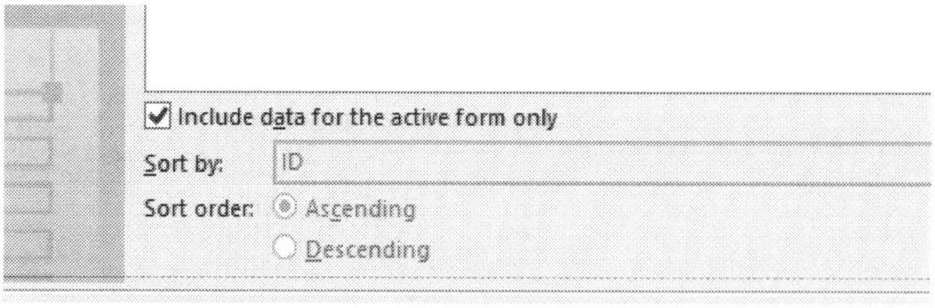

Figure 164. The 'Include data for the active form only' check box.

7. On the **Data Connection Wizard**, leave the **Store a copy of the data in the form template** check box deselected, and click **Next**.
8. On the **Data Connection Wizard**, name the data connection **NewOrExistingFormCheck**, leave the **Automatically retrieve data when form is opened** check box selected, and click **Finish**.
9. In this scenario, you will select a check box if the form is an existing form (for another usage of the technique described in this recipe, see recipe *60 Autonumber a form when it is submitted to a form library* or recipe *61 Create separate add and edit views in a form*). So add a **Check Box** control to the view of the form template and name it **isExistingForm**.
10. Click **Data ➤ Rules ➤ Form Load**.
11. On the **Rules** task pane, add an **Action** rule to the **Form Load** event with a **The expression** condition that says:

```
count(xdXDocument:GetDOM("NewOrExistingFormCheck")/dfs:myFields
/dfs:dataFields/d:SharePointListItem_RW/d:Title[. != ""]) != 0
```

and with an action that says:

```
Set a field's value: isExistingForm = "true"
```

This action rule counts the amount of non-blank **Title** fields in the **NewOrExistingFormCheck** secondary data source when the form opens, and if this amount is not equal to 0, it means that the form is an existing form, so the check box should be selected.

12. Republish the form template to the **NewOrNotLib** form library.

In SharePoint, navigate to the **NewOrNotLib** form library and add a new form. When the form opens, the **IsExistingForm** check box should be deselected as an indication that the form is a new form. Save or submit the form back to the form library, close it, and then reopen it. The second time the form opens, the **IsExistingForm** check box should be selected as an indication that the form is an existing form.

Discussion

In the solution described above you used the **Include data for the active form only** check box on the data connection for the SharePoint form library to retrieve the value of the **Title** field of a form stored in a form library (also see the discussion section of recipe *54 Retrieve a list of forms from a form library*).

The name of a form is stored in the **Title** field under the **d:SharePointListItem_RW** repeating group node under the **dataFields** group node in the secondary data source for the SharePoint form library. You could drag-and-drop this field onto the view of the form template to make it visible on the form and then retest the form to see how it behaves. When the form is new, the **Title** field will not exist. The solution described above uses this fact to determine whether a form is new or not.

60 Autonumber a form when it is submitted to a form library

Problem

You want to be able to generate a name that is guaranteed to be unique and use this name when submitting a new form to a SharePoint form library.

Solution

You can use a SharePoint list to generate items for every user who submits a form, retrieve the list item that has the highest ID for a particular user from the SharePoint list, and then use this ID in InfoPath to generate a form name right before a form is submitted to a form library.

To autonumber a form when it is submitted to a form library:

1. In SharePoint, create a new custom list named **FormIDs**. You do not have to add any extra columns to it; the **Title** column is enough.

2. Navigate to the **FormIDs** list, click **List ➤ Settings ➤ List Settings**, and then copy the GUID from the browser's address bar. The GUID should be listed after the **List** parameter in the URL and should look something like the following:

```
%7BB99B3779%2DB668%2D4F56%2D85D6%2DA94ACB2C41AE%7D
```

3. Convert the **%7B** characters to **{**, **%2D** to **-**, and **%7D** to **}**. The resulting list GUID should now resemble the following:

```
{B99B3779-B668-4F56-85D6-A94ACB2C41AE}
```

   Copy it to the Windows clipboard.

4. In Notepad, create a file with the following contents:

```
<Batch>
  <Method ID="1" Cmd="New">
    <Field Name="Title"></Field>
  </Method>
</Batch>
```

   Save the file to disk and name it **FormIDsBatch.xml**.

5. In InfoPath, create a new SharePoint form library form template or use an existing one.

6. On the **Fields** task pane, add a hidden field of type **Text (string)** and with the name **listName** to the Main data source, and set its **Default Value** to be equal to the list GUID from step 3.

7. Select **Data ➤ Get External Data ➤ From Other Sources ➤ From XML File** and follow the instructions to add an XML data connection for the **FormIDsBatch.xml** file. Leave the **Automatically retrieve data when form is opened** check box selected when you add the data connection and name the data connection **FormIDsBatch**.

8. The contents of the XML file should be submitted to the **Lists** web service of SharePoint to be able to add items to the **FormIDs** list. So select **Data ➤ Submit Form ➤ To Other Locations ➤ To Web Service**.

9. On the **Data Connection Wizard**, enter the URL of the **Lists** web service, for example:

```
http://servername/sitename/_vti_bin/Lists.asmx
```

and click **Next**. Here, **servername** is the name of the SharePoint server and **sitename** is the name of the site where the **FormIDs** SharePoint list is located.

10. On the **Data Connection Wizard**, select the **UpdateListItems** operation from the list of operations, and click **Next**.
11. On the **Data Connection Wizard**, select **listName** in the **Parameters** list, and then click the button behind the **Field or group** text box.
12. On the **Select a Field or Group** dialog box, leave **Main** selected in the drop-down list box, select **listName**, and click **OK**. With this you have set the **listName** parameter of the web service operation to be equal to the value of the **listName** field in the Main data source of the form, which contains the GUID of the **FormIDs** SharePoint list.
13. On the **Data Connection Wizard**, select **updates** in the **Parameters** list, and then click the button behind the **Field or group** text box.
14. On the **Select a Field or Group** dialog box, select **FormIDsBatch (Secondary)** from the drop-down list box, select the **Batch** group node, and click **OK**. With this you have set the **updates** parameter of the web service operation to be equal to the contents of the **Batch** group node in the secondary data source for the XML file you added earlier.
15. On the **Data Connection Wizard**, select **XML subtree, including selected element** from the **Include** drop-down list box, and click **Next**. This setting will submit the entire XML contents of the **Batch** group node including its child nodes and values to the web service.

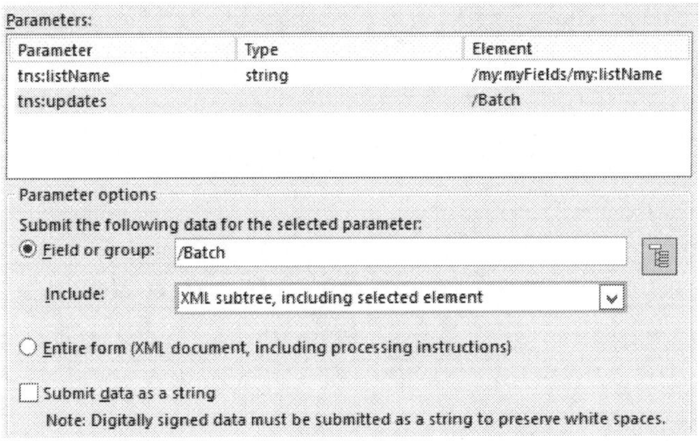

Figure 165. Parameter settings on the Data Connection Wizard.

16. Name the data connection **UpdateListItems**, deselect the **Set as the default submit connection** check box, and click **Finish**.
17. Publish the form template to a form library named **AutoNumberLib**.
18. Click **Data ➤ Get External Data ➤ From SharePoint List** and follow the instructions to add a data connection to the **FormIDs** SharePoint list (also see *Use a SharePoint list data connection* in recipe *43 2 Ways to retrieve data from a SharePoint list*). Ensure that you select the **ID** and **Title** fields to be included in the data source, name the data connection **FormIDs**, and deselect the **Automatically retrieve data when form is opened** check box.
19. Follow steps 3 through 8 of recipe *59 Determine whether a form is new or already exists* for the **AutoNumberLib** form library, and name the data connection **NewOrExistingFormCheck**.
20. Click **Data ➤ Submit Form ➤ To SharePoint Library**.
21. On the **Data Connection Wizard**, enter the URL of the form library (**AutoNumberLib**) to which you want to submit the form. The URL should have the following format:

    ```
    http://servername/sitename/AutoNumberLib
    ```

    where **servername** is the name of the SharePoint server and **sitename** is the name of the site where a form library named **AutoNumberLib** is located.
22. On the **Data Connection Wizard**, click the formula button behind the **File name** text box.
23. On the **Insert Formula** dialog box, enter a formula that generates a unique name for the form submitted based on the ID of the last item that was added by the current user to the **FormIDs** SharePoint list. For example:

    ```
    concat("Form_", max(ID))
    ```

    where **ID** is located under the **d:SharePointListItem_RW** repeating group node under the **dataFields** group node in the **FormIDs** secondary data source, and **concat()** and **max()** are InfoPath functions.
24. On the **Insert Formula** dialog box, click **OK**.

25. On the **Data Connection Wizard**, leave the **Allow overwrite if file exists** check box deselected, and click **Next**.

26. On the **Data Connection Wizard**, name the data connection **SubmitNewForm**, deselect the **Set as the default submit connection** check box, and click **Finish**.

27. Repeat steps 20 through 26 to add a second data connection named **SubmitExistingForm** that submits the form to the **AutoNumberLib** form library, but then using the following formula as the **File name**:

```
Title
```

where **Title** is located under the **d:SharePointListItem_RW** group node under the **dataFields** group node in the **NewOrExistingFormCheck** secondary data source. In addition, you must select the **Allow overwrite if file exists** check box, so that the existing form can be overwritten using the existing file name.

28. Click **Data** ➤ **Submit Form** ➤ **Submit Options**.

29. On the **Submit Options** dialog box, select the **Allow users to submit this form** check box, select the **Perform custom action using Rules** option, and then click **OK**. This should open the **Rules** task pane for the **Form Submit** event.

30. On the **Rules** task pane, if a rule is present, right-click it, and then select **Delete** from the drop-down menu that appears. Click **OK** on the message box that appears to confirm the deletion of the rule.

31. On the **Rules** task pane, add a new **Action** rule that has a **The expression** condition that says:

```
count(xdXDocument:GetDOM("NewOrExistingFormCheck")/dfs:myFields
/dfs:dataFields/d:SharePointListItem_RW/d:Title[. != ""]) != 0
```

and an action that says:

```
Submit using a data connection: SubmitExistingForm
```

This action rule counts the amount of non-blank **Title** fields in the **NewOrExistingFormCheck** secondary data source when the form is being submitted, and if this amount is not equal to 0, it means that the form is an existing form, so the form should be submitted to the form library using its existing name by calling the **SubmitExistingForm** data connection.

32. Add a second **Action** rule to the **Form Submit** event that has a **The expression** condition that says:

```
count(xdXDocument:GetDOM("NewOrExistingFormCheck")/dfs:myFields
/dfs:dataFields/d:SharePointListItem_RW/d:Title[. != ""]) = 0
```

and 5 actions that say:

```
Set a field's value: Field = userName()
```

where **Field** is a field that is located under the **Method** group node under the **Batch** group node in the **FormIDsBatch** secondary data source, and **userName()** is an InfoPath function. This action sets the value of the **Field** field in the XML batch file so that a new item that has the user name as its **Title** can be saved to the **FormIDs** SharePoint list.

```
Submit using a data connection: UpdateListItems
```

This action calls the **UpdateListItems** operation of the **Lists** web service to add a new list item to the **FormIDs** SharePoint list.

```
Set a field's value: Title = userName()
```

where **Title** is located under the **q:SharePointListItem_RW** group node under the **queryFields** group node in the **FormIDs** secondary data source, and **userName()** is an InfoPath function. This action prepares a query on the **FormIDs** SharePoint list to retrieve only those items that have the user name in their **Title** fields.

```
Query using a data connection: FormIDs
```

This action queries the **FormIDs** SharePoint list to retrieve the data.

```
Submit using a data connection: SubmitNewForm
```

This action rule counts the amount of non-blank **Title** fields in the **NewOrExistingFormCheck** secondary data source when the form is being submitted, and if this amount is equal to 0, it means that the form is a new form, so a new form name that is based on the **ID** of the item that has the highest **ID** in the **FormIDs** secondary data source should be generated before submitting the form to the form library by calling the **SubmitNewForm** data connection.

33. If your SharePoint environment is configured to use Claims Based authentication as opposed to Windows Classic authentication and the form is going to be filled out through the browser, you must set up UDC authentication for the **UpdateListItems** data connection that makes the web service call as described in *Configure a web service data connection for a web browser form* in the Appendix. But before you do this, test the form in InfoPath Filler 2013 to ensure that a list item is created in the **FormIDs** SharePoint list when you submit a form.
34. Republish the form template to the **AutoNumberLib** form library.

In SharePoint, navigate to the **AutoNumberLib** form library and add a new form. When the form opens, click the **Submit** button. A new form name should be generated and the form should appear with the generated form name in the form library. Open the form you just created and click **Submit** again. No new form should appear in the form library. Navigate to the **FormIDs** SharePoint list and check to see which items have been created there. Log on as another user and try submitting forms to the form library. Verify that the ID in the form name continues to be incremented with each form added to the form library.

Discussion

There are several solutions you can come up with to autonumber forms when they are submitted to a SharePoint form library. The challenge is to find a solution that minimizes the chance of two forms being submitted at exactly the same time and having form submission fail due to duplicate names in the SharePoint form library.

In the solution described above, a number (ID) is reserved for a particular user in a SharePoint list, and then this number is used to generate a form name that is almost guaranteed to be unique thereby minimizing the chance of duplicate names being assigned to forms. The only time the solution might fail is if a person has logged on multiple times as the same user or if one user name is being used by several people when submitting forms.

In the solution described above, you also filtered the secondary data source for the SharePoint list to be able to retrieve only those items that had a person's user name as their **Title**, and then afterwards used the **max()** function in the formula that generates the name of a form to find the ID of the item with the highest ID in the items that were returned.

61 Create separate add and edit views in a form

Problem

You want to be able to use one form template to add or edit data in forms that are submitted to a form library, but the form template should behave differently when a form is new compared to when a form is opened for editing.

Solution

You can use two views to add and edit data in one form, and add rules that take care of displaying the right view and data depending on whether the form is new or not.

To create separate add and edit views in a form:

1. In InfoPath, create a new SharePoint form library form template or use an existing one.
2. Add four **Text Box** controls named **firstName**, **lastName**, **city**, and **country**, respectively, to the view of the form template.
3. Click **Page Design ➤ Views ➤ New View** to add a new view to the form template. Name the view **Edit Data**.
4. Open the **View Properties** dialog box for the **Edit Data** view, and then on the **General** tab, deselect the **Show on the View menu when filling out this form** check box, and click **OK**.
5. On the **Fields** task pane, drag-and-drop each one of the four fields bound to the text box controls you added in step 2 onto the **Edit Data** view.
6. In this scenario, you will be making the **firstName** and **lastName** text boxes read-only on the **Edit Data** view to prevent users from editing

data in these two fields once a form has been previously saved or submitted to the form library. So select the **Read-Only** property on the **firstName** and **lastName** text boxes to make them read-only.

7. Click **Page Design** ➤ **Views** ➤ **View**, and select **View 1 (default)** from the **View** drop-down list box.
8. Open the **View Properties** dialog box for the **View 1** view, and then on the **General** tab, change the view's name to **Add Data**, deselect the **Show on the View menu when filling out this form** check box, and click **OK**.
9. Publish the form template to a form library named **AddEditViewLib**.
10. Follow steps 3 through 8 of recipe *59 Determine whether a form is new or already exists* to add a SharePoint list data connection to the **AddEditViewLib** form library, and name the data connection **NewOrExistingFormCheck**.
11. Click **Data** ➤ **Rules** ➤ **Form Load** and then add an **Action** rule to the **Form Load** event with a **The expression** condition that says:

```
count(xdXDocument:GetDOM("NewOrExistingFormCheck")/dfs:myFields
/dfs:dataFields/d:SharePointListItem_RW/d:Title[. != ""]) = 0
```

and with an action that says:

```
Switch to view: Add Data
```

This action rule switches to the **Add Data** view if the **NewOrExistingFormCheck** secondary data source does not contain an item with a **Title** field that is not blank, so if the form is new.

12. On the **Rules** task pane, add a second **Action** rule to the **Form Load** event with a **The expression** condition that says:

```
count(xdXDocument:GetDOM("NewOrExistingFormCheck")/dfs:myFields
/dfs:dataFields/d:SharePointListItem_RW/d:Title[. != ""]) != 0
```

and with an action that says:

```
Switch to view: Edit Data
```

This action rule switches to the **Edit Data** view if the **NewOrExistingFormCheck** secondary data source contains an item with a **Title** field that is not blank, so if the form already exists in the form library.

13. Click **Data** ➤ **Submit Form** ➤ **To SharePoint Library**.
14. On the **Data Connection Wizard**, enter the URL of the **AddEditViewLib** form library to which you want to submit the form. For example:

    ```
    http://servername/sitename/AddEditViewLib
    ```

    where **servername** is the name of the SharePoint server and **sitename** is the name of the site where the **AddEditViewLib** form library is located.
15. On the **Data Connection Wizard**, click the formula button behind the **File name** text box.
16. On the **Insert Formula** dialog box, construct a formula that would generate a unique form name, such as for example:

    ```
    concat("Form - ", now())
    ```

    and click **OK** (also see the discussion in step 8 of recipe *34 Submit a form to a form library and then close it*).
17. On the **Data Connection Wizard**, leave the **Allow overwrite if file exists** check box deselected, and click **Next**.
18. On the **Data Connection Wizard**, name the data connection **SubmitToFormLibraryIfNew**, leave the **Set as the default submit connection** check box selected, and click **Finish**.
19. Click **Data** ➤ **Submit Form** ➤ **To SharePoint Library**.
20. On the **Data Connection Wizard**, enter the URL of the **AddEditViewLib** form library to which you want to submit the form.
21. On the **Data Connection Wizard**, click the formula button behind the **File name** text box.
22. On the **Insert Formula** dialog box, click **Insert Field or Group**.
23. On the **Select a Field or Group** dialog box, select **NewOrExistingFormCheck (Secondary)** from the drop-down list box, expand all of the nodes under the **dataFields** group node, select

Title, and click **OK**. This formula allows you to use the existing form name to save the form back to the form library.

24. On the **Insert Formula** dialog box, click **OK**.
25. On the **Data Connection Wizard**, select the **Allow overwrite if file exists** check box, and click **Next**.
26. On the **Data Connection Wizard**, name the data connection **SubmitToFormLibraryIfExists**, leave the **Set as the default submit connection** check box deselected, and click **Finish**.
27. If the form is a new form, the **SubmitToFormLibraryIfNew** data connection should be executed and if the form already exists, the **SubmitToFormLibraryIfExists** data connection should be executed. To do this, you must submit the form using rules. So click **Data ➤ Submit Form ➤ Submit Options**.
28. On the **Submit Options** dialog box, the **Allow users to submit this form** check box should already be selected and **SharePoint document library** should be the selected item in the drop-down list box, because when you created the first submit data connection you indicated that it should be set as the default submit connection. Select the **Perform custom action using Rules** option, and click **OK**.
29. On the **Rules** task pane, there should already be one rule present with an action that submits the form to the form library. Add a **The expression** condition to this rule that says:

```
count(xdXDocument:GetDOM("NewOrExistingFormCheck")/dfs:myFields
/dfs:dataFields/d:SharePointListItem_RW/d:Title[. != ""]) = 0
```

This rule uses the **SubmitToFormLibraryIfNew** data connection to submit a new form to the form library.

30. On the **Rules** task pane, add a second **Action** rule with a **The expression** condition that says:

```
count(xdXDocument:GetDOM("NewOrExistingFormCheck")/dfs:myFields
/dfs:dataFields/d:SharePointListItem_RW/d:Title[. != ""]) != 0
```

and with an action that says:

```
Submit using a data connection: SubmitToFormLibraryIfExists
```

This rule uses the **SubmitToFormLibraryIfExists** data connection to submit an existing form back to the form library.

31. Republish the form template to the **AddEditViewLib** form library.

In SharePoint, navigate to the **AddEditViewLib** form library and add a new form. When the form opens, fill out the form and then submit it. Verify that a new form was created in the form library. Click the form to open it. Verify that the **firstName** and **lastName** fields are read-only, which means that the **Edit Data** view is being displayed. Change data in the **city** and/or **country** fields and submit the form again. Verify that no new form was created when you submitted the form for a second time.

Discussion

You can extend the solution described above by removing the **Save**, **Save As**, and **Close** commands from the Ribbon as described in recipe *33 Hide or show Ribbon commands for a form*, since users would be submitting and closing the form by clicking on the **Submit** command on the Ribbon.

Chapter 4: Use InfoPath Controls with Data from SharePoint

Drop-Down List Box

A drop-down list box is a control that takes up the space of only one row in a list and that can be temporarily expanded to display a list of items from which a user can select one item. Cascading or dependent drop-down list boxes are paired drop-down list boxes, where you select an item from one drop-down list box and then a second drop-down list box is automatically populated with items that depend on the selection made in the first drop-down list box.

Except for the first recipe, the recipes in this section take you through a couple of scenarios for creating cascading drop-down list boxes that are populated with data from one or several SharePoint lists.

62 Shrinking list in a repeating table using SharePoint list data

Problem

You have a drop-down list box in a repeating table that is being populated with items from a SharePoint list. You want users to be able to select an item only once from the drop-down list box. And once selected, that item should disappear from all of the drop-down list boxes in the other rows of the repeating table. In essence, you want to create a shrinking list of items.

Solution

You can use the **Filter Data** option on a secondary data source that is used to populate a drop-down list box to create shrinking list functionality in InfoPath.

Suppose you have a SharePoint list named **OfficeApplications** as described in *Create a SharePoint list form for an existing SharePoint list* in recipe *2 Customize a SharePoint list form from within InfoPath*.

To create a shrinking list in a repeating table using SharePoint list data:

1. In InfoPath, create a new SharePoint form library form template or use an existing one.
2. Add a **Receive** data connection to the **OfficeApplications** SharePoint list to the form template as described in *Use a SharePoint list data connection* in recipe *43 2 Ways to retrieve data from a SharePoint list*. Ensure that you select **ID** and **Title** as fields to include in the data source, and that you leave the **Automatically retrieve data when form is opened** check box selected.
3. Add a **Repeating Table** control with one column to the view of the form template, and rename the field in the repeating table to **officeApplication**.
4. Right-click the **officeApplication** text box in the repeating table, and then select **Change Control ➤ Drop-Down List Box** from the context menu that appears.
5. Open the **Drop-Down List Box Properties** dialog box.
6. On the **Drop-Down List Box Properties** dialog box on the **Data** tab, select the **Get choices from an external data source** option, select **OfficeApplications** from the **Data source** drop-down list box, and then click the button behind the **Entries** text box.
7. On the **Select a Field or Group** dialog box, select the **d:SharePointListItem_RW** repeating group node, and then click **Filter Data**.
8. On the **Filter Data** dialog box, click **Add**.
9. On the **Specify Filter Conditions** dialog box, select **ID** from the first drop-down list box, leave **is equal to** selected in the second drop-down list box, and then select **Select a field or group** from the third drop-down list box.

10. On the **Select a Field or Group** dialog box, select **Main** from the drop-down list box, expand the **group1** group node, expand the **group2** repeating group node, select **officeApplication**, and click **OK**.
11. On the **Specify Filter Conditions** dialog box, select **The expression** from the first drop-down list box, and then change the expression in the text box to say:

    ```
    not(d:ID = current()/my:officeApplication/../preceding-
    sibling::my:group2/my:officeApplication)
    ```

    This filter expression hides all of the items in the **OfficeApplications** secondary data source that have already been selected in any row preceding the current row in the repeating table. Note: You can refer to *InfoPath 2013 Cookbook* for an explanation of how the **current()** function works and how to navigate the DOM when constructing XPath expressions.
12. On the **Specify Filter Conditions** dialog box, click **And**.
13. On the **Specify Filter Conditions** dialog box, select **The expression** from the first drop-down list box for the second expression, select all of the text in the text box, press **Delete**, and then type the following expression into the text box for the second expression:

    ```
    not(d:ID = current()/my:officeApplication/../following-
    sibling::my:group2/my:officeApplication)
    ```

    Tip: You can copy and paste the first expression, and change **preceding-sibling** into **following-sibling**. This filter expression hides all of the items in the **OfficeApplications** secondary data source that have already been selected in any row following the current row in the repeating table.
14. On the **Specify Filter Conditions** dialog box, click **OK**.
15. On the **Filter Data** dialog box, click **OK**.
16. On the **Select a Field or Group** dialog box, click **OK**.
17. On the **Drop-Down List Box Properties** dialog box, set the **Value** property to be equal to the **ID** field and the **Display name** property to

be equal to the **Title** field in the **OfficeApplications** secondary data source, and then click **OK**.

18. On the **Fields** task pane, click **group1**, drag-and-drop it onto the view of the form template, and then delete the repeating table within the section control that is bound to **group1**.
19. Repeat the previous step, and place the second section control directly below the first without any spaces or empty lines between the two section controls.
20. Select the repeating table that was already present on the view, cut it, and then paste it inside of each section control. Delete all line-breaks and whitespaces that may be present around the two repeating tables within the section controls.
21. Configure the repeating table in the first section control to allow users to insert and delete rows. This is the default configuration of repeating tables, but verify that this is indeed the case.
22. Configure the repeating table in the second section control to allow users to only delete (not insert) rows. For this you must select the **Allow users to insert and delete rows** check box, deselect the **Show insert button and hint text** check box, and deselect all of the check boxes for the customizable commands except for the **Remove** command.
23. Add a **Formatting** rule to the first section control with a **The expression** condition that says:

```
count(xdXDocument:GetDOM("OfficeApplications")/dfs:myFields/dfs
:dataFields/d:SharePointListItem_RW) =
count(../my:group1/my:group2)
```

and with a formatting of **Hide this control**. **OfficeApplications** is the name of the secondary data source for the SharePoint list. This rule hides the first section control as soon as the user has added the maximum amount of rows that she is allowed to add to the repeating table.

24. Add a **Formatting** rule to the second section control with a **The expression** condition that says:

```
count(xdXDocument:GetDOM("OfficeApplications")/dfs:myFields/dfs
```

```
:dataFields/d:SharePointListItem_RW) !=
count(../my:group1/my:group2)
```

and with a formatting of **Hide this control**. This rule hides the second section control as long as the user has not yet reached the maximum amount of rows that she is allowed to add to the repeating table.

25. Publish the form template to a SharePoint form library.

In SharePoint, navigate to the form library where you published the form template and add a new form. When the form opens, all of the items from the **OfficeApplications** SharePoint list should be present in the drop-down list box in the first row of the repeating table. Select an item from the drop-down list box, and then click **Insert item** to add a second row to the repeating table. The item you selected in the first drop-down list box should not be present in the second drop-down list box. Continue adding rows until there are no items left in the drop-down list box. Also try removing rows from the repeating table to see items reappear in the drop-down list box.

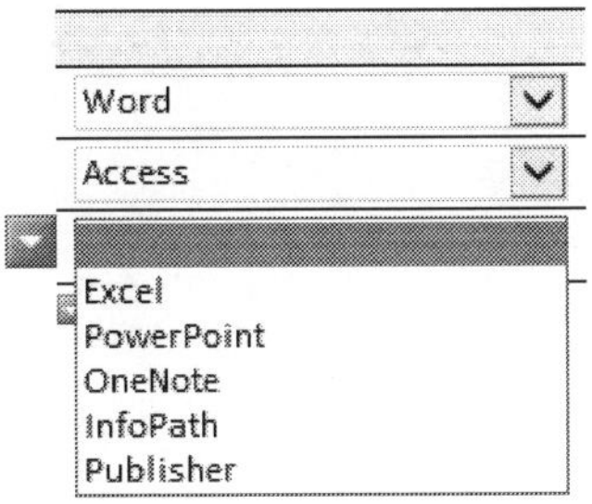

Figure 166. Drop-down list box containing less and less items as they are selected.

Discussion

In the solution described above, you saw that once you had selected all of the items from the drop-down list box, you were not able to continue adding rows to the repeating table. This technique of swapping a repeating table with another repeating table to which users cannot add rows as soon as a maximum amount of rows has been reached, was explained for the first time in recipe *114 Limit the amount of rows added to a repeating table to a maximum* of *InfoPath 2013 Cookbook*.

63 Cascading drop-down list boxes using one SharePoint list

Problem

You have a SharePoint list that contains the names and categories of software products. You want to add two drop-down list boxes to an InfoPath form, populate the first drop-down list box with all of the software categories, and populate the second drop-down list box with the software products that belong to the selected category in the first drop-down list box.

Solution

You can use the **Filter Data** option on the data source for a SharePoint list that is used to populate drop-down list boxes to filter data based on values that are entered or selected in the Main data source of a form.

Suppose you have a SharePoint list named **SoftwareProductsCategories** that contains the following data:

Title (Text)	SoftwareCategory (Text)
SQL Server	Servers
Word	Office Applications
Excel	Office Applications
Visual Studio	Development Tools

To create cascading drop-down list boxes using one SharePoint list:

1. In InfoPath, create a new SharePoint form library form template or use an existing one.
2. Add a **Receive** data connection to the **SoftwareProductsCategories** SharePoint list to the form template as described in *Use a SharePoint list data connection* in recipe *43 2 Ways to retrieve data from a SharePoint list*.

Include the **Title** and **SoftwareCategory** fields in the data source, leave the **Automatically retrieve data when form is opened** check box selected, and name the data connection **SoftwareProductsCategories**.

3. Add a **Drop-Down List Box** control to the view of the form template and name it **category**.
4. Open the **Drop-Down List Box Properties** dialog box.
5. On the **Drop-Down List Box Properties** dialog box on the **Data** tab, select the **Get choices from an external data source** option, and then select **SoftwareProductsCategories** from the **Data source** drop-down list box. The XPath expression for the **d:SharePointListItem_RW** repeating group should automatically appear in the **Entries** text box.
6. On the **Drop-Down List Box Properties** dialog box, click the button behind the **Value** text box.
7. On the **Select a Field or Group** dialog box, select **SoftwareCategory**, and click **OK**.
8. Repeat steps 6 and 7 for the **Display name** text box.
9. On the **Drop-Down List Box Properties** dialog box, select the **Show only entries with unique display names** check box, and click **OK**. This should prevent duplicate categories from appearing in the drop-down list box.
10. Add a second **Drop-Down List Box** control to the view of the form template and name it **product**.
11. Open the **Drop-Down List Box Properties** dialog box for the **product** drop-down list box.
12. On the **Drop-Down List Box Properties** dialog box on the **Data** tab, select the **Get choices from an external data source** option, select **SoftwareProductsCategories** from the **Data source** drop-down list box, and then click the button behind the **Entries** text box.
13. On the **Select a Field or Group** dialog box, select the **d:SharePointListItem_RW** repeating group node, and then click **Filter Data**.
14. On the **Filter Data** dialog box, click **Add**.
15. You must add a filter that will return the **Title** fields that fall under the same repeating group node as the selected **category** in the first drop-

down list box. For this you must add a filter that compares the value of the **SoftwareCategory** field in the SharePoint list with the value of the selected item in the **category** drop-down list box. So on the **Specify Filter Conditions** dialog box, select **SoftwareCategory** from the first drop-down list box. This **SoftwareCategory** field is located in the **SoftwareProductsCategories** secondary data source for the SharePoint list.

16. On the **Specify Filter Conditions** dialog box, leave **is equal to** selected in the second drop-down list box, and then select **Select a field or group** from the third drop-down list box.
17. On the **Select a Field or Group** dialog box, select **Main** from the drop-down list box, select **category**, and then click **OK**. Note: The **category** in the Main data source corresponds to the selected item in the **category** drop-down list box.
18. On the **Specify Filter Conditions** dialog box, click **OK**.
19. The filter on the **Filter Data** dialog box, should now say:

    ```
    SoftwareCategory = category
    ```

    Click **OK**.
20. On the **Select a Field or Group** dialog box, click **OK**. The XPath expression in the **Entries** text box on the **Drop-Down List Box Properties** dialog box should now say:

    ```
    /dfs:myFields/dfs:dataFields/d:SharePointListItem_RW[d:Software
    Category = xdXDocument:get-DOM()/my:myFields/my:category]
    ```

21. On the **Drop-Down List Box Properties** dialog box, ensure that both the **Value** and **Display name** properties have been set to be equal to the **Title** field in the **SoftwareProductsCategories** secondary data source (the product is stored in this field), and click **OK**. Note that because the products are expected to be unique in the SharePoint list, you do not have to select the **Show only entries with unique display names** check box.
22. Add an **Action** rule to the **category** drop-down list box with an action that says:

    ```
    Set a field's value: product = ""
    ```

where **product** is located in the Main data source of the form. This rule ensures that the selected item in the **product** drop-down list box is cleared whenever an item is selected from the **category** drop-down list box.

23. Publish the form template to a SharePoint form library.

In SharePoint, navigate to the form library where you published the form template and add a new form. When the form opens, verify that the second drop-down list box is empty. Select a category from the first drop-down list box. The second drop-down list box should now contain products.

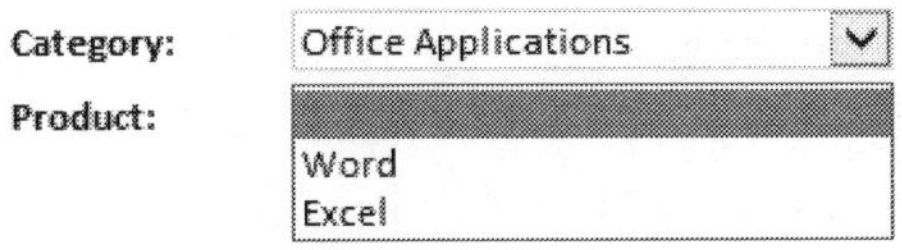

Figure 167. The cascading drop-down list boxes on the InfoPath form.

Discussion

To create cascading drop-down list boxes that make use of SharePoint list data in InfoPath, you must apply filtering. There are two basic ways to filter SharePoint list data in InfoPath when you make use of rules:

1. Use the **Filter Data** option on a secondary data source.
2. Use fields under the **queryFields** group node in the secondary data source.

If you use the first method, you must retrieve all of the data from SharePoint and then filter it locally in the InfoPath form. And if you use the second method, you generally filter the data as you retrieve it from SharePoint. The solution described above uses the first method and works best for populating drop-down list boxes from SharePoint lists that contain small amounts of data.

Because the data from both drop-down list boxes are coming from the same SharePoint list, you must pre-fetch all of the data from the SharePoint list and then use the **Filter Data** option on the secondary data source for the SharePoint list to filter the data and display it in the second drop-down list box. The pre-fetching of data takes place when the form opens, because you set the secondary data source to automatically retrieve the data when the form opened. However, you could also set the SharePoint list data to be retrieved on demand by deselecting the **Automatically retrieve data when form is opened** check box on the data connection and then adding a **Query for data** action in a rule on another control that should trigger populating the first drop-down list box.

You could have also used the second filter method in the solution above by adding two separate data connections to the same SharePoint list (instead of just one data connection) to the form template and then using query fields to filter and populate the data in each drop-down list box with each drop-down list box using its own (filtered) secondary data source. You will learn how to use query fields to filter SharePoint list data in cascading drop-down list boxes in recipe *65 Cascading drop-down list boxes using linked SharePoint lists*.

64 Cascading drop-down list boxes in a repeating table using linked lists

Problem

You have two SharePoint lists that are linked to each other through a lookup column and you want to use these lists to create cascading drop-down list boxes that are located within a repeating table on an InfoPath form.

Solution

You can use the **Filter Data** option on the data source for the SharePoint list used to populate the dependent drop-down list box to filter the data based on values that are entered or selected in the Main data source of the form.

Suppose you have two SharePoint lists named **SoftwareCategories** and **SoftwareProducts** as described in recipe *14 Master/detail with two linked SharePoint lists*.

To create cascading drop-down list boxes in a repeating table using linked SharePoint lists:

1. In InfoPath, create a new SharePoint form library form template or use an existing one.
2. Add a **Receive** data connection to the **SoftwareCategories** SharePoint list to the form template as described in *Use a SharePoint list data connection* in recipe *43 2 Ways to retrieve data from a SharePoint list*. Include the **ID** and **Title** fields in the data source, select **Title** as the field to sort the list by, leave the **Automatically retrieve data when form is opened** check box selected, and name the data connection **SoftwareCategories**.
3. Add a **Receive** data connection to the **SoftwareProducts** SharePoint list to the form template. Include the **ID**, **Title**, and **Category** fields in the data source, select **Title** as the field to sort the list by, leave the **Automatically retrieve data when form is opened** check box selected, and name the data connection **SoftwareProducts**.
4. Add a **Repeating Table** control with 2 columns to the view of the form template, and name the text boxes within the repeating table **category** and **product**, respectively.
5. Select the first text box within the repeating table, and then select **Control Tools ➤ Properties ➤ Modify ➤ Change Control ➤ Drop-Down List Box**.
6. Repeat the previous step for the second text box within the repeating table.
7. Populate the **category** drop-down list box with items from the **SofwareCategories** secondary data source, use **ID** as the **Value**, and use **Title** as the **Display name** for the drop-down list box.
8. Open the **Drop-Down List Box Properties** dialog box for the **product** drop-down list box.
9. On the **Drop-Down List Box Properties** dialog box on the **Data** tab, select the **Get choices from an external data source** option, select **SoftwareProducts** from the **Data source** drop-down list box, and then click the button behind the **Entries** text box.

10. On the **Select a Field or Group** dialog box, ensure that the **d:SharePointListItem_RW** repeating group node under the **dataFields** group is selected, and then click **Filter Data**.
11. On the **Filter Data** dialog box, click **Add**.
12. On the **Specify Filter Conditions** dialog box, select **Category** from the first drop-down list box, leave **is equal to** selected in the second drop-down list box, and then select **Select a field or group** from the third drop-down list box.
13. On the **Select a Field or Group** dialog box, select **Main** from the drop-down list box, expand all of the group nodes, select **category**, and click **OK**.
14. On the **Specify Filter Conditions** dialog box, click **OK**.
15. On the **Filter Data** dialog box, click **OK**.
16. On the **Select a Field or Group** dialog box, click **OK**. The XPath expression in the **Entries** text box on the **Drop-Down List Box Properties** dialog box should now say:

```
/dfs:myFields/dfs:dataFields/d:SharePointListItem_RW[d:Category
= current()/my:category]
```

17. On the **Drop-Down List Box Properties** dialog box, click the button behind the **Value** text box.
18. On the **Select a Field or Group** dialog box, select **ID**, and click **OK**. The **Display name** text box should already be set to be equal to the value of the **Title** field. If not, repeat this step to set it to be equal to the value of the **Title** field.
19. On the **Drop-Down List Box Properties** dialog box, click **OK**.
20. Add an **Action** rule to the **category** drop-down list box with an action that says:

```
Set a field's value: product = ""
```

    This action clears any previously selected value in the **product** drop-down list box whenever a new category is selected.
21. Publish the form template to a SharePoint form library.

In SharePoint, navigate to the form library where you published the form template and add a new form. When the form opens, the first drop-down list box should contain software categories and the second drop-down list box should be empty. Select a category from the first drop-down list box. The second drop-down list box should be populated with the software products belonging to the category you selected in the first drop-down list box. Add a second row to the repeating table and try selecting items again.

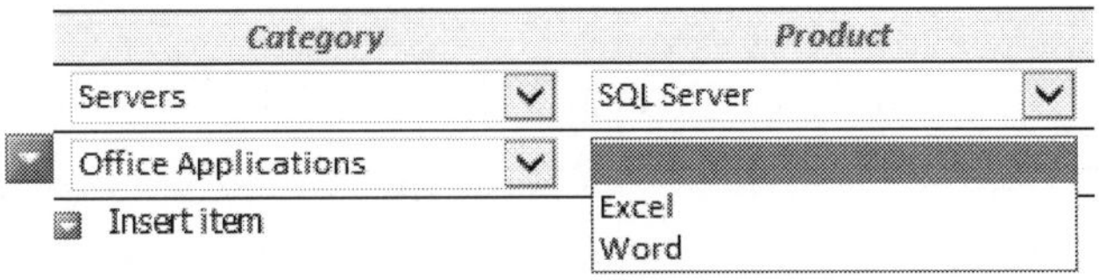

Figure 168. Repeating table with cascading drop-down list boxes on the InfoPath form.

Discussion

In step 12 of the solution described above, you selected **Select a field or group** from the third drop-down list box on the **Specify Filter Conditions** dialog box. Note that for this solution to work, you must not use the **Use a formula** option in the drop-down list box to select the **category** field from the Main data source. Doing so would have you wind up with the following expression for the entries of the **product** drop-down list box:

```
/dfs:myFields/dfs:dataFields/d:SharePointListItem_RW[d:Category =
xdXDocument:get-DOM()/my:myFields/my:group1/my:group2/my:category]
```

The expression above does not include the **current()** function in the XPath filter expression, and you need to use the **current()** function for the solution to work properly.

The solution described above uses filtering in InfoPath to create cascading drop-down list boxes. Note that you cannot use querying as described in for example recipe *65 Cascading drop-down list boxes using linked SharePoint lists*, because each time you requery the data connection, you would change the contents of the **SoftwareProducts** secondary data source. And since all of the **product** drop-down list boxes in the rows of the repeating table depend on that data, the list of available products in the drop-down list boxes would change every time you select an item from a **category** drop-down list box.

65 Cascading drop-down list boxes using linked SharePoint lists

Problem

You have two SharePoint lists that are linked to each other through a lookup column and you want to use these lists to create cascading drop-down list boxes on an InfoPath form.

Solution

You can use fields under the **queryFields** group node of a data source for a SharePoint list and rules to filter data and populate cascading drop-down list boxes.

Suppose you have two SharePoint lists named **SoftwareCategories** and **SoftwareProducts** as described in recipe *14 Master/detail with two linked SharePoint lists*.

To create cascading drop-down list boxes by querying linked SharePoint lists:

1. In InfoPath, create a new SharePoint form library form template or use an existing one.
2. Add a **Receive** data connection to the **SoftwareCategories** SharePoint list to the form template as described in *Use a SharePoint list data connection* in recipe *43 2 Ways to retrieve data from a SharePoint list*. Include the **ID** and **Title** fields in the data source, select **Title** as the field to sort the list by, leave the **Automatically retrieve data when form is opened** check box selected, and name the data connection **SoftwareCategories**.
3. Add a **Receive** data connection to the **SoftwareProducts** SharePoint list to the form template. Include the **ID**, **Title**, and **Category** fields in the data source, select **Title** as the field to sort the list by, deselect the

Automatically retrieve data when form is opened check box, and name the data connection **SoftwareProducts**.

4. Add a **Drop-Down List Box** control to the view of the form template and name it **category**.
5. Populate the **category** drop-down list box with items from the **SofwareCategories** secondary data source, use **ID** as the **Value**, and use **Title** as the **Display name** for the drop-down list box.
6. Add a second **Drop-Down List Box** control to the view of the form template and name it **product**.
7. Populate the **product** drop-down list box with items from the **SoftwareProducts** secondary data source, use **ID** as the **Value**, and use **Title** as the **Display name** for the drop-down list box.
8. The **product** drop-down list box should be populated with items when an item is selected from the **category** drop-down list box, so you have to add a rule that uses the selected value from the **category** drop-down list box to query the **SoftwareProducts** secondary data source, so that the **product** drop-down list box can be populated with filtered items. So add an **Action** rule to the **category** drop-down list box that has the following 3 actions:

```
Set a field's value: product = ""
Set a field's value: Category = .
Query using a data connection: SoftwareProducts
```

where **Category** is the **Category** field that is located under the **q:SharePointListItem_RW** group node under the **queryFields** group node in the **SoftwareProducts** secondary data source, and which contains the ID of a category that is linked to specific products. The dot (**.**) represents the **category** field in the Main data source. The first action clears any previously selected value in the **product** drop-down list box. The second action sets the value of the **Category** query field in the **SoftwareProducts** secondary data source to be equal to the value of the selected item in the **category** drop-down list box. The third action sends the query to SharePoint to filter and retrieve the data for the **SoftwareProducts** secondary data source and then populate the **product** drop-down list box with this data.

9. Because the **product** drop-down list box would be empty for a previously saved form, and because this would cause the **ID** (instead of

the **Title**) of a previously selected product to be shown in the **product** drop-down list box, you must add a rule for when the form opens that checks whether a category or a product has been previously selected, and if so, query the **SoftwareProducts** data source. So click **Data ➤ Rules ➤ Form Load**.

10. On the **Rules** task pane, add an **Action** rule to the **Form Load** event that has a **Condition** that says:

```
category is not blank
or
product is not blank
```

and that has the following 2 actions:

```
Set a field's value: Category = category
Query using a data connection: SoftwareProducts
```

where **Category** is the **Category** field that is located under the **q:SharePointListItem_RW** group node under the **queryFields** group node in the **SoftwareProducts** secondary data source, and **category** is a field that is located in the Main data source and that is bound to the **category** drop-down list box. The first action sets the value of the **Category** query field in the **SoftwareProducts** secondary data source to be equal to the value of the selected item in the **category** drop-down list box. The second action sends the query to SharePoint to filter and retrieve the data for the **SoftwareProducts** secondary data source and then populate the **product** drop-down list box with this data.

11. Publish the form template to a SharePoint form library.

In SharePoint, navigate to the form library where you published the form template and add a new form. When the form opens, the first drop-down list box should contain software categories and the second drop-down list box should be empty. Select a category from the first drop-down list box. The second drop-down list box should be populated with the software products for the category you selected in the first drop-down list box. Select another category from the first drop-down list box. The second drop-down list box should first be cleared and then refilled with the software products corresponding to the newly selected category.

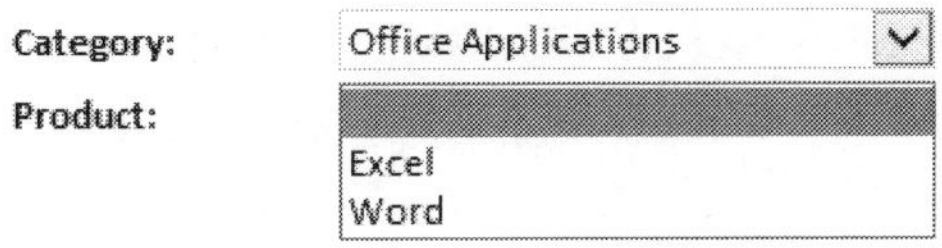

Figure 169. Cascading drop-down list boxes on the InfoPath form.

Discussion

The solution described above works best for populating drop-down list boxes from SharePoint lists that contain large amounts of data or which you want to populate on demand. Filtering data through query fields of a data connection is a two-step process:

1. You must set the values of one or more query fields of the data connection to be equal to the values you want to filter the data on.
2. You must (re)query the data connection to retrieve the filtered data.

These two steps were performed in step 8 through the use of rule actions.

To initiate the process of cascading the data, you must have some data to start with. So in the solution described above the data for the **SoftwareCategories** secondary data source was automatically retrieved when the form opened. You could have also set this data to be retrieved on demand by deselecting the **Automatically retrieve data when form is opened** check box on the **SoftwareCategories** data connection and then adding a **Query for data** action to a rule on an extra button or another field that should trigger populating the **category** drop-down list box.

Whether you use filtering within InfoPath as described in recipe *63 Cascading drop-down list boxes using one SharePoint list* or filtering in SharePoint through querying as described in the solution above for setting up cascading drop-down list boxes depends largely on your scenario and how you want to deal with data retrieval.

The advantage of using filtering within InfoPath is that the data is retrieved only once to populate the data sources and subsequently used for the rest of the session in the form and filtered to populate drop-down list boxes. So this method reduces the amount of queries sent to SharePoint to retrieve data. However, note that postbacks may still take place to be able to properly render the controls on the view whenever you select an item from a drop-down list box that affects the data in another drop-down list box. The disadvantage of using filtering within InfoPath is that the initial loading of data may take a long time, so affect the performance of the form, especially if the SharePoint lists being queried contain large amounts of data.

The advantage of using query fields of a data connection to create cascading drop-down list boxes is that only a subset of the data is retrieved, since it is filtered on the server. This positively affects the performance of forms. The disadvantage of using query fields of a data connection is that you must repeatedly make calls to SharePoint to retrieve the data to populate the drop-down list boxes. This may increase the amount of requests and load on the server.

If you have relatively small SharePoint lists that you want to use for populating cascading drop-down list boxes, you could choose to use the filtering within InfoPath method. However, if you have very large SharePoint lists to filter, it might be better to choose the query and filter on SharePoint method for creating cascading drop-down list boxes in InfoPath.

66 Cascading drop-down list box and repeating table using linked lists

Problem

You have two SharePoint lists that are linked to each other through a lookup column and you want to use these lists to design a form so that when an item is selected in a drop-down list box, the items that are linked to the selected item are displayed in a repeating table.

Solution

You can use fields under the **queryFields** group node of a data source for a SharePoint list and rules to filter data and populate a repeating table that is linked to a drop-down list box.

Suppose you have two SharePoint lists named **SoftwareCategories** and **SoftwareProducts** as described in recipe *14 Master/detail with two linked SharePoint lists*.

To create a repeating table that displays filtered data by selecting an item in a drop-down list box and querying linked SharePoint lists:

1. In SharePoint, add an item to the **SoftwareCategories** SharePoint list that has **X** as its **Title**.
2. You are going to use the **X** category to be able to clear the repeating table when an empty item is selected from the drop-down list box, since empty **queryField** values cannot be used to achieve this. When empty **queryField** values are used to retrieve data in InfoPath, all of the data from a SharePoint list is retrieved and displayed instead of no data. But if you query an item (category) that does not have any products linked to it, no products will be returned, so the repeating table will be empty. This is a workaround you can use to clear a repeating table that is bound to a secondary data source for a SharePoint list and that uses **queryFields** instead of data filtering as described in recipe *63 Cascading drop-down list boxes using one SharePoint list* to retrieve data to populate the repeating table. Users should not be able to see the **X** category in the SharePoint list. Therefore, you must set item-level permission on the item, so click on the ellipsis behind the item and select **Shared With** from the context menu that appears.
3. On the **Shared With** dialog, click **Advanced**.
4. On the **Permissions** page, click **Permissions ➤ Inheritance ➤ Stop Inheriting Permissions**.
5. Click **OK** on the message box that appears.
6. Select the top-most check box to select the check boxes in front of all of the users and groups, and then click **Permissions ➤ Modify ➤ Remove User Permissions**.
7. Click **OK** on the message box that appears. If you navigate back to the SharePoint list, you might still be able to see the **X** category if you are an administrator, but if you log on as a different user, you should not be able to see the list item anymore.
8. Follow steps 1 through 5 of recipe *65 Cascading drop-down list boxes using linked SharePoint lists*.

9. Open the **Drop-Down List Box Properties** dialog box, and click the button behind the **Entries** text box.
10. On the **Select a Field or Group** dialog box, click **Filter Data**.
11. On the **Filter Data** dialog box, click **Add**.
12. On the **Specify Filter Conditions** dialog box, construct a filter that says:

    ```
    Title is not equal to "X"
    ```

    and click **OK**. This filter condition ensures that the **X** category remains hidden from anybody who opens a form.
13. On the **Filter Data** dialog box, click **OK**.
14. On the **Select a Field or Group** dialog box, click **OK**.
15. On the **Drop-Down List Box Properties** dialog box, click **OK**.
16. Bind the **d:SharePointListItem_RW** repeating group node under the **dataFields** group node in the **SoftwareProducts** secondary data source to a **Repeating Table** control on the view of the form template as described in recipe *44 Display SharePoint list data in a repeating table*.
17. The repeating table should be populated with items when an item is selected from the **category** drop-down list box, so you have to add a rule that uses the selected value from the **category** drop-down list box to query the **SoftwareProducts** secondary data source, so that the repeating table can be populated with filtered items. So add an **Action** rule to the **category** drop-down list box that has a **Condition** that says:

    ```
    category is not blank
    ```

    and that has 2 actions that say:

    ```
    Set a field's value: Category = .
    Query using a data connection: SoftwareProducts
    ```

    where **Category** is the **Category** field that is located under the **q:SharePointListItem_RW** group node under the **queryFields** group node in the **SoftwareProducts** secondary data source, and which contains the ID of a category that is linked to specific products. The dot (**.**) represents the **category** field in the Main data source. The first action sets the value of the **Category** query field in the

SoftwareProducts secondary data source to be equal to the value of the selected item in the **category** drop-down list box. The second action sends the query to SharePoint to filter and retrieve the data for the **SoftwareProducts** secondary data source and then populate the repeating table with this data.

18. The repeating table should be cleared when an empty item is selected from the **category** drop-down list box, so you have to add a rule that uses the **X** category (hidden SharePoint list item linked to no products) to query the **SoftwareProducts** secondary data source, so that the repeating table can be cleared. So add a second **Action** rule to the **category** drop-down list box that has a **Condition** that says:

```
category is blank
```

and that has 2 actions that say:

```
Set a field's value: Category = "4"
Query using a data connection: SoftwareProducts
```

where **Category** is the **Category** field that is located under the **q:SharePointListItem_RW** group node under the **queryFields** group node in the **SoftwareProducts** secondary data source, and which contains the ID of a category that is linked to specific products. "4" is the ID of the **X** category. You can look up this ID in SharePoint by opening the list item that has **X** as its title, and then look at the number that is displayed behind the **ID** query string parameter in the browser's address bar. The first action sets the value of the **Category** query field in the **SoftwareProducts** secondary data source to be equal to the ID of the **X** category in the SharePoint list that is linked to no products. The second action sends the query to SharePoint to filter and retrieve no data, and then clear the repeating table.

19. Because the repeating table would be empty for a previously saved form, you must add a rule for when the form opens that checks whether a category has been previously selected, and if so, query the **SoftwareProducts** data source. So click **Data ➤ Rules ➤ Form Load**.

20. On the **Rules** task pane, add an **Action** rule to the **Form Load** event that has a **Condition** that says:

```
category is not blank
```

and that has the following 2 actions:

```
Set a field's value: Category = category
Query using a data connection: SoftwareProducts
```

where **Category** is the **Category** field that is located under the **q:SharePointListItem_RW** group node under the **queryFields** group node in the **SoftwareProducts** secondary data source, and **category** is a field that is located in the Main data source and that is bound to the **category** drop-down list box. The first action sets the value of the **Category** query field in the **SoftwareProducts** secondary data source to be equal to the value of the selected item in the **category** drop-down list box. The second action sends the query to SharePoint to filter and retrieve the data for the **SoftwareProducts** secondary data source and then populate the repeating table with this data.

21. Publish the form template to a SharePoint form library.

In SharePoint, navigate to the form library where you published the form template and add a new form. When the form opens, the drop-down list box should contain software categories and the repeating table should be empty. Select a category from the drop-down list box. The repeating table should be populated with the software products for the category you selected in the drop-down list box. Select the empty item from the drop-down list box. The repeating table should be cleared.

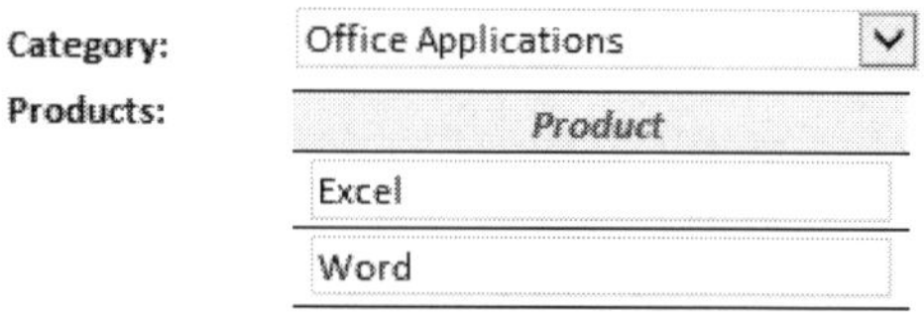

Figure 170. The linked drop-down list box and repeating table.

Discussion

The solution described above is similar to that in recipe *65 Cascading drop-down list boxes using linked SharePoint lists*, but then using a repeating table instead of a second drop-down list box, and is ideal to use if you have a scenario that would benefit from filtering SharePoint list data on the server due to the large amount of data that a linked list contains.

Picture

Picture controls are used to display images on an InfoPath form. You can add an image to a picture control on an InfoPath form either as an embedded base64 encoded string or as a hyperlink.

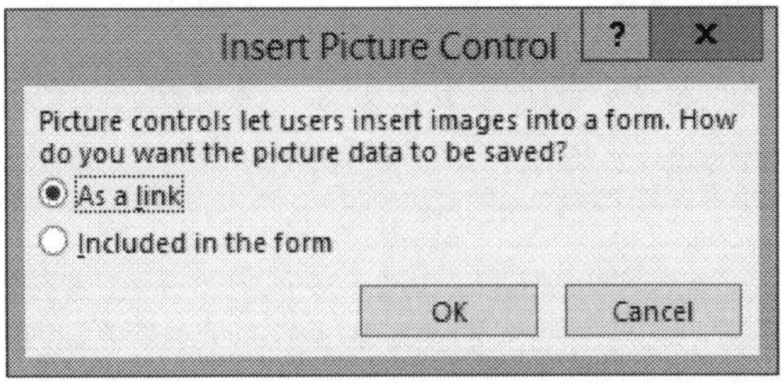

Figure 171. Dialog box that pops up when you add a Picture control.

When you retrieve an image from SharePoint, it is easier to store the URL of that image in a picture control that is configured to accept a hyperlink than it is to embed that image in a picture control. If you want to embed images from a SharePoint picture library on an InfoPath form, the most likely way to do this would be to write code to provide such functionality. So if you do not want to or cannot write code, always look for a way to link to images rather than embed them in InfoPath forms.

The following recipes discuss a few scenarios for retrieving and working with images that are stored in a SharePoint picture library or images that are attached to a SharePoint list item.

67 Upload an image as an attachment to a SharePoint list item

Problem

You want to be able to upload an image that is stored in a picture control on an InfoPath form to SharePoint and attach it to a particular item in a SharePoint list.

Solution

You can use the **Lists** web service of SharePoint to upload and attach an image to a SharePoint list item.

Suppose you have a SharePoint list named **OfficeApplications** as described in *Create a SharePoint list form for an existing SharePoint list* in recipe *2 Customize a SharePoint list form from within InfoPath* which you want to use to retrieve images.

To upload an image as an attachment to a SharePoint list item:

1. In SharePoint, navigate to the **OfficeApplications** list, click **List ➤ Settings ➤ List Settings**, and then copy the GUID that is listed after the **List** query string parameter in the URL in the browser's address bar. It should look something like the following:

   ```
   %7B88B1D952%2DE14A%2D470B%2D901C%2D156F4C315822%7D
   ```

2. Convert the **%7B** characters to **{**, **%2D** to **-**, and **%7D** to **}**. The resulting list GUID should now resemble the following:

   ```
   {88B1D952-E14A-470B-901C-156F4C315822}
   ```

   Copy it to the Windows clipboard.
3. In InfoPath, create a new SharePoint form library form template or use an existing one.
4. Add a **Receive** data connection to the **OfficeApplications** SharePoint list to the form template as described in *Use a SharePoint list data connection* in recipe *43 2 Ways to retrieve data from a SharePoint list*. Ensure that you select **ID** and **Title** as fields to include in the data source, and that you leave the **Automatically retrieve data when form is opened** check box selected.
5. Add a **Drop-Down List Box** control to the view of the form template and name it **officeApplication**.
6. Add a **Text Box** control to the view of the form template and name it **fileName**.

7. Add a **Picture** control named **image** to the view of the form template. Select the **Included in the form** option on the **Picture Control** dialog box when you add the control.
8. Add a **Button** control to the view of the form template and label it **Upload Image**.
9. Populate the **officeApplication** drop-down list box control with items from the **OfficeApplications** secondary data source by selecting the **d:SharePointListItem_RW** repeating group node that is located under the **dataFields** group node for the **Entries** property, the **ID** field for the **Value** property, and the **Title** field for the **Display name** property of the drop-down list box.
10. Select **Data ➤ Get External Data ➤ From Web Service ➤ From SOAP Web Service**.
11. On the **Data Connection Wizard**, enter the URL of the **Lists** web service that is located on the same site where the SharePoint list is located and where you will be publishing the InfoPath form template. For example:

    ```
    http://servername/sitename/_vti_bin/Lists.asmx
    ```

    where **servername** is the name of the SharePoint server, and **sitename** is the name of the site where the SharePoint list is located. Click **Next**.
12. On the **Data Connection Wizard**, select **AddAttachment** from the list of operations, and click **Next**.
13. On the **Data Connection Wizard**, leave all of the parameters as is, and click **Next**.
14. On the **Data Connection Wizard**, leave the **Store a copy of the data in the form template** check box deselected, and click **Next**.
15. On the **Data Connection Wizard**, leave the name of the data connection as **AddAttachment**, deselect the **Automatically retrieve data when form is opened** check box, and click **Finish**.
16. Add an **Action** rule to the **Upload Image** button with a **Condition** that says:

    ```
    officeApplication is not blank
    and
    fileName is not blank
    ```

```
and
image is not blank
```

and that has 5 actions that say:

```
Set a field's value: listName = "{88B1D952-E14A-470B-901C-156F4C315822}"
```

where **listName** is a field that is located under the **AddAttachment** group node under the **queryFields** group node in the **AddAttachment** secondary data source and `{88B1D952-E14A-470B-901C-156F4C315822}` is the GUID of the list you retrieved in step 2.

```
Set a field's value: listItemID = officeApplication
```

where **listItemID** is a field that is located under the **AddAttachment** group node under the **queryFields** group node in the **AddAttachment** secondary data source and **officeApplication** is the field that is bound to the drop-down list box.

```
Set a field's value: fileName = fileName
```

where the first **fileName** is a field that is located under the **AddAttachment** group node under the **queryFields** group node in the **AddAttachment** secondary data source and the second **fileName** is the field that is bound to the text box.

```
Set a field's value: attachment = image
```

where **attachment** is a field that is located under the **AddAttachment** group node under the **queryFields** group node in the **AddAttachment** secondary data source and **image** is the field that is bound to the picture control.

```
Query using a data connection: AddAttachment
```

This action queries the **AddAttachment** secondary data source to be able to upload the image stored in the picture control to SharePoint and attach it to the selected SharePoint list item in the drop-down list box.

17. If your SharePoint environment is configured to use Claims Based authentication as opposed to Windows Classic authentication and the form is going to be filled out through the browser, you must set up UDC authentication for the **AddAttachment** data connection that

makes the web service call as described in *Configure a web service data connection for a web browser form* in the Appendix. But before you do this, test the form in InfoPath Filler 2013 to ensure that the functionality is working properly.

18. Publish the form template to a SharePoint form library.

In SharePoint, navigate to the form library where you published the form template and add a new form. When the form opens, the drop-down list box should contain the names of Office applications. Select an Office application from the drop-down list box. Enter a name with file extension into the **fileName** text box, click the picture control and select an image, and then click the **Upload Image** button. Navigate to the **OfficeApplications** SharePoint list, open the list item to which you attached the image, and verify that the image is listed under the attachments for the list item.

Discussion

In the solution described above, you used the **AddAttachment** operation of the **Lists** web service to upload an image to SharePoint and attach it to a particular item in a SharePoint list. While you could have used a **Submit** data connection to achieve the same result as described in the solution above, using a **Receive** data connection allows you to bind the **AddAttachmentResult** field that is located under the **AddAttachmentResponse** group node under the **dataFields** group node in the **AddAttachment** secondary data source to a text box control or a calculated value control on the view of the InfoPath form so that you can display the URL of the attachment once the image has been uploaded to the SharePoint list item. The latter can also be used to give the user a sign that the image upload was successful.

Warning:

> While the solution described above works best for images, it can be abused to upload any type of file to a SharePoint list item when files are being uploaded via the browser. This is probably currently a bug in SharePoint, since the same is not possible when you use InfoPath Filler 2013. While the file may not appear in the picture control after you have selected it, its base64 encoded string should be present in the form, so that it can be uploaded to SharePoint; just remember to enter the correct file extension for the file in the **fileName** text box. For example, try using the solution above to upload a Word document (DOCX file) instead of an image.

68 Select and display an image attached to a SharePoint list item

Problem

You have a SharePoint list that contains items with images attached to them. You want to be able to retrieve and display the images that are linked to a particular SharePoint list item.

Solution

You can use the **SiteData** web service of SharePoint to retrieve images that are linked to a SharePoint list item.

Suppose you have a SharePoint list named **OfficeApplications** as described in *Create a SharePoint list form for an existing SharePoint list* in recipe *2 Customize a SharePoint list form from within InfoPath* which you want to use to retrieve images.

To select and display an image attached to a SharePoint list item:

1. In SharePoint, navigate to the **OfficeApplications** list, click **List ➤ Settings ➤ List Settings**, and then copy the GUID that is listed after the **List** query string parameter in the URL in the browser's address

bar. It should look something like the following:

```
%7B88B1D952%2DE14A%2D470B%2D901C%2D156F4C315822%7D
```

2. Convert the **%7B** characters to **{**, **%2D** to **-**, and **%7D** to **}**. The resulting list GUID should now resemble the following:

   ```
   {88B1D952-E14A-470B-901C-156F4C315822}
   ```

   Copy it to the Windows clipboard.

3. In InfoPath, create a new SharePoint form library form template or use an existing one.

4. Add a **Receive** data connection to the **OfficeApplications** SharePoint list to the form template as described in *Use a SharePoint list data connection* in recipe *43 2 Ways to retrieve data from a SharePoint list*. Ensure that you select **ID** and **Title** as fields to include in the data source, and that you leave the **Automatically retrieve data when form is opened** check box selected.

5. Select **Data ➤ Get External Data ➤ From Other Sources ➤ From XML File** and follow the instructions to add an XML data connection for an XML file named **OAHelper.xml** that has the following contents:

   ```
   <officeApplications>
     <officeApplication/>
   </officeApplications>
   ```

   to the form template. Ensure that you leave the **Automatically retrieve data when form is opened** check box selected on the data connection and that you name the data connection **OAHelper**.

6. On the **Fields** task pane, select **OAHelper (Secondary)** from the drop-down list box, right-click the **officeApplication** field, and then drag-and-drop it onto the view of the form template. Select **Drop-Down List Box** from the context menu that appears when you drop it.

7. Populate the **officeApplication** drop-down list box control with items from the **OfficeApplications** secondary data source by selecting the **d:SharePointListItem_RW** repeating group node that is located under the **dataFields** group node for the **Entries** property, the **ID** field for

the **Value** property, and the **Title** field for the **Display name** property of the drop-down list box.

8. Select **Data ➤ Get External Data ➤ From Web Service ➤ From SOAP Web Service**.
9. On the **Data Connection Wizard**, enter the URL of the **SiteData** web service that is located on the same site where the SharePoint list is located and where you will be publishing the InfoPath form template. For example:

```
http://servername/sitename/_vti_bin/SiteData.asmx
```

where **servername** is the name of the SharePoint server, and **sitename** is the name of the site where the SharePoint list is located. Click **Next**.

10. On the **Data Connection Wizard**, select **GetAttachments** from the list of operations, and click **Next**.
11. On the **Data Connection Wizard**, leave all of the parameters as is, and click **Next**.
12. On the **Data Connection Wizard**, leave the **Store a copy of the data in the form template** check box deselected, and click **Next**.
13. On the **Data Connection Wizard**, leave the name of the data connection as **GetAttachments**, deselect the **Automatically retrieve data when form is opened** check box, and click **Finish**.
14. On the **Fields** task pane, select **GetAttachments (Secondary)** from the drop-down list box, expand all of the group nodes under the **dataFields** group node, right-click the **string** repeating field that is located under the **vAttachments** group node, and then drag-and-drop it onto the view of the form template. Select **Repeating Table** from the context menu that appears when you drop it.
15. Right-click the text box within the repeating table, and then select **Change Control ➤ Picture** from the context menu that appears.
16. Add an **Action** rule to the **officeApplication** drop-down list box with a **Condition** that says:

```
officeApplication is not blank
```

and that has 3 actions that say:

```
Set a field's value: strListName = "{88B1D952-E14A-470B-901C-156F4C315822}"
```

where **strListName** is a field that is located under the **GetAttachments** group node under the **queryFields** group node in the **GetAttachments** secondary data source and `{88B1D952-E14A-470B-901C-156F4C315822}` is the GUID of the list you retrieved in step 2.

```
Set a field's value: strItemId = .
```

where **strItemId** is a field that is located under the **GetAttachments** group node under the **queryFields** group node in the **GetAttachments** secondary data source and the dot (**.**) represents the **officeApplication** field that is located in the **OAHelper** secondary data source and that is bound to the drop-down list box.

```
Query using a data connection: GetAttachments
```

This action queries the **GetAttachments** secondary data source to be able to retrieve the images pertaining to the selected list item in the drop-down list box.

17. Place the cursor behind the picture control within the repeating table, and then click **Table Tools ➤ Layout ➤ Rows & Columns ➤ Insert Right** to add a column to the repeating table.
18. Add a **Button** control to the table column you just added and label it **Select**.
19. Add a second **Picture** control **As a link** to the view of the form template and name it **selectedImage**.
20. With the picture control still selected, select **Control Tools ➤ Properties ➤ Modify ➤ Read-Only** to make the picture control read-only.
21. Add an **Action** rule to the **Select** button with an action that says:

```
Set a field's value: selectedImage = .
```

where **selectedImage** is the field that is bound to the second picture control and the dot (**.**) represents the **string** field within the repeating table that is located in the same row as where the **Select** button was clicked.

22. If your SharePoint environment is configured to use Claims Based authentication as opposed to Windows Classic authentication and the form is going to be filled out through the browser, you must set up UDC authentication for the **GetAttachments** data connection that makes the web service call as described in *Configure a web service data connection for a web browser form* in the Appendix. But before you do this, test the form in InfoPath Filler 2013 to ensure that the functionality is working properly.
23. Publish the form template to a SharePoint form library.

In SharePoint, navigate to the form library where you published the form template and add a new form. When the form opens, the drop-down list box should contain the names of Office applications. Select an Office application from the drop-down list box. The images that are attached to the SharePoint list item should appear in the repeating table. Click on the **Select** button behind one of the images. The selected image should appear in the second picture control.

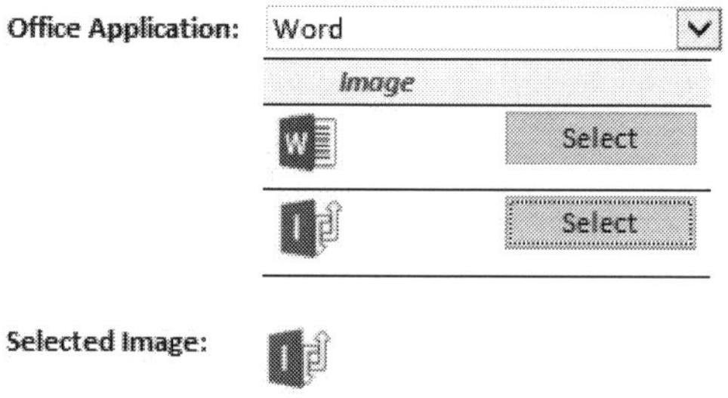

Figure 172. The InfoPath form displaying two images attached to a SharePoint list item.

Discussion

In the solution described above, you used the **GetAttachments** operation of the **SiteData** web service to retrieve one or more files that were attached to a particular item in a SharePoint list. Note that while this solution assumes that those attachments are images, they could be any type of file. But because a picture control is used here to display the attachments, if an attached file is not an image, the default image icon of InfoPath would be displayed for it. You could also replace the picture control with a hyperlink control to show links to files, which users can then click to download or open attachments.

In the solution described above you also used a secondary data source (**OAHelper**) to be able to add a drop-down list box to the view of the form template and display SharePoint list items in it without having the selected item be saved in the form when the form is saved or submitted. The sole purpose of the drop-down list box is to select a SharePoint list item and retrieve the images attached to that SharePoint list item. The actual image selection and storage takes place when a user clicks on a **Select** button in the repeating table. The URL of the selected image is then copied over to the second picture control where it is permanently stored in the form when the form is saved or submitted.

69 Upload an image to a picture library using an InfoPath form

Problem

You want to be able to upload an image that is stored in a picture control on an InfoPath form to a SharePoint picture library.

Solution

You can use the **Imaging** web service of SharePoint to upload an image to a picture library.

To upload an image to a SharePoint picture library using an InfoPath form:

1. In SharePoint, create a new **Picture Library** named **MyPics** or use an existing picture library.
2. In InfoPath, create a new SharePoint form library form template or use an existing one.
3. Add three **Text Box** controls named **listName**, **folder**, and **fileName**, respectively, to the view of the form template.
4. Add a **Picture** control named **bytes** to the view of the form template. Select the **Included in the form** option on the **Insert Picture Control** dialog box when you add the picture control.

5. Add an **Option Button** control named **overwrite** with 2 options to the view of the form template, label the first option **Yes** and the second option **No**, and change the **Value when selected** property of the **Yes** option to **true** (so type the text **true** in the text box for the property) and that of the **No** option to **false**, and select the **This button is selected by default** check box for the **No** option.
6. Add a **Button** control to the view of the form template and label it **Upload Image**.
7. Select **Data ➤ Submit Form ➤ To Other Locations ➤ To Web Service**.
8. On the **Data Connection Wizard**, enter the URL of the **Imaging** web service that is located on the same site where the picture library is located and where you will be publishing the InfoPath form template. For example:

   ```
   http://servername/sitename/_vti_bin/Imaging.asmx
   ```

   where **servername** is the name of the SharePoint server, and **sitename** is the name of the site where the picture library is located. Click **Next**.
9. On the **Data Connection Wizard**, select **Upload** from the list of operations, and click **Next**.
10. On the **Data Connection Wizard**, select **strListName** in the list of parameters, and then click the button behind the **Field or group** text box.
11. On the **Select a Field or Group** dialog box, select **listName**, and click **OK**.
12. On the **Data Connection Wizard**, leave **Text and child elements only** selected in the **Include** drop-down list box.
13. Repeat steps 10, 11, and 12 for the other parameters, but then bind **strFolder** to **folder**, **bytes** to **bytes**, **fileName** to **fileName**, and **fOverWriteIfExists** to **overwrite**. Click **Next** when you are done.
14. On the **Data Connection Wizard**, name the data connection **UploadImage**, leave the **Set as the default submit connection** check box selected, and then click **Finish**.

15. Add an **Action** rule to the **Upload Image** button with an action that says:

```
Submit using a data connection: UploadImage
```

16. If your SharePoint environment is configured to use Claims Based authentication as opposed to Windows Classic authentication and the form is going to be filled out through the browser, you must set up UDC authentication for the **UploadImage** data connection that makes the web service call as described in *Configure a web service data connection for a web browser form* in the Appendix. But before you do this, test the form in InfoPath Filler 2013 to ensure that the functionality is working properly.
17. Publish the form template to a SharePoint form library.

In SharePoint, navigate to the form library where you published the form template and add a new form. When the form opens, enter **MyPics** (or the name of the picture library from step 1) in the **listName** text box, leave the **folder** text box empty (or enter the name of a subfolder in the picture library if you want to upload the image to an existing subfolder), click the picture control and select the image you want to upload, and enter the file name of the image including its file extension in the **fileName** text box. If an image with the file name you entered already exists in the picture library, select the **Yes** option to overwrite the image; otherwise leave the **No** option selected. Note that the file name does not need to be the same as the original file name of the image. Click the **Upload Image** button to upload the image to the picture library.

Note: The same warning mentioned at the end of the discussion section of recipe *67 Upload an image as an attachment to a SharePoint list item* applies to the solution described above for picture libraries.

70 Select and display an image from a picture library

Problem

You have a SharePoint picture library from which you want to retrieve all of the images and then click a button to select one of those images.

Solution

You can use the **ListData** REST web service to retrieve images from a SharePoint picture library and then display those images in a repeating table for selection.

To select and display an image from a SharePoint picture library:

1. In SharePoint, ensure that you have a picture library that contains a couple of images.
2. In InfoPath, create a new SharePoint form library form template or use an existing one.
3. Select **Data** ➤ **Get External Data** ➤ **From Web Service** ➤ **From REST Web Service**.
4. On the **Data Connection Wizard**, enter the URL of the **ListData** REST web service that is located on the same site where the picture library is located and where you will be publishing the InfoPath form template. For example:

   ```
   http://servername/sitename/_vti_bin/ListData.svc/MyPics?$select
   =Path,Name
   ```

   where **servername** is the name of the SharePoint server, and **sitename** is the name of the site where a picture library named **MyPics** is located. Click **Next**.
5. On the **Data Connection Wizard**, enter a name for the data connection (for example **GetPictures**), leave the **Automatically retrieve data when form is opened** check box selected, and click **Finish**.
6. Add a **Drop-Down List Box** control to the view of the form template and name it **selectedImage**.
7. Populate the drop-down list box control with items from the **GetPictures** secondary data source by selecting the **entry** repeating group node for the **Entries** property and the **d:Name** field that is located under the **m:properties** group node under the **entry** repeating group node for both the **Value** and the **Display name** properties of the drop-down list box.

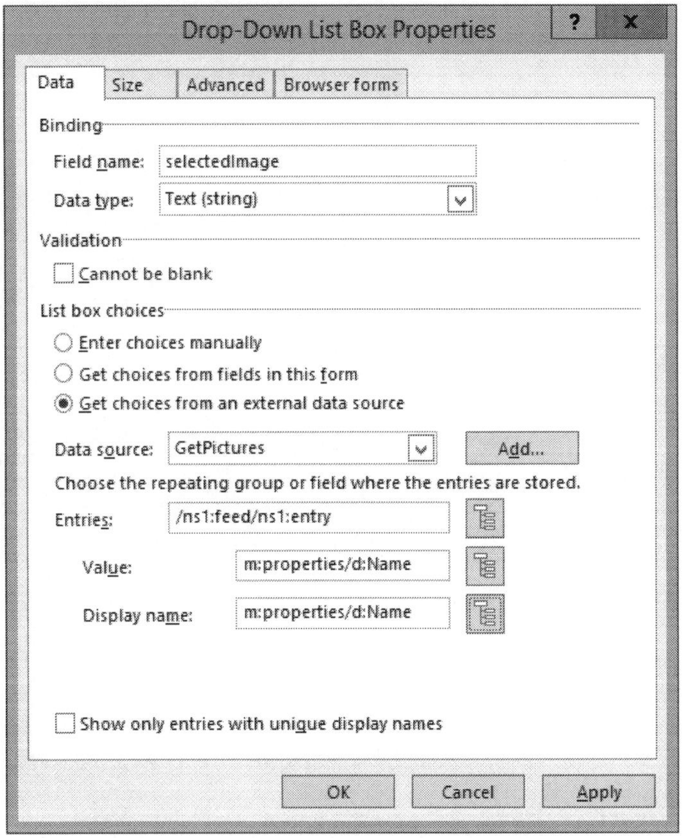

Figure 173. Settings on the Drop-Down List Box Properties dialog box in InfoPath.

8. Add a **Picture** control **As a link** to the view of the form template and name it **image**.
9. With the picture control still selected, select **Control Tools ➤ Properties ➤ Modify ➤ Read-Only** to make the picture control read-only.
10. Add an **Action** rule to the **selectedImage** drop-down list box with an action that says:

```
Set a field's value: image = concat("http://servername", Path,
"/", .)
```

where **servername** is the name of the SharePoint server, **Path** is a field that is located under the **m:properties** group node under the **entry** repeating group node in the **GetPictures** secondary data source, and the dot (.) represents the **selectedImage** field that is bound to the drop-down list box.

11. If your SharePoint environment is configured to use Claims Based authentication as opposed to Windows Classic authentication and the form is going to be filled out through the browser, you must set up UDC authentication for the **GetPictures** data connection that makes the web service call as described in *Configure a web service data connection for a web browser form* in the Appendix. But before you do this, test the form in InfoPath Filler 2013 to ensure that the functionality is working properly.
12. Publish the form template to a SharePoint form library.

In SharePoint, navigate to the form library where you published the form template and add a new form. When the form opens, the drop-down list box should contain the names of images. Select an image from the drop-down list box. The selected image should appear in the picture control.

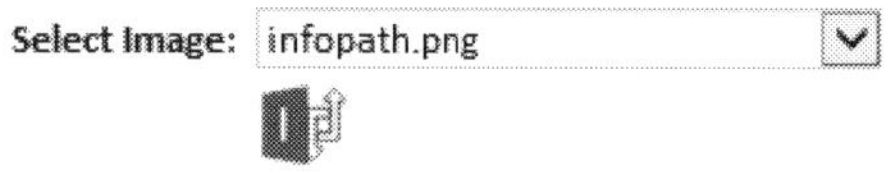

Figure 174. The InfoPath form displaying an image selected from the picture library.

Discussion

When you create a SharePoint list data connection to a SharePoint picture library in InfoPath, it does not normally offer a field that contains the URL to an image within the picture library. So in the solution described above, you used the **ListData** REST web service to retrieve the file name of an image to be able to construct an URL and use this with a picture control to display an image on an InfoPath form. The resulting XML of a call to this web service has a **Name** element that contains the file name (including the file extension) and a **Path** element in which the URL of the picture library where the file is located is stored.

71 Sequentially navigate through images in a picture library

Problem

You want to be able to select an image from a SharePoint picture library by sequentially clicking through all of the images in the picture library until you find the one you are looking for.

Solution

You can use the **ListData** REST web service to retrieve the URLs of all of the images in a SharePoint picture library and then use a counter to sequentially navigate through the images.

To sequentially navigate through images in a SharePoint picture library:

1. Follow steps 1 through 5 of recipe *70 Select and display an image from a picture library*.
2. Add a **Picture** control **As a link** to the view of the form template and name it **selectedImage**.
3. With the picture control still selected, select **Control Tools ➤ Properties ➤ Modify ➤ Read-Only** to make the picture control read-only.
4. On the **Fields** task pane, add a hidden **Field (element)** of type **Whole Number (integer)** to the Main data source, name it **position**, and set its **Default Value** to be equal to **1**. This field will serve as a counter for sequentially navigating through the images in the picture library.
5. Add two **Button** controls to the view of the form template and label them **Previous** and **Next**, respectively.
6. Add an **Action** rule to the **Previous** button with a **Condition** that says:

   ```
   position > 1
   ```

   and with an action that says:

   ```
   Set a field's value: position = position - 1
   ```

   This rule decreases the value of the **position** field by 1 every time the

Previous button is clicked and only if the value of the **position** field is greater than 1.

7. Add an **Action** rule to the **Next** button with a **Condition** that says:

```
position < count(entry)
```

where **entry** is the repeating group node that is located under the **feed** group node in the **GetPictures** secondary data source.

And add an action that says:

```
Set a field's value: position = position + 1
```

This rule increases the value of the **position** field by 1 every time the **Next** button is clicked and only if the value of the **position** field is less than the total amount of items in the SharePoint picture library.

8. Set the **Default Value** of the **selectedImage** field that is bound to the picture control to be equal to the following formula:

```
concat("http://servername",
xdXDocument:GetDOM("GetPictures")/ns1:feed/ns1:entry[count(prec
eding-sibling::ns1:entry) + 1 = xdXDocument:get-
DOM()/my:myFields/my:position]/m:properties/d:Path, "/",
xdXDocument:GetDOM("GetPictures")/ns1:feed/ns1:entry[count(prec
eding-sibling::ns1:entry) + 1 = xdXDocument:get-
DOM()/my:myFields/my:position]/m:properties/d:Name)
```

where **servername** is the name of the SharePoint server, and **GetPictures** is the name of the data source for the SharePoint picture library. This formula returns the concatenation of the **Path** and **Name** fields in the **GetPictures** secondary data source with a filter on the value specified in the **position** field to construct the URL of the image that should be displayed. The formula uses the **preceding-sibling** XPath axis and the **count()** function to count the amount of **entry** nodes preceding an **entry** node to find the position of an image in the list of images. Ensure that the **Refresh value when formula is recalculated** check box is selected on the **Field or Group Properties** dialog box for the **selectedImage** field.

9. Add a **Formatting** rule to the **Previous** button with a **Condition** that says:

```
position = 1
```

and that has a formatting of **Disable this control**. Here, **position** is the hidden field in the Main data source. This formatting rule disables the button when the first image is being displayed.

10. Add a **Formatting** rule to the **Next** button with a **Condition** that says:

```
position = count(entry)
```

and that has a formatting of **Disable this control**. Here, **position** is the hidden field in the Main data source and **entry** is the repeating group node that is located under the **feed** group node in the **GetPictures** secondary data source. This formatting rule disables the button when the last image is being displayed.

11. If your SharePoint environment is configured to use Claims Based authentication as opposed to Windows Classic authentication and the form is going to be filled out through the browser, you must set up UDC authentication for the **GetPictures** data connection that makes the web service call as described in *Configure a web service data connection for a web browser form* in the Appendix. But before you do this, test the form in InfoPath Filler 2013 to ensure that the functionality is working properly.

12. Publish the form template to a SharePoint form library.

In SharePoint, navigate to the form library where you published the form template and add a new form. When the form opens, the first image in the library should appear, and when you click on the **Previous** and **Next** buttons, you should be able to sequentially navigate through the images in the picture library.

Person/Group Picker

The person/group picker control (or people picker control) in InfoPath allows you to select one or more people from a SharePoint site.

Figure 175. Person/Group Picker control in InfoPath 2013.

The way the person/group picker control works is that you can either type in values that represent users or groups into the text box of the person/group picker control or click the **Browse** button (the second button behind the text box) to open a dialog box to search for and select users or groups.

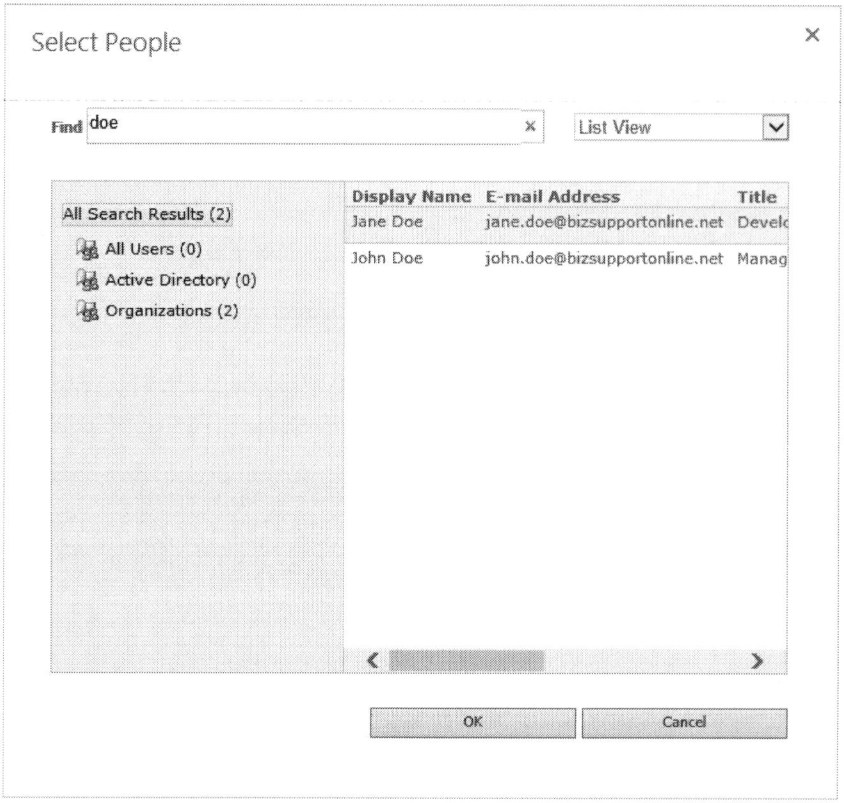

Figure 176. The Select People dialog in SharePoint 2013.

If you type names directly into the text box without performing a search via the **Select People** dialog, you can check whether those names are valid by clicking on the **Check Names** button (the first button behind the text box) of the person/group picker control.

When you place a person/group picker control on an InfoPath browser-compatible form template without explicitly configuring the control, publish the form template to SharePoint, and then open forms in the browser, the person/group picker control automatically uses the context of the SharePoint site where the form is located to find users and groups.

However, if you want to use the person/group picker control on a form in InfoPath Filler 2013, you must explicitly configure it to get its list of users and groups from a specific SharePoint site. You can specify the SharePoint site the person/group picker control should retrieve its list of users and groups from via the **SharePoint Server** tab on the **Person/Group Picker Properties** dialog box.

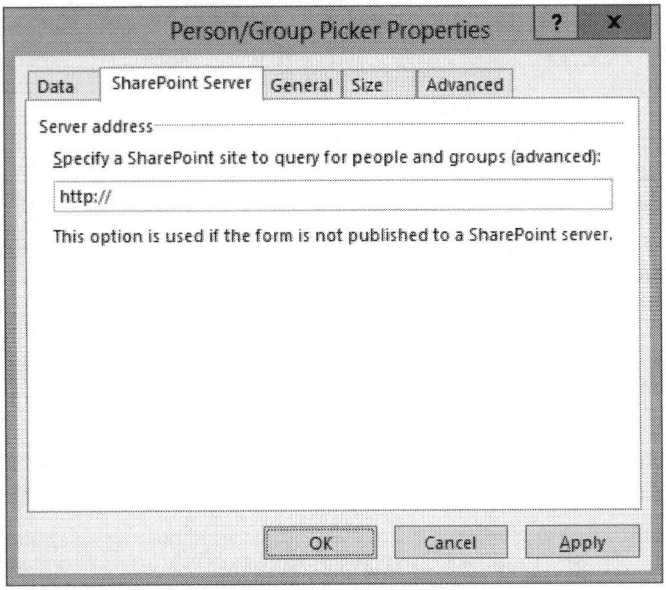

Figure 177. SharePoint Server tab on the Person/Group Picker Properties dialog box.

The person/group picker control allows you to select only one user by default, but you can specify whether the control should allow multiple users/groups to be entered or selected by selecting the **Allow multiple selections** check box on the **General** tab of the **Person/Group Picker Properties** dialog box.

Other configuration settings include:

- Specifying whether the control should allow people only or a combination of people and groups to be selected.
- Specifying whether all users should be shown or only users from a specific SharePoint group.

And finally, to make a person/group picker control mandatory, you can select the **Cannot be blank** check box that is located on the **Data** tab of the **Person/Group Picker Properties** dialog box or that is part of the **Modify** group on the **Properties** tab on the Ribbon in InfoPath.

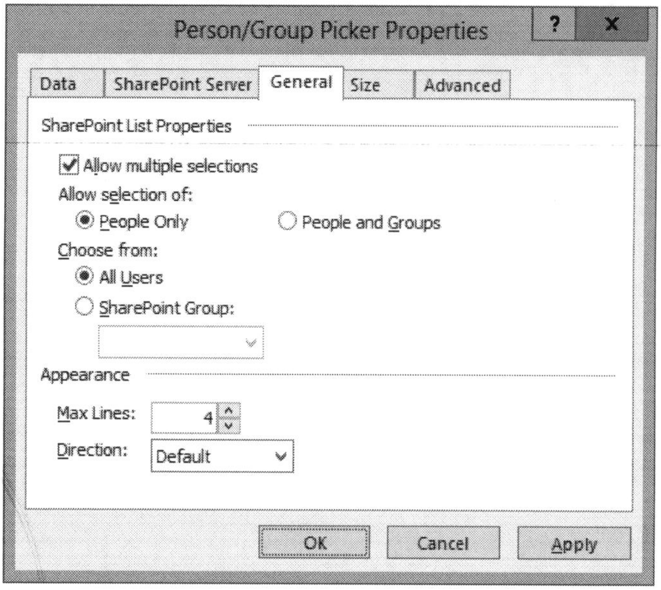

Figure 178. General tab of the Person/Group Picker Properties dialog box.

72 Display basic info of a user from a people picker in text boxes

Problem

You have a person/group picker control on an InfoPath form and want to use it to select a person and then display basic information such as the person's email address and department in text boxes.

Solution

You can use the **User Information List** SharePoint list to look up basic information for a selected person. Note that user information must have already been populated in SharePoint user profiles for this solution to work.

To display basic information of a user from a people picker in text boxes:

1. In InfoPath, create a new SharePoint form library form template or use an existing one.
2. Add a **Person/Group Picker** control to the view of the form template.
3. Add two **Text Box** controls named **email** and **department** to the view of the form template.
4. Add a **Button** control to the view of the form template and label it **Display User Info**.
5. Add a **Receive** data connection to the **User Information List** SharePoint list that is located on the site from which the person/group picker control should get its information and where you will be publishing the form template (also see *Use a SharePoint list data connection* in recipe *43 2 Ways to retrieve data from a SharePoint list*). Ensure that you select **Account**, **Work_email (Work email)** and **Department** as fields to include in the data source, and that you deselect the **Automatically retrieve data when form is opened** check box.
6. Add an **Action** rule to the **Display User Info** button with a **Condition** that says:

   ```
   AccountId is not blank
   ```

   where **AccountId** is located under the **pc:Person** repeating group node in the Main data source.

   And add 4 actions that say:

   ```
   Set a field's value: Name = AccountId
   ```

   where **Name** represents the **Account** field that is located under the **q:SharePointListItem_RW** group node under the **queryFields** group node in the **User Information List** secondary data source and **AccountId** is located under the **pc:Person** repeating group node in the Main data source.

   ```
   Query using a data connection: User Information List
   ```

   This action queries the **User Information List** secondary data source to retrieve the information for the user that was specified through the **Account** field.

```
Set a field's value: department = Department
```

where **department** is located in the Main data source and **Department** is located under the **d:SharePointListItem_RW** repeating group node under the **dataFields** group node in the **User Information List** secondary data source.

```
Set a field's value: email = EMail
```

where **email** is located in the Main data source and **EMail** represents the **Work email** field that is located under the **d:SharePointListItem_RW** repeating group node under the **dataFields** group node in the **User Information List** secondary data source.

7. Publish the form template to a SharePoint form library.

In SharePoint, navigate to the form library where you published the form template and add a new form. When the form opens, select a user from the person/group picker control and then click the button to check names. If the user is found to be a valid user, click the **Display User Info** button. The email address and department of the user you selected should appear in the text boxes.

Figure 179. The InfoPath form displaying basic information for a selected user.

Discussion

In the solution described above, you made use of the **User Information List** SharePoint list (see the discussion section of recipe *48 Display a list of people from the current user's department* for more information about the **User Information List** SharePoint list) to look up the email address and the department of a user. If you need more information about a user that the **User Information List** does not contain, you can use the User Profile Service to retrieve such information (see for example recipe *75 Get the details of the manager of a selected person in a people picker*).

73 Limit a person/group picker to a maximum of 3 selected people

Problem

You have a person/group picker control on an InfoPath form and want to use it to select one or more users, but you want to limit the selection of users to a maximum of 3.

Solution

You can use a text box that pulls data in from a person/group picker control to perform data validation for the person/group picker control and limit the amount of selections in the person/group picker control to a maximum of 3.

To limit a person/group picker control to a maximum of 3 selected people:

1. In InfoPath, create a new SharePoint form library form template or use an existing one.
2. Add a **Person/Group Picker** control to the view of the form template.
3. Open the **Person/Group Picker Properties** dialog box and then on the **General** tab, select the **Allow multiple selections** check box and leave the **People Only** option selected. With this you have configured the person/group picker control to allow multiple users to be selected. Click **OK** to close the dialog box.
4. Add a **Section** control to the view of the form template and write the text "Only 3 people max allowed" within the section control. Change the font color of the text to red. You are going to use this section control to display an error message to the user.
5. Add a **Text Box** control to the view of the form template, name it **peopleCount**, and change its data type to **Whole Number (integer)**.

6. Add a **Formatting** rule to the section control with a **Condition** that says:

   ```
   peopleCount ≤ 3
   ```

   and with a formatting of **Hide this control**. This formatting rule hides the section control if 3 people or less have been selected in the people picker.

7. Add a **Formatting** rule to the **peopleCount** text box control with a **The expression** condition that says:

   ```
   true()
   ```

   and with a formatting of **Hide this control**. This formatting rule always hides the text box control. The text box control needs to be present on the view (but remain invisible to the user) for the validation rule that you are going to set on it to work.

8. Add a **Validation** rule to the **peopleCount** text box with a **Condition** that says:

   ```
   peopleCount > 3
   ```

   and a **ScreenTip** that says: "Only 3 people max allowed". This rule prevents the form from being submitted if more than 3 people have been selected in the person/group picker control.

9. Set the **Default Value** of the **peopleCount** text box to be equal to the following formula:

   ```
   count(Person)
   ```

   or

   ```
   count(../my:group/pc:Person)
   ```

   if you have the **Edit XPath (advanced)** check box selected on the **Insert Formula** dialog box. **Person** refers to the repeating group node of the person/group picker control. This formula returns the amount of people that have been selected in the person/group picker control. Ensure that the **Refresh value when formula is recalculated** check box is selected on the **Properties** dialog box.

10. Publish the form template to a SharePoint form library.

In SharePoint, navigate to the form library where you published the form template and add a new form. When the form opens, enter more than 3 user names in the person/group picker control and click the button that checks names. The section control should appear. If you click the **Save** command on the Ribbon, a message box should appear. You can still go ahead and save the form if you wish. However, had you enabled the form to be submitted, then you would not be able to submit the form until you corrected the error. Remove one or more users from the person/group picker control and click away. The section control displaying the error should disappear.

Discussion

Because you cannot add **Validation** rules to a person/group picker control, the solution described above is a workaround for performing data validation on a people picker control. In this case, you added a text box control that pulled in data from the people picker control and performed the validation for the people picker control. You also used a section control that depended on the value of the text box control to display an error message to the user. Note that you can use this technique to perform any other type of validation on the data entered in a people picker control.

74 Get email addresses from a person/group picker

Problem

You have a person/group picker control on an InfoPath form and want to use it to select one or more users and then store the email address(es) of the selected user(s) in a hidden field that can be used to send emails to the selected user(s).

Solution

You can use the **eval()** function and the **User Information List** SharePoint list to look up email addresses for a selected group of people and concatenate them into a string separated by semi-colons. Note that email addresses must have already been populated in SharePoint user profiles for this solution to work.

To generate a list of email addresses from a person/group picker control:

1. In InfoPath, create a new SharePoint form library form template or use an existing one.
2. Add a **Person/Group Picker** control to the view of the form template.
3. Open the **Person/Group Picker Properties** dialog box and then on the **General** tab, select the **Allow multiple selections** check box and leave the **People Only** option selected. With this you have configured the person/group picker control to allow multiple users to be selected. Click **OK** to close the dialog box.
4. On the **Fields** task pane, add a hidden **Field (element)** with the data type **Text (string)** and the name **emailAddresses** to the Main data source.
5. Add a **Receive** data connection to the **User Information List** SharePoint list on the site from which the person/group picker control should get its information and where you will be publishing the form (also see *Use a SharePoint list data connection* in recipe *43 2 Ways to retrieve data from a SharePoint list*). Ensure that you select **Account** and **Work_email (Work email)** as fields to include in the data source, and that you leave the **Automatically retrieve data when form is opened** check box selected. You will use this data connection later to set the default value of the **emailAddresses** field. When the **emailAddresses** field retrieves its data from the **User Information List**, which takes place immediately after you select users from the person/group picker control, the **User Information List** should already contain data so that lookups can be performed. This is why you must populate the secondary data source for the **User Information List** either when the form opens (as you have done in this step) or ensure that you run a **Query for data** action rule before any users are selected from the person/group picker control.
6. Set the **Default Value** of the **emailAddresses** field to be equal to the following formula:

```
eval(eval(EMail[Name = AccountId and . != ""], 'concat(., ";
")'), "..")
```

or

```
xdMath:Eval(xdMath:Eval(xdXDocument:GetDOM("User Information
List")/dfs:myFields/dfs:dataFields/d:SharePointListItem_RW/d:EM
ail[../d:Name = xdXDocument:get-
DOM()/my:myFields/my:group/pc:Person/pc:AccountId and . != ""],
'concat(., "; ")'), "..")
```

if you have the **Edit XPath (advanced)** check box selected on the **Insert Formula** dialog box. Here, the inner **eval()** function returns the **Work email** fields that are located under the **d:SharePointListItem_RW** repeating group node under the **dataFields** group node in the **User Information List** secondary data source, filtered by the **Account** field in the secondary data source being equal to the **AccountId** field of the person/group picker in the Main data source and filtered by the value of the **Work email** field not being blank. The expression in the **eval()** function uses the **concat()** function to append a semi-colon to each email address returned:

```
eval(EMail[Name = AccountId and . != ""], 'concat(., "; ")')
```

You can construct the expression for the inner **eval()** function using the dialog boxes with the **Filter Data** option in InfoPath. Once you have constructed the inner **eval()** function, you can place the outer **eval()** function around the inner **eval()** function to return the value of the anonymous parent (`".."`), which is a concatenated string of all of the parent's children (email addresses with semi-colons in this case).

```
eval( [inner eval function goes here] , "..")
```

Ensure that the **Refresh value when formula is recalculated** check box is selected on the **Field or Group Properties** dialog box for the **emailAddresses** field.

7. On the **Fields** task pane, drag-and-drop the **emailAddresses** field onto the view of the form template to temporarily bind it to a text box control, so that you can display and check its value.
8. Publish the form template to a SharePoint form library.

In SharePoint, navigate to the form library where you published the form template and add a new form. When the form opens, enter a few usernames in the person/group picker control and then click the button that checks names. The email addresses of the users you entered should appear as a concatenated string of email addresses separated by semi-colons in the **emailAddresses** field.

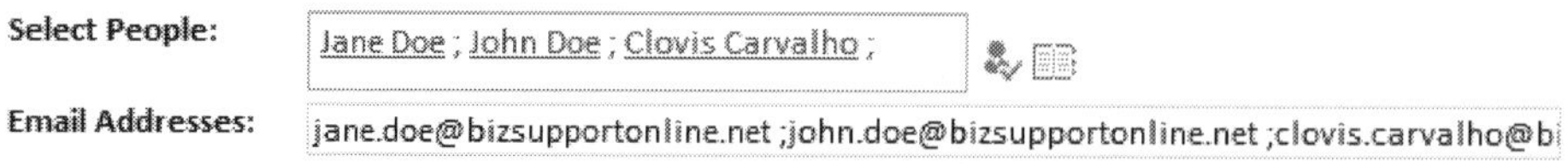

Figure 180. The InfoPath form displaying the email addresses of the selected users.

Now you should be able to use the concatenated string of email addresses as the value of the **To** field of for example an email submit data connection.

Discussion

In the solution described above, you made use of the **User Information List** SharePoint list (see the discussion section of recipe *48 Display a list of people from the current user's department* for more information about the **User Information List** SharePoint list) to look up email addresses of users. You also used the **eval()** function to generate a list of email addresses. The **eval()** function returns the values of a field or group. It takes two arguments, of which the second argument defines the expression to calculate for the field or group. You can use it on a repeating group or a repeating field to concatenate values of all of the fields or fields within the group. In the solution described above, it was used in a nested way to be able to not only concatenate email addresses, but also add semi-colons to separate those email addresses.

75 Get the details of the manager of a selected person in a people picker

Problem

You have a person/group picker control on an InfoPath form and want to retrieve the first name, last name, and email address of the manager of a user when you click a button.

Solution

You can use web service operations of the User Profile Service of SharePoint to retrieve the details of a person's manager.

To get the details of the manager of a selected person in a person/group picker control:

1. In InfoPath, create a new SharePoint form library form template or use an existing one.
2. Add a **Person/Group Picker** control to the view of the form template. Do not configure the control to **Allow multiple selections**; the control should allow only one user to be selected.
3. Add a **Button** control to the view of the form template and label it **Get Manager Details**.
4. Add a **Text Box** control to the view of the form template and name it **manager**.
5. Select **Data ➤ Get External Data ➤ From Web Service ➤ From SOAP Web Service**.
6. On the **Data Connection Wizard**, enter the URL of the User Profile Service. For example:

   ```
   http://servername/sitename/_vti_bin/UserProfileService.asmx
   ```

   where **servername** is the name of the SharePoint server and **sitename** is the name of the SharePoint site where you will be publishing the form template. Click **Next**.
7. On the **Data Connection Wizard**, select **GetUserPropertyByAccountName** from the list of operations, and click **Next**.

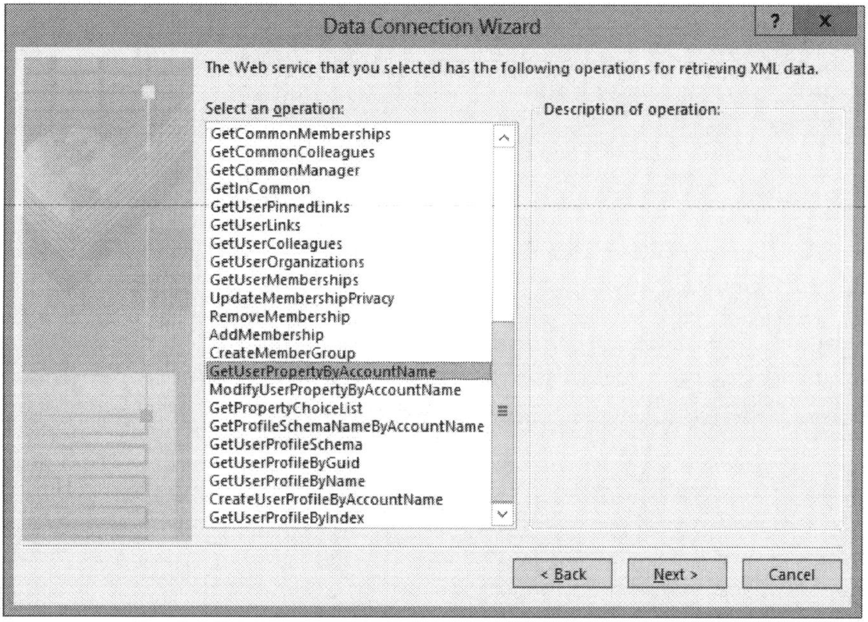

Figure 181. Selecting the GetUserPropertyByAccountName operation.

8. On the **Data Connection Wizard**, leave the parameter values as is, and click **Next**. You will be setting these values later through rules.
9. On the **Data Connection Wizard**, leave the **Store a copy of the data in the form template** check box deselected, and click **Next**.
10. On the **Data Connection Wizard**, leave the name of the data connection as **GetUserPropertyByAccountName**, deselect the **Automatically retrieve data when form is opened** check box, and click **Finish**.
11. Repeat steps 5 through 10 to add a second SOAP web service data connection, but this time, select **GetUserProfileByName** as the operation and name the data connection **GetUserProfileByName**.

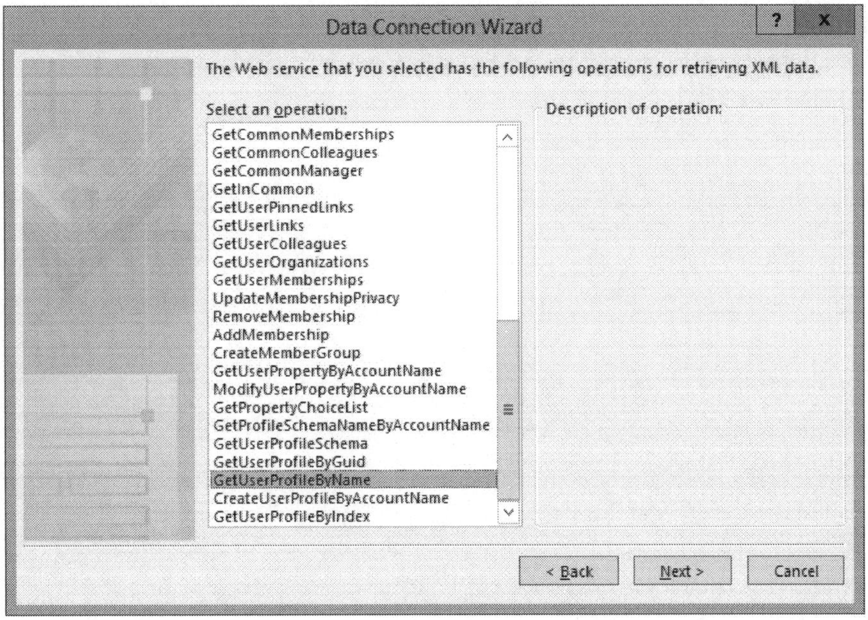

Figure 182. Selecting the GetUserProfileByName operation.

12. Add an **Action** rule to the **Get Manager Details** button with a **Condition** that says:

```
AccountId is not blank
```

where **AccountId** is the **AccountId** field of the person/group picker control.

And add the following 6 actions to the rule:

```
Set a field's value: accountName = AccountId
```

where **accountName** is a field that is located under the **GetUserPropertyByAccountName** group node under the **queryFields** group node in the **GetUserPropertyByAccountName** secondary data source, and **AccountId** is the **AccountId** field of the person/group picker control.

```
Set a field's value: propertyName = "Manager"
```

where **propertyName** is a field that is located under the

GetUserPropertyByAccountName group node under the **queryFields** group node in the **GetUserPropertyByAccountName** secondary data source, and **Manager** is a static piece of text that represents the name of the property for which you want to retrieve a value.

```
Query using a data connection: GetUserPropertyByAccountName
```

This action calls the **GetUserPropertyByAccountName** operation of the User Profile Service and passes the values of the **accountName** and **propertyName** parameters to it to be able to retrieve the value of the **Manager** property, which when returned should be located under the **dataFields** group node in the **GetUserPropertyByAccountName** secondary data source.

```
Set a field's value: AccountName = Value
```

where **AccountName** is a field that is located under the **GetUserProfileByName** group node under the **queryFields** group node in the **GetUserProfileByName** secondary data source, and **Value** is a field that is located under the **ValueData** repeating group node under the **Values** group node under the **GetUserPropertyByAccountNameResult** group node under the **GetUserPropertyByAccountNameResponse** group node under the **dataFields** group node in the **GetUserPropertyByAccountName** secondary data source. This action sets the value of the **AccountName** parameter of the **GetUserProfileByName** operation to be equal to the value of the **Manager** property you just retrieved when you queried the **GetUserPropertyByAccountName** data connection. Note that while **Value** is located under a repeating group node named **ValueData**, you queried the User Profile Service to retrieve only one property (**Manager**), so **ValueData** should contain only one row of data and the formula should return the value of the **Value** field in the first row of data.

```
Query using a data connection: GetUserProfileByName
```

This action calls the **GetUserProfileByName** operation of the User Profile Service and passes the value of the **AccountName** field to be able to retrieve the values of all of the properties of the manager.

```
Set a field's value: manager = normalize-
space(concat(Value[Name = "FirstName"], " ", Value[Name =
"LastName"], " [", Value[Name = "WorkEmail"], "]"))
```

where **manager** is the field that is bound to the text box and that is located in the Main data source, **Value** is a field that is located under the **ValueData** repeating group node under the **Values** group node under the **PropertyData** repeating group node under the **GetUserProfileByNameResult** group node under the **GetUserProfileByNameResponse** group node under the **dataFields** group node in the **GetUserProfileByName** secondary data source, and **Name** is a field that is located under the **PropertyData** repeating group node under the **GetUserProfileByNameResult** group node under the **GetUserProfileByNameResponse** group node under the **dataFields** group node in the **GetUserProfileByName** secondary data source. Note that the **Value** field is filtered by the **Name** of a property for each property you want to retrieve (**FirstName**, **LastName**, and **WorkEmail**). The formula looks like the following on the **Insert Formula** dialog box when you have selected the **Edit XPath (advanced)** check box:

```
normalize-
space(concat(xdXDocument:GetDOM("GetUserProfileByName")/dfs:myF
ields/dfs:dataFields/tns:GetUserProfileByNameResponse/tns:GetUs
erProfileByNameResult/tns:PropertyData/tns:Values/tns:ValueData
/tns:Value[../../../tns:Name = "FirstName"], " ",
xdXDocument:GetDOM("GetUserProfileByName")/dfs:myFields/dfs:dat
aFields/tns:GetUserProfileByNameResponse/tns:GetUserProfileByNa
meResult/tns:PropertyData/tns:Values/tns:ValueData/tns:Value[..
/../../tns:Name = "LastName"], " [",
xdXDocument:GetDOM("GetUserProfileByName")/dfs:myFields/dfs:dat
aFields/tns:GetUserProfileByNameResponse/tns:GetUserProfileByNa
meResult/tns:PropertyData/tns:Values/tns:ValueData/tns:Value[..
/../../tns:Name = "WorkEmail"], "]"))
```

13. If your SharePoint environment is configured to use Claims Based authentication as opposed to Windows Classic authentication and the form is going to be filled out through the browser, you must set up UDC authentication for the **GetUserProfileByName** and the **GetUserPropertyByAccountName** data connections that make the web service calls as described in *Configure a web service data connection for a web browser form* in the Appendix. But before you do this, test the form in InfoPath Filler 2013 to ensure that the functionality is working properly.

14. Publish the form template to a SharePoint form library.

In SharePoint, navigate to the form library where you published the form template and add a new form. When the form opens, type the account name of a user who has a manager in the person/group picker control, and click the **Check Names** button. Click the **Get Manager Details** button. The manager's first name, last name, and email address should appear in the text box.

Figure 183. Organization Chart showing that Jane Doe has John Doe as her manager.

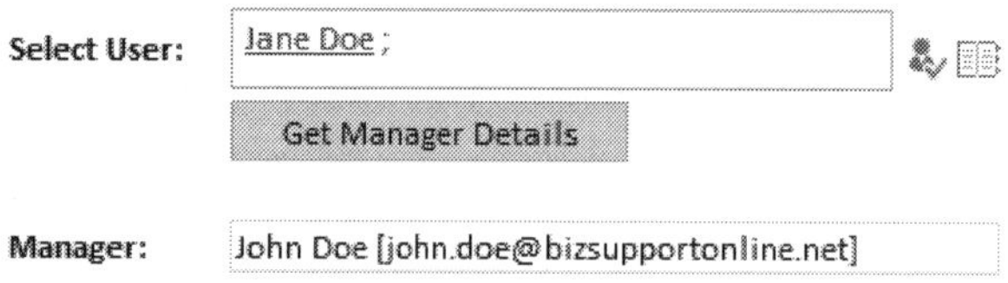

Figure 184. The InfoPath form showing the details of Jane Doe's manager.

Discussion

The solution described above used the User Profile Service of SharePoint to retrieve the details of a manager assigned to a particular user. Before you can call the User Profile Service, you must ensure that user profiles have been populated with data in SharePoint. An administrator must configure the population of user profiles in SharePoint through SharePoint Central Administration.

In the solution described above, you also saw that before you make a call to a web service, you must set the values of parameters. These parameters are located under the **queryFields** group node in the data source for the web service.

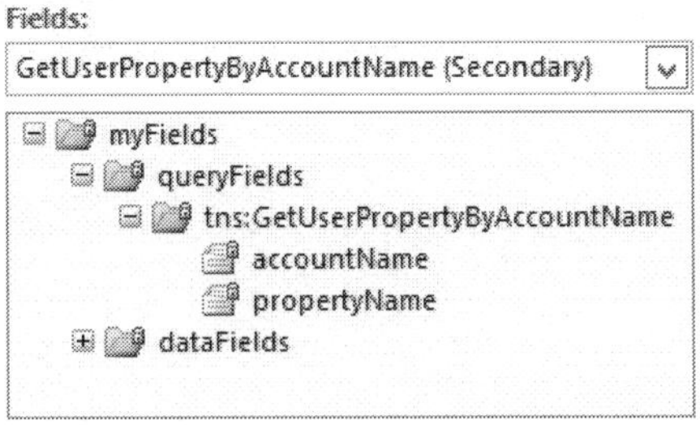

Figure 185. The queryFields group of the GetUserPropertyByAccountName data source.

And to retrieve the result of a call made to a web service, you have to retrieve the values of fields that are located under the **dataFields** group node of the data source for the web service.

Making a call to a web service is a 3-step process:

1. Set parameter values of the web service operation by setting the values of fields that are located under the **queryFields** group node in the secondary data source for the web service.
2. Use a **Query for data** action in an **Action** rule to call the web service operation.
3. Retrieve the result of the call from fields that are located under the **dataFields** group node in the secondary data source for the web service.

In the solution described above, you performed this 3-step process twice: Once to call the **GetUserPropertyByAccountName** operation and a second time to call the **GetUserProfileByName** operation of the User Profile Service.

You also retrieved the values of three properties: **FirstName**, **LastName**, and **WorkEmail**. While these are three well-known properties in a user's profile, you might not know the exact names of all of the properties returned by the **GetUserProfileByName** operation of the User Profile Service. If you do not know the exact property names, you can temporarily bind the **PropertyData** repeating group node that is located under the **dataFields** group node in the secondary data source for the web service to a repeating table on the form, preview the form, and then copy the names of the properties you want to use in your form.

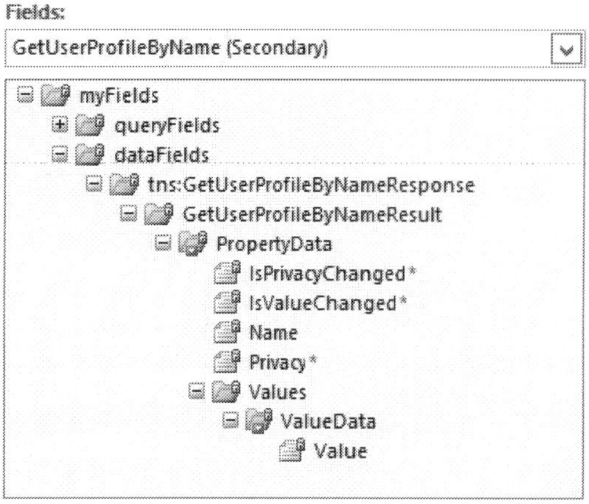

Figure 186. PropertyData repeating group node on the Fields task pane.

By temporarily binding the **PropertyData** repeating group node to a repeating table or a repeating section control (also see recipe *44 Display SharePoint list data in a repeating table*), you should get a list of all of the properties that are available for use. The **Name** field under the **PropertyData** repeating group node contains a property's name and the **Value** field under the **ValueData** repeating group node contains a property's value.

In the solution described above, the manager of a person was retrieved when the form was being filled out. If your scenario defers retrieving the manager of a person until after the form has been saved or submitted, you could make use of a SharePoint Designer workflow to retrieve the manager of a person (see recipe *89 Send an email to the manager of a selected person* for an example of how to retrieve a manager through a workflow) instead of making calls to the User Profile Service.

Multiple-Selection List Box

A multiple-selection list box combines the functionality of a normal list box control with check box controls. Instead of being able to select only one item as is the case with a list box control, a multiple-selection list box allows you to select and store multiple items.

The recipes in this section discuss a few scenarios for combining multiple-selection list boxes with SharePoint lists and person/group picker controls.

76 Fill a multi-select list box on a list form with SharePoint list data

Problem

You have a SharePoint list that contains a choice column. You customized the form for this SharePoint list in InfoPath and now you want to use a multiple-selection list box to fill the value of the choice column. The multiple-selection list box should get its values from another SharePoint list.

Solution

You can add a field of type **Choice (allow multiple selections)** to the SharePoint list form template from within InfoPath and then bind it to a multiple-selection list box that gets its entries from an external data source.

Suppose you have a SharePoint list named **OfficeApplications** as described in *Create a SharePoint list form for an existing SharePoint list* in recipe *2 Customize a SharePoint list form from within InfoPath* which you want to use to populate a multiple-selection list box on the SharePoint list form.

To populate a multiple-selection list box on a SharePoint list form with data from another SharePoint list:

1. In SharePoint, create a new custom SharePoint list or use an existing one. The SharePoint list need not contain any other columns than a **Title** column.
2. Start the customization of the SharePoint list form either from within SharePoint or from within InfoPath as described in recipe *1 Customize a SharePoint list form from within SharePoint* or recipe *2 Customize a SharePoint list form from within InfoPath*.
3. In InfoPath, on the **Fields** task pane, click **Show advanced view**.

4. On the **Fields** task pane, expand the **dataFields** group node, right-click the **my:SharePointListItem_RW** group node, and select **Add** from the drop-down menu that appears.
5. On the **Add Field or Group** dialog box, enter a **Display Name** and **Name** for the field (for example, **My Choices** and **MyChoices**), select **Choice (allow multiple selections)** from the **Data type** drop-down list box, and click **OK**.

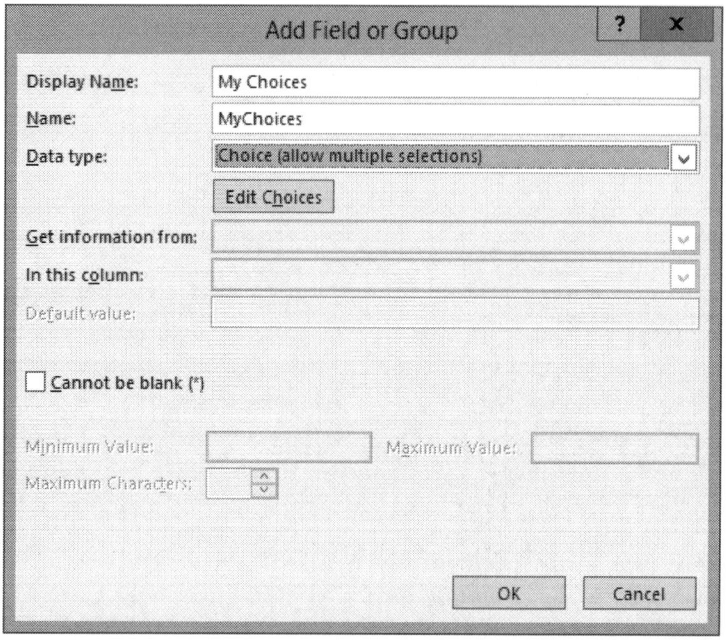

Figure 187. Adding a Choice field to a SharePoint list form in InfoPath Designer 2013.

6. On the **Fields** task pane, drag-and-drop the **:Value** repeating field from under the **My Choices** group node onto the view of the form template. InfoPath should automatically bind it to a multiple-selection list box.
7. Right-click the multiple-selection list box and select **Multiple-Selection List Box Properties** from the context menu that appears.
8. On the **Multiple-Selection List Box Properties** dialog box on the **Data** tab, select the **Get choices from an external data source** option, and then click **Add** behind the **Data source** drop-down list box.

9. On the **Data Connection Wizard**, follow the steps to add a **Receive** data connection to the **OfficeApplications** SharePoint list. Ensure that you select **ID** and **Title** as fields to include in the data source and that you leave the **Automatically retrieve data when form is opened** check box selected.

10. On the **Multiple-Selection List Box Properties** dialog box on the **Data** tab, ensure that **ID** is selected for the **Value** property and **Title** for the **Display name** property, and then click **OK**.

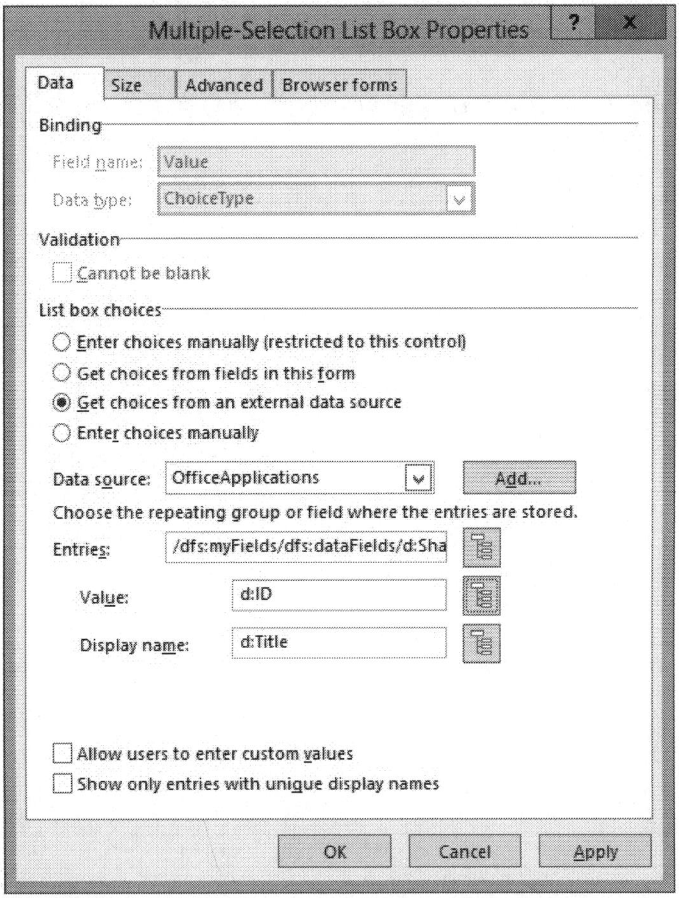

Figure 188. The multi-select list box configured to get items from an external list.

11. Publish the form template back to the SharePoint list.

In SharePoint, navigate to the SharePoint list for which you customized its form, and add a new item. When the SharePoint list form opens, verify that the multiple-selection list box is displaying items from the **OfficeApplications** SharePoint list.

Title	My Applications
Attachments	Click here to attach a file
My Choices	☑ Word ☐ Excel ☑ Access ☐ PowerPoint ☐ OneNote

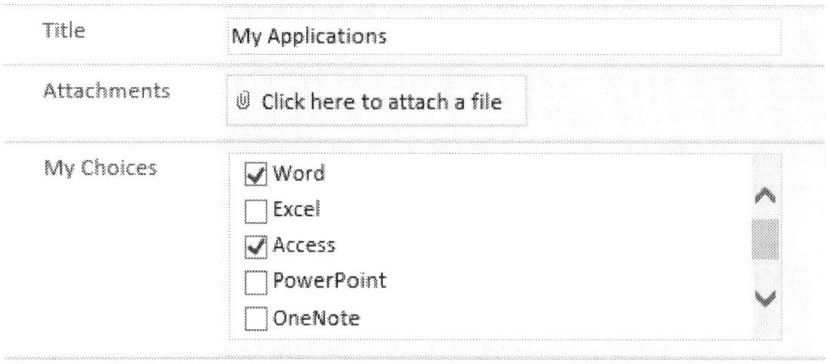

Figure 189. The SharePoint list form with a multiple-selection list box in SharePoint 2013.

Fill out the form and then save the item. Click on the item you just created to view it and verify that the form is displaying only the items you selected in the multiple-selection list box. Click the **Edit Item** command on the Ribbon to edit the item and verify that the multiple-selection list box displays the items you previously selected along with all of the other items from the **OfficeApplications** SharePoint list.

Discussion

In the solution described above you learned how to add a multiple-selection list box to a SharePoint list form to allow users to set the value of a choice column in a SharePoint list. You could have also first added a **Choice** column with a display type of **Checkboxes (allow multiple selections)** to the SharePoint list from within SharePoint and then bound this column to a multiple-selection list box in InfoPath to create functionality similar to the one described in the solution above.

SharePoint list forms come with the following **Choice** data types you can choose from when selecting the data type for a field you are adding to the Main data source of a SharePoint list form:

- Choice (menu to choose from)
- Choice (allow multiple selections)
- Choice with Fill-in (menu to choose from or text)

- Choice with Fill-in (allow multiple selections)

From these four data types, you can only bind the **Choice (allow multiple selections)** and **Choice with Fill-in (allow multiple selections)** to a multiple-selection list box. Because of the structure of the other two data types, you can only bind them to controls that accept a single value such as for example a drop-down list box control or an option button control. The difference between the **Choice (allow multiple selections)** and **Choice with Fill-in (allow multiple selections)** data types lies in whether you want to allow users to be able to manually add items to the multiple-selection list box or not. This option can also be switched on or off by selecting or deselecting the **Allow users to enter custom values** check box on the **Multiple-Selection List Box Properties** dialog box.

77 Fill a multi-select list box with email addresses from a people picker

Problem

You have a person/group picker control and a multiple-selection list box control on an InfoPath form. You want to be able to select one or more users from the person/group picker control and have their email addresses appear as selectable items in the multiple-selection list box control.

Solution

You can use the **User Information List** SharePoint list and the **Filter Data** option on a secondary data source to look up the email addresses of users and then have those email addresses appear as items in a multiple-selection list box.

To populate a multiple-selection list box with email addresses from users who were selected from a person/group picker control:

1. In InfoPath, create a new SharePoint form library form template or use an existing one.
2. Add a **Receive** data connection to the **User Information List** SharePoint list on the site from which the person/group picker control

should get its information (also see *Use a SharePoint list data connection* in recipe *43 2 Ways to retrieve data from a SharePoint list*). Ensure that you select **Account** and **Work_email (Work email)** as fields to include in the data source, and that you leave the **Automatically retrieve data when form is opened** check box selected. You will use this SharePoint list data connection to look up the email addresses of users.

3. Add a **Person/Group Picker** control to the view of the form template.
4. Open the **Person/Group Picker Properties** dialog box and then on the **General** tab, select the **Allow multiple selections** check box and leave the **People Only** option selected. With this you have configured the person/group picker control to allow multiple users to be selected. Click **OK** to close the dialog box.
5. Add a **Button** control to the view of the form template and set its **Action** property to **Update Form**.
6. Add a **Multiple-Selection List Box** control to the view of the form template and name its repeating field **emailAddress**.
7. Click **Data** ➤ **Form Data** ➤ **Default Values**.
8. On the **Edit Default Values** dialog box, expand the node for the multiple-selection list box, deselect the check box in front of the **emailAddress** repeating field, and click **OK**. This should prevent an empty selected item from appearing in the multiple-selection list box when a user creates a new form.

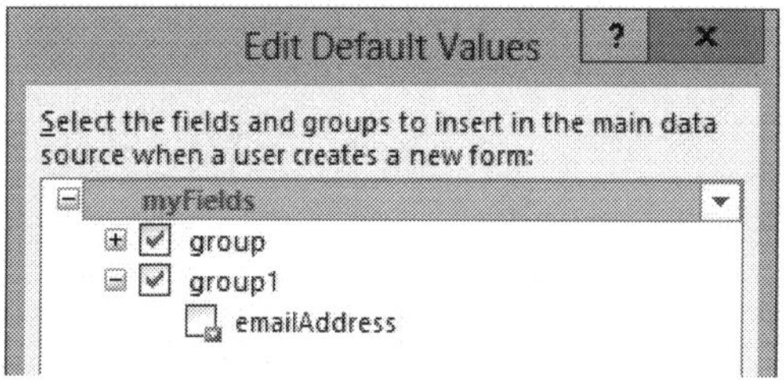

Figure 190. The emailAddress check box on the Edit Default Values dialog box.

9. Open the **Multiple-Selection List Box Properties** dialog box, configure it to get its items from the **User Information List** secondary data source, and then click the button behind the **Entries** text box.

10. On the **Select a Field or Group** dialog box, click **Filter Data**, click **Add**, and then add two filter conditions that say:

```
Account = AccountId
and
Work email is not blank
```

where **Account** and **Work email** are fields that are located under the **d:SharePointListItem_RW** repeating group node under the **dataFields** group node in the **User Information List** secondary data source and **AccountId** is the field that is located under the repeating group node of the person/group picker control in the Main data source. Click **OK** when closing all dialog boxes.

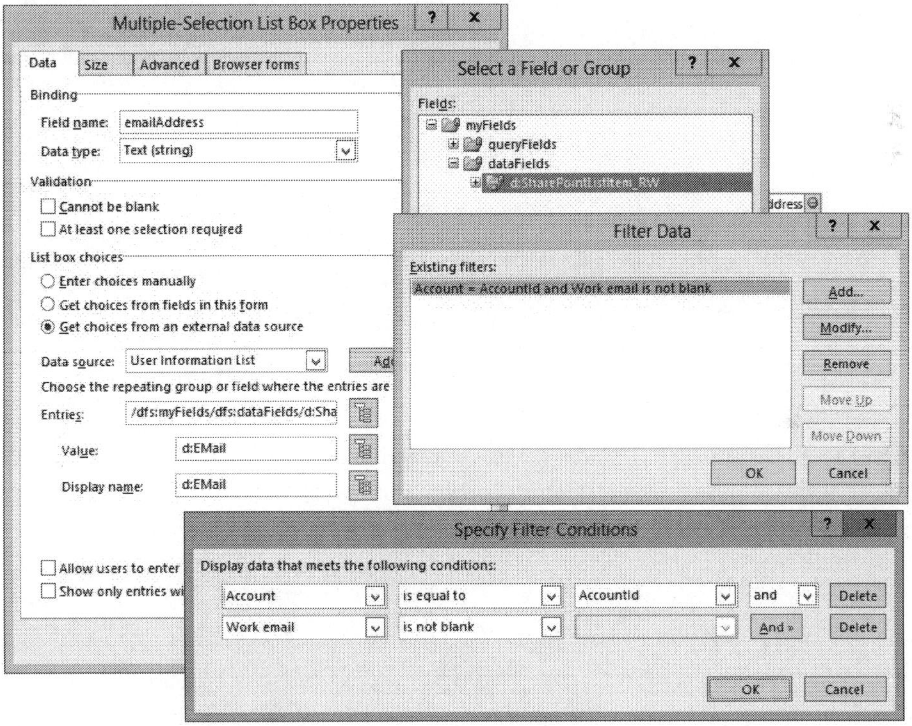

Figure 191. Configuring and filtering the items for the multiple-selection list box.

The resulting XPath expression for the **Entries** property on the **Multiple-Selection List Box Properties** dialog box should resemble the following expression:

```
/dfs:myFields/dfs:dataFields/d:SharePointListItem_RW[d:Name =
xdXDocument:get-
DOM()/my:myFields/my:group/pc:Person/pc:AccountId and d:EMail
!= ""]
```

Set the values of the **Value** and the **Display name** properties to be equal to the value of the **Work email** field that is located under the **d:SharePointListItem_RW** repeating group node in the **User Information List** secondary data source. Click **OK** when you are done.

11. Publish the form template to a SharePoint form library.

In SharePoint, navigate to the form library where you published the form template and add a new form. When the form opens, use the person/group picker to look up one or more users, and then click the **Check Names** button. Click the **Update Form** button. The multiple-selection list box should get populated with the email addresses of the people you selected.

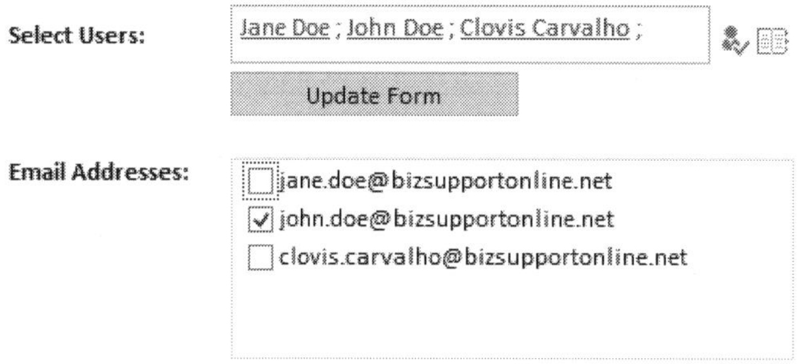

Figure 192. The InfoPath form displaying selected users and email addresses.

Discussion

In the solution described above you saw how to populate a multiple-selection list box by filtering a secondary data source on users that were selected via a person/group picker control on an InfoPath form. This technique is not limited to using SharePoint lists as data sources; you could also use a data source for the User Profile Service to populate the multiple-selection list box, for example, if you wanted to populate the multiple-selection list box with the names of the managers of the selected users (also see recipe *75 Get the details of the manager of a selected person in a people picker*), since the **User Information List** does not contain all SharePoint user profile information (see the discussion section of recipe *48 Display a list of people from the current user's department* to learn more about the **User Information List** SharePoint list).

You could extend the solution described above by adding a button and text box control named **emailAddresses** to the view of the form template with an **Action** rule on the button that says:

```
Set a field's value: emailAddresses = eval(eval(emailAddress,
'concat(., "; ")'), "..")
```

where **emailAddresses** is the field that is bound to the text box control and **emailAddress** is the repeating field of the multiple-selection list box control. This action sets the value of the **emailAddresses** text box to be equal to a concatenated string of email addresses that were selected from the **emailAddress** multiple-selection list box, separated by semi-colons. The resulting string would resemble:

```
jane.doe@bizsupportonline.net; john.doe@bizsupportonline.net;
```

if you selected the email addresses for Jane Doe and John Doe from the multiple-selection list box.

78 Cascading multi-select list boxes using linked SharePoint lists

Problem

You have two SharePoint lists that are linked to each other through a lookup column and you want to use these lists to create cascading multiple-selection list boxes on an InfoPath form.

Solution

You can use the **Filter Data** option on the data source for the SharePoint list used to populate the dependent multiple-selection list boxes to filter the data based on values that are entered or selected in the Main data source of the form.

Suppose you have two SharePoint lists named **SoftwareCategories** and **SoftwareProducts** as described in recipe *14 Master/detail with two linked SharePoint lists*.

To create cascading multiple-selection list boxes by using linked SharePoint lists:

1. In InfoPath, create a new SharePoint form library form template or use an existing one.
2. Add a **Receive** data connection to the **SoftwareCategories** SharePoint list to the form template as described in *Use a SharePoint list data connection* in recipe *43 2 Ways to retrieve data from a SharePoint list*. Include the **ID** and **Title** fields in the data source, select **Title** as the field to sort the list by, leave the **Automatically retrieve data when form is opened** check box selected, and name the data connection **SoftwareCategories**.
3. Add a **Receive** data connection to the **SoftwareProducts** SharePoint list to the form template. Include the **ID**, **Title**, and **Category** fields in the data source, leave the **Automatically retrieve data when form is opened** check box selected, and name the data connection **SoftwareProducts**.
4. Add two **Multiple-Selection List Box** controls to the view of the form template and name their repeating fields **category** and **product**, respectively.
5. Populate the **category** multiple-selection list box with items from the **SofwareCategories** secondary data source, use **ID** as the **Value**, and use **Title** as the **Display name** for the multiple-selection list box.
6. Populate the **product** multiple-selection list box with items from the **SoftwareProducts** secondary data source, use **ID** as the **Value**, use **Title** as the **Display name**, and then click the button behind the **Entries** text box on the **Multiple-Selection List Box Properties** dialog box.
7. On the **Select a Field or Group** dialog box, click **Filter Data**, click **Add**, and then add a filter condition that says:

   ```
   Category = category
   ```

   where **Category** is located under the **d:SharePointListItem_RW** repeating group node under the **dataFields** group node in the **SoftwareProducts** secondary data source and **category** is the repeating field of the first multiple-selection list box. Click **OK** when closing all dialog boxes when you are done.

8. Add a **Section** control to the view of the form template and then type the text "One or more selected products are missing a selected category. Please deselect those products before continuing." inside of the section control. You can change the color of the text to red if you wish.

9. Click anywhere behind the text on the section control to place the cursor, and then add a **Text Box** control within the section control. Name the text box **amountOfProductsMissingCategory**, change its data type to **Whole Number (integer)**, and select its **Cannot be blank** property. You are going to use this text box to keep track of the amount of selected products in the second multiple-selection list box that are missing a parent category in the first multiple-selection list box and perform data validation for the multiple-selection list box.

10. Add a **Formatting** rule to the **amountOfProductsMissingCategory** text box with a **The expression** condition that says:

    ```
    true()
    ```

    and with a formatting of **Hide this control**. Because you want the **amountOfProductsMissingCategory** text box to be present on the view of the form template, but always remain invisible to users, this rule makes use of the **true()** function to always run and hide the text box.

11. Because multiple-selection list boxes do not tend to trigger action rules when items are deselected, you are going to use a default value on the **amountOfProductsMissingCategory** text box to pull in data from the multiple-selection list box. So with the **amountOfProductsMissingCategory** text box still selected, click **Control Tools ➤ Properties ➤ Properties ➤ Default Value**.

12. On the **Field or Group Properties** dialog box, click the formula button behind the **Value** text box.

13. On the **Insert Formula** dialog box, type:

```
count(
```

and then click **Insert Field or Group**.

14. On the **Select a Field or Group** dialog box, select **SoftwareProducts (Secondary)** from the drop-down list box, expand the **dataFields** group node, expand the **d:SharePointListItem_RW** repeating group node, select the **ID** field, and then click **Filter Data**.
15. On the **Filter Data** dialog box, click **Add**.
16. On the **Specify Filter Conditions** dialog box, leave **ID** selected in the first drop-down list box, leave **is equal to** selected in the second drop-down list box, and then select **Use a formula** from the third drop-down list box.
17. On the **Insert Formula** dialog box, click **Insert Field or Group**.
18. On the **Select a Field or Group** dialog box, select **Main** from the drop-down list box, expand the **group2** group node, select the **product** repeating field, and then click **OK**.
19. On the **Insert Formula** dialog box, click **OK**.
20. On the **Specify Filter Conditions** dialog box, select **The expression** from the first drop-down list box. The expression should say:

```
. = xdXDocument:get-DOM()/my:myFields/my:group2/my:product
```

21. On the **Specify Filter Conditions** dialog box, click **And** to add a second condition.
22. On the **Specify Filter Conditions** dialog box, select **Category** from the first drop-down list box, leave **is equal to** selected in the second drop-down list box, and then select **Use a formula** from the third drop-down list box.
23. On the **Insert Formula** dialog box, click **Insert Field or Group**.
24. On the **Select a Field or Group** dialog box, select **Main** from the drop-down list box, expand the **group1** group node, select the **category** repeating field, and then click **OK**.

25. On the **Insert Formula** dialog box, click **OK**.
26. On the **Specify Filter Conditions** dialog box, select **The expression** from the first drop-down list box, and type the **not()** function around the entire expression. The final expression should say:

```
not(../d:Category = xdXDocument:get-
DOM()/my:myFields/my:group1/my:category)
```

27. On the **Specify Filter Conditions** dialog box, click **OK**.
28. On the **Filter Data** dialog box, click **OK**.
29. On the **Select a Field or Group** dialog box, click **OK**.
30. On the **Insert Formula** dialog box, type:

```
)
```

to close the **count()** function. The formula should now say:

```
count(ID[. = product and not(Category = category)])
```

Select the **Edit XPath (advanced)** check box. The formula should say:

```
count(xdXDocument:GetDOM("SoftwareProducts")/dfs:myFields/dfs:d
ataFields/d:SharePointListItem_RW/d:ID[. = xdXDocument:get-
DOM()/my:myFields/my:group2/my:product and not(../d:Category =
xdXDocument:get-DOM()/my:myFields/my:group1/my:category)])
```

This formula counts the amount of **IDs** in the **SoftwareProducts** secondary data source that have been selected in the **product** multiple-selection list box and that are linked to a **Category** field that has not been selected in the **category** multiple-selection list box.

31. On the **Insert Formula** dialog box, ensure that the **Edit XPath (advanced)** check box is selected, select the entire text for the formula, copy it to the Windows clipboard, and then click **OK**.

32. On the **Field or Group Properties** dialog box, ensure that the **Refresh value when formula is recalculated** check box is selected, and then click **OK**.

33. Add an **Action** rule to the **category** multiple-selection list box with an action that says:

```
Set a field's value: amountOfProductsMissingCategory =
count(ID[. = products and not(Category = categories)])
```

where **amountOfProductsMissingCategory** is the field that is bound to the text box. Note that you must manually paste the formula you copied earlier into the text box on the **Insert Formula** dialog box to get the correct expression:

```
count(ID[. = product and not(Category = category)])
```

This action rule does the same thing as the default value on the **amountOfProductsMissingCategory** text box, but then only when an item is selected in the **category** multiple-selection list box.

34. Click the section control to select it, ensure that **group3** is displayed under the title bar on the **Rules** task pane, and then add a **Formatting** rule to the **group3** section control with a formatting of **Hide this control** and with a **Condition** that says:

```
amountOfProductsMissingCategory = 0
```

This formatting rule hides the section control whenever no selected products in the **product** multiple-selection list box are missing a selected category in the **category** multiple-selection list box.

35. Add a **Validation** rule to the **amountOfProductsMissingCategory** text box with a **Condition** that says:

```
amountOfProductsMissingCategory > 0
```

and a **ScreenTip** that says: "One or more selected products are missing a selected category. Please deselect those products before continuing."

Because the **amountOfProductsMissingCategory** text box has been hidden (so users cannot enter any data into it), if one or more products selected in the **product** multiple-selection list box are missing a selected category in the **category** multiple-selection list box and a user tries to save or submit the form despite the section control telling her about the error, SharePoint should display an error to the user.

36. Publish the form template to a SharePoint form library.

In SharePoint, navigate to the form library where you published the form template and add a new form. When the form opens, select a couple of categories in the first multiple-selection list box. Corresponding products should appear in the second multiple-selection list box.

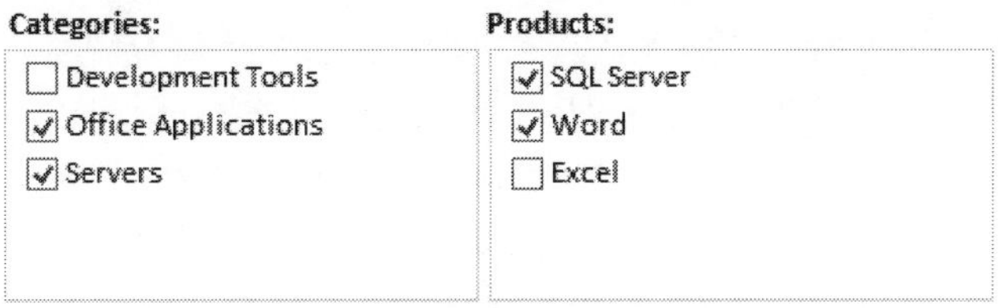

Figure 193. Categories with linked products in two multiple-selection list boxes.

Select a couple of products in the second multiple-selection list box, and then deselect one of the categories in the first multiple-selection list box. The ID of the product that is missing a category should appear in the second multiple-selection list box and the section containing the error message should also appear.

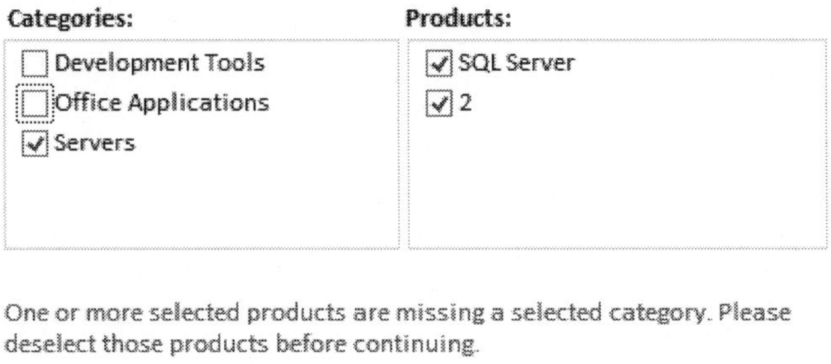

Figure 194. Word is missing Office Applications selected in the first multi-select list box.

Try saving the form back to the form library. SharePoint should display a validation error message box.

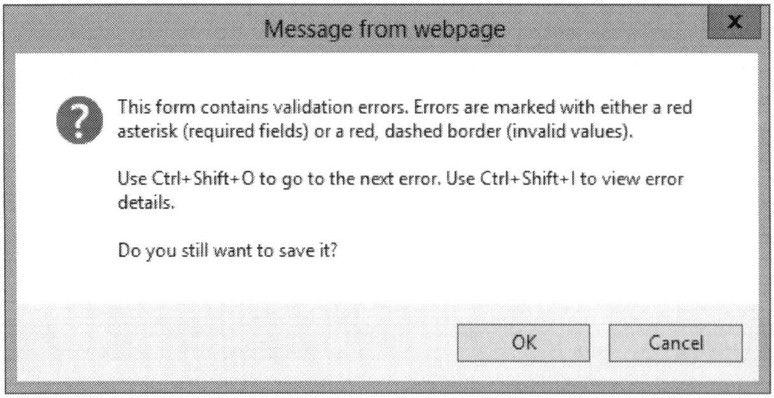

Figure 195. Validation error message box when trying to save the form.

Note that you can still go ahead and save the form with validation errors. However, if you configure the form to be submitted (and not saved), you would have to correct the validation errors before being able to submit the form.

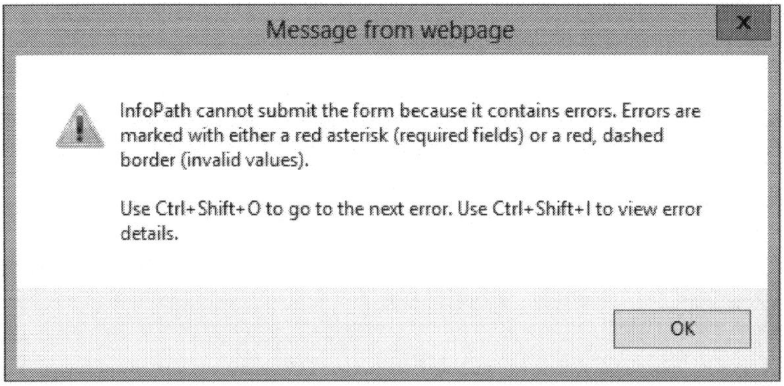

Figure 196. Validation error message box when trying to submit the form.

Discussion

Because InfoPath does not have actions you can use to remove items from a multiple-selection list box, you would either have to write code to programmatically remove orphaned items or use a workaround with data validation as described in the solution above.

In the solution described above, you also used a second workaround to count selected items. Because multiple-selection list boxes only seem to run action rules when items are selected (and not deselected), you used a default value on a text box to pull data in from a multiple-selection list box when items are deselected (and not selected).

79 Filter and display SharePoint list items using a multi-select list box

Problem

You have a SharePoint list that contains data you want to display in sections on a form, but you only want to display those sections that pertain to selected items in a multiple-selection list box.

Solution

You can use conditional formatting to show or hide sections displaying SharePoint list data based on items that are selected in a multiple-selection list box.

Suppose you have a SharePoint list named **OfficeApplications** as described in *Create a SharePoint list form for an existing SharePoint list* in recipe *2 Customize a SharePoint list form from within InfoPath* which you want to use to display data on an InfoPath form.

To filter and display SharePoint list items using a multiple-selection list box:

1. In InfoPath, create a new SharePoint form library form template or use an existing one.
2. Add a **Receive** data connection to the **OfficeApplications** SharePoint list to the form template as described in *Use a SharePoint list data connection* in recipe *43 2 Ways to retrieve data from a SharePoint list*. Include the **ID**, **Title**, and **Color** fields in the data source, select **Title** as the field to sort the list by, leave the **Automatically retrieve data when form is opened** check box selected, and name the data connection **OfficeApplications**.

3. Add a **Multiple-Selection List Box** control to the view of the form template and name its repeating field **selectedOfficeApplication**.
4. Populate the **selectedOfficeApplication** multiple-selection list box with items from the **OfficeApplications** secondary data source, configure the **Entries** to come from the **d:SharePointListItem_RW** repeating group node under the **dataFields** group node in the **OfficeApplications** secondary data source, use **ID** as the **Value**, and use **Title** as the **Display name** for the multiple-selection list box.
5. On the **Fields** task pane, select **OfficeApplications (Secondary)** from the drop-down list box, expand the **dataFields** group node, right-click the **d:SharePointListItem_RW** repeating group node, and then drag-and-drop it onto the view of the form template. Select **Repeating Section with Controls** from the context menu that appears when you drop it.
6. On the **Fields** task pane, ensure that the **d:SharePointListItem_RW** repeating group is selected, and then click **Home ➤ Rules ➤ Manage Rules**.
7. On the **Rules** task pane, click **New ➤ Formatting** to add a formatting rule.
8. On the **Rules** task pane, select the **Hide this control** check box, and then under **Condition**, click the text **None**.
9. On the **Condition** dialog box, select **ID** from the first drop-down list box, leave **is equal to** selected in the second drop-down list box, and then select **Select a field or group** from the third drop-down list box.
10. On the **Select a Field or Group** dialog box, select **Main** from the drop-down list box, expand the **group1** group node of the multiple-selection list box, select the **selectedOfficeApplication** repeating field, and click **OK**.
11. On the **Condition** dialog box, select **The expression** from the first drop-down list box, and then change the expression from

```
d:ID = xdXDocument:get-
DOM()/my:myFields/my:group1/my:selectedOfficeApplication
```

to

```
not(d:ID = xdXDocument:get-
DOM()/my:myFields/my:group1/my:selectedOfficeApplication)
```

by typing the **not()** function around the expression. The final expression evaluates to **true** when an ID in the **OfficeApplications** secondary data source is not equal to any of the selected IDs in the multiple-selection list box, so the section corresponding to that ID should be hidden.

12. On the **Condition** dialog box, click **OK**.
13. Publish the form template to a SharePoint form library.

In SharePoint, navigate to the form library where you published the form template and add a new form. When the form opens, select a couple of Office applications in the multiple-selection list box. The corresponding Office applications should appear in sections.

Figure 197. Selected Office applications displayed in sections.

Discussion

While you used the **not()** function in the solution described above to filter the repeating section and only display those sections that corresponded to the selected items in the multiple-selection list box, you could also use the

count() function to find IDs of Office applications that are present in the secondary data source but which have not been selected in the multiple-selection list box. The expression for the condition in step 11 would then become something like:

```
count(d:ID[. = xdXDocument:get-
DOM()/my:myFields/my:group1/my:selectedOfficeApplication]) = 0
```

Chapter 5: Use SharePoint Designer Workflows with InfoPath

SharePoint Designer 2013 can be used to perform several modifications in SharePoint, one of which is create and publish codeless workflows that can run in SharePoint 2013.

In SharePoint Designer 2013, you can create workflows that run on the SharePoint 2010 or SharePoint 2013 platform. Not all workflow actions that are available for the SharePoint 2010 platform are available for the SharePoint 2013 platform. And there are new workflow actions for the SharePoint 2013 platform that are not available for the SharePoint 2010 platform. Therefore you will notice a few recipes in this chapter creating a SharePoint 2010 workflow, while others require new features that are only available when creating a SharePoint 2013 workflow. Before you can create SharePoint 2013 workflows, you must install and configure Workflow Manager (see the article entitled *Set up and configure SharePoint 2013 Workflow Manager* on MSDN).

You can use InfoPath 2013 forms in one of the following two ways with SharePoint Designer workflows:

1. As workflow forms to pass data to SharePoint 2010 workflows.
2. As list items or content types SharePoint 2010 or 2013 workflows run on or use.

This chapter is not intended to give you an in-depth overview of how to create workflows in SharePoint Designer 2013, since an entire book could be written on the subject. However, because you do need some basic understanding of SharePoint Designer workflows before you move on to the InfoPath-related recipes in this chapter, I will first guide you through setting up a few simple workflows in SharePoint Designer 2013 and explain how to associate them with a list or content type before moving on to combining SharePoint Designer workflows with InfoPath 2013.

80 Create a workflow that runs on forms in a specific form library

Problem

You want to have a workflow run whenever a new form is added to a specific form library on a SharePoint site.

Solution

You can create a list workflow in SharePoint Designer 2013 and associate it with the form library on which the workflow should run.

To create a SharePoint 2010 workflow that runs on forms in a specific form library:

1. In InfoPath, create a new SharePoint form library form template or use an existing one, and publish it to either a form library or as a site content type. If published as a site content type, associate the content type with a form library as described in recipe *27 Create different types of forms in one form library*. We will call the form library you published the form template to **ListWorkflowLib**, so that we can easily refer to it in this solution.
2. Open SharePoint Designer 2013, and click **Sites ➤ Open Site**.

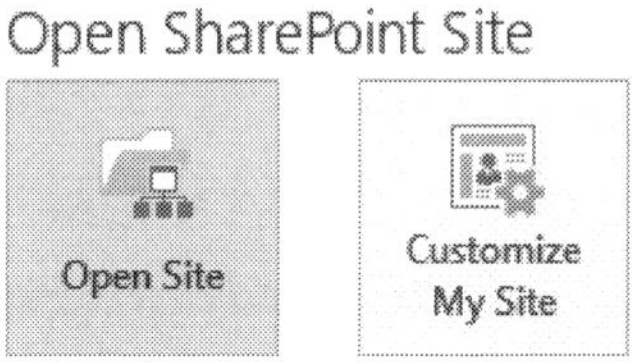

Figure 198. The Open Site command in SharePoint Designer 2013.

3. On the **Open Site** dialog box, browse to and select the site on which the **ListWorkflowLib** form library is located or enter the URL of the site in the **Site name** text box, and click **Open**.
4. Once the site has been opened in SharePoint Designer 2013, click **Site ➤ New ➤ List Workflow** or select **Workflows** in the left **Navigation** pane and then click **Workflows ➤ New ➤ List Workflow** on the

Ribbon, and then select **ListWorkflowLib** from the drop-down menu that appears.

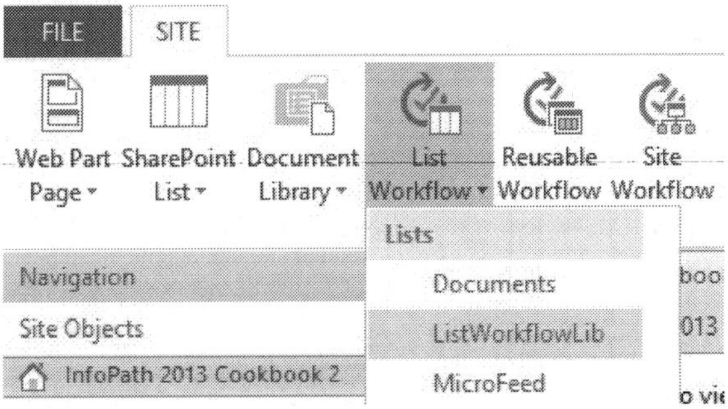

Figure 199. The List Workflow command on the Site tab in SharePoint Designer 2013.

5. On the **Create List Workflow** dialog box, type **ListWorkflowLibWF** in the **Name** text box, select **SharePoint 2010 Workflow** from the **Platform Type** drop-down list box, and click **OK**.

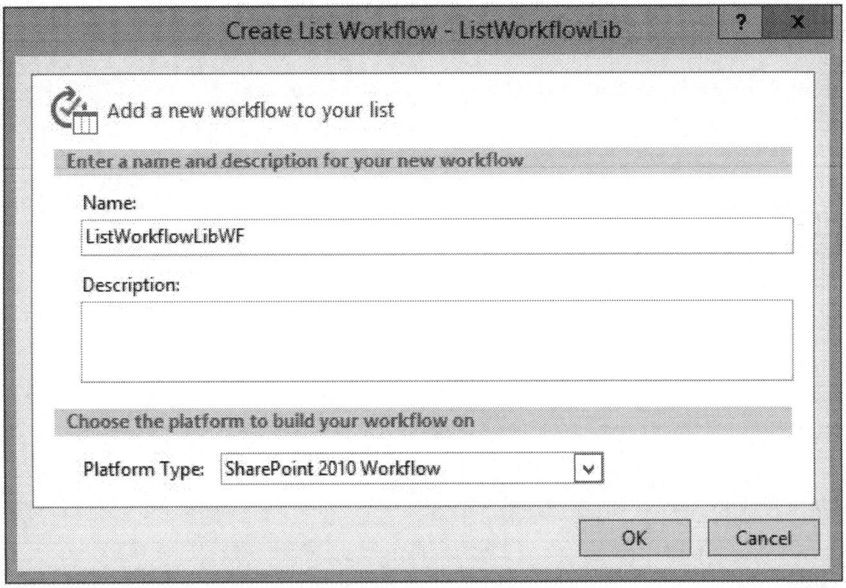

Figure 200. The Create List Workflow dialog box in SharePoint Designer 2013.

This should open the text-based designer with one step (**Step 1**) already added.

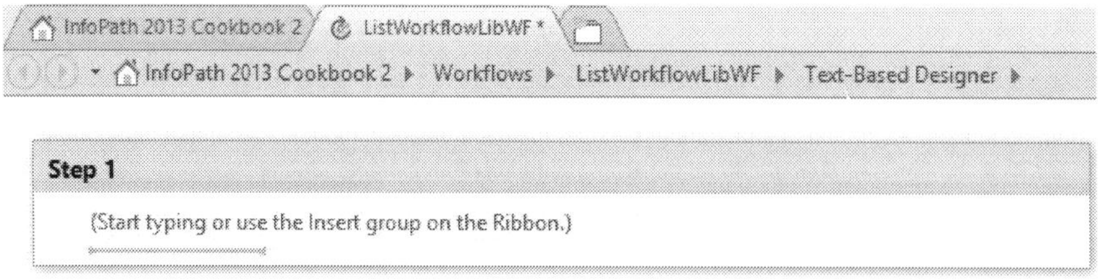

Figure 201. The text-based designer with one step already added.

6. You are going to keep this workflow very simple by just writing a message to the history list of the workflow whenever the workflow runs. This message will contain the URL of the form the workflow is running on. So click on the text in **Step 1** to place the cursor inside of **Step 1**, type **log**, and then press **Enter**. This should add a **Log to History List** workflow action.

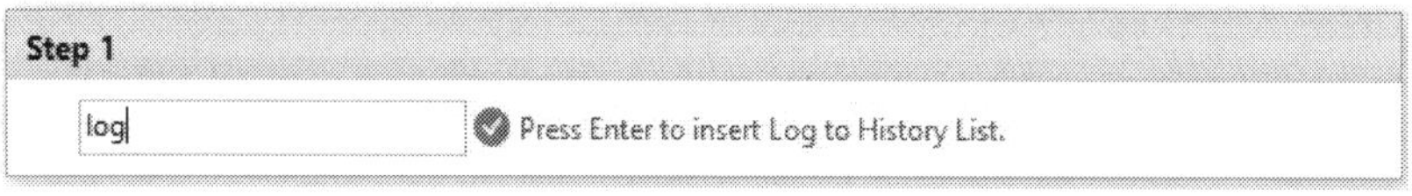

Figure 202. Typing to find and add a workflow action.

A second way to add a **Log to History List** workflow action is to click **Workflow ➤ Insert ➤ Action**, and then select **Log to History List** under the **Core Actions** category from the drop-down menu that appears.

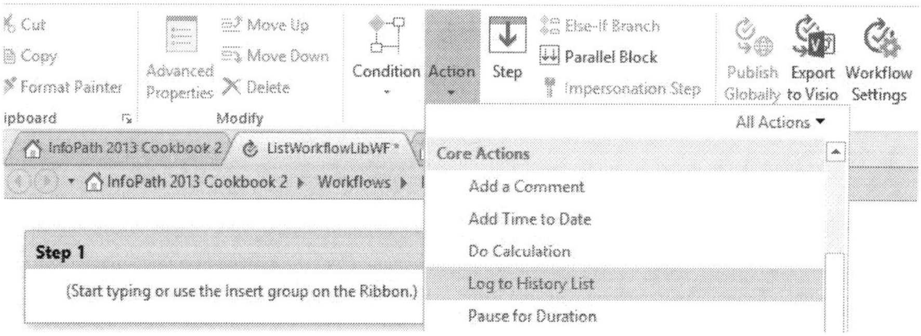

Figure 203. Selecting the Log to History List action in SharePoint Designer 2013.

7. Click **this message** in the sentence for the workflow action. A text box should appear in addition to two buttons behind the text box. The first button allows you to build a string, while the second button allows you to look up a string to set the message to. Click the second button (the formula button) behind the text box.

Figure 204. The workflow step after clicking 'this message' in the sentence.

8. On the **Lookup for String** dialog box, select **Workflow Context** from the **Data source** drop-down list box, select **Current Item URL** from the **Field from source** drop-down list box, and click **OK**.

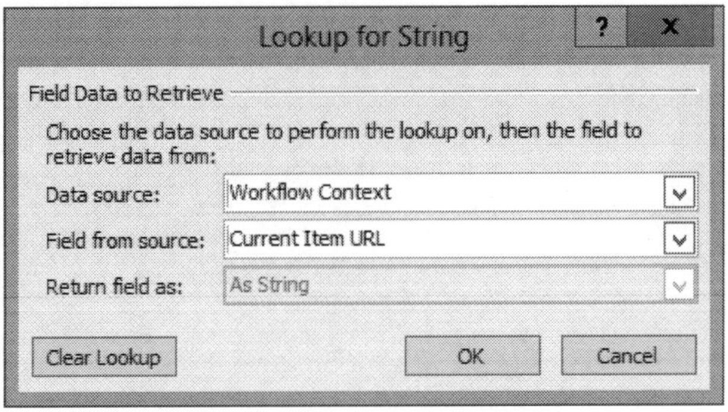

Figure 205. The Lookup for String dialog box in SharePoint Designer 2013.

The final sentence for the workflow action should say:

```
Log Workflow Context:Current Item URL to the workflow history
list
```

Note that the **Workflow Context** data source gives you access to the values of properties of the workflow that is running. SharePoint Designer 2013 has several data sources you can choose from, but the ones you are most likely to use are: **Current Item** (which gives you access to the item the workflow is running on), **Workflow Variables and Parameters** (which gives you access to the values of parameters and variables that have been defined and set in the workflow), and **Workflow Context**. Take a moment to go through the list of data sources to familiarize yourself with them.

9. Click **Workflow** ➤ **Save** ➤ **Check for Errors** to ensure that the workflow does not contain any errors. A message box saying that the workflow contains no errors should appear. If there are errors, you must fix them before publishing the workflow. Click **OK** to close the message box.

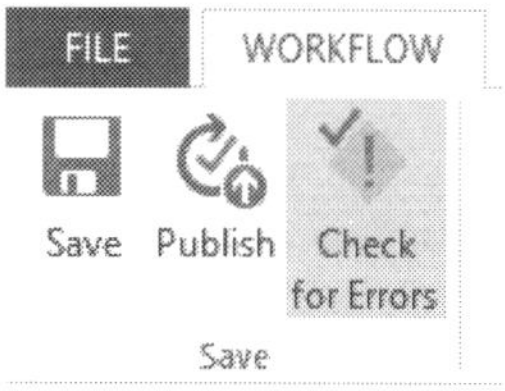

Figure 206. The Check for Errors command in SharePoint Designer 2013.

10. Click **Workflow** ➤ **Manage** ➤ **Workflow Settings**.

Figure 207. The Workflow Settings command in SharePoint Designer 2013.

11. On the workflow settings page under **Start Options**, select the **Start workflow automatically when an item is created** check box. This will allow the workflow to run whenever a new form is added to the form library. Leave the **Allow this workflow to be manually started** check box selected so that the workflow can also be manually started in case you want to run it again on a form or in case it failed to run.

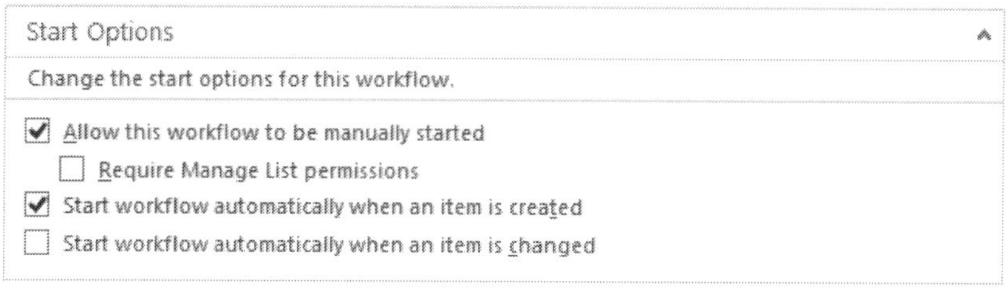

Figure 208. Configuring workflow start options in SharePoint Designer 2013.

12. Click **Workflow Settings ➤ Save ➤ Publish** to publish the workflow. Note: To go back to the text-based designer, you can click **Workflow Settings ➤ Edit ➤ Edit Workflow** or click the **Edit workflow** link under the **Customization** section on the workflow settings page. And from the text-based designer, you can also publish the workflow by clicking **Workflow ➤ Save ➤ Publish** on the Ribbon.

In SharePoint, navigate to the **ListWorkflowLib** form library and add a new form. Save the form to the form library and then close it. Soon after you save the form to the form library, you should see a column named **ListWorkflowLibWF** containing the text **In Progress** appear behind the new form in the form library. Wait a few seconds and then refresh the page. You should see the text **Completed** appear in the aforementioned column when the workflow has run and successfully completed.

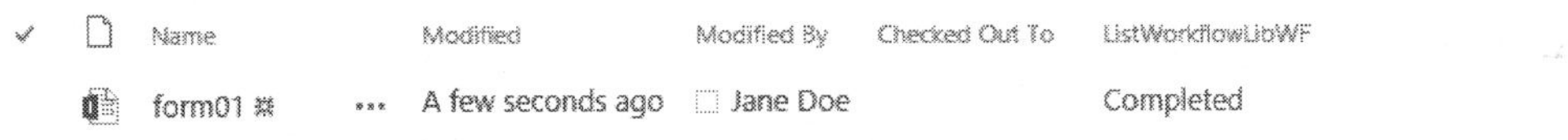

Name
Modified
Modified By
Checked Out To
ListWorkflowLibWF
form01
A few seconds ago
Jane Doe
Completed

Figure 209. The text 'Completed' appearing in a column after the workflow has run.

Click on the text **Completed** or any other workflow status text that may have appeared. This should take you to the **Workflow Status** page where under the **Workflow History** section you should see a comment with the URL of the form the workflow ran on listed in the **Description** column.

Workflow History
The workflow recorded these events.
Date Occurred
Event Type
User ID
Description
2/5/2014 12:07 PM
Comment
System Account
http://win-a5pj1269tfk/infopath2013cookbook2/ListWorkflowLib/form01.xml

Figure 210. Workflow History on the Workflow Status page in SharePoint 2013.

Discussion

You can use SharePoint Designer 2013 to create SharePoint 2010 workflows as well as SharePoint 2013 workflows that run in SharePoint 2013. You can visit MSDN to learn more about workflow support in SharePoint 2013.

The steps for creating a SharePoint 2013 workflow are similar to those for creating a SharePoint 2010 workflow. If you wanted to create a SharePoint 2013 workflow instead of a SharePoint 2010 workflow as described in the solution above, you would have to:

1. Follow steps 1 through 4 of the solution described above.
2. In step 5, select **SharePoint 2013 Workflow** as the **Platform Type**.

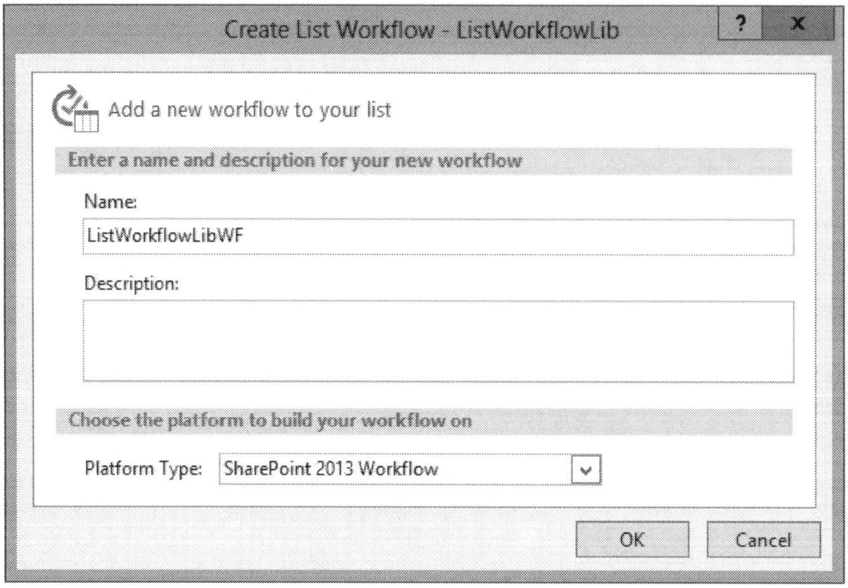

Figure 211. Creating a SharePoint 2013 workflow in SharePoint Designer 2013.

This should open the text-based designer with one stage (**Stage 1**) already added.

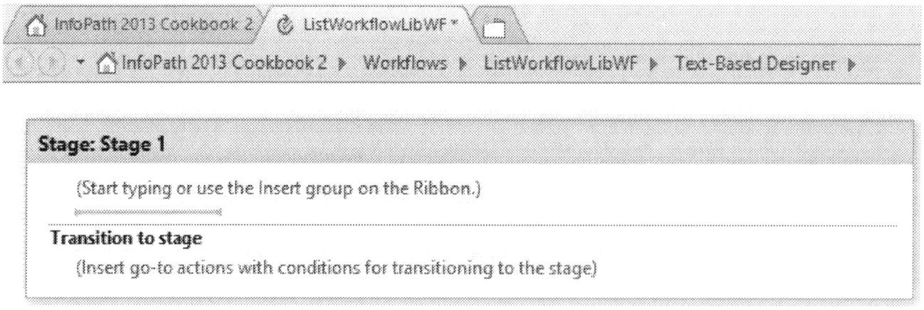

Figure 212. The text-based designer with one stage already added.

3. Follow steps 6 through 8 of the solution described above, thereby noting that a SharePoint 2013 workflow uses **Stages** instead of **Steps**.
4. Click inside of the **Transition to stage** section to place the cursor, and then select **Workflow ➤ Insert ➤ Action ➤ Go to a stage**.

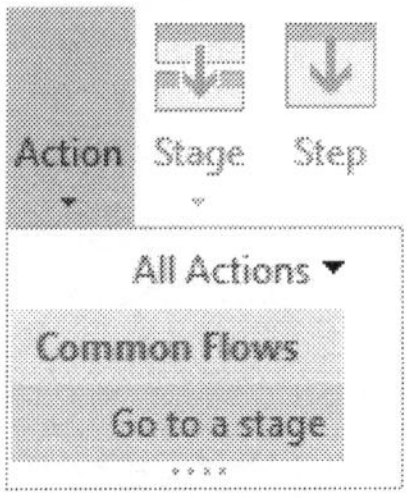

Figure 213. Inserting a 'Go to a stage' action in SharePoint Designer 2013.

5. Click **a stage** in the sentence for the workflow action, and then select **End of Workflow** from the drop-down list box that appears.

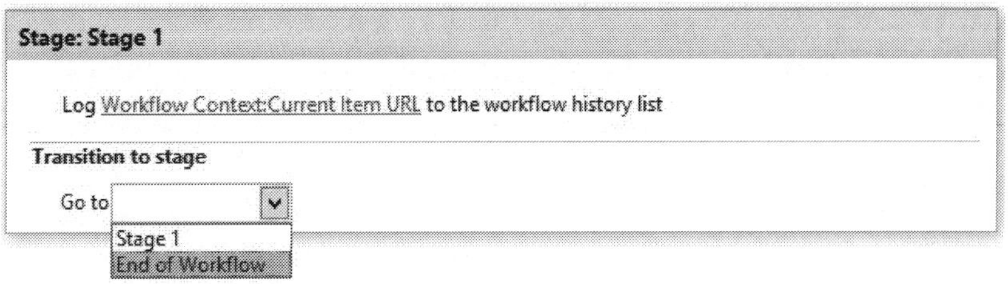

Figure 214. Selecting to end the workflow at the end of Stage 1.

6. Follow steps 9 through 12 of the solution described above.

After you have published and started the workflow by adding a new form to the **ListWorkflowLib** form library, you should see the name of the last stage that executed before the workflow ended appear in the **ListWorkflowLibWF** column of the form library.

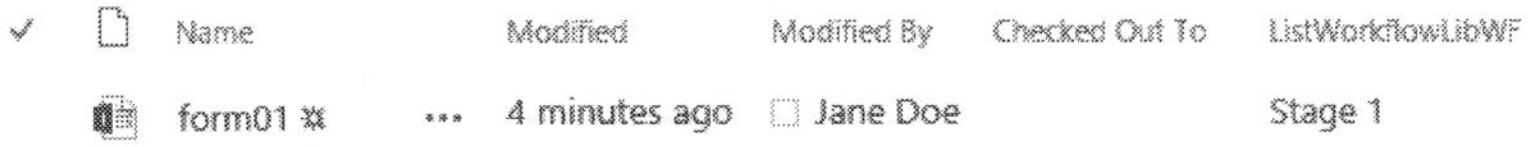

Figure 215. The name of the stage that last ran before the workflow ended.

Click on the stage's name to visit the **Workflow Status** page and see the **Workflow History**.

Workflow History

The workflow recorded these events.

☐ Date Occurred	Event Type	☐ User ID	Description
2/5/2014 12:23 PM	Comment	☐ Jane Doe	ListWorkflowLib/form01.xml

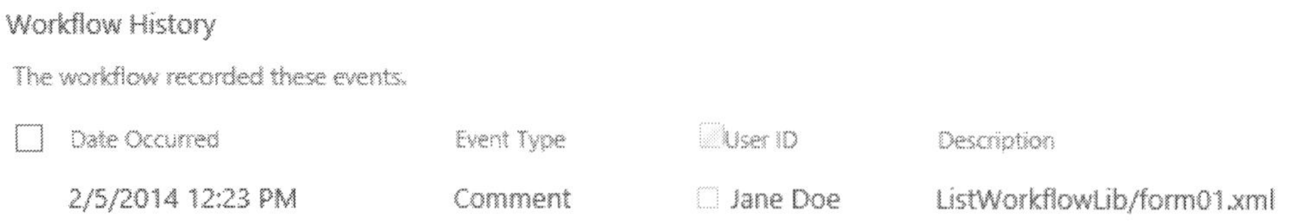

Figure 216. The workflow history in SharePoint 2013.

You can use SharePoint Designer to create workflow templates. A workflow template defines what a workflow does. And like a form template, a workflow template consists of several parts (steps or stages, actions, conditions, etc.), and can be configured so that any workflows that are created from that template are started automatically or manually.

A workflow consists of one or more workflow steps in a SharePoint 2010 workflow, or one or more stages in a SharePoint 2013 workflow. Each step or stage consists of one or more workflow actions. Optionally, you can add workflow conditions to workflow actions to get a workflow to execute certain actions only under certain conditions.

Actions are ordered by category in SharePoint Designer 2013. Click **Workflow ➤ Insert ➤ Action** and take a moment to scroll through the list of all of the categories and actions in SharePoint Designer 2013. Note that the cursor must be located inside of a step or stage for the **Action** command to become enabled on the Ribbon. The categories and actions are pretty self-explanatory and you will get a chance to work with several types of actions as you progress through this book. And as mentioned in the introduction of this chapter, the workflow actions that are available may differ depending on whether you are creating a SharePoint 2010 workflow or a SharePoint 2013 workflow.

In the solution described above, you used the **Log to History List** workflow action from the **Core Actions** category to write the URL of the InfoPath form on which the workflow ran as the description of a message to the history list. You can use the **Log to History List** workflow action anytime this way to debug a SharePoint Designer workflow. For example, if a workflow you created is showing unexpected behavior or producing incorrect values, you can add **Log to History List** workflow actions throughout the workflow to log the values of variables, parameters, etc. to the history list in order to verify that they are producing the values you expect them to produce.

Once you have created a workflow template in SharePoint Designer 2013, you must publish it. Depending on the type of workflow template you created, you may have to perform additional steps before you can create workflows that are based on that template in SharePoint.

There are three types of workflow templates you can create using SharePoint Designer 2013:

1. List
2. Reusable
3. Site

List workflows are workflows that can run on a particular list or library, are tightly bound to that list or library, and cannot be reused across multiple lists or libraries.

Reusable workflows are workflows that can run on one particular content type or a content type named **All**, which represents all of the content types associated with a list or library. Reusable workflows, as the name suggests, can be reused across multiple lists or libraries, so they are not tightly bound to only one list or library as is the case with list workflows. You will learn more about reusable workflows in recipe *81 Create a workflow that runs on a specific type of form*.

Site workflows are not bound to any content type, list, or library, but run in the context of a site.

When you first create a list workflow template in SharePoint Designer 2013, you must choose a SharePoint list or library to associate the workflow template with. Therefore, when you publish a list workflow template to SharePoint, a workflow that is based on that template is automatically added to the SharePoint list or library you selected when you created the workflow template; no further configuration is required in SharePoint and the workflow is ready to be started on items or documents in SharePoint.

Reusable workflows are different. Reusable workflows require extra configuration steps, which you will learn more about in recipe *81 Create a workflow that runs on a specific type of form*. And site workflows are automatically associated with the site for which you create the site workflow template.

In the solution described above, you created a simple list workflow that ran whenever a new form was added to a form library. If you have a form library on which you enabled multiple content types, so which contains different types of forms (also see recipe *27 Create different types of forms in one form library*), associating a list workflow with the form library would have the effect of the workflow running on any type of form that is added to that form library. If you want a workflow to run on a specific type of form in the form library, you must create a reusable workflow as described in recipe *81 Create a workflow that runs on a specific type of form*.

Note that while you configured the workflow to automatically run whenever a new form is added to the form library, you can also manually start the workflow to run on a form in the form library (also see recipe *83 Manually start a workflow to run on a form*), because you left the **Allow this workflow to be manually started** option enabled on the workflow.

81 Create a workflow that runs on a specific type of form

Problem

You want to have a workflow run whenever a form that is based on a specific form template (a specific type of form) is added as a new form to a form library.

Solution

You must publish the form template as a site content type and then in SharePoint Designer 2013, create a SharePoint 2010 reusable workflow that is associated with that particular content type.

To create a reusable workflow that can run on a specific type of form:

1. In InfoPath, create a new SharePoint form library form template or use an existing one, and publish it as a site content type as described in recipe *25 Create a content type for an InfoPath form from within InfoPath*. Name the content type **ReusableWFFormCT**.
2. Open SharePoint Designer 2013, and click **File** ➤ **Sites** ➤ **Open Site**.
3. On the **Open Site** dialog box, browse to and select the site on which the **ReusableWFFormCT** content type for the form template is located or enter the URL of the site in the **Site name** text box, and click **Open**.
4. Once the site has been opened, click **Site** ➤ **New** ➤ **Reusable Workflow**.
5. On the **Create Reusable Workflow** dialog box, type **ReusableWorkflowWF** in the **Name** text box, select **SharePoint 2010 Workflow** from the **Platform Type** drop-down list box, select **ReusableWFFormCT** from the **Content Type** drop-down list box, and click **OK**. This should open the text-based designer with one step (**Step 1**) already added to the workflow.

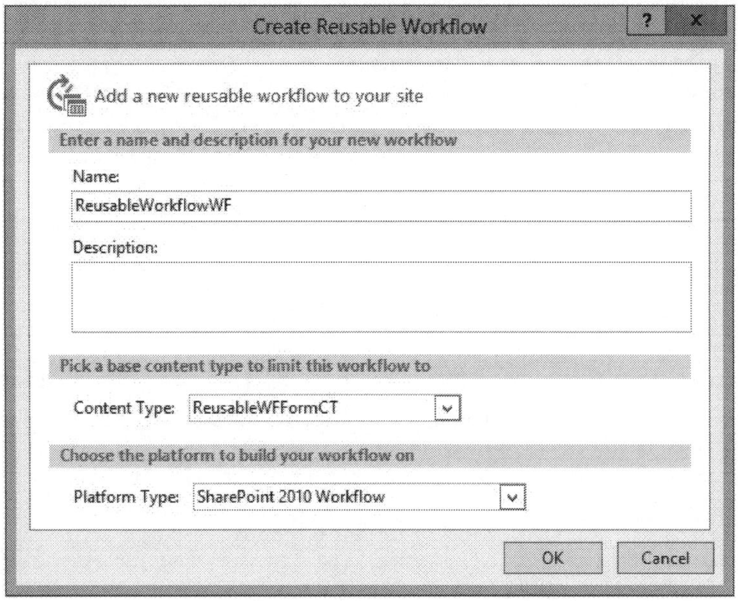

Figure 217. The Create Reusable Workflow dialog box in SharePoint Designer.

Note that if you already had SharePoint Designer 2013 open before you published the InfoPath form template as a site content type, the new content type may not be listed in the **Content Type** drop-down list box. If the content type is missing from the list of content types, close the dialog box, press **F5** or click the **Refresh** command on the **Quick Access Toolbar**, and then try creating the workflow again.

Figure 218. Refresh command on the Quick Access Toolbar in SharePoint Designer.

6. In recipe *80 Create a workflow that runs on forms in a specific form library*, you wrote the URL of the form the workflow was running on to the workflow history list. In this solution, you are going to write the name of the item (form) on which the workflow is running to the workflow history list. So place the cursor inside of **Step 1**, type **log**, and then press **Enter** to add a **Log to History List** action.
7. Click **this message** in the sentence for the workflow action, and then click the formula button (second button) behind the text box that appears.
8. On the **Lookup for String** dialog box, select **Workflow Context** from the **Data source** drop-down list box, select **Item Name** from the **Field from source** drop-down list box, and click **OK**. The final sentence for the workflow action should say:

```
Log Workflow Context:Item Name to the workflow history list
```

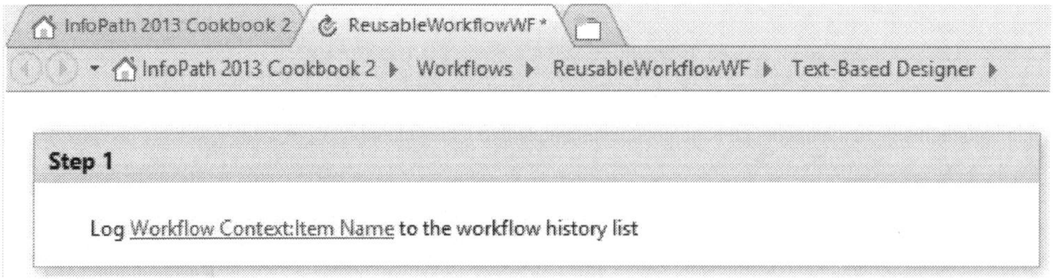

Figure 219. The configured action for the reusable workflow in SharePoint Designer.

9. Click **Workflow ➤ Save ➤ Check for Errors** to ensure that the workflow does not contain any errors. A message box saying that the workflow contains no errors should appear. If there are errors, you must fix them before publishing the workflow. Click **OK** to close the message box.
10. Click **Workflow ➤ Manage ➤ Workflow Settings**.
11. On the workflow settings page under **Start Options**, select the **Disable automatic start on item change option** check box. This prevents the user who adds the workflow to a form library from selecting the option that allows the workflow to run whenever an existing form is resubmitted or resaved to the form library.

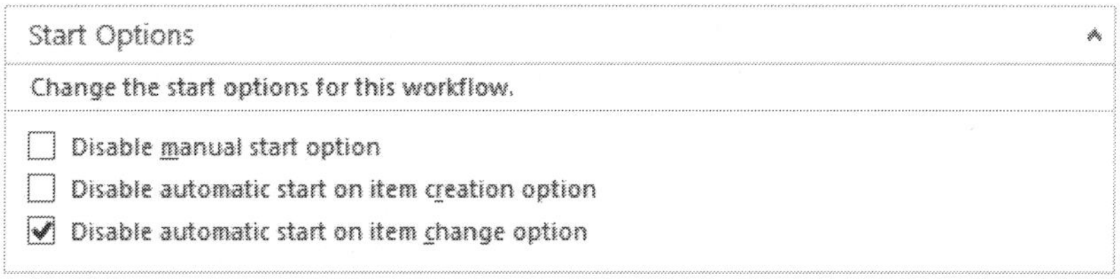

Figure 220. Start options for a reusable workflow in SharePoint Designer 2013.

Note that when you create a list workflow, you configure the way a user is allowed to start a workflow on an item by enabling start options on the workflow template (also see recipe *80 Create a workflow that runs on forms in a specific form library*). On the other hand, when you create a reusable workflow and select start options for it, you merely disable the start options check boxes a user is allowed to select when she adds the workflow to a list or library; the start options on the reusable workflow template are not meant to actually specify how a workflow should be started, but rather which options a user can select when the workflow is associated with a list or library. So the start options on list and reusable workflow templates mean slightly different things.

Figure 221 shows what the configuration of the start options on the **Add a Workflow** page in SharePoint would look like after you have selected the **Disable automatic start on item change option** in

SharePoint Designer 2013 and published the workflow template.

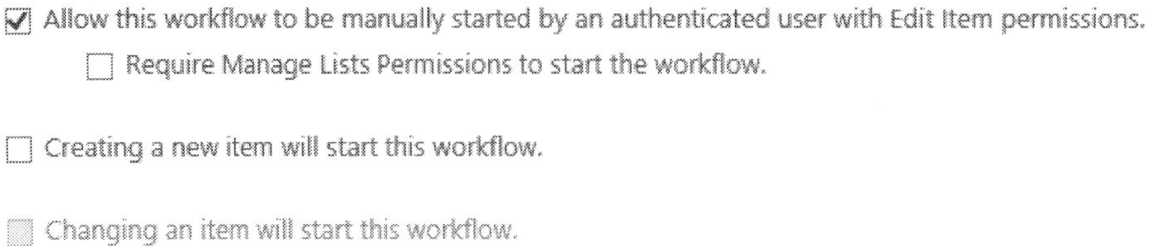

Figure 221. Start Options on the Add a Workflow page in SharePoint 2013.

As you can see from the figure above, the **Changing an item will start this workflow** check box has been dimmed (disabled) as an indication that the user is not allowed to select this option. You will be going through the steps for adding a reusable workflow to a form library next.

12. Click **Workflow Settings ➤ Save ➤ Publish** to publish the workflow.

Once you have created and published the workflow template in SharePoint Designer, you must then add a workflow that is based on that workflow template to the content type or to a form library that is associated with the content type before the workflow can run on forms that are based on the content type associated with the workflow.

To add a reusable workflow to a content type associated with a form library:

1. In SharePoint, associate the **ReusableWFFormCT** content type with a form library as described in recipe *27 Create different types of forms in one form library*.
2. Navigate to the form library that is associated with the **ReusableWFFormCT** content type, click **Library ➤ Settings ➤ Workflow Settings**, and then select **Add a Workflow** from the drop-down menu that appears.

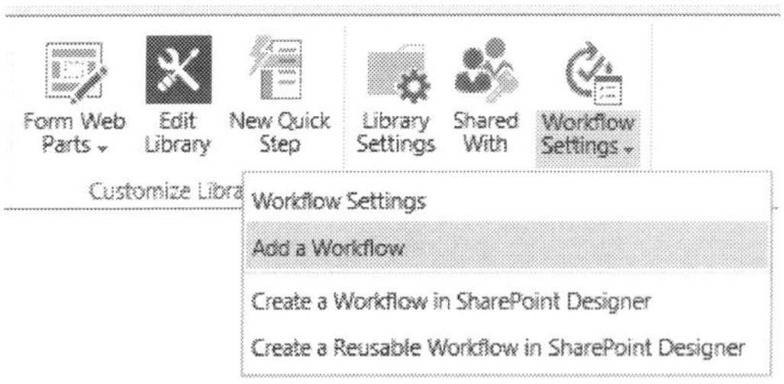

Figure 222. Add a Workflow drop-down menu item in SharePoint 2013.

3. On the **Add a Workflow** page, select the content type you associated the workflow with in SharePoint Designer 2013 from the **Run on items of this type** drop-down list box, select the name of the workflow template in the **Select a workflow template** list box, enter a unique name for the workflow in the **Type a unique name for this workflow** text box, select the **Creating a new item will start this workflow** check box, and click **OK**. Note that the name you give the workflow need not be the same as the name of the workflow template.

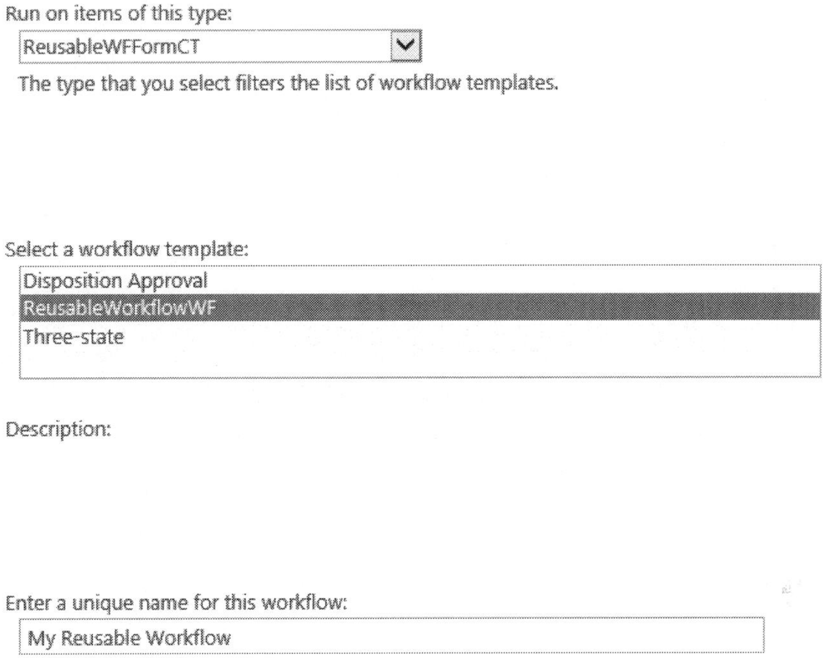

Figure 223. Adding a workflow to a content type of a form library in SharePoint 2013.

After you click **OK**, SharePoint should take you to the **Workflow Settings** page of the content type.

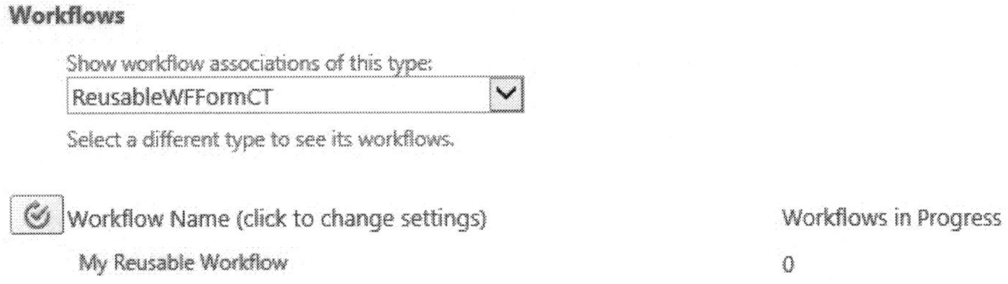

Figure 224. Workflow Settings page of the content type in SharePoint 2013.

On this page, you can also select any of the other content types that have been associated with the form library from the **Show workflow associations of this type** drop-down list box to view the list of workflows that have been added to those content types.

In SharePoint, navigate to the form library that is associated with the content type and add a new form that is based on the content type the workflow is linked to, to the form library. Fill out and then save the form back to the form library. Because you configured the workflow to start whenever a new item is added to the form library, the workflow should automatically start after you have saved the form to the form library. Once the workflow has completed, navigate to the workflow history list and verify that the name of the InfoPath form was logged to the history list.

Discussion

When you create a reusable workflow template in SharePoint Designer 2013, you must choose a content type to associate the workflow with. If you create a SharePoint 2010 workflow, you can choose to link a specific content type to the reusable workflow. However, if you create a SharePoint 2013 workflow, you cannot link a specific content type to the reusable workflow; the workflow will by default run on any content type.

In the solution described above, you chose to associate the workflow with a specific content type that had an InfoPath form template defined as its document template. And because content types are generally associated with a list or library in SharePoint, you must perform an extra step to manually attach a workflow that is based on the workflow template you created to lists or libraries on which you want the workflow to run. This step is called associating or adding a workflow to a list or library. And once you have added a workflow that is based on the workflow template to a form library, you should be able to run that workflow on forms that are based on the form template linked to the content type that the workflow was designed to run on.

Because content types can be associated with one or multiple libraries, you can add a reusable workflow to one or multiple libraries without having to recreate the workflow template. Had you created a list workflow as described in recipe *80 Create a workflow that runs on forms in a specific form library* instead of a reusable workflow, you would have had to recreate the list workflow template in SharePoint Designer 2013 for each form library on which you wanted to run the workflow. So a reusable workflow is recommended if you want to add a workflow to multiple lists or libraries instead of just one. There is where the term "reuse" comes from. Note however, that you can export a SharePoint 2013 list workflow (not a SharePoint 2010 list workflow) as a template to be reused on another site.

If you have a form library on which you enabled multiple content types, so which contains different types of forms (also see recipe *27 Create different types of forms in one form library*), associating a list workflow with the form library would have the same effect as the workflow running on any type of form in that form library. If on the other hand you associated a reusable workflow with one specific type of form (content type) in that form library, the workflow would only run on those forms that were based on the form template that corresponded to the content type the workflow was associated with, and not on all of the types of forms in the form library.

If you want a reusable workflow to run on all types of forms in a form library as is the case with a list workflow, you would have to associate the workflow template with the **All** content type, which you can select from the **Content Type** drop-down list box on the **Create Reusable Workflow** dialog box when you create the workflow template in SharePoint Designer 2013.

In the solution described above, you added the reusable workflow to a list content type that was associated with a form library. Note that you could have also added the workflow to the site content type the list content type was copied from when you added it to the form library. By adding the workflow to the site content type instead of a list content type, you would not have to add the workflow to form libraries every time you associated them with the content type linked to the workflow. List content types that you copy onto form libraries would then automatically be associated with the workflow you added to the site content type the list content types are based on. The quickest way to add a workflow to a site content type is by clicking **Workflow Settings ➤ Manage ➤ Associate to Content Type** in

SharePoint Designer 2013, and then selecting the content type to add the workflow to from the drop-down menu that appears.

Figure 225. Adding a workflow to a content type from within SharePoint Designer.

You can also add a workflow to a list or site content type in SharePoint 2013 by clicking **Workflow settings** under the **Settings** section on the **List Content Type** or **Site Content Type** page, and then clicking **Add a workflow** on the **Workflow Settings** page.

Tip:

> While a list workflow is quick and easy to create and publish, if you suspect that you will want to use a workflow on multiple form libraries in the future, consider creating a reusable workflow instead of a list workflow.

82 Delete a workflow that runs on forms in a form library

Problem

You have previously added a workflow to a form library, but now you do not want the workflow to run anymore on the form library.

Solution

You can delete a workflow from a form library either from within SharePoint 2013 or from within SharePoint Designer 2013.

To delete a workflow from a form library from within SharePoint 2013:

1. In SharePoint, navigate to the form library that has the workflow associated with it, click **Library ➤ Settings ➤ Workflow Settings**, and select **Workflow Settings** from the drop-down menu that appears.

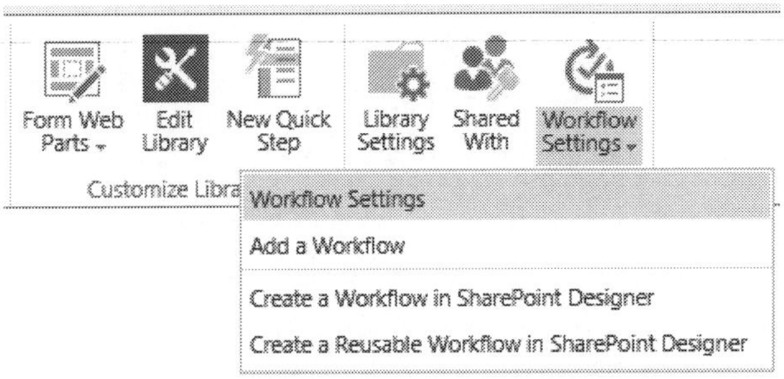

Figure 226. Workflow Settings drop-down menu item in SharePoint 2013.

2. On the **Workflow Settings** page, select **This List** from the **Show workflow associations of this type** drop-down list box if the workflow you want to delete is a list workflow or select the name of a content type from the drop-down list box if the workflow you want to delete is a reusable workflow, and then click **Remove, Block, or Restore a Workflow**.

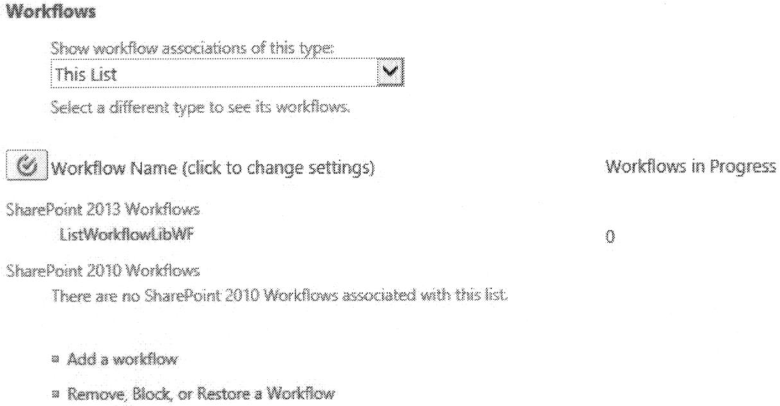

Figure 227. Workflow Settings page of a form library in SharePoint 2013.

3. On the **Remove Workflows** page, select the **Remove** option for the workflow you want to remove, and then click **OK**.

SharePoint 2013 Workflows	Workflow	Instances	Allow	No New Instances	Remove
Select the workflows to remove from this document library. Removing a workflow association cancels its running workflows. Select No New Instances to allow running workflows to complete.	ListWorkflowLibWF	0	○	○	●

Figure 228. The Remove Workflows page of a form library in SharePoint 2013.

Note that deleting a workflow as described above only disassociates the workflow from the form library or content type, but does not delete the actual workflow template that was used to associate the workflow to the form library or content type. So if you wanted to, you could republish the workflow from within SharePoint Designer 2013 at a later stage to add the workflow back to the form library, or reassociate the workflow to a content type if the workflow is a reusable workflow.

If you want to get rid of all traces of the workflow, you must delete the workflow template from within SharePoint Designer 2013. This action removes the workflow from the form library or content type, but also deletes the actual workflow template.

To delete a workflow from a form library and its corresponding workflow template from within SharePoint Designer 2013:

1. In SharePoint Designer 2013, click **Workflows** in the left **Navigation** pane.

2. On the **Workflows** page, right-click the workflow you want to delete, and select **Delete** from the context menu that appears.

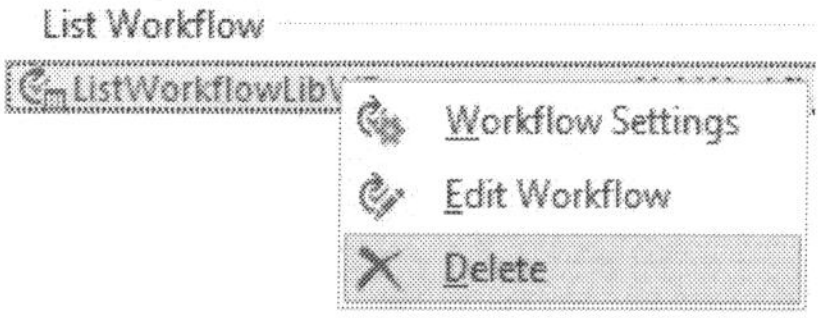

Figure 229. Deleting a list workflow template in SharePoint Designer 2013.

3. On the **Confirm Delete** message box, click **Yes**.

83 Manually start a workflow to run on a form

Problem

You have configured a workflow that runs on forms in a form library to be manually started. Now you want to manually start the workflow on an existing form in the form library.

Solution

You must access the workflow start page to manually start a workflow on a form in a form library. The steps for starting a SharePoint 2010 workflow differ from those for starting a SharePoint 2013 workflow.

To manually start a SharePoint 2010 workflow to run on a form:

1. If you have not already published a list workflow, follow the instructions in recipe *80 Create a workflow that runs on forms in a specific form library* to create a SharePoint 2010 **List Workflow** that is associated with a form library named **ListWorkflowLib**.
2. In SharePoint, navigate to the **ListWorkflowLib** form library.
3. Select the check mark in front of a form on which you want to start the workflow, and then click **Files** ➤ **Workflows** ➤ **Workflows**.

Figure 230. Workflows command under the Workflows group on the Files tab.

Or click the ellipsis behind the name of the form, click the ellipsis behind **Share** on the context menu that appears, and then select **Workflows** from the drop-down menu that appears.

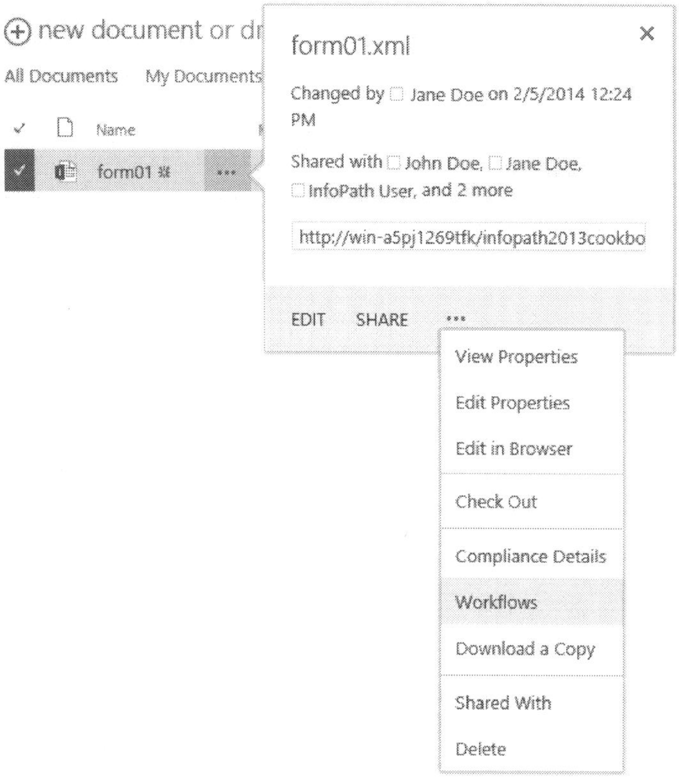

Figure 231. Accessing the Workflows page of an InfoPath form in a form library.

4. On the **Workflows** page of the form under the **Start a New Workflow** section, click **ListWorkflowLibWF**.

Figure 232. Manually starting a workflow on an InfoPath form in SharePoint.

5. On the **Start** page of the workflow, you will see a **Start** and a **Cancel** button. These buttons are located on an InfoPath form called a workflow initiation form, which you will learn how to customize in recipe *88 Send a form's link in an email to selected users at workflow startup*. For now, click **Start** to manually start the workflow.

Figure 233. Workflow initiation form with Start and Cancel buttons.

After you click the **Start** button, you should be redirected back to the form library. Wait a few seconds and then refresh the page. You should see the text **Completed** appear in the workflow column after the workflow has run and successfully completed.

To manually start a SharePoint 2013 workflow to run on a form:

1. If you have not already published a list workflow, follow the instructions in the discussion section of recipe *80 Create a workflow that runs on forms in a specific form library* to create a SharePoint 2013 **List Workflow** that is associated with a form library named **ListWorkflowLib**.
2. Follow steps 2 through 4 of the solution described above.

After you click the name of the workflow you want to start, you should be redirected back to the form library. Wait a few seconds and then refresh the page. You should see the name of a stage appear in the workflow column after the workflow has run and successfully completed.

Discussion

A workflow can be started in one of four ways:

1. Manually.
2. Automatically when a new item is created.
3. Automatically when an item is changed.
4. From a coordination action within a SharePoint 2013 workflow.

For list workflows you must configure the start options when you create the workflow template in SharePoint Designer 2013. For reusable workflows you must define which start options should become available for a workflow when you create the workflow template and then configure the start options when you associate the workflow with a list, library, or content type (see recipe *81 Create a workflow that runs on a specific type of form*). Site workflows can be manually started via the **Site Workflows** link on the **Site Contents** page. And finally, you can use a **Start a List Workflow** action or a **Start a Site Workflow** action in a SharePoint 2013 workflow to start a list or a site workflow.

If a workflow is manually started, you can allow the user who started the workflow to pass extra information to the workflow at startup by using a workflow initiation form, which is an InfoPath form in the case of a SharePoint 2010 workflow (also see recipe *88 Send a form's link in an email to selected users at workflow startup*) or an ASP.NET form in the case of a SharePoint 2013 workflow.

In the solution described above you saw that starting a SharePoint 2010 workflow manually on an item is a 5-click process and a 4-click process for a SharePoint 2013 workflow. You can reduce the amount of clicks to start a particular workflow on an InfoPath form in a form library by adding a custom action to the drop-down menu of forms in the form library as described in the next recipe.

84 Start a workflow from a custom action in a library

Problem

You want to be able to start a workflow on a form by selecting an item from the menu of an InfoPath form in a form library.

Solution

You can use SharePoint Designer 2013 to add a custom action to the drop-down menu of InfoPath forms in a form library, so that users can easily start a list workflow on a form.

To start a list workflow from a custom action on a form:

1. If you have not already published a list workflow, follow the instructions in recipe *80 Create a workflow that runs on forms in a specific form library* to create a SharePoint 2010 or SharePoint 2013 **List**

Workflow that is associated with a form library named **ListWorkflowLib**.

2. In SharePoint Designer 2013, in the left **Navigation** pane, click **Lists and Libraries**.

Figure 234. List and Libraries in the Navigation pane in SharePoint Designer 2013.

3. On the **Lists and Libraries** page under **Document Libraries**, click on the name of the form library to which you want to add a custom action.

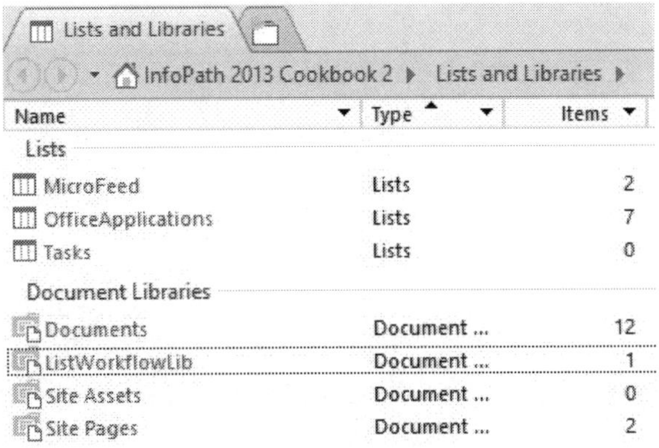

Figure 235. List and Libraries page in SharePoint Designer 2013.

4. On the form library page under the **Custom Actions** section, click **New**.

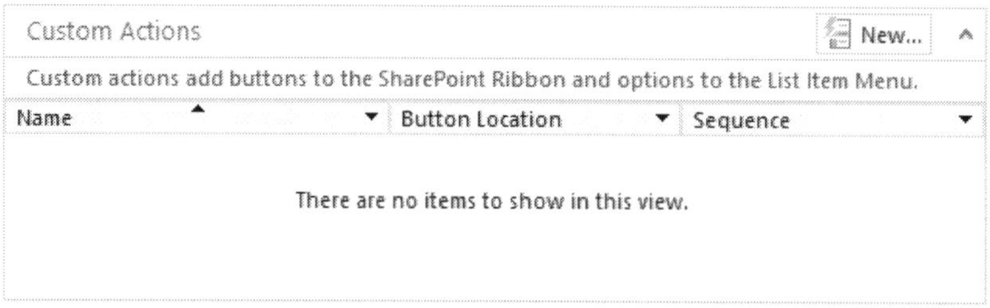

Figure 236. Custom Actions section in SharePoint Designer 2013.

5. On the **Create Custom Action** dialog box, enter a **Name** for the custom action (for example **Show Form URL**), select the **Initiate workflow** option, select the list workflow you want to start from the drop-down list box, and click **OK**.

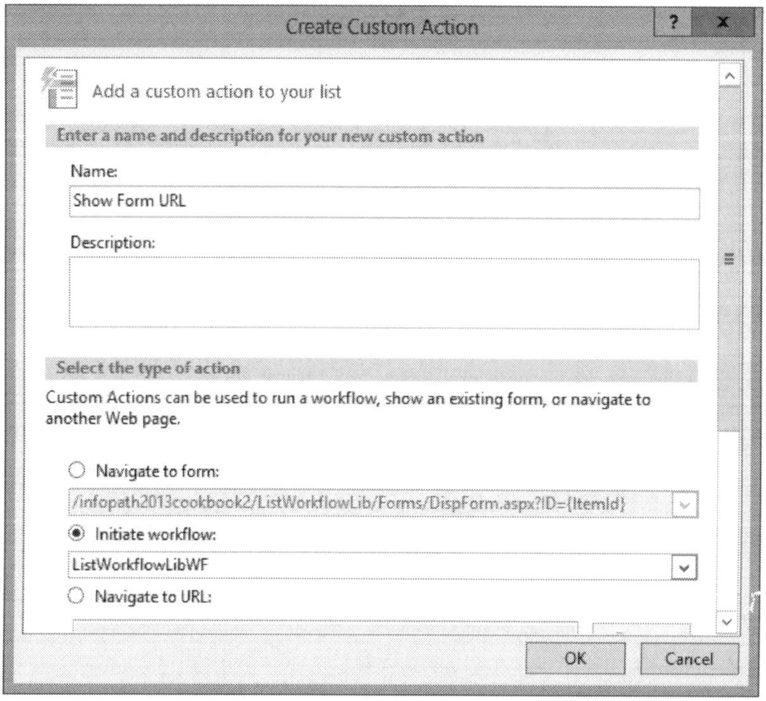

Figure 237. The Create Custom Action dialog box in SharePoint Designer 2013.

In SharePoint, navigate to the form library where you added the custom action. Click the ellipsis behind the name of a form, and then click the ellipsis behind **Share** on the context menu that appears to open the form's drop-down menu. The **Show Form URL** custom action you added should be listed as the first item on the drop-down menu.

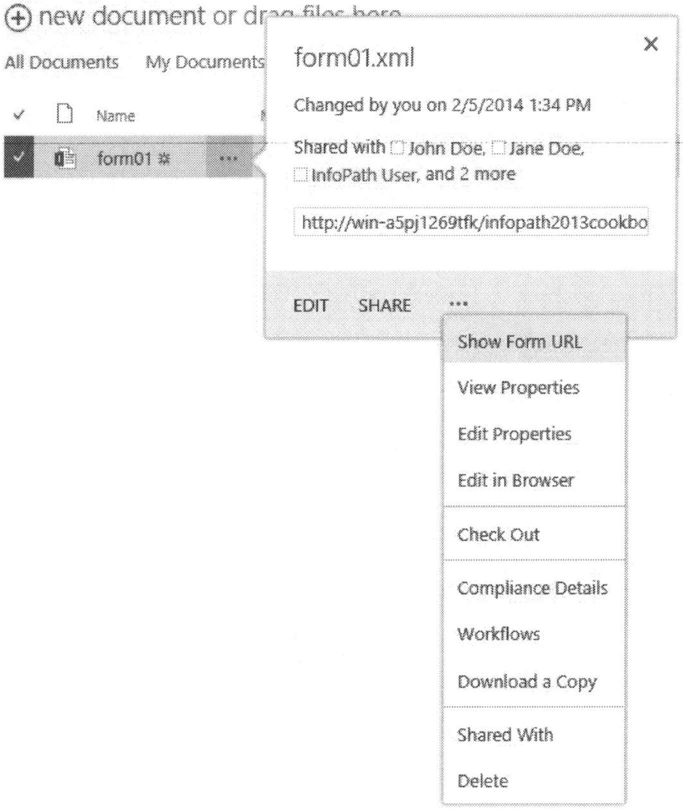

Figure 238. The newly added Show Form URL custom action on the menu of a form.

Select the **Show Form URL** menu item. You should be taken directly to the workflow start page of a SharePoint 2010 workflow where you can start the workflow, or the workflow should immediately start to run for a SharePoint 2013 workflow that does not make use of an initiation form. Navigate to the form library and verify that the workflow ran.

Discussion

In the solution described above, you learned how to add a custom action to the drop-down menu of forms in a form library.

To delete the custom action you added:

1. In SharePoint Designer 2013, follow steps 2 and 3 of the solution described above.
2. On the form library page under the **Custom Actions** section, select the custom action you want to delete, and then click **Custom Actions ➤ Edit ➤ Delete** on the Ribbon.
3. On the **Confirm Delete** message box, click **Yes**.

In SharePoint, navigate to the form library from which you deleted the custom action. Open the menu of a form and verify that the custom action has been removed from the drop-down menu.

Note that custom actions as described in the solution above apply to list or reusable workflows you have added to a list or library.

85 Start a workflow by clicking on a button on an InfoPath form

Problem

You want to click a button on an InfoPath form to start and run a workflow in SharePoint.

Solution

You can use the **UpdateListItems** operation of SharePoint's **Lists** web service and a helper list in SharePoint to start a workflow when an item is added to that list.

To start and run a workflow by clicking on a button on an InfoPath form:

1. In SharePoint, create a new custom list named **StartWorkflow** that has a **Title** column.
2. Navigate to the **StartWorkflow** list, click **List ➤ Settings ➤ List Settings**, and then copy the GUID that is listed after the **List** query string parameter in the URL in the browser's address bar. It should look something like the following:

```
%7BADFA2558%2DB237%2D491B%2D8E86%2D1F8A7ADFF3E0%7D
```

3. Convert the **%7B** characters to **{**, **%2D** to **-**, and **%7D** to **}**. The resulting list GUID should now resemble the following:

```
{ADFA2558-B237-491B-8E86-1F8A7ADFF3E0}
```

Copy it to the Windows clipboard.

4. In Notepad, create a file with the following contents:

```
<Batch>
  <Method ID="1" Cmd="New">
    <Field Name="Title">Start Workflow</Field>
  </Method>
</Batch>
```

and save it to disk with the name **StartWorkflowBatch.xml**.

5. In InfoPath, create a new SharePoint form library form template or use an existing one.
6. On the **Fields** task pane, add a hidden field named **listName** to the Main data source, and then set its **Default Value** to be equal to the list GUID from step 3.
7. Select **Data ➤ Get External Data ➤ From Other Sources ➤ From XML File** and follow the instructions to add an XML data connection for the **StartWorkflowBatch.xml** file. Leave the **Automatically retrieve data when form is opened** check box selected and name the data connection **StartWorkflowBatch**.
8. The contents of the XML file should be submitted to the **Lists** web service in SharePoint to add a new item to the **StartWorkflow** list. So select **Data ➤ Submit Form ➤ To Other Locations ➤ To Web Service**.
9. On the **Data Connection Wizard**, enter the URL of the **Lists** web service, for example:

```
http://servername/sitename/_vti_bin/Lists.asmx
```

and click **Next**. Here, **servername** is the name of the SharePoint server and **sitename** is the name of the site where the **StartWorkflow** SharePoint list is located.

10. On the **Data Connection Wizard**, select the **UpdateListItems** operation from the list of operations, and click **Next**.
11. On the **Data Connection Wizard**, select **listName** in the **Parameters** list, and then click the button behind the **Field or group** text box.
12. On the **Select a Field or Group** dialog box, leave **Main** selected in the drop-down list box, select **listName**, and click **OK**. With this you have set the **listName** parameter of the web service operation to be equal to the value of the **listName** field in the Main data source of the form that contains the GUID of the **StartWorkflow** SharePoint list.

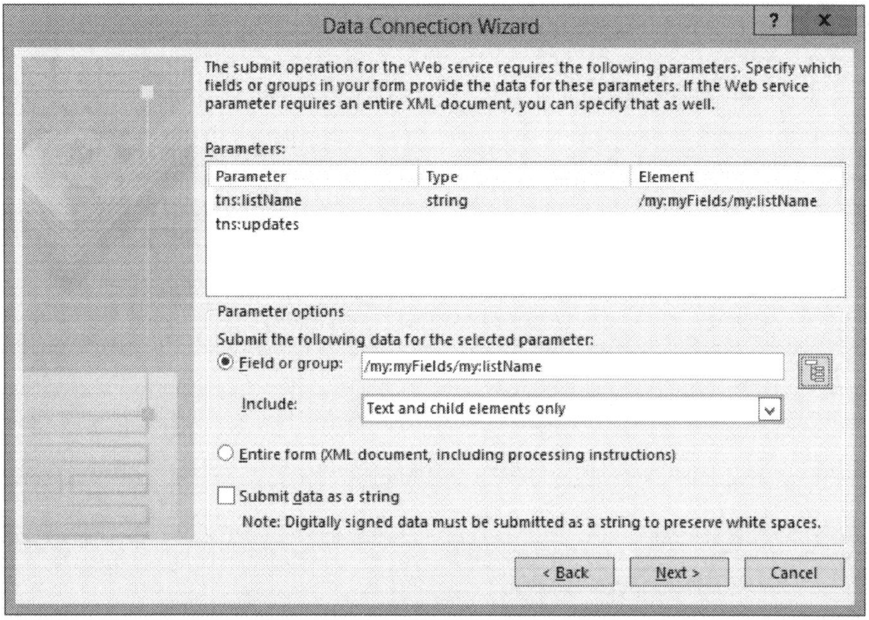

Figure 239. The Data Connection Wizard after setting the value of the first parameter.

13. On the **Data Connection Wizard**, select **updates** in the **Parameters** list, and then click the button behind the **Field or group** text box.
14. On the **Select a Field or Group** dialog box, select **StartWorkflowBatch (Secondary)** from the drop-down list box, select the **Batch** group node, and click **OK**. With this you have set the **updates** parameter of the web service operation to be equal to the contents of the entire **Batch** node in the secondary data source for the XML file you added earlier.

15. On the **Data Connection Wizard**, select **XML subtree, including selected element** from the **Include** drop-down list box, and click **Next**. This setting will submit the entire XML contents of the **Batch** node including its child nodes and values to the web service.

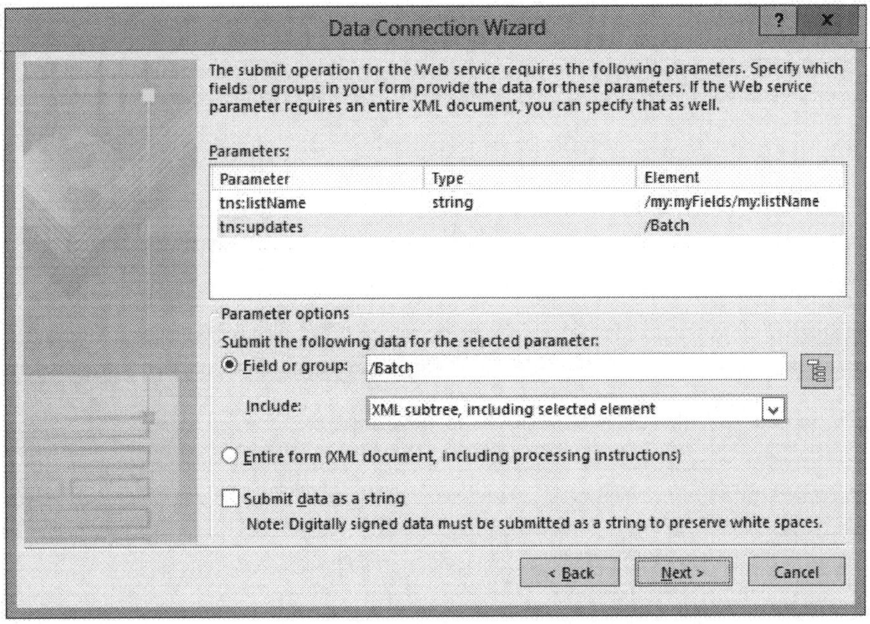

Figure 240. The Data Connection Wizard after setting the second parameter.

16. Name the data connection **UpdateListItems**, deselect the **Set as the default submit connection** check box, and click **Finish**. Note that while you have created a submit data connection to call the **Lists** web service, you should add another submit data connection to the form template that does the actual submitting of the form, for example to a SharePoint form library (also see recipe *34 Submit a form to a form library and then close it*). The submit data connection for the web service is not meant to submit the form; it is only meant to call the web service to add a new item to the **StartWorkflow** SharePoint list.

17. Add a **Button** control to the view of the form template and label it **Start Workflow**.

18. Add an **Action** rule to the button with an action that says:

```
Submit using a data connection: UpdateListItems
```

This action rule calls the **UpdateListItems** operation of the **Lists** web service to add a new list item to the **StartWorkflow** SharePoint list.

19. If your SharePoint environment is configured to use Claims Based authentication as opposed to Windows Classic authentication and the form is going to be filled out through the browser, you must set up UDC authentication for the **UpdateListItems** data connection that makes the web service call as described in *Configure a web service data connection for a web browser form* in the Appendix. But before you do this, test the form in InfoPath Filler 2013 to ensure that the functionality is working properly.
20. Publish the form template to a SharePoint form library.
21. In SharePoint Designer 2013, create a SharePoint 2010 **List Workflow** that runs on the **StartWorkflow** SharePoint list (also see recipe *80 Create a workflow that runs on forms in a specific form library*, but select the **StartWorkflow** SharePoint list to associate the workflow to instead of a SharePoint form library) and that performs actions of your choice, for example creates a list item in another list, logs a message to the workflow history list, or sends an email. Ensure that you set the start options for the workflow to **Start workflow automatically when an item is created** before you publish the workflow.

In SharePoint, navigate to the form library where you published the form template and add a new form. When the form opens, click the **Start Workflow** button. Close the form. Navigate to the **StartWorkflow** SharePoint list and check whether a new item was created and that the workflow was started. Once the workflow has completed, verify that the workflow performed the actions you wanted it to perform.

If no new item was added to the **StartWorkflow** SharePoint list after you clicked the **Start Workflow** button, you should get an administrator to check for any error messages that could be related to the form via **Applications and Services Logs ➤ Microsoft ➤ SharePoint Products ➤ Shared ➤ Operational** in the Windows event log on the SharePoint server.

Discussion

The solution described above is based on two principles:

1. You can add a new item to a SharePoint list from within an InfoPath form by calling the **UpdateListItems** operation of the **Lists** web service through a web service submit data connection.
2. You can automatically start and run a workflow in SharePoint whenever a new item is added to a SharePoint list.

Because there is no direct way to start a workflow from within an InfoPath form without writing code, the solution described above can be seen as a workaround, so should be used sparingly.

86 Get the value of an InfoPath form field in a workflow

Problem

You want to be able to retrieve data from an InfoPath form field in a SharePoint Designer workflow and use this data to create a new item in a SharePoint list.

Solution

You can promote the form field from which you want to retrieve data, to a column in a form library when you publish the form template to SharePoint, and then use a lookup in a SharePoint Designer workflow to retrieve the value of the form field and use it to create a new SharePoint list item.

To get the value of an InfoPath form field from within a workflow:

1. In InfoPath, create a new SharePoint form library form template or use an existing one that contains the field you want to access from within the workflow, and publish the form template to SharePoint. When publishing the form template, promote the field you want to access either as a list column or a site column (see recipe *22 Promote form fields to columns of a form library* and recipe *23 Promote form fields to existing site columns*). You do not have to select the **Allow users to edit data in this field by using a datasheet or properties page** check box when you promote the field, because in this case you only want to retrieve a

value of a form field and not set the value of a form field. Name the promoted field **GetValueInWorkflow**.

2. In SharePoint, create a new SharePoint list named **Contacts** in which you can store names. The SharePoint list only needs to have a **Title** column.
3. In SharePoint Designer 2013, create a SharePoint 2010 or a SharePoint 2013 **List Workflow** and associate it with the form library to which you published the form template that has the promoted field (also see recipe *80 Create a workflow that runs on forms in a specific form library*). You are going to create a workflow that adds a new item to the **Contacts** SharePoint list and sets the value of the **Title** field of the new item to be equal to the value of the **GetValueInWorkflow** promoted field.
4. On the text-based designer, place the cursor within a step or stage, type **create list**, and then press **Enter** to add a **Create List Item** action.
5. Click **this list** in the sentence for the workflow action.
6. On the **Create New List Item** dialog box, select **Contacts** from the **List** drop-down list box, select **Title (*)** in the list of fields, and then click **Modify**.
7. On the **Value Assignment** dialog box, click the formula button (second button) behind the **To this value** text box.
8. On the **Lookup for Single line of text** dialog box, leave **Current Item** selected in the **Data source** drop-down list box, select **GetValueInWorkflow** from the **Field from source** drop-down list box, and click **OK**.

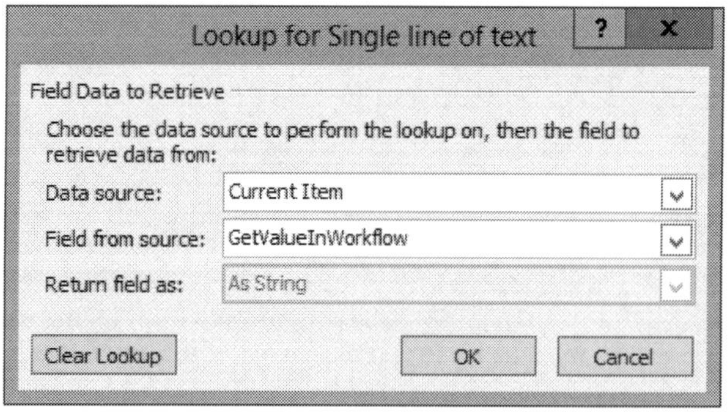

Figure 241. Setting the promoted field to be the value of the Title of the new list item.

9. On the **Value Assignment** dialog box, click **OK**. With this you have set the value of the **Title** field of the new item in the **Contacts** list to be equal to the value of the **GetValueInWorkflow** promoted field.
10. On the **Create New List Item** dialog box, click **OK**.
11. If you created a SharePoint 2013 **List Workflow**, add a **Go to a stage** action to the **Transition to stage** section, and select to go to **End of Workflow**.

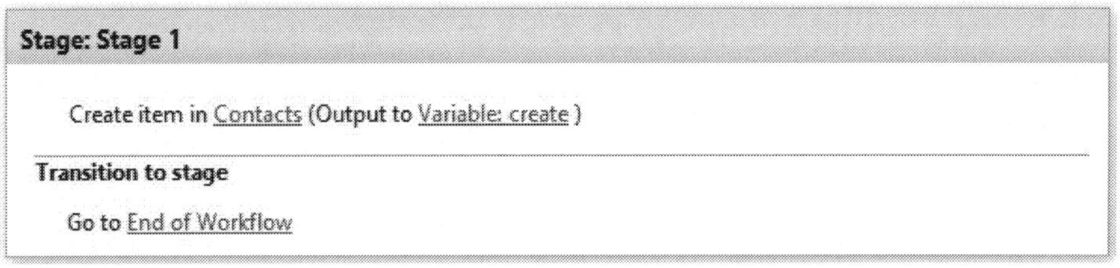
Stage: Stage 1
Create item in Contacts (Output to Variable: create)
Transition to stage
Go to End of Workflow

Figure 242. The completed workflow in SharePoint Designer 2013.

12. Click **Workflow ➤ Manage ➤ Workflow Settings**.
13. On the workflow setting page under **Start Options**, select the **Start workflow automatically when an item is created** check box. You can leave the **Allow this workflow to be manually started** check box selected so that users are still able to rerun the workflow on the InfoPath form in case the workflow failed to create a new list item or if a list item needs to be created for forms that were created before the workflow was associated with the form library.
14. Click **Workflow Settings ➤ Save ➤ Publish** to publish the workflow.

In SharePoint, navigate to the form library where you published the form template and add a new form. Fill out the form and then save or submit it back to the form library. Once the workflow has run, navigate to the **Contacts** list and check whether a new item was created with a **Title** that has the same value as the one you entered into the **GetValueInWorkflow** promoted field while filling out the form.

Discussion

In the solution described above, you promoted a field to a column in a SharePoint form library to be able to run a workflow and retrieve the value of this field from within a SharePoint Designer workflow. The only requirement for a SharePoint Designer workflow to be able to retrieve the value of a field from an InfoPath form stored in a form library is that the field is a promoted field and present as a column on the form library. It does not matter whether you use a list column or a site column to promote the field, neither does it matter whether you select the **Allow users to edit data in this field by using a datasheet or properties page** check box or not when your promote the field. You only need to select the **Allow users to edit data in this field by using a datasheet or properties page** check box when you want a SharePoint Designer workflow to write data to promoted InfoPath fields as demonstrated in the next recipe.

Note:

> Because you cannot promote all types of InfoPath fields to SharePoint (see the discussion section of recipe *22 Promote form fields to columns of a form library*), the solution described above is limited to the types of fields you can promote.

87 Set the value of an InfoPath form field through a workflow

Problem

You want to be able to select a person from a person/group picker control on an InfoPath form, have a SharePoint Designer workflow look up the manager of the selected person, and then from within the workflow, write the name of the manager to a field on the InfoPath form.

Solution

You can promote the form field you want to write to, make it editable when you publish the form template to SharePoint, and then access the field from within a SharePoint Designer workflow to set its value to be equal to the manager's name. Note that users must have managers assigned to them and those values must have been populated in their SharePoint user profiles, otherwise manager lookups via the SharePoint Designer workflow you create in this solution will fail. Contact your administrator about the presence of manager information in SharePoint user profiles.

To set the value of an InfoPath form field from within a workflow:

1. In InfoPath, create a new SharePoint form library form template or use an existing one.
2. Add a **Person/Group Picker** control and a **Text Box** control to the view of the form template. Name the text box control **manager**. You will be using the person/group picker control to select a person, which the workflow will retrieve. The workflow should then look up the manager of the selected person and write this value back to the **manager** field on the form. So the workflow must be able to get the value of the field bound to the person/group picker control and set the value of the **manager** field. Therefore, you must promote both fields.
3. Publish the form template to a new SharePoint form library named **SetFormFieldValueLib** and while publishing, promote the first **AccountId** field of the person/group picker as a list column named **Employee**, promote the **manager** field as a list column named **Manager**, and select the **Allow users to edit data in this field by using a datasheet or properties page** check box when you promote the **manager** field. Also see recipe *22 Promote form fields to columns of a form library* for information on how to promote form fields.

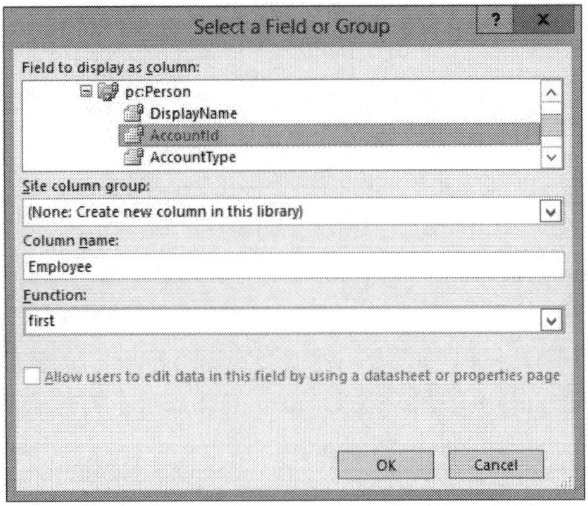

Figure 243. Promoting the AccountId field in InfoPath Designer 2013.

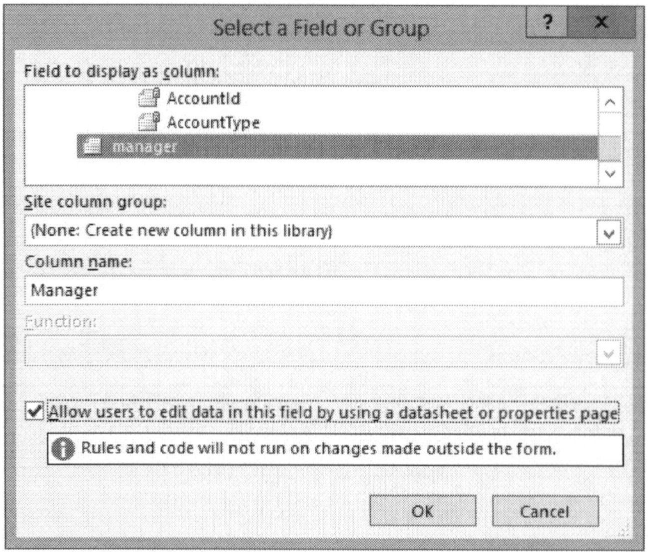

Figure 244. Promoting the manager field in InfoPath Designer 2013.

4. In SharePoint Designer 2013, open the site where the **SetFormFieldValueLib** form library is located, create a new **List Workflow**, associate it with the **SetFormFieldValueLib** form library, name it **SetFormFieldValueWF**, and select **SharePoint 2010 Workflow** as the **Platform Type** (also see recipe *80 Create a workflow that runs on forms in a specific form library*). Note: If you already had the site open in SharePoint Designer when you published the form template and created the new form library, the new form library may not be present in the list of lists or libraries you can associate the workflow with. If the form library is not present in SharePoint Designer, click the **Refresh** command on the **Quick Access Toolbar** at the top of screen or press **F5**, and try again.
5. The workflow must retrieve the manager of the selected employee and then write the name of the manager to the **manager** field on the InfoPath form. So on the text-based designer, click to place the cursor inside of **Step 1**, type **manager**, and then press **Enter** to add a **Lookup Manager of a User** action.
6. Click **this user** in the sentence for the workflow action.
7. On the **Select User** dialog box, select **Workflow Lookup for a User** in the existing users and groups list, and then click **Add**.

8. On the **Lookup for Person or Group** dialog box, leave **Current Item** selected in the **Data source** drop-down list box, select **Employee** from the **Field from source** drop-down list box, and click **OK**.

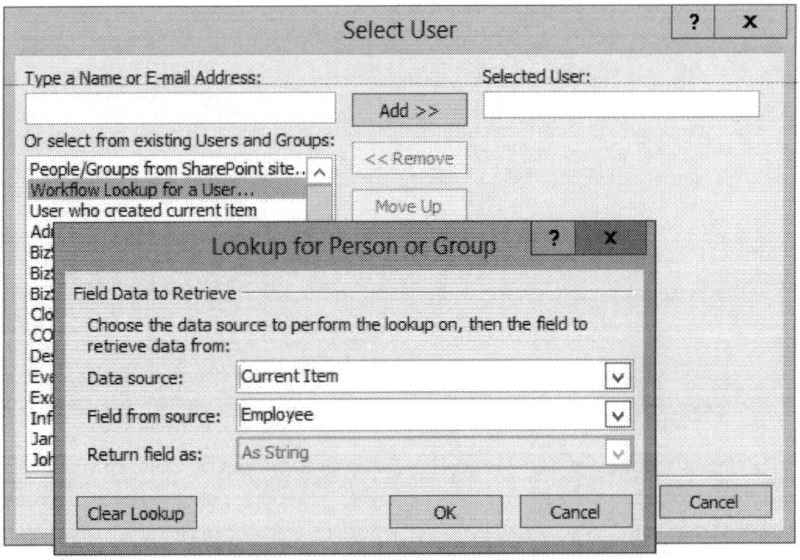

Figure 245. Dialog boxes to configure selecting a person to look up a manager.

9. On the **Select User** dialog box, click **OK**. The account ID of the manager of the person should automatically be stored in a variable that is listed after the **output to Variable** text in the sentence for the workflow action. By default, this should be a variable named **manager**. The sentence for the workflow action should now say:

```
Find Manager of Current Item:Employee (output to Variable:
manager)
```

10. Once you have retrieved the manager, you can use the value to set the manager field in the InfoPath form. So click to place the cursor below the previous workflow action, type **update**, and then press **Enter** to add an **Update List Item** action.
11. Click **this list** in the sentence for the workflow action you just added.
12. On the **Update List Item** dialog box, leave **Current Item** selected in the **List** drop-down list box, and then click **Add**.

13. On the **Value Assignment** dialog box, select **Manager** from the **Set this field** drop-down list box, and then click the formula button (second button) behind the **To this value** text box.

14. On the **Lookup for Single line of text** dialog box, select **Workflow Variables and Parameters** from the **Data source** drop-down list box, select **Variable: manager** from the **Field from source** drop-down list box, select **Display Name** from the **Return field as** drop-down list box, and click **OK**.

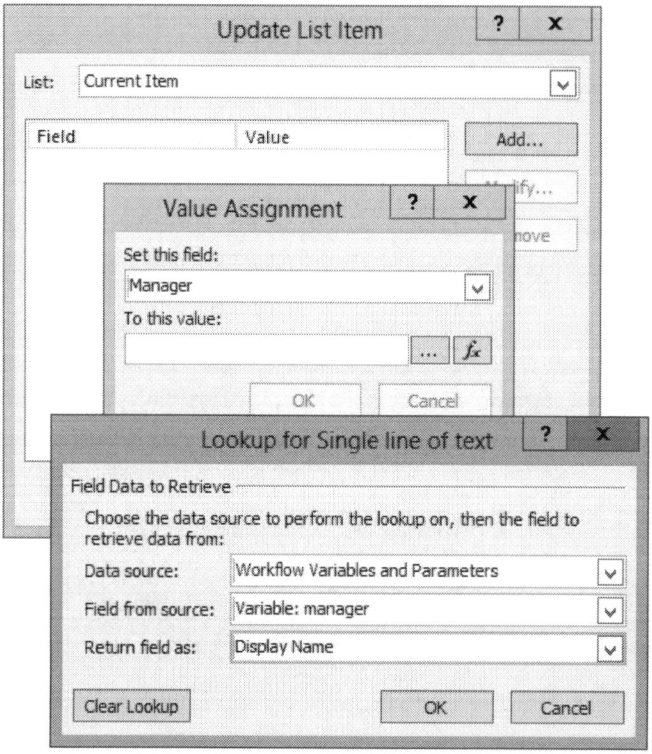

Figure 246. Dialog boxes to configure updating the manager field on the form.

15. On the **Value Assignment** dialog box, click **OK**. With this you have set the value of the manager field in the InfoPath form to be equal to the value of the manager the workflow searched for based on the value of the field bound to the person/group picker control on the InfoPath form.

16. On the **Update List Item** dialog box, click **OK**. The sentence for the workflow action should now say:

```
Find Manager of Current Item:Employee (output to Variable:
manager)

then Update item in Current Item
```

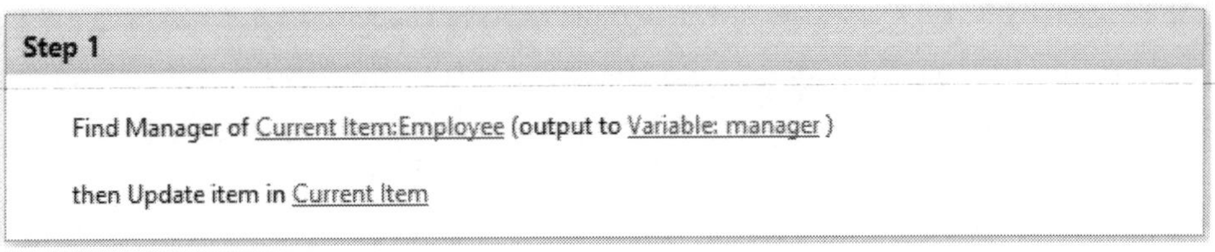

Figure 247. The completed workflow in SharePoint Designer 2013.

17. Click **Workflow ➤ Manage ➤ Workflow Settings**.
18. On the workflow settings page under **Start Options**, select the **Start workflow automatically when an item is created** check box. You can leave the **Allow this workflow to be manually started** check box selected so that users are still able to rerun the workflow on the InfoPath form in case the workflow fails to update the form field.
19. Click **Workflow Settings ➤ Save ➤ Publish** to publish the workflow.

In SharePoint, navigate to the **SetFormFieldValueLib** form library and add a new form. When the form opens, select a user that has a manager from the person/group picker control, and then save or submit the form. Wait until the workflow has run and completed, and once it has, open the form and verify that the name of the manager was retrieved by the workflow and written to the **manager** form field.

Discussion

If you want a SharePoint Designer workflow to be able to get as well as set the value of a field on an InfoPath form, you must:

1. Promote the field to a list column or a site column (also see recipe *22 Promote form fields to columns of a form library* and recipe *23 Promote form fields to existing site columns*).
2. Select the **Allow users to edit data in this field by using a datasheet or properties page** check box for the field when you publish the form template.

Once a field has been promoted either as a list column or a site column and made editable, it is automatically added to the view of the form library. However, the promoted field does not have to be part of the view of the form library for a SharePoint Designer workflow to have access to it; it must just be part of the schema of the form library for the workflow to have read and/or write access to the field. So you could remove columns from the view of the form library and the workflow should still be able to get and set the values of those columns.

Note that you cannot set the values of all types of fields in InfoPath from within a SharePoint Designer workflow, because not all types of fields can be promoted as editable fields. For example, the following types of fields cannot be promoted as editable fields:

- Rich text fields
- Date-only fields
- Repeating fields (e.g. fields in a repeating table, a repeating section, a multiple-selection list box, or a numbered list)
- Base64 encoded fields (e.g. a file attachment or embedded picture)
- Hyperlink fields

Since the **Lookup Manager of a User** action is not available for SharePoint 2013 workflows, you created a SharePoint 2010 workflow in the solution described above to be able to perform a lookup for a manager. Had you not had such a requirement, then you could have also used a SharePoint 2013 workflow to write data to InfoPath form fields.

88 Send a form's link in an email to selected users at workflow startup

Problem

You want to allow users to start a workflow on a form in a SharePoint form library thereby specifying a list of recipients to whom an email containing a link to the form the workflow is started on should be sent, and a value for the urgency with which the form should be processed. The values for the urgency field should be retrieved from a SharePoint list.

Solution

You can create a list or a reusable SharePoint 2010 workflow in SharePoint Designer 2013 and then modify the workflow's initiation form in InfoPath Designer 2013 so that it retrieves a list of urgency values from a SharePoint list. The solution described below makes use of a list workflow.

To send a form's link in an email to selected users at workflow startup:

1. In InfoPath, create a new SharePoint form library form template or use an existing one, and publish it to a SharePoint form library named **SendEmailLib**.
2. In SharePoint, create a custom list named **Urgency** that contains a list of urgency values, for example **Not Urgent**, **Semi-Urgent**, and **Very Urgent**.
3. In SharePoint Designer 2013, create a **List Workflow**, associate it with the **SendEmailLib** form library, name it **SendEmailWF**, and select **SharePoint 2010 Workflow** as the **Platform Type** (also see recipe *80 Create a workflow that runs on forms in a specific form library*).

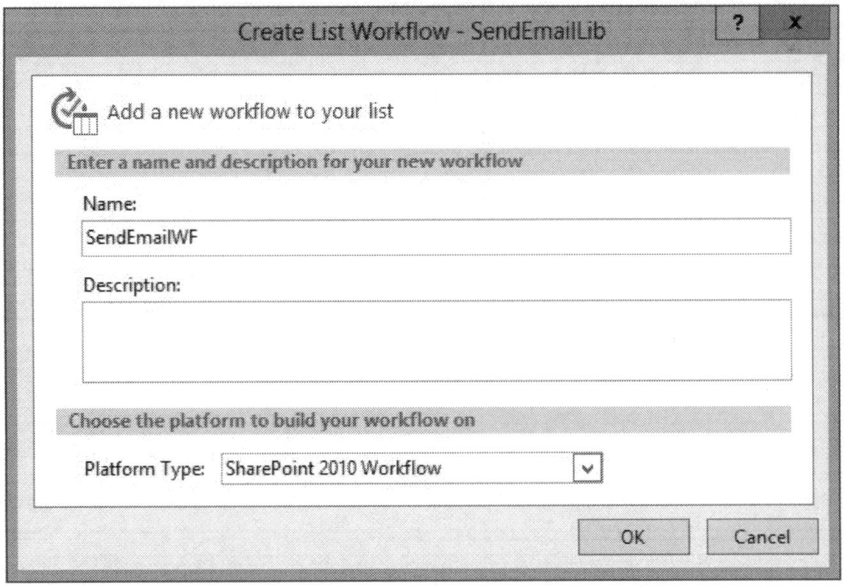

Figure 248. Creating the SharePoint 2010 list workflow in SharePoint Designer 2013.

4. Click **Workflow ➤ Variables ➤ Initiation Form Parameters**. Initiation form parameters serve as input parameters for a workflow and are automatically hooked up by SharePoint Designer to controls on the initiation form you will modify later in InfoPath Designer 2013.

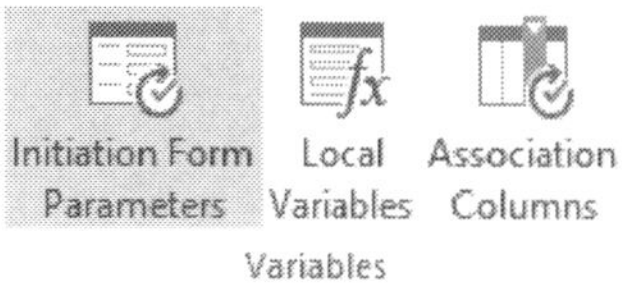

Figure 249. Initiation Form Parameters command on the Workflow tab.

5. On the **Association and Initiation Form Parameters** dialog box, click **Add**.
6. On the **Add Field** dialog box, type **EmailRecipients** in the **Field name** text box, select **Person or Group** from the **Information type** drop-down list box, and click **Next**.

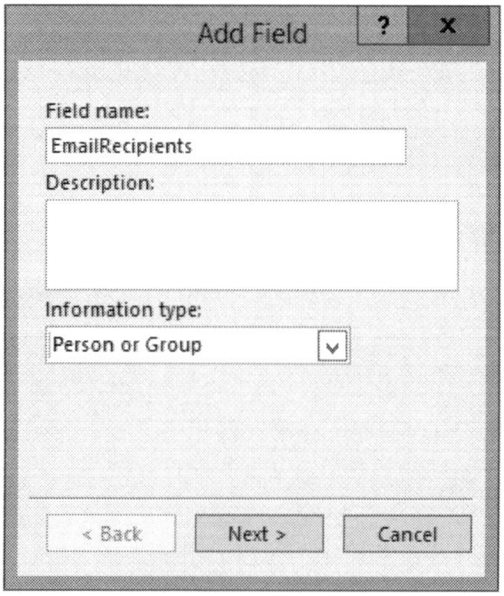

Figure 250. Adding an initiation form parameter in SharePoint Designer 2013.

7. On the **Column Settings** dialog box, leave **Account** selected in the **Show Field** drop-down list box, select the **People Only** option, select the **All Users** option, deselect the **Allow blank values** check box, select the **Allow multiple values** check box, and then click **Finish**.

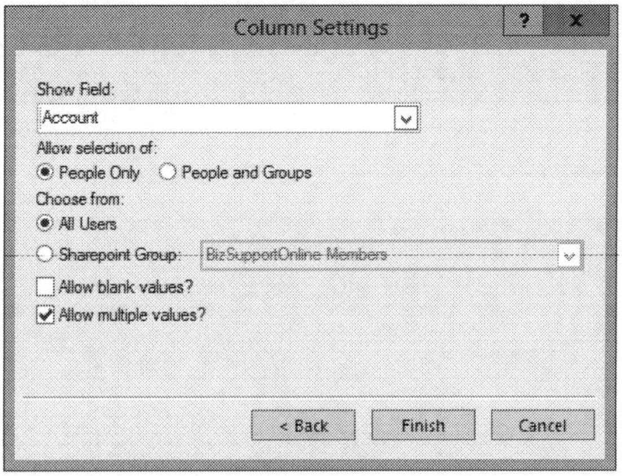

Figure 251. Configuring the properties for the initiation form parameter.

8. On the **Association and Initiation Form Parameters** dialog box, click **Add**.
9. On the **Add Field** dialog box, type **Urgency** in the **Field name** text box, leave **Single line of text** selected in the **Information type** drop-down list box, and click **Next**. Note that you could have also selected **Choice (menu to choose from)** as the **Information type**, but this would have forced you to specify a fixed list of options. In this scenario, you do not want a fixed list of options, but rather want the values to come from a specific SharePoint list.
10. On the **Column Settings** dialog box, leave the **Default value** text box empty, and click **Finish**.
11. On the **Association and Initiation Form Parameters** dialog box, click **OK**.

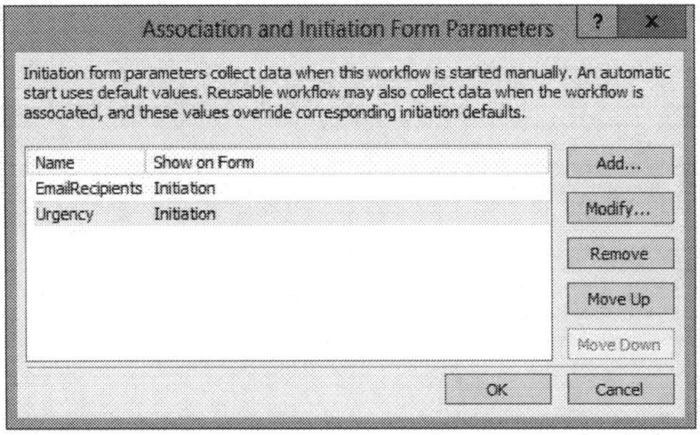

Figure 252. The Association and Initiation Form Parameters dialog box.

12. The workflow must send an email to a list of recipients that is specified by a user at startup and that is stored in the **EmailRecipients** initiation form parameter. The email must include the selected urgency that is stored in the **Urgency** parameter and a link to the form in the body of the email. So place the cursor inside of **Step 1**, type **email**, and then press **Enter** to add a **Send an Email** action.
13. Click **these users** in the sentence for the workflow action.
14. On the **Define E-mail Message** dialog box, click the button behind the **To** text box.
15. On the **Select Users** dialog box, select **Workflow Lookup for a User** from the list of existing users and groups, and then click **Add**.
16. On the **Lookup for Person or Group** dialog box, select **Workflow Variables and Parameters** from the **Data source** drop-down list box, select **Parameter: EmailRecipients** from the **Field from source** drop-down list box, select **Email Addresses, Semicolon Delimited** from the **Return field as** drop-down list box, and click **OK**.

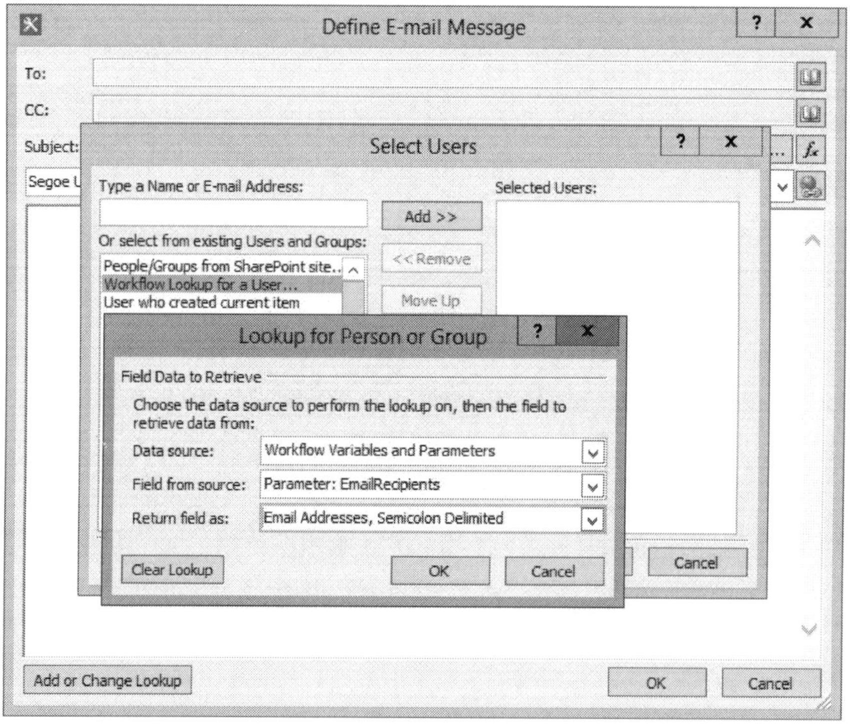

Figure 253. Configuring the email recipients to send an email to.

Note that you can always retrieve the value of any variable or parameter you have defined for the workflow from the **Workflow Variables and Parameters** data source. Here you are retrieving the value of an initiation form parameter.

17. On the **Select Users** dialog box, click **OK**.
18. On the **Define E-mail Message** dialog box, enter the text "InfoPath form requires your attention" in the **Subject** text box. Note that you can use the buttons behind the **Subject** text box to dynamically build a string for the subject line if your scenario calls for it. In this solution you should just type in the text as a static piece of text.
19. On the **Define E-mail Message** dialog box, click anywhere in the text box for the body of the email, type the text **InfoPath Form:**, and then click **Add or Change Lookup**.
20. On the **Lookup for String** dialog box, select **Workflow Context** from the **Data source** drop-down list box, select **Current Item URL** from the **Field from source** drop-down list box, and click **OK**.

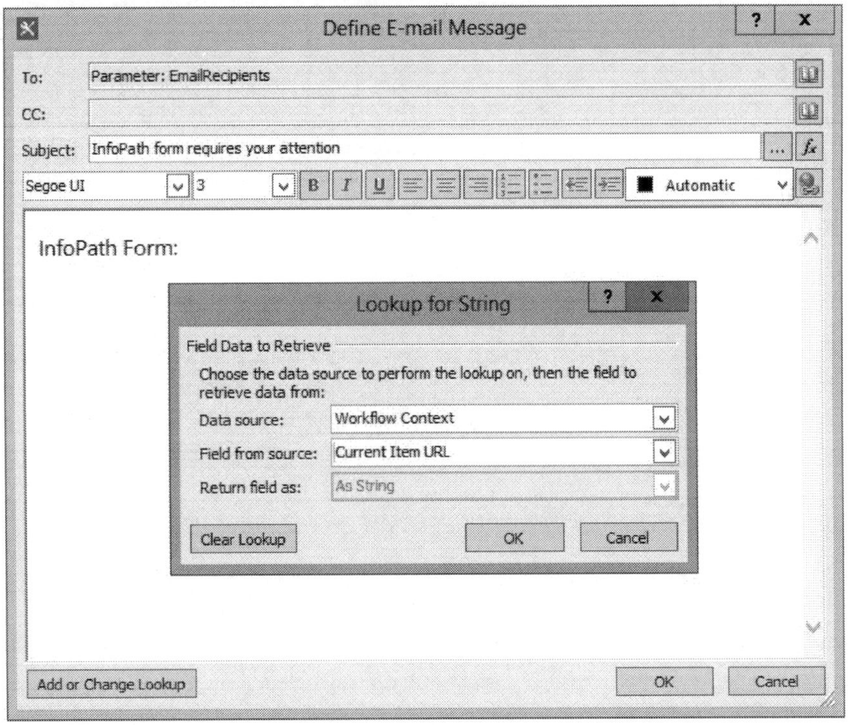

Figure 254. Constructing the body of the email message.

The **Current Item URL** field contains the full URL of the InfoPath form (XML file). When a user clicks this URL in an email, it will not automatically open the form in the browser, but will rather prompt the user to download the file. If you want the form to open in the browser when a user clicks the link, you must modify the URL to contain the **FormServer.aspx** page and the **OpenIn=Browser** query string parameter (see the discussion section for more details). The text in the body of the email should now say:

```
InfoPath Form: [%Workflow Context:Current Item URL%]
```

21. On the **Define E-mail Message** dialog box, press **Enter**, type the text **Urgency:** on the new line, and then click **Add or Change Lookup**.
22. On the **Lookup for String** dialog box, select **Workflow Variables and Parameters** from the **Data source** drop-down list box, select **Parameter: Urgency** from the **Field from source** drop-down list box, and click **OK**.

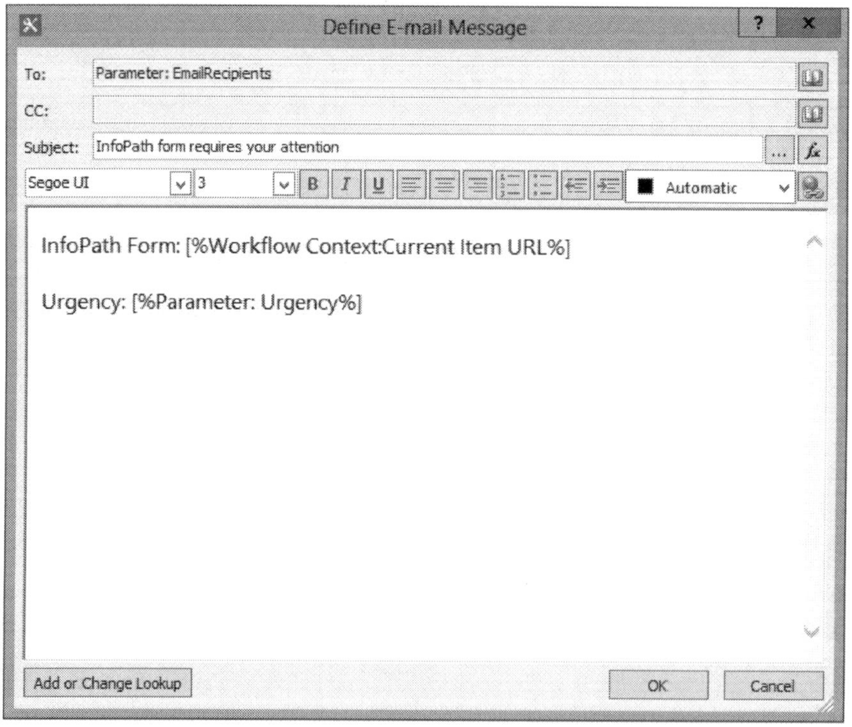

Figure 255. The completed Define E-mail Message dialog box.

The text in the body of the email should now say:

```
InfoPath Form: [%Workflow Context:Current Item URL%]

Urgency: [%Parameter: Urgency%]
```

23. On the **Define E-mail Message** dialog box, click **OK**. The sentence for the workflow action should now say:

```
Email Parameter: EmailRecipients
```

Figure 256. The completed workflow in SharePoint Designer 2013.

24. Click **Workflow ➤ Save ➤ Publish** to publish the workflow.
25. Click **Workflow ➤ Manage ➤ Workflow Settings**.
26. Because a user must manually enter a list of email recipients and choose the urgency with which the form should be processed, the workflow must be manually started. So on the workflow settings page under **Start Options**, ensure that only the **Allow this workflow to be manually started** check box has been selected.
27. On the workflow settings page under the **Forms** section, click **SendEmailWF.xsn**. This should open the form template for the initiation form in InfoPath Designer 2013.
28. In InfoPath, you should see that SharePoint Designer already bound the **EmailRecipients** field to a person/group picker control and the **Urgency** field to a text box control. Because you want to select the **Urgency** from a SharePoint list, you must change the text box control into a drop-down list box control and then populate it with values from the **Urgency** SharePoint list. So right-click the text box control and select **Change Control ➤ Drop-Down List Box** from the context menu that appears.
29. Add a **Receive** data connection to the **Urgency** SharePoint list as described in *Use a SharePoint list data connection* in recipe *43 2 Ways to retrieve data from a SharePoint list*. Ensure that you include the **Title** and

ID fields in the secondary data source, sort the list by **Title**, leave the **Automatically retrieve data when form is opened** check box selected, and name the data connection **GetUrgency**.

30. Open the **Drop-Down List Box Properties** dialog box and configure the drop-down list box to get its items from the **GetUrgency** secondary data source, and set both the **Value** and **Display name** properties to come from the **Title** field in the data source.

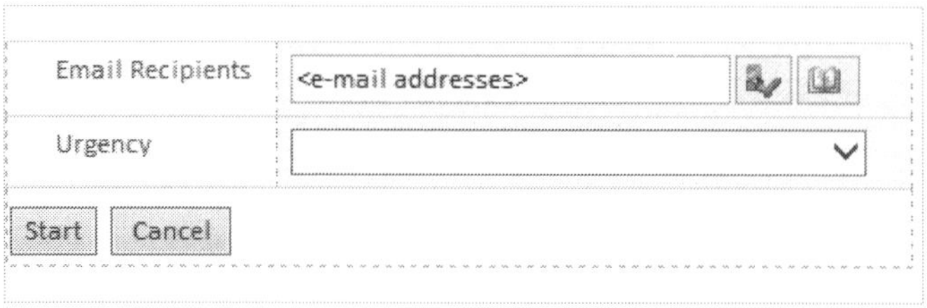

Figure 257. The completed InfoPath form template in InfoPath Designer 2013.

31. Preview the form and check whether the drop-down list box is being populated.
32. Click **Quick Publish** on the **Quick Access Toolbar** at the top of the screen in InfoPath Designer 2013, click **File** ➤ **Info** ➤ **Quick Publish**, or click **File** ➤ **Publish** ➤ **Workflow** to republish the form template. Note: InfoPath may prompt you to save the form template.

In SharePoint, navigate to the **SendEmailLib** form library and add a new form. Save or submit the form back to the form library. Manually start the **SendEmailWF** workflow as described in recipe *83 Manually start a workflow to run on a form*. On the **Start** page of the workflow, enter one or more user names in the **Email Recipients** people picker, select a value for the urgency from the **Urgency** drop-down list box, and click **Start**. Once the workflow has run and completed, verify that the email message was sent (see Figure 259).

Discussion

In the solution described above, you used an InfoPath form as a workflow initiation form to pass data to a workflow at startup. Because SharePoint

2013 workflows do not support InfoPath forms, you created a SharePoint 2010 workflow instead.

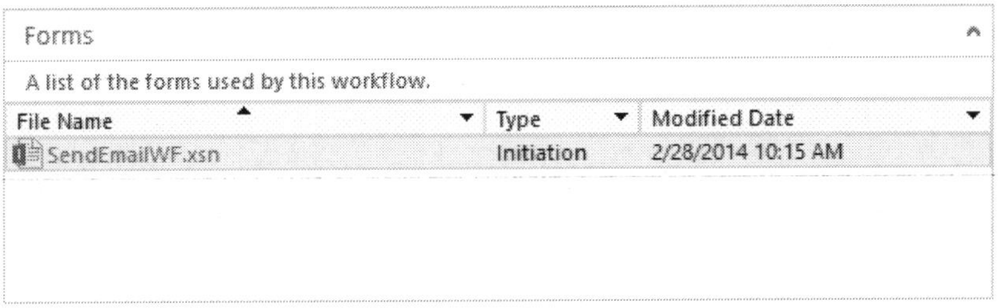

Figure 258. Workflow initiation form as listed in SharePoint Designer 2013.

The initiation form of a SharePoint Designer workflow is an InfoPath form that has an InfoPath form type of **Workflow Form**. You can verify this in InfoPath by looking at the **Form type** in the **Compatibility** section on the **Form Options** dialog box.

Workflow forms cannot be created from scratch from within InfoPath Designer 2013, because there is no **Workflow Form** template available when you open InfoPath Designer 2013 to create an InfoPath form template from scratch. However, workflow forms can be customized in InfoPath Designer 2013 after you have published a workflow from within SharePoint Designer 2013. Workflow forms are similar to other types of forms in InfoPath in that you can add rules, conditional formatting, data connections, etc. to them just like you would do with any other type of form in InfoPath.

Controls on a workflow initiation form are automatically bound to initiation form parameters that you set up for the workflow in SharePoint Designer 2013, and you can retrieve the value of any parameter passed to the workflow from the **Workflow Variables and Parameters** data source.

You also learned that you can dynamically retrieve the URL of the form a workflow is running on from the **Current Item URL** field of the **Workflow Context** data source. The **Current Item URL** field returns the full path of the XML file that represents the InfoPath form. Therefore, when a user clicks on a link that references this URL, an XML file is downloaded instead of the InfoPath form opened in the browser. If you want the InfoPath form to open in the browser, you must dynamically construct the URL to contain a reference to the **FormServer.aspx** page in addition to the **OpenIn** query string parameter and optionally the **Source** query string parameter. You can construct the URL the same way you did in steps 19 through 22 of the solution described above. The final text in the body of the email should say:

```
InfoPath Form: [%Workflow Context:Current Site
URL%]/_layouts/15/FormServer.aspx?XmlLocation=[%Workflow
Context:Current Item URL%]&OpenIn=Browser&Source=[%Workflow
Context:Current Site URL%]

Urgency: [%Parameter: Urgency%]
```

Note that the **Current Site URL** field in the **Workflow Context** data source is used to dynamically retrieve the URL of the site where the workflow is running. Also note that the **Source** query string parameter at the end of the form's URL redirects the user back to the home page of the site when the form is closed (also see the discussion section of recipe *38 Add a link to open a form from a SharePoint page* to learn more about constructing the URL of an InfoPath form).

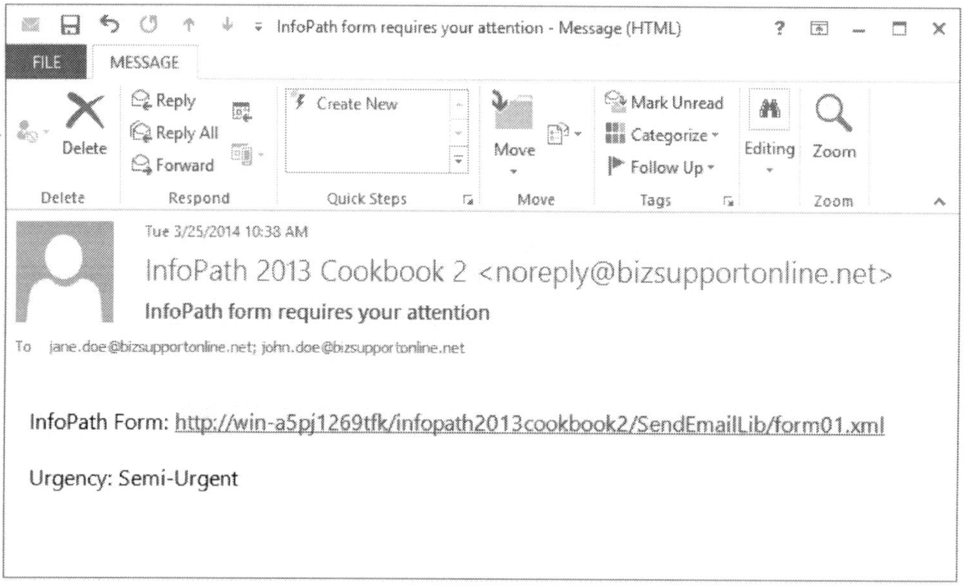

Figure 259. The email message as it appears in Outlook 2013 after the workflow has run.

89 Send an email to the manager of a selected person

Problem

You have a person/group picker control on an InfoPath form and you want to be able to select a person and then send an email to the manager of the selected person immediately after the form is saved or submitted to a form library.

Solution

You can promote the field that is bound to the person/group picker control, use a SharePoint Designer workflow to retrieve the value of that field, lookup the manager of the person, and then send an email to the manager.

To send an email to the manager of a selected person:

1. In InfoPath, create a new SharePoint form library form template or use an existing one.
2. Add a **Person/Group Picker** control to the view of the form template.
3. Publish the form template to a SharePoint form library named **SendEmailToManagerLib** and promote the first **AccountId** field of the person/group picker as a column named **Employee** as described in recipe *22 Promote form fields to columns of a form library*.

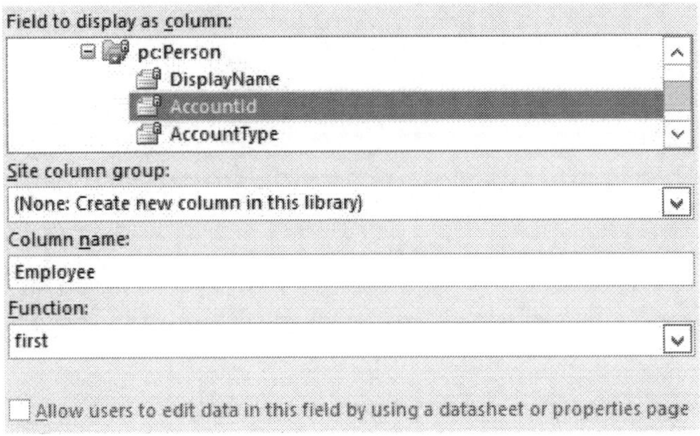

Figure 260. Promoting the first AccountId field in InfoPath.

4. In SharePoint Designer 2013, open the site where the **SendEmailToManagerLib** form library is located, create a new **List Workflow**, associate it with the **SendEmailToManagerLib** form library, name it **SendManagerEmailWF**, and select **SharePoint 2010 Workflow** as the **Platform Type** (also see recipe *80 Create a workflow that runs on forms in a specific form library*).
5. On the text-based designer, click to place the cursor inside of **Step 1**, type **manager**, and then press **Enter** to add a **Lookup Manager of a User** action.
6. Click **this user** in the sentence for the workflow action.
7. On the **Select User** dialog box, select **Workflow Lookup for a User** in the existing users and groups list, and then click **Add**.
8. On the **Lookup for Person or Group** dialog box, leave **Current Item** selected in the **Data source** drop-down list box, select **Employee** (the field you promoted earlier) from the **Field from source** drop-down list box, and click **OK**.
9. On the **Select User** dialog box, click **OK**. The sentence for the workflow action should now say:

   ```
   Find Manager of Current Item:Employee (output to Variable:
   manager)
   ```

   The account ID of the manager of the person should automatically be stored in a variable that is listed after the **output to Variable** text in the sentence for the workflow action. By default, this should be a variable named **manager**.
10. Once you have retrieved the manager, you can use the value to send an email. Because a person might not have a manager, you should perform a check before sending an email. So click below the previous workflow action to place the cursor, and then click **Workflow ➤ Insert ➤ Condition** and select **If any value equals value** from the drop-down menu that appears.

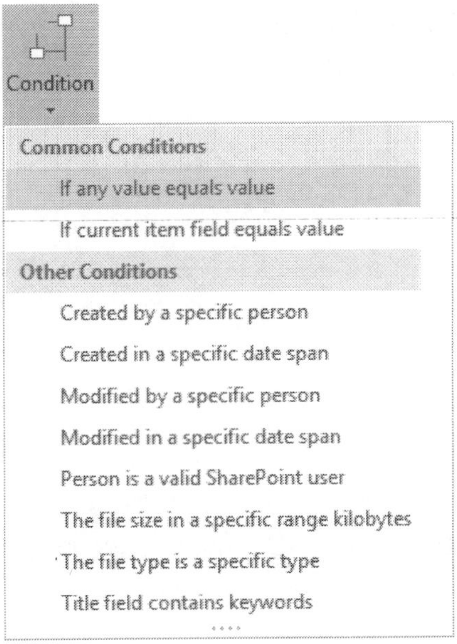

Figure 261. Adding a workflow condition.

11. Click the first **value** in the sentence for the workflow condition, and then click the formula button that appears behind the text box.
12. On the **Define Workflow Lookup** dialog box, select **Workflow Variables and Parameters** from the **Data source** drop-down list box, select **Variable: manager** from the **Field from source** drop-down list box, and click **OK**.
13. Click **equals** in the sentence for the workflow condition, and select **is not empty** from the drop-down menu that appears. The condition should now say:

```
If Variable: manager is not empty
```

14. Click within the **If**-branch of the workflow condition to place the cursor, type **email**, and then press **Enter** to add a **Send an Email** action.
15. Click **these users** in the sentence for the workflow action you just added.
16. On the **Define E-mail Message** dialog box, click the button behind the **To** text box.

17. On the **Select Users** dialog box, select **Workflow Lookup for a User** in the existing users and groups list, and then click **Add**.
18. On the **Lookup for Person or Group** dialog box, select **Workflow Variables and Parameters** from the **Data source** drop-down list box, select **Variable: manager** from the **Field from source** drop-down list box, select **Email Address** from the **Return field as** drop-down list box, and click **OK**.
19. On the **Select Users** dialog box, click **OK**. With this you have set the email to be sent to the email address of the manager.
20. On the **Define E-mail Message** dialog box, enter a **Subject**, define a body for the email message, and then click **OK**.
21. Click to place the cursor below the action you added within the **If**-branch of the workflow condition, and then click **Workflow ➤ Insert ➤ Else-If Branch** to add an **Else**-branch to the workflow condition.

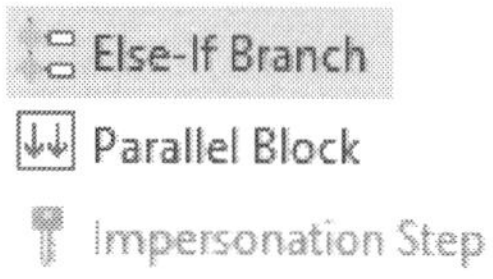

Figure 262. Else-If Branch command highlighted on the Workflow tab.

22. Repeat steps 14 through 20 for the **Else**-branch to add an action that sends an email to the administrator reporting that the user does not have a manager. Use the **Add or Change Lookup** button on the **Define E-mail Message** dialog box to construct a body with a text similar to the following:

```
Cannot send an email, because [%Current Item:Employee%] does
not have a manager.
```

where **[%Current Item:Employee%]** performs a lookup for the account ID (**Employee** promoted field) of the selected person in the current form (**Current Item**).

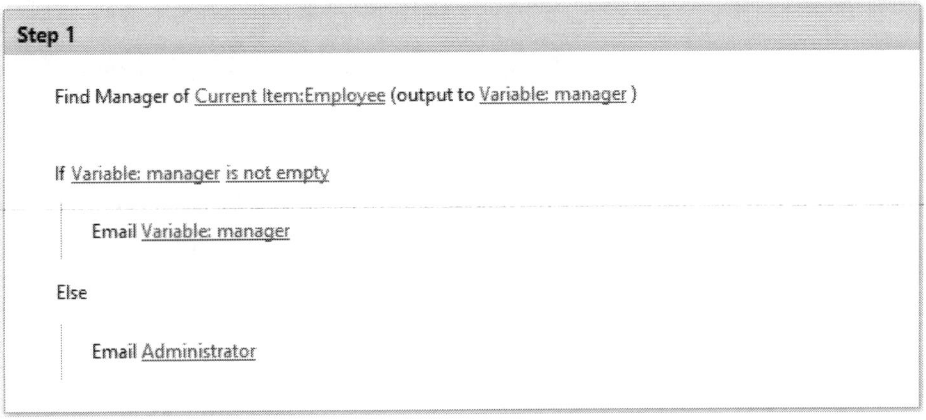

Figure 263. The completed workflow in SharePoint Designer 2013.

23. Click **Workflow ➤ Manage ➤ Workflow Settings**.
24. On the workflow settings page under **Start Options**, select the **Start workflow automatically when an item is created** check box.
25. Click **Workflow Settings ➤ Save ➤ Publish** to publish the workflow.

In SharePoint, navigate to the **SendEmailToManagerLib** form library and add a new form. Select a person from the person/group picker control whose manager you want to send an email, and then save or submit the form. Wait until the workflow has run and completed, and then verify that the manager of the person you selected from the person/group picker control received an email. Also test the workflow for a person who does not have a manager and verify that the administrator received an email.

Discussion

In recipe *75 Get the details of the manager of a selected person in a people picker* you learned how to use the User Profile Service to retrieve the details of the manager of a selected person. While you could have used a similar technique to retrieve the email address in the InfoPath form itself, in the solution described above you let SharePoint take care of performing the lookup and sending the email.

If your scenario requires doing more with the details of the manager than just performing a lookup and sending an email, it would make sense to retrieve those details in the InfoPath form and not let the workflow do the work. In all other cases, it might be quicker and easier to implement a SharePoint Designer workflow that takes care of performing the lookup and sending the email.

Because the **Lookup Manager of a User** action is not available for SharePoint 2013 workflows, you created a SharePoint 2010 workflow in the solution described above to be able to perform a lookup for a manager.

90 Send an email to a list of people in a people picker

Problem

You have a person/group picker control on an InfoPath form and you want to be able to select one or more people and then send an email to those people immediately after the form is saved or submitted to a form library.

Solution

You can promote the account ID field of the person/group picker control as a merged field, and then use a SharePoint 2013 workflow to send an email to the people that were selected from the person/group picker control.

To send an email to a list of people in a people picker:

1. In InfoPath, create a new SharePoint form library form template or use an existing one.
2. Add a **Person/Group Picker** control to the view of the form template.
3. Open the **Person/Group Picker Properties** dialog box, select the **General** tab, select the **Allow multiple selections** check box, and then click **OK**.
4. Click **File** ➤ **Info** ➤ **Form Options**.
5. On the **Form Options** dialog box, select **Property Promotion** in the **Category** list, and then click **Add** on the right-hand side of the list box at the top of the dialog box.

6. On the **Select a Field or Group** dialog box, expand all of the group nodes in the tree view, select **AccountId**, type **PeopleToEmail** in the **Column name** text box, select **merge** from the **Function** drop-down list box, and then click **OK**. The **merge** function should place each account ID on a separate line in the **PeopleToEmail** field in the form library.

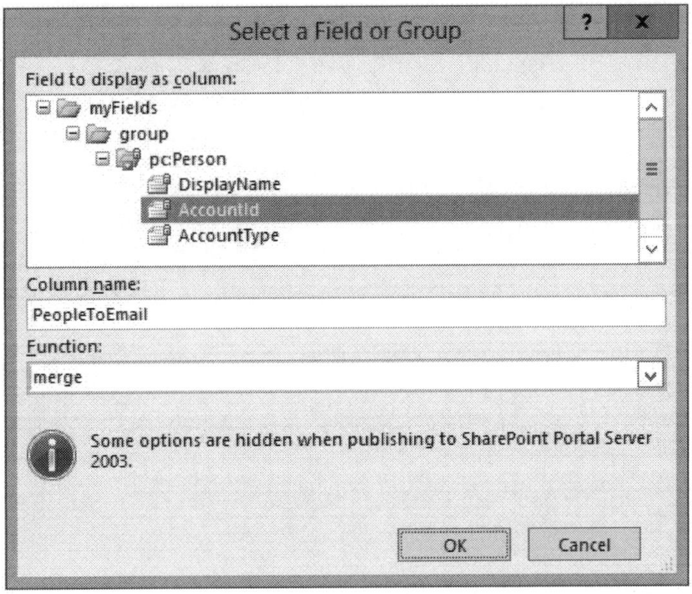

Figure 264. Configuring the field to promote and merge its contents.

7. On the **Form Options** dialog box, click **OK**.
8. Publish the form template to a form library named **SendAlertsLib**.
9. In SharePoint Designer 2013, open the site where the **SendAlertsLib** form library is located, create a new **List Workflow**, associate it with the **SendAlertsLib** form library, name it **SendEmailAlertsWF**, and select **SharePoint 2013 Workflow** as the **Platform Type** (also see recipe *80 Create a workflow that runs on forms in a specific form library*).
10. On the text-based designer, click to place the cursor inside of **Stage 1**, type **replace**, and then press **Enter** to add a **Replace Substring in String** action.
11. Click the first **string** in the sentence for the workflow action, and then click the ellipsis button (first button) behind the text box.

12. On the **String Builder** dialog box, click to place the cursor in the **Name** text box, press **Enter**, and then click **OK**. This should add a line-break to be recognized and replaced.
13. Click the second **string** in the sentence for the workflow action, type a semi-colon (**;**) in the text box, and then press **Enter**.
14. Click the third **string** in the sentence for the workflow action, and then click the formula button (second button) behind the text box.
15. On the **Lookup for String** dialog box, leave **Current Item** selected in the **Data source** drop-down list box, select **PeopleToEmail** from the **Field from source** drop-down list box, leave **As String** selected in the **Return field as** drop-down list box, and click **OK**. The workflow sentence should now say:

```
Replace _ with ; in Current Item:PeopleToEmail (Output to
Variable: output)
```

16. Click below the workflow sentence to place the cursor, type **email**, and then press **Enter** to add a **Send an Email** action.
17. Click **these users** in the sentence for the workflow action you just added.
18. On the **Define E-mail Message** dialog box, click the button behind the **To** text box.
19. On the **Select Users** dialog box, select **Workflow Lookup for a User** in the existing users and groups list, and then click **Add**.
20. On the **Lookup for Person or Group** dialog box, select **Workflow Variables and Parameters** from the **Data source** drop-down list box, select **Variable: output** from the **Field from source** drop-down list box, leave **As String** selected in the **Return field as** drop-down list box, and click **OK**.
21. On the **Select Users** dialog box, click **OK**.
22. On the **Define E-mail Message** dialog box, enter a **Subject**, define a body for the email message, and then click **OK**.
23. Click to place the cursor in the **Transition to stage** section, and then select **Workflow ➤ Insert ➤ Action ➤ Go to a stage**.

24. Click **a stage** in the sentence for the workflow action, and then select **End of Workflow** from the drop-down list box that appears.
25. Click **Workflow ➤ Manage ➤ Workflow Settings**.
26. On the workflow settings page under **Start Options**, select the **Start workflow automatically when an item is created** check box.
27. Click **Workflow Settings ➤ Save ➤ Publish** to publish the workflow.

In SharePoint, navigate to the **SendAlertsLib** form library and add a new form. When the form opens, select two people from the person/group picker control, and then save the form back to the form library. Once the workflow has run and completed, verify that the users you selected from the person/group picker control received an email.

Discussion

While the solution described above used a SharePoint Designer 2013 workflow to send emails, if you do not require a customized email message to be sent, you could let users use the **Alerts** option on a form library as described in recipe *37 Send an alert when a new form is added to a form library*. And if you are not allowed to use SharePoint Designer, you could use the technique described in recipe *74 Get email addresses from a person/group picker* with an email submit data connection to send an email on submit.

In the solution described above, you used a **Replace Substring in String** action to replace line-breaks with semi-colons. Because this workflow action is not available when you create a SharePoint 2010 workflow, you would have to concatenate the account IDs of the selected users in the people picker using for example the **eval()** function (also see *74 Get email addresses from a person/group picker*), store the result in a hidden field, promote the hidden field to the SharePoint form library, retrieve the value of the promoted field in the SharePoint 2010 workflow, and then use it in a **Send an Email** workflow action to send an email.

SharePoint Designer should automatically find email addresses based on account IDs, but if it fails, you can always perform email address lookups in InfoPath using the **User Information List**, and then pass the data to the workflow to send an email.

Note that strings in SharePoint Designer workflows allow a maximum of 255 characters. This means that you must ensure that any strings you pass to a workflow do not exceed this limit. In the solution above, this would mean checking the length of the merged account IDs or the amount of people selected in the people picker in InfoPath and displaying a data validation error to the user if the limit is exceeded (see for example recipe *73 Limit a person/group picker to a maximum of 3 selected people*).

91 Create SharePoint list items for multiple people in a people picker

Problem

You have a person/group picker control on an InfoPath form from which you want to select one or more people and create new SharePoint list items containing the display names and email addresses from all of those people immediately after the form is saved or submitted to a form library.

Solution

You can promote the account ID field of the person/group picker control as a merged field, and then use a SharePoint 2013 workflow to create SharePoint list items containing the display names and email addresses of the people that were selected in the person/group picker control.

To create SharePoint list items for multiple people in a people picker:

1. In SharePoint, create a new custom list named **People**, and add a **Single line of text** column named **EmailAddress** to the SharePoint list.
2. In InfoPath, create a new SharePoint form library form template or use an existing one.
3. Add a **Person/Group Picker** control to the view of the form template.
4. Open the **Person/Group Picker Properties** dialog box, select the **General** tab, select the **Allow multiple selections** check box, and click **OK**.
5. Click **File** ➤ **Info** ➤ **Form Options**.
6. On the **Form Options** dialog box, select **Property Promotion** in the **Category** list, and then click **Add** on the right-hand side of the list box at the top of the dialog box.

7. On the **Select a Field or Group** dialog box, expand all of the group nodes in the tree view, select **AccountId**, type **PeopleList** in the **Column name** text box, select **merge** from the **Function** drop-down list box, and then click **OK**. The **merge** function should place each account ID on a separate line in the **PeopleList** field in the form library.

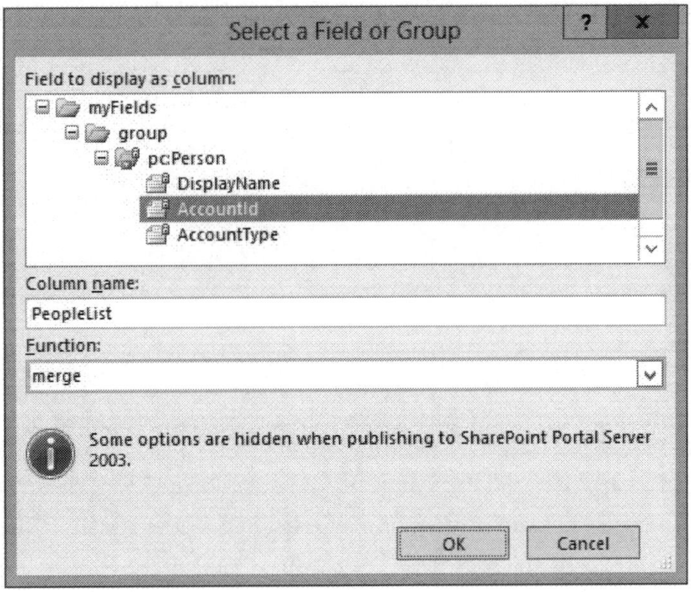

Figure 265. Promoting the AccountId field as a merged field.

8. On the **Form Options** dialog box, click **OK**.
9. Publish the form template to a form library named **PeopleLib**.
10. In SharePoint Designer 2013, open the site where the **PeopleLib** form library is located, create a new **List Workflow** that is associated with the **PeopleLib** form library, name it **CreatePeopleListItemsWF**, and select **SharePoint 2013 Workflow** as the **Platform Type** (also see recipe *80 Create a workflow that runs on forms in a specific form library*).
11. On the text-based designer, click to place the cursor inside of **Stage 1**, type **replace**, and then press **Enter** to add a **Replace Substring in String** action.
12. Click the first **string** in the sentence for the workflow action, and then click the ellipsis button (first button) behind the text box that appears.

13. On the **String Builder** dialog box, click to place the cursor in the **Name** text box, press **Enter**, and then click **OK**. This should add a line-break to be recognized and replaced.
14. Click the second **string** in the sentence for the workflow action, type a semi-colon (**;**) in the text box that appears, and then press **Enter**.
15. Click the third **string** in the sentence for the workflow action, and then click the formula button (second button) behind the text box.
16. On the **Lookup for String** dialog box, leave **Current Item** selected in the **Data source** drop-down list box, select **PeopleList** from the **Field from source** drop-down list box, leave **As String** selected in the **Return field as** drop-down list box, and click **OK**. The workflow sentence should now say:

```
Replace _ with ; in Current Item:PeopleList (Output to
Variable: output)
```

17. Because the **output** variable will not have a semi-colon at the end (because there is no line-break after the last account ID coming from the promoted field for the people picker), you must add a semi-colon at the end. So click to place the cursor below the last action you added, type **set**, press **Enter**, and select **Set Workflow Variable** from the drop-down menu.
18. Click **workflow variable** in the sentence for the workflow action, and select **Variable: output** from the drop-down list box that appears.
19. Click **value** in the sentence for the workflow action, and then click the ellipsis button (first button) behind the text box that appears.
20. On the **String Builder** dialog box, click **Add or Change Lookup**.
21. On the **Lookup for String** dialog box, select **Workflow Variables and Parameters** from the **Data source** drop-down list box, select **Variable: output** from the **Field from source** drop-down list box, leave **As String** selected in the **Return field as** drop-down list box, and click **OK**.
22. On the **String Builder** dialog box, type a semi-colon (**;**) at the end. The text should look as follows:

```
[%Variable: output%];
```

23. On the **String Builder** dialog box, click **OK**. The workflow sentence should say:

```
then Set Variable: output to [%Variable: output%];
```

24. Click **Workflow ➤ Variables ➤ Local Variables**.
25. On the **Workflow Local Variables** dialog box, click **Add**.
26. On the **Edit Variable** dialog box, type **Person** in the **Name** text box, leave **String** selected in the **Type** drop-down list box, and click **OK**.
27. On the **Workflow Local Variables** dialog box, click **OK**.
28. The workflow must loop through all of the account IDs in the **PeopleList** string. You can find the first account ID by looking for the first semi-colon in the **output** variable. So click to place the cursor below the last action you added, type **find sub**, and then press **Enter** to add a **Find Substring in String** action.
29. Click **substring** in the sentence for the workflow action, type a semi-colon (**;**) in the text box, and then press **Enter**.
30. Click **string** in the sentence for the workflow action, and then click the formula button (second button) behind the text box that appears.
31. On the **Lookup for String** dialog box, select **Workflow Variables and Parameters** from the **Data source** drop-down list box, select **Variable: output** from the **Field from source** drop-down list box, leave **As String** selected in the **Return field as** drop-down list box, and click **OK**. The final sentence should say:

```
then Find ; in Variable: output (Output to Variable: index)
```

32. Click to place the cursor below the last action you added, and then select **Workflow ➤ Insert ➤ Loop ➤ Loop with Condition**.

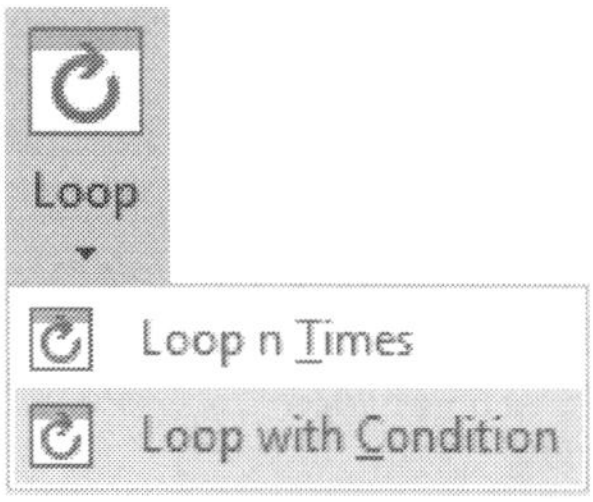

Figure 266. Inserting a Loop with Condition in SharePoint Designer 2013.

33. Click the first **value** in the sentence inside the loop.
34. On the **LoopCondition Properties** dialog box, select the first **Value**, and then click the formula button behind the text box.
35. On the **Define Workflow Lookup** dialog box, select **Workflow Variables and Parameters** from the **Data source** drop-down list box, select **Variable: index** from the **Field from source** drop-down list box, and click **OK**.
36. On the **LoopCondition Properties** dialog box, select **Operator**, and then select **not equals** from the drop-down list box.
37. On the **LoopCondition Properties** dialog box, select the second **Value**, type **-1** in the text box, and then click **OK**.

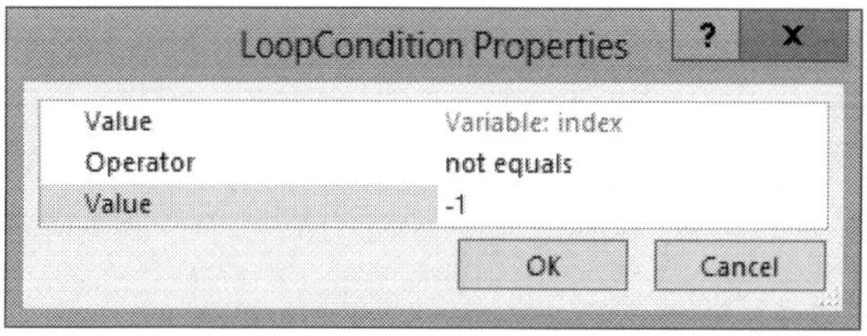

Figure 267. The LoopCondition Properties dialog box in SharePoint Designer 2013.

Note that if a semi-colon is not found, the value of the index will be equal to **-1**. The sentence within the loop should now say:

```
The contents of this loop will run repeatedly while Variable:
index not equals -1
```

38. Once you have the position of a semi-colon in the **output** variable, you can extract the first account ID and store it in the **Person** variable. So click to place the cursor below the first sentence within the loop, type **extract**, press **Enter**, and then select **Extract Substring of String from Index with Length** from the drop-down menu that appears.

39. Set **string** in the sentence for the workflow action to be equal to the **output** workflow variable, replace the second **0** in the sentence for the workflow action with the **index** workflow variable, and have the output written to the **Person** workflow variable. To have the output written to the **Person** workflow variable you must click on **Variable: substring** in the sentence and then select **Variable: Person** from the drop-down list box that appears. The final sentence should say:

```
Copy from Variable: output , starting at 0 for Variable: index
characters (Output to Variable: Person)
```

40. Once you have an account ID, you can create a new item in the **PeopleList** SharePoint list. So click to place the cursor below the last workflow action within the loop, type **create list**, and then press **Enter** to add a **Create List Item** action.

41. Click **this list** in the sentence for the workflow action.

42. On the **Create New List Item** dialog box, select **People** from the **List** drop-down list box, select **Title** in the list of fields, and then click **Modify**.

43. On the **Value Assignment** dialog box, click the formula button (second button) behind the **To this value** text box.

44. On the **Lookup for Single line of text** dialog box, select **Workflow Variables and Parameters** from the **Data source** drop-down list box, select **Variable: Person** from the **Field from source** drop-down list box, select **Display Name** from the **Return field as** drop-down list box, and click **OK**.

45. On the **Value Assignment** dialog box, click **OK**.

46. On the **Create New List Item** dialog box, click **Add**.

47. On the **Value Assignment** dialog box, select **EmailAddress** from the **Set this field** drop-down list box, and then click the formula button (second button) behind the **To this value** text box.

48. On the **Lookup for Single line of text** dialog box, select **Workflow Variables and Parameters** from the **Data source** drop-down list box, select **Variable: Person** from the **Field from source** drop-down list box, select **Email Address** from the **Return field as** drop-down list box, and click **OK**.
49. On the **Value Assignment** dialog box, click **OK**.
50. On the **Create New List Item** dialog box, click **OK**.

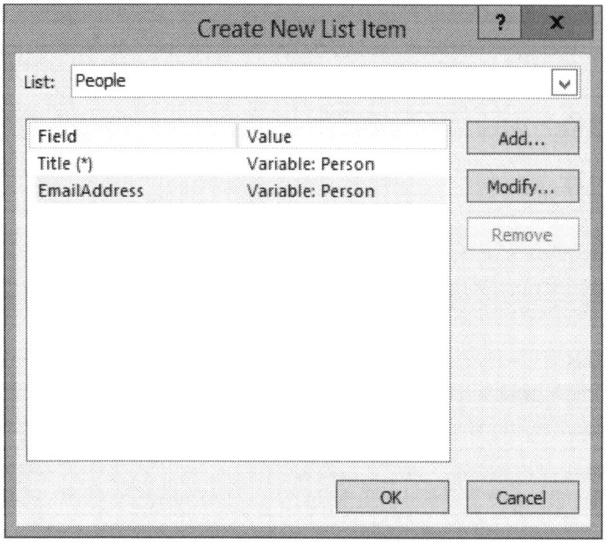

Figure 268. The Create New List Item dialog box in SharePoint Designer 2013.

51. Next, you must find the next semi-colon in the **output** variable to retrieve the next account ID. To find the next semi-colon in the **output** variable, you must first reposition the index to be one character after the previous semi-colon. So click to place the cursor below the last workflow action within the loop, type **calc**, and then press **Enter** to add a **Do Calculation** action.
52. Configure the workflow action to say:

```
then Calculate Variable: index plus 1 (Output to Variable:
calc)
```

53. To make it easier to extract the next account ID starting from the beginning of the string stored in the **output** variable, you must remove

the substring for the previous account ID from the string. So click to place the cursor below the last workflow action within the loop, type **extract**, press **Enter**, and then select **Extract Substring from Index of String** from the drop-down menu that appears.

54. Configure the workflow action to say:

```
then Copy from Variable: output , starting at Variable: calc
(Output to Variable: output)
```

55. Now you can look for the next semi-colon in what is left of the string in the **output** variable. So click to place the cursor below the last workflow action within the loop, type **find sub**, and then press **Enter** to add a **Find Substring in String** action.

56. Configure the workflow action to say:

```
then Find ; in Variable:output (Output to Variable: index)
```

57. Click to place the cursor in the **Transition to stage** section, and then select **Workflow ➤ Insert ➤ Action ➤ Go to a stage**.

58. Click **a stage** in the sentence for the workflow action, and then select **End of Workflow** from the drop-down list box that appears. The completed workflow should resemble Figure 269.

59. Click **Workflow ➤ Manage ➤ Workflow Settings**.

60. On the workflow settings page under **Start Options**, select the **Start workflow automatically when an item is created** check box.

61. Click **Workflow Settings ➤ Save ➤ Publish** to publish the workflow.

In SharePoint, navigate to the **PeopleLib** form library and add a new form. When the form opens, select two people from the person/group picker control, and then save the form back to the form library. Once the workflow has run and completed, verify that the people you selected from the person/group picker control were created in the **People** SharePoint list (see Figure 270).

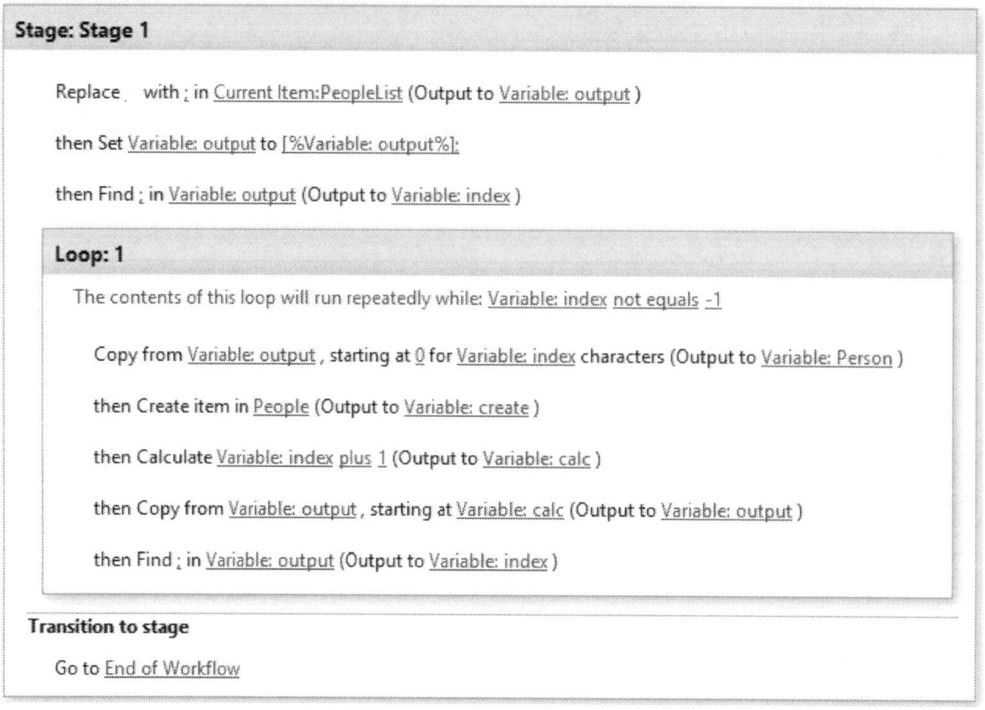

Stage: Stage 1
Replace with ; in Current Item:PeopleList (Output to Variable: output)
then Set Variable: output to [%Variable: output%];
then Find ; in Variable: output (Output to Variable: index)
Loop: 1
The contents of this loop will run repeatedly while: Variable: index not equals -1
Copy from Variable: output , starting at 0 for Variable: index characters (Output to Variable: Person)
then Create item in People (Output to Variable: create)
then Calculate Variable: index plus 1 (Output to Variable: calc)
then Copy from Variable: output , starting at Variable: calc (Output to Variable: output)
then Find ; in Variable: output (Output to Variable: index)
Transition to stage
Go to End of Workflow

Figure 269. The completed workflow in SharePoint Designer 2013.

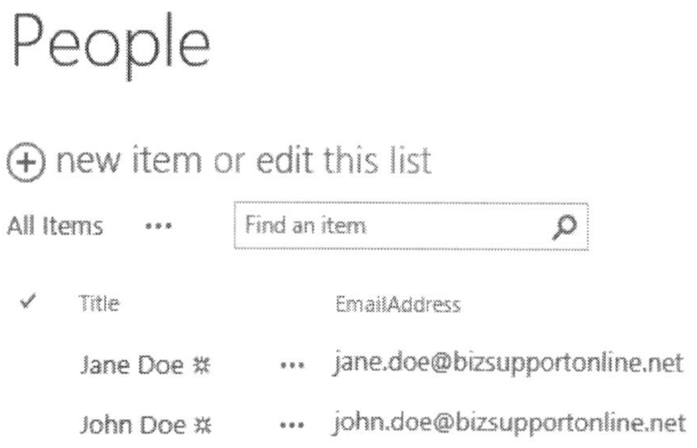

Figure 270. Selected people from people picker added as new SharePoint list items.

Discussion

In the solution described above, you used a **Replace Substring in String** workflow action to replace line-breaks with semi-colons. You also used a **Loop** to loop through the account IDs of the people that were selected from the people picker. The **Replace Substring in String** action and **Loop** are not available when you create a SharePoint 2010 workflow, which is why you had to create a SharePoint 2013 workflow.

Note that strings in SharePoint Designer workflows allow a maximum of 255 characters. This means that you must ensure that any strings you pass to a workflow do not exceed this limit. In the solution above, this would mean checking the length of the merged account IDs or the amount of people selected in the people picker in InfoPath and displaying a data validation error to the user if the limit is exceeded (see for example recipe *73 Limit a person/group picker to a maximum of 3 selected people*).

92 Submit rows of a repeating table to a SharePoint list

Problem

You have a repeating table on an InfoPath form, which you want to use to create new list items in a SharePoint list.

Solution

You can promote a hidden field that contains all of the data (or a maximum of 255 characters) from the repeating table in a certain format that can be parsed to extract rows and columns from the repeating table, and then use a SharePoint 2013 workflow to create SharePoint list items containing the data from the repeating table.

To submit rows of a repeating table to a SharePoint list:

1. In InfoPath, create a new SharePoint form library form template or use an existing one.
2. Add a **Repeating Table** control with 2 columns to the view of the form template. Name the field in the first column **fruitName** and the field in the second column **fruitColor**.
3. Add a hidden field of data type **Text (string)** and with the name **repeatingTableData** to the Main data source of the form.
4. Add an **Action** rule to the **fruitName** field with an action that says:

```
Set a field's value: repeatingTableData = eval(eval(group2,
```

```
'concat(my:fruitName, "|", my:fruitColor, ";")'), "..")
```

where you must manually type the following formula in the **Formula** text box on the **Insert Formula** dialog box:

```
eval(eval(../../my:group2, 'concat(my:fruitName, "|",
my:fruitColor, ";")'), "..")
```

5. Repeat the previous step for the **fruitColor** field (do not copy and paste the rule). Now when values are entered in the repeating table, the value of the **repeatingTableData** field should look something like for example:

   ```
   Apple|Red;Banana|Yellow;
   ```

   where **Apple** and **Red** have been entered in the first row of the repeating table, and **Banana** and **Yellow** in the second row.
6. Promote the **repeatingTableData** field to a column named **Repeating Table Data** as described in recipe *22 Promote form fields to columns of a form library*. Note that the column will be a single line of text column that can contain up to 255 characters. This means that you must apply restrictions to the repeating table, so that users do not go over this amount of characters by for example restricting the length of text boxes (see recipe 31 of *InfoPath 2013 Cookbook*) and the amount of rows that can be added to the repeating table (see recipe 114 of *InfoPath 2013 Cookbook*).
7. Publish the form template to a SharePoint form library named **RepTblLib**.
8. In SharePoint, create a new **Custom List** named **RepTblList**. Rename the **Title** column to **FruitName** and add a second **Single line of text** column named **FruitColor** to the list.
9. In SharePoint Designer 2013, create a **List Workflow** that is associated with the **RepTblLib** form library you published the form template to, name the workflow **ExtractRepTblDataWF**, and select **SharePoint 2013 Workflow** as the **Platform Type** (also see recipe *80 Create a workflow that runs on forms in a specific form library*).

10. The first step is to create a local variable in which you can store the contents of the repeating table, so click **Workflow ➤ Variables ➤ Local Variables**.
11. On the **Workflow Local Variables** dialog box, click **Add**.
12. On the **Edit Variable** dialog box, enter **RepeatingTableData** in the **Name** text box, leave **String** selected in the **Type** drop-down list box, and click **OK**.
13. On the **Workflow Local Variables** dialog box, click **OK**.
14. On the text-based designer, click to place the cursor inside of **Stage 1**, type **var**, and then press **Enter** to add a **Set Workflow Variable** action.
15. Click **workflow variable** in the sentence for the workflow action, and then select **Variable: RepeatingTableData** from the drop-down list box that appears.
16. Click **value** in the sentence for the workflow action, and then click the formula button (second button) behind the text box that appears.
17. On the **Lookup for String** dialog box, leave **Current Item** selected in the **Data source** drop-down list box, select **Repeating Table Data** from the **Field from source** drop-down list box, and click **OK**. The workflow action should now say:

```
Set Variable: RepeatingTableData to Current Item:Repeating
Table Data
```

18. The workflow must loop through all of the rows of the repeating table and then for each row, loop through the columns of the row. You can find the first row by looking for the first semi-colon (;) in the **RepeatingTableData** variable. First you will add a loop to find the rows of the repeating table, and then within that loop, you will parse the string that represents a row to find the columns in each row. Click to place the cursor below the first action, type **find sub**, and then press **Enter** to add a **Find Substring in String** action.
19. Click **substring** in the sentence for the workflow action, enter a semi-colon (;) in the text box, and then press **Enter**.
20. Click **string** in the sentence for the workflow action, and then click the formula button (second button) behind the text box that appears.

21. On the **Lookup for String** dialog box, select **Workflow Variables and Parameters** from the **Data source** drop-down list box, select **Variable: RepeatingTableData** from the **Field from source** drop-down list box, leave **As String** selected in the **Return field as** drop-down list box, and click **OK**. The workflow action should now say:

```
then Find ; in Variable:RepeatingTableData (Output to Variable:
index)
```

22. Click to place the cursor below the last action, and then select **Workflow** ➤ **Insert** ➤ **Loop** ➤ **Loop with Condition**.
23. Click the first **value** in the sentence inside the loop.
24. On the **LoopCondition Properties** dialog box, select the first **Value**, and then click the formula button behind the text box.
25. On the **Define Workflow Lookup** dialog box, select **Workflow Variables and Parameters** from the **Data source** drop-down list box, select **Variable: index** from the **Field from source** drop-down list box, and click **OK**.
26. On the **LoopCondition Properties** dialog box, select **Operator**, and then select **not equals** from the drop-down list box.
27. On the **LoopCondition Properties** dialog box, select the second **Value**, type **-1** in the text box, and then click **OK**.

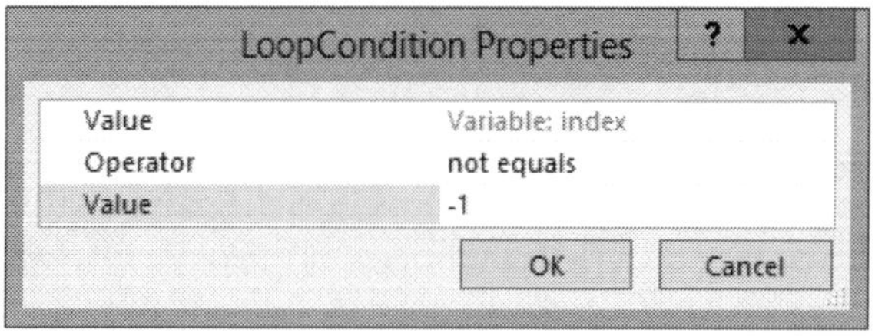

Figure 271. Settings on the LoopCondition Properties dialog box.

Note that if a semi-colon is not found, the value of the index will be equal to **-1**. The sentence within the loop should now say:

```
The contents of this loop will run repeatedly while Variable:
index not equals -1
```

28. Once you have the position of a semi-colon in the **RepeatingTableData** variable, you can extract the contents of a row and store it in another string variable named **Row**. So click **Workflow ➤ Variables ➤ Local Variables** and add a second local variable named **Row** of type **String** to the workflow.

29. Click to place the cursor below the first sentence within the loop, type **extract**, press **Enter**, and then select **Extract Substring of String from Index with Length** from the drop-down menu that appears.

30. Set **string** in the sentence for the workflow action to be equal to the **RepeatingTableData** workflow variable, replace the second **0** in the sentence for the workflow action with the **index** workflow variable, and have the output written to the **Row** workflow variable. To have the output written to the **Row** workflow variable you must click on **Variable: substring** in the sentence for the workflow action and then select **Variable: Row** from the drop-down list box that appears. The workflow action should now say:

```
Copy from Variable: RepeatingTableData , starting at 0 for
Variable: index characters (Output to Variable: Row)
```

31. Next, you must find the next semi-colon in the **RepeatingTableData** variable to retrieve the next row. To find the next semi-colon in the **RepeatingTableData** variable, you must first reposition the index to be one character after the previous semi-colon. So click to place the cursor below the last workflow action within the loop, type **calc**, and then press **Enter** to add a **Do Calculation** action.

32. Configure the workflow action to say:

```
then Calculate Variable: index plus 1 (Output to Variable:
calc)
```

33. To make it easier to extract the next row starting from the beginning of the string stored in the **RepeatingTableData** variable, you must remove the substring for the previous row from the string. So place the cursor below the last workflow action within the loop, type **extract**, press **Enter**, and then select **Extract Substring from Index of String** from the drop-down menu that appears.

34. Configure the workflow action to say:

```
then Copy from Variable: RepeatingTableData , starting at
Variable: calc (Output to Variable: RepeatingTableData)
```

35. Now you can look for the next semi-colon in what is left of the string in the **RepeatingTableData** variable. So place the cursor below the last workflow action within the loop, type **find sub**, and then press **Enter** to add a **Find Substring in String** action.

36. Configure the workflow action to say:

```
then Find ; in Variable: RepeatingTableData (Output to
Variable: index)
```

The workflow should now resemble the following:

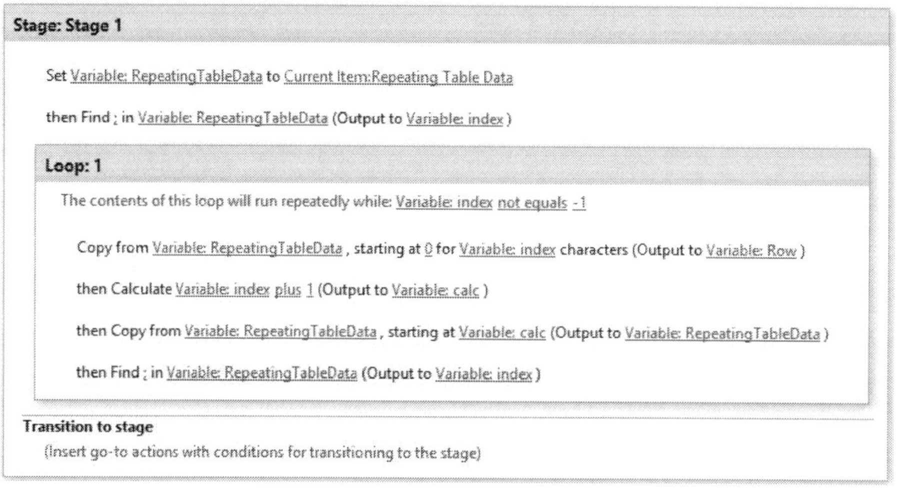
Stage: Stage 1
Set Variable: RepeatingTableData to Current Item:Repeating Table Data
then Find ; in Variable: RepeatingTableData (Output to Variable: index)
Loop: 1
The contents of this loop will run repeatedly while: Variable: index not equals -1
Copy from Variable: RepeatingTableData , starting at 0 for Variable: index characters (Output to Variable: Row)
then Calculate Variable: index plus 1 (Output to Variable: calc)
then Copy from Variable: RepeatingTableData , starting at Variable: calc (Output to Variable: RepeatingTableData)
then Find ; in Variable: RepeatingTableData (Output to Variable: index)
Transition to stage
(Insert go-to actions with conditions for transitioning to the stage)

Figure 272. Workflow to loop through rows of a repeating table.

37. You could add a second loop within the first loop that does the same thing for the columns within each row to retrieve the value of each column in each row. You would then have to look for the column separator (a pipe symbol in this case) instead of the row separator (a semi-colon). However, in this case we want to create list items using the values retrieved and because the repeating table only contains two columns we want to retrieve, we are going to keep things simple by just parsing the string and storing the values of the columns in two separate

variables, so that they can be used with the **Create List Item** action. So add two local variables with the names **Column1** and **Column2** of type **String** to the workflow.

38. The value of the first column is found by looking for the pipe symbol (|) in the string representing a row and then extracting a substring up until the pipe symbol. The value of the second column is found by extracting a substring starting from one character after the pipe symbol until the end of the string representing a row. So click to place the cursor immediately below the workflow action within the loop that says:

```
Copy from Variable: RepeatingTableData , starting at 0 for
Variable: index characters (Output to Variable: Row)
```

and then add a **Find Substring in String** action and configure it to say:

```
then Find | in Variable: Row (Output to Variable: index2)
```

39. To extract the value of the first column, add an **Extract Substring from Start of String** action immediately after the last workflow action you added and configure it to say:

```
then Copy Variable: index2 characters from start of Variable:
Row (Output to Variable: Column1)
```

40. To extract the value of the second column, you must first move **index2** one character position up. So add a **Do Calculation** action immediately after the last workflow action you added and configure it to say:

```
the Calculate Variable: index2 plus 1 (Output to Variable:
calc1)
```

41. Now you can extract the value of the second column by adding an **Extract Substring from Index of String** action immediately after the last workflow action you added and configuring it to say:

```
then Copy from Variable: Row , starting at Variable: calc1
(Output to Variable: Column2)
```

42. And finally, you can create a new SharePoint list item using the values of the first and the second column of a row. So click to place the cursor immediately below the last workflow action you added, type **create list**, and then press **Enter** to add a **Create List Item** action.
43. Click **this list** in the sentence for the workflow action.
44. On the **Create New List Item** dialog box, select **RepTblList** from the **List** drop-down list box, select **FruitName** in list of fields, and click **Modify**.
45. On the **Value Assignment** dialog box, click the formula button (second button) behind the **To this value** text box.
46. On the **Lookup for Single line of text** dialog box, select **Workflow Variables and Parameters** from the **Data source** drop-down list box, select **Variable: Column1** from the **Field from source** drop-down list box, leave **As String** selected in the **Return field as** drop-down list box, and click **OK**.
47. On the **Value Assignment** dialog box, click **OK**.
48. On the **Create New List Item** dialog box, click **Add**.
49. On the **Value Assignment** dialog box, select **FruitColor** from the **Set this field** drop-down list box, and then click the formula button (second button) behind the **To this value** text box.
50. On the **Lookup for Single line of text** dialog box, select **Workflow Variables and Parameters** from the **Data source** drop-down list box, select **Variable: Column2** from the **Field from source** drop-down list box, leave **As String** selected in the **Return field as** drop-down list box, and click **OK**.
51. On the **Value Assignment** dialog box, click **OK**.

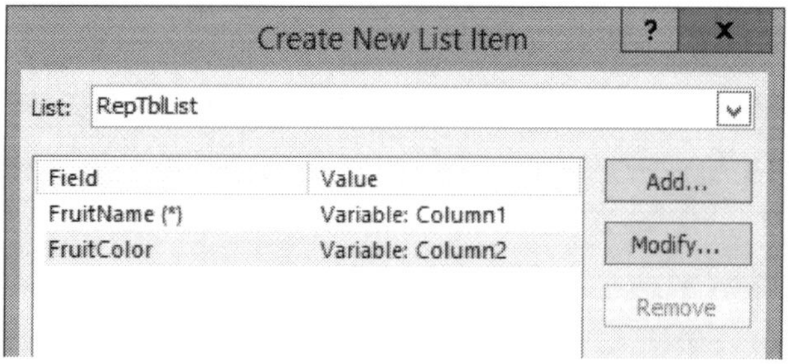

Figure 273. Settings on the Create New List Item dialog box.

52. On the **Create New List Item** dialog box, click **OK**.
53. Click to place the cursor in the **Transition to stage** section, and then select **Workflow ➤ Insert ➤ Action ➤ Go to a stage**.
54. Click **a stage** in the sentence for the workflow action, and then select **End of Workflow** from the drop-down list box that appears. The completed workflow should now resemble the following:

Stage: Stage 1
Set Variable: RepeatingTableData to Current Item:Repeating Table Data
then Find ; in Variable: RepeatingTableData (Output to Variable: index)
Loop: 1
The contents of this loop will run repeatedly while: Variable: index not equals -1
Copy from Variable: RepeatingTableData , starting at 0 for Variable: index characters (Output to Variable: Row)
then Find | in Variable: Row (Output to Variable: index2)
then Copy Variable: index2 characters from start of Variable: Row (Output to Variable: Column1)
then Calculate Variable: index2 plus 1 (Output to Variable: calc1)
then Copy from Variable: Row , starting at Variable: calc1 (Output to Variable: Column2)
then Create item in RepTblList (Output to Variable: create)
then Calculate Variable: index plus 1 (Output to Variable: calc)
then Copy from Variable: RepeatingTableData , starting at Variable: calc (Output to Variable: RepeatingTableData)
then Find ; in Variable: RepeatingTableData (Output to Variable: index)
Transition to stage
Go to End of Workflow

Figure 274. The completed workflow in SharePoint Designer 2013.

55. Click **Workflow ➤ Manage ➤ Workflow Settings**.
56. On the workflow settings page under **Start Options**, select the **Start workflow automatically when an item is created** check box.
57. Click **Workflow Settings ➤ Save ➤ Publish** to publish the workflow.

In SharePoint, navigate to the **RepTblLib** form library and add a new form. Add a couple of rows with data to the repeating table and then save the form back to the form library. Once the workflow has run and completed, navigate to the SharePoint list and check whether the repeating table rows were added as new items to the SharePoint list.

Discussion

The solution described above is limited to passing 255 characters in total from the repeating table to the SharePoint Designer workflow. If the total amount of data in the repeating table exceeds 255 characters, you must find a way to split the data and pass it to the workflow. You can use the **string-length()** function in InfoPath to check the length of the string that contains data from the repeating table.

93 Create a new InfoPath form through a workflow

Problem

You want to use a SharePoint 2010 workflow to create a new InfoPath form in a particular form library and also have the workflow fill out the values of fields in the form it creates.

Solution

You can add a site content type that inherits from the **Form** content type to a SharePoint site and then set a copy of the XML file for the form you want to create a new instance of as the document template of the content type. Once you have added the content type to the SharePoint site, you can use this content type and a SharePoint Designer workflow to create a new InfoPath form.

There are two parts to this solution: First you must add a site content type to a SharePoint site, and then you must create a SharePoint Designer workflow.

To add a new site content type for creating InfoPath documents:

1. In InfoPath, create a new SharePoint form library form template or use an existing one, ensure that it contains a text field named **lastName**, and publish the form template as a site content type named **CreateFormsCT** (also see recipe *25 Create a content type for an InfoPath form from within InfoPath*). When you publish the form template to SharePoint, ensure that you promote the **lastName** field as a site column named **Last Name** (also see recipe *23 Promote form fields to existing site columns*) and that you select the **Allow users to edit data in**

this field by using a datasheet or properties page check box for the promoted field.

2. In SharePoint, create a new form library named **CreateFormsLib**, and then add the **CreateFormsCT** content type to this form library (also see recipe *27 Create different types of forms in one form library*). When you add the site content type to the form library, the **Last Name** site column should automatically appear on the form library as a column.

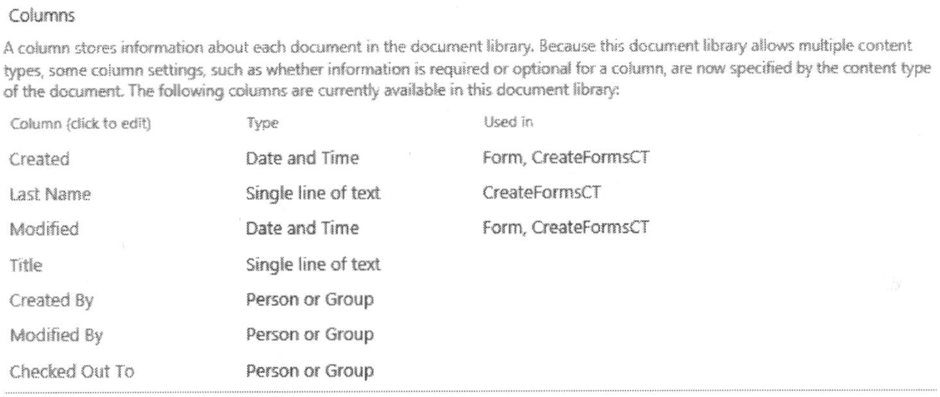

Columns

A column stores information about each document in the document library. Because this document library allows multiple content types, some column settings, such as whether information is required or optional for a column, are now specified by the content type of the document. The following columns are currently available in this document library:

Column (click to edit)	Type	Used in
Created	Date and Time	Form, CreateFormsCT
Last Name	Single line of text	CreateFormsCT
Modified	Date and Time	Form, CreateFormsCT
Title	Single line of text	
Created By	Person or Group	
Modified By	Person or Group	
Checked Out To	Person or Group	

Figure 275. The Last Name column has become available in the form library.

3. Navigate to the **CreateFormsLib** form library and add a new form that is based on the **CreateFormsCT** content type to the form library. You can prefill this form with data or leave all fields empty; whichever fits your scenario. Save the form to the form library and name it **template**. Close the form.

4. Click the ellipsis behind the name of the new form you just added to the form library, click the ellipsis behind **Share** on the context menu that appears, and then select **Download a Copy** from the drop-down menu that appears. Once you have downloaded the **template.xml** file, you can delete it from the form library.

5. Now you must create a second site content type that uses the InfoPath form you just downloaded. So follow steps 1 through 4 of recipe *26 Create a content type for an InfoPath form from within SharePoint* to create a new site content type named **CreateFormsWFCT**.

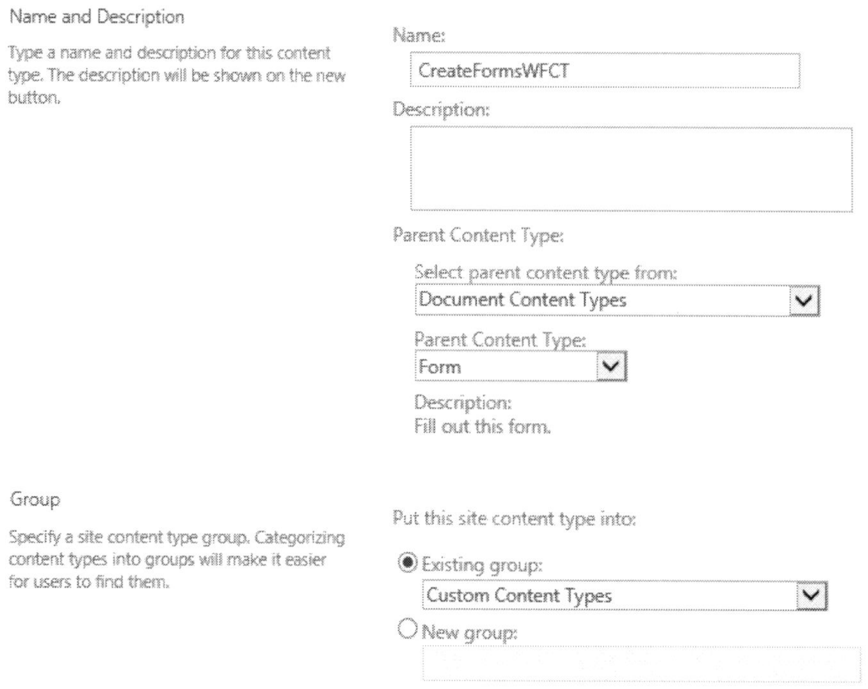

Figure 276. Creating a new Form content type in SharePoint 2013.

6. On the **Site Content Type** page under **Settings**, click **Advanced settings**.
7. On the **Advanced Settings** page under **Document Template**, select the **Upload a new document template** option, and then click **Browse**.
8. On the **Choose a File to Upload** dialog box, browse to and select the **template.xml** file you downloaded earlier, and click **Open**.

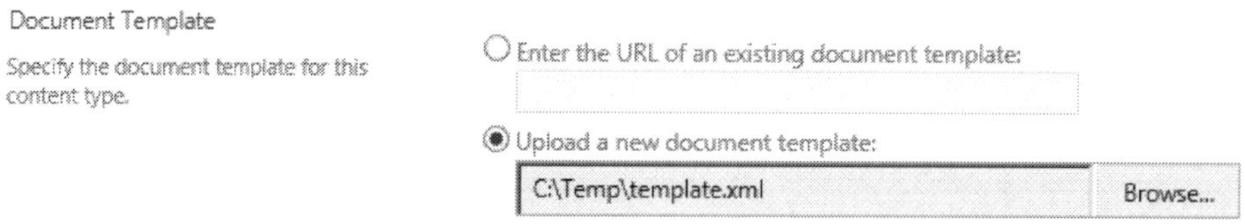

Figure 277. Setting the InfoPath form as the document template for the content type.

9. On the **Advanced Settings** page, click **OK**. With this you have set the new site content type to use an XML file (InfoPath form) instead of an XSN file (InfoPath form template) as its document template.
10. On the **Site Content Type** page under **Columns**, click **Add from existing site columns**.
11. On the **Add Columns** page, search for the **Last Name** site column you used in step 1 in the **Available columns** list, click **Add** to add it to the **Columns to add** list, and then click **OK**.
12. Navigate to the **Settings** page of the **CreateFormsLib** form library, and add the **CreateFormsWFCT** content type to the form library.
13. On the **Settings** page of the **CreateFormsLib** form library under **Content Types**, click the **Change new button order and default content type** link, and then deselect the **Visible** check boxes for the **Form** and **CreateFormsWFCT** content types, so that users cannot use them to add forms to the form library. This should automatically make the **CreateFormsCT** the **Default Content Type** of the form library (also see recipe *28 Configure a form library to create a certain type of form by default*). Note that the **CreateFormsWFCT** content type should only be used by the SharePoint 2010 workflow (and not by users) to create InfoPath forms. Click **OK** when you are done.

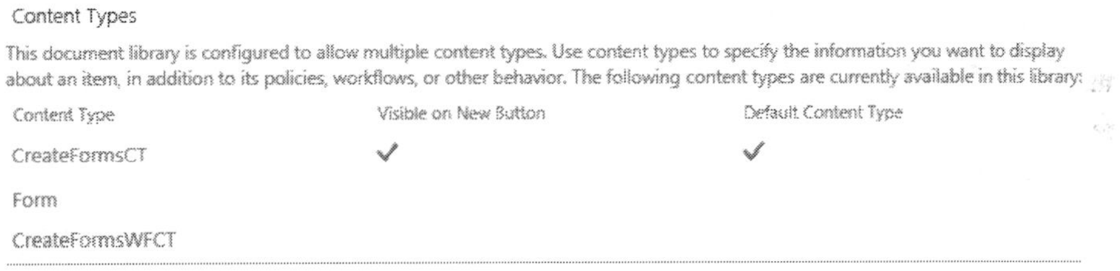

Content Types
This document library is configured to allow multiple content types. Use content types to specify the information you want to display about an item, in addition to its policies, workflows, or other behavior. The following content types are currently available in this library:
Content Type
Visible on New Button
Default Content Type
CreateFormsCT
Form
CreateFormsWFCT

Figure 278. Content types associated with the form library in SharePoint 2013.

After adding the **CreateFormsWFCT** content type to the form library, you should notice that the **Last Name** column is now shared by the **CreateFormsCT** and the **CreateFormsWFCT** content types.

Columns

A column stores information about each document in the document library. Because this document library allows multiple content types, some column settings, such as whether information is required or optional for a column, are now specified by the content type of the document. The following columns are currently available in this document library:

Column (click to edit)	Type	Used in
Created	Date and Time	CreateFormsCT, Form, CreateFormsWFCT
Last Name	Single line of text	CreateFormsCT, CreateFormsWFCT
Modified	Date and Time	CreateFormsCT, Form, CreateFormsWFCT
Title	Single line of text	
Created By	Person or Group	
Modified By	Person or Group	
Checked Out To	Person or Group	

Figure 279. Columns available in the form library in SharePoint 2013.

With this you have added a site content type that can be used by a workflow to create new InfoPath forms based on the form template you published earlier to the form library. Note that if you change and republish the form template in the future, you will have to go through all of the steps (except for creating a new site content type) again to replace the old **template.xml** file of the **CreateFormsWFCT** content type with a new form that is based on the modified form template.

Let us say you have a SharePoint list named **Contacts**, which contains last names stored in its **Title** column. Whenever a new item is added to this list, you want to have a SharePoint Designer workflow create a new InfoPath form in the **CreateFormsLib** form library with the same name you entered into the **Title** column, and also write this name to the **lastName** text field on the form, which you promoted as a site column named **Last Name**.

To create a SharePoint 2010 workflow that creates an InfoPath form:

1. In SharePoint, create a custom list named **Contacts** that has a column named **Title**.
2. In SharePoint Designer 2013, open the site on which the **Contacts** list and **CreateFormsLib** form library are located.
3. Create a new **List Workflow** that is associated with the **Contacts** list, name the workflow **CreateFormWF**, and select **SharePoint 2010 Workflow** as the **Platform Type** (also see recipe *80 Create a workflow that runs on forms in a specific form library*).

4. On the text-based designer, click to place the cursor inside of **Step 1**, type **create list**, and then press **Enter** to add a **Create List Item** action.
5. Click **this list** in the sentence for the workflow action.
6. On the **Create New List Item** dialog box, select **CreateFormsLib** from the **List** drop-down list box, select **Content Type ID** in the list of fields, and then click **Modify**.
7. On the **Value Assignment** dialog box, leave **Content Type ID** selected in the **Set this field** drop-down list box, select **CreateFormsWFCT** from the **To this value** drop-down list box, and click **OK**. With this you have set the workflow to use the document template of the **CreateFormsWFCT** content type to create a list item or InfoPath form in this case.

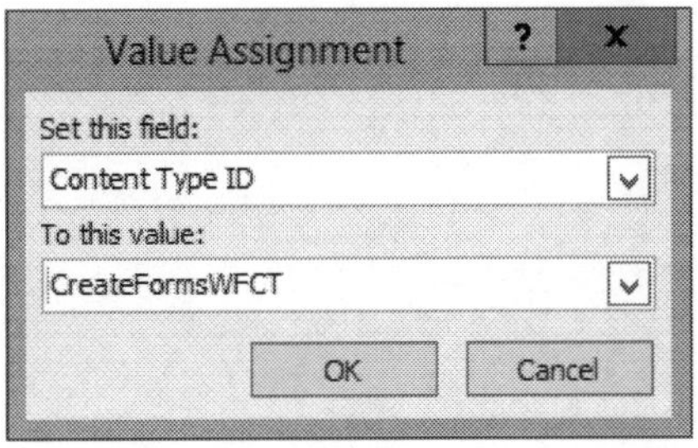

Figure 280. Selecting CreateFormsWFCT as the content type to use.

8. On the **Create New List Item** dialog box, select **Path and Name (*)** in the list of fields, and then click **Modify**.
9. On the **Value Assignment** dialog box, click the formula button (second button) behind the **To this value** text box.
10. On the **Lookup for String** dialog box, leave **Current Item** selected in the **Data source** drop-down list box (this is the **Contacts** list item the workflow is running on), select **Title** from the **Field from source** drop-down list box, and click **OK**.

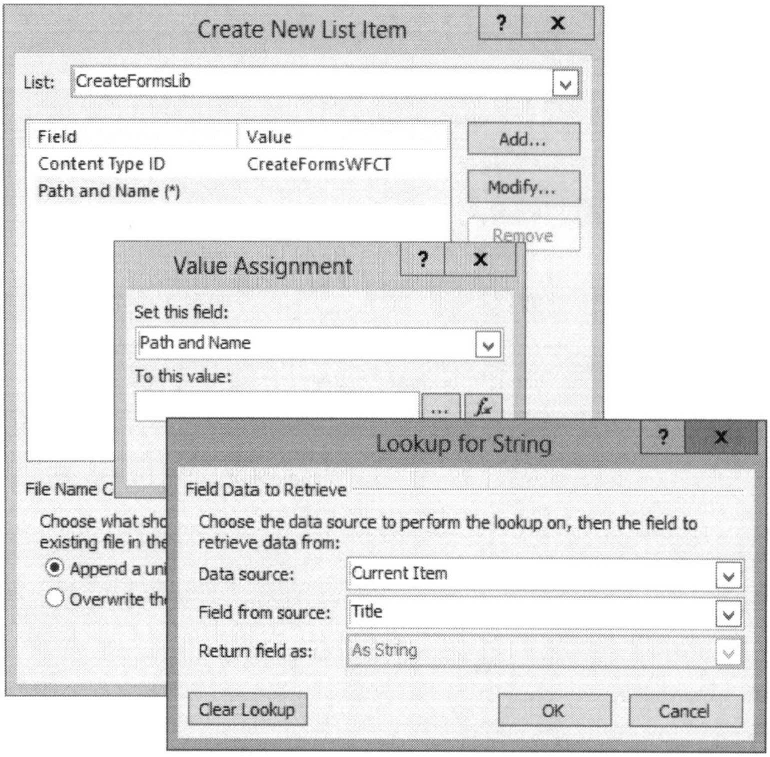

Figure 281. Setting the path and name of the new item in SharePoint Designer 2013.

Note that the path and name field should not contain any periods, since this would interfere with the newly created InfoPath form being recognized as a valid file type. And since it is difficult to prevent users from adding periods to any text they enter unless you customize the SharePoint list form and add data validation to the InfoPath form for the SharePoint list to prevent faulty data entry, you may want to use something other than the value of the **Title** field of the list item as the path and name for the newly created InfoPath form (see for example steps 27 through 30 of recipe *94 Create a new form and link it to an existing form through a workflow*).

11. On the **Value Assignment** dialog box, click **OK**.
12. On the **Create New List Item** dialog box, click **Add**.

13. On the **Value Assignment** dialog box, select **Last Name** from the **Set this field** drop-down list box, and then click the formula button (second button) behind the **To this value** text box.
14. On the **Lookup for Single line of text** dialog box, leave **Current Item** selected in the **Data source** drop-down list box, select **Title** from the **Field from source** drop-down list box, and click **OK**.
15. On the **Value Assignment** dialog box, click **OK**. With this you have set the value of the **Last Name** column (**lastName** field on the InfoPath form) to be equal to the value of the **Title** field in the **Contacts** list.
16. On the **Create New List Item** dialog box, click **OK**.

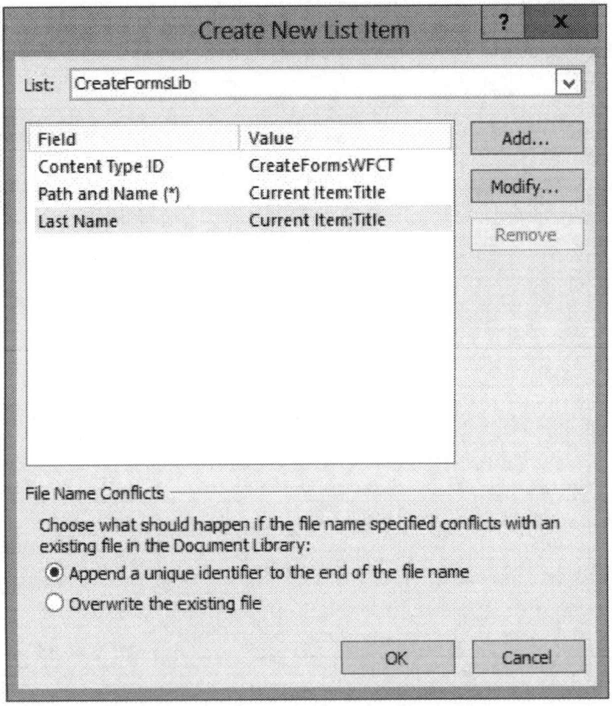

Figure 282. The Create New List Item dialog box in SharePoint Designer 2013.

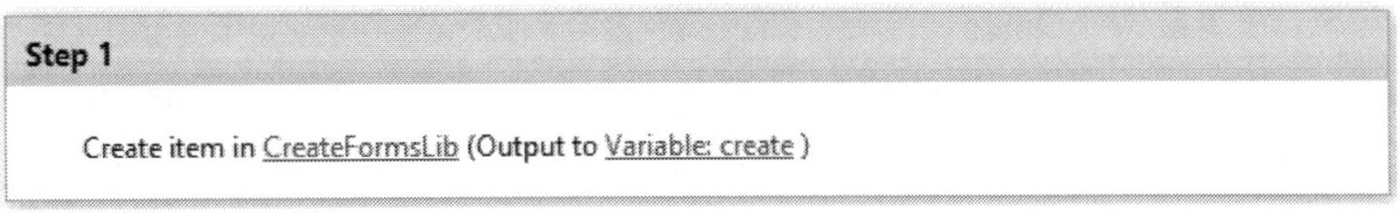

Figure 283. The completed workflow in SharePoint Designer 2013.

17. Click **Workflow ➤ Manage ➤ Workflow Settings**.
18. On the workflow settings page under **Start Options**, select the **Start workflow automatically when an item is created** check box.
19. Click **Workflow Settings ➤ Save ➤ Publish** to publish the workflow.

If you are using SharePoint 2013 without Service Pack 1 installed, you must perform the following additional steps for the SharePoint Designer workflow to use the correct XML file:

1. In SharePoint, navigate to the **Settings** page of the **CreateFormsLib** form library.
2. On the **Settings** page of the **CreateFormsLib** form library under **General Settings**, click **Advanced settings**.
3. On the **Advanced Settings** page, select the **No** option for **Allow management of content types**.
4. On the **Advanced Settings** page under **Document Template**, change the **Template URL** to point to the same XML file as the **CreateFormsWFCT** content type is pointing to. So change

    ```
    CreateFormsLib/Forms/template.xml
    ```

    to

    ```
    CreateFormsLib/Forms/CreateFormsWFCT/template.xml
    ```

5. On the **Advanced Settings** page, click **OK**.
6. On the **Settings** page of the **CreateFormsLib** form library under **General Settings**, click **Advanced settings**.
7. On the **Advanced Settings** page, leave the **Document Template** pointing to the same XML file as the **CreateFormsWFCT** content type, select the **Yes** option for **Allow management of content types**, and then click **OK**.

In SharePoint, navigate to the **Contacts** list and add a new list item. Enter a piece of text in the **Title** text box and save the item back to the list. The workflow should automatically start. After the workflow has run and completed, navigate to the **CreateFormsLib** form library to see whether a new InfoPath form was created. Open the InfoPath form and check whether the **lastName** field was populated with the piece of text you entered as the title for the item in the **Contacts** list.

Discussion

In the solution described above you made use of two different content types to create InfoPath forms: One content type (**CreateFormsCT**) was used by users to manually create InfoPath forms within SharePoint, while the other content type (**CreateFormsWFCT**) was used by a SharePoint 2010 workflow to automatically create InfoPath forms in a form library.

The main difference between the two content types used in the solution described above is that the content type that is used by users in SharePoint to create InfoPath forms (**CreateFormsCT**) has an InfoPath form template (XSN file) defined as its document template, while the content type that is used by SharePoint Designer 2013 to create InfoPath forms (**CreateFormsWFCT**) has an XML file defined as its document template. The XML file of the second content type is an InfoPath form that is linked to the same InfoPath form template that is defined as the document template of the first content type. You can see that this is the case by switching to the **Relink Documents** view (**Library ➤ Manage Views ➤ Current View ➤ Relink Documents**) of the form library.

Type	Name	Relink	Content Type	Template Link
	CreatedByWF NEW	☐	CreateFormsWFCT	http://win-a5pj1269tfk/infopath2013cookbook2/Shared%20Documents/CreateFormsCT.xsn
	ManuallyCreated NEW	☐	CreateFormsCT	http://win-a5pj1269tfk/infopath2013cookbook2/Shared%20Documents/CreateFormsCT.xsn

Figure 284. The Relink Documents view of the form library displaying two forms.

In the figure above, the **Modified** and **Modified By** columns have been removed from the **Relink Documents** view for clarity. The **CreatedByWF** form was created by the SharePoint Designer workflow and is based on the **CreateFormsWFCT** content type, while the **ManuallyCreated** form was created by a user via the browser and is based on the **CreateFormsCT** content type. Both forms are linked to a template named

CreateFormsCT.xsn that is located in the **Shared Documents** document library.

Note that if you ever update and republish the InfoPath form template linked to the **CreateFormsCT** content type, you must recreate the XML file and update the document template of the **CreateFormsWFCT** content type to keep them in sync with each other.

Also note that the sole purpose of the SharePoint Designer workflow in the solution described above is to create and fill out a new InfoPath form with data. The SharePoint Designer workflow cannot run rules and other business logic that are contained within an InfoPath form.

94 Create a new form and link it to an existing form through a workflow

Problem

You have a form in which project information is entered, and you want to be able to submit this form to a form library and automatically create a related form in which project approval information is entered, in another form library.

Solution

You can use a combination of property promotion in forms and a SharePoint Designer workflow to create related forms in two separate form libraries.

It is recommended that you go through recipe ***93 Create a new InfoPath form through a workflow*** before going through this recipe, since recipe 93 explains the basics of creating InfoPath forms through a SharePoint Designer workflow and this recipe expands on the concepts learned in recipe 93.

To create a new form and link it to an existing form through a SharePoint Designer workflow:

1. In InfoPath, create a new SharePoint form library form template and save it locally as **ProjectInfo.xsn**.

2. Add two **Text Box** controls to the view of the form template, and name them **projectName** and **projectDescription**, respectively.
3. Publish the form template to a form library named **ProjectInfoLib** and promote the **projectName** field as a readable but not editable field to the form library during the publishing process (also see recipe *22 Promote form fields to columns of a form library*).

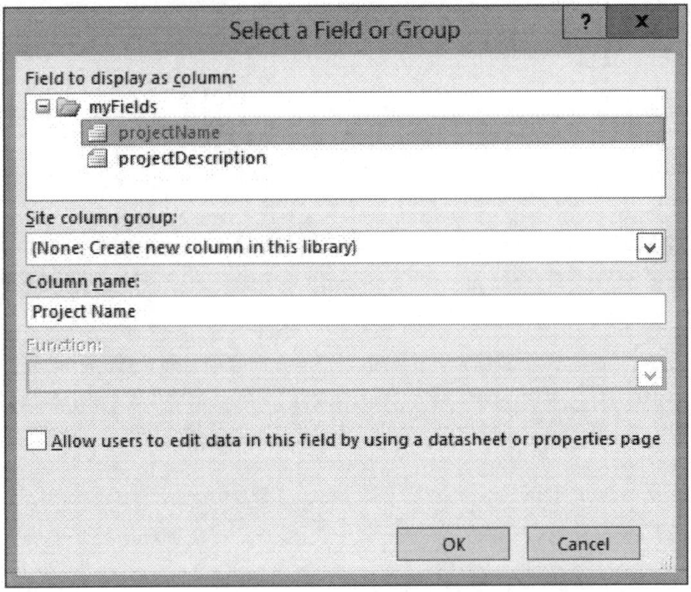

Figure 285. Promoting the projectName field as a new column of the form library.

4. Create a second SharePoint form library form template and save it locally as **ProjectApproval.xsn**.
5. Add a **Receive** data connection to the **ProjectInfoLib** form library to the form template (also see recipe *54 Retrieve a list of forms from a form library*). Ensure that you select **ID** and **Project_Name (Project Name)** as fields to include in the data source, and that you deselect the **Automatically retrieve data when form is opened** check box.
6. On the **Fields** task pane, add a hidden **Field (element)** of type **Text (string)** and with the name **projectID** to the Main data source. You are going to use this field to store the **ID** of the **ProjectInfo** form that should be linked to the **ProjectApproval** form.
7. On the **Fields** task pane, select **ProjectInfoLib (Secondary)** from the **Fields** drop-down list box, and then drag-and-drop the **Project Name**

field from under the **d:SharePointListItem_RW** repeating group node under the **dataFields** group node onto the view of the form template and bind it to a **Repeating Section with Controls** control.

8. Click **Data** ➤ **Rules** ➤ **Form Load** and add an **Action** rule that has a **Condition** that says:

```
projectID is not blank
```

and that has 2 actions that say:

```
Set a field's value: ID = projectID
Query using a data connection: ProjectInfoLib
```

where **ID** is the **ID** field that is located under the **q:SharePointListItem_RW** group node under the **queryFields** group node in the **ProjectInfoLib** secondary data source, and **projectID** is the hidden field located in the Main data source. This action rule queries the secondary data source to retrieve the project that corresponds to the ID stored in the **projectID** field. The **projectID** field serves as the link between the two forms.

9. Add any other controls that you would like to place on the project approval form.
10. Publish the form template to a form library named **ProjectApprovalLib**, and promote the **projectID** field as an editable field to the form library (select the **Allow users to edit data in this field by using a datasheet or properties page** check box) during the publishing process.

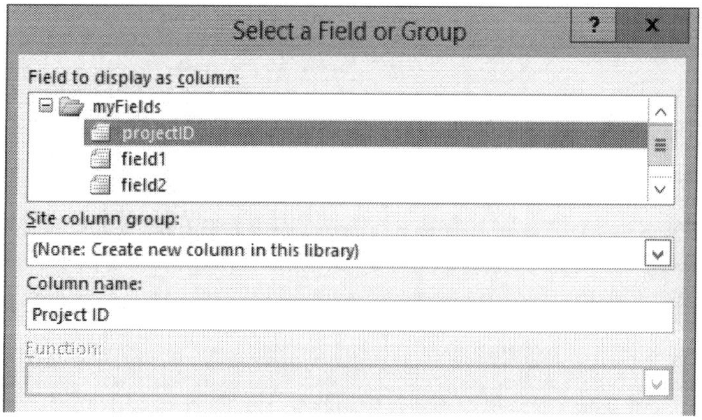

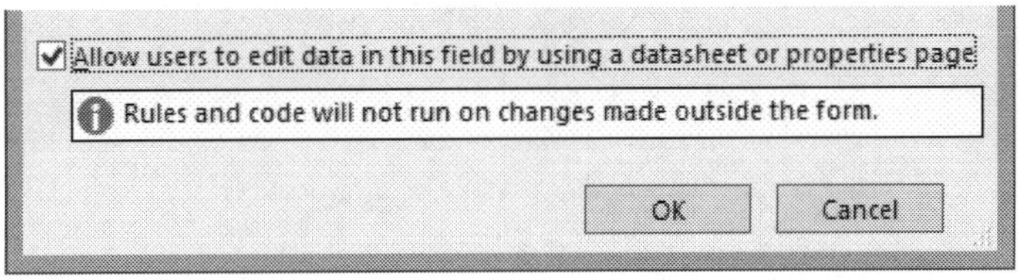

Figure 286. Promoting the project ID field as a new column in the form library.

11. In SharePoint, navigate to the **ProjectApprovalLib** form library and add a new form to it. Save the form back to the form library and name it **template**. Close the form.
12. Download a copy of the newly created form, save it locally on disk, and then delete it from the **ProjectApprovalLib** form library.
13. Manually create a new site content type named **ApprovalFormWFCT** as described in steps 1 through 4 of recipe *26 Create a content type for an InfoPath form from within SharePoint* that inherits from the **Form** parent content type. Do not set its document template or add any columns to the new site content type.
14. Add the **ApprovalFormWFCT** content type to the **ProjectApprovalLib** form library as described in recipe *27 Create different types of forms in one form library*.
15. On the **Settings** page of the **ProjectApprovalLib** form library under **Content Types**, click **ApprovalFormWFCT** to navigate to the **List Content Type** page.
16. On the **List Content Type** page under **Columns**, click **Add from existing site or list columns**.
17. On the **Add Columns** page, leave **List Columns** selected in the **Select columns from** drop-down list box, select **Project ID** in the **Available columns** list, click **Add**, and then click **OK**. This action copies the **Project ID** column of the form library, which is also the column the **projectID** field was promoted to, onto the content type.

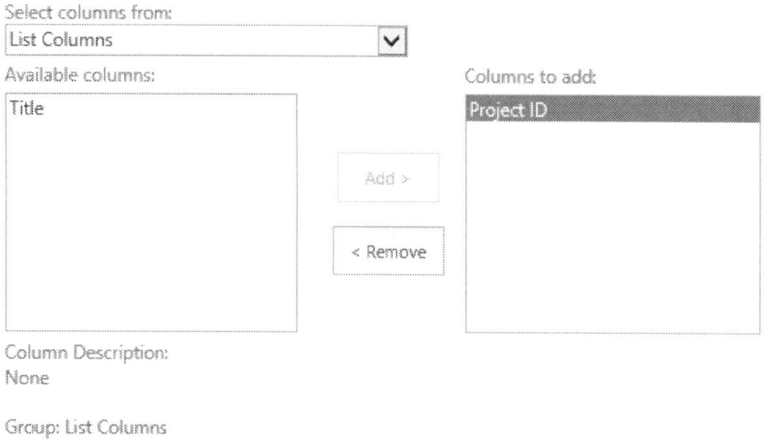

Figure 287. Adding the Project ID column of the form library to the list content type.

18. On the **List Content Type** page under **Settings**, click **Advanced settings**.
19. On the **Advanced Settings** page under **Document Template**, select the **Upload a new document template** option, click **Browse**, and then browse to and open the InfoPath form you downloaded earlier as the document template for the content type. Click **OK** when you are done.
20. Navigate back to the **Settings** page of the **ProjectApprovalLib** form library, and then under **Content Types**, click the **Change new button order and default content type** link, and then make the **ApprovalFormWFCT** content type invisible.

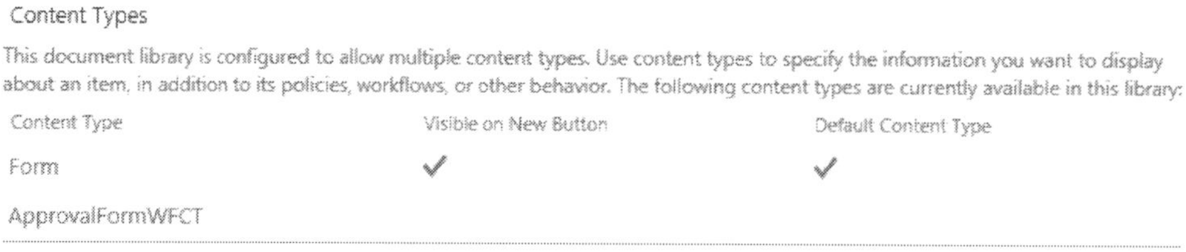

Figure 288. Content types associated with the SharePoint form library.

Columns

A column stores information about each document in the document library. Because this document library allows multiple content types, some column settings, such as whether information is required or optional for a column, are now specified by the content type of the document. The following columns are currently available in this document library:

Column (click to edit)	Type	Used in
Created	Date and Time	Form, ApprovalFormWFCT
Modified	Date and Time	Form, ApprovalFormWFCT
Project ID	Single line of text	Form, ApprovalFormWFCT
Title	Single line of text	
Created By	Person or Group	
Modified By	Person or Group	
Checked Out To	Person or Group	

Figure 289. Columns available in the SharePoint form library.

As shown in the figure above, the default content type (**Form**) of the form library, the invisible **ApprovalFormWFCT** list content type associated with the form library, and the form library share the same **Project ID** column.

21. In SharePoint Designer 2013, create a **List Workflow** that is associated with the **ProjectInfoLib** form library, name the workflow **CreateApprovalFormWF**, and select **SharePoint 2010 Workflow** as the **Platform Type** (also see recipe *80 Create a workflow that runs on forms in a specific form library*).
22. On the text-based designer, click inside of **Step 1** to place the cursor, type **create list**, and then press **Enter** to add a **Create List Item** action.
23. Click **this list** in the sentence for the workflow action.
24. On the **Create New List Item** dialog box, select **ProjectApprovalLib** from the **List** drop-down list box, select **Content Type ID** in the list of fields, and then click **Modify**.
25. On the **Value Assignment** dialog box, leave **Content Type ID** selected in the **Set this field** drop-down list box, select **ApprovalFormWFCT** from the **To this value** drop-down list box, and click **OK**. With this you have set the workflow to use the document template of the **ApprovalFormWFCT** content type to create a list item or InfoPath form in this case.

26. On the **Create New List Item** dialog box, select **Path and Name (*)** in the list of fields, and then click **Modify**.
27. On the **Value Assignment** dialog box, leave **Path and Name** selected in the **Set this field** drop-down list box, and click the ellipsis button (first button) behind the **To this value** text box.
28. On the **String Builder** dialog box, type **ApprovalForm_** in the **Name** text box, and then click **Add or Change Lookup**.
29. On the **Lookup for String** dialog box, leave **Current Item** selected in the **Data source** drop-down list box, select **ID** from the **Field from source** drop-down list box, and click **OK**. The text on the **String Builder** dialog box should now say:

```
ApprovalForm_[%Current Item:ID%]
```

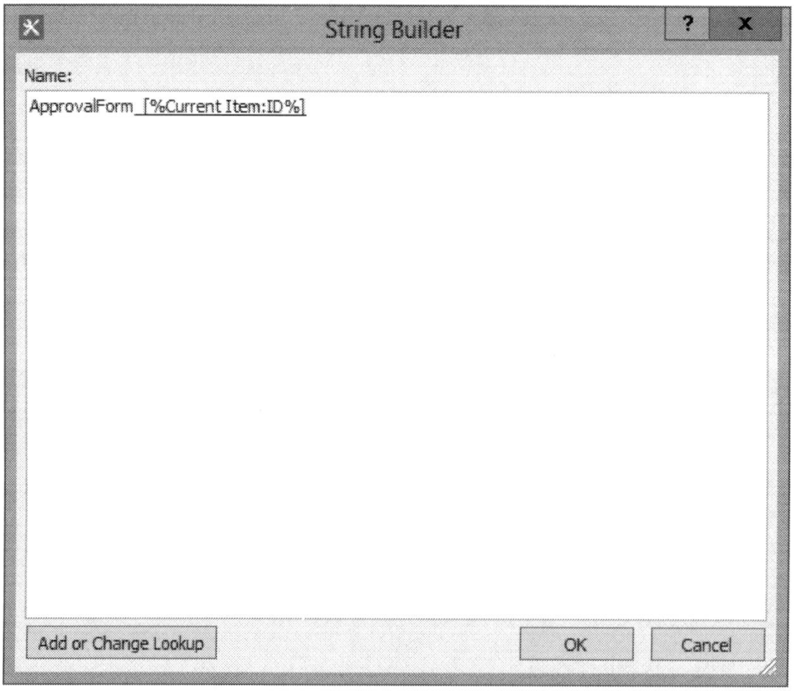

Figure 290. The String Builder dialog box in SharePoint Designer 2013.

30. On the **String Builder** dialog box, click **OK**.
31. On the **Value Assignment** dialog box, click **OK**. With this you have set the name of the new item (**ProjectApprovalLib** InfoPath form) to

be equal to the text "ApprovalForm_" plus the **ID** of the **ProjectInfoLib** InfoPath form the workflow is running on.

32. On the **Create New List Item** dialog box, click **Add**.
33. On the **Value Assignment** dialog box, select **Project ID** from the **Set this field** drop-down list box, and then click the formula button (second button) behind the **To this value** text box.
34. On the **Lookup for Single line of text** dialog box, leave **Current Item** selected in the **Data source** drop-down list box, select **ID** from the **Field from source** drop-down list box, and click **OK**.
35. On the **Value Assignment** dialog box, click **OK**. With this you have set the **Project ID** field of the new item (**ProjectApprovalLib** InfoPath form) to be equal to the **ID** of the **ProjectInfoLib** InfoPath form the workflow is running on.
36. On the **Create New List Item** dialog box, leave the **Append a unique identifier to the end of the file name** option selected, and click **OK**.

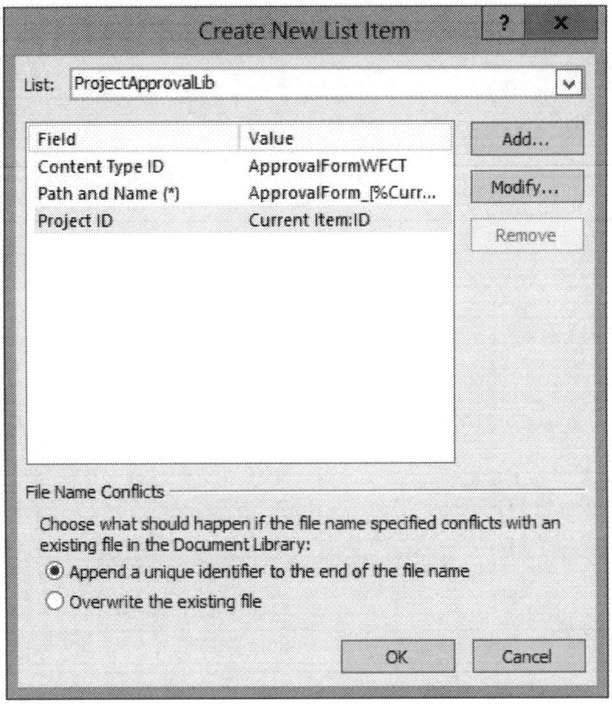

Figure 291. The Create New List Item dialog box in SharePoint Designer 2013.

37. Click **Workflow** ➤ **Manage** ➤ **Workflow Settings**.
38. On the workflow settings page under **Start Options**, select the **Start workflow automatically when an item is created** check box.
39. Click **Workflow Settings** ➤ **Save** ➤ **Publish** to publish the workflow.

If you are using SharePoint 2013 without Service Pack 1 installed, you must perform the following additional steps for the SharePoint Designer workflow to use the correct XML file:

1. In SharePoint, navigate to the **Settings** page of the **ProjectApprovalLib** form library.
2. On the **Settings** page of the **ProjectApprovalLib** form library under **General Settings**, click **Advanced settings**.
3. On the **Advanced Settings** page, select the **No** option for **Allow management of content types**.
4. On the **Advanced Settings** page under **Document Template**, change the **Template URL** to point to the same XML file as the **ApprovalFormWFCT** content type is pointing to. So change

   ```
   ProjectApprovalLib/Forms/template.xml
   ```

   to

   ```
   ProjectApprovalLib/Forms/ApprovalFormWFCT/template.xml
   ```

5. On the **Advanced Settings** page, click **OK**.
6. On the **Settings** page of the **ProjectApprovalLib** form library under **General Settings**, click **Advanced settings**.
7. On the **Advanced Settings** page, leave the **Document Template** pointing to the same XML file as the **ApprovalFormWFCT** content type, select the **Yes** option for **Allow management of content types**, and then click **OK**.

In SharePoint, navigate to the **ProjectInfoLib** form library and add a new form. When the form opens, enter data in the text boxes and then save the form back to the form library. Wait until the **CreateApprovalFormWF** workflow has run and completed, navigate to the **ProjectApprovalLib** form library, and verify that a new form was created. Open the form and verify that the project name you entered in the project information form has been loaded in the project name text box on the approval form.

Discussion

In the solution described above you saw how to use a SharePoint 2010 workflow to set the value of a field in a newly created InfoPath form so that it is linked to an existing form in a different form library. You also used a similar technique as the one described in recipe *93 Create a new InfoPath form through a workflow* to be able to automatically create new InfoPath forms in the **ProjectApprovalLib** form library whenever a new **ProjectInfo** InfoPath form is added to the **ProjectInfoLib** form library. But in this recipe you made use of a list column instead of a site column on the form library to promote a form field to and which was copied onto a list content type (**ApprovalFormWFCT**) used by the workflow to create new InfoPath forms. You also published the form templates directly to form libraries instead of as site content types.

95 Move a form from one form library to another using a workflow

Problem

You want to be able to select an item from the drop-down menu of a form and then automatically move that form to another form library on the same site.

Solution

You can publish a form template as a site content type, so that the form template can be associated with two form libraries between which you can move forms, create a SharePoint Designer workflow that can copy and delete a form, and then add a custom action to the source form library to be able to easily start the workflow.

To move a form from one library to another using a workflow:

1. In InfoPath, create a new SharePoint form library form template or use an existing one, and publish the form template as a site content type named **FormToMoveCT** (also see recipe *25 Create a content type for an InfoPath form from within InfoPath*) on the site where you will be creating the form libraries.
2. In SharePoint, create two form libraries named **SourceFormLib** and **DestinationFormLib**.
3. Add the **FormToMoveCT** content type to the **SourceFormLib** form library (also see recipe *27 Create different types of forms in one form library*).
4. In SharePoint Designer 2013, create a **List Workflow** that is associated with the **SourceFormLib** form library, name it **MoveFormWF**, and select **SharePoint 2013 Workflow** as the **Platform Type** (also see recipe *80 Create a workflow that runs on forms in a specific form library*).
5. Moving an InfoPath form from one form library to another entails copying the form to the destination form library and then deleting it from the source form library. So on the text-based designer, click to place the cursor inside of **Stage 1**, type **copy**, and then press **Enter** to add a **Copy Document** action.
6. Click the first **this library** in the sentence for the workflow action.
7. On the **Choose List Item** dialog box, leave **Current Item** (which represents the current InfoPath form the workflow is running on) selected in the **List** drop-down list box, and click **OK**.
8. Click the second **this library** in the sentence for the workflow action, and select **DestinationFormLib** from the drop-down list box that appears. With this you have set the workflow to copy the InfoPath form it is currently running on to the **DestinationFormLib** form library. The workflow action should now say:

   ```
   Copy document in Current Item to DestinationFormLib
   ```

9. Click to place the cursor below the previous workflow action, type **delete**, and then press **Enter** to add a **Delete Item** action.
10. Click **this list** in the sentence for the workflow action.

11. On the **Choose List Item** dialog box, leave **Current Item** selected in the **List** drop-down list box, and click **OK**. With this you have set the workflow to delete the InfoPath form it is currently running on from the **SourceFormLib** form library.
12. Click to place the cursor in the **Transition to stage** section, and then select **Workflow ➤ Insert ➤ Action ➤ Go to a stage**.
13. Click **a stage** in the sentence for the workflow action, and select **End of Workflow** from the drop-down list box that appears. The completed workflow should now resemble the following:

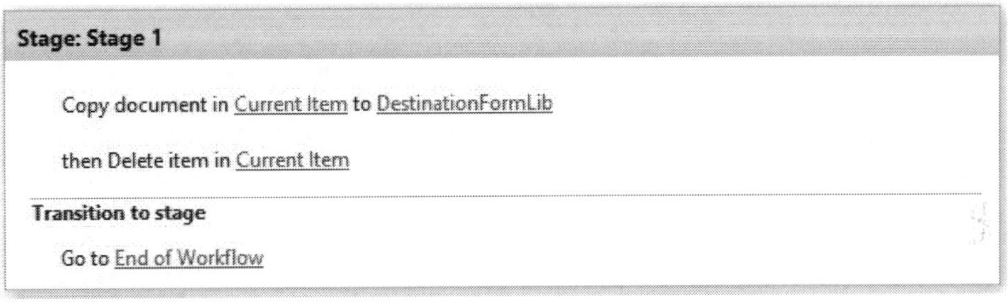

Figure 292. The completed workflow in SharePoint Designer 2013.

14. Click **Workflow ➤ Manage ➤ Workflow Settings**.
15. On the workflow settings page under **Start Options**, leave the **Allow this workflow to be manually started** check box selected as the only selected option, to allow users to manually move forms from one form library to the next.
16. Click **Workflow Settings ➤ Save ➤ Publish** to publish the workflow.
17. In the left **Navigation** pane, click **List and Libraries** to bring up all of the lists and libraries on the site.
18. On the **List and Libraries** page under **Document Libraries**, click **SourceFormLib**, and then follow the instructions in recipe *84 Start a workflow from a custom action in a library* to add a custom action named **Move to DestinationFormLib** that initiates the **MoveFormWF** workflow to move forms from the **SourceFormLib** form library to the **DestinationFormLib** form library.

In SharePoint, navigate to the **SourceFormLib** form library and add a new form that is based on the **FormToMoveCT** content type. Fill out the form and then save or submit it back to the form library. Click the ellipsis behind the name of the newly added form, click the ellipsis behind **Share** on the context menu that appears, and then select **Move to DestinationFormLib** from the drop-down menu that appears.

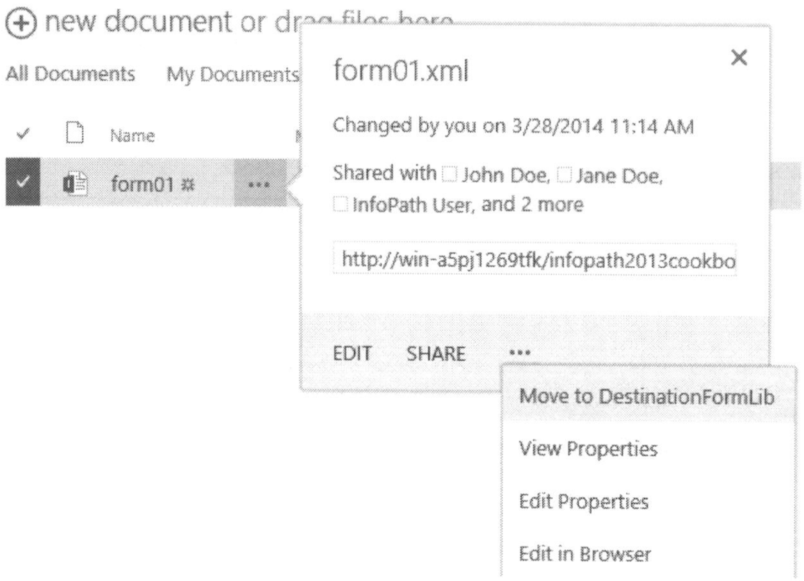

Figure 293. Selecting to start a workflow from a custom action on a form's menu.

Once the workflow has run and completed, the form should disappear from the **SourceFormLib** form library and appear in the **DestinationFormLib** form library. Navigate to the **DestinationFormLib** form library to check whether this is the case and open the form to ensure that it can be opened.

Discussion

By publishing a form template as a site content type, and then adding that site content type to the source form library that is involved in moving the forms, you minimize the likelihood of form template links being broken when forms are moved.

In the solution described above you also added a custom action to InfoPath forms in a form library to make it easier for users to start a workflow. By adding a custom action you remove a couple of extra steps a user would have to perform to manually start the workflow as described in recipe *83 Manually start a workflow to run on a form*.

96 Set a task form field from an initiation form in an approval workflow

Problem

You have a person/group picker control on a leave request form from which an employee name is selected. The leave request form is submitted to a form library and then a custom approval workflow is manually started on the form. When the approval workflow is started, the initiator of the workflow should be able to enter a textual request in a multi-line text box. A task should then be created and assigned to the manager of the employee, and when the manager opens the task form of the approval workflow, the request entered at startup of the workflow should appear on the task form for the manager to read. The manager should then be able to approve or reject the leave request.

Solution

You can use a combination of initiation parameters and task form fields to pass the value of an initiation parameter to a task form by using the Task list as an intermediary for the communication between the workflow initiation and task forms.

To pass an initiation parameter value to a task form in a leave request approval workflow:

1. In InfoPath, create a new SharePoint form library form template or use an existing one.
2. Add a **Person/Group Picker** control to the view of the form template.
3. Promote the first **AccountId** field of the person/group picker control as a column named **Employee** via the **Form Options** dialog box as described in the discussion section of recipe *22 Promote form fields to columns of a form library*.

4. Publish the form template to a SharePoint form library named **LeaveRequestFormsLib**.

5. In SharePoint Designer 2013, create a **List Workflow** that is associated with the **LeaveRequestFormsLib** form library, name the workflow **GetManagerApprovalWF**, and select **SharePoint 2010 Workflow** as the **Platform Type** (also see recipe *80 Create a workflow that runs on forms in a specific form library*).

6. Because you want anyone who starts the workflow to have the ability to enter a textual request, you must create an initiation parameter to capture this request. So click **Workflow ➤ Variables ➤ Initiation Form Parameters** and add a parameter named **StartupRequest** of type **Multiple lines of text** to the workflow.

7. Because an approval workflow assigns tasks to users and these tasks should have an expiration date, you will create a local variable that stores a date that is 7 days from the date the workflow was started. So click **Workflow ➤ Variables ➤ Local Variables**, and add a variable named **expirationDate** of type **Date/Time** to the workflow.

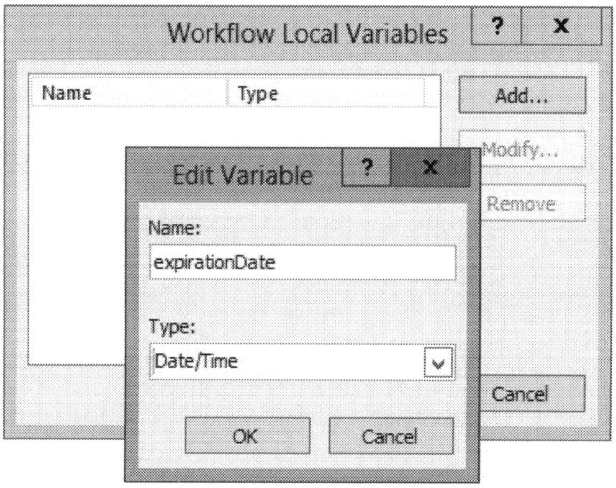

Figure 294. Adding a local variable to a workflow in SharePoint Designer 2013.

8. To set the **expirationDate** variable to a date in the future, you must perform a date calculation. So on the text-based designer, click to place the cursor inside of **Step 1**, type **add time**, and then press **Enter** to add an **Add Time to Date** action.

9. Click **0** in the sentence for the workflow action and type **7** in the text box that appears.
10. Click **minutes** in the sentence for the workflow action and select **days** from the drop-down list box that appears.
11. Click **date** in the sentence for the workflow action, and then click the formula button (second button) behind the text box that appears.
12. On the **Lookup for Date/Time** dialog box, select **Workflow Context** from the **Data source** drop-down list box, select **Date and Time Started** from the **Field from source** drop-down list box, and click **OK**.
13. Click **Variable: date** in the sentence for the workflow action and select **Variable: expirationDate** from the drop-down list box that appears. You have now set the value of the **expirationDate** variable to be equal to a date that lies 7 days in the future starting from the date the workflow was started. The workflow action should now say:

```
Add 7 days to Workflow Context:Date and Time Started (Output to
Variable: expirationDate)
```

14. For a manager to be able to approve or reject a leave request, a task must be assigned to the manager. And before you can assign a task to the manager, you must know who the manager of the employee is, so you must perform a lookup. So click to place the cursor below the previous workflow action, type **manager**, and then press **Enter** to add a **Lookup Manager of a User** action.
15. Click **this user** in the sentence for the second workflow action.
16. On the **Select User** dialog box, select **Workflow Lookup for a User** in the existing users and groups list, and then click **Add**.
17. On the **Lookup for Person or Group** dialog box, leave **Current Item** selected in the **Data source** drop-down list box, select **Employee** from the **Field from source** drop-down list box, and click **OK**.
18. On the **Select User** dialog box, click **OK**. The account ID of the manager of the employee should automatically be stored in a variable that is listed after **output to Variable** in the sentence for the workflow action. By default, this should be a variable named **manager**. The workflow action should now say:

```
then Find Manager of Current Item:Employee (output to Variable:
```

`manager)`

19. Tasks are stored in the **Tasks** SharePoint list. You could either use the **Tasks** list that is added to a site by default or you could create a new **Tasks** list for the workflow. Here you will create a new **Tasks** list to see how you would go about doing this. So click **Workflow ➤ Manage ➤ Workflow Settings**.
20. On the workflow settings page under **Settings**, select **New Task List** from the **Task List** drop-down list box, and when prompted, confirm that you want to create a new task list. A new **Tasks** list that has the name of the workflow as part of its own name should be created. You could perform a similar step to create a new **History List** for the workflow if you wanted to.
21. Click **Workflow Settings ➤ Edit ➤ Edit Workflow** to go back to the text-based designer.
22. Under the action that retrieves the manager, you can assign a task to that manager. So click to place the cursor below the last workflow action you added, type **task**, and then press **Enter** to add a **Start Custom Task Process** action.
23. Click **these users** in the sentence for the third workflow action.
24. On the **Select Task Process Participants** dialog box, click the button behind the **Participants** text box.
25. On the **Select Users** dialog box, select **Workflow Lookup for a User** in the existing users and groups list, and then click **Add**.
26. On the **Lookup for Person or Group** dialog box, select **Workflow Variables and Parameters** from the **Data source** drop-down list box, select **Variable: manager** from the **Field from source** drop-down list box, select **Email Address** from the **Return field as** drop-down list box, and click **OK**.

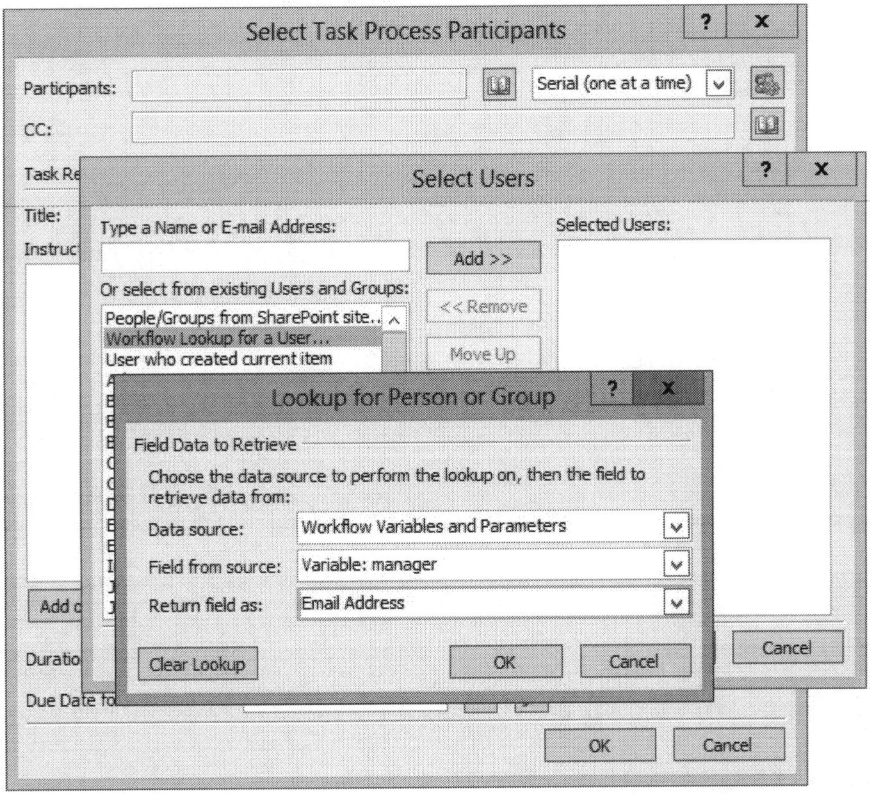

Figure 295. Selecting the manager as a workflow participant in an approval workflow.

27. On the **Select Users** dialog box, click **OK**.
28. On the **Select Task Process Participants** dialog box, enter a **Title** (for example **Leave request approval required**), enter a few **Instructions**, select a **Duration per Task** of **1 Day(s)**, and click the formula button (second button) behind the **Due Date for Task Process** text box.
29. On the **Lookup for Date/Time** dialog box, select **Workflow Variables and Parameters** from the **Data source** drop-down list box, select **Variable: expirationDate** from the **Field from source** drop-down list box, and click **OK**. With this you have set the task to be due within 7 days from the day the workflow was started.
30. On the **Select Task Process Participants** dialog box, click **OK**. With this you have assigned a task to the manager who should approve the leave request.

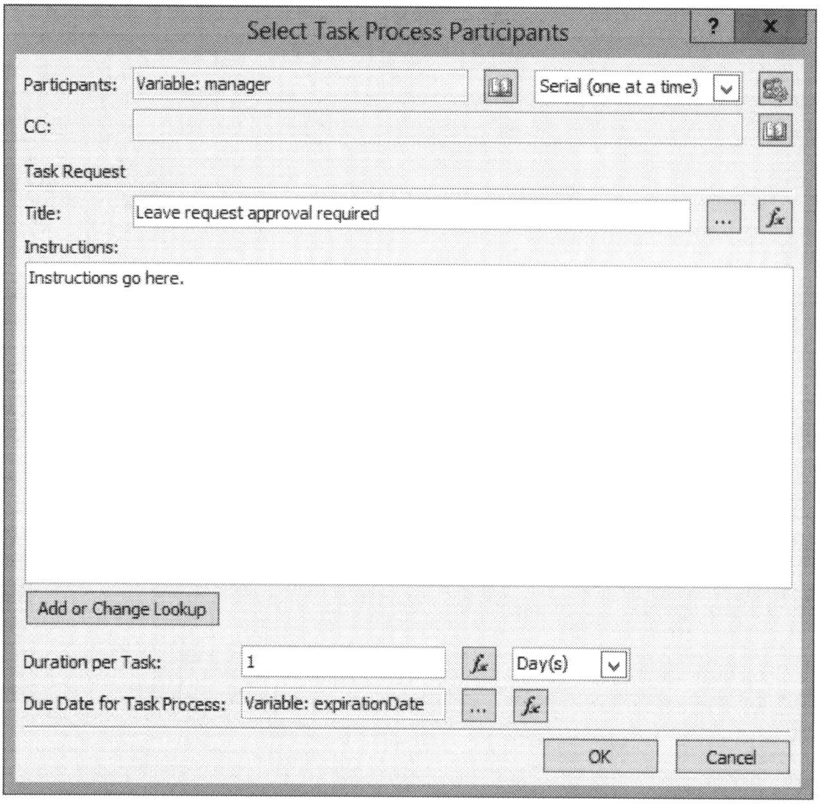

Figure 296. The completed Select Task Process Participants dialog box.

31. Now you must configure the task so that it contains a field in which the value of the **StartupRequest** initiation parameter can be stored and subsequently displayed on the task form. So click **Task ([number])** in the sentence for the third workflow action.
32. On the task process page under **Task Form Fields**, click **New** to add a new task form field.
33. On the **Add Field** dialog box, type **StartupRequest** in the **Field name** text box, select **Multiple lines of text** from the **Information type** drop-down list box, leave the **Add to default view** check box selected, click **Next**, and then click **Finish**. This step should also automatically add a column named **StartupRequest** to the **Tasks** list.

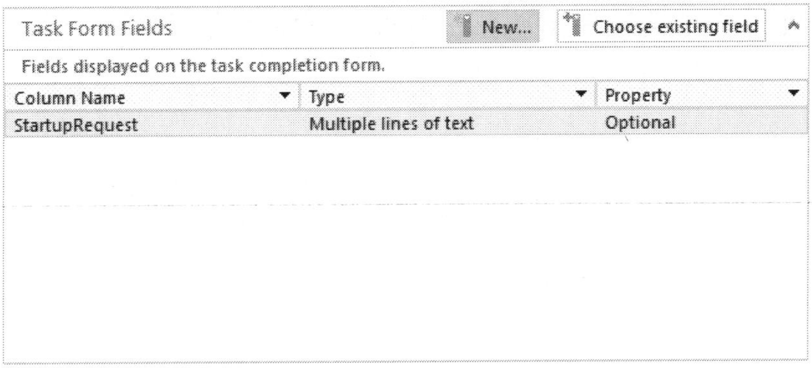

Figure 297. The newly added StartupRequest task form field in SharePoint Designer.

34. When you publish the workflow, the initiation and task forms will be created, and then you can edit them. For now, continue configuring the task by clicking **Change the behavior of a single task** under the **Customization** section on the task process page.
35. You must set the value of the **StartupRequest** field in the **Tasks** list to be equal to the value of the **StartupRequest** initiation parameter before the task is assigned, so click to place the cursor inside of the **Before a Task is Assigned** task behavior, type **task field**, and then press **Enter** to add a **Set Task Field** action.
36. Click **field** in the sentence for the workflow action you just added and select **StartupRequest** from the drop-down list box that appears.
37. Click **value** in the sentence for the workflow action, and then click the formula button (second button) behind the text box that appears.
38. On the **Lookup for Multiple lines of text** dialog box, select **Workflow Variables and Parameters** from the **Data source** drop-down list box, select **Parameter: StartupRequest** from the **Field from source** drop-down list box, and then click **OK**. The workflow action should now say:

```
Set Task Field StartupRequest to Parameter: StartupRequest
```

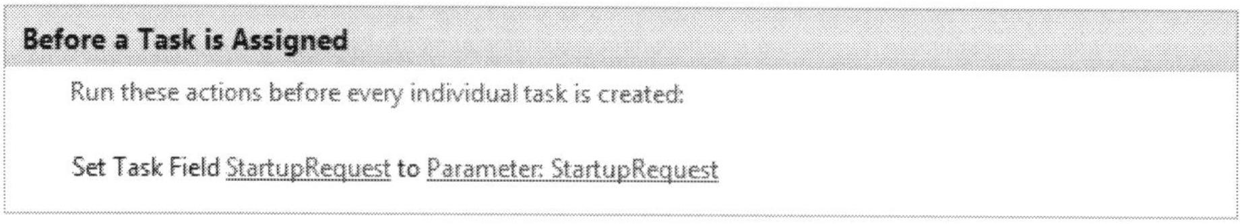

Figure 298. The completed Before a Task is Assigned task behavior.

39. Currently, the task is set to expire after 7 days. When the task expires, you could let the workflow take an appropriate action such as escalate the task to the manager of the manager. To do this, click to place the cursor inside of the **When a Task Expires** task behavior, type **escalate**, and then press **Enter** to add an **Escalate Task** action. The workflow action should say:

```
Escalate this task to the current assignee's manager
```

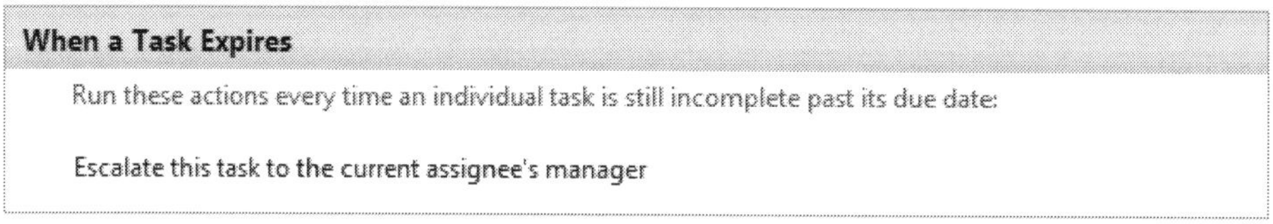

When a Task Expires
Run these actions every time an individual task is still incomplete past its due date:
Escalate this task to the current assignee's manager

Figure 299. The completed When a Task Expires task behavior.

40. Click **Task ([number])** in the breadcrumbs to return to the task process page.
41. On the task process page under **Customization**, click **Change the completion conditions for this task process**.
42. On the **Completion Conditions** page, click to place the cursor inside of the completion condition, and then select **Workflow ➤ Insert ➤ Condition ➤ Other Conditions ➤ If task outcome equals value**.
43. Click the first **value** in the sentence for the workflow condition and select **Number of Approved** from the drop-down list box that appears.
44. Click the second **value** in the sentence for the workflow condition and type **1** in the text box that appears.

45. Click to place the cursor within the **If**-branch of the workflow condition, type **log**, and then press **Enter** to add a **Log to History List** action.
46. Click **this message** in the sentence for the workflow action and type **approved** in the text box that appears.
47. Click to place the cursor below the action you added within the **If**-branch of the workflow condition, and then click **Workflow ➤ Insert ➤ Else-If Branch** to add an **Else**-branch to the workflow condition.
48. Click to place the cursor within the **Else**-branch of the workflow condition, type **log**, and then press **Enter** to add a **Log to History List** action.
49. Click **this message** in the sentence for the workflow action you just added and type **rejected** in the text box that appears.

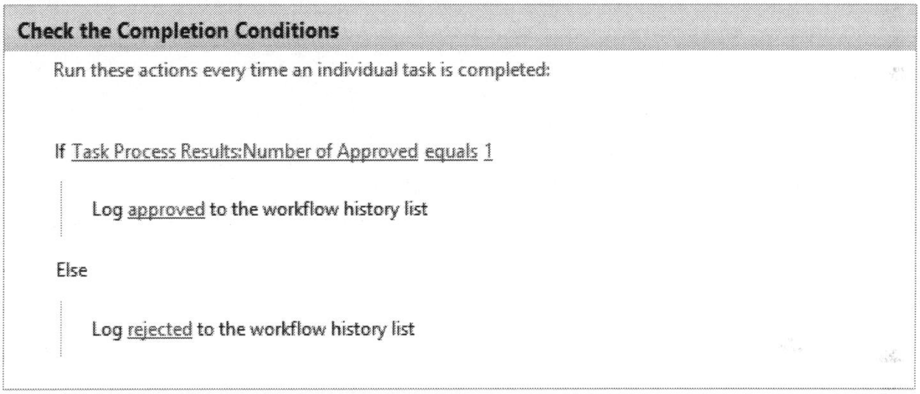

Figure 300. The completed workflow completion conditions in SharePoint Designer.

50. Click **Workflow ➤ Save ➤ Publish** to publish the workflow and create the InfoPath form templates for the workflow.
51. Click **Workflow ➤ Manage ➤ Workflow Settings**.
52. On the workflow settings page under **Forms**, click the task form (XSN file of type **Task**) to open it in InfoPath Designer 2013.

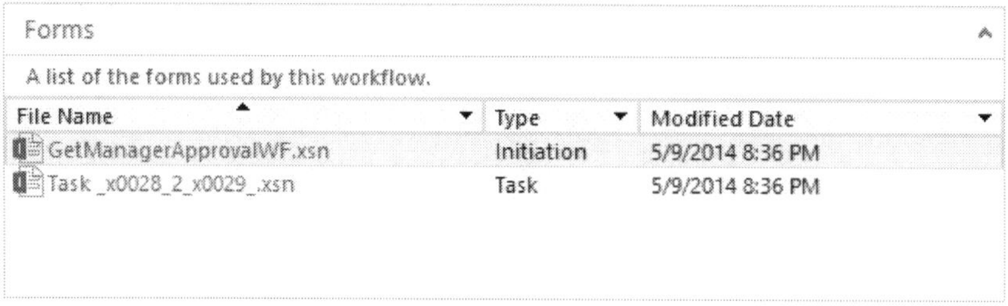

Figure 301. The workflow forms created by SharePoint Designer.

53. In InfoPath, a text box that is bound to the **StartupRequest** field should have already been added to the view of the form template. Click the text box for the **StartupRequest** field, select **Control Tools ➤ Properties ➤ Modify ➤ Read-Only** on the Ribbon to make the text box read-only, and then give the text box a different background color through the **Properties ➤ Color ➤ Shading** setting on the Ribbon to make it distinguishable from the other fields on the form.

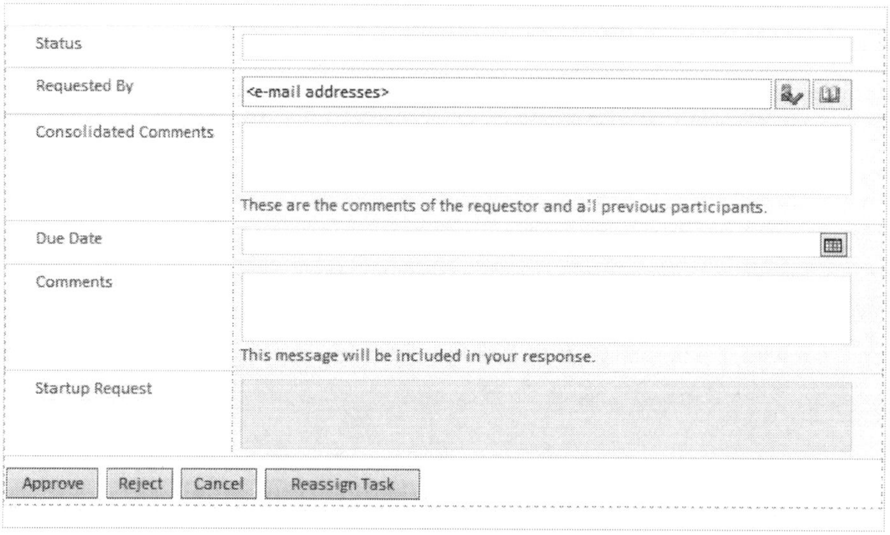

Figure 302. The workflow task form template in InfoPath Designer 2013.

54. Click **Quick Publish** on the **Quick Access Toolbar** at the top of the screen in InfoPath Designer 2013, click **File ➤ Info ➤ Quick Publish**, or click **File ➤ Publish ➤ Workflow** to republish the form template. Note: InfoPath may prompt you to save the form template.

In SharePoint, navigate to the **LeaveRequestFormsLib** form library and add a new form. When the form opens, select a user that has a manager from the person/group picker control, and then save the form back to the form library. Close the form. Manually start the **GetManagerApprovalWF** workflow on the form you just added as described in recipe *83 Manually start a workflow to run on a form*. When the initation form opens, type a textual request in the **StartupRequest** text box before clicking **Start**. Click the text **In Progress** behind the form, and then on the workflow status page under **Tasks**, click the **GetmanagerApprovalWF Tasks** link.

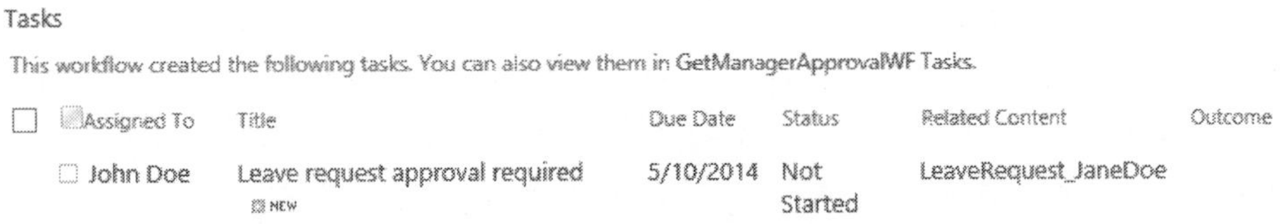

Tasks
This workflow created the following tasks. You can also view them in GetManagerApprovalWF Tasks.
Assigned To
Title
Due Date
Status
Related Content
Outcome
John Doe
Leave request approval required
NEW
5/10/2014
Not Started
LeaveRequest_JaneDoe

Figure 303. Tasks section on the workflow status page in SharePoint 2013.

In the **GetManagerApprovalWF Tasks** list, click on the title of the task to open the task. When the workflow task page opens, you should see the startup request text you entered earlier.

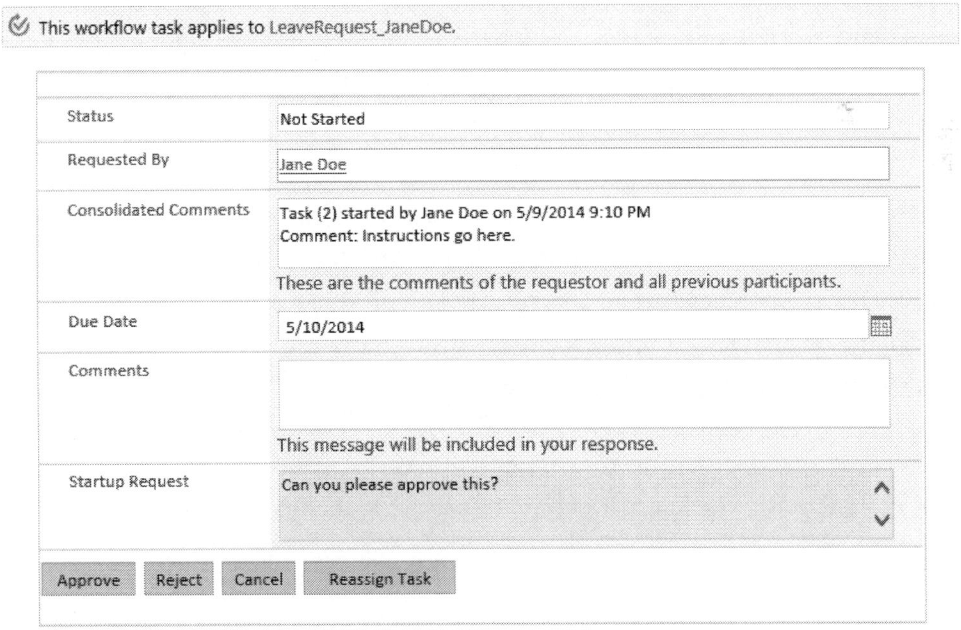

Figure 304. Workflow task form in SharePoint 2013.

Click **Approve** or **Reject**. Navigate back to the **LeaveRequestFormsLib** form library and verify that the workflow has **Completed**. Click on the text **Completed** and verify that the correct value ("approved" or "rejected") was written to the workflow history list.

Discussion

When you create a workflow that allows an approval process that contains tasks to be assigned, you can use workflow task forms to pass data to the workflow for completing or further progressing the task. In recipe *88 Send a form's link in an email to selected users at workflow startup* you saw how to modify a workflow initiation form. In the solution described above you not only learned how to modify a workflow task form, but also how to pass a value that was specified at startup via an initiation parameter to that workflow task form through the use of task form fields and the **Set Task Field** task behavior action.

The workflow created above was kept simple in order not to clutter the demonstration of the concepts. Therefore you logged the result of the workflow to the workflow history list instead of performing more complex actions. In addition, you added actions to only 2 of the 5 task behaviors that are available on an approval workflow, but you could have extended the workflow by adding actions to the rest of the task behaviors; for example, used a **Send an Email** action to send an email to the employee when the task completes or used a combination of the **Copy List Item** and **Delete Item** actions to move the leave request form to another form library when the task completes. The possibilities with approval workflows are endless and this recipe only served as a practical introduction to them. For a thorough explanation of approval workflows, consult the SharePoint Designer documentation on the Microsoft Office web site, and in particular the article entitled *Use the task process editor for approval workflows.*

Chapter 6: Use Word with InfoPath via SharePoint

Users are sometimes required to enter additional information when saving their documents for the purpose of managing documents across an organization. An example of this would be a Word document template that is used to create release notes for a software product. A document containing release notes generally has common fields such as project name, document author, release date, etc. that are required to be filled out whenever a new version of a software product is released. These fields can be added to a Word document template as document properties that have to be filled out.

A document information panel is a template that can be displayed in Microsoft Office applications to enable users to easily fill out document properties. While a document information panel is not required for users to be able to fill out document properties, because there are several other ways to fill out document properties, a document information panel that has been customized in InfoPath Designer 2013 can provide additional InfoPath functionality such as data validation, data retrieval, and business logic to users when filling out document property fields.

In the recipes in this chapter, you will go through the process of creating a document information panel for a release notes document from beginning to end, so that you get a feel for where the document information panel fits in the broader picture of what you can do with InfoPath in SharePoint.

97 Use a Word document as a template for documents in a library

Problem

You have a standard Word document template that your company uses to streamline the creation of release notes for the deployment of software products. You want to use this document template as the base template from which all documents are created and stored in a document library.

Solution

You can set a Word document to be the document template of the default content type that is associated with the document library, so that the Word document can be used as a starter template for documents that are created in the document library.

To use a Word document as the template for documents in a document library:

1. In SharePoint, create a new **Document Library** named **ReleaseNotes**. By default, when you create a document library, the default content type it is associated with is linked to a blank Word document.
2. Navigate to the **ReleaseNotes** document library, and click **Library ➤ Settings ➤ Library Settings**, or on the **Site Contents** page, click the ellipsis button behind the name of the **ReleaseNotes** document library, and then click **Settings** on the context menu that appears to navigate to the **Settings** page of the document library.
3. On the **Settings** page under **Columns**, click **Create column** and repeat this step to add the following columns to the **ReleaseNotes** document library:

Column Name	Data Type
ProjectName	Single line of text
DocumentAuthor	Person or Group
ReleaseDate	Date and Time

4. On the **Settings** page under **General Settings**, click **Advanced settings**.
5. On the **Advanced Settings** page under **Document Template**, click **Edit Template**.

6. In Word 2013, modify the document to suit your needs. In the figure shown below, text and formatting was copied from another Word document and pasted into the document template that will be used by SharePoint.

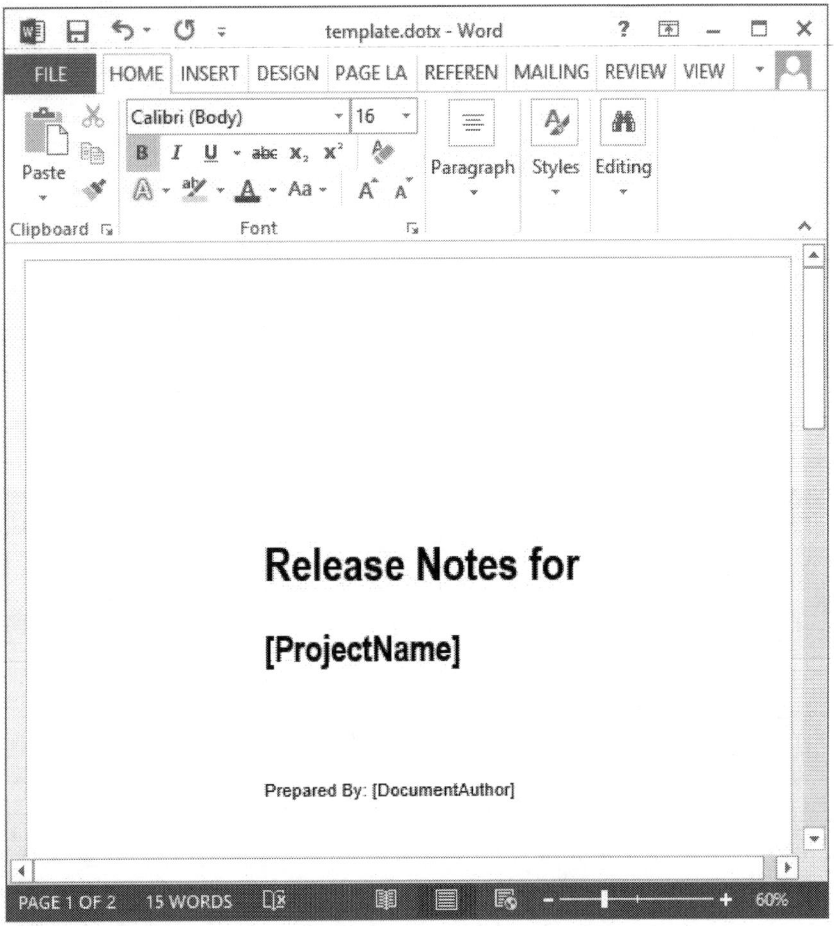

Figure 305. Sample release notes document in Word 2013.

7. When you are done editing the document template, click **File ➤ Save As ➤ SharePoint**, and then click **Browse**.

8. On the **Save As** dialog box, select **Word document (*.docx)** from the **Save as type** drop-down list box, leave everything else as is, and click **Save**. Close Word once the document has been saved back to SharePoint.

9. In SharePoint, on the **Advanced Settings** page under **Document Template**, change the file extension of the document in the **Template URL** text box from **dotx** to **docx**, and then click **OK**.

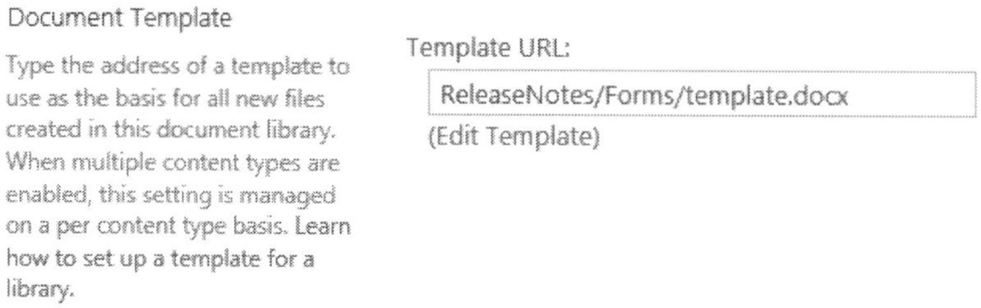
Document Template
Type the address of a template to use as the basis for all new files created in this document library. When multiple content types are enabled, this setting is managed on a per content type basis. Learn how to set up a template for a library.
Template URL:
ReleaseNotes/Forms/template.docx
(Edit Template)

Figure 306. The new template URL on the Advanced Settings page in SharePoint.

In SharePoint, navigate to the **ReleaseNotes** document library, and click **Files ➤ New ➤ New Document**. The release notes document should open in Word.

Discussion

In the solution described above you learned how to set a Word document to be the document template of the default **Document** content type of a document library.

You have the following 3 options for setting a document template:

1. Set the Word document to be the document template of the document library as described in the solution above.
2. Enable management of content types as described in steps 3 through 5 of recipe *27 Create different types of forms in one form library*, and then set the Word document to be the document template of the default **Document** list content type associated with the document library via the **Advanced Settings** page of the list content type.
3. Create a new site content type that is based on the **Document** parent content type similar to the steps described in recipe *26 Create a content type for an InfoPath form from within SharePoint*, add new site columns (**ProjectName**, **DocumentAuthor**, and **ReleaseDate**) to the site content type as described in *Create a new site column* and *Add a site column to a site content type* in the Appendix, set the Word

document to be the document template of the site content type via the **Advanced Settings** page of the site content type, and then add the content type to the document library similar to what you did in recipe *27 Create different types of forms in one form library*. Note that in this case you would not have to create the columns on the document library, since they should automatically be copied onto the document library when you add the content type to the document library.

While the first option is quick and easy to implement, document management in SharePoint would typically involve implementing the third option.

98 Link Word document fields to document panel fields

Problem

You have a standard Word document template that your company uses to streamline the creation of release notes for the deployment of software products. The release notes document has common fields such as project name, document author, release date, etc. that are required to be filled out whenever a new version of a software product is released. You want to make the process of filling out these document properties easier by linking them to the fields on the document information panel, so that whenever the document information panel fields are filled out, the data automatically appears in fields throughout the Word document.

Solution

After you have added columns to a document library that is used to create Word documents and set a DOCX file to be used as the document template for that document library, you can use **Quick Parts** in Word to link document properties to columns of the document library (document information panel fields).

To link Word document fields to document information panel fields:

1. If you have already gone through recipe 97, in SharePoint, navigate to the **Advanced Settings** page of the **ReleaseNotes** document library, and then under **Document Template**, click **Edit Template** to open the document template in Word. Otherwise, follow steps 1 through 6 of recipe *97 Use a Word document as a template for documents in a library* to create a document library named **ReleaseNotes**, and add a Word document as a template to it.
2. In Word 2013, on a location where you want to add a document property field, select the piece of text you want to replace with a document property field (for example **[ProjectName]**), click **Insert ➤ Text ➤ Quick Parts**, select **Document Property**, and then select the name of the field you want to add as a document property from the drop-down menu that appears.

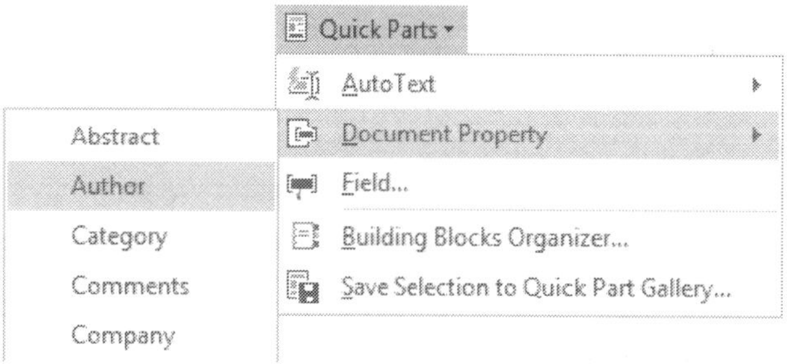

Figure 307. Inserting a document property Quick Part in Word 2013.

Note that the **Quick Parts** command places a content control on the document that should automatically make use of the formatting of the text you replaced. So ensure that you format the text before you replace it with a content control for any textual formatting to be used by the content control. Repeat this step for each document property you want to add.

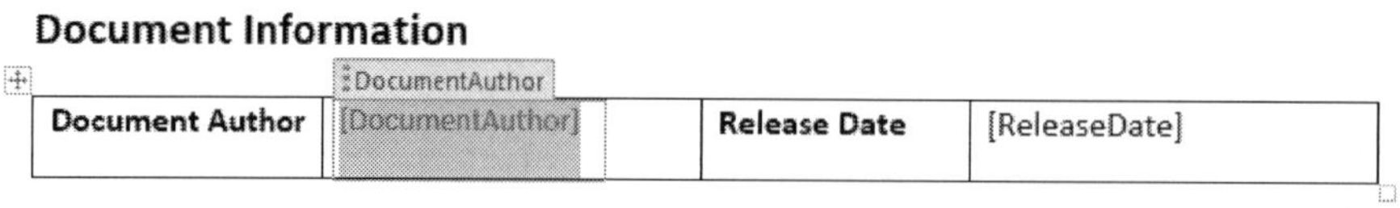

Figure 308. Text replaced by a content control on the document template.

3. When you are done editing the document template, click **File ➤ Save As ➤ SharePoint**, and then click **Browse**.
4. If you did not go through recipe 97 before going through this recipe, follow steps 8 and 9 of recipe *97 Use a Word document as a template for documents in a library*. Otherwise, on the **Save As** dialog box, leave everything as is, and click **Save**. Click **Yes** on the message box that appears to ask you whether you want to replace the existing file named **template.docx**, and then close Word once the document has been saved back to SharePoint.
5. In SharePoint, on the **Advanced Settings** page, click **OK**.

In SharePoint, navigate to the **ReleaseNotes** document library and click **Files ➤ New ➤ New Document** to add a new document. When the document opens in Word, open the document information panel (**File ➤ Info ➤ Properties ➤ Show Document Panel**) if it does not automatically appear.

Figure 309. Opening the document information panel in Word 2013.

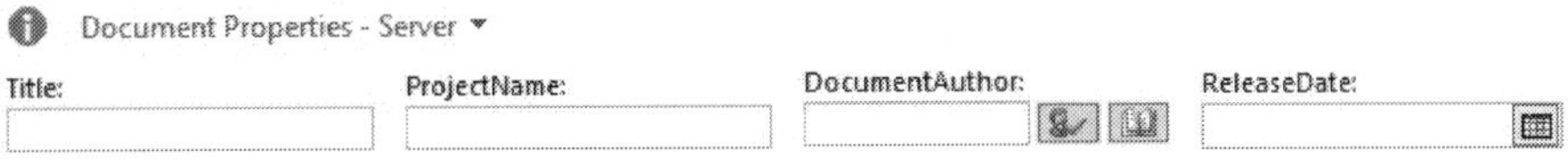

Figure 310. The document information panel in Word 2013.

Fill out the fields on the document information panel, and verify that the values you entered into the fields on the document information panel also appear in the corresponding fields (content controls) on the document. Save the document back to the document library and close Word. Back in SharePoint, refresh the document library, and then verify that the values you entered in the fields in the Word document also appear in the columns of the document library.

Discussion

In the solution described above, you linked columns of a document library, which became fields on the default document information panel generated by SharePoint, to content controls on a Word document template used to create documents in the document library.

The usefulness of document information panels becomes clear when you notice how easy it is to fill out all of the document properties by just filling out one form at the top of a Word document and then automatically populate the fields (content controls) on the Word document with the information you entered.

However, you do not have to use a document information panel if you do not want to. For example, if you wanted to fill out document properties in Word on the standard way, you could go to the **Info** tab (**File ➤ Info**) and then on the right-hand side of the screen, fill out the properties listed there. You could also enter values directly in the fields (content controls) that are located throughout the document. And because the document property fields are also accessible through columns of the document library, you could also fill them out by selecting **Edit Properties** on the menu of a document.

Tip:

> If you have added a new column to a document library or to the content type linked to a Word document template and the new column is not showing up on the **Quick Parts** command drop-down menu in Word as a document property, click **File ➤ Save As ➤ SharePoint ➤ Browse** and overwrite the existing Word document template in SharePoint. Close Word and then in SharePoint, click the **Edit Template** link on the **Advanced Settings** page of the document library or of the content type to reopen the Word document template and check whether the new column shows up in Word.

99 Create a document information panel from within SharePoint

Problem

You have a standard Word document template that your organization uses to streamline the creation of release notes for the deployment of software products. This release notes document contains document properties, which you want users to be able to easily fill out through the document information panel in Word.

Solution

You can use the **Create a new custom template** link on the **Document Information Panel Settings** page in SharePoint to start the process of creating a document information panel from within SharePoint.

To create a new document information panel form template from within SharePoint:

1. Follow the instructions in recipe *98 Link Word document fields to document panel fields* to create a **ReleaseNotes** document library that uses a Word document as its template, which is linked to fields in the document library.
2. In SharePoint, navigate to the **ReleaseNotes** document library and enable management of content types as described in steps 3 through 5 of recipe *27 Create different types of forms in one form library*.
3. On the **Settings** page under **Content Types**, click **Document**.
4. On the **List Content Type** page under **Settings**, click **Document Information Panel settings**.
5. On the **Document Information Panel Settings** page under the **Document Information Panel Template** section, click **Create a new custom template**. This should open the **Data Source Wizard** in InfoPath Designer 2013.

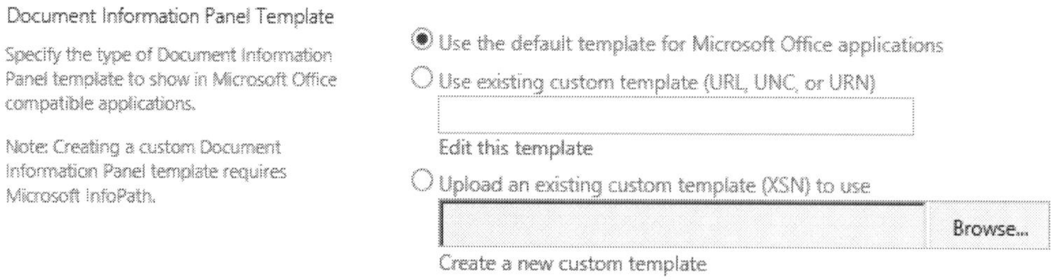

Figure 311. The document information panel template settings in SharePoint 2013.

6. In InfoPath, on the **Data Source Wizard**, click **Finish**. The InfoPath form template for the document information panel should appear.
7. Customize the form template as you would do with any other type of form template in InfoPath.
8. Click the **Quick Publish** command on the **Quick Access Toolbar**, click **File ➤ Info ➤ Quick Publish**, or click **File ➤ Publish ➤ Document Information Panel** to publish the form template back to SharePoint. Note: InfoPath may prompt you to save the form template.
9. Close InfoPath Designer 2013.
10. In SharePoint, click the link that says **Go back to the Document Information Panel settings page**. The **Use existing custom template (URL, UNC, or URN)** option should now be selected and you should see the URL of the form template you customized and published listed in the text box as an indication that the document information panel template has been customized. SharePoint automatically assigns a name to the customized form template and stores it in a folder that has the same name as the content type (**Document** in this case) which is located under the **Forms** folder of the document library.

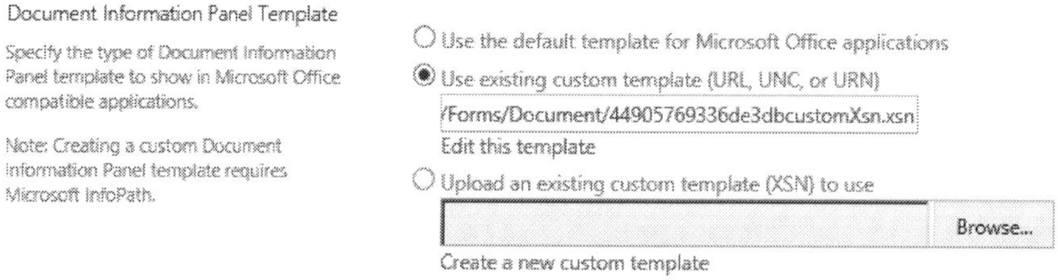

Figure 312. Settings for a customized document information panel in SharePoint 2013.

11. On the **Document Information Panel Settings** page, click **OK**.

In SharePoint, navigate to the **ReleaseNotes** document library and click **Files ➤ New ➤ New Document** to add a new document. The Word document should open and the customized document information panel should appear. If it does not appear, click **File ➤ Info**, and then select **Properties ➤ Show Document Panel**.

Discussion

Once you have created a custom template as you have done in the solution described above, you can go back to the **Document Information Panel Settings** page and click the **Edit this template** link to edit the existing form template in InfoPath Designer 2013.

Note that you could also open the document library in SharePoint Designer 2013 via **Navigation ➤ All Files ➤ ReleaseNotes ➤ Forms**, navigate to the **Document** folder (or a folder that has the same name as the content type for which you customized the document information panel in SharePoint) under the **Forms** folder, and then click on the XSN file located in the content type's folder to open and modify the form template in InfoPath Designer 2013.

Figure 313. The document information panel template in SharePoint Designer 2013.

To revert back to the default (uncustomized) document information panel used by SharePoint, you can select the **Use the default template for Microsoft Office applications** option on the **Document Information Panel Settings** page. Note that this action does not delete the existing template and that if you wanted to, you could switch back to using the custom form template at a later stage by selecting the **Use existing custom template (URL, UNC, or URN)** on the **Document Information Panel Settings** page.

Tip:

> If changes you made to a document information panel are not showing up when you open a new document in Word: In SharePoint, open the Word document template by clicking on the **Edit Template** link on the **Advanced Settings** page of the document library or the content type linked to the Word document template, and then in Word, click **File ➤ Save As ➤ SharePoint ➤ Browse** and overwrite the existing Word document template in SharePoint. Close Word and then in SharePoint, add a new document and check whether the latest changes you applied to the document information panel are showing up in Word.

100 Create a document information panel from within InfoPath

Problem

You have a standard Word document template that your organization uses to streamline the creation of release notes for the deployment of software products. This release notes document contains document properties, which you want users to be able to easily fill out through the document information panel in Word.

Solution

You can use the **Document Information Panel** advanced form template in InfoPath Designer 2013 to create a new document information panel form template from within InfoPath.

To create a document information panel from within InfoPath:

1. Follow the instructions in recipe *98 Link Word document fields to document panel fields* to create a **ReleaseNotes** document library that

uses a Word document as its template, which is linked to fields in the document library.

2. In InfoPath, click **File ➤ New**.
3. On the **New** tab under **Advanced Form Templates**, click **Document Information Panel**, and then click **Design Form**.
4. On the **Data Source Wizard**, enter the URL of the document library for which you want to create a document information panel for a content type associated with the document library, and click **Next**. The URL should have a format such as:

   ```
   http://servername/sitename/libraryname
   ```

   where **servername** is the name of the SharePoint server and **sitename** is the name of the site where a document library named **libraryname** is located.
5. On the **Data Source Wizard**, select a content type from the list of content types that are associated with the document library, and click **Next**. If a custom form template has already been specified for the content type you selected, InfoPath will display a message telling you that this is the case, but that you can still go ahead and create a new form template. When you publish the new form template, it will replace the existing form template. Click **OK** if this message appears. Note that this action creates a new form template and does not modify the existing form template. If you want to edit an existing form template, you must use the **Edit this template** link that was mentioned in the discussion section of the previous recipe.
6. On the **Data Source Wizard**, click **Finish**.
7. Customize the form template as you would do with any other type of form template in InfoPath.
8. Click the **Quick Publish** command on the **Quick Access Toolbar**, click **File ➤ Info ➤ Quick Publish**, or click **File ➤ Publish ➤ Document Information Panel** to publish the form template back to SharePoint. Note: InfoPath may prompt you to save the form template.

In SharePoint, navigate to the **ReleaseNotes** document library and click **Files ➤ New ➤ New Document** to add a new document. The Word document should open and the customized document information panel should appear. If it does not appear, click **File ➤ Info**, and then select **Properties ➤ Show Document Panel**.

Discussion

In recipe *99 Create a document information panel from within SharePoint* you learned how to create a document information panel from within SharePoint and then customize it in InfoPath Designer 2013. In the solution described above you learned how to create a new document information panel starting from within InfoPath Designer 2013.

In step 5 of the solution described above, you also had to select a content type for which you wanted to create a document information panel, since document information panels are created on a per content type basis, and not on a per document library basis. And because a document information panel form template is based on the schema of a content type, you could also create a document information panel form template by using the **XML or Schema** form template as follows:

1. In InfoPath, click **File ➤ New**.
2. On the **New** tab under **Advanced Form Templates**, click **XML or Schema**, and then click **Design Form**.
3. On the **Data Source Wizard**, enter the URL of the document library for which you want to create a document information panel for a content type associated with the document library, and click **Next**. The URL should have a format such as:

   ```
   http://servername/sitename/libraryname
   ```

   where **servername** is the name of the SharePoint server and **sitename** is the name of the site where a document library named **libraryname** is located.
4. On the **Data Source Wizard**, select a content type from the list of content types that are associated with the document library, and click **Next**. If a message appears saying that a custom form template has already been specified for the content type you selected, click **OK**.
5. On the **Data Source Wizard**, click **Finish**.

One thing to note about document information panel form templates is that the **Compatibility** is set to **Document Information Panel**, which is a form type that does not appear when you create any of the other types of form templates in InfoPath. In addition, you cannot change a document information panel form template to be a Web Browser Form or InfoPath Filler Form.

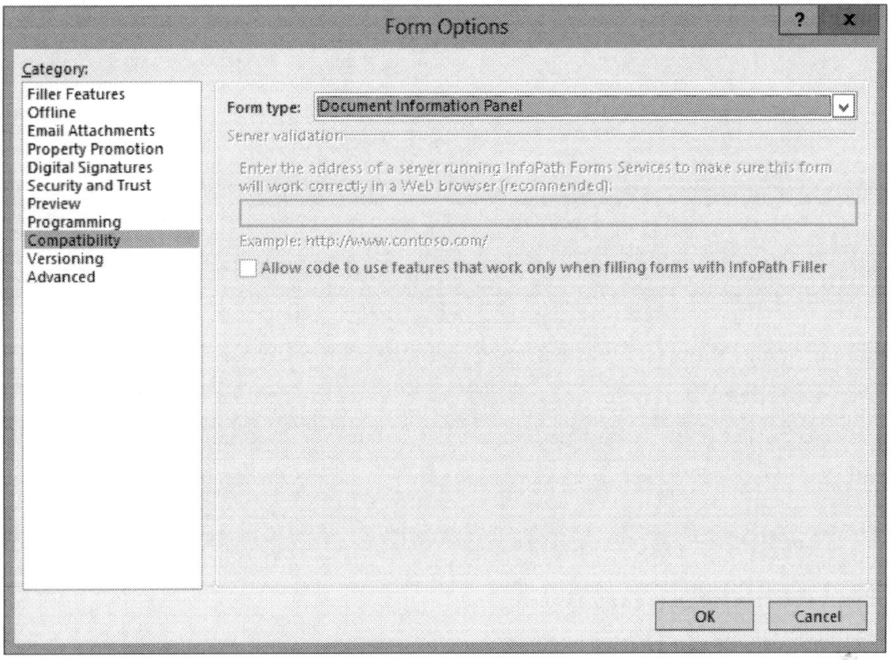

Figure 314. The compatibility setting for a document information panel form template.

If you customize a document information panel and then afterwards add a new column to the content type of the document information panel, the document information panel may not be able to load when you open a new Word document that makes use of the document information panel, and you may see the following message appear:

The Document Information Panel was unable to load. The document will continue to open. For more information, contact your system administrator.

with the following details:

Document Information Panel cannot open a new form.

The form contains schema validation errors.

Element '{98f12a62-5a6c-420d-bbc1-98d8981e03f1}NewCol' is unexpected according to content model of parent element 'documentManagement'.

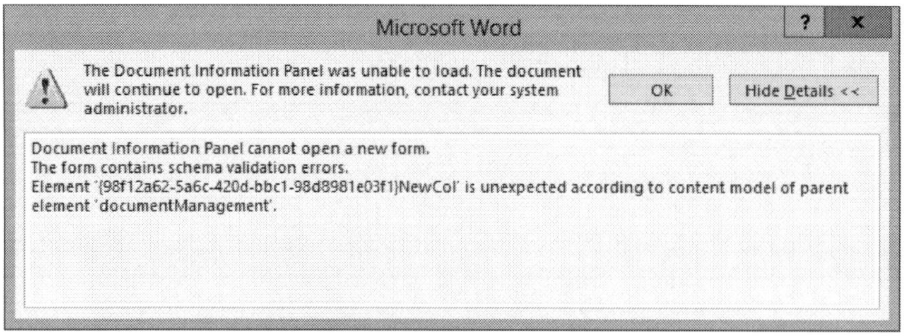

Figure 315. Message that appears when a document information panel cannot load.

In the example above, a column named **NewCol** was added to the document library after customizing the document information panel. To solve the problem, click the **Edit this template** link on the **Document Information Panel Settings** page in SharePoint, and then republish the form template from within InfoPath.

101 Auto-generate a simple Word document from an InfoPath form

Problem

You have a standard Word document template that your organization uses to streamline the creation of release notes for the deployment of software products. You want to be able to automatically create and fill out documents that are based on this Word document template whenever a new InfoPath form is saved or submitted to a form library.

Solution

You can use a SharePoint 2010 workflow that runs whenever a new form is submitted or saved to a form library to create a Word document that is based on the values of fields on the form.

Important:

> This solution assumes that you already know the basics of creating SharePoint Designer workflows as discussed in Chapter 5.

To automatically generate a Word document that is based on data from an InfoPath form:

1. Follow the instructions in recipe *98 Link Word document fields to document panel fields* to create a **ReleaseNotes** document library that uses a Word document as its template, which is linked to fields in the document library.
2. In InfoPath, create a new SharePoint form library form template or use an existing one.
3. Add a **Text Box** control to the view of the form template and name it **projectName**.
4. Add a **Person/Group Picker** control to the view of the form template and name its main group node **documentAuthor**.
5. Add a **Date and Time Picker** control to the view of the form template and name it **releaseDate**.
6. Promote all of the fields to columns as described in recipe *22 Promote form fields to columns of a form library*. Ensure that you promote the first **AccountId** field of the person/group picker control and name it **Document Author**.

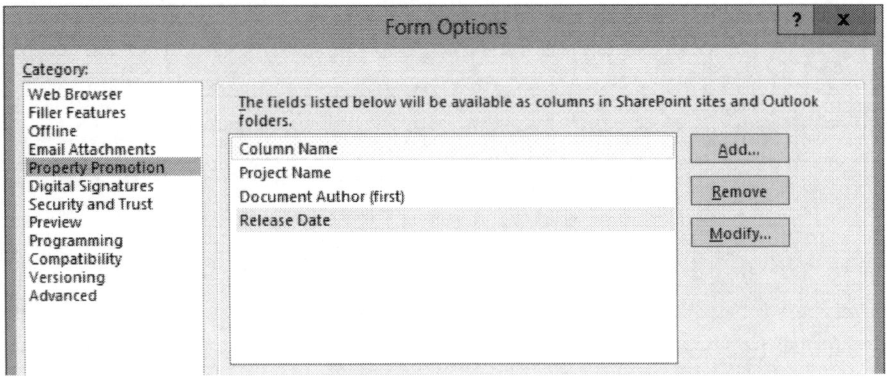

Figure 316. Promoted fields on the Form Options dialog box in InfoPath.

7. Publish the form template to a SharePoint form library named **ReleaseNotesFormLib**.
8. In SharePoint Designer 2013, create a **List Workflow** that is associated with the **ReleaseNotesFormLib** form library you published the form template to, name the workflow **CreateWordDocWF**, and select **SharePoint 2010 Workflow** as the **Platform Type** (also see recipe *80 Create a workflow that runs on forms in a specific form library*).
9. Creating a Word document using a workflow entails creating an item that is based on the Word document template that is linked to a document library. So click to place the cursor inside of **Step 1**, type **create list**, and then press **Enter** to add a **Create List Item** action.
10. Click **this list** in the sentence for the workflow action.
11. On the **Create New List Item** dialog box, select **ReleaseNotes** from the **List** drop-down list box, select **Path and Name (*)** in the list of fields, and then click **Modify**.
12. On the **Value Assignment** dialog box, click the formula button (second button) behind the **To this value** text box.
13. On the **Lookup for String** dialog box, leave **Current Item** selected in the **Data source** drop-down list box, select **Name** from the **Field from source** drop-down list box, and then click **OK**.
14. On the **Value Assignment** dialog box, click **OK**. With this you have set the name of the newly created Word document to be the same as the name of the InfoPath form.
15. On the **Create New List Item** dialog box, click **Add**.
16. On the **Value Assignment** dialog box, select **ProjectName** from the **Set this field** drop-down list box, and then click the formula button (second button) behind the **To this value** text box.
17. On the **Lookup for Single line of text** dialog box, leave **Current Item** selected in the **Data source** drop-down list box, select **Project Name** from the **Field from source** drop-down list box, and then click **OK**.
18. On the **Value Assignment** dialog box, click **OK**. With this you have set the value of the **ProjectName** field (content control) on the Word document to be equal to the value of the promoted **Project Name** field on the InfoPath form.

19. Repeat steps 15 through 18 for the **DocumentAuthor** and **ReleaseDate** fields.

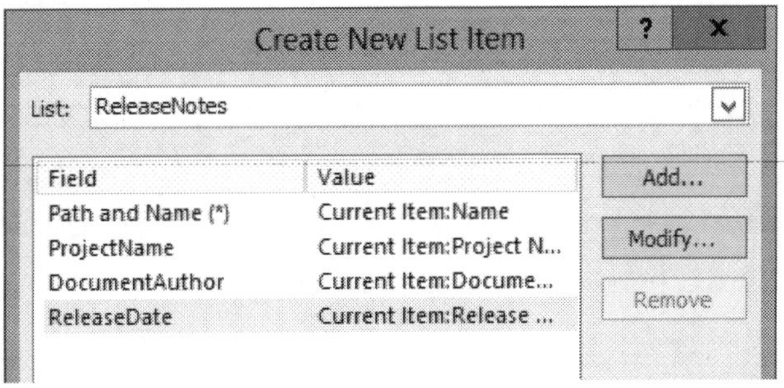

Figure 317. The final Create New List Item dialog box in SharePoint Designer 2013.

20. On the **Create New List Item** dialog box, click **OK**.
21. Click **Workflow ➤ Manage ➤ Workflow Settings**.
22. On the workflow settings page under **Start Options**, select the **Start workflow automatically when an item is created** check box. This should start the workflow whenever a new InfoPath form is saved or submitted to the form library. Leave the **Allow this workflow to be manually started** check box selected so that users can manually start the workflow on an InfoPath form in case the workflow failed to create the Word document.
23. Click **Workflow Settings ➤ Save ➤ Publish** to publish the workflow.

In SharePoint, navigate to the **ReleaseNotesFormLib** form library and add a new form. Fill out the form and save or submit it. Once you have saved the form to the form library, the workflow should automatically start to run. Once the workflow has completed, navigate to the **ReleaseNotes** document library and check whether a Word document that has the same name as the InfoPath form you saved, was created in the document library. Open the Word document and verify that the fields (content controls) have been filled out with the information you entered on the InfoPath form.

Discussion

An often requested functionality regarding InfoPath and Word is the conversion of InfoPath forms into Word documents. Because InfoPath does not offer an easy way to generate Word documents that use InfoPath form data, you would have to write code to implement such functionality.

If you have an InfoPath form that contains simple data such as text and date fields, you can use the technique described in the solution above to automatically generate Word documents that are based on InfoPath form data through a SharePoint 2010 workflow. If on the other hand you have an InfoPath form that contains complex data such as repeating tables, bulleted lists, pictures, file attachments, etc., you will most likely have to write code to be able to convert the InfoPath form into a Word document.

Note:

> If you are using SharePoint 2013 with Service Pack 1 installed, you can also create documents that are based on a particular content type using a SharePoint 2010 workflow. Without Service Pack 1 installed, a SharePoint 2010 workflow may ignore document templates defined on content types, and use the document template that is located in the **Forms** folder of the document library and that was last set on the **Advanced Settings** page of the document library, to create documents when you use the **Create List Item** action. The solution described above should work for SharePoint 2013, with or without Service Pack 1 installed.

102 Bulk convert selected InfoPath forms into Word documents

Problem

You have several InfoPath forms in a SharePoint form library. You want to be able to select one or more forms from that form library, and then automatically generate Word documents that contain data for each one of those forms and store the Word documents in a document library.

Solution

You can use a SharePoint list form with a multiple-selection list box that displays the names of forms that are stored in a SharePoint form library, select items from the multiple-selection list box, save a new item to the SharePoint list, and then have a SharePoint 2013 list workflow run on the list item to extract the selected forms and for each form extracted call a SharePoint 2010 site workflow to generate a Word document and store it in a document library.

Important:

> This solution assumes that you already know the basics of creating SharePoint Designer workflows as discussed in Chapter 5.

To bulk convert selected InfoPath forms into Word documents:

1. Follow the instructions in recipe *76 Fill a multi-select list box on a list form with SharePoint list data* to create a SharePoint list form for a SharePoint list named **GenerateReleaseNotes** that has a **Multiple-Selection List Box** control on it that has **InfoPath Forms** as its **Display Name** and that displays the names of forms from the **ReleaseNotesFormLib** form library as its items. Ensure that you set the **Value** property of the multiple-selection list box to be equal to the **ID** field and the **Display name** property to be equal to the **Title** field in the secondary data source for the **ReleaseNotesFormLib** form library.
2. Follow steps 1 through 7 of recipe *101 Auto-generate a simple Word document from an InfoPath form*.
3. First you are going to create a workflow that accepts an ID as a parameter, uses this ID to look up a form in the **ReleaseNotesFormLib** form library, and then uses its data to generate a Word document in the **ReleaseNotes** document library. Because such a workflow would not run on items in a list or library, you must create a site workflow. So in SharePoint Designer 2013, open the site on which the **ReleaseNotesFormLib** and **ReleaseNotes** libraries are located, and click **Site ➤ New ➤ Site Workflow**.

4. On the **Create Site Workflow** dialog box, type **GenerateDocWF** in the **Name** text box, select **SharePoint 2010 Workflow** from the **Platform Type** drop-down list box, and click **OK**.

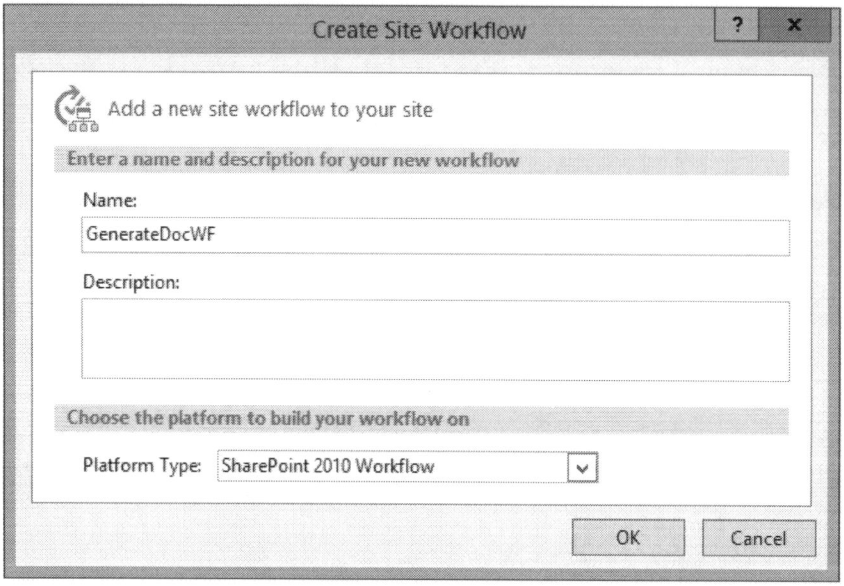

Figure 318. Creating a site workflow in SharePoint Designer 2013.

5. For the workflow to be able to accept an ID as a parameter, you must add an initiation parameter to the workflow. So click **Workflow** ➤ **Variables** ➤ **Initiation Form Parameters**.
6. On the **Association and Initiation Form Parameters** dialog box, click **Add**.
7. On the **Add Field** dialog box, type **ID** in the **Field name** text box, select **Number (1, 1.0, 100)** from the **Information type** drop-down list box, and click **Next**.
8. On the **Column Settings** dialog box, leave everything as is, and click **Finish**.
9. On the **Association and Initiation Form Parameters** dialog box, click **OK**.
10. On the text-based designer, click to place the cursor inside of **Step 1**, type **create list**, and then press **Enter** to add a **Create List Item** action.

11. Click **this list** in the sentence for the workflow action.
12. On the **Create New List Item** dialog box, select **ReleaseNotes** from the **List** drop-down list box, select **Path and Name (*)** in the list of fields, and then click **Modify**.
13. On the **Value Assignment** dialog box, click the formula button (second button) behind the **To this value** text box.
14. On the **Lookup for String** dialog box, select **ReleaseNotesFormLib** from the **Data source** drop-down list box, select **Name** from the **Field from source** drop-down list box, select **ID** from the **Field** drop-down list box, and then click the formula button behind the **Value** text box.
15. On the **Lookup for Integer** dialog box, select **Workflow Variables and Parameters** from the **Data source** drop-down list box, select **Parameter: ID** from the **Field from source** drop-down list box, and click **OK**.

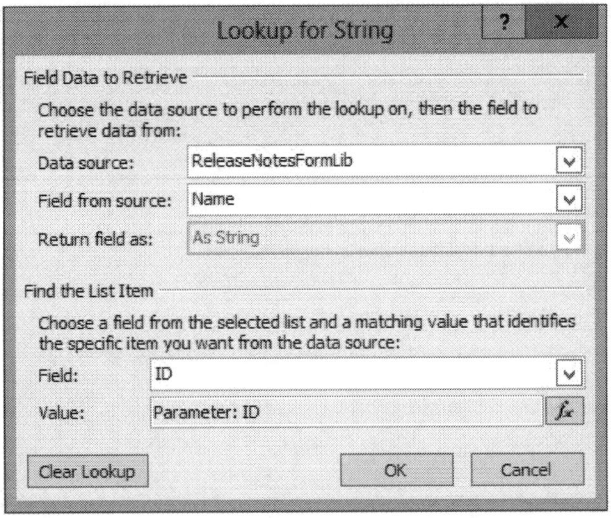

Figure 319. A lookup for a form's Name based on the ID passed to the workflow.

16. On the **Lookup for String** dialog box, click **OK**.
17. On the **Value Assignment** dialog box, click **OK**.
18. On the **Create New List Item** dialog box, click **Add**.

19. On the **Value Assignment** dialog box, select **ProjectName** from the **Set this field** drop-down list box, and then click the formula button (second button) behind the **To this value** text box.
20. On the **Lookup for Single line of text** dialog box, select **ReleaseNotesFormLib** from the **Data source** drop-down list box, select **Project Name** from the **Field from source** drop-down list box, select **ID** from the **Field** drop-down list box, and then click the formula button behind the **Value** text box.
21. On the **Lookup for Integer** dialog box, select **Workflow Variables and Parameters** from the **Data source** drop-down list box, select **Parameter: ID** from the **Field from source** drop-down list box, and click **OK**.
22. On the **Lookup for Single line of text** dialog box, click **OK**.
23. On the **Value Assignment** dialog box, click **OK**.
24. Repeat steps 18 through 23 to configure the **DocumentAuthor** and **ReleaseDate** fields for the new list item.

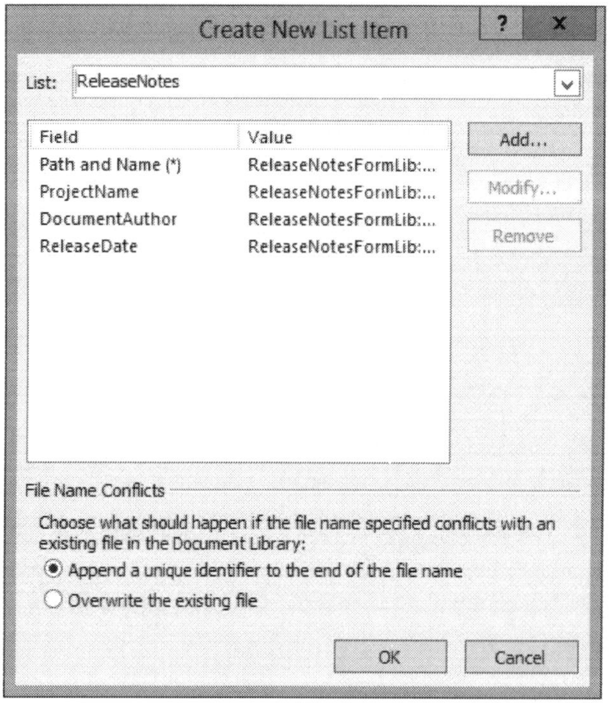

Figure 320. The final Create New List Item dialog box in SharePoint Designer 2013.

25. On the **Create New List Item** dialog box, click **OK**.

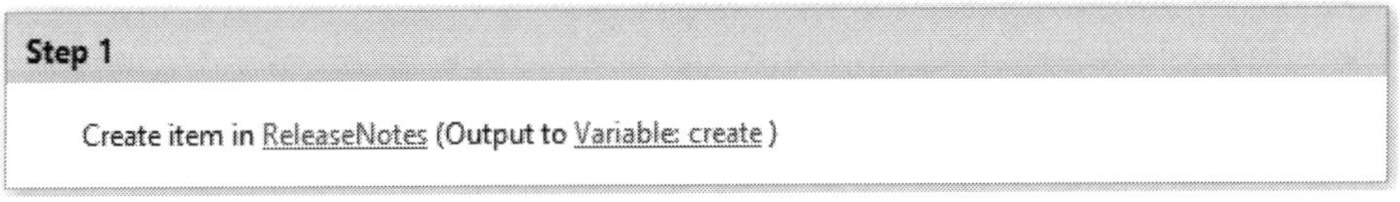
Step 1
Create item in ReleaseNotes (Output to Variable: create)

Figure 321. The completed site workflow in SharePoint Designer 2013.

26. Click **Workflow ➤ Save ➤ Publish** to publish the workflow.
27. Once you have created a site workflow that can generate a Word document based on an ID of a form in the **ReleaseNotesFormLib** form library, you must create a second workflow that can loop through the IDs of the selected forms in the multiple-selection list box on the list form of the **GenerateReleaseNotes** SharePoint list. And because you require a loop, you must create a SharePoint 2013 workflow. So in SharePoint Designer 2013, create a **List Workflow** that is associated with the **GenerateReleaseNotes** SharePoint list, name the workflow **GenerateDocsWF**, and select **SharePoint 2013 Workflow** as the **Platform Type** (also see recipe *80 Create a workflow that runs on forms in a specific form library*).
28. When items are selected from the multiple-selection list box and saved in the column of the SharePoint list, they are saved as a string that resembles the following:

    ```
    1,2,5
    ```

    where **1**, **2**, and **5** are the IDs of the selected items in the multiple-selection list box. So to retrieve the IDs, you must find commas in the string. You are going to store the IDs in a variable named **IDs** and slowly strip away IDs from the string once they have been processed. So click **Workflow ➤ Variables ➤ Local Variables**.
29. On the **Workflow Local Variables** dialog box, click **Add**.
30. On the **Edit Variable** dialog box, enter **IDs** in the **Name** text box, leave **String** selected in the **Type** drop-down list box, and click **OK**.
31. On the **Workflow Local Variables** dialog box, click **OK**.
32. On the text-based designer, click to place the cursor inside of **Stage 1**, type **var**, and then press **Enter** to add a **Set Workflow Variable** action.

33. Click **workflow variable** in the sentence for the workflow action, and select **Variable: IDs** from the drop-down list box that appears.
34. Click **value** in the sentence for the workflow action, and then click the formula button (second button) behind the text box that appears.
35. On the **Lookup for String** dialog box, leave **Current Item** selected in the **Data source** drop-down list box, select **InfoPath Forms** (the field that represents the multiple-selection list box on the SharePoint list form) from the **Field from source** drop-down list box, select **Choices, Comma Delimited** from the **Return field as** drop-down list box, and click **OK**.

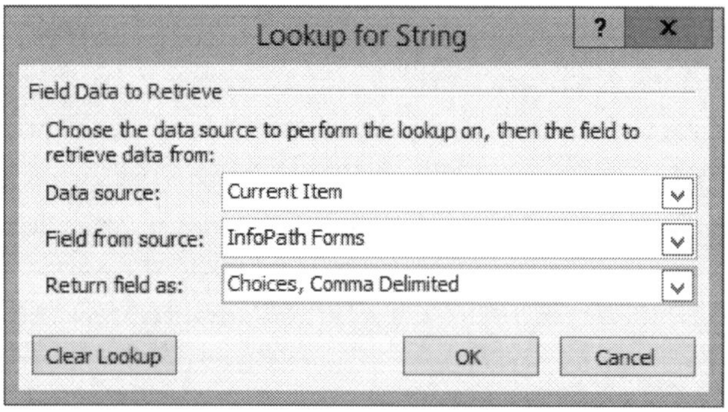

Figure 322. The Lookup for String dialog box in SharePoint Designer 2013.

The workflow action should say:

```
Set Variable: IDs to Current Item:InfoPath Forms
```

36. To make it easier to parse the string in its entirety, you must add a comma at the end, since the string will be missing one. So click to place the cursor below the last action you added, type **var**, and then press **Enter** to add a **Set Workflow Variable** action.
37. Click **workflow variable** in the sentence for the workflow action, and select **Variable: IDs** from the drop-down list box that appears.
38. Click **value** in the sentence for the workflow action, and then click the ellipsis button (first button) behind the text box that appears.
39. On the **String Builder** dialog box, click **Add or Change Lookup**.
40. On the **Lookup for String** dialog box, select **Workflow Variables and Parameters** from the **Data source** drop-down list box, select

Variable: IDs from the **Field from source** drop-down list box, leave **As String** selected in the **Return field as** drop-down list box, and click **OK**.

41. On the **String Builder** dialog box, type a comma at the end. The text should look as follows:

```
[%Variable: IDs%],
```

42. On the **String Builder** dialog box, click **OK**. The workflow action should now say:

```
then Set Variable: IDs to [%Variable: IDs%],
```

43. The workflow must loop through all of the form IDs in the **IDs** variable. You can find the first ID by looking for the first comma in the **IDs** variable. So click to place the cursor below the last action you added, type **find sub**, and then press **Enter** to add a **Find Substring in String** action.

44. Configure the workflow action to say:

```
then Find , in Variable: IDs (Output to Variable: index)
```

45. Click to place the cursor below the last action you added, and then select **Workflow** ➤ **Insert** ➤ **Loop** ➤ **Loop with Condition**.

46. Configure the sentence within the loop to say:

```
The contents of this loop will run repeatedly while Variable:
index not equals -1
```

47. Once you have the position of the first comma in the **IDs** variable, you can extract the first form ID and store it in a string variable named **ID**. So click **Workflow** ➤ **Variables** ➤ **Local Variables** and add a local variable with the name **ID** and of type **String** to the workflow.

48. Click to place the cursor below the first sentence within the loop, type **extract**, press **Enter**, and then select **Extract Substring of String from Index with Length** from the drop-down menu that appears.

49. Configure the workflow action to say:

```
Copy from Variable: IDs , starting at 0 for Variable: index
characters (Output to Variable: ID)
```

50. Once you have a form ID, you can call the **GenerateDocWF** site workflow to generate a release notes document. But because the site workflow accepts a number as a parameter, you must first convert the string for the form ID into a number. So click **Workflow ➤ Variables ➤ Local Variables** and add a local variable with the name **formID** and of type **Integer** to the workflow.
51. Click to place the cursor below the last action you added, type **var**, and then press **Enter** to add a **Set Workflow Variable** action.
52. Configure the workflow action to say:

```
Set Variable: formID to Variable: ID
```

Ensure that you select **As Integer** from the **Return field as** drop-down list box on the **Lookup for Integer** dialog box when performing the lookup for the **ID** variable.

53. Click to place the cursor below the last workflow action within the loop, type **site**, and then press **Enter** to add a **Start a Site Workflow** action.
54. Click **SharePoint 2010 site workflow** in the sentence for the workflow action.
55. On the **Choose a Workflow** dialog box, select **GenerateDocWF** from the **Choose a workflow** drop-down list box, and click **OK**.

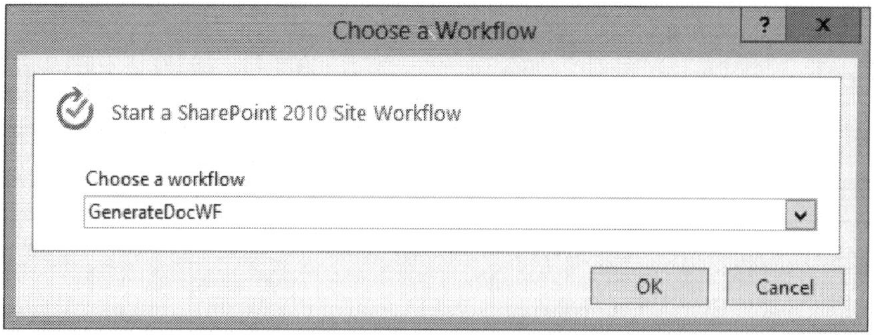

Figure 323. Selecting to start a SharePoint 2010 site workflow.

56. Click **parameters** in the sentence for the workflow action.

57. On the **Set Values for Initiation Parameters** dialog box, click **0** in the **Value** column.

58. On the **Set Value for ID** dialog box, configure the value to be equal to the **formID** workflow variable, and click **Set**.

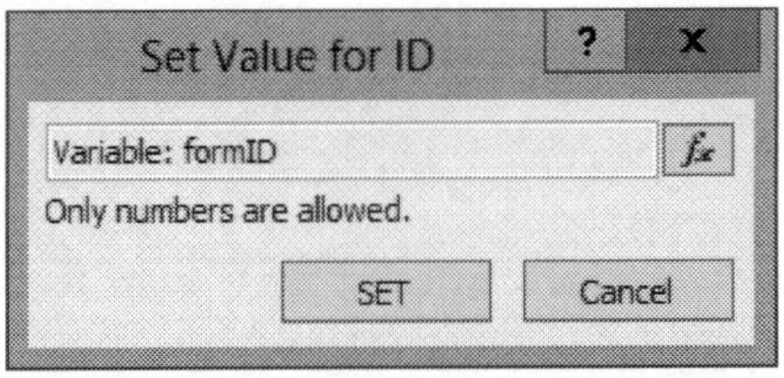

Figure 324. The Set Value for ID dialog box in SharePoint Designer 2013.

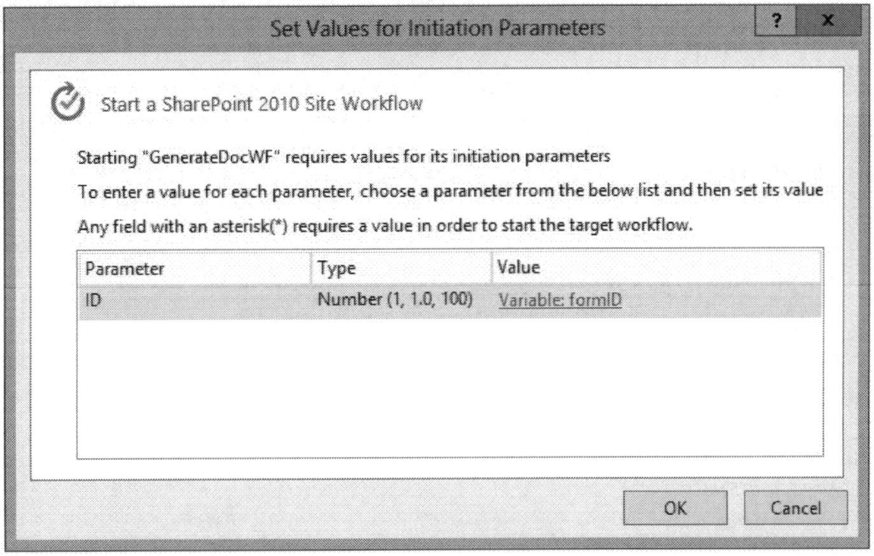

Figure 325. Setting the value of the parameter passed to the site workflow.

59. On the **Set Values for Initiation Parameters** dialog box, click **OK**. The workflow action should now say:

```
then Start GenerateDocWF with 1 out of 1 parameter (Output to
Data source)
```

60. Next, you must find the next comma in the **IDs** variable to retrieve the next form ID. To find the next comma in the **IDs** variable, you must first reposition the index to be one character after the previous comma. So click to place the cursor below the last workflow action within the loop, type **calc**, and then press **Enter** to add a **Do Calculation** action.
61. Configure the workflow action to say:

```
then Calculate Variable: index plus 1 (Output to Variable:
calc)
```

62. To make it easier to extract the next form ID starting from the beginning of the string stored in the **IDs** variable, you must remove the substring for the previous form ID from the string. So click to place the cursor below the last workflow action within the loop, type **extract**, press **Enter**, and then select **Extract Substring from Index of String** from the drop-down menu that appears.
63. Configure the workflow action to say:

```
then Copy from Variable: IDs , starting at Variable: calc
(Output to Variable: IDs)
```

64. Now you can look for the next comma in what is left of the string in the **IDs** variable. So click to place the cursor below the last workflow action within the loop, type **find sub**, and then press **Enter** to add a **Find Substring in String** action.
65. Configure the workflow action to say:

```
then Find , in Variable: IDs (Output to Variable: index)
```

66. Click to place the cursor in the **Transition to stage** section, and then select **Workflow ➤ Insert ➤ Action ➤ Go to a stage**.
67. Click **a stage** in the sentence for the workflow action, and then select **End of Workflow** from the drop-down list box that appears. The completed workflow should now resemble Figure 326.
68. Click **Workflow ➤ Manage ➤ Workflow Settings**.
69. On the workflow settings page under **Start Options**, select the **Start workflow automatically when an item is created** check box.

70. Click **Workflow Settings** ➤ **Save** ➤ **Publish** to publish the workflow.

In SharePoint, ensure that you have added and filled out a couple of forms in the **ReleaseNotesFormLib** form library, and then navigate to the **GenerateReleaseNotes** list and add a new item to it. Fill out the form, select one or more names of InfoPath forms from the multiple-selection list box on the form, and then save the item back to the SharePoint list. The SharePoint 2013 workflow should automatically start. Wait until it has completed, and then navigate to the **ReleaseNotes** document library and verify that release notes documents were created for the InfoPath forms you selected for the **GenerateReleaseNotes** list item.

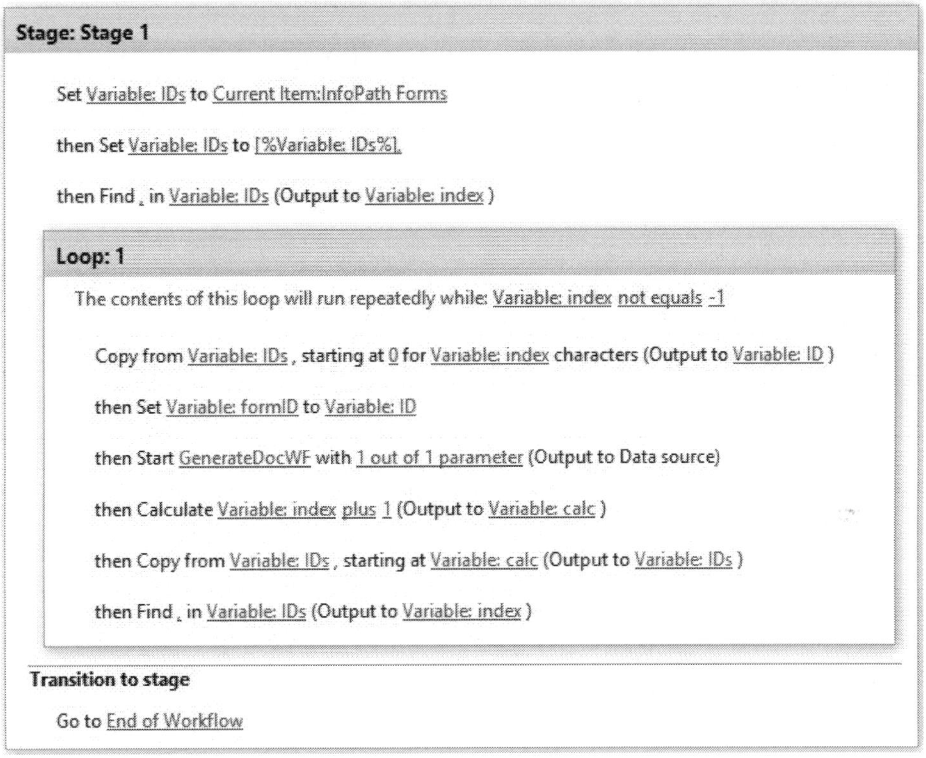

Figure 326. The completed workflow in SharePoint Designer 2013.

Discussion

In the solution described above you used a SharePoint 2013 workflow to loop through selected items from a multiple-selection list box on a SharePoint list form, and pass data to a SharePoint 2010 site workflow to be able to create Word documents for each item that was selected from the multiple-selection list box.

If no items are selected from the multiple-selection list box, no IDs will be passed to the workflow, so the workflow will be canceled due to an exception taking place. You can avoid such an exception by extending the solution by selecting **Control Tools ➤ Properties ➤ Modify ➤ Cannot Be Blank** for the multiple-selection list box on the SharePoint list form to force users to select at least one item from the multiple-selection list box.

Note that the technique described in the solution above is not limited to starting a SharePoint workflow, but you could also use it for example to create SharePoint list items based on data from InfoPath forms stored in a form library, to delete InfoPath forms from a form library, or to send emails containing data from InfoPath forms stored in a form library.

Chapter 7: Use Excel (Services) with InfoPath via SharePoint

SharePoint 2013 offers several ways to integrate InfoPath 2013 with Excel 2013, a couple of which include:

- Exporting Excel data to a SharePoint list and then creating a data connection to that SharePoint list in InfoPath.
- Connecting InfoPath to an Excel workbook through the SOAP web services offered by Excel Services.
- Connecting an InfoPath Form Web Part to an Excel Web Access web part to send data from an InfoPath form to an Excel workbook.

The recipes in this chapter are meant to provide ideas for solutions that combine InfoPath forms with Excel workbooks through SharePoint.

103 Export data from Excel to SharePoint for display in InfoPath

Problem

You have data in a table on an Excel 2013 spreadsheet, which you want to display in a repeating table on an InfoPath form.

Solution

You can export the Excel spreadsheet to a SharePoint list and then add a data connection to that SharePoint list in InfoPath.

Suppose you have an Excel workbook named **Fruits.xlsx** that has the following contents:

FruitName	FruitColor
Apple	Red
Banana	Yellow

FruitName	FruitColor
Kiwi	Brown
Plum	Purple
Orange	Orange

To display data from an Excel spreadsheet in an InfoPath browser form:

1. In Excel 2013, open the **Fruits.xlsx** workbook.
2. Select all of the data in the table including headers by clicking in the top-left cell, holding the mouse button pressed down, dragging the cursor to the bottom-right cell, and then releasing the mouse button.
3. Click **Home** ➤ **Styles** ➤ **Format as Table** and select a table format from the drop-down menu of table formats.
4. On the **Format As Table** dialog box, the **Where is the data for your table?** text box should already contain a correct reference to the cells on the spreadsheet. Select the **My table has headers** check box and click **OK**.
5. Click on any cell in the table, and then select **Table Tools** ➤ **Design** ➤ **External Table Data** ➤ **Export** ➤ **Export Table to SharePoint List**.

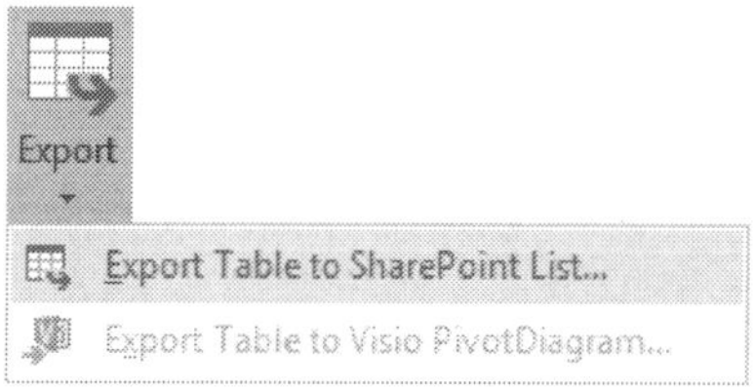

Figure 327. Export Table to SharePoint List command in Excel 2013.

6. On the **Export Table to SharePoint List** dialog box, enter the URL of the SharePoint site (where you want to publish the table) in the **Address** combo box, enter a **Name** and **Description** for the SharePoint list, and click **Next**.

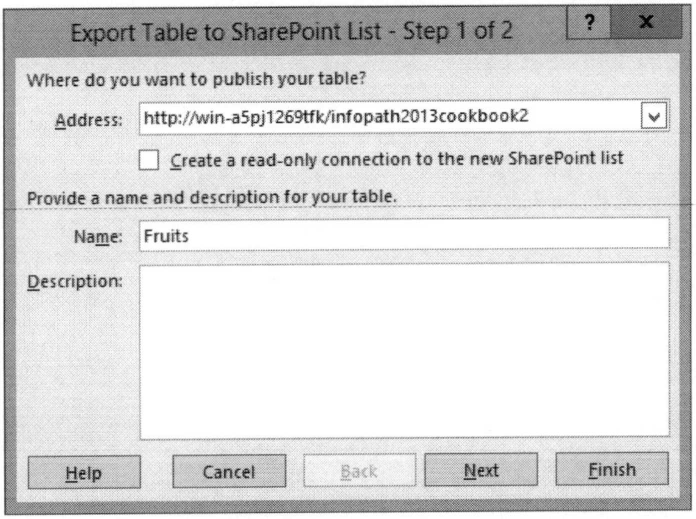

Figure 328. Selecting the SharePoint site to which to export the Excel data.

7. On the **Export Table to SharePoint List** dialog box, read the information that is displayed, and then click **Finish**. A confirmation message box should appear once the data has been exported to SharePoint.

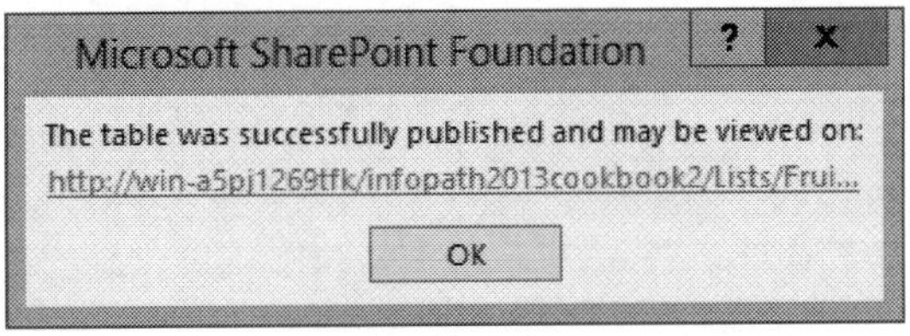

Figure 329. Confirmation message box that table was successfully published.

You can verify whether the data was successfully exported to SharePoint by clicking on the link that Excel provides on the confirmation message box or by going to the SharePoint site and searching for the SharePoint list on the **Site Contents** page in SharePoint.

8. In InfoPath, create a new SharePoint form library form template or use an existing one.

9. Add a **Receive** data connection to the SharePoint list you just created for the data in Excel to the form template as described in *Use a SharePoint list data connection* in recipe *43 2 Ways to retrieve data from a SharePoint list*.
10. Bind the secondary data source for the SharePoint list to a repeating table as described in recipe *44 Display SharePoint list data in a repeating table*.
11. Publish the form template to a SharePoint form library.

In SharePoint, navigate to the form library where you published the form template and add a new form. When the form opens, the data from the Excel spreadsheet should appear in the repeating table.

Discussion

In the solution described above, you exported data from a table on an Excel spreadsheet to SharePoint. Excel does not maintain a live connection with SharePoint when you export data to a SharePoint list. However, you could make changes in SharePoint and then recreate the Excel file from the SharePoint list via the **List ➤ Connect & Export ➤ Export to Excel** command of the SharePoint list to export the data in the SharePoint list to an IQY file, which you could then open in Excel 2013.

Another feature worth mentioning is that once you have exported Excel data to a SharePoint 2013 list, you can create a SharePoint list form with which you can add and edit items in the SharePoint list (also see recipe *1 Customize a SharePoint list form from within SharePoint* or recipe *2 Customize a SharePoint list form from within InfoPath*).

104 Export data from forms in a form library to Excel

Problem

You want to be able to export the data that is contained in InfoPath forms that are stored in a SharePoint form library to an Excel spreadsheet.

Solution

You can use the **Export to Excel** command of a SharePoint form library to export the contents of a form library to Excel.

To export data from forms in a form library to Excel:

1. In InfoPath, create a new SharePoint form library form template or use an existing one.
2. Add a **Text Box** control, a **Date Picker** control, and a **Repeating Table** control that has 3 columns to the view of the form template. Name the text box **myText**, name the date picker **myDate**, and name the 3 fields in the repeating table **field1**, **field2**, and **rows**, respectively.
3. Add an **Action** rule to **field1** in the repeating table with an action that says:

   ```
   Set a field's value: rows = concat(., "|", field2)
   ```

   This rule concatenates the values of **field1** and **field2** in a row of the repeating table thereby separating them with a pipe symbol (**|**) and stores the result in the **rows** field that is located in the same row as **field1** and **field2**.
4. Add an **Action** rule to **field2** in the repeating table with an action that says:

   ```
   Set a field's value: rows = concat(field1, "|", .)
   ```

   This rule concatenates the values of **field1** and **field2** in a row of the repeating table thereby separating them with a pipe symbol (**|**) and stores the result in the **rows** field that is located in the same row as **field1** and **field2**.
5. Click **File ➤ Info ➤ Form Options**.
6. On the **Form Options** dialog box, select **Property Promotion** in the **Category** list.
7. On the **Form Options** dialog box, click **Add** on the right-hand side of the list box at the top of the dialog box.
8. On the **Select a Field or Group** dialog box, select **myText** in the **Field to display as column** tree view, leave **My Text** in the **Column name** text box, and then click **OK**.

9. Repeat steps 7 and 8 for the **myDate** field, and leave **My Date** in the **Column name** text box.
10. On the **Form Options** dialog box, click **Add** on the right-hand side of the list box at the top of the dialog box.
11. On the **Select a Field or Group** dialog box, expand the **group1** group node, expand the **group2** repeating group node, select **rows**, leave **Rows** in the **Column name** text box, select **merge** from the **Function** drop-down list box, and then click **OK**. The **merge** function should place each concatenated row containing **field1** and **field2** on a separate line in the **Rows** field in the form library.

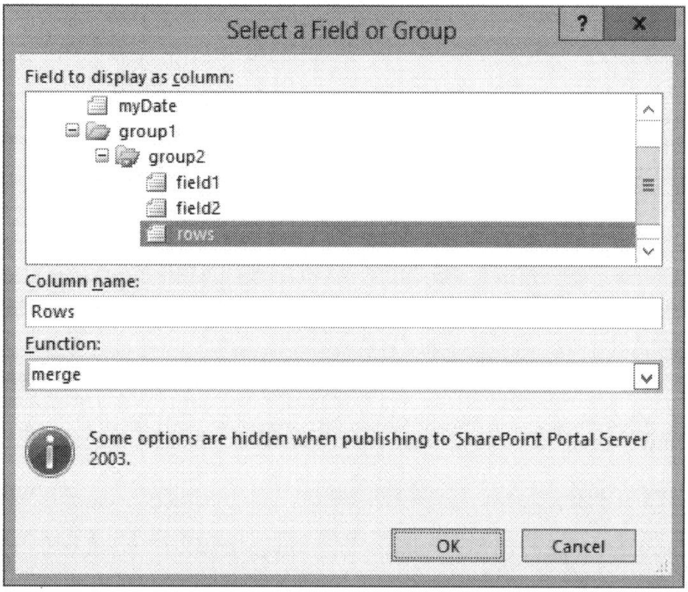

Figure 330. Promoting the 'rows' repeating field as a column with merged data.

12. On the **Form Options** dialog box, click **OK**.
13. Publish the form template to a SharePoint form library.
14. In SharePoint, navigate to the form library where you published the form template, and then click **Library ➤ Manage Views ➤ Create View**.
15. On the **View Type** page, click **Standard View**.
16. On the **Create View** page, type **Excel View** in the **View Name** text box, deselect all of the check boxes under the **Columns** section except

for the check boxes in front of the **Type (icon linked to document)**, **Name (linked to document with edit menu)**, **My Text**, **My Date**, and **Rows** columns, and then click **OK**.

In SharePoint, navigate to the form library where you published the form template and add a couple of forms with data to the form library. Select **Library ➤ Manage Views ➤ Current View ➤ Excel View** to change the view to the standard view you created earlier. Click **Library ➤ Connect & Export ➤ Export to Excel** to export the form library contents to an IQY file named **owssvr.iqy** that can be opened in Excel 2013. Open the **owssvr.iqy** file in Excel 2013 to view the form library contents and data stored in the InfoPath forms that were exported.

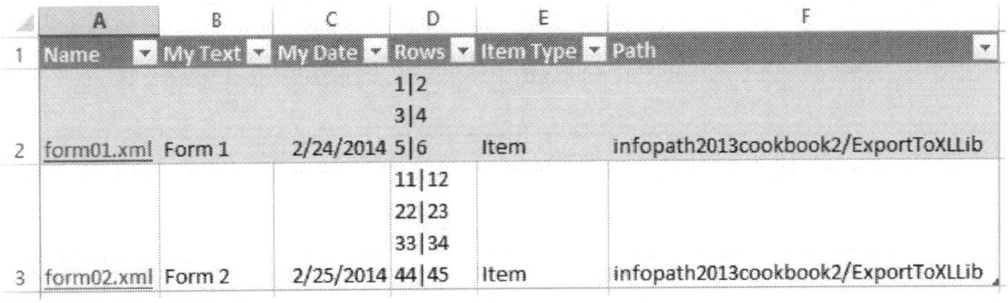

	A	B	C	D	E	F
1	Name	My Text	My Date	Rows	Item Type	Path
2	form01.xml	Form 1	2/24/2014	1|2 3|4 5|6	Item	infopath2013cookbook2/ExportToXLLib
3	form02.xml	Form 2	2/25/2014	11|12 22|23 33|34 44|45	Item	infopath2013cookbook2/ExportToXLLib

Figure 331. Excel spreadsheet displaying the data contained in two InfoPath forms.

Discussion

In the solution described above, you saw how to design and publish an InfoPath form template in such a way that data from forms that are based on that form template and stored in a form library could be exported to Excel. You thereby made use of property promotion to expose the data from the InfoPath forms in columns of the form library. You also created an extra view for the form library that you could use to export the columns you wanted to see in Excel.

Note that not all types of fields can be promoted to SharePoint form library columns (also see the discussion section of recipe *23 Promote form fields to existing site columns*), so the solution described above is limited to those types of fields that can be promoted.

105 Publish an Excel workbook for use with InfoPath in SharePoint

Configure browser view options for an Excel workbook

Problem

You have an Excel workbook, which you want to access through Excel Services in SharePoint.

Solution

You can publish an entire workbook or parts of a workbook to a trusted file location in SharePoint so that it can be used with Excel Services.

This solution assumes that you have never previously published an Excel workbook to SharePoint and that the **SharePoint** command to save an Excel workbook to SharePoint is missing from the **Save As** tab in Excel.

To publish an Excel workbook to SharePoint:

1. In Excel, create a new **Blank workbook** that has 3 sheets (**Sheet1**, **Sheet2**, and **Sheet3**), and save it locally on disk as **MyWorkbook.xlsx**. Close Excel when you are done.
2. In SharePoint, navigate to a document library where you want to store the Excel workbook (for example the **Documents** library) on the SharePoint site to which the InfoPath form will be connecting, and click **Files** ➤ **New** ➤ **Upload Document**.
3. On the **Add a document** dialog, click **Browse**.
4. On the **Choose File to Upload** dialog box, browse to the location where you saved the Excel file, select the file, and then click **Open**.
5. On the **Add a document** dialog, click **OK**.
6. Once the Excel workbook has been uploaded, click the ellipsis button behind its name in the document library, and click **Edit** on the context menu that appears to open the workbook in Excel.
7. If the document opens in **Protected View**, click **Enable Editing**.

8. Click **File ➤ Save As ➤ SharePoint** and then click **Browse**.

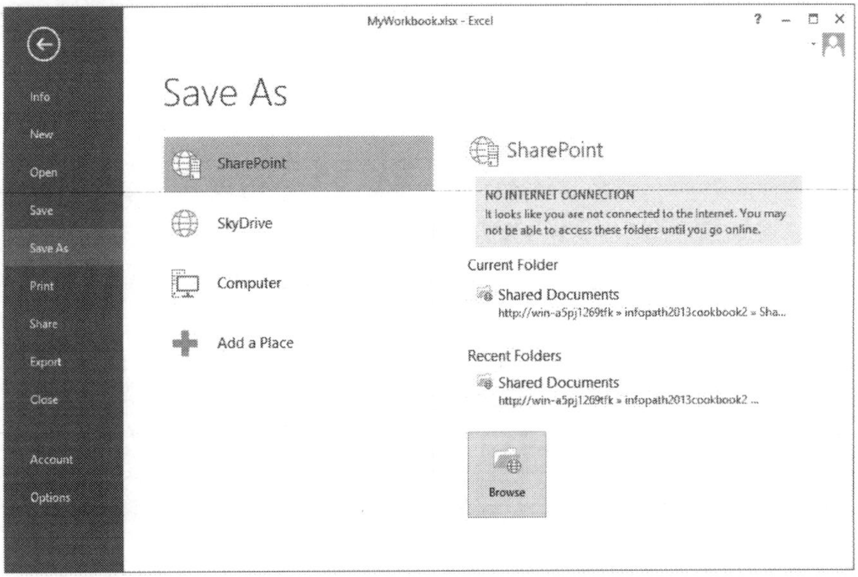

Figure 332. Saving a workbook to SharePoint in Excel 2013.

9. On the **Save As** dialog box, click **Browser View Options**.

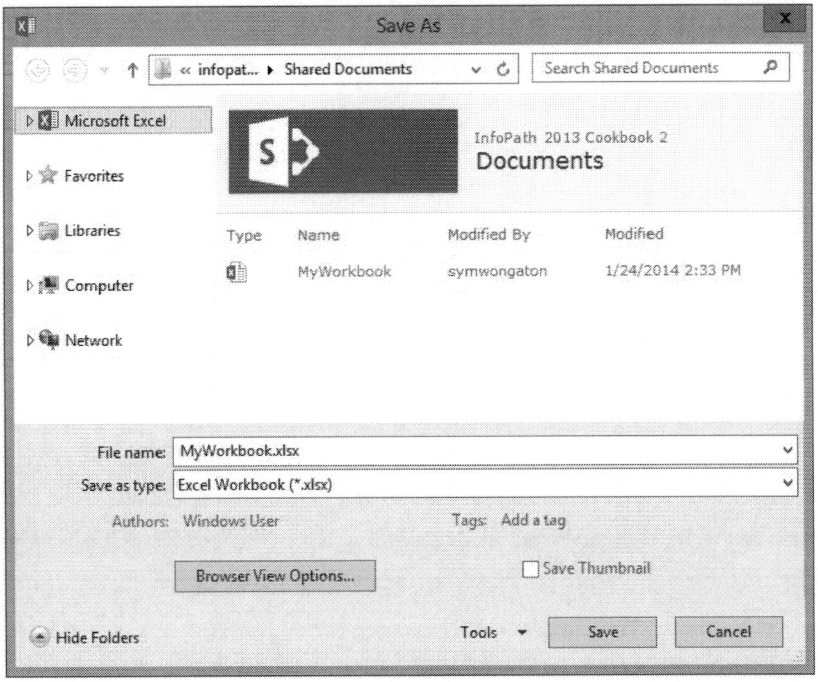

Figure 333. The Browser View Options button on the Save As dialog box in Excel.

10. On the **Browser View Options** dialog box on the **Show** tab, select **Sheets** from the drop-down list box, select the check box(es) for the sheet(s) that have data you want to make viewable in the browser via SharePoint, and then click **OK**.

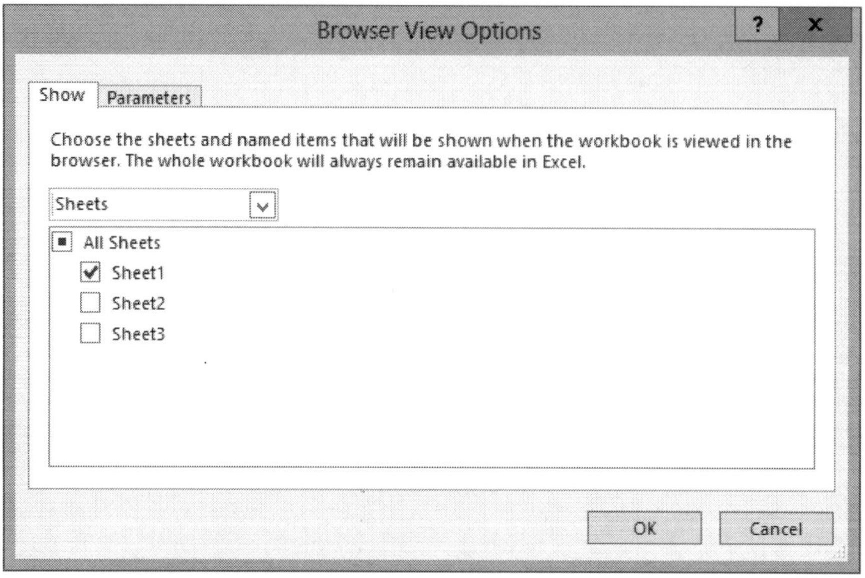

Figure 334. The Browser View Options dialog box in Excel 2013.

Alternatively, if you want to display all of the data in the entire workbook in the browser via SharePoint, select **Entire Workbook** from the drop-down list box. And if you only want to display certain items, for example a chart, select **Items in the Workbook** from the drop-down list box, and then select the check boxes for the individual items you want to display.

Note that the browser view options only apply to viewing a workbook in the browser and not to the Excel Services web services, which means that if for example you only publish **Sheet1** in a workbook to SharePoint, you will only be able to view the data on **Sheet1** if you use Excel Web Access (that is, view the Excel workbook in the browser or in an Excel Web Access web part), but you will still be able to access data from other worksheets through the Excel Services web services. So if you are going to use the Excel Services web services, it does not really matter which browser view options you select.

Refer to *Configure parameters for an Excel workbook* later in this recipe for the meaning and use of the **Parameters** tab on the **Browser View Options** dialog box.

11. On the **Save As** dialog box, click **Save**. If a message box pops up asking you to confirm replacing the file, click **Yes**.
12. Close Excel.

In SharePoint, navigate to the document library where you saved the Excel workbook and click on the name of the Excel workbook. It should open in the browser and you should only be able to view the items you configured through the browser view options.

Discussion

In the solution described above, you saw how to publish an Excel workbook to SharePoint so that it could be viewed using Excel Web Access or accessed through the Excel Services web services. If you want to provide interactivity with the Excel workbook through Excel Web Access (the browser or the web part), you must expose workbook cells through parameters as discussed in *Configure parameters for an Excel workbook* later in this recipe, so that data can be passed to and used by the Excel workbook when it is being viewed using Excel Web Access.

All SharePoint sites are configured by default as trusted file locations when SharePoint is first installed, so you need not explicitly define the document library to which you publish an Excel workbook as a trusted file location. But if a solution that makes use of Excel Services is not working for you, you may want to have your administrator check whether the document library in which you saved the Excel file is indeed a trusted file location.

Your administrator can verify the existence of trusted file locations as follows:

1. In SharePoint 2013 Central Administration under **Application Management**, click **Manage service applications**.

2. On the **Manage Service Applications** page, ensure that **Excel Services Application** has a status of **Started**, and then click **Excel Services Application**.
3. On the **Manage Excel Services Application** page, click **Trusted File Locations**.
4. On the **Trusted File Locations** page, ensure that **http://** has been added as a trusted file location, or click **Add Trusted File Location** and follow the instructions to add a trusted file location.

Configure parameters for an Excel workbook

Problem

You have an Excel workbook to which you want to pass data to certain cells in the workbook via Excel Web Access (the browser or the web part).

Solution

You can define names for cells in an Excel workbook to which you want to pass values and then add the named ranges as parameters to the workbook when setting browser view options for the workbook when you are saving it to SharePoint.

To configure an Excel workbook cell to receive input data:

1. Follow steps 1 through 7 of *Configure browser view options for an Excel workbook* in this recipe to create a new Excel workbook.
2. Select a cell on a worksheet in the workbook to which data should be passed. For example, cell **B3** on **Sheet3**. Note: To expose a cell through a parameter, you must use a single cell (not multiple cells) and the cell must not be used to perform a calculation using a formula. Named ranges that span multiple cells or that contain formulas cannot be added as parameters to an Excel workbook.
3. Click **Formulas** ➤ **Defined Names** ➤ **Define Name**.
4. On the **New Name** dialog box, enter a **Name** for the cell (for example **InputParam1**), leave **Workbook** selected in the **Scope** drop-down list box, and click **OK**.
5. Click **File** ➤ **Save As** ➤ **SharePoint** and then click **Browse**.

6. On the **Save As** dialog box, click **Browser View Options**.
7. On the **Browser View Options** dialog box, select the **Parameters** tab, and then click **Add**.

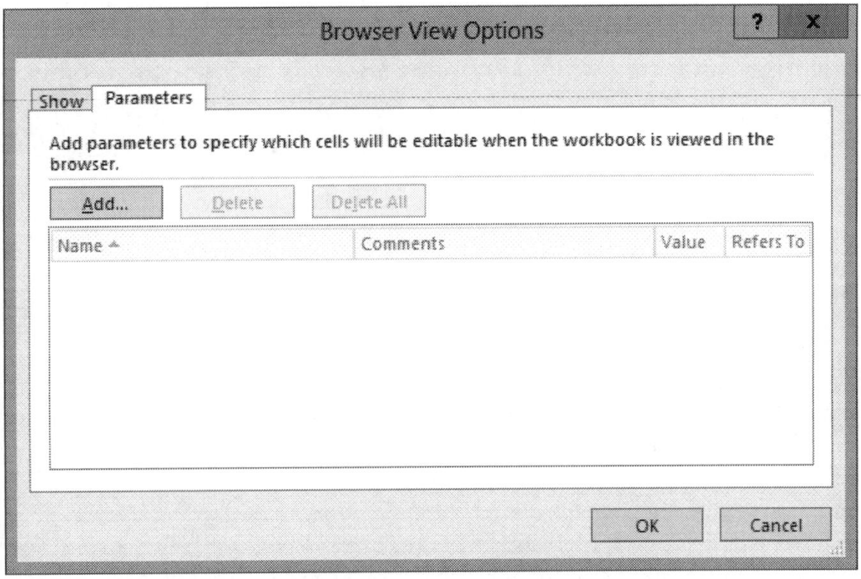

Figure 335. Adding a parameter to a workbook in Excel 2013.

8. On the **Add Parameters** dialog box, select the check box in front of the **InputParam1** named range you defined earlier, and click **OK**.

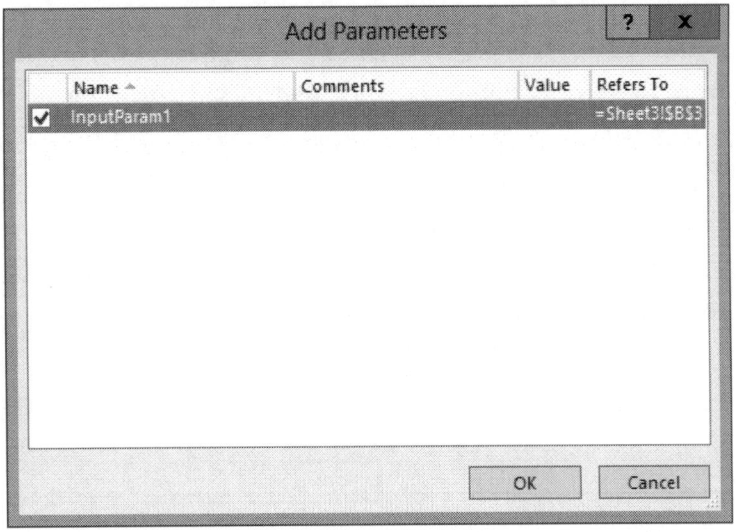

Figure 336. Selecting a named range to be used as a parameter in Excel 2013.

9. On the **Browser View Options** dialog box, click **OK**.
10. On the **Save As** dialog box, click **Save**. If a message box pops up asking you to confirm replacing the file, click **Yes**.
11. Close Excel.

In SharePoint, navigate to the document library where you saved the Excel workbook and click on the name of the Excel workbook. When the Excel workbook opens in the browser, a **Parameters** task pane with a text box for the input parameter should appear on the right-hand side of the browser window.

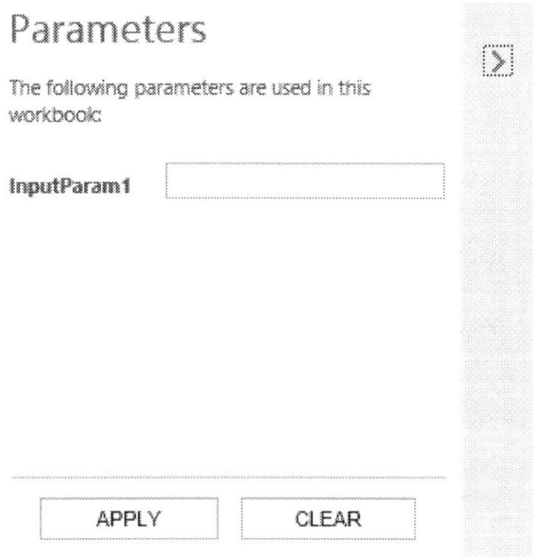

Figure 337. Parameters task pane displayed by Excel Services in SharePoint 2013.

On the **Parameters** task pane, type a piece of text in the **InputParam1** text box, and then click **Apply**. The text you entered should appear in cell **B3** on **Sheet3**. Note that while the worksheet on which the named range is located need not be viewable in the browser for you to be able to set the value of the parameter, you must make the worksheet viewable if you want users to be able to see the value they entered for the parameter, or use the value of the parameter on another worksheet that is viewable by users.

106 Send an InfoPath form value to an Excel workbook

Problem

You have an InfoPath form and an Excel workbook, and you want to enter data in a field on the InfoPath form, click a button to send the data to the Excel workbook, and then use the data passed to the Excel workbook in a formula to perform a calculation and display the result on a worksheet in the Excel workbook.

Solution

You can embed both an InfoPath form and an Excel workbook in web parts on a SharePoint page and then set up web part connections to pass data from the InfoPath form to the Excel workbook.

To set up an Excel workbook to receive parameters:

1. In Excel, create a new **Blank workbook** or use an existing one.
2. Place the cursor in cell **A1** on **Sheet1**, enter a date such as for example **2014-07-02**, and then click in another cell. The data type for the cell should automatically change to **Date**.
3. Place the cursor again in cell **A1** on **Sheet1**, and then click **Formulas ➤ Defined Names ➤ Define name**.
4. On the **New Name** dialog box, type **startDate** in the **Name** text box, leave **Workbook** selected in the **Scope** drop-down list box, ensure that

   ```
   =Sheet1!$A$1
   ```

   has been entered in the **Refers to** text box, and click **OK**. You will use this named range later as a parameter.
5. Place the cursor in cell **A2** on **Sheet1**, and enter the following formula:

   ```
   =WEEKNUM(startDate,2)
   ```

   where **startDate** refers to cell **A1**. This formula returns the week number for a specific date with the 2 indicating that the week begins on a Monday.

6. Click **File ➤ Save As ➤ SharePoint** and then click **Browse** to publish the Excel workbook with the name **WeekNumber.xlsx** to SharePoint thereby making the **startDate** named range a parameter. Note that if the **File ➤ Save As ➤ SharePoint** command is not available, you can follow steps 2 through 7 of *Configure browser view options for an Excel workbook* in recipe *105 Publish an Excel workbook for use with InfoPath in SharePoint* to publish an Excel workbook named **WeekNumber.xlsx** to SharePoint, and then after you have reopened the workbook in Excel, configure the parameter as described in *Configure parameters for an Excel workbook* in recipe *105 Publish an Excel workbook for use with InfoPath in SharePoint*.

Once you have published the Excel workbook with parameters to SharePoint, you can design an InfoPath form template that sends data to this Excel workbook.

To create an InfoPath form template that can send data to an Excel workbook:

1. In InfoPath, create a new SharePoint form library form template or use an existing one.
2. Add a **Date Picker** control and a **Button** control to the view of the form template. Name the date picker control **startDate** and label the button control **Send Data to Excel**.
3. Add an **Action** rule to the **Send Data to Excel** button with an action that says:

   ```
   Send data to Web Part
   ```

   and then on the **Rule Details** dialog box, click **Property Promotion**.
4. On the **Form Options** dialog box, click **Add** in the section for managing SharePoint Web Part connection parameters (the bottom section).
5. On the **Select a field** dialog box, select **startDate** in the **Field to use as Web Part Connection Parameter** tree view, leave **Start Date** in the **Parameter name** text box, select the **Output** option, and click **OK**.

With this you have created an output web part connection parameter for the **startDate** field.

6. On the **Form Options** dialog box, click **OK**.
7. On the **Rule Details** dialog box, click **OK**.
8. Publish the form template to a SharePoint form library that is located on the same site where the Excel workbook is stored.

Once you have created and published both the Excel workbook and the InfoPath form template to SharePoint, you can embed them in web parts on a SharePoint page and set up web part connections between them to send or receive data.

To send a value from the InfoPath form to the Excel workbook:

1. In SharePoint, navigate to a page on which you want to place the InfoPath form and Excel workbook, and click **Page ➤ Edit ➤ Edit** or click the small **Edit** command on the Ribbon.
2. Add an **InfoPath Form Web Part** (located under the **Forms** category of web parts) to the page as described in steps 3 and 4 of recipe *13 Embed a SharePoint list form on a SharePoint page*.
3. Add an **Excel Web Access** web part (located under the **Business Data** category of web parts) to the page.
4. On the **InfoPath Form Web Part**, click the **Click here to open the tool pane** link.
5. On the web part tool pane, select the SharePoint form library to which you published the InfoPath form template from the **List or Library** drop-down list box, and then click **OK**.
6. On the **Excel Web Access** web part, click the **Click here to open the tool pane** link.
7. On the web part tool pane, click the ellipsis button behind the **Workbook** text box.
8. On the **Select an Asset** dialog, navigate to the location where you published the Excel workbook, select the **WeekNumber.xlsx** Excel workbook, and click **Insert**.
9. On the web part tool pane under **Navigation and Interactivity**, deselect the **Display Parameters Task Pane** check box, and click **OK**.

10. Hover over the **InfoPath Form Web Part**, click the drop-down arrow in the top-right corner, and then select **Edit Web Part** from the drop-down menu that appears.
11. Hover over the **InfoPath Form Web Part** again, click the drop-down arrow in the top-right corner, and then select **Connections ➤ Send Data To ➤ Excel Web Access** from the drop-down menu that appears.
12. On the **Configure Connection** webpage dialog, select **Start Date** from the **Provider Field Name** drop-down list box, select **startDate** from the **Consumer Field Name** drop-down list box, and click **Finish**. With this you have configured the **InfoPath Form Web Part** to send data to the **Excel Web Access** web part.
13. On the web part tool pane, click **OK**.
14. Click **Page ➤ Edit ➤ Save** or click the small **Save** command on the Ribbon to save and stop editing the page.

In SharePoint, navigate to the page on which you placed the two web parts. Select a date from the date picker control on the InfoPath form and then click the **Send Data to Excel** button. The date you selected should appear in cell **A1** and its corresponding week number should appear in cell **A2** on **Sheet1** in the Excel workbook.

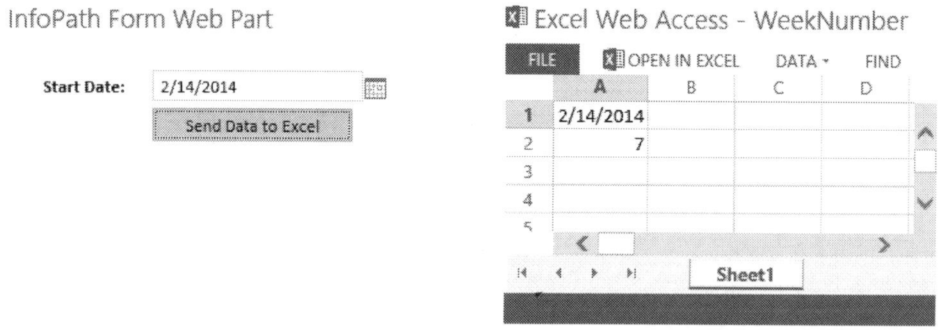

Figure 338. The InfoPath form and Excel workbook embedded on a SharePoint page.

Discussion

In the solution described above, you saw how to use the Excel Web Access web part to embed an Excel workbook on a SharePoint page and send data from an InfoPath form embedded in an InfoPath Form Web Part to that Excel workbook through a web part connection parameter.

You thereby used the **Send data to Web Part** action in InfoPath to send the value of one InfoPath form field to the Excel workbook. If your scenario calls for passing multiple parameters to an Excel workbook, you could set up multiple web part connection parameters in InfoPath, define multiple parameters in the Excel workbook, and then use SharePoint Designer 2013 as described in recipe *42 Pass data from a selected row in a repeating table to another form* to set up the web part connections between the InfoPath Form Web Part and the Excel Web Access web part in SharePoint.

The power of Excel lies in its ability to perform complex calculations. The formula used in the solution described above was kept simple for demonstration purposes, but you could make it as complex as you like.

107 Get the value of an Excel cell in InfoPath

Problem

You have an Excel workbook from which you want to retrieve the value of a particular cell so that you can display this value on an InfoPath form.

Solution

You can create an Excel workbook that contains data, publish this Excel workbook to a trusted file location for Excel Services in SharePoint, and then call Excel Services SOAP web service operations from within an InfoPath form to perform data retrieval.

To get the value of an Excel cell in InfoPath:

1. In Excel, create a new **Blank workbook** that has login names of employees in column **A** of **Sheet1** and their corresponding leave balances in column **B** of **Sheet1**.

   Sample data on **Sheet1** in the Excel workbook:

	A	B	C
1	jane.doe	25	
2	john.doe	15	
3	clovis.carvalho	33	
4			

2. Click **File ➤ Save As ➤ SharePoint** and then click **Browse** to publish the entire workbook with the name **LeaveBalances.xlsx** to a document library (for example the **Documents** library) on the SharePoint site to which the InfoPath form will be connecting. Note that if the **File ➤ Save As ➤ SharePoint** command is not available, you can follow steps 2 through 5 of *Configure browser view options for an Excel workbook* in recipe *105 Publish an Excel workbook for use with InfoPath in SharePoint*.
3. In InfoPath, create a new SharePoint form library form template or use an existing one.
4. Select **Data ➤ Get External Data ➤ From Web Service ➤ From SOAP Web Service**.

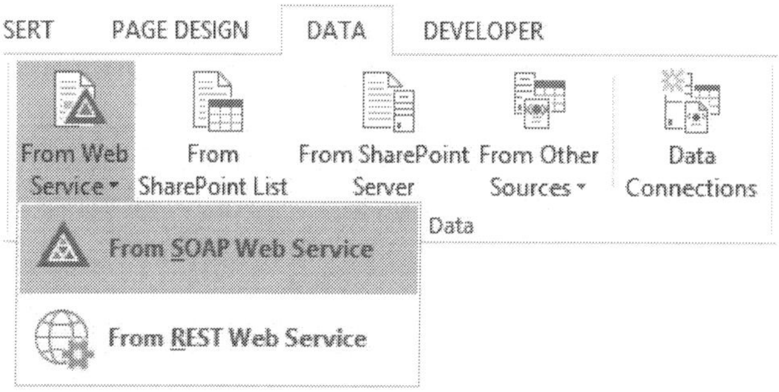

Figure 339. The From SOAP Web Service command on the Data tab in InfoPath 2013.

5. On the **Data Connection Wizard**, enter the URL of the Excel Services SOAP web service on the site where the Excel workbook is located, for example:

```
http://servername/sitename/_vti_bin/ExcelService.asmx
```

where **servername** is the name of the SharePoint server, **sitename** is the name of the site where the Excel workbook is located, and **ExcelService.asmx** is the Excel Services SOAP web service ASMX file. Click **Next**.

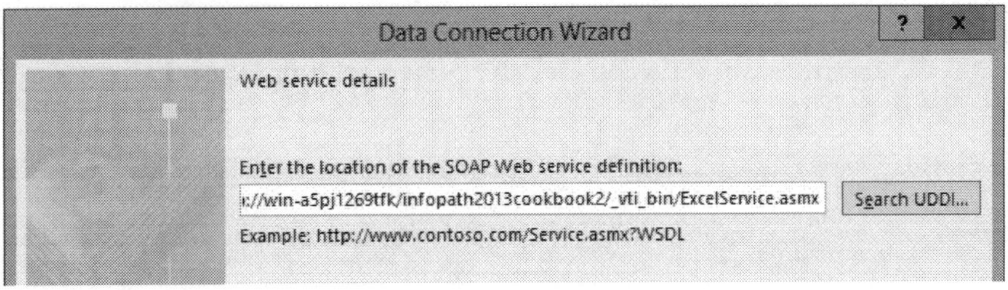

Figure 340. Entering the URL of the web service on the Data Connection Wizard.

6. On the **Data Connection Wizard**, select **OpenWorkbook** from the list of operations, and click **Next**.

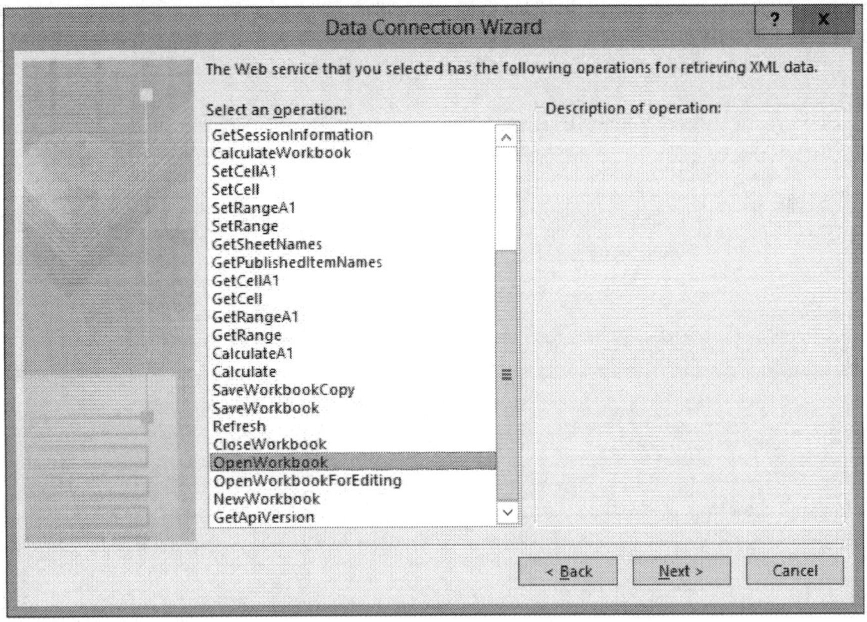

Figure 341. Selecting the OpenWorkbook web service operation in InfoPath 2013.

7. On the **Data Connection Wizard**, leave **workbookPath** selected in the **Parameters** list, and click **Set Value**.

8. On the **Parameter Details** dialog box, enter the full URL of the Excel workbook location, for example:

```
http://servername/sitename/libraryname/LeaveBalances.xlsx
```

where **servername** is the name of the SharePoint server, **sitename** is the name of the site, and **libraryname** is the name of the document library and Excel Services trusted file location where the **LeaveBalances.xlsx** Excel workbook is located. Click **OK** when you are done.

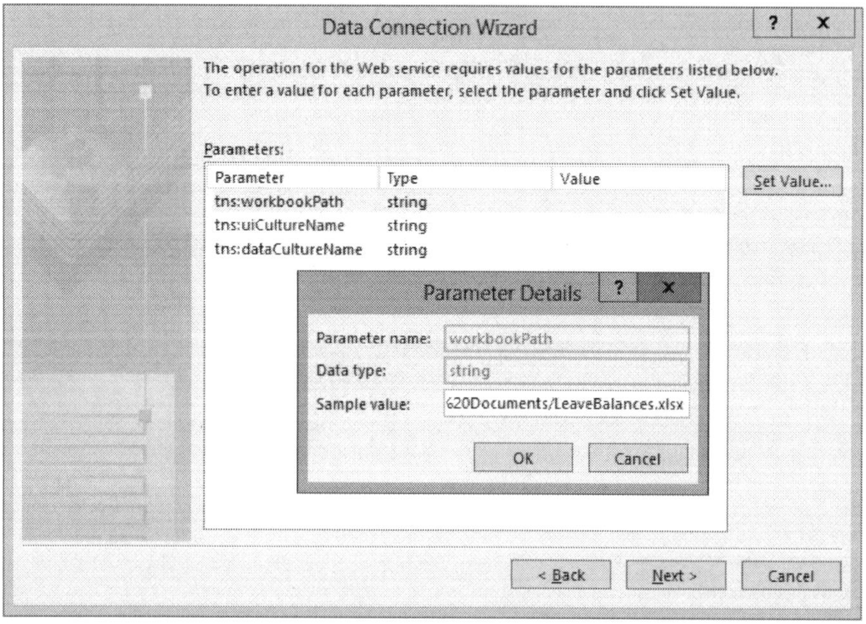

Figure 342. Entering the path of the Excel workbook to open.

9. On the **Data Connection Wizard**, leave the other two parameters as is, and click **Next**.
10. On the **Data Connection Wizard**, leave the **Store a copy of the data in the form template** check box deselected, and click **Next**.
11. On the **Data Connection Wizard**, accept the default name for the data connection (**OpenWorkbook**), deselect the **Automatically retrieve data when form is opened** check box, and click **Finish**. You will use this data connection to open the Excel workbook and get a session ID that you can use for all subsequent calls you make to Excel Services.

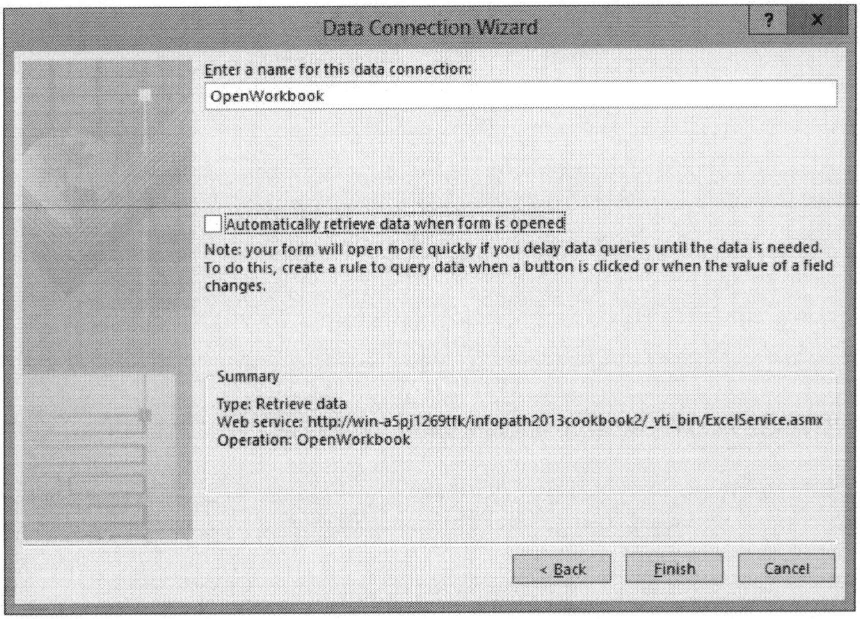

Figure 343. The final screen of the Data Connection Wizard in InfoPath 2013.

12. Repeat steps 4 through 11 to add a SOAP web service data connection for the **GetCellA1** operation of the Excel Services SOAP web service. Do not set any values for the parameters (you will be using a rule later to set their values), name the data connection **GetCellA1**, and deselect the **Automatically retrieve data when form is opened** check box. You will use this data connection to retrieve the amount of leave for a particular employee from the Excel workbook.
13. Repeat steps 4 through 11 to add a SOAP web service data connection for the **CloseWorkbook** operation of the Excel Services SOAP web service. Do not set the value of the **sessionId** parameter (you will be using a rule later to set its value), name the data connection **CloseWorkbook**, and deselect the **Automatically retrieve data when form is opened** check box. You will use this data connection to close the Excel workbook and the Excel Services session.
14. On the **Fields** task pane, select **GetCellA1 (Secondary)** from the drop-down list box, expand the **dataFields** group node, expand the **GetCellA1Response** group node, and then drag-and-drop the **GetCellA1Result** field onto the view of the form template. The field should automatically get bound to a text box control.

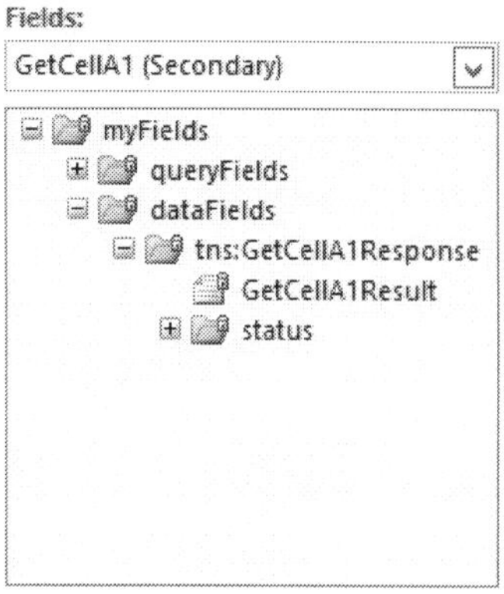

Figure 344. The secondary data source for the GetCellA1 web service operation.

15. Add a **Button** control to the view of the form template and label it **Get Leave Balance**.
16. Add an **Action** rule to the **Get Leave Balance** button with the following 7 actions:

```
Query using a data connection: OpenWorkbook
```

This action calls the **OpenWorkbook** web service operation to retrieve a session ID.

```
Set a field's value: sessionId = OpenWorkbookResult
```

where **sessionId** is located under the **GetCellA1** group node under the **queryFields** group node in the **GetCellA1** secondary data source and **OpenWorkbookResult** is located under the **OpenWorkbookResponse** group node under the **dataFields** group node in the **OpenWorkbook** secondary data source.

```
Set a field's value: sheetName = "Sheet1"
```

where **sheetName** is located under the **GetCellA1** group node under the **queryFields** group node in the **GetCellA1** secondary data source and **Sheet1** is a static piece of text representing the name of the worksheet in the Excel workbook where the leave balances are located.

```
Set a field's value: rangeName = "B1"
```

where **rangeName** is located under the **GetCellA1** group node under the **queryFields** group node in the **GetCellA1** secondary data source and **B1** is a static piece of text representing cell **B1** on **Sheet1** in the Excel workbook that contains the leave balances.

```
Query using a data connection: GetCellA1
```

This action calls the **GetCellA1** web service operation to retrieve the value of cell **B1**.

```
Set a field's value: sessionId = OpenWorkbookResult
```

where **sessionId** is located under the **CloseWorkbook** group node under the **queryFields** group node in the **CloseWorkbook** secondary data source and **OpenWorkbookResult** is located under the **OpenWorkbookResponse** group node under the **dataFields** group node in the **OpenWorkbook** secondary data source.

```
Query using a data connection: CloseWorkbook
```

This action closes the workbook and the Excel Services session.

17. If your SharePoint environment is configured to use Claims Based authentication as opposed to Windows Classic authentication and the form is going to be filled out through the browser, you must set up UDC authentication for all of the data connections that make web service calls as described in *Configure a web service data connection for a web browser form* in the Appendix. But before you do this, test the form in InfoPath Filler 2013 to ensure that the functionality is working properly.
18. Publish the form template to a SharePoint form library.

In SharePoint, navigate to the form library where you published the form template and add a new form. When the form opens, click the **Get Leave Balance** button. **25** should appear in the text box. If the InfoPath form is not working for you, see *Troubleshooting InfoPath with Excel Services* in the Appendix.

Discussion

In the solution described above, you saw how to use Excel Services SOAP web service operations to retrieve the value of a cell in an Excel workbook that was stored in a SharePoint document library. The sequence of Excel Services SOAP web service calls to retrieve the value of a cell in an Excel workbook was as follows:

1. Call **OpenWorkbook** to get an Excel Services session ID, which allowed you to read data from the Excel workbook and change but not permanently store data in the Excel workbook.
2. Call **GetCellA1** to retrieve the value of a cell in the Excel workbook.
3. Call **CloseWorkbook** to close the workbook and end the Excel Services session.

Before calling either the **GetCellA1** or **CloseWorkbook** operation, you had to set values of parameters to query them. In the case of **GetCellA1**, you had to set the value of the following 3 parameters:

1. sessionId
2. sheetName
3. rangeName

While you could have set the values of **sheetName** and **rangeName** through the **Data Connection Wizard** when you added the data connection for the web service operation, you used actions in a rule in step 16 of the solution described above to set their values. Actions in a rule allow you to dynamically (when the form is being filled out) set the values of parameters of a web service operation, while the **Data Connection Wizard** only allows you to set parameter values statically (when designing the form template). And because the session ID becomes available after you call the **OpenWorkbook** operation, you cannot use the **Data Connection Wizard** to set the **sessionId** parameter of the **GetCellA1** operation, but instead must use an action in a rule. Note that all query parameters are located under the **queryFields** group node in the secondary data source for the web service operation.

In the case of **CloseWorkbook**, you only had to set the value of a **sessionId** parameter, which you retrieved from the **dataFields** group node in the secondary data source for the **OpenWorkbook** web service operation. Note that because **CloseWorkbook** only returns a status, it can be seen as a submit operation for sending data to Excel Services, so you could have also created a **Submit** data connection to call it instead of a **Receive** data connection. But because a **Submit** data connection may produce an error when used in a browser-compatible form template, you used a **Receive** data connection instead.

The Excel Services SOAP web service provides two web service operations you can use to retrieve the value of a cell:

1. GetCellA1
2. GetCell

The difference between **GetCellA1** and **GetCell** is that you must specify the name of a cell when using the **GetCellA1** operation, while you must specify a row number and a column number of a particular cell when using the **GetCell** operation.

You can set the **rangeName** parameter of the **GetCellA1** operation to have a particular value, for example **B1** as in the solution described above. In terms of a row number and a column number, cell **B1** would correspond to row number **0** and column number **1** when you use the **GetCell** operation. Note that row and column numbers always start at **0** for Excel Services SOAP web service operations with cell **A1** having row number **0** and column number **0**.

The **GetCell** operation is good to use if you do not want to use a specific name of a cell, but rather want to dynamically change the row and column numbers of a cell at runtime from within InfoPath (see for example recipe *108 Set the value of an Excel cell in InfoPath* or recipe *118 Sequentially navigate through rows of an Excel table*).

108 Set the value of an Excel cell in InfoPath

Problem

You have an Excel workbook in which you want to set the value of a cell so that a calculation can be performed and the result returned to an InfoPath form for display.

Solution

You can create an Excel workbook that contains data and a formula, publish this Excel workbook to a trusted file location for Excel Services in SharePoint, and then call Excel Services SOAP web service operations from within the InfoPath form to perform data submission and retrieval.

To set the value of a cell in an Excel workbook from within an InfoPath form:

1. Follow step 1 of recipe *107 Get the value of an Excel cell in InfoPath*.
2. In Excel, add a second worksheet, rename the new worksheet to **Calculations**, and add the following formula to cell **A2** on the **Calculations** worksheet:

   ```
   =VLOOKUP(A1, Sheet1!A1:B3, 2, FALSE)
   ```

3. Click **File ➤ Save As ➤ SharePoint** and then click **Browse** to publish the entire workbook with the name **LeaveBalances.xlsx** to a document library (for example the **Documents** library) on the SharePoint site to which the InfoPath form will be connecting. Note that if the **File ➤ Save As ➤ SharePoint** command is not available, you can follow steps 2 through 5 of *Configure browser view options for an Excel workbook* in recipe *105 Publish an Excel workbook for use with InfoPath in SharePoint*.
4. In InfoPath, create a new SharePoint form library form template or use an existing one.
5. Add a **Receive** data connection for the **OpenWorkbook** operation of the Excel Services web service as described in recipe *107 Get the value of an Excel cell in InfoPath* and configure its parameters as follows:

Parameter	Value
tns:workbookPath	`http://servername/sitename/libraryname/LeaveBalances.xlsx` where **servername** is the name of the SharePoint server, **sitename** is the name

	of the site, and **libraryname** is the name of the document library and Excel Services trusted file location where the **LeaveBalances.xlsx** Excel workbook is located.
tns:uiCultureName	
tns:dataCultureName	

Leave the **Store a copy of the data in the form template** check box deselected, name the data connection **OpenWorkbook**, and deselect the **Automatically retrieve data when form is opened** check box. You will use this data connection to open the Excel workbook and get a session ID that you can use for all subsequent calls you make to Excel Services.

6. Add a **Receive** data connection for the **SetCellA1** operation of the Excel Services web service and configure its parameters as follows:

Parameter	Value
tns:sessionId	
tns:sheetName	Calculations where **Calculations** is the name of the worksheet in the **LeaveBalances.xlsx** Excel workbook that has a **VLOOKUP** formula defined on it.
tns:rangeName	A1 where **A1** is the name of the cell that is used as input for the **VLOOKUP** formula on the **Calculations** worksheet in the

	LeaveBalances.xlsx Excel workbook.
tns:cellValue	

Leave the **Store a copy of the data in the form template** check box deselected, name the data connection **SetCellA1**, and deselect the **Automatically retrieve data when form is opened** check box. You will use this data connection to set the value of cell **A1** on the **Calculations** worksheet in the Excel workbook. At this point, the **sessionId** and **cellValue** parameters are still blank; you will use a rule later to set their values before making the web service call.

7. Add a **Receive** data connection for the **GetCell** operation of the Excel Services web service and configure its parameters as follows:

Parameter	Value
tns:sessionId	
tns:sheetName	Calculations where **Calculations** is the name of the worksheet in the **LeaveBalances.xlsx** Excel workbook that has a **VLOOKUP** formula defined on it.
tns:row	1 Because the result of the calculation is stored in cell **A2** on the **Calculations** worksheet in the Excel workbook, you must use number **1** to access the row for cell **A2**.
tns:column	0 Because the result of the calculation is stored

	in cell **A2** on the **Calculations** worksheet in the Excel workbook, you must use number **0** to access the column for cell **A2**.
tns:formatted	false

Leave the **Store a copy of the data in the form template** check box deselected, name the data connection **GetCell**, and deselect the **Automatically retrieve data when form is opened** check box. You will use this data connection to get the result of the **VLOOKUP** calculation in the Excel workbook. Note that at this stage the **sessionId** parameter is still blank, since you will set its value later through a rule.

8. Add a **Receive** data connection for the **CloseWorkbook** operation of the Excel Services web service. Leave the **sessionId** parameter as is, leave the **Store a copy of the data in the form template** check box deselected, name the data connection **CloseWorkbook**, and deselect the **Automatically retrieve data when form is opened** check box. You will use this data connection to close the workbook and the Excel Services session. Note that at this stage the **sessionId** parameter is still blank, since you will set its value later through a rule.
9. On the **Fields** task pane, select **SetCellA1 (Secondary)** from the drop-down list box, expand the **queryFields** group node, expand the **SetCellA1** group node, and then drag-and-drop the **cellValue** field onto the view of the form template. It should automatically get bound to a text box control.
10. Add a **Button** control to the view of the form template and label it **Get Leave Balance**.
11. Add an **Action** rule to the **Get Leave Balance** button control with the following 7 actions:

```
Query using a data connection: OpenWorkbook
```

This action calls the **OpenWorkbook** web service operation to retrieve a session ID.

```
Set a field's value: sessionId = OpenWorkbookResult
```

where **sessionId** is located under the **SetCellA1** group node under the **queryFields** group node in the **SetCellA1** secondary data source and **OpenWorkbookResult** is located under the **OpenWorkbookResponse** group node under the **dataFields** group node in the **OpenWorkbook** secondary data source.

```
Query using a data connection: SetCellA1
```

This action calls the **SetCellA1** web service operation to set the value of cell **A1** on the **Calculations** worksheet to be able to perform a **VLOOKUP** calculation in the Excel workbook.

```
Set a field's value: sessionId = OpenWorkbookResult
```

where **sessionId** is located under the **GetCell** group node under the **queryFields** group node in the **GetCell** secondary data source and **OpenWorkbookResult** is located under the **OpenWorkbookResponse** group node under the **dataFields** group node in the **OpenWorkbook** secondary data source.

```
Query using a data connection: GetCell
```

This action calls the **GetCell** web service operation to retrieve the result of the **VLOOKUP** calculation.

```
Set a field's value: sessionId = OpenWorkbookResult
```

where **sessionId** is located under the **CloseWorkbook** group node under the **queryFields** group node in the **CloseWorkbook** secondary data source and **OpenWorkbookResult** is located under the **OpenWorkbookResponse** group node under the **dataFields** group node in the **OpenWorkbook** secondary data source.

```
Query using a data connection: CloseWorkbook
```

This action closes the workbook and the Excel Services session.

12. On the **Fields** task pane, select **GetCell (Secondary)** from the drop-down list box, expand the **dataFields** group node, expand the **GetCellResponse** group node, and then drag-and-drop the **GetCellResult** field onto the view of the form template. It should automatically get bound to a text box control.

13. If your SharePoint environment is configured to use Claims Based authentication as opposed to Windows Classic authentication and the form is going to be filled out through the browser, you must set up UDC authentication for all of the data connections that make web service calls as described in *Configure a web service data connection for a web browser form* in the Appendix. But before you do this, test the form in InfoPath Filler 2013 to ensure that the functionality is working properly.
14. Publish the form template to a SharePoint form library.

In SharePoint, navigate to the form library where you published the form template and add a new form. When the form opens, enter an employee name (for example **john.doe**) into the **cellValue** text box, and then click the **Get Leave Balance** button. **15** should appear in the **GetCellResult** text box. If the InfoPath form is not working for you, see *Troubleshooting InfoPath with Excel Services* in the Appendix.

Discussion

In the solution described above, you used Excel Services SOAP web service operations to perform a **VLOOKUP** calculation in an Excel workbook and return the result to an InfoPath form.

Note that you could have also used the **GetCellA1** web service operation instead of the **GetCell** web service operation to get the value of the calculation. Refer to the discussion section of recipe *107 Get the value of an Excel cell in InfoPath* to learn about the difference between the **GetCell** and **GetCellA1** web service operations. Likewise, you could have also used the **SetCell** web service operation instead of the **SetCellA1** web service operation to set the value of a cell in the Excel workbook. It all depends on what you want to pass to the web service operation, that is, a cell name, or row and column numbers representing a cell on a worksheet.

The sequence of Excel Services SOAP web service calls to update the value of a cell in an Excel workbook and then retrieve the result of a calculation is as follows:

1. Call **OpenWorkbook** to get an Excel Services session ID, which allows you to read data from the Excel workbook and change but not permanently store data in the Excel workbook.
2. Call **SetCell** or **SetCellA1** to update the value of a cell in the Excel workbook that is used to perform a calculation. Note that such a change is not permanent unless you open the Excel workbook for editing using the **OpenWorkbookForEditing** web service operation (also see recipe *112 Update an Excel workbook when submitting a form to SharePoint*) instead of the **OpenWorkbook** web service operation.
3. Call **GetCell** or **GetCellA1** to retrieve the result of the calculation from a cell in the Excel workbook.
4. Call **CloseWorkbook** to close the workbook and end the Excel Services session.

Note that the solution described above uses **Receive** data connections to call the web service operations. While you can also use **Submit** data connections to call for example an operation like **CloseWorkbook**, such a data connection may produce an error when used in a browser-compatible form template.

109 Populate a drop-down list box with data from an Excel workbook

Problem

You have data on an Excel spreadsheet, which you would like to use to populate a drop-down list box on an InfoPath form. In addition, whenever a user selects an item from the drop-down list box, you want a text box to display additional information for the selected item.

Solution

You can create an Excel workbook that contains data in a table and a calculation for performing a lookup in the data, publish this Excel workbook to a trusted file location for Excel Services, and then call Excel Services SOAP web service operations from within an InfoPath form to perform data retrieval and lookups so that you can populate controls on the InfoPath form.

To populate a drop-down list box in InfoPath with data from an Excel workbook:

1. In Excel, create a new **Blank workbook** that contains a list of Office applications and their corresponding colors as described in recipe *2 Customize a SharePoint list form from within InfoPath*. Do not add headers; only enter data. Add the following formula to cell **C2** on **Sheet1**:

   ```
   =VLOOKUP(C1, A1:B7, 2, FALSE)
   ```

   where cell **C1** on **Sheet1** contains a static piece of text from column **A** and cells **A1** through **B7** contain the names and colors of Office applications. The value of cell **C1** will be set from within InfoPath, so that whenever an Office application is selected from the drop-down list box, its corresponding color can be retrieved using the **VLOOKUP** function in Excel.

2. Select cells **A1** through **A7**, and then click **Formulas ➤ Defined Names ➤ Define Name**.

3. On the **New Name** dialog box, type **OfficeApplicationNames** in the **Name** text box, leave **Workbook** selected in the **Scope** drop-down list box, ensure that

   ```
   =Sheet1!$A$1:$A$7
   ```

   has been entered in the **Refers to** text box, and click **OK**. This named range will be used by one of the web service operations to be able to retrieve the Office application names for the drop-down list box. The advantage of using named ranges instead of static cell names is that after you have designed your InfoPath form template and published it to SharePoint and later want to update the data in the Excel workbook, you can do so without having to make any changes in InfoPath. Just remember to also edit the named ranges to contain the updated data or cells. After you republish the Excel workbook to SharePoint, all InfoPath forms should then automatically display the newly updated Excel data in the drop-down list box.

4. Click **File ➤ Save As ➤ SharePoint** and then click **Browse** to publish the entire workbook with the name **OfficeApplications.xlsx** to a document library (for example the **Documents** library) on the SharePoint site to which the InfoPath form will be connecting. Note that if the **File ➤ Save As ➤ SharePoint** command is not available, you can follow steps 2 through 5 of *Configure browser view options for an Excel workbook* in recipe *105 Publish an Excel workbook for use with InfoPath in SharePoint*.
5. In InfoPath, create a new SharePoint form library form template or use an existing one.
6. Add a **Drop-Down List Box** control to the view of the form template and name it **officeApplication**.
7. Add a **Text Box** control to the view of the form template and name it **applicationColor**.
8. Add a **Button** control to the view of the form template and label it **Get Office Applications**.
9. Add a **Receive** data connection for the **OpenWorkbook** operation of the Excel Services web service as described in recipe *107 Get the value of an Excel cell in InfoPath* and configure its parameters as follows:

Parameter	Value
tns:workbookPath	`http://servername/sitename/libraryname/OfficeApplications.xlsx` where **servername** is the name of the SharePoint server, **sitename** is the name of the site, and **libraryname** is the name of the document library and Excel Services trusted file location where the **OfficeApplications.xlsx** Excel workbook is located.
tns:uiCultureName	
tns:dataCultureName	

Leave the **Store a copy of the data in the form template** check box deselected, name the data connection **OpenWorkbook**, and deselect the **Automatically retrieve data when form is opened** check box. You will use this data connection to open the Excel workbook and get a session ID that you can use for all subsequent calls you make to Excel Services.

10. Add a **Receive** data connection for the **GetRangeA1** operation of the Excel Services web service and configure its parameters as follows:

Parameter	Value
tns:sessionId	
tns:sheetName	Sheet1 where **Sheet1** is a static piece of text representing the name of the worksheet in the Excel workbook where the list of Office application names and colors is located.
tns:rangeName	OfficeApplicationNames where **OfficeApplicationNames** is a static piece of text representing the name of the named range on **Sheet1** in the Excel workbook that contains the list of Office application names.
tns:formatted	false

Leave the **Store a copy of the data in the form template** check box deselected, name the data connection **GetRangeA1**, and deselect the **Automatically retrieve data when form is opened** check box. You will use this data connection to retrieve the list of Office application names. Note that at this stage the **sessionId** parameter is still blank, since you will set its value later through a rule.

11. Add a **Receive** data connection for the **SetCellA1** operation of the Excel Services web service and configure its parameters as follows:

Parameter	Value
tns:sessionId	
tns:sheetName	Sheet1 where **Sheet1** is a static piece of text representing the name of the worksheet in the Excel workbook where the list of Office application names and colors is located.
tns:rangeName	C1 where **C1** is a static piece of text representing the name of the cell that accepts the input for the **VLOOKUP** calculation that looks up the color of an Office application based on its name.
tns:cellValue	

Leave the **Store a copy of the data in the form template** check box deselected, name the data connection **SetCellA1**, and deselect the **Automatically retrieve data when form is opened** check box. You will use this data connection to set the value of cell **C1** which should receive the name of an Office application and that is subsequently used to perform a **VLOOKUP** calculation to find a color. At this point, the **sessionId** and **cellValue** parameters are still blank; you will use a rule later to set their values before making the web service call.

12. Add a **Receive** data connection for the **GetCellA1** operation of the Excel Services web service and configure its parameters as follows:

Parameter	Value
tns:sessionId	
tns:sheetName	Sheet1 where **Sheet1** is a static piece of text representing the name of the worksheet in the Excel workbook where the list of Office application names and colors is located.
tns:rangeName	C2 where **C2** is a static piece of text representing the name of the cell that contains the result of the **VLOOKUP** calculation that looks up the color of an Office application based on its name.
tns:formatted	false

Leave the **Store a copy of the data in the form template** check box deselected, name the data connection **GetCellA1**, and deselect the **Automatically retrieve data when form is opened** check box. You will use this data connection to retrieve the result of the **VLOOKUP** calculation from the Excel workbook. Note that at this stage the **sessionId** parameter is still blank, since you will set its value later through a rule.

13. Add a **Receive** data connection for the **CloseWorkbook** operation of the Excel Services web service. Leave the **sessionId** parameter as is, leave the **Store a copy of the data in the form template** check box deselected, name the data connection **CloseWorkbook**, and deselect the **Automatically retrieve data when form is opened** check box.

You will use this data connection to close the workbook and the Excel Services session. Note that at this stage the **sessionId** parameter is still blank, since you will set its value later through a rule.

14. Add an **Action** rule to the **Get Office Applications** button with the following 5 actions:

```
Query using a data connection: OpenWorkbook
```

This action calls the **OpenWorkbook** web service operation to retrieve a session ID.

```
Set a field's value: sessionId = OpenWorkbookResult
```

where **sessionId** is located under the **GetRangeA1** group node under the **queryFields** group node in the **GetRangeA1** secondary data source and **OpenWorkbookResult** is located under the **OpenWorkbookResponse** group node under the **dataFields** group node in the **OpenWorkbook** secondary data source.

```
Query using a data connection: GetRangeA1
```

This action calls the **GetRangeA1** web service operation to retrieve the list of Office application names.

```
Set a field's value: sessionId = OpenWorkbookResult
```

where **sessionId** is located under the **CloseWorkbook** group node under the **queryFields** group node in the **CloseWorkbook** secondary data source and **OpenWorkbookResult** is located under the **OpenWorkbookResponse** group node under the **dataFields** group node in the **OpenWorkbook** secondary data source.

```
Query using a data connection: CloseWorkbook
```

This action closes the workbook and the Excel Services session.

15. Add an **Action** rule to the drop-down list box with the following 9 actions:

```
Query using a data connection: OpenWorkbook
```

This action calls the **OpenWorkbook** web service operation to retrieve a session ID.

```
Set a field's value: sessionId = OpenWorkbookResult
```

where **sessionId** is located under the **SetCellA1** group node under the **queryFields** group node in the **SetCellA1** secondary data source and **OpenWorkbookResult** is located under the **OpenWorkbookResponse** group node under the **dataFields** group node in the **OpenWorkbook** secondary data source.

```
Set a field's value: cellValue = .
```

where **cellValue** is located under the **SetCellA1** group node under the **queryFields** group node in the **SetCellA1** secondary data source and the dot (**.**) represents the value of the selected item in the **officeApplication** drop-down list box.

```
Query using a data connection: SetCellA1
```

This action calls the **SetCellA1** web service operation to set the value of the cell in the Excel workbook that contains the name of the Office application for which a color should be retrieved.

```
Set a field's value: sessionId = OpenWorkbookResult
```

where **sessionId** is located under the **GetCellA1** group node under the **queryFields** group node in the **GetCellA1** secondary data source and **OpenWorkbookResult** is located under the **OpenWorkbookResponse** group node under the **dataFields** group node in the **OpenWorkbook** secondary data source.

```
Query using a data connection: GetCellA1
```

This action calls the **GetCellA1** web service operation to retrieve the color of the Office application that was selected in the drop-down list box.

```
Set a field's value: applicationColor = GetCellA1Result
```

where **applicationColor** is a field that is located in the Main data source and that is bound to the text box control on the form and **GetCellA1Result** is located under the **GetCellA1Response** group node under the **dataFields** group node in the **GetCellA1** secondary data source.

```
Set a field's value: sessionId = OpenWorkbookResult
```

where **sessionId** is located under the **CloseWorkbook** group node under the **queryFields** group node in the **CloseWorkbook** secondary data source and **OpenWorkbookResult** is located under the **OpenWorkbookResponse** group node under the **dataFields** group node in the **OpenWorkbook** secondary data source.

```
Query using a data connection: CloseWorkbook
```

This action closes the workbook and the Excel Services session.

16. Open the **Drop-Down List Box Properties** dialog box, and then on the **Data** tab, select the **Get choices from an external data source** option, select **GetRangeA1** from the **Data Source** drop-down list box, and then click the button behind the **Entries** text box.
17. On the **Select a Field or Group** dialog box, expand the **GetRangeA1Response** group node, expand the **GetRangeA1Result** group node, select the **anyType** repeating field, and click **OK**.
18. On the **Drop-Down List Box Properties** dialog box, ensure that a dot (`.`) is selected for both the **Value** property and the **Display name** property, and then click **OK**.
19. If your SharePoint environment is configured to use Claims Based authentication as opposed to Windows Classic authentication and the form is going to be filled out through the browser, you must set up UDC authentication for all of the data connections that make web service calls as described in *Configure a web service data connection for a web browser form* in the Appendix. But before you do this, test the form in InfoPath Filler 2013 to ensure that the functionality is working properly.
20. Publish the form template to a SharePoint form library.

In SharePoint, navigate to the form library where you published the form template and add a new form. When the form opens, verify that the drop-down list box does not contain any items. Click the **Get Office Applications** button and then verify that the drop-down list box was populated with the names of Office applications from the Excel workbook. Select an Office application from the drop-down list box. The color of the selected Office application should appear in the text box. If the InfoPath form is not working for you, see *Troubleshooting InfoPath with Excel Services* in the Appendix.

Discussion

In the solution described above, you saw how to call Excel Services SOAP web service operations to populate a drop-down list box on an InfoPath form with data from an Excel workbook and also perform a lookup for data in the workbook to populate a text box control on the InfoPath form.

You thereby used a sequence of Excel Services web service calls on a button control to:

1. Call **OpenWorkbook** to get an Excel Services session ID, which allowed you to open an Excel workbook to be able to read data from it.
2. Call **GetRangeA1** to retrieve a list of Office application names from the Excel workbook thereby making use of a named range in the Excel workbook.
3. Call **CloseWorkbook** to close the workbook and end the Excel Services session.

You then used the data that was retrieved by this sequence of Excel Services web service calls to populate a drop-down list box on the InfoPath form. Note that you could have used the data that was returned by Excel Services to populate any type of list box (normal list box, combo box, and multiple-selection list box) that you can bind to a secondary data source.

You then used a second sequence of Excel Services web service calls on the drop-down list box control to:

1. Call **OpenWorkbook** to get an Excel Services session ID, which allowed you to open the Excel workbook again to be able to run a calculation and return its result.
2. Call **SetCellA1** to set the value of cell **C1** on **Sheet1** in the Excel workbook, so that it could be used to perform a **VLOOKUP** calculation using the Office application name passed to the Excel workbook.
3. Call **GetCellA1** to retrieve the value of cell **C2** on **Sheet1** in the Excel workbook that contained the result of the **VLOOKUP**

calculation. You then used this value to set the value of the text box control on the InfoPath form.

4. Call **CloseWorkbook** to close the workbook and end the Excel Services session.

110 Calculate business days between two dates excluding holidays

Problem

You have two date picker controls on an InfoPath form and want to calculate the difference in days between these two dates excluding holidays and weekends.

Solution

You can create an Excel workbook that contains the calculation for the amount of business days between two dates and a list of dates for holidays, publish this Excel workbook to a trusted file location for Excel Services, and then call Excel Services SOAP web service operations from within an InfoPath form to perform the calculation.

To calculate the amount of business days between two dates excluding holidays:

1. In Excel, create a new **Blank workbook**, add a second worksheet named **Sheet2** to it, add a list of dates for holidays in column **A** of **Sheet2**, and add the following formula in cell **A3** on **Sheet1**:

```
=NETWORKDAYS(A1,A2,Sheet2!A1:A3)
```

where cell **A1** on **Sheet1** contains a start date that has a format of **yyyy-MM-dd** and a default value of **2014-01-01**, cell **A2** on **Sheet1** contains an end date that has a format of **yyyy-MM-dd** and a default value of **2015-01-01**, and cells **A1** to **A3** on **Sheet2** contain a range of dates that represent holidays. The dates have the **Date** data type in Excel. You will be changing the default values of cells **A1** and **A2** on **Sheet1** later through InfoPath. The Excel formula uses the **NETWORKDAYS** function to calculate the amount of business days minus holidays.

2. Click **File ➤ Save As ➤ SharePoint** and then click **Browse** to publish the entire workbook with the name **WorkdaysCalculator.xlsx** to a document library (for example the **Documents** library) on the SharePoint site to which the InfoPath form will be connecting. Note that if the **File ➤ Save As ➤ SharePoint** command is not available, you can follow steps 2 through 5 of *Configure browser view options for an Excel workbook* in recipe *105 Publish an Excel workbook for use with InfoPath in SharePoint*.
3. In InfoPath, create a new SharePoint form library form template or use an existing one.
4. Add two **Date Picker** controls to the view of the form template and name them **startDate** and **endDate**, respectively.
5. Add a **Text Box** control to the view of the form template and name it **workdaysDiff**. Make the text box read-only or change it into a calculated value control, since the user should not be able to change the value of this field.
6. Add a **Button** control to the view of the form template and label it **Calculate**.
7. Add a **Receive** data connection for the **OpenWorkbook** operation of the Excel Services web service as described in recipe *107 Get the value of an Excel cell in InfoPath* and configure its parameters as follows:

Parameter	Value
tns:workbookPath	`http://servername/sitename/libraryname /WorkdaysCalculator.xlsx` where **servername** is the name of the SharePoint server, **sitename** is the name of the site, and **libraryname** is the name of the document library and Excel Services trusted file location where the **WorkdaysCalculator.xlsx** Excel workbook is located.

tns:uiCultureName	
tns:dataCultureName	

Leave the **Store a copy of the data in the form template** check box deselected, name the data connection **OpenWorkbook**, and deselect the **Automatically retrieve data when form is opened** check box. You will use this data connection to open the Excel workbook and get a session ID that you can use for all subsequent calls you make to Excel Services.

8. Add a **Receive** data connection for the **SetCellA1** operation of the Excel Services web service and configure its parameters as follows:

Parameter	Value
tns:sessionId	
tns:sheetName	Sheet1 where **Sheet1** is the name of the worksheet in the **WorkdaysCalculator.xlsx** Excel workbook that has a **NETWORKDAYS** formula defined on it.
tns:rangeName	
tns:cellValue	

Leave the **Store a copy of the data in the form template** check box deselected, name the data connection **SetCellA1**, and deselect the **Automatically retrieve data when form is opened** check box. You will use this data connection to set the value of cell **A1** or **A2** on the **Sheet1** worksheet in the Excel workbook. At this point, the **sessionId**, **rangeName**, and **cellValue** parameters are still blank; you will use a rule later to set their values before making the web service call.

9. Add a **Receive** data connection for the **GetCellA1** operation of the Excel Services web service and configure its parameters as follows:

Parameter	Value
tns:sessionId	
tns:sheetName	Sheet1 where **Sheet1** is the name of the worksheet in the **WorkdaysCalculator.xlsx** Excel workbook that has a **NETWORKDAYS** formula defined on it.
tns:rangeName	A3 where **A3** is the name of the cell that contains the result of the calculation using the **NETWORKDAYS** formula on the **Sheet1** worksheet in the **WorkdaysCalculator.xlsx** Excel workbook.
tns:formatted	false

Leave the **Store a copy of the data in the form template** check box deselected, name the data connection **GetCellA1**, and deselect the **Automatically retrieve data when form is opened** check box. You will use this data connection to get the result of the **NETWORKDAYS** calculation in the Excel workbook. Note that at this stage the **sessionId** parameter is still blank, since you will set its value later through a rule.

10. Add a **Receive** data connection for the **CloseWorkbook** operation of the Excel Services web service. Leave the **sessionId** parameter as is, leave the **Store a copy of the data in the form template** check box deselected, name the data connection **CloseWorkbook**, and deselect the **Automatically retrieve data when form is opened** check box.

You will use this data connection to close the workbook and the Excel Services session. Note that at this stage the **sessionId** parameter is still blank, since you will set its value later through a rule.

11. Add an **Action** rule to the **Calculate** button control with a **Condition** that says:

```
startDate is not blank
and
endDate is not blank
```

and that has the following 13 actions:

```
Query using a data connection: OpenWorkbook
```

This action calls the **OpenWorkbook** web service operation to retrieve a session ID.

```
Set a field's value: sessionId = OpenWorkbookResult
```

where **sessionId** is located under the **SetCellA1** group node under the **queryFields** group node in the **SetCellA1** secondary data source and **OpenWorkbookResult** is located under the **OpenWorkbookResponse** group node under the **dataFields** group node in the **OpenWorkbook** secondary data source.

```
Set a field's value: rangeName = "A1"
```

where **rangeName** is located under the **SetCellA1** group node under the **queryFields** group node in the **SetCellA1** secondary data source and **A1** is a static piece of text.

```
Set a field's value: cellValue = startDate
```

where **cellValue** is located under the **SetCellA1** group node under the **queryFields** group node in the **SetCellA1** secondary data source and **startDate** is located in the Main data source.

```
Query using a data connection: SetCellA1
```

This action calls the **SetCellA1** web service operation to set the value of cell **A1** on the **Sheet1** worksheet to be able to perform the **NETWORKDAYS** calculation in the Excel workbook.

```
Set a field's value: rangeName = "A2"
```

where **rangeName** is located under the **SetCellA1** group node under the **queryFields** group node in the **SetCellA1** secondary data source and **A2** is a static piece of text.

```
Set a field's value: cellValue = endDate
```

where **cellValue** is located under the **SetCellA1** group node under the **queryFields** group node in the **SetCellA1** secondary data source and **endDate** is located in the Main data source.

```
Query using a data connection: SetCellA1
```

This action calls the **SetCellA1** web service operation to set the value of cell **A2** on the **Sheet1** worksheet to be able to perform the **NETWORKDAYS** calculation in the Excel workbook.

```
Set a field's value: sessionId = OpenWorkbookResult
```

where **sessionId** is located under the **GetCellA1** group node under the **queryFields** group node in the **GetCellA1** secondary data source and **OpenWorkbookResult** is located under the **OpenWorkbookResponse** group node under the **dataFields** group node in the **OpenWorkbook** secondary data source.

```
Query using a data connection: GetCellA1
```

This action calls the **GetCellA1** web service operation to retrieve the result of the **NETWORKDAYS** calculation.

```
Set a field's value: workDaysDiff = GetCellA1Result
```

where **workDaysDiff** is located in the Main data source and **GetCellA1Result** is located under the **GetCellA1Response** group node under the **dataFields** group node in the **GetCellA1** secondary data source. **GetCellA1Result** contains the result of the **NETWORKDAYS** calculation.

```
Set a field's value: sessionId = OpenWorkbookResult
```

where **sessionId** is located under the **CloseWorkbook** group node under the **queryFields** group node in the **CloseWorkbook** secondary data source and **OpenWorkbookResult** is located under the **OpenWorkbookResponse** group node under the **dataFields** group node in the **OpenWorkbook** secondary data source.

```
Query using a data connection: CloseWorkbook
```

This action closes the workbook and the Excel Services session.

12. If your SharePoint environment is configured to use Claims Based authentication as opposed to Windows Classic authentication and the form is going to be filled out through the browser, you must set up UDC authentication for all of the data connections that make web service calls as described in ***Configure a web service data connection for a web browser form*** in the Appendix. But before you do this, test the form in InfoPath Filler 2013 to ensure that the functionality is working properly.
13. Publish the form template to a SharePoint form library.

In SharePoint, navigate to the form library where you published the form template and add a new form. When the form opens, enter a start date, enter an end date, and then click the **Calculate** button. Check whether the result for the date difference calculation took the holidays that were specified in the Excel workbook and weekends into account. If the InfoPath form is not working for you, see ***Troubleshooting InfoPath with Excel Services*** in the Appendix.

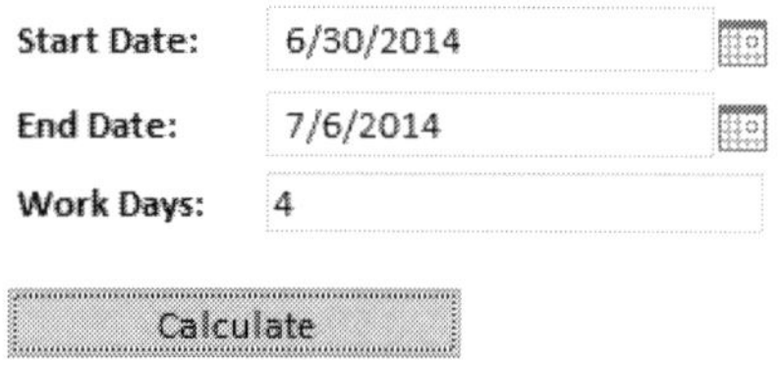

Figure 345. The form displaying the amount of business days with July 4 being a holiday.

Discussion

In the solution described above you used operations of the Excel Services SOAP web service in SharePoint 2013 to:

1. Open an Excel workbook.
2. Set the value of a cell containing a start date.
3. Set the value of a cell containing an end date.

4. Perform a calculation and retrieve the result.
5. Close the Excel workbook.

While all of these steps were executed by one action rule on the **Calculate** button on the form, you could have also created 5 separate action rules for you to be able to easily disable any of the rules should you have to debug the calls made to the web service in order to resolve any errors.

You also used Excel's **NETWORKDAYS** function to calculate the amount of business days between two dates and take holidays and weekends into account. In step 1 you specified the dates in the Excel workbook in the ISO date format (**yyyy-MM-dd**), which is also used by default in InfoPath.

The list of dates for holidays specified in the Excel formula does not affect the web service calls made by the InfoPath form, so if you want to update the list of holidays in the Excel workbook afterwards by adding more dates to it or by removing dates from it, you can freely do so. Just remember to also update the range (third argument) specified in the **NETWORKDAYS** formula to include more or less cells depending on the updates you make. Note that in the solution above, the list of holidays is located on **Sheet2** instead of **Sheet1**, but you could have also placed the dates on **Sheet1** if you wanted to; just remember to update the Excel formula accordingly if you make such a change. If you want to update the list of holidays in the Excel workbook, you can do so by opening and editing the file that is stored in the SharePoint document library, in Excel, and then saving the file back to the document library.

111 Use an InfoPath form to create a new Excel workbook in SharePoint

Problem

You want to use an InfoPath form to create a new Excel workbook in a SharePoint document library.

Solution

You can call Excel Services SOAP web service operations from within an InfoPath form to copy an existing blank Excel workbook and store a copy of it with a new name in a SharePoint document library.

To use an InfoPath form to create a new Excel workbook in SharePoint:

1. In Excel, create a new **Blank workbook** that contains a worksheet but no data, click **File ➤ Save As ➤ SharePoint**, and then click **Browse** to save the entire workbook with the name **BlankWorkbook.xlsx** to a document library (for example the **Documents** library) on the SharePoint site to which the InfoPath form will be connecting. Note that if the **File ➤ Save As ➤ SharePoint** command is not available, you can follow steps 2 through 5 of *Configure browser view options for an Excel workbook* in recipe *105 Publish an Excel workbook for use with InfoPath in SharePoint*.
2. In InfoPath, create a new SharePoint form library form template or use an existing one.
3. Add a **Text Box** control to the view of the form template and name it **filename**.
4. Add a **Button** control to the view of the form template and label it **Create New Workbook**.
5. Add a **Receive** data connection for the **OpenWorkbook** operation of the Excel Services web service as described in recipe *107 Get the value of an Excel cell in InfoPath* and configure its parameters as follows:

Parameter	Value
tns:workbookPath	`http://servername/sitename/libraryname /BlankWorkbook.xlsx` where **servername** is the name of the SharePoint server, **sitename** is the name of the site, and **libraryname** is the name of the document library and Excel Services trusted file location where the

	BlankWorkbook.xlsx Excel workbook is located.
tns:uiCultureName	
tns:dataCultureName	

Leave the **Store a copy of the data in the form template** check box deselected, name the data connection **OpenWorkbook**, and deselect the **Automatically retrieve data when form is opened** check box. You will use this data connection to open the Excel workbook and get a session ID that you can use for all subsequent calls you make to Excel Services.

6. Add a **Receive** data connection for the **SaveWorkbookCopy** operation of the Excel Services web service and configure its parameters as follows:

Parameter	Value
tns:sessionId	
tns:workbookPath	
tns:workbookType	FullWorkbook where **FullWorkbook** is one of three values you can select for the type of Excel workbook to create. Other possible values are **FullSnapshot** and **PublishedItemsSnapshot**.
tns:saveOptions	None where **None** is a static piece of text representing a save option. You could also

---

use **AllowOverwrite** as a save option.

Leave the **Store a copy of the data in the form template** check box deselected, name the data connection **SaveWorkbookCopy**, and deselect the **Automatically retrieve data when form is opened** check box. You will use this data connection to make a copy of the existing Excel workbook in SharePoint and save it with a new name.

7. Add a **Receive** data connection for the **CloseWorkbook** operation of the Excel Services web service. Leave the **sessionId** parameter as is, leave the **Store a copy of the data in the form template** check box deselected, name the data connection **CloseWorkbook**, and deselect the **Automatically retrieve data when form is opened** check box. You will use this data connection to close the workbook and the Excel Services session. Note that at this stage the **sessionId** parameter is still blank, since you will set its value later through a rule.
8. Add an **Action** rule to the **Create New Workbook** button control with the following 6 actions:

```
Query using a data connection: OpenWorkbook
```

This action calls the **OpenWorkbook** web service operation to retrieve a session ID.

```
Set a field's value: sessionId = OpenWorkbookResult
```

where **sessionId** is located under the **SaveWorkbookCopy** group node under the **queryFields** group node in the **SaveWorkbookCopy** secondary data source and **OpenWorkbookResult** is located under the **OpenWorkbookResponse** group node under the **dataFields** group node in the **OpenWorkbook** secondary data source.

```
Set a field's value: workbookPath =
concat("http://servername/sitename/libraryname/", filename)
```

where **workbookPath** is located under the **SaveWorkbookCopy** group node under the **queryFields** group node in the **SaveWorkbookCopy** secondary data source, `http://servername/sitename/libraryname/` is the URL of the SharePoint document library where you want to save the new Excel workbook (this URL can point to a different SharePoint library on a different site than where the **BlankWorkbook.xlsx** Excel workbook is located), and **filename** is the field that is bound to the text box control on the form. The **concat()** function is used here to generate the full URL for the new Excel workbook.

```
Query using a data connection: SaveWorkbookCopy
```

This action calls the **SaveWorkbookCopy** web service operation to save a copy of the **BlankWorkbook.xlsx** Excel workbook in SharePoint.

```
Set a field's value: sessionId = OpenWorkbookResult
```

where **sessionId** is located under the **CloseWorkbook** group node under the **queryFields** group node in the **CloseWorkbook** secondary data source and **OpenWorkbookResult** is located under the **OpenWorkbookResponse** group node under the **dataFields** group node in the **OpenWorkbook** secondary data source.

```
Query using a data connection: CloseWorkbook
```

This action closes the workbook and the Excel Services session.

9. If your SharePoint environment is configured to use Claims Based authentication as opposed to Windows Classic authentication and the form is going to be filled out through the browser, you must set up UDC authentication for all of the data connections that make web service calls as described in *Configure a web service data connection for a web browser form* in the Appendix. But before you do this, test the form in InfoPath Filler 2013 to ensure that the functionality is working properly.
10. Publish the form template to a SharePoint form library.

In SharePoint, navigate to the form library where you published the form template and add a new form. When the form opens, enter a name (including the **.xlsx** file extension) for the new Excel workbook in the **filename** text box, and then click the **Create New Workbook** button. Navigate to the SharePoint document library where the new Excel workbook should have been created and verify that it is indeed present in the document library. If the InfoPath form is not working for you, see *Troubleshooting InfoPath with Excel Services* in the Appendix.

Discussion

In the solution described above, you saw how to use a browser-compatible form template to call Excel Services SOAP web service operations with which you can create a new Excel workbook in a SharePoint document library. You thereby copied an existing blank Excel workbook and saved it with a different name in either the same or a different SharePoint document library than where the original Excel workbook was located.

The sequence of Excel Services SOAP web service calls to create a new Excel workbook based on an existing Excel workbook was as follows:

1. Call **OpenWorkbook** to get an Excel Services session ID, which allowed you to open an existing Excel workbook.
2. Call **SaveWorkbookCopy** to copy the Excel workbook that was opened using **OpenWorkbook** and save it with a new name.
3. Call **CloseWorkbook** to close the workbook and end the Excel Services session.

While you added a normal button control to the view of the form template with an action rule to create the new Excel workbook in SharePoint, you could have also added a rule to the **Form Submit** event of the form to submit the form and create a new Excel workbook.

You could have also created a **SharePoint List** form template as described in recipe *113 Submit SharePoint list form values to a new Excel workbook* to create and save a new Excel workbook in SharePoint.

Note that an error will occur if a workbook that has the same name already exists in the document library, because you set the **saveOptions** of the **SaveWorkbookCopy** operation to **None** instead of **AllowOverwrite**.

112 Update an Excel workbook when submitting a form to SharePoint

Problem

You have an Excel workbook that is stored in a SharePoint document library and want to have the ability to update specific cells on worksheets within the workbook when an InfoPath form is submitted to a SharePoint form library.

Solution

You can call Excel Services SOAP web service operations from within an InfoPath form to perform updates in an Excel workbook that is stored in a SharePoint document library.

To update an Excel workbook when submitting an InfoPath form to SharePoint:

1. In Excel, create a new **Blank workbook** that contains the following two named ranges: **firstName** and **lastName**. Each named range should span only one cell, must have a scope of **Workbook**, and can be located on any worksheet in the Excel workbook.
2. Click **File** ➤ **Save As** ➤ **SharePoint** and then click **Browse** to publish the entire workbook with the name **Contacts.xlsx** to a document library (for example the **Documents** library) on the SharePoint site to which the InfoPath form will be connecting. Note that if the **File** ➤ **Save As** ➤ **SharePoint** command is not available, you can follow steps 2 through 5 of *Configure browser view options for an Excel workbook* in recipe *105 Publish an Excel workbook for use with InfoPath in SharePoint*.
3. In InfoPath, create a new SharePoint form library form template or use an existing one.
4. Add two **Text Box** controls to the view of the form template and name them **firstName** and **lastName**, respectively.
5. Click **Data** ➤ **Submit Form** ➤ **To SharePoint Library** and follow the instructions to add a data connection to submit the InfoPath form to a SharePoint form library (if you do not have an existing form library,

create one in SharePoint before adding the data connection to the InfoPath form template). Accept the default name for the data connection (**SharePoint Library Submit**) and leave the **Set as the default submit connection** check box selected. Also see recipe *34 Submit a form to a form library and then close it*.

6. Click **File** ➤ **Info** ➤ **Form Options** to open the **Form Options** dialog box, deselect the **Save** and **Save As** check boxes under the **Web Browser** category, and then click **OK**.
7. Add a **Receive** data connection for the **OpenWorkbookForEditing** operation of the Excel Services web service as described in recipe *107 Get the value of an Excel cell in InfoPath* and configure its parameters as follows:

Parameter	Value
tns:workbookPath	`http://servername/sitename/libraryname/Contacts.xlsx` where **servername** is the name of the SharePoint server, **sitename** is the name of the site, and **libraryname** is the name of the document library and Excel Services trusted file location where the **Contacts.xlsx** Excel workbook is located.
tns:uiCultureName	
tns:dataCultureName	

Leave the **Store a copy of the data in the form template** check box deselected, name the data connection **OpenWorkbookForEditing**, and deselect the **Automatically retrieve data when form is opened** check box. You will use this data connection to open the Excel workbook and get a session ID that you can use for all subsequent calls you make to Excel Services.

8. Add a **Receive** data connection for the **SetCellA1** operation of the Excel Services web service (also see recipe *108 Set the value of an Excel cell in InfoPath*). Leave all parameters as is, leave the **Store a copy of the data in the form template** check box deselected, name the data connection **SetCellA1**, and deselect the **Automatically retrieve data when form is opened** check box. You will use this data connection to set the values of the named ranges in the Excel workbook.
9. Add a **Receive** data connection for the **CloseWorkbook** operation of the Excel Services web service. Leave the **sessionId** parameter as is, leave the **Store a copy of the data in the form template** check box deselected, name the data connection **CloseWorkbook**, and deselect the **Automatically retrieve data when form is opened** check box. You will use this data connection to close the workbook and the Excel Services session. Note that at this stage the **sessionId** parameter is still blank, since you will set its value later through a rule.
10. Click **Data ➤ Submit Form ➤ Submit Options**.
11. On the **Submit Options** dialog box, select the **Perform custom action using Rules** option, and then click **OK**.
12. On the **Rules** task pane, there should already be one rule present for submitting the form to the SharePoint form library. Add a new **Action** rule and then move it up so that it is executed before the rule that was already present for submitting the form.
13. Add the following 11 actions to the new **Action** rule you just added:

```
Query using a data connection: OpenWorkbookForEditing
```

This action calls the **OpenWorkbookForEditing** web service operation to retrieve a session ID.

```
Set a field's value: sessionId = OpenWorkbookForEditingResult
```

where **sessionId** is located under the **SetCellA1** group node under the **queryFields** group node in the **SetCellA1** secondary data source and **OpenWorkbookForEditingResult** is located under the **OpenWorkbookForEditingResponse** group node under the **dataFields** group node in the **OpenWorkbookForEditing** secondary data source.

```
Set a field's value: sheetName = ""
```

where **sheetName** is located under the **SetCellA1** group node under the **queryFields** group node in the **SetCellA1** secondary data source. The worksheet name is set to be equal to an empty string, because you will be using named ranges, which can be located anywhere in the workbook (not on a specific worksheet) to submit data to the Excel workbook.

```
Set a field's value: rangeName = "firstName"
```

where **rangeName** is located under the **SetCellA1** group node under the **queryFields** group node in the **SetCellA1** secondary data source and **firstName** is a static piece of text representing the name of a named range in the Excel workbook.

```
Set a field's value: cellValue = firstName
```

where **cellValue** is located under the **SetCellA1** group node under the **queryFields** group node in the **SetCellA1** secondary data source and **firstName** is located in the Main data source.

```
Query using a data connection: SetCellA1
```

This action calls the **SetCellA1** web service operation to update the value of the **firstName** named range in the Excel workbook.

```
Set a field's value: rangeName = "lastName"
```

where **rangeName** is located under the **SetCellA1** group node under the **queryFields** group node in the **SetCellA1** secondary data source and **lastName** is a static piece of text representing the name of a named range in the Excel workbook.

```
Set a field's value: cellValue = lastName
```

where **cellValue** is located under the **SetCellA1** group node under the **queryFields** group node in the **SetCellA1** secondary data source and **lastName** is located in the Main data source.

```
Query using a data connection: SetCellA1
```

This action calls the **SetCellA1** web service operation to update the value of the **lastName** named range in the Excel workbook.

```
Set a field's value: sessionId = OpenWorkbookForEditingResult
```

where **sessionId** is located under the **CloseWorkbook** group node under the **queryFields** group node in the **CloseWorkbook** secondary data source and **OpenWorkbookForEditingResult** is located under the **OpenWorkbookForEditingResponse** group node under the **dataFields** group node in the **OpenWorkbookForEditing** secondary data source.

```
Query using a data connection: CloseWorkbook
```

This action closes the workbook and the Excel Services session.

14. If your SharePoint environment is configured to use Claims Based authentication as opposed to Windows Classic authentication and the form is going to be filled out through the browser, you must set up UDC authentication for all of the data connections that make web service calls as described in *Configure a web service data connection for a web browser form* in the Appendix. But before you do this, test the form in InfoPath Filler 2013 to ensure that the functionality is working properly.
15. Publish the form template to the form library you specified in the data connection in step 5.

In SharePoint, navigate to the form library where you published the form template and add a new form. When the form opens, enter values in all of the text boxes, and then click the **Submit** button on the Ribbon. Once you have submitted the form, navigate to the document library where the Excel workbook is stored, open the workbook, and verify that the data you submitted from within the InfoPath form was written to the named ranges in the Excel workbook. If the InfoPath form is not working for you, see *Troubleshooting InfoPath with Excel Services* in the Appendix.

Discussion

In the solution described above, you saw how to update cells that were defined with names in an Excel workbook with data from an InfoPath form when submitting the form to a SharePoint form library.

The sequence of Excel Services SOAP web service calls to update the values of cells in an Excel workbook with data from an InfoPath form when the form is submitted to a SharePoint form library is as follows:

1. Call **OpenWorkbookForEditing** to get an Excel Services session ID, which allows you to edit the Excel workbook.
2. Call **SetCell** or **SetCellA1** to edit the value of a cell in the Excel workbook. You can call these operations repeatedly for each cell you need to update in the workbook. Note that in the solution described above, the **sheetName** parameter of the **SetCellA1** web service operation was set to be equal to an empty string, because the named ranges in the Excel workbook were defined with a scope of **Workbook**, so they should automatically be found through their names and not a particular worksheet in the Excel workbook.
3. Call **CloseWorkbook** to save the changes made to the workbook, close the workbook, and end the Excel Services session.

When you use the **OpenWorkbookForEditing** web service operation to open an Excel workbook for editing, you generally do not need to explicitly call the **SaveWorkbook** operation to save the changes made to the workbook before calling the **CloseWorkbook** operation to close the workbook, since any changes made to the workbook should automatically and permanently be stored in the workbook when you close it. But if the changes you made are not being saved in the workbook, you may want to try adding the **SaveWorkbook** operation just before calling the **CloseWorkbook** operation to see whether the additional operation solves the issue.

While the Excel workbook and the SharePoint form library need not be on the same SharePoint site for the solution to work, if you place them on different SharePoint sites, you must ensure that users can access the InfoPath form and Excel workbook on both SharePoint sites.

Note that when Excel Services is updating a workbook, the workbook is locked for a period of time. If you are trying to open a workbook for editing and Excel tells you that you can only open a read-only copy, wait between 5 to 15 minutes for Excel Services to release the workbook if the workbook was just updated by Excel Services.

113 Submit SharePoint list form values to a new Excel workbook

Problem

You have a SharePoint list form which you want to use to create a new Excel workbook and then submit values from the form to the newly created Excel workbook.

Solution

You can call Excel Services SOAP web service operations from within a SharePoint list form to copy an existing blank Excel workbook, store a copy of it with a new name in a SharePoint document library, and then edit the newly created Excel workbook to contain values from the SharePoint list form.

To submit SharePoint list form values to a new Excel workbook:

1. In Excel, create a new **Blank workbook**, click **File ➤ Save As ➤ SharePoint**, and then click **Browse** to publish the entire workbook with the name **BlankWorkbook.xlsx** to a document library (for example the **Documents** library) on the SharePoint site to which the InfoPath form will be connecting. Note that if the **File ➤ Save As ➤ SharePoint** command is not available, you can follow steps 2 through 5 of *Configure browser view options for an Excel workbook* in recipe *105 Publish an Excel workbook for use with InfoPath in SharePoint*.
2. In SharePoint, create a new custom SharePoint list named **Employees** that has 4 columns with the data type **Single line of text** and the names **Title**, **FirstName**, **LastName**, and **ExcelFileName**, respectively.
3. Click **List ➤ Customize List ➤ Customize Form** to create a SharePoint list form and open it in InfoPath Designer 2013.
4. Add a **Receive** data connection for the **OpenWorkbook** operation of the Excel Services web service as described in recipe *107 Get the value of an Excel cell in InfoPath* and configure its parameters as follows:

Parameter	Value
tns:workbookPath	`http://servername/sitename/libraryname /BlankWorkbook.xlsx` where **servername** is the name of the SharePoint server, **sitename** is the name of the site, and **libraryname** is the name of the document library and Excel Services trusted file location where the **BlankWorkbook.xlsx** Excel workbook is located.
tns:uiCultureName	
tns:dataCultureName	

Leave the **Store a copy of the data in the form template** check box deselected, name the data connection **OpenWorkbook**, and deselect the **Automatically retrieve data when form is opened** check box. You will use this data connection to open the Excel workbook and get a session ID that you can use in subsequent calls you make to Excel Services.

5. Add a **Receive** data connection for the **SaveWorkbookCopy** operation of the Excel Services web service and configure its parameters as follows:

Parameter	Value
tns:sessionId	
tns:workbookPath	
tns:workbookType	FullWorkbook where **FullWorkbook** is one of three values

	you can select for the type of Excel workbook to create. Other possible values are **FullSnapshot** and **PublishedItemsSnapshot**.
tns:saveOptions	None where **None** is a static piece of text representing a save option. You could also use **AllowOverwrite** as a save option.

Leave the **Store a copy of the data in the form template** check box deselected, name the data connection **SaveWorkbookCopy**, and deselect the **Automatically retrieve data when form is opened** check box. Note that you left the **sessionId** and **workbookPath** parameters blank, since you will be using a rule to set them later. You will use this data connection to save a copy of the **BlankWorkbook.xlsx** Excel workbook.

6. Add a **Receive** data connection for the **CloseWorkbook** operation of the Excel Services web service. Leave the **sessionId** parameter as is, leave the **Store a copy of the data in the form template** check box deselected, name the data connection **CloseWorkbook**, and deselect the **Automatically retrieve data when form is opened** check box. You will use this data connection to close the Excel workbook and Excel Services session.
7. Add a **Receive** data connection for the **OpenWorkbookForEditing** operation of the Excel Services web service. Leave all parameters as is, leave the **Store a copy of the data in the form template** check box deselected, name the data connection **OpenWorkbookForEditing**, and deselect the **Automatically retrieve data when form is opened** check box. You will use this data connection to open the Excel workbook for editing and get a session ID that you can use in subsequent calls you make to Excel Services.
8. Add a **Receive** data connection for the **SetCellA1** operation of the Excel Services web service (also see recipe *108 Set the value of an Excel*

cell in InfoPath). Leave all parameters as is, leave the **Store a copy of the data in the form template** check box deselected, name the data connection **SetCellA1**, and deselect the **Automatically retrieve data when form is opened** check box. You will use this data connection to set the value of a cell in the Excel workbook.

9. Click **Data** ➤ **Submit Form** ➤ **Submit Options**.
10. On the **Submit Options** dialog box, select the **Perform custom action using Rules** option, and click **OK**.
11. On the **Fields** task pane, click **Show advanced view**. This is to make it easier for you to select fields when adding actions in the next step.
12. On the **Rules** task pane, one **Action** rule should already be present. This **Action** rule is used to save the item back to the SharePoint list, so leave the rule as is. Add a new **Action** rule with the following 18 actions:

```
Query using a data connection: OpenWorkbook
```

This action calls the **OpenWorkbook** web service operation to retrieve a session ID.

```
Set a field's value: sessionId = OpenWorkbookResult
```

where **sessionId** is located under the **SaveWorkbookCopy** group node under the **queryFields** group node in the **SaveWorkbookCopy** secondary data source and **OpenWorkbookResult** is located under the **OpenWorkbookResponse** group node under the **dataFields** group node in the **OpenWorkbook** secondary data source.

```
Set a field's value: workbookPath =
concat("http://servername/sitename/libraryname/",
ExcelFileName)
```

where **workbookPath** is located under the **SaveWorkbookCopy** group node under the **queryFields** group node in the **SaveWorkbookCopy** secondary data source and **ExcelFileName** is located under the **SharePointListItem_RW** group node under the **dataFields** group node in the Main data source. Note that you must replace **servername**, **sitename**, and **libraryname** in the formula with the correct values for your own scenario. The URL in the **concat()** function represents the location where the newly created Excel workbook should be stored. This location can be a different document library than where the original Excel workbook is located.

```
Query using a data connection: SaveWorkbookCopy
```

This action calls the **SaveWorkbookCopy** web service operation to save the workbook.

```
Set a field's value: sessionId = OpenWorkbookResult
```

where **sessionId** is located under the **CloseWorkbook** group node under the **queryFields** group node in the **CloseWorkbook** secondary data source and **OpenWorkbookResult** is located under the **OpenWorkbookResponse** group node under the **dataFields** group node in the **OpenWorkbook** secondary data source.

```
Query using a data connection: CloseWorkbook
```

This action closes the workbook and the Excel Services session.

```
Set a field's value: workbookPath =
concat("http://servername/sitename/libraryname/",
ExcelFileName)
```

where **workbookPath** is located under the **OpenWorkbookForEditing** group node under the **queryFields** group node in the **OpenWorkbookForEditing** secondary data source and **ExcelFileName** is located under the **SharePointListItem_RW** group node under the **dataFields** group node in the Main data source. Note that you must replace **servername**, **sitename**, and **libraryname** in the formula with the correct values for your own scenario. The URL in the **concat()** function represents the location where the newly created Excel workbook was stored.

```
Query using a data connection: OpenWorkbookForEditing
```

This action calls the **OpenWorkbookForEditing** web service operation to retrieve a session ID.

```
Set a field's value: sessionId = OpenWorkbookForEditingResult
```

where **sessionId** is located under the **SetCellA1** group node under the **queryFields** group node in the **SetCellA1** secondary data source and

OpenWorkbookForEditingResult is located under the **OpenWorkbookForEditingResponse** group node under the **dataFields** group node in the **OpenWorkbookForEditing** secondary data source.

```
Set a field's value: sheetName = "Sheet1"
```

where **sheetName** is located under the **SetCellA1** group node under the **queryFields** group node in the **SetCellA1** secondary data source and **Sheet1** is a static piece of text representing the worksheet in the Excel workbook where the cell that should be written to is located.

```
Set a field's value: rangeName = "A1"
```

where **rangeName** is located under the **SetCellA1** group node under the **queryFields** group node in the **SetCellA1** secondary data source and **A1** is a static piece of text representing the name of the cell that should receive data.

```
Set a field's value: cellValue = FirstName
```

where **cellValue** is located under the **SetCellA1** group node under the **queryFields** group node in the **SetCellA1** secondary data source and **FirstName** is located under the **SharePointListItem_RW** group node under the **dataFields** group node in the Main data source.

```
Query using a data connection: SetCellA1
```

This action sets the value of cell **A1** in the Excel workbook to be equal to the value of the **FirstName** text box on the InfoPath form.

```
Set a field's value: rangeName = "B1"
```

where **rangeName** is located under the **SetCellA1** group node under the **queryFields** group node in the **SetCellA1** secondary data source and **B1** is a static piece of text representing the name of the cell that should receive data.

```
Set a field's value: cellValue = LastName
```

where **cellValue** is located under the **SetCellA1** group node under the **queryFields** group node in the **SetCellA1** secondary data source and **LastName** is located under the **SharePointListItem_RW** group node under the **dataFields** group node in the Main data source.

```
Query using a data connection: SetCellA1
```

This action sets the value of cell **B1** in the Excel workbook to be equal to the value of the **LastName** text box on the InfoPath form.

```
Set a field's value: sessionId = OpenWorkbookForEditingResult
```

where **sessionId** is located under the **CloseWorkbook** group node under the **queryFields** group node in the **CloseWorkbook** secondary data source and **OpenWorkbookForEditingResult** is located under the **OpenWorkbookForEditingResponse** group node under the **dataFields** group node in the **OpenWorkbookForEditing** secondary data source.

```
Query using a data connection: CloseWorkbook
```

This action closes the workbook and the Excel Services session.

13. If your SharePoint environment is configured to use Claims Based authentication as opposed to Windows Classic authentication, you must set up UDC authentication for all of the data connections that make web service calls as described in *Configure a web service data connection for a web browser form* in the Appendix. But before you do this, test the form in InfoPath Filler 2013 to ensure that the functionality is working properly.
14. Publish the form template back to the SharePoint list.

In SharePoint, navigate to the **Employees** SharePoint list for which you customized its form and add a new item. When the form opens, enter values into the **Title**, **FirstName**, and **LastName** text boxes, enter a file name with file extension (for example **JaneDoe.xlsx**) in the **ExcelFileName** text box, and then click **Save**. The item should appear in the SharePoint list and a new Excel workbook should have been created. Navigate to the document library where the new Excel workbook should have been created, open the Excel workbook, and verify that the values from the SharePoint list form were written to and saved in the new Excel workbook. If the InfoPath form is not working for you, see *Troubleshooting InfoPath with Excel Services* in the Appendix.

Discussion

In the solution described above, you saw how to combine the techniques from recipe ***111 Use an InfoPath form to create a new Excel workbook in SharePoint*** and recipe ***112 Update an Excel workbook when submitting a form to SharePoint*** to call Excel Services SOAP web service operations to submit values that were entered into a SharePoint list form to an Excel workbook stored in a SharePoint document library. You thereby copied an existing blank Excel workbook, saved it with a different name in either the same or a different SharePoint document library than where the original Excel workbook was located, and then edited it afterwards to contain the values from the SharePoint list form.

While you used rules in the **Form Submit** event of the form to submit the form and create a new Excel workbook containing values from the form, you could have also added a normal button control to the view of the form template with an action rule to perform the same actions as the rule in the **Form Submit** event.

114 Add a form's URL as a link to an Excel workbook from within InfoPath

Problem

You have a few Excel workbooks stored in a SharePoint document library and you want to add a link of an existing InfoPath browser form to any one of those Excel workbooks by clicking on a button on the InfoPath form.

Solution

You can use the Excel Services SOAP web service to send a formula that makes use of the **HYPERLINK** function with the URL of an existing InfoPath form to an Excel workbook and then save the Excel workbook from within the InfoPath form.

To add the URL of a browser form as a link to an Excel workbook from within InfoPath:

1. In Excel, create a couple of workbooks, add a named range that spans one cell, that has a scope of **Workbook**, and that has the name **InfoPathLink** to each one of the workbooks.
2. In SharePoint, upload the Excel workbooks to a document library (for example the **Documents** library) on the site to which the InfoPath form will be connecting. Ensure that the **Title** properties of all of the workbooks contain the actual file name (including the file extension) of each workbook.
3. In InfoPath, create a new SharePoint form library form template or use an existing one.
4. Click **Data** ➤ **Get External Data** ➤ **From SharePoint List** and follow the instructions to add a data connection to the SharePoint document library that contains the Excel workbooks (also see recipe *54 Retrieve a list of forms from a form library*). Ensure that you select the **ID** and **Title** fields to be included in the data source, name the data connection **ExcelWorkbooks**, and leave the **Automatically retrieve data when form is opened** check box selected.
5. Add a **Drop-Down List Box** control to the view of the form template, name it **excelWorkbook**, and configure it to get its items from the **ExcelWorkbooks** secondary data source with the **Title** field configured for both its **Value** and **Display name** properties.
6. Publish the form template to a SharePoint form library.
7. Click **Data** ➤ **Get External Data** ➤ **From SharePoint List** and follow the instructions to add a data connection to the SharePoint form library to which you published the form template. Ensure that you select the **ID** and **Title** fields to be included in the data source, select the **Include data for the active form only** check box, name the data connection **CurrentFormData**, and leave the **Automatically retrieve data when form is opened** check box selected. You will use this data connection to retrieve the name of the current form when a user opens an existing form in the browser. This name will be used to construct the link that should be added to the Excel workbook the user selects from the drop-down list box.

8. Add a **Receive** data connection for the **OpenWorkbookForEditing** operation of the Excel Services web service as described in recipe *107 Get the value of an Excel cell in InfoPath*. Leave all of the parameters as is, leave the **Store a copy of the data in the form template** check box deselected, name the data connection **OpenWorkbookForEditing**, and deselect the **Automatically retrieve data when form is opened** check box. You will use this data connection to open an Excel workbook and get a session ID that you can use for all subsequent calls you make to Excel Services. Note that you will set the **workbookPath** parameter later through a rule, since the URL depends on the workbook that is selected from the drop-down list box.
9. Add a **Receive** data connection for the **SetCellA1** operation of the Excel Services web service. Leave all parameters as is, leave the **Store a copy of the data in the form template** check box deselected, name the data connection **SetCellA1**, and deselect the **Automatically retrieve data when form is opened** check box. You will use this data connection to set the value of a named range named **InfoPathLink** that should exist in the Excel workbooks that a user can select from the drop-down list box to be equal to the URL of the form that the user currently has open. You will use a rule later to set the values of the parameters for the **SetCellA1** operation before making the web service call.
10. Add a **Receive** data connection for the **CloseWorkbook** operation of the Excel Services web service. Leave the **sessionId** parameter as is, leave the **Store a copy of the data in the form template** check box deselected, name the data connection **CloseWorkbook**, and deselect the **Automatically retrieve data when form is opened** check box. You will use this data connection to close the Excel workbook and Excel Services session.
11. Add a **Button** control to the view of the form template and label it **Add Form Link**.
12. Add an **Action** rule to the **Add Form Link** button with the following 9 actions:

    ```
    Set a field's value: workbookPath =
    concat("http://servername/sitename/libraryname/",
    excelWorkbook)
    ```

    where **workbookPath** is located under the

OpenWorkbookForEditing group node under the **queryFields** group node in the **OpenWorkbookForEditing** secondary data source and **excelWorkbook** is the field in the Main data source that is bound to the drop-down list box containing the titles of Excel workbooks. Note that the **concat()** function is used to construct the full URL of an Excel workbook that is selected from the drop-down list box. You must replace **servername**, **sitename**, and **libraryname** with the correct values for the SharePoint document library where the Excel workbooks are located and which you chose in step 2.

```
Query using a data connection: OpenWorkbookForEditing
```

This action calls the **OpenWorkbookForEditing** web service operation to retrieve a session ID.

```
Set a field's value: sessionId = OpenWorkbookForEditingResult
```

where **sessionId** is located under the **SetCellA1** group node under the **queryFields** group node in the **SetCellA1** secondary data source and **OpenWorkbookForEditingResult** is located under the **OpenWorkbookForEditingResponse** group node under the **dataFields** group node in the **OpenWorkbookForEditing** secondary data source.

```
Set a field's value: sheetName = ""
```

where **sheetName** is located under the **SetCellA1** group node under the **queryFields** group node in the **SetCellA1** secondary data source. This will clear the value of the **sheetName** query field in the **SetCellA1** secondary data source. Because you defined a specific named range (**InfoPathLink**) with a scope of **Workbook** in each workbook and this named range could be located on any sheet in the workbook, you do not have to pass a worksheet name to Excel; the named range that was defined should automatically be found.

```
Set a field's value: rangeName = "InfoPathLink"
```

where **rangeName** is located under the **SetCellA1** group node under the **queryFields** group node in the **SetCellA1** secondary data source and **InfoPathLink** is a static piece of text representing the name of the cell on the worksheet in the Excel workbook that should receive data.

```
Set a field's value: cellValue = concat('=HYPERLINK("',
"http://servername/sitename/_layouts/15/FormServer.aspx?XmlLoca
tion=/sitename/libraryname/", Title, "&DefaultItemOpen=1", '",
"InfoPathForm"')
```

where **cellValue** is located under the **SetCellA1** group node under the **queryFields** group node in the **SetCellA1** secondary data source, and **Title** is the **Title** field under the **SharePointListItem_RW** repeating group node under the **dataFields** group node in the **CurrentFormData** secondary data source. Note that the **concat()** function is used to construct an Excel formula that makes use of the **HYPERLINK** function. The first argument passed to the **HYPERLINK** function is the URL of the form that is currently open and which is constructed using a browser form URL where **libraryname** is the SharePoint form library to which you published the form template in step 6 (you must replace **servername**, **sitename**, and **libraryname** with the correct values for your own scenario). The second argument passed to the **HYPERLINK** function is a static piece of text (**InfoPathForm**) representing the friendly name that the hyperlink should get in the Excel workbook. Note that in this case an entire formula is sent to Excel instead of a value that should be used in a formula.

```
Query using a data connection: SetCellA1
```

This action calls the **SetCellA1** web service operation to update the value of the **InfoPathLink** named range in the Excel workbook.

```
Set a field's value: sessionId = OpenWorkbookForEditingResult
```

where **sessionId** is located under the **CloseWorkbook** group node under the **queryFields** group node in the **CloseWorkbook** secondary data source and **OpenWorkbookForEditingResult** is located under the **OpenWorkbookForEditingResponse** group node under the **dataFields** group node in the **OpenWorkbookForEditing** secondary data source.

```
Query using a data connection: CloseWorkbook
```

This action closes the workbook and the Excel Services session.

13. Add a **Formatting** rule to the **Add Form Link** button with a condition that says:

```
Number of occurrences of SharePointListItem_RW = 0
```

and a formatting of **Disable this control**. Here **SharePointListItem_RW** is the repeating group node under the **dataFields** group node in the **CurrentFormData** secondary data source. You can construct the condition for the rule by using an expression such as the following:

```
count(xdXDocument:GetDOM("CurrentFormData")/dfs:myFields/dfs:da
taFields/d:SharePointListItem_RW) = 0
```

This formatting rule disables the button if the InfoPath form is a new form instead of an existing form.

14. Copy and paste the **Formatting** rule you just added onto the drop-down list box that contains the names of Excel workbooks.
15. If your SharePoint environment is configured to use Claims Based authentication as opposed to Windows Classic authentication and the form is going to be filled out through the browser, you must set up UDC authentication for all of the data connections that make web service calls as described in *Configure a web service data connection for a web browser form* in the Appendix.
16. Republish the form template to the same SharePoint form library you published it to in step 6.

In SharePoint, navigate to the form library where you published the form template and add a new form. When the form opens, the drop-down list box and button should be disabled. Save the form back to the form library, close it, and then reopen it. When the form opens, the drop-down list box and button should be enabled. Select an Excel workbook from the drop-down list box and click the **Add Form Link** button. Close the form. Navigate to the document library where the Excel workbook you added the form link to is located and open the workbook. Verify that it contains the link to the InfoPath form. Click on the link and verify that the form opens in the browser. If the InfoPath form is not working for you, see *Troubleshooting InfoPath with Excel Services* in the Appendix.

Discussion

In the solution described above, you used the **HYPERLINK** function in Excel and Excel Services SOAP web service operations to add a link for an existing InfoPath browser form to an Excel workbook.

In this case, you selected an existing Excel workbook from a list of workbooks to add a link to. However, you could have also first created a new Excel workbook as described in recipe ***111 Use an InfoPath form to create a new Excel workbook in SharePoint*** and then updated the newly created workbook to contain a link to the existing InfoPath browser form with which the Excel workbook was created. This way you can easily use an InfoPath form to create a new Excel workbook that contains a link back to the original InfoPath form that created it.

The **HYPERLINK** function creates a shortcut or jump that opens a document stored on a network server, an intranet, or the Internet. When you click the cell that contains the **HYPERLINK** function, Excel opens the file that is stored at the location specified by the first argument of the function.

Note that while you used the **SetCell** or **SetCellA1** in other recipes in this chapter to set the value of a cell in an Excel workbook that could then be used to perform a calculation using an Excel formula in another cell in the Excel workbook (see for example recipe ***108 Set the value of an Excel cell in InfoPath***), in this recipe you used the **SetCellA1** operation to directly set the value of a cell in an Excel workbook to be equal to an Excel formula.

```
Set a field's value: cellValue = concat('=HYPERLINK("',
"http://servername/sitename/_layouts/15/FormServer.aspx?XmlLocation
=/sitename/libraryname/", Title, "&DefaultItemOpen=1", '",
"InfoPathForm"')
```

115 Send a repeating table row to Excel

Problem

You have a repeating table on an InfoPath form and want to send data that is contained in fields of a specific row of the repeating table to an Excel workbook for storage.

Solution

You can use Excel Services SOAP web service operations to send data to an Excel workbook and then in the Excel workbook, use Excel formulas to retrieve and parse the data that was sent from a repeating table on an InfoPath form.

To send a repeating table row to Excel:

1. In Excel, create a new **Blank workbook**, and add a new worksheet named **Sheet2** to the workbook.
2. Select cells **A1**, **B1**, and **C1** on **Sheet1** and then add the following horizontal array formula to them:

   ```
   =MID(Sheet2!A1, VALUE(LEFT(MID(RIGHT(Sheet2!A1, 21), (COLUMN()
   - 1) * 7 + 1, 7),3)), VALUE(RIGHT(MID(RIGHT(Sheet2!A1, 21),
   (COLUMN() - 1) * 7 + 1, 7),3)))
   ```

   Note that you must press **Shift+Ctrl+Enter** after entering the formula to create an array formula. Once you have defined the array formula, select cells **A1**, **B1**, and **C1**, hover over the bottom-right corner of cell **C1** until the cursor becomes a cross, and then click and pull the cursor downwards to cover more rows. For example, the horizontal array formula should say:

   ```
   =MID(Sheet2!A2, VALUE(LEFT(MID(RIGHT(Sheet2!A2, 21), (COLUMN()
   - 1) * 7 + 1, 7),3)), VALUE(RIGHT(MID(RIGHT(Sheet2!A2, 21),
   (COLUMN() - 1) * 7 + 1, 7),3)))
   ```

   for cells **A2**, **B2**, and **C2**, and it should say:

   ```
   =MID(Sheet2!A3, VALUE(LEFT(MID(RIGHT(Sheet2!A3, 21), (COLUMN()
   - 1) * 7 + 1, 7),3)), VALUE(RIGHT(MID(RIGHT(Sheet2!A3, 21),
   (COLUMN() - 1) * 7 + 1, 7),3)))
   ```

for cells **A3**, **B3**, and **C3**, etc. As you can see, the value of the first argument of the **MID** function now depends on the row in which the horizontal array formula is located. For example, the horizontal array formula in the first row gets its value from cell **A1** on **Sheet2**, the horizontal array formula in the second row gets its value from cell **A2** on **Sheet2**, etc. You will be passing strings to cells **A1**, **A2**, **A3**, etc. on **Sheet2** from a repeating table on an InfoPath form and then the horizontal array formulas should parse the data and place them in columns **A**, **B**, and **C** of **Sheet1**.

3. Click **File** ➤ **Save As** ➤ **SharePoint** and then click **Browse** to publish the entire workbook with the name **SendRepeatingTableToExcel.xlsx** to a document library (for example the **Documents** library) on the SharePoint site to which the InfoPath form will be connecting. Note that if the **File** ➤ **Save As** ➤ **SharePoint** command is not available, you can follow steps 2 through 5 of *Configure browser view options for an Excel workbook* in recipe *105 Publish an Excel workbook for use with InfoPath in SharePoint*.
4. In InfoPath, create a new SharePoint form library form template or use an existing one.
5. Add a **Repeating Table** control with 4 columns to the view of the form template and name the fields within the repeating table **field1**, **field2**, **field3**, and **field4**, respectively.
6. Replace **field4** in the repeating table with a **Button** control and label the button **Send To Excel**. You can delete **field4** from the Main data source since you will not be using it.
7. Add a **Text Box** control to the view of the form template and name it **cellReference**. This text box will serve to enter a cell reference, for example **A1**, **A2**, **A3**, etc.
8. Add a **Receive** data connection for the **OpenWorkbookForEditing** operation of the Excel Services web service as described in recipe *107 Get the value of an Excel cell in InfoPath* and configure its parameters as follows:

Parameter	Value
tns:workbookPath	`http://servername/sitename/libraryname /SendRepeatingTableToExcel.xlsx` where **servername** is the name of the SharePoint server, **sitename** is the name of the site, and **libraryname** is the name of the document library and Excel Services trusted file location where the **SendRepeatingTableToExcel.xlsx** Excel workbook is located.
tns:uiCultureName	
tns:dataCultureName	

Leave the **Store a copy of the data in the form template** check box deselected, name the data connection **OpenWorkbookForEditing**, and deselect the **Automatically retrieve data when form is opened** check box. You will use this data connection to open the Excel workbook and get a session ID that you can use for all subsequent calls you make to Excel Services.

9. Add a **Receive** data connection for the **SetCellA1** operation of the Excel Services web service (also see recipe *108 Set the value of an Excel cell in InfoPath*). Leave all parameters as is, leave the **Store a copy of the data in the form template** check box deselected, name the data connection **SetCellA1**, and deselect the **Automatically retrieve data when form is opened** check box. You will use this data connection to send the values from a row of the repeating table to a cell in the Excel workbook. You will use a rule later to set the values of the parameters of the **SetCellA1** operation before making the web service call.
10. Add a **Receive** data connection for the **CloseWorkbook** operation of the Excel Services web service. Leave the **sessionId** parameter as is, leave the **Store a copy of the data in the form template** check box deselected, name the data connection **CloseWorkbook**, and deselect

the **Automatically retrieve data when form is opened** check box. You will use this data connection to close the Excel workbook and Excel Services session.

11. Add an **Action** rule to the **Send To Excel** button in the repeating table with the following 8 actions:

```
Query using a data connection: OpenWorkbookForEditing
```

This action calls the **OpenWorkbookForEditing** web service operation to retrieve a session ID.

```
Set a field's value: sessionId = OpenWorkbookForEditingResult
```

where **sessionId** is located under the **SetCellA1** group node under the **queryFields** group node in the **SetCellA1** secondary data source and **OpenWorkbookForEditingResult** is located under the **OpenWorkbookForEditingResponse** group node under the **dataFields** group node in the **OpenWorkbookForEditing** secondary data source.

```
Set a field's value: sheetName = "Sheet2"
```

where **sheetName** is located under the **SetCellA1** group node under the **queryFields** group node in the **SetCellA1** secondary data source and **Sheet2** is a static piece of text representing the worksheet in the Excel workbook where the data is stored. In this case, the data of a repeating table row should be sent to a cell in column **A** of **Sheet2** in the Excel workbook.

```
Set a field's value: rangeName = cellReference
```

where **rangeName** is located under the **SetCellA1** group node under the **queryFields** group node in the **SetCellA1** secondary data source and **cellReference** is located in the Main data source of the form.

```
Set a field's value: cellValue = concat(field1, field2, field3,
concat("001.", substring(concat("000", string-length(field1)),
string-length(concat("000", string-length(field1))) - 2, 3)),
concat(substring(concat("000", string-length(field1) + 1),
string-length(concat("000", string-length(field1) + 1)) - 2,
3), ".", substring(concat("000", string-length(field2)),
string-length(concat("000", string-length(field2))) - 2, 3)),
concat(substring(concat("000", string-length(field1) + string-
```

```
length(field2) + 1), string-length(concat("000", string-
length(field1) + string-length(field2) + 1)) - 2, 3), ".",
substring(concat("000", string-length(field3)), string-
length(concat("000", string-length(field3))) - 2, 3)))
```

where **cellValue** is located under the **SetCellA1** group node under the **queryFields** group node in the **SetCellA1** secondary data source and the formula is used to concatenate the values of **field1**, **field2**, and **field3** that are located in the repeating table row with their starting positions and lengths appended at the end of the string. For example, if the repeating table contains the values "1" in **field1**, "test 1" in **field2**, and "test 2" in **field3**, the string resulting from the formula would be "1test 1test 2001.001002.006008.006" where the last 21 characters of the string represent the starting position and length of each one of the 3 strings in the concatenated string. For example **002.006** means starting position 2 with a length of 6 characters. Such a string is fairly easy to parse in Excel.

```
Query using a data connection: SetCellA1
```

This action calls the **SetCellA1** web service operation to send the concatenated string for the repeating table row to a cell in the Excel workbook.

```
Set a field's value: sessionId = OpenWorkbookForEditingResult
```

where **sessionId** is located under the **CloseWorkbook** group node under the **queryFields** group node in the **CloseWorkbook** secondary data source and **OpenWorkbookForEditingResult** is located under the **OpenWorkbookForEditingResponse** group node under the **dataFields** group node in the **OpenWorkbookForEditing** secondary data source.

```
Query using a data connection: CloseWorkbook
```

This action closes the workbook and the Excel Services session.

12. If your SharePoint environment is configured to use Claims Based authentication as opposed to Windows Classic authentication and the form is going to be filled out through the browser, you must set up UDC authentication for all of the data connections that make web service calls as described in *Configure a web service data connection for a* *web browser form* in the Appendix. But before you do this, test the form in InfoPath Filler 2013 to ensure that the functionality is working properly.

13. Publish the form template to a SharePoint form library.

In SharePoint, navigate to the form library where you published the form template and add a new form. When the form opens, enter the name of a cell in the Excel workbook to which you want to send data (for example **A1**) in the **cellReference** text box. Add a row to the repeating table, fill its fields with data, and then click the **Send To Excel** button in the same row. Enter the name of another cell (for example **A2**) in the **cellReference** text box. Add another row to the repeating table, fill its fields with data, and then click the **Send To Excel** button in the same row. Navigate to the document library that contains the **SendRepeatingTableToExcel.xlsx** Excel workbook, open the workbook, and verify that the workbook contains the data sent from the repeating table rows and that the formulas correctly parsed and stored the data in the different columns of **Sheet1**. If the InfoPath form is not working for you, see *Troubleshooting InfoPath with Excel Services* in the Appendix.

Discussion

In the solution described above, you used a combination of string concatenation in InfoPath and string parsing in Excel to send values from a particular row in a repeating table on an InfoPath form to a particular cell in an Excel workbook. You thereby used the **COLUMN** function to parse a string passed from InfoPath and place the extracted values in a row of the Excel workbook through a horizontal array formula. In addition, you added the starting position and length of the value of each field in the repeating table row at the end of the concatenated string to make it easier to parse the data in Excel. The formula in InfoPath used a combination of the **concat()**, **substring()**, and **string-length()** functions to generate a concatenated string.

Note that instead of opening an Excel Services session, saving the workbook, and closing the workbook and Excel Services session every time a button in the repeating table is clicked, you could also for example:

1. Call **OpenWorkbookForEditing** to open the Excel Services session when the form loads.
2. Call **SetCellA1** when the button in a repeating table row is clicked.
3. Provide a separate button that calls **CloseWorkbook** to save the changes made to the workbook, close the workbook, and close the Excel Services session. Another option is to call **CloseWorkbook** when you submit the form.

When you use the **OpenWorkbookForEditing** web service operation to open an Excel workbook for editing, you generally do not need to explicitly call the **SaveWorkbook** operation to save the changes made to the workbook before calling the **CloseWorkbook** operation to close the workbook, since any changes made to the workbook should automatically and permanently be stored in the workbook when you close it. But if the changes you made are not being saved in the workbook, you may want to try adding the **SaveWorkbook** operation just before calling the **CloseWorkbook** operation to see whether the additional operation solves the issue.

Note that all cells for which no value can be calculated will be filled with the **#VALUE!** error value. You can replace this error value with a blank value by checking for errors using the **IF** and **ISERROR** functions as follows:

```
IF(ISERROR([original formula goes here]), "", [original formula
goes here])
```

where you must replace **[original formula goes here]** with the Excel formulas from step 2. For example, the formula for cells **A1**, **B1**, and **C1** on **Sheet1** in the Excel workbook would then become:

```
=IF(ISERROR(MID(Sheet2!A1, VALUE(LEFT(MID(RIGHT(Sheet2!A1, 21),
(COLUMN() - 1) * 7 + 1, 7),3)), VALUE(RIGHT(MID(RIGHT(Sheet2!A1,
21), (COLUMN() - 1) * 7 + 1, 7),3)))), "", MID(Sheet2!A1,
VALUE(LEFT(MID(RIGHT(Sheet2!A1, 21), (COLUMN() - 1) * 7 + 1,
7),3)), VALUE(RIGHT(MID(RIGHT(Sheet2!A1, 21), (COLUMN() - 1) * 7 +
1, 7),3))))
```

116 Send an entire repeating table to Excel

Problem

You have a repeating table on an InfoPath form and want to send the data that is contained in rows and columns of the repeating table to an Excel workbook that is stored in SharePoint.

Solution

You can use Excel Services SOAP web service operations to send data to an Excel workbook and then in the Excel workbook, use an array formula to parse the data that was sent from a repeating table on an InfoPath form and place that data in cells in the Excel workbook.

To send an entire repeating table to Excel:

1. In Excel, create a new **Blank workbook**, and add a new worksheet named **Sheet2** to the workbook.
2. Repeating table data is going to be sent to cells **A1**, **B1**, and **C1** on **Sheet2** in the Excel workbook. These cells expect to receive data in the following format:

   ```
   Value 1Value 2Value 3001.007008.007015.007003
   ```

   This data represents a row in the repeating table, where **Value 1** is the value of the first cell, **Value 2** that of the second cell, and **Value 3** that of the third cell. **001.007** indicates that the first value starts at position 1 and is 7 characters long. **008.007** indicates that the second value starts at position 8 and is 7 characters long. **015.007** indicates that the third value starts at position 15 and is 7 characters long. **003** at the end of the string indicates that there are 3 values in the string.

   Add the following vertical array formula to cells **A1** through **A10** on **Sheet1**:

   ```
   =MID(Sheet2!A1, LEFT(MID(MID(Sheet2!A1, LEN(Sheet2!A1) - 3 -
   VALUE(RIGHT(Sheet2!A1, 3))*7 + 1, VALUE(RIGHT(Sheet2!A1,
   3))*7), (ROW()-1)*7+1, 7), 3), RIGHT(MID(MID(Sheet2!A1,
   LEN(Sheet2!A1) - 3 - VALUE(RIGHT(Sheet2!A1, 3))*7 + 1,
   VALUE(RIGHT(Sheet2!A1, 3))*7), (ROW()-1)*7+1, 7), 3))
   ```

Note that you must select cells **A1** through **A10**, enter the formula, and then press **Shift+Ctrl+Enter** to create the array formula. Cells **A1** through **A10** on **Sheet1** will contain all of the values from the rows in the first column of the repeating table on the InfoPath form.

Add the following vertical array formula to cells **B1** through **B10** on **Sheet1**:

```
=MID(Sheet2!B1, LEFT(MID(MID(Sheet2!B1, LEN(Sheet2!B1) - 3 -
VALUE(RIGHT(Sheet2!B1, 3))*7 + 1, VALUE(RIGHT(Sheet2!B1,
3))*7), (ROW()-1)*7+1, 7), 3), RIGHT(MID(MID(Sheet2!B1,
LEN(Sheet2!B1) - 3 - VALUE(RIGHT(Sheet2!B1, 3))*7 + 1,
VALUE(RIGHT(Sheet2!B1, 3))*7), (ROW()-1)*7+1, 7), 3))
```

Note that you must select cells **B1** through **B10**, enter the formula, and then press **Shift+Ctrl+Enter** to create the array formula. Cells **B1** through **B10** on **Sheet1** will contain all of the values from the rows in the second column of the repeating table on the InfoPath form.

Add the following vertical array formula to cells **C1** through **C10** on **Sheet1**:

```
=MID(Sheet2!C1, LEFT(MID(MID(Sheet2!C1, LEN(Sheet2!C1) - 3 -
VALUE(RIGHT(Sheet2!C1, 3))*7 + 1, VALUE(RIGHT(Sheet2!C1,
3))*7), (ROW()-1)*7+1, 7), 3), RIGHT(MID(MID(Sheet2!C1,
LEN(Sheet2!C1) - 3 - VALUE(RIGHT(Sheet2!C1, 3))*7 + 1,
VALUE(RIGHT(Sheet2!C1, 3))*7), (ROW()-1)*7+1, 7), 3))
```

Note that you must select cells **C1** through **C10**, enter the formula, and then press **Shift+Ctrl+Enter** to create the array formula. Cells **C1** through **C10** on **Sheet1** will contain all of the values from the rows in the third column of the repeating table on the InfoPath form.

3. Click **File ➤ Save As ➤ SharePoint** and then click **Browse** to publish the entire workbook with the name **ParseRepeatingTable.xlsx** to a document library (for example the **Documents** library) on the SharePoint site to which the InfoPath form will be connecting. Note that if the **File ➤ Save As ➤ SharePoint** command is not available, you can follow steps 2 through 5 of *Configure browser view options for an Excel workbook* in recipe *105 Publish an Excel workbook for use with InfoPath in SharePoint*.

4. In InfoPath, create a new SharePoint form library form template or use an existing one.
5. Add a **Repeating Table** control with 3 columns to the view of the form template and name the fields within the repeating table **field1**, **field2**, and **field3**, respectively.
6. Add a **Button** control to the view of the form template and label it **Send To Excel**.
7. Add a **Receive** data connection for the **OpenWorkbookForEditing** operation of the Excel Services web service as described in recipe *107 Get the value of an Excel cell in InfoPath* and configure its parameters as follows:

Parameter	Value
tns:workbookPath	`http://servername/sitename/libraryname/ParseRepeatingTable.xlsx` where **servername** is the name of the SharePoint server, **sitename** is the name of the site, and **libraryname** is the name of the document library and Excel Services trusted file location where the **ParseRepeatingTable.xlsx** Excel workbook is located.
tns:uiCultureName	
tns:dataCultureName	

Leave the **Store a copy of the data in the form template** check box deselected, name the data connection **OpenWorkbookForEditing**, and deselect the **Automatically retrieve data when form is opened** check box. You will use this data connection to open the Excel workbook and get a session ID that you can use for all subsequent calls you make to Excel Services.

8. Add a **Receive** data connection for the **SetCellA1** operation of the Excel Services web service (also see recipe *108 Set the value of an Excel cell in InfoPath*). Leave all parameters as is, leave the **Store a copy of the data in the form template** check box deselected, name the data connection **SetCellA1**, and deselect the **Automatically retrieve data when form is opened** check box. You will use this data connection to set the values of cells **A1**, **B1**, and **C1** on **Sheet2** in the Excel workbook to be equal to the concatenated values from the repeating table on the InfoPath form. You will use a rule later to set the values of the parameters of the **SetCellA1** operation before making the web service call.

9. Add a **Receive** data connection for the **CloseWorkbook** operation of the Excel Services web service. Leave the **sessionId** parameter as is, leave the **Store a copy of the data in the form template** check box deselected, name the data connection **CloseWorkbook**, and deselect the **Automatically retrieve data when form is opened** check box. You will use this data connection to close the Excel workbook and Excel Services session.

10. Add an **Action** rule to the **Send To Excel** button with the following 14 actions:

```
Query using a data connection: OpenWorkbookForEditing
```

This action calls the **OpenWorkbookForEditing** web service operation to retrieve a session ID.

```
Set a field's value: sessionId = OpenWorkbookForEditingResult
```

where **sessionId** is located under the **SetCellA1** group node under the **queryFields** group node in the **SetCellA1** secondary data source and **OpenWorkbookForEditingResult** is located under the **OpenWorkbookForEditingResponse** group node under the **dataFields** group node in the **OpenWorkbookForEditing** secondary data source.

```
Set a field's value: sheetName = "Sheet2"
```

where **sheetName** is located under the **SetCellA1** group node under the **queryFields** group node in the **SetCellA1** secondary data source and **Sheet2** is a static piece of text representing the name of the worksheet in the Excel workbook where the original data from the repeating table is stored.

```
Set a field's value: rangeName = "A1"
```

where **rangeName** is located under the **SetCellA1** group node under the **queryFields** group node in the **SetCellA1** secondary data source and **A1** is a static piece of text representing the name of the cell on the worksheet in the Excel workbook that should receive data.

```
Set a field's value: cellValue = concat(eval(eval(group2,
"my:field1"), ".."), eval(eval(group2,
'concat(substring(concat("000",
sum(xdMath:Eval(preceding::my:field1, "string-length(.)")) +
1), string-length(concat("000",
sum(xdMath:Eval(preceding::my:field1, "string-length(.)")) +
1)) - 2, 3), ".", substring(concat("000", string-
length(my:field1)), string-length(concat("000", string-
length(my:field1))) - 2, 3))'), ".."), substring(concat("000",
count(group2)), string-length(concat("000", count(group2))) -
2, 3))
```

where you must enter the following formula on the **Insert Formula** dialog box:

```
concat(xdMath:Eval(xdMath:Eval(my:group1/my:group2,
"my:field1"), ".."),
xdMath:Eval(xdMath:Eval(my:group1/my:group2,
'concat(substring(concat("000",
sum(xdMath:Eval(preceding::my:field1, "string-length(.)")) +
1), string-length(concat("000",
sum(xdMath:Eval(preceding::my:field1, "string-length(.)")) +
1)) - 2, 3), ".", substring(concat("000", string-
length(my:field1)), string-length(concat("000", string-
length(my:field1))) - 2, 3))'), ".."), substring(concat("000",
count(my:group1/my:group2)), string-length(concat("000",
count(my:group1/my:group2))) - 2, 3))
```

Here, **cellValue** is located under the **SetCellA1** group node under the **queryFields** group node in the **SetCellA1** secondary data source. The basic idea of the formula is to loop through all of the **field1** fields in the rows of the repeating table using the **eval()** function and concatenate them using the **concat()** function to form a string such as for example "First sentenceSecond sentenceLast sentence001.014015.015030.013003", which can then be parsed in the Excel workbook.

```
Query using a data connection: SetCellA1
```

This action calls the **SetCellA1** web service operation to update the value of cell **A1** on **Sheet2** in the Excel workbook.

```
Set a field's value: rangeName = "B1"
```

where **rangeName** is located under the **SetCellA1** group node under the **queryFields** group node in the **SetCellA1** secondary data source and **B1** is a static piece of text representing the name of the cell on the worksheet in the Excel workbook that should receive data.

```
Set a field's value: cellValue = concat(eval(eval(group2,
"my:field2"), ".."), eval(eval(group2,
'concat(substring(concat("000",
sum(xdMath:Eval(preceding::my:field2, "string-length(.)")) +
1), string-length(concat("000",
sum(xdMath:Eval(preceding::my:field2, "string-length(.)")) +
1)) - 2, 3), ".", substring(concat("000", string-
length(my:field2)), string-length(concat("000", string-
length(my:field2))) - 2, 3))'), ".."), substring(concat("000",
count(group2)), string-length(concat("000", count(group2))) -
2, 3))
```

where you must enter the following formula on the **Insert Formula** dialog box:

```
concat(xdMath:Eval(xdMath:Eval(my:group1/my:group2,
"my:field2"), ".."),
xdMath:Eval(xdMath:Eval(my:group1/my:group2,
'concat(substring(concat("000",
sum(xdMath:Eval(preceding::my:field2, "string-length(.)")) +
1), string-length(concat("000",
sum(xdMath:Eval(preceding::my:field2, "string-length(.)")) +
1)) - 2, 3), ".", substring(concat("000", string-
length(my:field2)), string-length(concat("000", string-
length(my:field2))) - 2, 3))'), ".."), substring(concat("000",
count(my:group1/my:group2)), string-length(concat("000",
count(my:group1/my:group2))) - 2, 3))
```

Here, **cellValue** is located under the **SetCellA1** group node under the **queryFields** group node in the **SetCellA1** secondary data source and the formula concatenates values from all of the **field2** fields in the repeating table.

```
Query using a data connection: SetCellA1
```

This action calls the **SetCellA1** web service operation to update the value of cell **B1** on **Sheet2** in the Excel workbook.

```
Set a field's value: rangeName = "C1"
```

where **rangeName** is located under the **SetCellA1** group node under the **queryFields** group node in the **SetCellA1** secondary data source and **C1** is a static piece of text representing the name of the cell on the worksheet in the Excel workbook that should receive data.

```
Set a field's value: cellValue = concat(eval(eval(group2,
"my:field3"), ".."), eval(eval(group2,
'concat(substring(concat("000",
sum(xdMath:Eval(preceding::my:field3, "string-length(.)")) +
1), string-length(concat("000",
sum(xdMath:Eval(preceding::my:field3, "string-length(.)")) +
1)) - 2, 3), ".", substring(concat("000", string-
length(my:field3)), string-length(concat("000", string-
length(my:field3))) - 2, 3))'), ".."), substring(concat("000",
count(group2)), string-length(concat("000", count(group2))) -
2, 3))
```

where you must enter the following formula on the **Insert Formula** dialog box:

```
concat(xdMath:Eval(xdMath:Eval(my:group1/my:group2,
"my:field3"), ".."),
xdMath:Eval(xdMath:Eval(my:group1/my:group2,
'concat(substring(concat("000",
sum(xdMath:Eval(preceding::my:field3, "string-length(.)")) +
1), string-length(concat("000",
sum(xdMath:Eval(preceding::my:field3, "string-length(.)")) +
1)) - 2, 3), ".", substring(concat("000", string-
length(my:field3)), string-length(concat("000", string-
length(my:field3))) - 2, 3))'), ".."), substring(concat("000",
count(my:group1/my:group2)), string-length(concat("000",
count(my:group1/my:group2))) - 2, 3))
```

Here, **cellValue** is located under the **SetCellA1** group node under the **queryFields** group node in the **SetCellA1** secondary data source and the formula concatenates values from all of the **field3** fields in the repeating table.

```
Query using a data connection: SetCellA1
```

This action calls the **SetCellA1** web service operation to update the value of cell **C1** on **Sheet2** in the Excel workbook.

```
Set a field's value: sessionId = OpenWorkbookForEditingResult
```

where **sessionId** is located under the **CloseWorkbook** group node under the **queryFields** group node in the **CloseWorkbook** secondary data source and **OpenWorkbookForEditingResult** is located under the **OpenWorkbookForEditingResponse** group node under the **dataFields** group node in the **OpenWorkbookForEditing** secondary data source.

```
Query using a data connection: CloseWorkbook
```

This action closes the workbook and the Excel Services session.

11. If your SharePoint environment is configured to use Claims Based authentication as opposed to Windows Classic authentication and the form is going to be filled out through the browser, you must set up UDC authentication for all of the data connections that make web service calls as described in *Configure a web service data connection for a web browser form* in the Appendix. But before you do this, test the form in InfoPath Filler 2013 to ensure that the functionality is working properly.
12. Publish the form template to a SharePoint form library.

In SharePoint, navigate to the form library where you published the form template and add a new form. Add a couple of rows to the repeating table, fill out the fields, and then click the **Send To Excel** button. Close the form and then navigate to the SharePoint document library where the **ParseRepeatingTable.xlsx** Excel workbook is located. Open the Excel workbook and verify that cells contain the data from the repeating table. Note: It may take a little while before the values are written to the workbook, so wait a few minutes before opening the Excel workbook. If the InfoPath form is not working for you, see *Troubleshooting InfoPath with Excel Services* in the Appendix.

Discussion

In the solution described above, you saw how to use Excel Services SOAP web service operations to send the data from columns in a repeating table to separate cells in an Excel workbook, which then used vertical array formulas to parse and extract the data from the repeating table.

Note that all cells for which no value can be calculated will be filled with the **#VALUE!** error value. You can replace this error value with a blank value by checking for errors using the **IF** and **ISERROR** functions as follows:

```
IF(ISERROR([original formula goes here]), "", [original formula
goes here])
```

where you must replace **[original formula goes here]** with the Excel formulas from step 2. For example, the formula for column **A** on **Sheet1** in the Excel workbook would then become:

```
=IF(ISERROR(MID(Sheet2!A1,LEFT(MID(MID(Sheet2!A1,LEN(Sheet2!A1)-3-
VALUE(RIGHT(Sheet2!A1,3))*7+1,VALUE(RIGHT(Sheet2!A1,3))*7),(ROW()-
1)*7+1,7),3),RIGHT(MID(MID(Sheet2!A1,LEN(Sheet2!A1)-3-
VALUE(RIGHT(Sheet2!A1,3))*7+1,VALUE(RIGHT(Sheet2!A1,3))*7),(ROW()-
1)*7+1,7),3))), "",
MID(Sheet2!A1,LEFT(MID(MID(Sheet2!A1,LEN(Sheet2!A1)-3-
VALUE(RIGHT(Sheet2!A1,3))*7+1,VALUE(RIGHT(Sheet2!A1,3))*7),(ROW()-
1)*7+1,7),3),RIGHT(MID(MID(Sheet2!A1,LEN(Sheet2!A1)-3-
VALUE(RIGHT(Sheet2!A1,3))*7+1,VALUE(RIGHT(Sheet2!A1,3))*7),(ROW()-
1)*7+1,7),3)))
```

117 Add a new row to an Excel table from within InfoPath

Problem

You have a table in an Excel workbook to which you would like to add a new row from within an InfoPath form.

Solution

You can use Excel Services SOAP web service operations to retrieve the total amount of rows in a table in an Excel workbook, calculate a new row number to use, and then use this row number to add a new row to the Excel table from within an InfoPath form.

Suppose you have an Excel workbook named **Fruits.xlsx** as described in recipe *103 Export data from Excel to SharePoint for display in InfoPath*.

To add a new row to an Excel table from within an InfoPath form:

1. In Excel, open the **Fruits.xlsx** Excel workbook, select all of the cells that contain data, and then select **Home ➤ Styles ➤ Format as Table** to convert the data into a table. Ensure that you select the **My table has headers** check box on the **Format As Table** dialog box if your table contains a header row and enter **Fruits** in the **Table Name** text box under the **Properties** group on the **Design** tab on the Ribbon.
2. Add a new worksheet named **RowCount** to the Excel workbook and then add the following formula to cell **A1** on the **RowCount** worksheet:

   ```
   =ROWS(Fruits)
   ```

   This formula returns the amount of rows in the **Fruits** table.
3. Click **File ➤ Save As ➤ SharePoint** and then click **Browse** to publish the entire workbook with the name **Fruits.xlsx** to a document library (for example the **Documents** library) on the SharePoint site to which the InfoPath form will be connecting. Note that if the **File ➤ Save As ➤ SharePoint** command is not available, you can follow steps 2 through 5 of *Configure browser view options for an Excel workbook* in recipe *105 Publish an Excel workbook for use with InfoPath in SharePoint*.
4. In InfoPath, create a new SharePoint form library form template or use an existing one.
5. Add two **Text Box** controls to the view of the form template and name them **fruitName** and **fruitColor**, respectively. You will use these text boxes to set the values of the fruit's name and color in the new row of the Excel table.
6. Add a **Button** control to the view of the form template and label it **Add New Row**.
7. Add a **Receive** data connection for the **OpenWorkbookForEditing** operation of the Excel Services web service as described in recipe *107 Get the value of an Excel cell in InfoPath* and configure its parameters as follows:

Parameter	Value
tns:workbookPath	`http://servername/sitename/libraryname/Fruits.xlsx` where **servername** is the name of the SharePoint server, **sitename** is the name of the site, and **libraryname** is the name of the document library and Excel Services trusted file location where the **Fruits.xlsx** Excel workbook is located.
tns:uiCultureName	
tns:dataCultureName	

Leave the **Store a copy of the data in the form template** check box deselected, name the data connection **OpenWorkbookForEditing**, and deselect the **Automatically retrieve data when form is opened** check box. You will use this data connection to open the Excel workbook and get a session ID that you can use for all subsequent calls you make to Excel Services.

8. Add a **Receive** data connection for the **GetCellA1** operation of the Excel Services web service and configure its parameters as follows:

Parameter	Value
tns:sessionId	
tns:sheetName	RowCount where **RowCount** is the name of the worksheet in the **Fruits.xlsx** Excel workbook that has a **ROWS** formula defined on it.

tns:rangeName	A1 where **A1** is the name of the cell that contains the result of the **ROWS** formula on the **RowCount** worksheet in the **Fruits.xlsx** Excel workbook.
tns:formatted	false

Leave the **Store a copy of the data in the form template** check box deselected, name the data connection **GetCellA1**, and deselect the **Automatically retrieve data when form is opened** check box. You will use this data connection to get the result of the **ROWS** calculation in the Excel workbook. Note that at this stage the **sessionId** parameter is still blank, since you will set its value later through a rule.

9. Add a **Receive** data connection for the **SetCell** operation of the Excel Services web service (also see recipe *108 Set the value of an Excel cell in InfoPath*). Leave all parameters as is, leave the **Store a copy of the data in the form template** check box deselected, name the data connection **SetCell**, and deselect the **Automatically retrieve data when form is opened** check box. You will use this data connection to set a value in the new Excel table row. At this point, the fields in the **SetCell** secondary data source are still blank; you will use a rule later to set their values before making the web service call.
10. Add a **Receive** data connection for the **CloseWorkbook** operation of the Excel Services web service. Leave the **sessionId** parameter as is, leave the **Store a copy of the data in the form template** check box deselected, name the data connection **CloseWorkbook**, and deselect the **Automatically retrieve data when form is opened** check box. You will use this data connection to close the Excel workbook and Excel Services session.
11. Add an **Action** rule to the **Add New Row** button with the following 14 actions:

```
Query using a data connection: OpenWorkbookForEditing
```

This action calls the **OpenWorkbookForEditing** web service operation to retrieve a session ID.

```
Set a field's value: sessionId = OpenWorkbookForEditingResult
```

where **sessionId** is located under the **GetCellA1** group node under the **queryFields** group node in the **GetCellA1** secondary data source and **OpenWorkbookForEditingResult** is located under the **OpenWorkbookForEditingResponse** group node under the **dataFields** group node in the **OpenWorkbookForEditing** secondary data source.

```
Query using a data connection: GetCellA1
```

This action calls the **GetCellA1** web service operation to retrieve the result of the **ROWS** calculation.

```
Set a field's value: sessionId = OpenWorkbookForEditingResult
```

where **sessionId** is located under the **SetCell** group node under the **queryFields** group node in the **SetCell** secondary data source and **OpenWorkbookForEditingResult** is located under the **OpenWorkbookForEditingResponse** group node under the **dataFields** group node in the **OpenWorkbookForEditing** secondary data source.

```
Set a field's value: sheetName = "Sheet1"
```

where **sheetName** is located under the **SetCell** group node under the **queryFields** group node in the **SetCell** secondary data source and **Sheet1** is a static piece of text representing the name of the worksheet in the Excel workbook where the table is located. Note that you could also provide an extra field on the form so that the value of the name of the worksheet can be dynamically changed by users at runtime.

```
Set a field's value: row = GetCellA1Result + 2 - 1
```

where **row** is located under the **SetCell** group node under the **queryFields** group node in the **SetCell** secondary data source and **GetCellA1Result** is located under the **GetCellA1Response** group node under the **dataFields** group node in the **GetCellA1** secondary data source. A **2** is added to the value of **GetCellA1Result**, because the table rows start at row number **2** on the **Sheet1** worksheet. And a **1** is subtracted to apply a correction to get the correct row number to use when calling the **SetCell** operation (also see the discussion section for more information). Note that you can also use a formula such as **GetCellA1Result + 1** instead of **GetCellA1Result + 2 – 1**. The **2 – 1** is kept here to make it clear which row number the table starts at (row number **2**), since you can also replace the **2** with a field in a secondary data source for a second web service call that can be used to dynamically retrieve the number of the first row of a table using the **ROW** function (see the discussion section for more information).

```
Set a field's value: column = 0
```

where **column** is located under the **SetCell** group node under the **queryFields** group node in the **SetCell** secondary data source and **0** is a number representing the first column of the worksheet, so the first field in the Excel table row.

```
Set a field's value: cellValue = fruitName
```

where **cellValue** is located under the **SetCell** group node under the **queryFields** group node in the **SetCell** secondary data source and **fruitName** is located in the Main data source of the form.

```
Query using a data connection: SetCell
```

This action calls the **SetCell** web service operation to set the value of the first field in a new row in the table in the Excel workbook.

```
Set a field's value: column = 1
```

where **column** is located under the **SetCell** group node under the **queryFields** group node in the **SetCell** secondary data source and **1** is a number representing the second column of the worksheet, so the second field in the Excel table row.

```
Set a field's value: cellValue = fruitColor
```

where **cellValue** is located under the **SetCell** group node under the **queryFields** group node in the **SetCell** secondary data source and **fruitColor** is located in the Main data source of the form.

```
Query using a data connection: SetCell
```

This action calls the **SetCell** web service operation to set the value of the second field in a new row in the table in the Excel workbook.

```
Set a field's value: sessionId = OpenWorkbookForEditingResult
```

where **sessionId** is located under the **CloseWorkbook** group node under the **queryFields** group node in the **CloseWorkbook** secondary data source and **OpenWorkbookForEditingResult** is located under the **OpenWorkbookForEditingResponse** group node under the **dataFields** group node in the **OpenWorkbookForEditing** secondary data source.

```
Query using a data connection: CloseWorkbook
```

This action closes the workbook and the Excel Services session.

12. If your SharePoint environment is configured to use Claims Based authentication as opposed to Windows Classic authentication and the form is going to be filled out through the browser, you must set up UDC authentication for all of the data connections that make web service calls as described in *Configure a web service data connection for a web browser form* in the Appendix. But before you do this, test the form in InfoPath Filler 2013 to ensure that the functionality is working properly.
13. Publish the form template to a SharePoint form library.

In SharePoint, navigate to the form library where you published the form template and add a new form. Enter data in the **fruitName** and **fruitColor** text boxes, and then click the **Add New Row** button. Repeat the process to add a second fruit. Close the form. Navigate to the SharePoint document library where the Excel workbook that contains the table is located. Open the Excel workbook and verify that the table contains two new records. If the InfoPath form is not working for you, see *Troubleshooting InfoPath with Excel Services* in the Appendix.

Discussion

In the solution described above, you used the Excel Services SOAP web service to be able to first determine the row number that should be used to add a new row to a table in an Excel workbook, and then submit data to the table. You thereby used the **ROWS** function in an Excel workbook to retrieve the amount of rows contained in a table in the Excel workbook. The **ROWS** function in Excel returns the number of rows in a reference or array.

You also made an assumption that the records in the Excel table started at row number **2**. If you want to dynamically determine which row number an Excel table starts at, you can use the **ROW** function to do so. For example **ROW(Fruits)** would return **2** as its value. You can add this formula to a cell on the **RowCount** worksheet in the Excel workbook and retrieve the calculated value dynamically through Excel Services just like you retrieved the total amount of rows (**ROWS(Fruits)**) in the Excel table. You would then have to change the **Set a field's value** action in step 11 from

```
Set a field's value: row = GetCellA1Result + 2 - 1
```

to

```
Set a field's value: row = GetCellA1Result + GetCellA1Result - 1
```

where the first **GetCellA1Result** refers to the total amount of rows from the **GetCellA1** secondary data source and the second **GetCellA1Result** refers to the starting row number from the second secondary data source you would have to add to dynamically retrieve the starting row number of the Excel table using the **ROW** function.

And if you wanted to do the same for the columns, you could have to use **COLUMN(Fruits)** to determine the column number the Excel table starts at and **COLUMNS(Fruits)** to determine how many columns the Excel table spans.

The **ROW** function returns the row number of a reference, the **ROWS** function returns the number of rows in a reference or array, the **COLUMN** function returns the column number of a reference, and the **COLUMNS** function returns the number of columns in a reference or array.

Because it is much easier to work with row and column numbers instead of cell names such as **A1**, **B2**, etc. when adding rows to an Excel table, the solution described above used the **SetCell** operation instead of the

SetCellA1 operation to set the value of a cell in the Excel table. The only thing you have to remember is that **SetCell** starts its row and column numbers at **0** (so the row and column numbers for cell **A1** would be equal to **0** and **0**, respectively), while an Excel worksheet starts counting at **1** (so the row and column numbers for cell **A1** are equal to **1** and **1**, respectively). This means that you must apply a correction of **-1** when using the **SetCell** operation.

For example, if the row numbers for an Excel table on a worksheet start at **2** and there are **20** rows in the table, the new row number would be **22** (2 + 20), but because row numbers start at **0** when using the **SetCell** operation, the new row number to use with the **SetCell** operation would be **21** (22 - 1).

118 Sequentially navigate through rows of an Excel table

Problem

You have an Excel workbook that contains a table. You want to sequentially navigate through the rows that are present in the table from within an InfoPath form.

Solution

You can use Excel Services SOAP web service operations to retrieve data from a specific row and column in an Excel table and return this data to an InfoPath form for display while using a counter to navigate forward and backward through the table records.

To sequentially navigate through rows of an Excel table from within an InfoPath form:

1. Follow steps 1 through 4 of recipe *117 Add a new row to an Excel table from within InfoPath*.
2. In InfoPath, add a **Receive** data connection for the **OpenWorkbook** operation of the Excel Services web service as described in recipe *107 Get the value of an Excel cell in InfoPath* and configure its parameters as

follows:

Parameter	Value
tns:workbookPath	`http://servername/sitename/libraryname/Fruits.xlsx` where **servername** is the name of the SharePoint server, **sitename** is the name of the site, and **libraryname** is the name of the document library and Excel Services trusted file location where the **Fruits.xlsx** Excel workbook is located.
tns:uiCultureName	
tns:dataCultureName	

Leave the **Store a copy of the data in the form template** check box deselected, name the data connection **OpenWorkbook**, and deselect the **Automatically retrieve data when form is opened** check box. You will use this data connection to open the Excel workbook and get a session ID that you can use for all subsequent calls you make to Excel Services.

3. Add a **Receive** data connection for the **GetCell** operation of the Excel Services web service. Leave all parameters as is, leave the **Store a copy of the data in the form template** check box deselected, name the data connection **GetCell**, and deselect the **Automatically retrieve data when form is opened** check box. You will use this data connection to retrieve values from the Excel workbook.
4. Add a **Receive** data connection for the **CloseWorkbook** operation of the Excel Services web service. Leave the **sessionId** parameter as is, leave the **Store a copy of the data in the form template** check box deselected, name the data connection **CloseWorkbook**, and deselect the **Automatically retrieve data when form is opened** check box.

You will use this data connection to close the Excel workbook and Excel Services session.

5. Add two **Text Box** controls to the view of the form template and name them **fruitName** and **fruitColor**, respectively.
6. On the **Fields** task pane, add a **Field (element)** with the name **pos**, the data type **Whole Number (integer)**, and a default value equal to **1** to the Main data source.
7. On the **Fields** task pane, add another **Field (element)** with the name **amountOfRows**, the data type **Whole Number (integer)**, and a default value equal to **0** to the Main data source.
8. Add two **Button** controls to the view of the form template and label them **Previous** and **Next**, respectively.
9. Add a **Formatting** rule to the **Previous** button with a **Condition** that says:

   ```
   pos = 1
   ```

   and a formatting of **Disable this control**. This formatting rule disables the **Previous** button if the value of the **pos** field is pointing to the first record in the Excel table.
10. Add a **Formatting** rule to the **Next** button with a **Condition** that says:

    ```
    pos ≥ amountOfRows
    ```

    and a formatting of **Disable this control**. Here **amountOfRows** is located in the Main data source. This formatting rule disables the **Next** button if the value of the **pos** field is greater than or equal to the amount of records in the Excel table.
11. Add an **Action** rule to the **Next** button with the following 17 actions:

    ```
    Set a field's value: pos = pos + 1
    ```

    This action increases the value of the **pos** field in the Main data source by **1**.

    ```
    Query using a data connection: OpenWorkbook
    ```

    This action calls the **OpenWorkbook** web service operation to retrieve a session ID.

```
Set a field's value: sessionId = OpenWorkbookResult
```

where **sessionId** is located under the **GetCell** group node under the **queryFields** group node in the **GetCell** secondary data source and **OpenWorkbookResult** is located under the **OpenWorkbookResponse** group node under the **dataFields** group node in the **OpenWorkbook** secondary data source.

```
Set a field's value: sheetName = "RowCount"
```

where **sheetName** is located under the **GetCell** group node under the **queryFields** group node in the **GetCell** secondary data source and **RowCount** is a static piece of text representing the worksheet on which the **ROWS** formula is located.

```
Set a field's value: row = 0
```

where **row** is located under the **GetCell** group node under the **queryFields** group node in the **GetCell** secondary data source and **0** represents the row number for cell **A1** in the Excel workbook.

```
Set a field's value: column = 0
```

where **column** is located under the **GetCell** group node under the **queryFields** group node in the **GetCell** secondary data source and **0** represents the column number for cell **A1** in the Excel workbook.

```
Query using a data connection: GetCell
```

This action calls the **GetCell** web service operation to retrieve the value of cell **A1** on the **RowCount** worksheet in the Excel workbook.

```
Set a field's value: amountOfRows = GetCellResult
```

where **amountOfRows** is located in the Main data source and **GetCellResult** is located under the **GetCellResponse** group node under the **dataFields** group node in the **GetCell** secondary data source.

```
Set a field's value: sheetName = "Sheet1"
```

where **sheetName** is located under the **GetCell** group node under the **queryFields** group node in the **GetCell** secondary data source and

Sheet1 is a static piece of text representing the worksheet on which the Excel table is located.

```
Set a field's value: row = pos
```

where **row** is located under the **GetCell** group node under the **queryFields** group node in the **GetCell** secondary data source and **pos** is located in the Main data source.

```
Query using a data connection: GetCell
```

This action calls the **GetCell** web service operation to retrieve the value of the cell that is located in the first column and in the row specified by the value of **pos** on the **Sheet1** worksheet in the Excel workbook.

```
Set a field's value: fruitName = GetCellResult
```

where **fruitName** is located in the Main data source and **GetCellResult** is located under the **GetCellResponse** group node under the **dataFields** group node in the **GetCell** secondary data source.

```
Set a field's value: column = 1
```

where **column** is located under the **GetCell** group node under the **queryFields** group node in the **GetCell** secondary data source and **1** represents the column number for the second column in the Excel workbook.

```
Query using a data connection: GetCell
```

This action calls the **GetCell** web service operation to retrieve the value of the cell that is located in the second column and in the row specified by the value of **pos** on the **Sheet1** worksheet in the Excel workbook.

```
Set a field's value: fruitColor = GetCellResult
```

where **fruitColor** is located in the Main data source and **GetCellResult** is located under the **GetCellResponse** group node under the **dataFields** group node in the **GetCell** secondary data source.

```
Set a field's value: sessionId = OpenWorkbookResult
```

where **sessionId** is located under the **CloseWorkbook** group node under the **queryFields** group node in the **CloseWorkbook** secondary data source and **OpenWorkbookResult** is located under the **OpenWorkbookResponse** group node under the **dataFields** group node in the **OpenWorkbook** secondary data source.

```
Query using a data connection: CloseWorkbook
```

This action closes the workbook and the Excel Services session.

12. On the **Rules** task pane, copy the **Action** rule from the **Next** button, paste it onto the **Previous** button, and then change the first action of the newly pasted rule on the **Previous** button to say:

```
Set a field's value: pos = pos - 1
```

This action decreases the value of the **pos** field in the Main data source by **1**.

13. Click **Data ➤ Rules ➤ Form Load** to switch to the **Rules** task pane for the **Form Load** event, and then click **Paste Rule** to paste the rule you copied earlier from the **Next** button. Delete the first action (`Set a field's value: pos = pos + 1`) of the newly pasted rule, since the **pos** field has a default value equal to **1** set on it, and if a form has been previously saved, the **pos** field should have a value when the form is reopened.
14. If your SharePoint environment is configured to use Claims Based authentication as opposed to Windows Classic authentication and the form is going to be filled out through the browser, you must set up UDC authentication for all of the data connections that make web service calls as described in *Configure a web service data connection for a web browser form* in the Appendix. But before you do this, test the form in InfoPath Filler 2013 to ensure that the functionality is working properly.
15. Publish the form template to a SharePoint form library.

In SharePoint, navigate to the form library where you published the form template and add a new form. When the form opens, the first record from the Excel table should appear. Click the **Next** and **Previous** buttons to navigate through the records. When you reach the last record, the **Next** button should be disabled, and when you navigate back to the first record, the **Previous** button should be disabled. If the InfoPath form is not working for you, see *Troubleshooting InfoPath with Excel Services* in the Appendix.

Discussion

In the solution described above, you saw how to use Excel Services SOAP web service operations to sequentially navigate through data that was stored in a table in an Excel workbook.

While you could have also used the **GetCellA1** operation instead of the **GetCell** operation, the **GetCell** operation makes it easier to pass data to and retrieve data from the Excel workbook using a counter (the value of the **pos** field in this case) that represents a specific number for a row. Had you used the **GetCellA1** operation, then you would have had to construct the name of the cell that should be retrieved.

Because the amount of requests a user is allowed to make via an InfoPath browser form is capped by default, too many clicks while navigating back and forth through Excel data may cause InfoPath Forms Services to eventually raise an error. Therefore, it is recommended that you find a way to reduce the amount of requests made by not continuously opening and closing the workbook with each click of a button, or provide the user with a way to search the data instead of sequentially navigate through it.

Chapter 8: Use Access with InfoPath via SharePoint

SharePoint 2013 offers several ways to integrate InfoPath 2013 with Access 2013, a couple of which include:

- Moving Access data to a SharePoint list and then creating a data connection to that SharePoint list in InfoPath.
- Using a SharePoint list form to maintain data in an Access database table.
- Using a SharePoint list form to maintain data and then exporting the SharePoint list data to Access for reporting purposes.

The recipes in this chapter are meant to provide ideas for solutions that combine InfoPath forms with Access database tables through SharePoint.

119 Display Access data in an InfoPath browser form

Problem

You have an Access database table which you want to be able to use in an InfoPath browser form to display data in a repeating table, but InfoPath does not allow you to directly connect to an Access database table from an InfoPath browser form. You get an error message saying that

The selected database is not supported in Web browser forms. Select a Microsoft SQL Server database.

when you try to connect to an Access database from an InfoPath browser-compatible form template.

Solution

You can publish the Access database table to a SharePoint list and then use a SharePoint list data connection in InfoPath to be able to read data from the Access table bound to the SharePoint list.

To display data from an Access database table in an InfoPath browser form:

1. In Access 2013, create a new **Blank desktop database** that contains a table named **Fruits** with data that has the same structure and data as the Excel spreadsheet from recipe *103 Export data from Excel to SharePoint for display in InfoPath*. When you create the table, leave the **ID** column intact as an **AutoNumber** column.
2. Click **Database Tools ➤ Move Data ➤ SharePoint**.

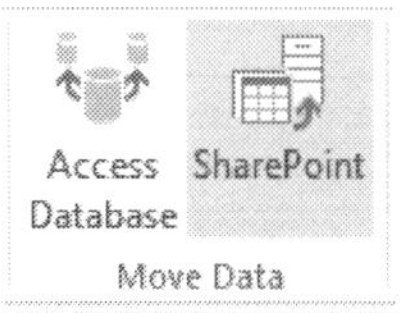

Figure 346. The Move Data group on the Database Tools tab in Access 2013.

3. On the **Export Tables to SharePoint Wizard**, enter the URL of the SharePoint site to which you want to export the table (or select the URL from the list if you have already previously connected to the site), and click **Next**.

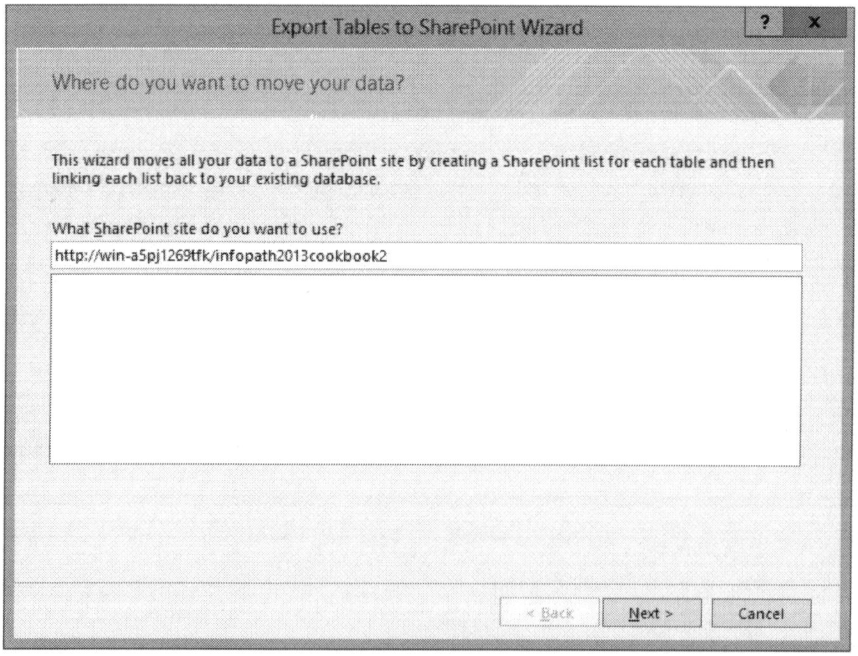

Figure 347. The Export Tables to SharePoint Wizard in Access 2013.

After this, Access should back up the database by creating a copy of the original database, connect to SharePoint to create the SharePoint list, and convert the existing table into a linked table in the database.

4. On the **Export Tables to SharePoint Wizard**, click **Finish**.
5. In SharePoint, navigate to the site to which you exported the Access database table, click **Site Contents**, and then under **Lists, Libraries, and other Apps**, verify that the SharePoint list was created for the Access database table.
6. In InfoPath, create a new SharePoint form library form template or use an existing one.
7. Add a **Receive** data connection to the SharePoint list that you created for the Access database table as described in *Use a SharePoint list data connection* in recipe *43 2 Ways to retrieve data from a SharePoint list*. Ensure that you select **FruitName** and **FruitColor** as fields to be included in the data source, and that you leave the **Automatically retrieve data when form is opened** check box selected.
8. Bind the secondary data source for the SharePoint list to a repeating table on the view of the form template as described in recipe *44 Display SharePoint list data in a repeating table*.
9. Add a **Button** control to the view of the form template and change its **Action** property to **Refresh**.
10. Publish the form template to a SharePoint form library.

In SharePoint, navigate to the form library where you published the form template and add a new form. When the form opens, the repeating table should contain the same rows that are present in the Access database table. Open the database in Access and add a new row to the table. Then go back to the form, and click the **Refresh** button. The row you just added in Access should appear in the repeating table.

Discussion

In the solution described above, you connected an InfoPath browser form to an Access database table through SharePoint. You also used the **Refresh** button action to refresh the data in the secondary data source for the SharePoint list.

The **Export Tables to SharePoint Wizard** in Access 2013 allows you to move data to SharePoint lists and maintain a "live link" with this data. The latter means that you can update the data locally in the Access database and have those changes automatically reflected in the SharePoint list. You can use this method to centralize and make data from an Access database available over the network using SharePoint as the solution above demonstrates.

Because direct connections to Access databases from within an InfoPath browser-compatible form template are not supported, whether you want to have read-only access or read/write access, you can only connect to SQL Server databases from within an InfoPath browser-compatible form template. Therefore, the solution described above is a workaround for connecting InfoPath browser forms to Access databases by going through SharePoint.

120 Maintain Access data through an InfoPath browser form

Problem

You have an Access database table which you want to connect to from an InfoPath browser form to add, edit, and delete records in it, but InfoPath does not allow you to connect to an Access database table from an InfoPath browser form. You get an error message saying that

The selected database is not supported in Web browser forms. Select a Microsoft SQL Server database.

when you try to connect to an Access database from an InfoPath browser-compatible form template.

Solution

You can create a SharePoint list form that has been enabled for editing multiple list items to be able to add, edit, and delete records in an Access database table from within an InfoPath browser form.

To perform create, update, and delete (CRUD) operations on an Access database table using an InfoPath browser form:

1. In Access 2013, follow steps 1 through 4 of recipe *119 Display Access data in an InfoPath browser form*.
2. In InfoPath, create a new SharePoint list form for the SharePoint list to which you exported the Access database table and enable it to manage multiple list items as described in recipe *3 Create a SharePoint list form to manage multiple list items*.
3. On the view of the form template, right-click the **Repeating Section** that InfoPath automatically added, and select **Repeating Section Properties** from the context menu that appears.
4. On the **Repeating Section Properties** dialog box on the **Data** tab, select the **Allow users to insert and delete the sections** check box, select the **Show insert button and hint text** check box, and then click **OK**.

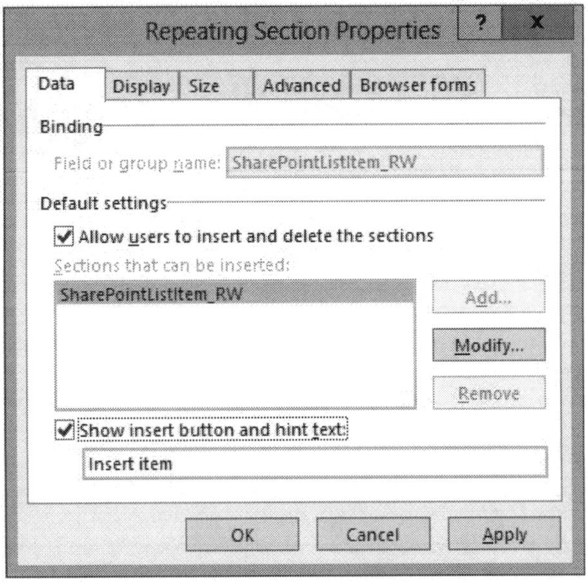

Figure 348. Setting the repeating table to allow insertion and deletion of sections.

5. Delete the **Title** and **_OldID** rows from the table within the repeating section control on the view. **_OldID** contains the value of the **ID** field from the Access database table, while **Title** is a SharePoint field that you are not required to fill out.

6. Add a **Button** control to the view of the form template, and change its **Action** property to **Run Query**.
7. Publish the form template back to the SharePoint list.

In SharePoint, navigate to the SharePoint list that is connected to the Access database table and add a new item. When the form opens, click the **Run Query** button to retrieve all of the items from the SharePoint list. Click **Insert item** to insert a new section. Enter some values, and then click **Save** on the Ribbon. Note that you can delete items from the SharePoint list by deleting the sections for those items and then saving your changes. Verify that the new item was added to the SharePoint list. Open the Access database table and verify that the changes you made were written back to the database.

Discussion

In the solution described above you learned how to create an InfoPath browser form with which you could manage all of the records in an Access database table through a SharePoint list form.

Because a SharePoint list form displays only one section to enter or modify a list item when you add or edit a list item, you must either add a **Run Query** button to the form or add a **Query for data** action rule that runs for example during the **Form Load** event to query the **Main Data Connection**, so that all of the list items are retrieved whenever the form opens.

While this and the previous recipe showed you how to export only one Access database table to SharePoint, you could export multiple tables including the relationships between those tables in order to create linked lists in SharePoint, and then customize the SharePoint list forms for those lists to simulate master/detail functionality across SharePoint lists (see recipe *14 Master/detail with two linked SharePoint lists*).

You could also go in the opposite direction (from SharePoint to Access) and use an InfoPath form to maintain data in a SharePoint list and then export that SharePoint list to Access by using the **Open with Access** command on the Ribbon (**List ➤ Connect & Export ➤ Open with**

Access) in order to use Access to create reports based on the data in the SharePoint list.

When you create a SharePoint form library form template and publish it to a SharePoint form library, it becomes a bit more difficult to export data from InfoPath forms to create a report in Access, since the **Open with Access** command is not available on SharePoint form libraries. One workaround would be to use the **Export to Excel** command instead and then import the Excel data in Access to create a report. However, you must promote fields from the InfoPath form to the SharePoint form library as columns to be able to export the values of the InfoPath form fields to an Excel file (see recipe *104 Export data from forms in a form library to Excel*) and then use that data for reporting purposes in Access.

121 Import data from an InfoPath form into Access database tables

Problem

You have an InfoPath form, which you want to import into an Access database and split its data for storage in one or more tables.

Solution

You can use the **Import & Link** functionality in Access 2013 for an XML file together with an XSL stylesheet to import InfoPath form data into several tables in an Access database.

To import data from an InfoPath form into Access database tables:

1. In InfoPath, create a new SharePoint form library form template or use an existing one.
2. Add two **Text Box** controls named **customerNo** and **lastName**, respectively, to the view of the form template.
3. Add a **Repeating Table** control with 3 columns to the view of the form template, and rename the fields in the repeating table to **street**, **city**, and **country**, respectively. In addition, rename the **group1** group node to **addresses**, and the **group2** repeating group node to **address**.

4. Publish the form template to a SharePoint form library.
5. In SharePoint, navigate to the form library where you published the form template and add a new form. When the form opens, fill it out with some data by entering a customer name, a customer number, and two addresses for the customer in the repeating table. Save the form back to the form library. Download a copy of the form and name the downloaded XML file **form01.xml**. You are going to import data from this InfoPath form into an Access database.
6. In Access 2013, create a new **Blank desktop database**.
7. Add a table named **Customer** that has the following fields:

Field Name	Data Type
ID	AutoNumber (Primary Key)
CustomerNo	Short Text
LastName	Short Text

8. Add a table named **Address** that has the following fields:

Field Name	Data Type
ID	AutoNumber (Primary Key)
Street	Short Text
City	Short Text
Country	Short Text
CustomerNo	Short Text

9. In Notepad, create a new XSL file named **ImportInfoPathForm.xsl** that has the following contents:

```
<?xml version="1.0" encoding="UTF-8" standalone="yes"?>
<xsl:stylesheet
xmlns:xsl="http://www.w3.org/1999/XSL/Transform" version="1.0"
xmlns:my="http://schemas.microsoft.com/office/infopath/2003/myX
SD/2014-05-25T23:53:01">
<xsl:output method="xml"/>
  <xsl:template match="/">
    <dataroot>
      <Customer>
        <CustomerNo>
          <xsl:value-of select="/my:myFields/my:customerNo"/>
        </CustomerNo>
        <LastName>
          <xsl:value-of select="/my:myFields/my:lastName"/>
        </LastName>
      </Customer>
      <xsl:for-each select=
        "/my:myFields/my:addresses/my:address">
        <Address>
          <Street><xsl:value-of select="my:street"/></Street>
          <City><xsl:value-of select="my:city"/></City>
          <Country>
            <xsl:value-of select="my:country"/>
          </Country>
          <CustomerNo>
            <xsl:value-of select="/my:myFields/my:customerNo"/>
          </CustomerNo>
        </Address>
      </xsl:for-each>
    </dataroot>
  </xsl:template>
</xsl:stylesheet>
```

where you must replace the value of the **my** namespace prefix with the correct value used by the InfoPath form that will be imported into Access. For this you must open the **form01.xml** file in Notepad, search for the declaration of the **my** namespace (`xmlns:my="..."`), copy it, and then replace it in the XSL file. Note that the transformed XML will contain a root element named **dataroot** that contains two elements (**Customer** and **Address**) that have the same names and structure as the tables in the Access database.

10. In Access 2013, click **External Data ➤ Import & Link ➤ XML File**.
11. On the **Get External Data - XML File** dialog box, click **Browse**, browse to and select the **form01.xml** file, and then click **OK**.

12. On the **Import XML** dialog box, select the **Append Data to Existing Table(s)** option, and then click **Transform**.

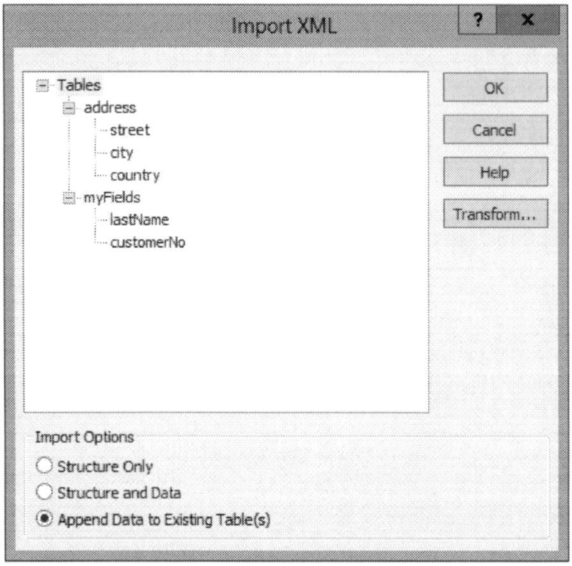

Figure 349. The Import XML dialog box in Access 2013 before selecting an XSL file.

13. On the **Import Transforms** dialog box, click **Add**, and then browse to and select the **ImportInfoPathForm.xsl** file you created earlier.

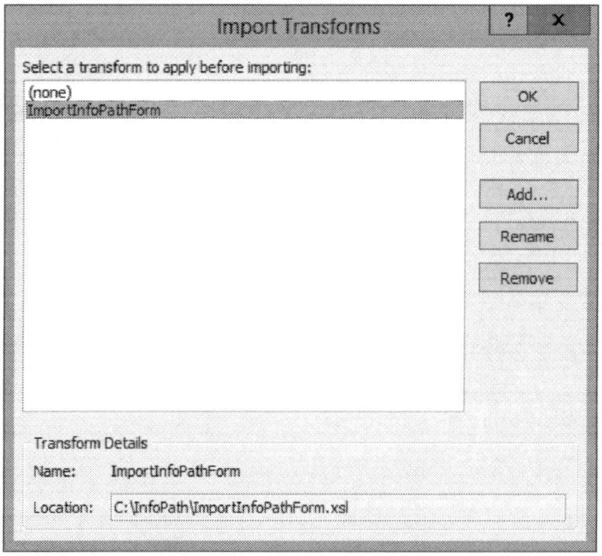

Figure 350. The Import Transforms dialog box in Access 2013.

14. On the **Import Transforms** dialog box, ensure that **ImportInfoPathForm** has been selected in the list box, and click **OK**.
15. On the **Import XML** dialog box, click **OK**.

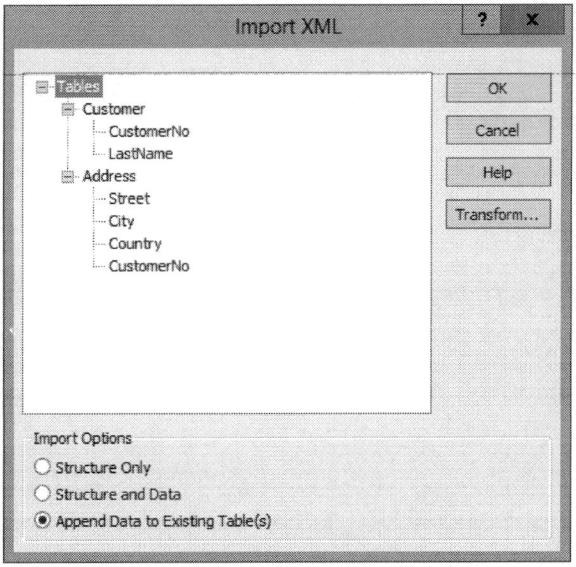

Figure 351. The Import XML dialog box in Access 2013 after selecting the XSL file.

16. On the **Get External Data - XML File** dialog box, click **Close**.

In Access 2013, open the tables and verify that the data from the InfoPath form was correctly imported. If you do not see the newly imported data and you had the tables open before you imported the data, close and reopen the tables or click **Home ➤ Records ➤ Refresh All** to see whether the data was imported.

Note: After you have imported the data, you could assign the **CustomerNo** field to be the primary key of the **Customer** table, and then add a relationship that links the **CustomerNo** field in the **Customer** table to the **CustomerNo** field in the **Address** table.

Discussion

In the solution described above, you imported data from an InfoPath form, which is an XML file, into two tables in an Access database. Access can import XML files that have the following structure:

```
<dataroot>
  <TableName>
    <Field1Name>Value</Field1Name>
    <Field2Name>Value</Field2Name>
    ...
  </TableName>
  <TableName>
    <Field1Name>Value</Field1Name>
    <Field2Name>Value</Field2Name>
    ...
  </TableName>
  ...
</dataroot>
```

where a **TableName** element represents a record in an Access database table, and each **TableName** element contains child elements for the fields in a record.

While you can import an InfoPath form without applying an XSL transformation, the form would not have a structure that is suitable to be properly imported into Access, especially if you have precreated tables. In the case of the InfoPath form used in this recipe, the XSL transformation would produce the following XML data, which would be suitable to be imported into the two Access database tables.

```
<dataroot>
  <Customer>
    <CustomerNo>123</CustomerNo>
    <LastName>Doe</LastName>
  </Customer>
  <Address>
    <Street>One Microsoft Way</Street>
    <City>Redmond</City>
    <Country>United States of America</Country>
    <CustomerNo>123</CustomerNo>
  </Address>
  <Address>
    <Street>157 Lambton Quay</Street>
    <City>Wellington</City>
    <Country>New Zealand</Country>
    <CustomerNo>123</CustomerNo>
  </Address>
</dataroot>
```

In the example shown above, the data that would be imported is indicated in bold. As you can see, there are two **Address** elements representing two rows in the repeating table on the InfoPath form.

If you want to modify the XSL transformation to suit your needs, you must first ensure that you specify the correct namespace for your InfoPath form at the top of the XSL file.

```
<xsl:stylesheet xmlns:xsl="http://www.w3.org/1999/XSL/Transform"
version="1.0"
xmlns:my="http://schemas.microsoft.com/office/infopath/2003/myXSD/2
014-05-25T23:53:01">
```

Then you must construct a table record containing fields, for example:

```
<Customer>
  <CustomerNo>
    ...
  </CustomerNo>
  <LastName>
    ...
  </LastName>
</Customer>
```

where **Customer** is the name of a table, and **CustomerNo** and **LastName** are the names of fields in the table. Once you have the structure of a table record, you can fill the values of the fields using XSL.

```
<CustomerNo>
  <xsl:value-of select="/my:myFields/my:customerNo"/>
</CustomerNo>
```

In the snippet shown above, the `xsl:value-of` element creates a text node. You must specify an XPath expression for its `select` attribute to be able to retrieve the value of a field from the InfoPath form. In the example above, the XPath expression retrieves the value of the **customerNo** field on the InfoPath form.

```
/my:myFields/my:customerNo
```

Note that if you do not know what the XPath expression of a field is, you can right-click the field on the **Fields** task pane in InfoPath, select **Copy XPath** from the context menu that appears, and then paste the XPath expression in the XSL file.

The second example of using an XSL element is on a repeating table. To be able to loop through the rows of a repeating table, you can use an `xsl:for-each` element and specify the repeating node of the repeating table in its `select` attribute. For example:

```
<xsl:for-each select="/my:myFields/my:addresses/my:address">
  ...
</xsl:for-each>
```

where

```
/my:myFields/my:addresses/my:address
```

is the XPath expression for the repeating group node of the repeating table. Once you are in the loop, the context becomes the repeating group node, so then you must specify a relative XPath expression for a field in an `xsl:value-of` element to retrieve the value of a field in the repeating table.

```
<xsl:for-each select="/my:myFields/my:addresses/my:address">
  <Address>
    <Street><xsl:value-of select="my:street"/></Street>
    ...
  </Address>
</xsl:for-each>
```

You can do much more with XSL than has been specified in this recipe. To learn more about XSL transformations, refer to the article entitled *XSL Transformations (XSLT)* on the W3C web site (w3c.org).

Note that in the solution described above, you manually imported one InfoPath form into Access. If you want to import multiple InfoPath forms and automate the process, you would have to write code.

Appendix

Content types and site columns

A content type is a collection of settings that define a particular type of information. A site column is a column that has been defined on a particular SharePoint site. Columns can be used to define the properties or attributes of content types.

Content types follow a hierarchichal structure that enables them to inherit characteristics from parent content types. When you create a content type on a particular SharePoint site, that site content type becomes available to all of the subsites of that SharePoint site where it can be reused. The same applies to site columns.

A site content type can be added to or associated with a particular list or library where it then becomes what is called a list content type, which can be defined as an instance of the site content on the list or library. When you associate a site content type with a list or library, you enable users to create items or documents that are based on that content type.

The use of content types in SharePoint is important to understand, not only because content types are a core element of lists and libraries, but also because they are pivotal for creating and using InfoPath forms in SharePoint. As far as InfoPath goes, it is good to know a bit about content types, because:

- When you create a SharePoint list form template, you base it on a content type that is associated with a SharePoint list.
- When you publish an InfoPath form template to a form library or as a site content type, the form template becomes the document template of the form library and/or of the content type.
- Content types enable form libraries to contain different types of InfoPath forms.
- Content types allow you to run SharePoint 2010 workflows on specific types of InfoPath forms.

Since a thorough explanation of content types is beyond the scope of this book, this book instead focuses on providing you with the basic knowledge you need to be able to work with content types as they relate to InfoPath forms in SharePoint.

Add existing content types to a SharePoint list

Problem

You want a custom SharePoint list to be able to contain tasks, contacts, and custom items, so you want the SharePoint list to contain three different types of list items.

Solution

You can enable management of content types on a SharePoint list and then add a **Task** and a **Contact** content type to the list, so that users can create items that are based on those content types.

To add existing content types to a SharePoint list:

1. In SharePoint, create a new custom SharePoint list or use an existing one.
2. Click **List** ➤ **Settings** ➤ **List Settings**.
3. When you create a custom SharePoint list, an **Item** content type is added to it by default. But you will not be able to see that this is the case unless you enable management of content types, which is disabled by default. So on the **Settings** page under **General Settings**, click **Advanced settings**.
4. On the **Advanced Settings** page, select the **Yes** option for **Allow management of content types**, and then click **OK**.
5. Back on the **Settings** page, you should now see a **Content Types** section present on the page and the **Item** content type should be listed under that section. This is the default content type of the list. Click **Add from existing site content types** under the **Content Types** section to add more content types to the list.

6. Content types are ordered in groups in SharePoint. You can find those groups listed in the **Select site content types from** drop-down list box on the **Add Content Types** page. Because you want to add **Task** and **Contact** content types to the SharePoint list and these content types are generally added to SharePoint lists, you can select **List Content Types** from the **Select site content types from** drop-down list box, click **Contact**, hold the **Ctrl** key on your keyboard pressed down, and then click **Task** to select both content types in the **Available Site Content Types** list box. Click **Add** to add the content types to the **Content types to add** list box, and then click **OK**. Back on the **Settings** page, you should now see three content types listed: **Item**, **Contact**, and **Task**, of which **Item** is marked as the **Default Content Type**.

Content Types

This list is configured to allow multiple content types. Use content types to specify the information you want to display about an item, in addition to its policies, workflows, or other behavior. The following content types are currently available in this list:

Content Type	Visible on New Button	Default Content Type
Item	✓	✓
Contact	✓	
Task	✓	

▫ Add from existing site content types
▫ Change new button order and default content type

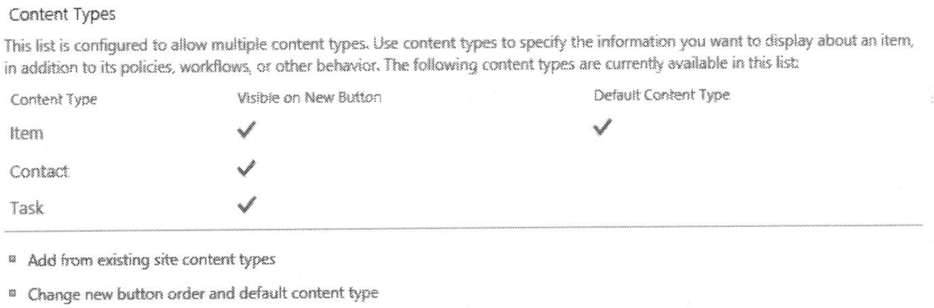

Figure 352. The three content types associated with the SharePoint list.

In SharePoint, navigate to the SharePoint list. Click **new item** to add a new item that is based on the **Item** content type to the list. Select **Items ➤ New ➤ New Item ➤ Contact** to add a new contact that is based on the **Contact** content type to the list. Select **Items ➤ New ➤ New Item ➤ Task** to add a new task that is based on the **Task** content type to the list.

Discussion

SharePoint comes with an entire range of content types right out-of-the-box, so you do not always have to create content types yourself, but can make use of the ones that already exist in SharePoint.

In the solution described above, you added a **Contact** and a **Task** content type to a custom SharePoint list that already had an **Item** content type associated with it. Before you can add additional content types to a SharePoint list or library, you must enable management of content types on that list or library. And once enabled, you can choose to add content types from different groups of content types that are available in SharePoint. You can navigate to the **Site Content Types** page via the site's **Settings** menu (**Site settings** ➤ **Web Designer Galleries** ➤ **Site content types**) to see the list of content types that are available on a SharePoint site.

The method described in this recipe applies to both SharePoint lists and libraries. To create a new content type that can be used with InfoPath, see recipe *26 Create a content type for an InfoPath form from within SharePoint*.

Create a new site column

Problem

You want to add a site column to a SharePoint site so that you can use it later as a column on a list, library, or content type.

Solution

You can create a new site column via the settings page of a SharePoint site.

To create a new site column:

1. In SharePoint, navigate to the site on which you want to create the new site column, and select **Site settings** from the **Settings** menu (the gear icon in the top-right corner).
2. On the **Site Settings** page under **Web Designer Galleries**, click **Site columns**.
3. On the **Site Columns** page, click **Create**.
4. On the **Create Column** page, enter a name for the column, select a data type, configure any other settings on the page as you require for the column, and then click **OK**.

The new site column should now be listed under the **Custom Columns** group (if you accepted the default group setting) on the **Site Columns** page.

Discussion

Site columns are reusable columns that can be added to one or more lists, libraries, or content types. Site columns differ from list columns in that list columns are created within the context of a list or library, so are private to that list or library, while site columns are created within the context of a site, so are available to all lists or libraries on a site or its subsites.

Add a site column to a site content type

Problem

You want to add an existing site column to an existing site content type in SharePoint.

Solution

You can use the **Site Content Type** page to add a new or an existing site column to a content type.

To add an existing site column to an existing site content type:

1. In SharePoint, navigate to the site where the site content type to which you want to add a site column is located, and click **Site settings** on the **Settings** menu (the gear icon in the top-right corner).
2. On the **Site Settings** page under **Web Designer Galleries**, click **Site content types**.
3. On the **Site Content Types** page, locate the content type you want to add a site column to, and then click it to open its **Site Content Type** page. If you do not have a site content type and would like to create a new one, see for example recipe *26 Create a content type for an InfoPath form from within SharePoint*.
4. On the **Site Content Type** page under **Columns**, click **Add from existing site columns**. Note: If you want to add a new site column to the content type, you must click **Add from new site column** instead, which should open the **Create Column** page where you can add a new column as described in *Create a new site column*.

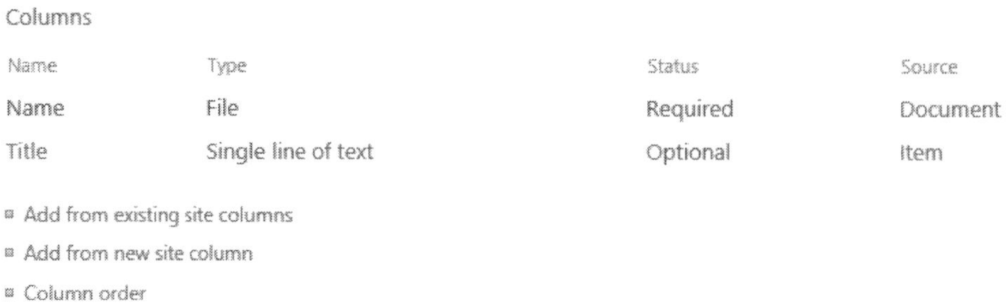

Columns
Name
Type
Status
Source
Name
File
Required
Document
Title
Single line of text
Optional
Item
Add from existing site columns
Add from new site column
Column order

Figure 353. Links to add an existing or a new site column to a content type.

5. On the **Add Columns** page, select the site column you want to add in the **Available columns** list box, and click **Add** to add it to the **Columns to add** list box.
6. On the **Add Columns** page, click **OK**.

The site column should now appear under the **Columns** section on the **Site Content Type** page.

Discussion

In the solution described above, you learned how to add an existing or a new site column to a site content type. While you can add columns to a content type, a content type may already have columns defined on it. Such columns have most likely been inherited from the parent content type when you created the content type based on a parent content type. If a column was inherited from a parent content type, the name of that parent content type should be listed in the **Source** column under the **Columns** section on the **List Content Type** or **Site Content Type** page.

Troubleshooting and solving errors from browser forms in SharePoint

The first place to look when you receive an error message from an InfoPath form in SharePoint is in the **Operational** log, which you can access via **Applications and Services Logs ➤ Microsoft ➤ SharePoint Products ➤ Shared** in Windows Event Viewer on the SharePoint server.

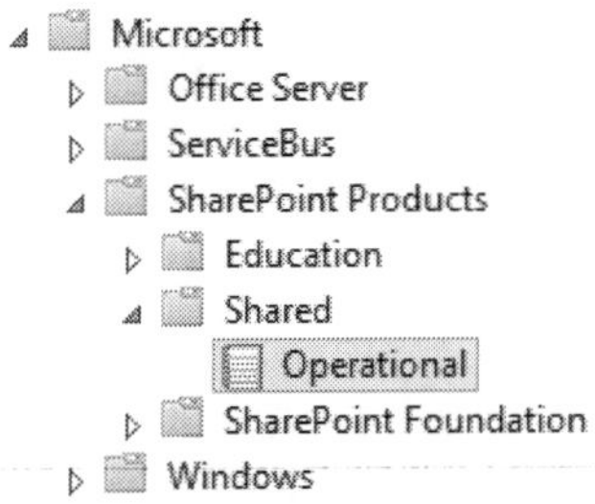

Figure 354. Operational log in Windows Event Viewer.

InfoPath form errors should be listed under the *InfoPath Forms Services* **Source**. Other sources you may be interested in for troubleshooting solutions are:

- Secure Store Service
- Excel Services Application

The second place to look when you receive an error message from an InfoPath form in SharePoint and have a correlation ID, is in the log files in the SharePoint root, which you can access via Windows File Explorer at the following location:

```
C:\Program Files\Common Files\microsoft shared\Web Server
Extensions\15\LOGS
```

When an error occurs, start searching for the correlation ID in the most recent log files to see what the error message says and hopefully resolve the issue.

The third thing you can do to resolve errors coming from browser forms is to open the form template that is linked to an InfoPath form in InfoPath Designer 2013, preview it, and try to reproduce the error in InfoPath Filler 2013. Generally, InfoPath Filler 2013 will produce more meaningful error messages than those displayed in the browser via SharePoint.

Configure a web service data connection for a web browser form

To configure a web service data connection for a web browser form:

1. In SharePoint Central Administration, configure the Secure Store Service and create a target application that can be used for InfoPath forms (see the article entitled *Configure the Secure Store Service in SharePoint 2013* on TechNet and see *Secure Store Target Application example* here in the Appendix for screenshots of the configuration of a sample target application). This is a one-off configuration, unless you want to use different target applications for different data connections.
2. In SharePoint Central Administration, enable the use of UDC authentication (see *Enable the use of UDC authentication* here in the Appendix). This is a one-off configuration.
3. In SharePoint, create a Data Connection Library on the site where the InfoPath forms are located (see *Create a Data Connection Library* here in the Appendix).
4. In InfoPath, convert the data connection for a web service into a UDCX file (see *Convert a data connection to a data connection file* here in the Appendix).
5. In SharePoint, download the UDCX file from the data connection library, add the Secure Store Service app ID to the authentication section in the file (see *Configure authentication for a data connection file* here in the Appendix), save the file, and then upload the file back to the data connection library.

Enable the use of UDC authentication

To enable the use of UDC authentication:

1. In SharePoint Central Administration, click **General Application Settings**.
2. On the **General Application Settings** page under **InfoPath Forms Services**, click **Configure InfoPath Forms Services**.

3. On the **Configure InfoPath Forms Services** page, select the **Allow user form templates to use authentication information contained in data connection files** check box, and click **OK**.

Create a Data Connection Library

To create a data connection library:

1. In SharePoint, navigate to the site on which you want to create a data connection library, and select **Add an app** from the **Settings** menu (the gear icon in the top-right corner).
2. On the **Your Apps** page, click **Data Connection Library**. Note that you may have to navigate to the second page of apps to find the **Data Connection Library** app.

Figure 355. The Data Connection Library app on the Your Apps page in SharePoint.

3. On the **Adding Data Connection Library** dialog, enter a name for the data connection library in the **Name** text box, and then click **Create**.

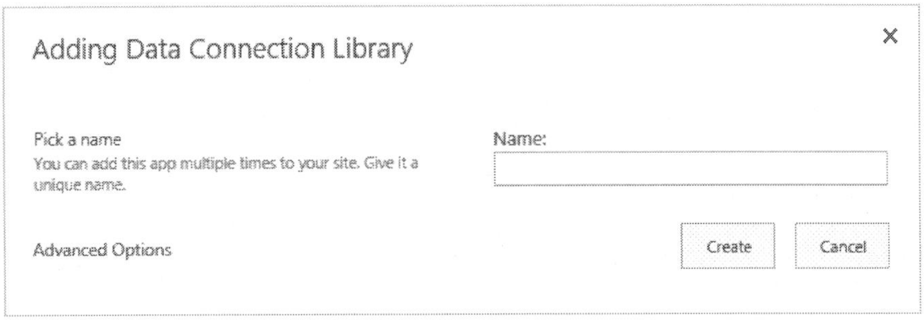

Figure 356. The Adding Data Connection Library dialog in SharePoint 2013.

Convert a data connection to a data connection file

To convert a data connection to a data connection file:

1. In SharePoint, ensure that you have a data connection library available.
2. In InfoPath, click **Data ➤ Data Connections**.
3. On the **Data Connections** dialog box, select the data connection you want to convert, and then click **Convert to Connection File**. Note that the **Convert to Connection File** button will be disabled if a data connection has already been converted.
4. On the **Convert Data Connection** dialog box, click **Browse**.
5. On the **Browse** dialog box, click in the location combo box at the top of the dialog box, type the URL of the SharePoint site on which the data connection library is located, and then press **Enter**. This action should display the contents of the SharePoint site.
6. On the **Browse** dialog box, navigate to the data connection library where you want to store the UDCX file, type a name for the UDCX file in the **File name** text box, and then click **Save**.
7. On the **Convert Data Connection** dialog box, leave the **Relative to site collection (recommended)** option selected, and click **OK**.

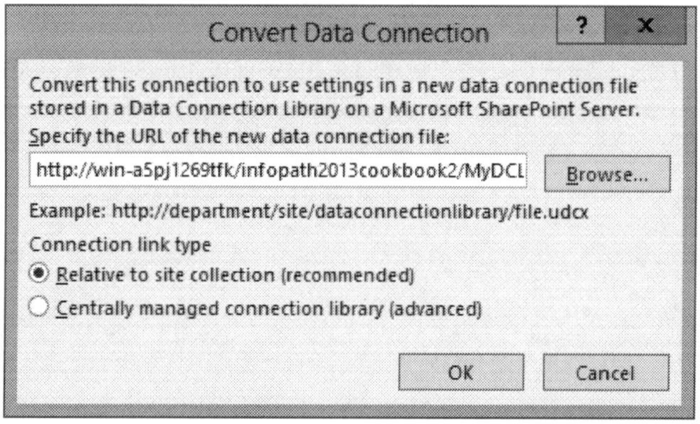

Figure 357. Converting a data connection and storing the file in SharePoint.

8. On the **Data Connections** dialog box, click **Close**.
9. Publish or republish the form template.

Configure authentication for a data connection file

To configure authentication for a data connection file:

1. In SharePoint, navigate to the data connection library in which you stored the UDCX file and download a copy of the file.
2. In Notepad, open the UDCX file you downloaded and then uncomment and change the line that configures authentication. For example, to have the UDCX file use an Secure Store target application named **IPWSSSO** with NTLM, change

```
<!--udc:Authentication>
  <udc:SSO AppId='' CredentialType='' />
</udc:Authentication-->
```

   into

```
<udc:Authentication>
  <udc:SSO AppId='IPWSSSO' CredentialType='Ntlm' />
</udc:Authentication>
```

3. Click **File ➤ Save** to save the UDCX file, and then close Notepad.
4. In SharePoint, navigate to the data connection library that contains the old UDCX file, and click **Files ➤ New ➤ Upload Document**.
5. On the **Add a document** dialog, click **Browse**.
6. On the **Choose File to Upload** dialog box, browse to and select the UDCX file you modified earlier, and then click **Open**.
7. On the **Add a document** dialog, leave the **Add as a new version to existing files** check box selected, and then click **OK**.

Discussion

Once you have stored a data connection in a data connection library and configured it, you can reuse it in InfoPath as follows:

1. In InfoPath, click **Data ➤ Get External Data ➤ From SharePoint Server**.
2. On the **Data Connection Wizard**, click **Manage Sites**.
3. On the **Manage Sites** dialog box, click **Add**.

4. On the **Site Details** dialog box, enter the URL of the site on which the data connection library is located into the **URL** text box, and click **OK**.
5. On the **Manage Sites** dialog box, click **Close**.

The data connection library should now appear in the tree view on the **Data Connection Wizard**, where you can expand it to select the data connection you would like to reuse.

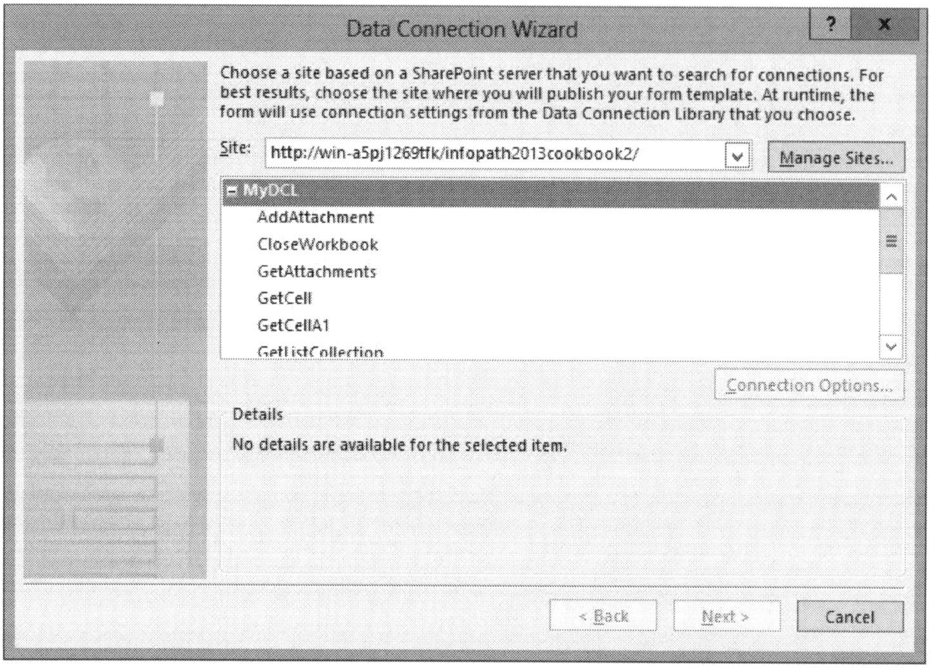

Figure 358. Data Connection Wizard displaying data connections in a DCL on a site.

Secure Store Target Application example

The sample target application shown in the figures below runs under a specific domain user named **InfoPathUser**, which is used as the credentials for any of the users specified under **Members**.

	Target Application ID↑	Type	Target Application Name
☐	IPWSSSO	Group	InfoPath Web Services SSO

Figure 359. IPWSSSO is a Secure Store Target Application ID.

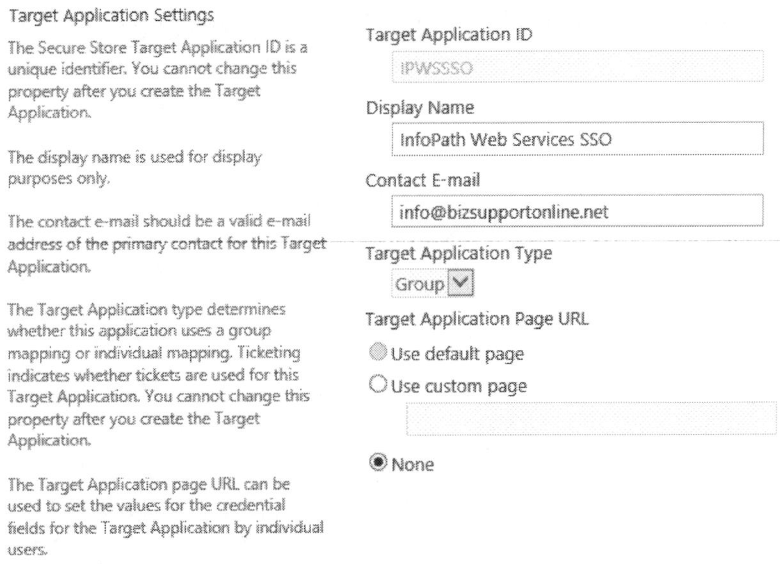
Target Application Settings
The Secure Store Target Application ID is a unique identifier. You cannot change this property after you create the Target Application.
The display name is used for display purposes only.
The contact e-mail should be a valid e-mail address of the primary contact for this Target Application.
The Target Application type determines whether this application uses a group mapping or individual mapping. Ticketing indicates whether tickets are used for this Target Application. You cannot change this property after you create the Target Application.
The Target Application page URL can be used to set the values for the credential fields for the Target Application by individual users.
Target Application ID
IPWSSSO
Display Name
InfoPath Web Services SSO
Contact E-mail
info@bizsupportonline.net
Target Application Type
Group
Target Application Page URL
Use default page
Use custom page
None

Figure 360. First configuration screen of the Secure Store Target Application.

Field Name
Field Type
Masked
Windows User Name
Windows User Name
Windows Password
Windows Password

Figure 361. Second configuration screen of the Secure Store Target Application.

Target Application Administrators
The list of users who have access to manage the Target Application settings. The farm administrator will have access by default.
CORP\administrator;
Users who have Full Control or All Target Applications privileges can administer this Secure Store Target Application.
Members
The users and groups that are mapped to the credentials defined for this Target Application.
CORP\bizsuportonline users;

Figure 362. Third configuration screen of the Secure Store Target Application.

Troubleshooting InfoPath with Excel Services

Excel Services generally writes more detailed error messages to the Windows event log than the error that is displayed in SharePoint. So if an error occurs while an Excel Services web service operation is being called, the error should be listed in the **Operational** log, which you can access via **Applications and Services Logs ➤ Microsoft ➤ SharePoint Products ➤ Shared** in Windows Event Viewer on the SharePoint server.

You can also disable action rules in InfoPath and then enable them one-by-one to check the values that are returned to try to narrow down which rule (or action) is causing the error. You can disable a rule by clicking on the drop-down arrow on the right-hand side of the rule on the **Rules** task pane, and then selecting **Disable** from the drop-down menu that appears.

And finally, always test a form template in InfoPath Filler 2013 before converting any data connections and before publishing the form template to SharePoint, since InfoPath Filler tends to display more meaningful error messages than SharePoint does.

A few of the most common reasons for getting errors while using the Excel Services SOAP web service have been listed below.

There was a time-out

Excel Services tends to need to "warm-up" the first time a user calls it. You may see an error such as:

An error occurred while querying the data source.

displayed in a dialog box or on a page.

Solution: Close the InfoPath form, reopen it, and try again. Or open an Excel workbook in the browser for Excel Services to "warm up" before trying to fill out any InfoPath forms that make use of the Excel Services SOAP web service.

Authentication information could not be used

You may see the following error in the Windows event log:

Authentication information in the UDC file could not be used for this connection because user forms are not allowed to use UDC authentication. To change this settings, use the InfoPath Forms Services configuration page in SharePoint Central Admin.

Solution: Follow the instructions in *Enable the use of UDC authentication* earlier in the Appendix.

(401) Unauthorized

You may see the following error in the Windows event log:

The remote server returned an error: (401) Unauthorized.

Solution: If you are using the Secure Store Service to make web service calls, you must give the user you used to set the credentials for the Secure Store Service target application read and/or write permission in SharePoint or on the Excel workbook being accessed.

Access to an Excel workbook is denied

The Excel workbook you are trying to access has been either opened or locked by another user. To check whether the Excel workbook has been locked by another user, open it in the Excel client application from within SharePoint. If Excel displays a dialog box saying that you can only get a read-only copy, then the file is in use by another user or locked by Excel Services.

Solution: If locked by a user, ask the user to close the Excel workbook. If locked by Excel Services (for example because an error took place while a user was submitting data to the Excel Services SOAP web service), wait 5 to 15 minutes for Excel Services to release the Excel workbook.

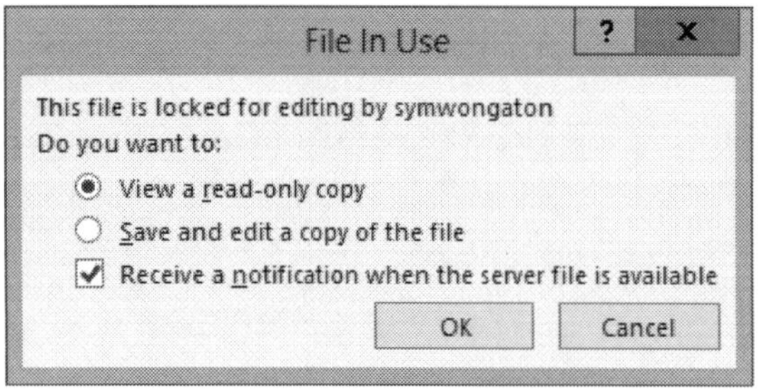

Figure 363. File In Use dialog box in Excel 2013.

The Excel workbook cannot be found

The URL for the Excel workbook used in the InfoPath form template is incorrect or the Excel workbook does not exist at the location specified in the InfoPath form template.

Solution: Double-check whether the data connection (most likely for the **OpenWorkbook** or **OpenWorkbookForEditing** web service operation) in the InfoPath form template is referencing the correct URL for the Excel workbook, change it if necessary, and then republish the form template.

The form template failed to work

The InfoPath form is not working as intended, is not doing what it is supposed to do, or an error is being displayed.

Solution: Open and fill out the InfoPath form in InfoPath Filler 2013 to get a better error message with details, and possibly solve the issue.

Index

A

B

C

D

E

F

G

H

I

L

M

Q

R

S

T

U

V

W

X